# GLOBAL ST...ES

# THE MIDDLE EAST

**THIRTEENTH EDITION**

**Dr. Azzedine Layachi**

**OTHER BOOKS IN THE GLOBAL STUDIES SERIES**
- Africa
- China
- Europe
- India and South Asia
- Islam and the Muslim World
- Japan and the Pacific Rim
- Latin America and the Caribbean
- Russia and the Near Abroad
- The World at a Glance

Mc Graw Hill   Connect Learn Succeed™

GLOBAL STUDIES: THE MIDDLE EAST, THIRTEENTH EDITION

Published by McGraw-Hill, a business unit of The McGraw-Hill Companies, Inc., 1221 Avenue of the Americas, New York, NY 10020. Copyright © 2011 by The McGraw-Hill Companies, Inc. All rights reserved. Previous edition(s) © 2009, 2007, and 2005. No part of this publication may be reproduced or distributed in any form or by any means, or stored in a database or retrieval system, without the prior written consent of The McGraw-Hill Companies, Inc., including, but not limited to, in any network or other electronic storage or transmission, or broadcast for distance learning.

Some ancillaries, including electronic and print components, may not be available to customers outside the United States.

Global Studies® is a registered trademark of The McGraw-Hill Companies, Inc.

Global Studies is published by the **Contemporary Learning Series** group within the McGraw-Hill Higher Education division.

1 2 3 4 5 6 7 8 9 0 QDB/QDB 1 0 9 8 7 6 5 4 3 2 1 0

ISBN 978-0-07-352775-8
MHID 0-07-352775-0
ISSN 1056-6848 (print)

Managing Editor: *Larry Loeppke*
Senior Developmental Editor: *Jade Benedict*
Permissions Coordinator: *Shirley Lanners*
Senior Marketing Communications Specialist: *Mary Klein*
Senior Project Manager: *Jane Mohr*
Design Coordinator: *Brenda Rolwes*
Cover Graphics: *Rick D. Noel*

Compositor: Laserwords Private Limited
Cover Image: © Royalty-Free/CORBIS

**Library in Congress Cataloging-in-Publication Data**
Main entry under title: Global Studies: Middle East. 13th ed.
        1. Middle East—History. 2. Arab countries—History. 3. Israel—History.
I. Title: Middle East. II. Layachi, Azzedine, *comp.*

www.mhhe.com

# THE MIDDLE EAST

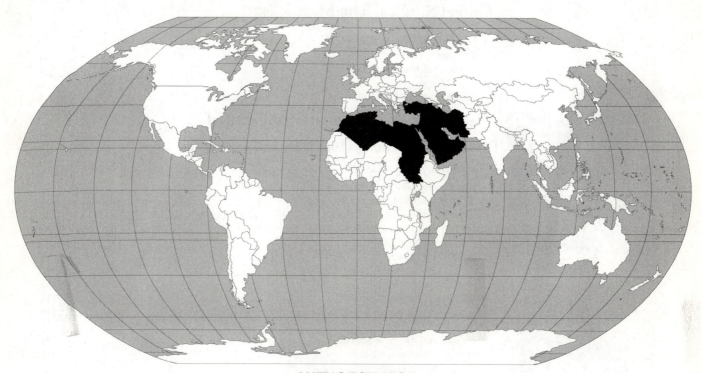

## AUTHOR/EDITOR

### Dr. Azzedine Layachi

The author/editor for Global Studies: The Middle East is specialized in, and has been teaching politics and political economy of the Middle East and North Africa for a quarter century. He is Professor of Politics at St. John's University in New York City and Rome, Italy. He is the author of several books, book chapters, and journal articles on the region. He is a member of the Executive Board of the American Institute of Maghrebi Studies (AIMS) and a member of the Advisory Board of Maghreb Center (USA). In recent years, he served as Associate Editor of the Bulletin of the Middle East Studies Association (MESA,) Associate Director of the Center for Global Studies, New York; President of the U.S. Northeastern Political Science Association; and President of the New York State Political Science Association. Dr. Layachi is also a consultant to private and public institutions, and makes appearances on national and international radio and television, and in seminars and international conferences.

## SERIES CONSULTANT

### Chris J. Sutton

Western Illinois University

# Contents

## Articles from the World Press

# Using *Global Studies: The Middle East*

## THE GLOBAL STUDIES SERIES

The Global Studies series was created to help readers acquire a basic knowledge and understanding of the regions and countries in the world. Each volume provides a foundation of information—geographic, cultural, economic, political, historical, artistic, and religious—that will allow readers to better assess the current and future problems within these countries and regions and to comprehend how events there might affect their own well-being. In short, these volumes present the background information necessary to respond to the realities of our global age.

Each of the volumes in the Global Studies series is crafted under the careful direction of an author/editor—an expert in the area under study. The author/editors teach and conduct research and have traveled extensively through the regions about which they are writing.

In *Global Studies: The Middle East,* the author/editor has written several regional essays and country reports for each of the countries included.

## MAJOR FEATURES OF THE GLOBAL STUDIES SERIES

The Global Studies volumes are organized to provide concise information on the regions and countries within those areas under study. The major sections and features of the books are described here.

## Regional Essays

For *Global Studies: The Middle East,* the author/editor has written several essays focusing on the religious, cultural, sociopolitical, and economic differences and similarities of the countries and peoples in the various regions of the Middle East. Regional maps accompany the essays.

## Country Reports

Concise reports are written for each of the countries within the region under study. These reports are the heart of each Global Studies volume. *Global Studies: The Middle East, Thirteenth Edition,* contains 22 country reports.

The country reports are composed of five standard elements. Each report contains a detailed map visually positioning the country among its neighboring states; a summary of statistical information; a current essay providing important historical, geographical, political, cultural, and economic information; a historical timeline, offering a convenient visual survey of a few key historical events; and four "graphic indicators," with summary statements about the country in terms of development, freedom, health/welfare, and achievements.

### A Note on the Statistical Reports

The statistical information provided for each country has been drawn from a wide range of sources. Every effort has been made to provide the most current and accurate information available. However, sometimes the information cited by these sources differs to some extent; and, all too often, the most current information

available for some countries is somewhat dated. Aside from these occasional difficulties, the statistical summary of each country is generally quite complete and up to date. Care should be taken, however, in using these statistics (or, for that matter, any published statistics) in making hard comparisons among countries. We have also provided comparable statistics for the United States and Canada, which can be found on pages viii and ix.

## World Press Articles

Within each Global Studies volume is reprinted a number of articles carefully selected by our editorial staff and the author/editor from a broad range of international periodicals and newspapers. The articles have been chosen for currency, interest, and their differing perspectives on the subject countries. There are 13 articles in *Global Studies: The Middle East, Thirteenth Edition.*

The articles section is preceded by an annotated table of contents. This resource offers a brief summary of each article.

## WWW Sites

An extensive annotated list of selected World Wide Web sites can be found on page vii in this edition of *Global Studies: The Middle East.* In addition, the URL addresses for country-specific Web sites are provided on the statistics page of most countries. All of the Web site addresses were correct and operational at press time. Instructors and students alike are urged to refer to those sites often to enhance their understanding of the region and to keep up with current events.

## Glossary, Bibliography, Index

At the back of each Global Studies volume, readers will find a glossary of terms and abbreviations, which provides a quick reference to the specialized vocabulary of the area under study and to the standard abbreviations used throughout the volume.

Following the glossary is a bibliography that lists general works, national histories, and current-events publications and periodicals that provide regular coverage on The Middle East.

The index at the end of the volume is an accurate reference to the contents of the volume. Readers seeking specific information and citations should consult this standard index.

## Currency and Usefulness

*Global Studies: The Middle East,* like the other Global Studies volumes, is intended to provide the most current and useful information available to understand the events that are shaping the cultures of the region today.

This volume is revised on a regular basis. The statistics are updated, regional essays and country reports revised, and world press articles replaced. In order to accomplish this task, we turn to our author/editor, our advisory boards, and—hopefully—to you, the users of this volume. Your comments are more than welcome. If you have an idea that you think will make the next edition more useful, an article or bit of information that will make it more current, or a general comment on its organization, content, or features that you would like to share with us, please send it in for serious consideration.

# Selected World Wide Web Sites for *Global Studies: The Middle East*

**(Some web sites continually change their structure and content,
so the information listed here may not always be available.)**

## GENERAL SITES

### BBC News
*http://news.bbc.co.uk/hi/english/world/middle_east/default.stm*

Access current Middle East news from this BBC site.

### C-SPAN Online
*www.c-span.org*

See especially C-SPAN International on the Web for International Programming Highlights and archived C-SPAN programs.

### Library of Congress
*www.loc.gov*

An invaluable resource for facts and analysis of 100 countries' political, economic, social, and national-security systems and installations.

### ReliefWeb
*www.reliefweb.int/w/rwb.nsf*

UN's Department of Humanitarian Affairs clearinghouse for international humanitarian emergencies. It has daily updates, including Reuters and Voice of America.

### United Nations
*www.unsystem.org*

The official website for the United Nations system of organizations. Everything is listed alphabetically, and data on UNICC and Food and Agriculture Organization are available.

### UN Development Programme (UNDP)
*www.undp.org*

Publications and current information on world poverty, Mission Statement, UN Development Fund for Women, and much more. Be sure to see the Poverty Clock.

### UN Environmental Programme (UNEP)
*www.unep.org*

Official site of UNEP with information on UN environmental programs, products, services, events, and a search engine.

### U.S. Central Intelligence Agency Home Page
*www.cia.gov/index.htm*

This site includes publications of the CIA, such as the World Factbook, Factbook on Intelligence, Handbook of International Economic Statistics, CIA Maps and Publications, and much more.

### U.S. Department of State Home Page
*www.state.gov/www/ind.html*

Organized alphabetically (i.e., Country Reports, Human Rights, International Organizations, and more).

### World Health Organization (WHO)
*www.who.ch*

Maintained by WHO's headquarters in Geneva, Switzerland, the site uses Excite search engine to conduct keyword searches.

## MIDDLE EAST SITES

### The Abraham Fund
*www.abrahamfund.org/main/siteNew/index.php*

The goal of peaceful coexistence between Jews and Arabs is the theme of this site. It offers information on various projects and links to related sites.

### Arab Political Systems: Baseline Information and Reforms
*www.carnegieendowment.org/publications/index.cfm?fa=view&id=16918*

This website provides information on the political systems of Arab countries, with links to official documents and websites. It is produced by the Carnegie Endowment for International Peace and the Fundación para las Relaciones Internacionales y el Diálogo Exterior (FRIDE) in Spain.

### The Arab American National Museum
*www.arabamericanmuseum.org/About-the-Museum.id.3.htm*

The Arab American National Museum is the first museum in the world devoted to Arab American history and culture. It has an online library and resource catalog.

### Arab News
*http://arabnews.com/middleeast/*

Daily news on the Arab and other Middle East countries

### Camera Media Report
*www.camera.org*

This site is run by the Committee for Accuracy in Middle East Reporting in America, and it is devoted to fair and accurate coverage of Israel and the Middle East.

### Central Zionist Archives
*www.zionistarchives.org.il/ZA/pMainE.aspx*

This site is the official historical archives of the World Zionist Organization, the Jewish Agency, the Jewish National Fund, Karen Hayesod, and the World Jewish Congress.

### CNN Interactive—World Regions: Middle East
*www.cnn.com/MIDDLEEAST/*

This 24-hour news channel often focuses on the Middle East and is updated every few hours.

### Institute for Middle Eastern and Islamic Studies
*www.dur.ac.uk/sgia/imeis/*

The University of Durham in England maintains this site. It offers links to the University's extensive library of Middle East information; the Sudan Archive is the largest collection of documentation outside of Sudan itself.

### The Middle East Institute
*www.mideasti.org*

The Middle East Institute is dedicated to educating Americans about the Middle East. The site offers links to publications, media resources, and other links of interest.

### Middle East Policy Council
*www.mepc.org*

The purpose of the Middle East Policy Council's website is to expand public discussion and understanding of issues affecting U.S. policy in the Middle East.

### Middle East Times
*http://metimes.com*

The *Middle East Times* is a source for independent analysis of politics, business, religion, and culture in the Middle East. It requires a subscription.

**We highly recommend that you review our website for expanded information and our other product lines. We are continually updating and adding links to our website in order to offer you the most usable and useful information that will support and expand the value of your book. You can reach us at: *www.mhhe.com/cls*.**

# The United States (United States of America)

## GEOGRAPHY

*Area in Square Miles (Kilometers):*
3,794,085 (9,826,630) (about 1/2 the size of Russia)

*Capital (Population):* Washington, DC (591,833)

*Environmental Concerns:* air and water pollution; limited freshwater resources, desertification; loss of habitat; waste disposal; acid rain

*Geographical Features:* vast central plain, mountains in the west, hills and low mountains in the east; rugged mountains and broad river valleys in Alaska; volcanic topography in Hawaii

*Climate:* mostly temperate, but ranging from tropical to arctic

## PEOPLE
### Population
*Total:* 304,059,724

*Annual Growth Rate:* 0.89%

*Rural/Urban Population Ratio:* 19/81

*Major Languages:* predominantly English; a sizable Spanish-speaking minority; many others

*Ethnic Makeup:* 82% white; 13% black; 4% Asian; 1% Amerindian and others

*Religions:* 52% Protestant; 24% Roman Catholic; 1% Jewish; 13% others; 10% none or unaffiliated

### Health
*Life Expectancy at Birth:* 75 years (male); 81 years (female)

*Infant Mortality:* 6.37/1,000 live births

*Physicians Available:* 2.3/1000 people

*HIV/AIDS Rate in Adults:* 0.6%

### Education
*Adult Literacy Rate:* 97% (official)

*Compulsory (Ages):* 7–16

## COMMUNICATION
*Telephones:* 177,900,000 main lines

*Daily Newspaper Circulation:* 196.3/1,000 people

*Televisions:* 844/1,000 people

*Internet Users:* 208,000,000 (2006)

## TRANSPORTATION
*Highways in Miles (Kilometers):* 3,986,827 (6,430,366)

*Railroads in Miles (Kilometers):* 140,499 (226,612)

*Usable Airfields:* 14,947

*Motor Vehicles in Use:* 229,620,000

## GOVERNMENT
*Type:* federal republic

*Independence Date:* July 4, 1776

*Head of State/Government:* President George W. Bush is both head of state and head of government

*Political Parties:* Democratic Party; Republican Party; others of relatively minor political significance

*Suffrage:* universal at 18

## MILITARY
*Military Expenditures (% of GDP):* 4.06%

*Current Disputes:* various boundary and territorial disputes; Iraq and Afghanistan; "war on terrorism"

## ECONOMY
*Per Capita Income/GDP:* $43,800/$13.06 trillion

*GDP Growth Rate:* 2.9% (2006)

*Inflation Rate:* 3.2%

*Unemployment Rate:* 4.8%

*Population Below Poverty Line:* 12%

*Natural Resources:* many minerals and metals; petroleum; natural gas; timber; arable land

*Agriculture:* food grains; feed crops; fruits and vegetables; oil-bearing crops; livestock; dairy products

*Industry:* diversified in both capital and consumer-goods industries

*Exports:* $1.023 trillion (primary partners Canada, Mexico, Japan, China, U.K.)

*Imports:* $1.861 trillion (primary partners Canada, Mexico, Japan, China, Germany)

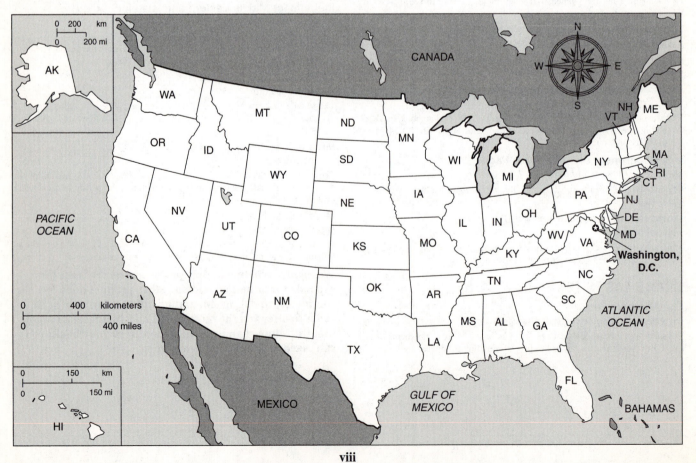

# Canada

## GEOGRAPHY

*Area in Square Miles (Kilometers):*
3,855,103 (9,984,670) (slightly larger than the United States)
*Capital (Population):* Ottawa (1,560,000)
*Environmental Concerns:* air and water pollution; acid rain; industrial damage to agriculture and forest productivity
*Geographical Features:* permafrost in the north; mountains in the west; central plains; lowlands in the southeast
*Climate:* varies from temperate to arctic

## PEOPLE

### Population

*Total:* 33,390,141(2007)
*Annual Growth Rate:* 0.87%
*Rural/Urban Population Ratio:* 20/80
*Major Languages:* both English and French are official
*Ethnic Makeup:* 28% British Isles origin; 23% French origin; 15% other European; 6% others; 2% indigenous; 26% mixed
*Religions:* 42.6% Roman Catholic; 27.7% Protestant; 12.7% others; 16% none.

### Health

*Life Expectancy at Birth:* 77 years (male); 84 years (female)
*Infant Mortality:* 4.63/1,000 live births
*Physicians Available:* 2.1/1,000 people

*HIV/AIDS Rate in Adults:* 0

### Education

*Adult Literacy Rate:* 97%
*Compulsory (Ages):* 6–16

## COMMUNICATION

*Telephones:* 20,780,000 main lines
*Daily Newspaper Circulation:* 167.9/1,000 people
*Televisions:* 709/1,000 people
*Internet Users:* 22,000,000 (2006)

## TRANSPORTATION

*Highways in Miles (Kilometers):* 646,226 (1,042,300)
*Railroads in Miles (Kilometers):* 29,802 (48,068)
*Usable Airfields:* 1,343
*Motor Vehicles in Use:* 18,360,000

## GOVERNMENT

*Type:* federation with parliamentary democracy
*Independence Date:* July 1, 1867
*Head of State/Government:* Queen Elizabeth II; Prime Minister Stephen Harper
*Political Parties:* Conservative Party of Canada; Liberal Party; New Democratic Party; Bloc Québécois; Green Party
*Suffrage:* universal at 18

## MILITARY

*Military Expenditures (% of GDP):* 1.1%
*Current Disputes:* maritime boundary disputes with the United States and Denmark (Greenland)

## ECONOMY

*Currency ($U.S. equivalent):* 0.97 Canadian dollars = $1 (Oct. 2007)
*Per Capita Income/GDP:* $35,700/$1.181 trillion
*GDP Growth Rate:* 2.8%
*Inflation Rate:* 2%
*Unemployment Rate:* 6.4% (2006)
*Labor Force by Occupation:* 75% services; 14% manufacturing; 2% agriculture; and 8% others
*Natural Resources:* petroleum; natural gas; fish; minerals; cement; forestry products; wildlife; hydropower
*Agriculture:* grains; livestock; dairy products; potatoes; hogs; poultry and eggs; tobacco; fruits and vegetables
*Industry:* oil production and refining; natural-gas development; fish products; wood and paper products; chemicals; transportation equipment
*Exports:* $401.7 billion (primary partners United States, Japan, United Kingdom)
*Imports:* $356.5 billion (primary partners United States, China, Japan)

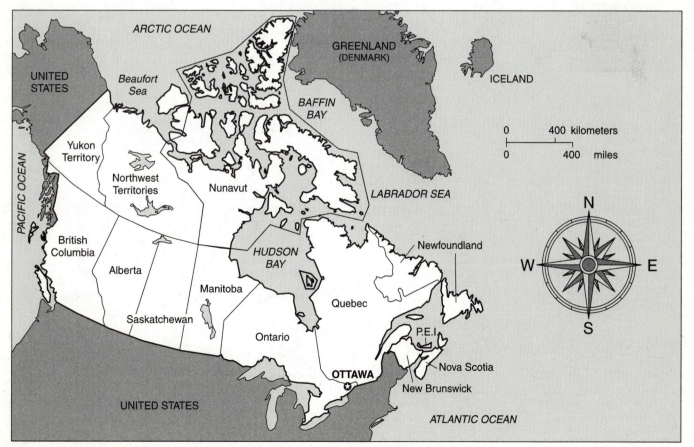

# GLOBAL ● STUDIES

This map is provided to give you a graphic picture of where the countries of the world are located, the relationship they have with their region and neighbors, and their positions relative to major powers and power blocs. We have focused on certain areas to illustrate these crowded regions more clearly.

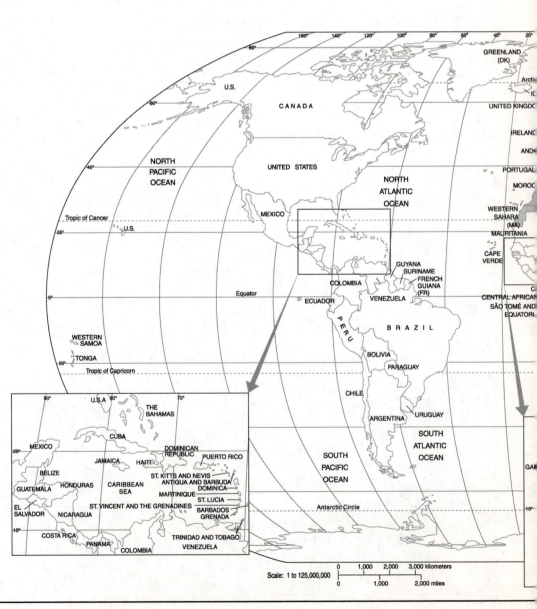

Scale: 1 to 125,000,000

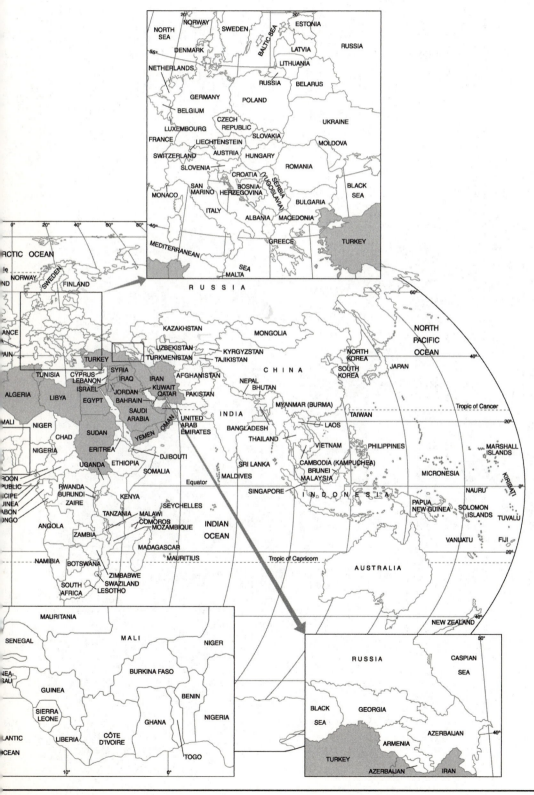

# The Middle East

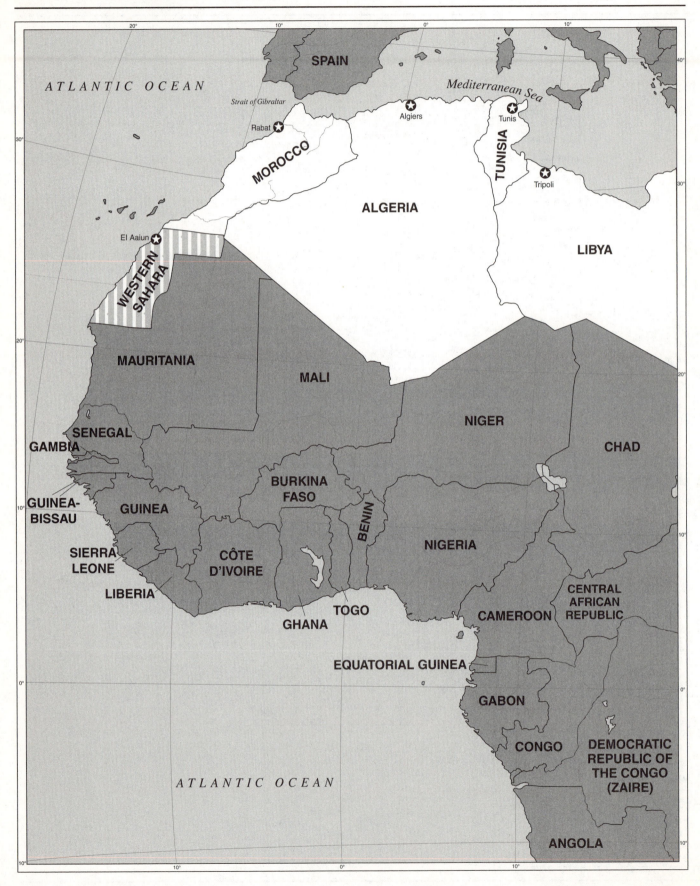

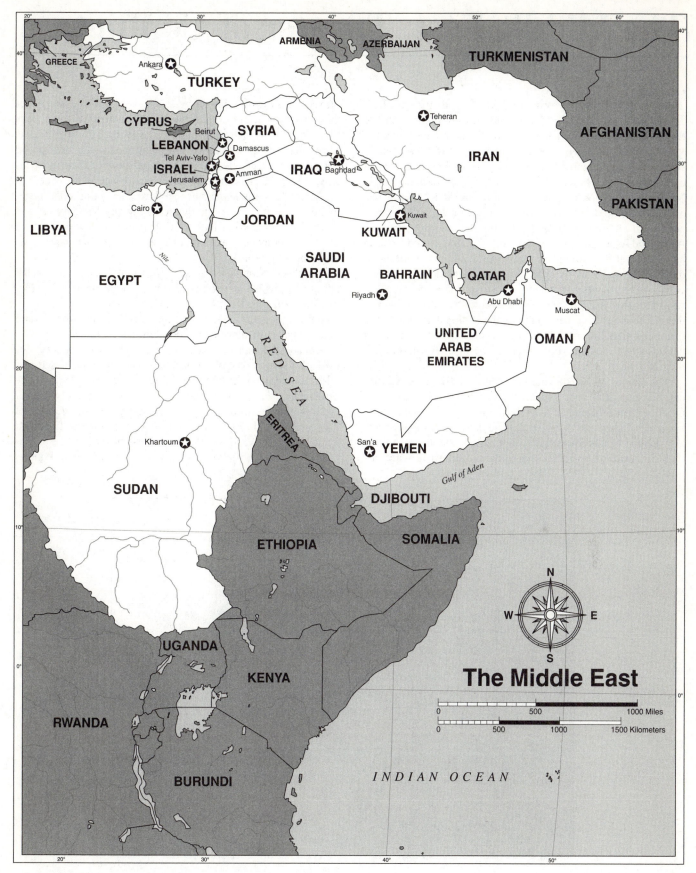

The Middle East

# The Middle East: Theater of Conflict

The Middle East was formerly divided, in British and U.S. diplomatic parlance, into "Near" and "Middle" (plus the Far East) covering the rest of Asia, but in common present-day usage, it describes the geographical region approximately equal in size to the continental U.S. and extends from the Atlantic coast of Morocco to the Iranian-Afghan border. The Middle East and North Africa region is thus intercontinental rather than continental, with the diversity of topography, climate, and physical and social environments characteristic of the two continents, Africa and Asia, that define its territory. Geography and location have dictated a significant role in world affairs for the Middle East throughout recorded history; humankind's earliest cities, governments, organized societies, and state conflicts were probably located there. In the twentieth century, this traditional role has been confirmed by the exploitation of mineral resources vital to the global economy and by the rivalries of nations that regard the Middle East as strategically important to their national interests.

The nations of the contemporary Middle East are very different, however, from their predecessors of 100 or 200 years ago. One important difference is political. When the United States became independent of England, there were three more or less "sovereign" Middle Eastern nation-states and empires: the Sherifian Sultanate of Morocco; the Ottoman Turkish Empire; and Iran, (also previously known as Persia) reunited by force under the new Qajar Dynasty, which would remain in power until it was succeeded by the Pahlavi Dynasty in the 1920s. These three states were still in place late in the nineteenth century, but European powers had effectively robbed them of most of their independence. Since then—a process accelerated since World War II—the Middle Eastern map has been redrawn many times. The result of the redrawing process is the contemporary Middle East and North Africa region, 21 independent states with diverse political systems overlaying a pastiche of ethnic groups, languages, customs, and traditions.

The diversity of these states is compensated for, in part, by the cohesion provided by various unifying factors. One of these factors is geography. The predominance of deserts, with areas suitable for agriculture compressed into small spaces where water was available in dependable flow, produced the *oasis-village* type of social organization and agricultural life. Beyond the oases evolved a second type of social organization suited to desert life, a less settled lifestyle termed *nomadism*. Another type of village settlement evolved in plateau and mountain regions, wherever the topography afforded physical protection for the defense of the community. In Egypt, and to a lesser extent in the Tigris and Euphrates River Valleys, *villages* were established to take advantage of a dependable water supply for crop irrigation. Peoples

(Visit Algeria/Mostefa Brahim (BRA001))

Traditionally the world's earliest civilizations organized into societies with a social structure, governments, urban centers, agricultural surpluses, and such technological essentials as a written language, accounting procedures and a hierarchical system of divinities, developed first in Mesopotamia and then in China. However recent research has added the civilizations of Mesoamerica to the list.[1]

living in the region mirrored these lifestyles, with the Middle Eastern city developing as an urban refinement of the same traditions.

The broad set of values, traditions, historical experiences, kinship structures, and so on, usually defined as "culture," is a second cohesive factor for the Middle East's peoples. Islam, for example, is either the official state religion or the leading religion in all but one (Israel) of the states. The Arabic language, due to its identification with Islam, is a bond even for those peoples who use another spoken and/or written language (such as Turkish, Hebrew, or Farsi); and, in any case, the social order of Islam is another unifying force.

Subjoined to this factor of cultural cohesion, for Americans and other Western peoples, is the element of religion. In recent years, and particularly under the administration of George Bush, foreign policy has often been guided by a "Higher Authority," one which motivated the invasion of Iraq and reinforced a long-term alliance with the Jewish state of Israel.[2]

A third unifying factor, while it is intangible and difficult to define, is a common historical experience. Without exception, the states of the Middle East are the products of twentieth-century international politics and the conflict of interests of outside powers. Clashing national interests and external involvement in regional affairs have set the tone for the internal and regional conflicts of Middle Eastern states. Thus, the intercommunal violence in modern Lebanon has its roots in foreign (French and British) support for various communal groups in the 1860s, setting the groups against one another under the guise of protecting them from the Ottoman government. European intervention contributed significantly to the conflict process. Robert Aumann, the Israeli scholar who shared the Nobel Peace Prize in Economics with a U.S. scholar for their work on game theory, noted in his acceptance speech that the Arab-Israeli conflict had been going on for 80 years, roughly the period of European rule in the region. But that one is only among the more recent millennial conflicts, as invaders swept across the Middle East, conquering, being conquered by other invaders, eventually being absorbed into the larger society.

## THE LAND ISLAND

Until recently, the Middle East was compartmentalized. Its peoples had little awareness of one another and even less of the outside world. Peoples who lived on or near the shores of the Mediterranean had more contact with each other and with Europeans, forming in general a broad trading community. But in the inland areas distances were great and communications poor. Often residents of one village knew nothing of those who lived in villages a few miles away. Travel throughout the region was slow and often dangerous. Caravans crossing the Sahara, for example, needed escorts from the nomadic Tuareg, the "Blue Men" so-called from their indigo robes, who would provide protection and guidance across the unmarked desert for a fee. It took several months, sometimes longer, for edicts from the Caliph in Baghdad to reach his governors in Spain or North Africa.

Consequently, the combination of vast distances, poor communications, and geographical isolation brought about the early development of subregions within the larger Middle East. As early as the tenth century A.D., three such subregions had been defined: North Africa, the Arab lands traditionally known to

(Ghardaia, Algeria—United Nations Photo (UN152627))

Life in the Sahara Desert is often perceived as nomadic, with the people living in tents and riding camels. To some extent this is still true, but there are many towns that offer a more settled way of life, such as this town in the Algerian Sahara.

Europeans as the Near East, and the highland plateaus of Turkey and Iran. In the twentieth century, these three areas were further separated from one another by foreign political control with the establishment of League of Nations mandates over the Arab lands and recognition of French protectorates over Morocco and Tunisia. Algeria, originally a French colony, became a department of metropolitan France in 1871. With Egypt already a British protectorate (as of 1882), only the truncated Ottoman empire and Qajar Iran remained as more or less sovereign entities on the eve of World War I.

In some respects the Middle East illustrates the theory developed by Admiral Alfred Thayer Mahan, distinguished naval officer and historian, many years ago. Mahan viewed the region from a naval perspective as a "land island" vulnerable to control by outside powers when their national interests seemed to be at stake. He based his theory on his study of the contest between Britain and imperial Russia for control of land and sea routes across those areas of Asia not under their rule. The key area, for both powers, was the Middle East, which was then shared between Persia and the Ottoman Turkish Empire. This contest has often been described as "The Great Game" or more imaginatively as "The Tournament of Shadows," as if the two powers were knights jousting in a tournament or engaged in moves on a chessboard. Thus the British sought to protect India, their imperial prize, by a land barrier extending northward through Afghanistan to Central Asia. On their side the Russians worked to expand their land empire southward in search of a warm-water port. The overthrow of the Czarist rule and more recently the collapse of the Soviet Union essentially ended the Great Game, which was in any case unwinnable. However, in recent years U.S. involvement in Iraq and rivalry with Iran over regional hegemony have to some extent regenerated "The Game" in a Middle Eastern setting.

The Ronald Reagan administration's commitment to a strongly anti-Communist policy revived the Great Game in new locations in the 1980s. Thus President Reagan insisted in 1983–1984 that American marines were in Lebanon to defend vital U.S. interests. In 1987, the United States accepted a request from Kuwait to "reflag" Kuwaiti tankers in the Persian Gulf and provide them with naval protection, ostensibly to thwart Iran but also to forestall a Soviet move into the region. The U.S. "national interest" has been invoked on numerous occasions to justify military intervention (as in Iraq in 2003) or warning of imminent intervention as in the case of the Iranian nuclear program (2007–2008).

## SUBREGIONAL CONFLICTS

The periodic outbreak of local or subregional conflicts in the Middle East has brought the region to the forefront of world affairs in recent years. Several of these conflicts have generated international involvement, in particular the 1991 Gulf War and the long-running Arab-Israeli conflict. Others, such as the internal war in Lebanon and Algeria remained essentially internal in nature.

Although thus far these Middle Eastern conflicts have been confined to their areas of origin or mediated by outside powers to reduce tension levels, some government policy makers continue to fear that they might spread and involve other countries in a wider war. The uninvolved state may then become involved, as the particular dispute becomes tied to the rivalry of competing national interests. At some point, a specific incident ignites a general war, as country after country become involved in the widening conflict. The classic analogy of this is World War I.

Regional conflict, however, has, so far, not affected long-term global commerce or national survival, and international terrorist acts identified with Middle Eastern sources remain sporadic and uncoordinated. But there are very real limits to involvement or effective management of conflict, even by the superpowers. President Reagan recognized these limits implicitly by withdrawing American marines from Lebanon in 1984; and when Egypt's President Anwar al-Sadat ordered the withdrawal of all Soviet military advisers from his country in 1972, home they went.

A final point about these conflicts is that they are all direct results of European intervention in the Middle East. For much of its history, the Middle East was a region without defined borders, other than the intangible limits fixed for Muslims by their religion. Even the Ottoman Empire, the major power in the region for more than five centuries, did not mark off its territories into

## IRANIANS AND ARABS

Iranians (or Persians) and Arabs are nearly all Muslims. But they have very different ethnic origins, linguistic and geographical backgrounds, and histories.

The Iranians were a loosely organized nomadic people from Central Asia who migrated into the Iranian plateau some 3,000 years ago, settling in the province of Parsa (hence the name Persian) as sedentary farmers and herders. They gradually expanded their territory at the expense of the earlier inhabitants, and in about 600 B.C. they joined forces with the Medes, another tribal people, under the leadership of the Persian chief Cyrus. In a few years they conquered other Near Eastern peoples to form the world's first true empire, in the sense of many different peoples ruled by a single ruler. Cyrus's successors, the Achaemenian Dynasty, expanded Iranian territory east to the Indus River and westward to the edge of Asia on the Mediterranean Sea. Iranians have retained a lofty sense of their many important contributions to civilization beginning with this period. Except in Iraq and the Persian Gulf states, where there are significant Iranian communities, Iranians have largely remained in their country of origin.

The Arabs, whose Semitic language is different in roots and structure from Farsi (Persian) although they share alphabets, were the original population of the Arabian Peninsula. Historically they were divided into often-competing tribal clans and groups, the majority nomads (Bedouin) roaming the deserts but with a small urban element in trading cities such as Mecca. The element which eventually united them as a people was religion. Islam was brought to them by the Prophet Muhammad in the seventh century A.D. After his death, they expanded into other areas of the Middle East, first as conquerors, and then as settlers. Arabs form the majority in the broad area stretching from Morocco on the west, across North Africa, eastward to Egypt, Sudan, the "Arab states" and Arabia proper. There are also large Arab minorities in Iran and Israel.

provinces with precise boundaries until well into the 1800s. But the European powers brought a different set of rules into the area. They laid down fixed borders sanctified by treaties, played ruler against ruler, divided and conquered. It was this European ascendancy, building on old animosities while creating new ones, that laid the groundwork for today's conflicts.

## THE IRAN–IRAQ WAR: BATTLE OF ISLAMIC BROTHERS

The Iran–Iraq War broke out in September 1980, when Iraqi forces invaded Iran and occupied large portions of Khuzestan Province. This measure was in retaliation for Iranian artillery attacks across the border, and efforts by Iranian agents to subvert the Iraqi Shia Muslim population, along with propaganda broadcasts urging Iraqis to overthrow the Iraqi regime of Saddam Hussein. But, as is the case with most conflicts, the causes of the war are complex.

One factor is the ancient animosity between Iranians and Arabs, which dates back to the seventh century A.D., when invading Arab armies overran the once powerful Sassanid Empire of Iran, defeating the Iranian Army at the famous Battle of Qadisiya in 637. The Iranians were converted to Islam with relative ease, yet they looked down on the Arabs as uncivilized

(Courtesy of informationwar.org (INFOWAR001))

A group of Iraqi prisoners being indoctrinated in Iran's Islamic revolution.

## UN PEACEKEEPING MISSIONS

Out of some thousands of UN peacekeepers from 97 countries deployed in peacekeeping and border control missions in 18 locations worldwide, five are based presently in the Middle East. The longest-established in the United Nations Truce Observer Force (UNTSO), established in 1948 to monitor the truce between Israel and its Arab neighbors. Despite periodic violations it is still in existence. Others are UNIFIL (13,000 personnel, based on the Lebanese-Israeli border, the Golan Heights (1,247) established in 1974, the Western Sahara (459) established in 1993, and southern Sudan (13,021), established in 2005 to monitor the peace agreement between the north and the south regions of that country. In August 2007 the Security Council approved a 26,000-member peacekeeping force for Darfur province, Sudan, to replace the 7,000-member African Union which has been trying unsuccessfully to end the 4-year conflict there, and has caused some 200,000 casualties there as well as displacement of refugees to Chad and elsewhere (see Sudan Country Report). The peacekeeping force, called UNAMID, is to be deployed speedily, but given the stalling techniques of the Sudanese government there is presently no guarantee that it will be deployed there, and recurring attacks on peacekeeping units suggest further destabilization in the battered province.

nomads who needed to be taught the arts of government and refined social behavior. The Arabs, in turn, despised the Iranians for what they considered their effeminateness—their love of gardens and flowers, their appreciation of wine and fine banquets. These attitudes have never entirely disappeared.[3] After the 1980 invasion, Iraq's government-controlled press praised it as Saddam Hussein's Qadisiya, reminding readers of the earlier Arab success.

Iran and Iraq have been at odds over a number of issues in recent years. One is occupation of three small islands at the mouth of the Persian Gulf. The British had included these islands in their protectorate over eastern Arabia and transferred them to the United Arab Emirates after that country became independent. But Shah Mohammed Reza Pahlavi, then the leader of Iran, contested the transfer, on the grounds that historically they had belonged to Iran. In 1971, an Iranian commando force seized the islands. Although the islands had never belonged to Iraq, the Iraqis denounced the occupation as a violation of *Arab* sovereignty and mounted a campaign among the predominantly Arab population of Iran's Khuzestan Province, adjacent to the border, to encourage them to revolt against the central government. The campaign failed, as would a later effort made by Saddam when his forces invaded Iran, and the islands remain under Iranian control.

Another issue was the shah's support for Kurdish guerrillas who had been fighting the Iraqi government for years to obtain autonomy for their mountain region. The shah also resented Iraq's grant of asylum to the Ayatollah Khomeini in 1963, because of the religious leader's continued anti-shah activities and propaganda broadcasts into Iran.

These disagreements intensified after the overthrow of the shah in 1979. Iraq accused the Khomeini regime of mistreatment of Khuzestan Arabs and of sending agents to incite its own Shi'a Muslim population to rebel. As noted in the Iraq Country Report in this book, some three-fourths of its population is Shi'a. However, the Sunni minority has ruled the country since independence. During his rule Saddam Hussein was ruthless in crushing opposition, particularly among Shi'a.[4]

The personal hatred between Saddam and Khomeini certainly contributed to the war. The two had been bitter enemies since 1978, when Saddam ordered Khomeini expelled from Iraq and accused him of working with Iraqi Shi'a Muslim leaders to undermine the regime. But differences in their views on the nature of authority and of social development also set the two leaders in opposition. For Saddam Hussein, the development of Islamic society to the fullest is best achieved by a secular Socialist party (e.g., the Ba'th); Islam is tangential. Khomeini, in the republic that he fashioned for Iran based on his Islamic political philosophy, argued for authority to be vested in religious leaders like himself, since they are qualified by wisdom, moral uprightness, and insight to know what is best for the Islamic community.

One issue often overlooked as a cause of the war is a territorial dispute, dating back many centuries, that has been aggravated by European intervention in the Middle East. The dispute concerns the Shatt al-Arab, the 127-mile waterway from the junction of the Tigris and Euphrates Rivers south to the Persian Gulf. The waterway was a bone of contention between the Ottoman and Iranian Empires for centuries, due to its importance as a trade outlet to the Gulf. It came entirely under Ottoman control in the nineteenth century. But with the collapse of the Ottoman Empire in World War I, the new kingdom of Iraq, set up by Britain, came in conflict with a revitalized Iran over navigation and ownership rights. Iran demanded ownership of half the Shatt al-Arab under international law, which would mean to mid-channel at the deepest point. Iraq claimed the entire waterway across to the Iranian side. Conflict intensified as both countries built up their oil exports in the 1960s and 1970s. In 1969, the shah of Iran threatened to occupy Iran's side of the waterway with gunboats, and he began a program of military support to Kurdish (Sunni Muslim) rebels fighting the Iraqi government.

Iran was much wealthier and militarily stronger than Iraq at that time, and Iraq could do little about Iranian support for the Kurds. But the Iraqis did have the Shatt al-Arab as a bargaining chip, in that their rights to it were embodied in several treaties. In 1975, after lengthy negotiations, Houari Boumedienne, then the president of Algeria, interrupted an oil ministers' conference in Algiers to announce that "our fraternal countries Iran and Iraq have reached agreement on their differences."[5] Iraq agreed to recognize Iranian ownership of the Shatt from bank to mid-channel, and Iran agreed to stop supporting Kurdish rebels in Iraq.

The advantage to Iraq of bringing an end to the Kurdish rebellion was offset by the humiliation felt by Iraqi leaders because they had bartered away a part of the sacred Arab territory. Hussain considered the agreement a personal humiliation because he had been the chief negotiator. When he became president, he said that he had negotiated it under duress and that Iraq would one day be strong enough to revoke it.[6]

The overthrow of the Shah and the consequent weakening of his army after the establishment of the Islamic Republic seemed to Saddam Hussain an excellent opportunity to restore Iraqi pride at the expense of an inferior adversary. In September 1980, he announced that the 1975 treaty was null and void, and he demanded Iran's recognition of Iraqi sovereignty over the entire Shatt al-Arab. He also called for the return of the three islands seized by the shah's forces in 1971 and the transfer of predominantly Arab areas of Khuzestan to Iraqi control. Although the two countries were roughly equal in military strength at the time, purges in Iranian Army leadership, low morale, and lack of spare parts for weapons due to the U.S. economic boycott convinced Saddam that a limited attack on Iran would almost certainly succeed.

However, the quick and easy victory anticipated by the Iraqis did not materialize. Political expectations proved equally erroneous. Iraq had expected the Arabs of Khuzestan to support the invasion, but they remained loyal to Iran's Khomeini regime. The Iraqi forces failed to capitalize on their early successes and were stopped by determined Iranian resistance. The war quickly turned into a stalemate.

In 1981–1982, the momentum shifted strongly in Iran's favor. The war became a patriotic undertaking as thousands of volunteers, some barely teenagers, headed for the front. An Iranian operation, appropriately code-named Undeniable Victory, routed three Iraqi divisions. Iran's blockade of Iraqi oil exports put a severe strain on the Iraqi economy. After the defeat, Saddam withdrew all Iraqi forces from Iranian territory and asked for a cease-fire. But Iran refused; Khomeini set the ouster of "the traitor Saddam" as a precondition for peace.

Iraqi forces fared better on their own soil and threw back a number of large-scale Iranian assaults, with huge casualties. Subsequent Soviet deliveries of missiles and new aircraft gave Iraq total air superiority. In early 1985, the Iraqis launched a campaign of "total war, total peace," combining air raids on Iranian ports and cities with an all-out effort to bring international pressure on Iran to reach a settlement.

In March 1985, Iranian forces launched another major offensive toward Basra from their forward bases in the Majnoon Islands, deep in the marshes, which they had captured by surprise in 1984. Although they were driven back with heavy losses, a year later, the Iranian forces captured the Fao (Faw) Peninsula southeast of Basra in another surprise attack and moved to within artillery range of Iraq's second city.

With the ground war stalemated, conflict shifted in 1986 and 1987 to the sky and sea lanes. Iraq's vast air superiority enabled the country to carry the war deep into Iranian territory, with almost daily bombing raids on Iranian cities, industrial plants, and oil installations.

But the most dangerous aspect of the conflict stemmed from Iraqi efforts to interdict Iranian oil supplies in order to throttle its enemy's economy. The war had a high-risk potential for broader regional conflict from the start, and in 1984, Iraqi missile attacks on tanker traffic in the Persian Gulf came close to involving other states in the region in active participation.

The internationalization of the war, which had been predicted by many analysts, became a reality in its seventh year. The secret dealings with the United States (revealed in the 1987 Iran–Contra hearings) had immeasurably strengthened Iran's air power and defenses; Iraq lost one fifth of its aircraft in a series of battles in the marshes. Iranian arms dealers were successful in purchasing weaponry from many sources. One of their major suppliers was China, from which they purchased a number of Silkworm missiles, which were installed at secret launching sites along the coast facing the Strait of Hormuz and the Fao Peninsula. At the same time, Iranian Revolutionary Guards established bases in various small harbors from whence they could mount missile and grenade attacks in fast patrol boats against ships passing in the Gulf. The government warned that tankers bound for Kuwait and other Gulf ports would be attacked if Iraq continued its air raids.

The direct cause of the internationalization of the war, however, was an Iraqi air raid on the U.S. naval frigate *Stark* on May 17, 1987. Thirty-seven American sailors were killed in the raid. (Although more than 200 ships had been attacked by Iraq or Iran since 1984, the *Stark* was the first warship attacked, and it suffered the heaviest casualties.) Saddam apologized, calling the attack a "tragic mistake." The United States drastically increased its naval forces in the Gulf and, in the following month, accepted a request from Kuwait for tanker protection under the American flag, along with naval escorts. In June 1987, the first convoy of "reflagged" Kuwaiti tankers traversed the Gulf without incident, escorted by U.S. warships and overflying jets from the aircraft carrier *Constellation*.

Predictably, Iran's threat to make the Gulf "safe for every one or no one," following the U.S. buildup in the region, affected nearby countries as well as international shipping. Saboteurs blew up oil installations and factories in the United Arab Emirates, Bahrain, and Saudi Arabia. Revolutionary Guardsmen carried out their earlier threats with hit-and-run strafing and grenade attacks on passing tankers. But the most serious danger came from floating mines strewn at random in shipping lanes. After a number of tankers had been damaged, the United States and several European countries previously uninvolved in the conflict, notably Italy, began sending minesweepers to the area.

With the Gulf in a state of high tension, the United Nations (UN) Security Council mounted a major effort to end the war. In July 1987, the Security Council unanimously approved *Resolution*

*598.* It called for an immediate cease-fire, the withdrawal of all forces to within recognized international boundaries, repatriation of all prisoners, and negotiations under UN auspices for a permanent peace settlement. Iraq accepted the resolution, but Iran temporized. Its leader, Ali Khamenei, told the UN General Assembly: "The Security Council's stance in relation to the war imposed on us has not changed up to this moment."[7]

A year later, though, Iran accepted *Resolution 598,* in an abrupt about-face. A number of factors combined to bring about this change, but the principal one was probably Iraqi success on the battlefield. Early in 1988, Republican Guard units specially trained in chemical warfare recaptured Fao in a massive assault, using nerve gases such as tabun and sarin along with mustard gas to thwart counterattacks. These chemical weapons worked with deadly effectiveness against the "human wave" tactics of teenage Iranian volunteers. Meanwhile, Saddam Hussein's crash program of development of long-range missiles enabled his forces to hit cities and military installations deep inside Iran and bring a further drop in Iranian morale.

Khomeini's death in June 1989 removed a major obstacle to peace negotiations. He had been persuaded only with great difficulty to approve the cease-fire, and his uncompromising hatred of Saddam Hussein was not shared by many of his associates.

A real peace settlement would enable both regimes to turn their full attention to the enormous problems of reconstruction. Unfortunately, their diametrically opposed positions on war gains worked against dialogue. Iran insisted on the withdrawal of Iraqi troops from its territory as a first step, while Iraq demanded that prisoner exchanges and clearing of the Shatt al-Arab should precede withdrawal.

The 1990 Iraqi invasion of Kuwait brought about an important change in the relationship. Urgently in need of allies, Saddam Hussein abruptly agreed to the original peace terms set by the United States and accepted by Iran. These terms required Iraqi troop withdrawal from occupied Iranian territory along with prisoner exchanges and clearance of mines and other obstacles from the Shatt al-Arab. Iran stayed neutral during the Gulf War and provided sanctuary for Iraqi pilots fleeing Allied air attacks, although it impounded their aircraft, which as of this writing have not been returned. (Presumably they are no longer serviceable). Although the two countries have not yet signed a formal peace treaty, the removal of Saddam Hussein has brought significant improvements in their relations with each other. In addition to an exchange of prisoners (such as 2,939 Iraqis repatriated in 2000), trade between them reached $4 billion in 2008. Iran also provided a $1 billion loan in 2007 for specific investment projects and spent several millions of dollars to help Iraq develop religious tourism in the holy shiite cities such Dajaf and Karbala and in general infrastructure (roads and airports).[8] Furthermore, more than 200 Iranian companies have started doing business in various fields in Iraq and an Iranian National Bank was established in Baghdad.

## The Gulf War and its Aftermath

On August 2, 1990, the Iraqi Army, which had been mobilized along the border, invaded and occupied Kuwait, quickly overcoming light resistance as the ruling Kuwaiti emir and his family escaped into exile. The invasion was the climax of a long dispute between the two Arab neighbors over oil-production quotas, division of output from the oil fields of the jointly controlled Neutral Zone along the border, and repayment of Iraqi debts to Kuwait from the war with Iran. Saddam Hussein had criticized Kuwait for producing more than its quota as allotted by the Organization of Petroleum Exporting Countries (OPEC), thus driving down the price per barrel and costing Iraq $7 to $8 billion in lost revenues. The Iraqi leader also charged Kuwait with taking more than its share of the output of the Neutral Zone. The Iraqi charges found considerable support from other Arab states, most of which consider the Kuwaitis to be greedy and arrogant. An Arab League summit meeting of oil ministers failed to resolve the dispute. Kuwait agreed only to a month-long adherence to its OPEC quota and continued to press for repayment of Iraqi debts owed for aid during the war with Iran.

What had been initially an inter-Arab conflict was internationalized by the invasion. Although Iraq called its occupation a recovery of part of the Arab homeland, which had been "stolen" from the Arabs by the British and given its independence under false premises, the action was viewed as aggression by nearly all the countries in the world. The UN Security Council on August 6 approved *Resolution 660,* calling for an immediate withdrawal of Iraqi forces from Kuwait and restoration of the country's legitimate government. Pending withdrawal, a worldwide embargo would be imposed on Iraq, covering both exports and imports and including medical and food supplies as well as military equipment. A similar resolution approved by the League of Arab States denounced Iraq's aggression against the "brotherly Arab state of Kuwait" and demanded immediate Iraqi withdrawal and restoration of Kuwaiti independence.

The invasion divided the Arab states, as several, notably Yemen and Sudan, agreed with Iraq's contention that Kuwait was historically part of Iraq and that Kuwaiti arrogance was partly responsible for the conflict. Others took the opposite view. Egyptian president Hosni Mubarak accused Saddam Hussain of breaking a solemn pledge not to invade Kuwait. Saudi Arabia, fearing that it might be Iraq's next victim, requested U.S. help under the bilateral defense treaty to protect its territory. U.S. president George Bush and Soviet president Mikhail Gorbachev issued a joint pledge for action to expel Iraqi forces from Kuwait. A massive military buildup followed, largely made up of U.S. forces, but with contingents from a number of other countries, including several Arab states. Although led by U.S. military commanders, the collective force operated under the terms of UN *Resolution 660* and was responsible ultimately to the Security Council as a military coalition.

The UN embargo continued in effect for six months but failed to generate an Iraqi withdrawal from Kuwait, despite its severe impact on the civilian population. (The only concession made by Saddam Hussein during that period was the release of foreign technicians who had been working in Kuwait at the time of the invasion). As a result, the coalition forces launched the so-called Operation Desert Storm on January 16, 1991. With their total air and technological superiority, they made short work of Iraq's army, as thousands of Iraqi soldiers fled into the desert or surrendered where they were. Subsequently, on the express orders of President George Bush, the campaign was halted on February 7, after Iraqi forces had been expelled from Kuwait. Yet Saddam remained in power, and uprisings of the

Kurdish and Shi'a populations in Iraq were ruthlessly crushed by the reorganized Iraqi. Although the Bush administration was unwilling to commit American forces to assist these populations and presumably risk significant casualties in unfamiliar territory, the United States and other members of the UN Security Council established "no-fly zones" north of the 36th parallel and south of the 33rd parallel of longitude, which would be off limits to Iraqi airforce. The zones effectively limited Iraq's sovereignty to approximately two thirds of its own territory.

Saddam Hussain's running battle with the United Nations kept world attention focused on Iraq in 1992–1993. Despite his country's sound defeat in the Gulf War, the Iraqi leader had gained the support not only of some other Arab states but also of many developing-world leaders, for what was to them an infringement on Iraq's sovereignty by the United Nations in its zeal to destroy Iraq's weapons of mass destruction. But for the United Nations and the United States, the main issue involved Iraq's noncompliance with UN resolutions. Thus *Resolution 687* directed the country to destroy all its long-range ballistic missiles and dismantle its chemical- and nuclear-weapons facilities, while *Resolution 715* would establish a permanent UN monitoring system, with surveillance cameras, for all missile test sites and installations as well as nuclear facilities. Iraq's compliance with these resolutions would end the embargo imposed after the invasion of Kuwait and would enable Iraq to sell $1.6 billion in oil to finance imports of badly needed medicines, medical supplies, and foodstuffs. Iraqi representatives argued that their country had complied with *Resolution 687* by demolishing under international supervision the al-Atheer nuclear complex outside Baghdad and by opening all missile sites to UN inspectors. However, they said that *Resolution 715* was illegal under international law, since it infringed on national sovereignty.

For the next four years Saddam held firm in his refusal to accept the resolution, along with a later one, *Resolution 986,* which would allow Iraq to sell 700,000 barrels per day (b/d) for six months, in return for compliance. The embargo and the standoff between Saddam and the United Nations placed a terrible burden on the Iraqi people who suffered from extreme shortages of food, medical and other humanitarian supplies. In 1996, the Iraqi government accepted UN terms to allow it to sell $2 billion worth of oil every six months, in return for opening all missile-testing sites and biological- and chemical-weapons facilities to inspectors. The oil revenues would be used for purchases of critically needed food, medicines, and children's supplies. However, the UN Security Council was divided, with the United States insisting on Iraq's adherence to all its obligations specified in *Resolution 715,* while other Council members argued that the embargo was hurting the most vulnerable groups in the population without affecting the leadership.

The standoff hardened in late 1997, when Saddam ordered the American members of the inspection team to leave his country, saying that they were spies. The Clinton administration threatened to use force to compel their return and beefed up U.S. military strength in the Persian Gulf.

Iraq's adamant refusal to accept renewed inspections along with the patrolling by U.S. and British aircraft of the "no-fly zones" led to increased attacks on the aircraft by Iraqi gunners. The United States and Britain reacted by bombing military targets within the country. The conflict escalated in December 1998, when some 100 such installations were either damaged or destroyed. The bombings were also used to destroy installations alleged to produce weapons of mass destruction. In 2001, the attacks were scaled back. By that time Iraqi gunners were firing surface-to-air missiles (SAMS) at the aircrafts. However, in the course of 200,000 sorties none were hit.

In August 2001 both overflights and Iraqi anti-aircraft fire increased significantly as the U.S. and Britain expanded their attacks on the country's air defense system. Saddam Hussain's determination to end the sanctions without preconditions, along with elimination of the no-fly zones as unwarranted interference in Iraq's internal affairs, generated a deadlock between the UN and its most recalcitrant member state. In December 2001 the Security Council renewed the sanctions for an additional six months, under a compromise resolution backed by the U.S. and Britain. It revised the oil-for-food program to establish a "goods review list." Items on the list that could be used for either civilian or military purposes would have to be approved by all Council members states before they could be imported into Iraq. Items not on the list could be imported without restrictions.

The September 11, 2001 attacks on mainland America changed the equation. President George Bush included Iraq in his "axis of evil" of states sponsoring terrorism as part of a global campaign against Osama bin Laden and his Al-Qaeda terrorist network. At the same time his administration began a massive buildup of military forces in the Middle East in preparation for an attack on Iraq as a part of that "axis."

The military buildup, among other factors, led Saddam to change his mind and admit the inspection team of the UN Monitoring, Verification and Inspection Commission (UNMOVIC) which was set up in 1999. The inspectors then proceeded to Iraq, and this time received greater cooperation, than in 1999, even to opening of Saddam's palaces for inspection. Subsequently, in January 2003 Hans Blix (Norway), head of the team, reported that Iraq had destroyed 40 of its Al-Samoud 2 missiles, which have a range of 93-plus miles, above UN-set limits. The government stated that the remainder were in the process of being destroyed. The team had found no evidence of weapons of mass destruction, he said. Saddam Hussain then announced a ban on production or importation of these weapons and the materials used to make them.

## America Invades

Following this development the great majority of Security Council member states favored the continuation of the inspections until either evidence of the existence of Iraqi weapons emerged or there was absolute proof to the contrary. However the Bush administration's foreign policy architects had privately determined to invade Iraq, as the only feasible means of removing Saddam Hussain as a "threat to world peace." In October 2002 Congress, with little debate, approved a resolution to allow the president "to use the armed forces of the United States as necessary to defend the national interest against the continuing threat posed by Iraq." Efforts to develop a coalition similar to that set up by the first President Bush in the Security Council, however, foundered under the determined opposition of most member states, notably Russia and long-term allies France and Germany. The Turkish parliament refused to allow the U.S. to use its bases for an attack on Iraq, and of all the Council's member states, only Britain supported an invasion and agreed to send troops.

With the buildup of 140,000 U.S. forces in various Middle Eastern bases essentially complete, President Bush issued a warning to Saddam Hussain: go into exile within 48 hours or face the consequences. There was no response, and on March 19 Anglo-American forces invaded Iraq.

There is as yet little agreement between those who argue that Saddam Hussain needed to be removed as a threat to world peace or those who feel that the U.S. invasion was an arrant violation of international law. It has also been said that by doing so, the U.S. tore apart the delicate fabric that has held the nation-state system together since the Peace of Westphalia in 1848. Other scholars have questioned the use of the "just war" theory first propounded by St. Augustine to support the U.S. invasion. But in military terms, the invasion was a textbook example of technological perfection. With control of the skies, coalition aircraft carried out pinpoint bombing raids on strategic targets; they were followed by a land assault by tanks and mobile units and then by infantry moving swiftly through the desert. Basra, Iraq's southernmost city and only seaport, was taken first. Special teams captured key oil installations before they could be sabotaged. The Iraqi capital, Baghdad, offered little resistance, perhaps on Saddam's orders or those of his military commanders. The Iraqi army simply melted into the civilian population. Many Ba'th leaders were captured or killed in the weeks that followed. Those killed included Saddam's two sons, Uday and Qusay. Ultimately Saddam himself was captured, hiding in a small subterranean chamber in a house in the village of Dujail, near Tikrit. He was held for trial in December 2005, and after intermittent delays, he was found guilty of a specific crime, the massacre of villagers in a particular location, and was sentenced to death. The death sentence was carried out in December 2006.

### Stumbling Toward Self-Government

It had taken Coalition forces eighteen days to capture Baghdad; the only slowdown came from sandstorms in the desert; there was almost no organized resistance. A terrifying amount of air and ground firepower more thoroughly destroyed Baghdad than the Mongols had. In some respects the war was somewhat internationalized, with the participation of troops from a number of states.

Iraq's misfortune was to be seen as the first stage in the Bush administration's "crusade" against the terrorism let loose in 9/11 and coincidentally to establish democratic regimes where needed in the Middle East. But as a long-time scholar and observer of the region noted, "the establishment of democracy happens indigenously or it does not happen at all. It has never been imposed on governments or nations at the point of a bayonet."[9] Since the invasion was based on faulty intelligence (or the wilful disregard of warnings in sound intelligence reports), and the invaders arrived with no long-term plan for the political and economic reconstruction of a society battered by years of crippling sanctions and international isolation, U.S. forces faced not only a hostile population but also a well-organized insurgency.

As of August 17, 2008, U.S. casualties from the war which "officially" ended in 2003 have totaled 4,332, of whom 3,465 died of insurgent action; there were over 30,000 injured. Other Coalition casualty figures include Britain (179), Italy (33), Poland (21), and Ukraine (18). Iraqi casualty figures are incomplete but, according to different sources, they could be anywhere between 100,000 and 1 million people killed. An added problem for its population is the high mortality for Iraqis who have served the occupation authorities since invasion. Working for Americans has become a "death sentence" because they are seen as collaborators, working for the enemy, i.e., the forces of occupation. Some 1,500 among them have been given asylum status and admitted to the United States, on top of the 30,000 who have been resettled in America since 2003. However, these are very small numbers in comparison to the 4 million Iraqis who fled the country due to the war and ended up as refugees mostly in the neighboring countries.

It is a strange irony, that the U.S. invasion and occupation of Iraq were foreshadowed by the observations of a British general 88 years ago, then commanding British forces as they entered Baghdad in 1917. He wrote, "Our armies do not come into your cities and lands as conquerors but as liberators." An Iraqi voter echoed these very words, with the same theme, during the January, 2005 elections for a Transitional Assembly that would govern the country under U.S. control. He said: "The future of Iraq is a line that goes through the occupation. If you ask me why I was voting, it is because I want to find something to pull me out of this mud."[10]

## THE ARAB–ISRAELI CONFLICT

Until very recently, the Arab–Israeli conflict involved two peoples: those grouped into the modern Arab states, for the most part products of European colonialism, and Israel. Israel's military superiority over its Arab neighbors seemed to remove the likelihood of another Arab–Israeli war, and the peace treaties with Jordan and Egypt were further deterrents to renewal of armed conflict. The Arab states that surround Israel, although politically new, are heirs to a proud and ancient tradition, reaching back to when Islamic–Arab civilization was far superior to

| COALITION FORCES IN IRAQ (AS OF 12/05) | |
| --- | --- |
| U.S. | 148,000 |
| Britain | 9,000 |
| South Korea | 3,600 |
| Italy | 3,000 |
| Poland | 2,400 |
| Ukraine | 1,650 |
| Netherlands | 1,345 |
| Romania | 700 |
| Denmark | 525 |
| Japan | 500 |
| Bulgaria | 480 |
| El Salvador | 380 |
| Georgia | 300 |
| Australia | 250 |
| Mongolia | 173 |
| Azerbaijan | 151 |
| Portugal | 120 |
| Latvia | 110 |
| Slovakia | 105 |
| Other countries | 421 in all |

that of the Western world. This tradition and the self-proclaimed commitment to Arab brotherhood, however, have yet to bring them together in a united front toward Israel.

A major obstacle to Arab unity is the variety of political systems that exist in the individual Arab states. These range from patriarchal absolute rule in Saudi Arabia by a ruling family to the multiparty system of Lebanon. Other Arab states reflect a variety of political systems—constitutional and patriarchal monarchies, authoritarian single-party governments, and regimes dependent on a single individual, to name a few examples. The United Arab Emirates provides one model of successful unification, mainly because the individual emirates are patriarchally ruled; in addition, aside from large expatriate work forces their populations are ethnically and linguistically similar. The Yemen Arab Republic, the other successful example, resulted from unification of the Marxist People's Republic of Yemen (South Yemen) and the tribal Arab Republic of Yemen (North Yemen). Their unification nearly collapsed in 1994 due to civil war, but the triumph of northern over southern forces and subsequent coalition government, confirmed by national elections, seem to have assured its survival. However, in 2009, a rising separatist rebellion, along with violent religious and tribal challenges to the northern-dominated central authority, threaten that unity and the stability of the country.

In the past several decades the conflict between the Arab states and Israel has shifted from an essentially external one involving sovereign entities to an Israeli-Palestinian one. In its essentials the conflict stems from opposing views of land ownership. The land in question is Palestine, ancient Judea and Samaria for Jews, claimed by modern Israel on historical, emotional, and symbolic grounds. The Jewish claim to possession is to fulfill God's original covenant with Abraham, patriarch of the ancient Jewish tribes. To the Jews, it is a sacred homeland. The modern Israelis are the returned Jews, immigrants from many lands, plus the small Jewish community that remained there during the centuries of dispersion (diaspora). The Palestinians, mostly descendants of peoples who settled there over the centuries, were formerly 80 percent Muslim and 20 percent Christian, but emigration and displacement under the Jewish state in its wars have reduced the latter to 20 percent of the population. For most of its history, the territory was ruled by outside powers—Persians, Syrians, Rome, the Byzantine Empire, and from the 1400s to 1917 by the Ottoman Empire. Under Ottoman rule it was divided into two *vilayets* (provinces) plus the separate Sanjak of Jerusalem (a more or less self-governing district). When Britain was given the League of Nations mandate over the southern vilayet, named Acre from its principal town, the British named the territory "Palestine," possibly from biblical associations with the ancient Philistine inhabitants.

During its existence as an Ottoman vilayet (province), Palestine was essentially a tranquil place with a mixed Christian-Muslim population and a small Jewish minority. The advent of Zionism, as mentioned below, brought Jews in increasing numbers there, many of them victims of Russian or Polish persecution. Few of them were skilled in agriculture or other vocational knowledge needed to build a viable Jewish state, but over time their energy and hard work, coupled with outside funding, brought into existence a number of Jewish communities. These included collective settlements called kibbutzes as well as Jewish

## ZIONISM

*Zionism* may be defined as the collective expression of the will of dispersed Jews to have their own modern homeland. This nationalist feeling was given concrete form by European Jews in the nineteenth century.

In 1882, a Jewish law student, Leon Pinsker, published *Auto-Emancipation,* a book that called on Jews, who were being pressed at the time between the twin dangers of anti-Semitism and assimilation into European society, to resist by establishing a Jewish homeland *somewhere.* Subsequently, a Viennese journalist, Theodor Herzl, published *Der Judenstaat (The Jewish State)* in 1896. Herzl argued that Jews could never hope to be fully accepted into the societies of nations where they lived; anti-Semitism was too deeply rooted. The only solution would be a homeland for immigrant Jews as a secular commonwealth of farmers, artisans, traders, and shopkeepers. In time, he said, it would become a model for all nations through its restoration of the ancient Jewish nation formed under a covenant with God.

Herzl's vision of the Zionist state would give equal rights and protection to people of other nationalities who came there. This secular view generated conflict with Orthodox Jews, who felt that only God could ordain a Jewish state and that, therefore, Zionism would have to observe the rules and practices of Judaism in establishing such a state.

neighborhoods in existing Palestinian cities. Thus an area of empty sand dunes near the city of Jaffa evolved into the bustling metropolis of Tel Aviv, which today has swallowed up Jaffa.[11]

*Arab nationalism,* slower to develop, grew out of the contacts of Arab subject peoples in the Ottoman Empire with Europeans, particularly missionary-educators sent by their various churches to work with the Christian Arab communities. It developed political overtones during World War I, when British agents such as T. E. Lawrence encouraged the Arabs to revolt against the Ottomans, their "Islamic brothers." In return, Britain promised to support the establishment of an independent Arab state in the Arab lands of the empire. An Anglo–Arab army entered Jerusalem in triumph in 1917 and Damascus in 1918, where an independent Arab kingdom was proclaimed, headed by the Emir Faisal, the leader of the revolt.

The Arab population of Palestine took relatively little part in these events, but European rivalries and conflicting commitments for disposition of the provinces of the defeated Ottoman Empire soon involved them directly in conflict over Palestine. The most important document affecting the conflict was the Balfour Declaration, a letter of British support for a Jewish homeland in Palestine written by Foreign Secretary Arthur Balfour to Lord Rothschild, a prominent Jewish banker and leader of the Zionist Organization.

Although the Zionists interpreted the statement as permission to proceed with their plans for a Jewish National Home in Palestine, neither they nor the Arabs were fully satisfied with the World War I peace settlement, in terms of the disposition of territories. The results soon justified their pessimism. The Arab kingdom of Syria was dismantled by the French, who then established a mandate over Syria under the League of Nations. The British set up a mandate over Palestine, attempting to balance support for Jewish aspirations with a commitment to develop self-government for the Arab population, in accordance with the terms of the mandate as approved by the League of Nations. The British mandate was opposed by both Jews and Arabs, the former because immigration would be limited, the latter due to the dismantling of the proposed Arab state which would have included Palestine. While some Arab leaders, notably the president of the Arab Higher Committee, which represented the Palestinian community under the terms of the mandate, put their faith in "the government of Great Britain, with its concern for the well-being of Palestinians and safeguarding of their rights," the Zionists not only encouraged immigration in violation of mandate restrictions but began smuggling arms to the Jewish communities to "protect them from Arab reprisals."[12] On their side, the Palestinians engaged in often violent protests, first against the mandatory authorities and then against the Jews. These protests culminated in the 1929 riots, and later Palestinian leaders called a general strike, the so-called "Arab Revolt" of 1936–1939, against British rule.

On its part, Britain attempted to placate both communities at various times, placing limits on Jewish immigration and in 1939 halting it entirely. World War II, with its appalling slaughter by the Germans of the Jewish population of occupied Europe, made Britain's task even more difficult. Boatloads of desperate Jews escaping Nazism were turned back, a number of them sinking while in sight of the Palestinian shore. As violence between the Jewish and Arab communities became endemic, the British decided that the mandate was unworkable. They turned over the "Palestine problem" to the newly-formed United Nations, successor to the League. Britain set May 14, 1948 as the departure date for its forces from Palestine. The UN had formed a committee, the Special Committee on Palestine (UNSCOP) in 1947 to deal with the issue, and it approved by majority vote a plan for the partition of Palestine into two states, one Arab and the other Jewish. On May 14 the last British soldier left Palestine, the Union Jack was lowered, and David Ben Gurion's Zionist Organization proclaimed the birth of the state of Israel.

Most state-to-state disputes are susceptible to arbitration and outside mediation, particularly when they involve borders or territory, but Palestine is a special case. Its location astride communication links between the eastern and western sections of the Arab world made it essential to the building of a unified Arab nation-state, the goal of Arab leaders since World War I. Its importance to Muslims as the site of one of their holiest shrines, the Dome of the Rock in Jerusalem, is underscored by Jewish control—a control made possible, in the Arab Muslim view, by the "imperialist enemies of Islam," and reinforced by the relatively lenient treatment given by an Israeli court to Jewish terrorists arrested for trying to blow up the shrines on the Dome and build a new temple on the site. Also, since they lack an outside patron, both the dispersed Palestinians and those remaining in Israel look to the Arab states as the natural champions of their cause.

Yet the Arab states have never been able to develop a coherent, unified policy toward Israel in support of the Palestinian cause. There are several reasons for this failure, including the historic rivalry of Arab leaders, the overall immaturity of the modern Arab political system, and the difficulty of distinguishing between rhetoric and fact. The Arabic language lends itself more to the former than the latter. Thus the repeated declarations

of Arab leaders that with God's help "we will drive the Jews into the sea. . . ." are not meant to be taken literally. But because rhetoric urged them to subscribe to the ideal of a single Arab nation, they were torn between the ideal of this nation and the reality of separate states. Inasmuch as their populations are mostly Muslim, a further obstacle to their coming to terms with Israel is that of disagreements within their societies over the nature and purpose of "political Islam," interpreted by many Muslims as the restoration of the fundamentals of the religion in these states. The Arab states surrounding Israel see their regimes as under attack from radical practitioners of political Islam. Israel's very existence and its development as a modern state underline their own weakness and lack of political unity.

Another reason for Arab disunity stems from the relationship of the Arab states with the Palestinians. During the British mandate, the Arab Higher Committee—the nexus of what became the Palestine national movement—aroused the anger of Arab leaders in neighboring countries by refusing to accept their authority over the committee's policies in return for financial support. After the 1948 Arab–Israeli War, the dispersal of Palestinians into Arab lands caused further conflict. To this day the Palestinians are haunted by their forced departure from their homes and villages by that event, which they call *an-Naqba* ("the catastrophe"). Further disillusionment resulted from the poor performance of Arab armies in the wars with Israel. Constantine Zurayk of the American University of Beirut expressed their shame in his book *The Meaning of Disaster:*

> Seven Arab states declare war on Zionism, stop impotent before it and turn on their heels. . . . Declarations fall like bombs from the mouths of officials at meetings of the Arab League, but when action becomes necessary, the fire is still and quiet.[13]

It should be noted that the aspirations of the Palestinians for a state of their own in Palestine were the focal point for Arab-Israeli conflict as this conflict developed after 1948. An important difference between the two communities was the degree of their organization. By the time of independence, the Israelis had developed all the necessary institutions of government plus a strong sense of national identity. The Palestinians had little sense of their identity as part of a Palestinian *nation;* they had always lived there, generation after generation, in compact self-supporting villages, authority (such as it was) held by a handful of leading families, one of whose members was the village *muhtar* (headman). A Palestinian national identity as such developed eventually, but its main cause was the establishment of a Jewish national identity and state in their midst.

The opposition of Israelis to any form of return of Palestinian refugees to their former lands, or to compensation thereof, has hardened in recent years to be essentially out of the question, especially as two intifadas and a steady diet of suicide bombings set the two communities even farther apart. This was not always the case. Even before the establishment of Israel, many prominent Jews, Zionist and non-Zionist, sought an accommodation of the two peoples. Chaim Weizmann, founder of the WZO and later Israel's first president, once expressed in a letter to a friend his belief that Palestine should be shared by the two "nations." Others, notably Dr. Judah Magnes and the brilliant theologian Martin Buber, argued tirelessly on behalf of Jewish-Arab harmony. On the eve of the UN partition resolution Buber warned: "What is really needed by each of the two peoples living one alongside the other in Palestine is self-determination, autonomy, the chance to decide for itself. But this most certainly does not mean that each is in need of a state for itself. . . . Its realization on both sides can be guaranteed within the framework of a joint bi-national socio-political entity."[14]

More recently, Uri Avnery, a prominent Zionist and Knesset (Israeli Parliament) member, writing in the afterglow of Israel's triumph over the Arab states in the 1967 Six-Day War, said, "The government [should] offer the Palestine Arabs assistance in setting up a national republic of their own . . . [which] will become the natural bridge between Israel and the Arab world."

Many scholars and experts have argued that Israel's great mistake after the war lay in not pursuing "peace of the brave" in order to provide an equitable solution for the Palestinians and establish a peaceful relationship with its defeated enemies. Aside from Moshe Dayan's famous comment to Arab leaders that "we are waiting for your telephone call" (which never came), Israel's staggering success ironically united the Palestinians of both the West Bank and Gaza against the Zionist occupation. But military success, though it enhances the ego, is seldom followed by political solutions. In that sense 1967 has been a political failure for the Jewish state. Along with two intifadas it has helped spawn Hamas, an organization as uncompromising in its hostility to Israel as is the latter in terms of security.

## Israel and the Palestinians

The effort to distinguish between a rightful Jewish "homeland" and the occupied territories gained momentum in 1977 with the formation of Peace Now, a movement initiated by army officers who felt that the government of Menachem Begin should not miss the opportunity to negotiate peace with Egypt. Peace Now gradually became the engine of the Israeli peace movement, leading public opposition to invasion of Lebanon and establishment of Jewish settlements in the occupied territories. However, Peace Now's policy of "exchanging land for peace" was rejected by the Likud Bloc after it had defeated Labor in the 1996 elections and held power in the Knesset until 1999.

Domestic political pressures, the broad sympathy of Americans for Israel, and support for the country as a dependable ally in the Middle East have been passed along from one U.S. administration to another. This innate preference has not been

helped by the position taken on the issue by the Palestine Liberation Organization (PLO), the international exponent organization of the Palestinian cause, which has sometimes resorted to terrorism. The PLO, upon its founding in 1964, issued a charter calling for the destruction of Israel and the establishment of a sovereign Palestinian Arab state. The PLO until recently was also ambivalent about its acceptance of UN *Resolutions 242* and *338,* which call for Israeli withdrawal from the West Bank and Gaza Strip as a prelude to peace negotiations.

For the first two decades of the Israeli occupation, the Palestinians who remained in the territories were largely helpless. An entire generation grew up under Israeli control, living in squalid refugee camps or towns little changed since Ottoman times and deprived of even the basic human rights guaranteed to an occupied population under international law. In December 1987, a series of minor clashes between Palestinian youths and Israeli security forces escalated into a full-scale revolt against the occupying power. This single event, called in Arabic the *intifada* (literally, "a shaking off"), has changed the context of the Israeli–Palestinian conflict more decisively than any other in recent history.

The intifada caught not only the Israelis but also the PLO by surprise. Having lost their Beirut base due to the Israeli invasion of 1982, PLO leaders found themselves in an unusual situation, identified internationally with a conflict from which they were physically separated and could not control directly or even influence to any great degree. As more and more Palestinians in the territories were caught up in the rhythm of struggle, the routine of stone-throwings, waving of forbidden Palestinian flags, demonstrations, and cat-and-mouse games with Israeli troops, the PLO seemed increasingly irrelevant to the Palestinian cause.

In view of its isolation from the intifada, the only role the PLO could play was to keep the Palestinian cause prominently focussed in the global spotlight, via the media and before international organizations. Its leader, the late Yassir Arafat, ended a meeting of the PLO National Council, the organization's executive body, in Tunis, Tunisia, with the historic statement that, in addition to formal acceptance of *Resolutions 242* and *338* as the basis for peace negotiations, the PLO would recognize Israel's right to exist. Arafat amplified the statement at a special UN General Assembly session in Geneva, Switzerland, formally accepting Israeli sovereignty over its own territory and renouncing the use of armed struggle by the PLO.

The PLO's return to the West Bank and Gaza Strip, and its reconstitution as the Palestine National Authority (PNA, known also as PA) in accordance with the Oslo Accords refocused the attention of the Arab states on the Palestine refugees, an Arab people exiled from its Arab homeland. The PA now emerged as an international political actor in its own right. Nonetheless, its leadership faced the prospect of having to put years of armed struggle behind it and concentrate on state-building. This would be difficult under ordinary circumstances, but in the PA's case it would have to be done in ways acceptable to Israel and the United States as Israel's principal sponsor.

Although evidence of five Israeli-Arab wars and periodic border conflicts suggest that this conflict will remain localized. The Palestinian people, unlike the Kurds, the world's other stateless people, have come to weigh heavily on the conscience of the world. Mohammed Shadid contends that "Palestine is the conscience of the Arab world and a pulsating vein of the Islamic

## THE BALFOUR DECLARATION

The text of the Balfour Declaration is as follows: "I have much pleasure in conveying to you on behalf of His Majesty's Government the following declaration of sympathy with Jewish Zionist aspirations which has been submitted to and approved by the Cabinet:

"His Majesty's Government view with favor the establishment in Palestine of a National Home for the Jewish people and will use their best endeavors to facilitate the achievement of this project, it being clearly understood that nothing shall be done which may prejudice the civil and religious rights of existing non-Jewish communities in Palestine or the rights and political status enjoyed by Jews in any other country."

world . . . perhaps the only issue where Arab nationalism and Islamic revivalism are joined."[15] In 1995, Libya's leader, Muammar al-Qadhafi, the Arab world's most fervent advocate of Arab unity since Gamal Abdel Nasser of Egypt, abruptly expelled 1,500 Palestinian workers that were long residents in his country. He did so, he said, to protest the Palestinian–Israeli peace agreements, which he called a sellout of Arab interests.

Libya is not the only Arab state affected by the Palestinians and their goal of return to their homeland. Israel's 1982 invasion of Lebanon, formulated and led by Ariel Sharon with the concurrence of Prime Minister Begin, was intended to drive the PLO leadership out of Beirut. It succeeded in that goal but led to the collapse of the Begin government after Christian militiamen, allied with Israelis, massacred Palestinians in the Sabra and Shatila refugee camps. An internal committee of inquiry placed the blame for the massacre on Sharon, because he had not prevented it. The other unintended result was the emergence in southern Lebanon of an anti-Israeli guerrilla force, Hizbullah, which eventually forced the Israelis to withdraw after years of attrition and guerrilla attacks that seriously affected troop morale.

An accomplishment of sorts was the convening by the first President Bush of direct peace talks in Madrid, Spain, between Israeli, Arab and Palestinian representatives in 1991. As the second President Bush would do years later with his "road map to peace," the first Bush declared in a speech that the time had come to put an end to the conflict. In international terms the time was right, with the collapse of the Soviet Union leaving the United States as the sole power capable of moving these intractable opponents toward an equitable solution. For a number of reasons however, the Madrid talks produced no results.

## Oslo and After

A major breakthrough took place in September 1993, as negotiations conducted in secret by Palestinian and Israeli negotiators in Norway, a neutral country, resulted in a historic agreement. The agreement, although it fell far short of Palestinian objectives of an independent state, provided for Israeli recognition of Palestinian territorial rights and acceptance of a Palestinian "mini-state" in the Gaza Strip and an area around the West Bank city of Jericho, which would be its capital. It would be governed by an elected Council and would have limited self-rule for a five-year transitional period, after which discussions would begin on its permanent status.

After many false starts and delays that were caused by extremist violence on both sides, Israel and the PLO reached an interim agreement for additional land transfers to Palestinian self-rule in 1995. However, the election of Benjamin Netanyahu as Israel's prime minister in that year put a hold on the process. Netanyahu did meet with Arafat at the Wye River Plantation in Maryland in October 1998, with President Bill Clinton and Jordan's King Hussein as mediators. Arafat and Netanyahu signed the "Wye Agreement," which provided for three more land transfers and a "safe passage route" for Palestinians between the Gaza Strip and the West Bank. In addition, 750 Palestinian prisoners held in Israel were released, bringing the number to 7,000 since 1993 although Netanyahu later put a moratorium on the implementation of these provisions.

Ehud Barak's election as Israeli prime minister in May 1999 breathed new life into the peace process after a long hiatus under Netanyahu. In January 2000, Barak met with Syrian foreign minister Farouk al-Atassi in Shepherdstown, West Virginia, in a renewed effort to bring about a Syrian–Israeli peace treaty. President Clinton served as moderator and mediator. However, Israel and Syria remained far apart on issues of mutual concern, notably the control of the Golan Heights, and the talks adjourned without agreement. The renewal of violent Israeli–Palestinian confrontation in 2000 made any further moves toward peace between Israel and its last hostile state neighbor impossible.

Barak brought partial peace with Lebanon by ordering the withdrawal of Israeli forces from their self-declared "security zone" just inside the Lebanese border in April 2000, ahead of schedule. Peacekeeping units of the United Nations Interim Force in Lebanon (UNIFIL) assumed the responsibility for border control, leaving only Shab'a Farms contested between the two countries. (See Lebanon Country Report). This contested area was going to become a serious point of contention between Israel and Lebanon and will contribute to yet another war in 2006.

## THE ISRAEL–HEZBOLLAH WAR OF 2006

The war known also as "the 2006 Israel–"Hezbollah War" or "the Second Lebanon War," started when Israeli forces entered Lebanon on July 14 following Hezbollah's rocket attacks on Northern Israel and incursion into the Israeli side of the border fence, killing three soldiers and abducting two others. Hezbollah, the "Party of God," is a Lebanese paramilitary group and a political party with representation in the legislature and the government. Its two immediate aims in the conflict with Israel are the return of all remaining Lebanese territory (Shebaa Farms) still controlled by Israel and the release of all Lebanese prisoners. It also supports the struggle of the Palestinians against the Israeli occupation and is known to have close ties with Iran and Syria.

The government of Ehud Olmert reacted to Hezbollah's actions by bombarding most of Lebanon after it became evident that Hezbollah's forces were intractable. The response included also a ground invasion and an air and naval blockade of Lebanon. Over the 34-day war, Hezbollah responded to the Israeli by engaging the enemy ground forces and by sustaining a daily and intense barrage of rockets fired into Israel. The casualties included the death of around 1,000 Lebanese—mostly civilians—500 Hezbollah fighters, 118 Israeli soldiers and 43 Israeli civilians. Around 1 million Lebanese civilians and some 300,000 Israelis were temporarily displaced by the conflict. Most of Lebanon's infrastructure—electricity and water plants, roads and bridges—were heavily damaged by Israel's bombs.

None of the protagonists could win the war; however, Hezbollah's ability to survive the Israeli air and ground assault, while inflicting significant damage on the Israeli Defense Forces (IDF), led it to claim victory after Israel agreed to a ceasefire resolution passed by the Security Council on August 14. The resolution, however, was approved by the Israelis because it called for the deployment of an expanded UNIFIL peacekeeping force of 15,000 individuals in order to deny the Lebanese territory south of the Litani River to both Israeli and Lebanese "hostile activities of any kind." In their respective countries, Hezbollah's political stature increased tremendously, while the

Olmert government and its military high officers were fiercely criticized for having rushed into war, for not having planned it well, and for having underestimated Hezbollah's military capabilities. An investigation commission, the Winograd Commission, established by the Israeli government, acknowledged in its final report "serious failures of the decision-making process."

# ISRAEL AND THE PALESTINIANS

With Israeli–Arab relations in a state of temporary peace, the focus of Middle East conflict centered on the Palestinian population of the occupied West Bank and Gaza Strip. Following Barak's election, several steps were taken to implement the 1993 Oslo Agreement. Another 12 percent of the West Bank was turned over to the Palestine National Authority in late 1999 and early 2000. In the summer of 2000, Barak met with PA head Yassir Arafat at Camp David, Maryland, with President Clinton again serving as moderator. In what seemed at the time to be a generous proposal, Barak offered to turn over 94 percent of the West Bank, along with administrative control over the Dome of the Rock (exclusive of the Wailing Wall) and the Old City of Jerusalem, with its separate Jewish, Muslim, Christian, and Armenian quarters. Arafat, for his part, agreed that Jewish settlements outside of Jerusalem built illegally on Palestinian land would be exempt from Palestinian control. However, he insisted that the "right of return" of dispossessed Palestinians to their former homes and villages in what is now Israel be included in the agreement. This right of return has been an article of faith for them since the establishment of the Israeli state.

In retrospect, it seems doubtful that Barak's proposals would have been acceptable to the Israeli public and given the necessary approval by a bitterly divided Knesset. But in any case, they were doomed by Arafat's insistence on the right of refugee return. Subsequently, in 2001, Barak was defeated in elections for the office of prime minister, called prematurely after several no-confidence votes in the Knesset. His successor, former general Ariel Sharon, said he would not be bound by the proposals and would consider only interim agreements with the PA, with no additional transfers of land to the Palestinians.

## Intifada II

A recent profile of Sharon by a respected Israeli journalist described him as "as a man with no moral brakes; as Defense Minister and architect of the Lebanon invasion he said he had no idea that such a thing (as the massacres at the Sabra and Shatila refugee camps) could take place; he is known for deftly pretending to be doing what he is not doing."[16]

Intifada II (also called the Al-Aqsa Intifada, from its immediate cause) broke out in September 2000, after Sharon made a widely-publicized visit to the Islamic shrines of the Dome of the Rock in Jerusalem. Although he was not a member of the government at that time, he said his visit was peaceful but was intended to emphasize Israel's right to sovereignty over its entire territory. But the visit enraged the Palestinians, who also hated Sharon for his indirect role in the massacres of Palestinians in the Sabra and Shatila refugee camps in Lebanon in 1982. It was as if a shoe had been flung in their faces.

Intifada II also grew from the Palestinian conviction that Israel had no intention of honoring its commitment to a Palestinian sovereign state. From a psychoanalytic viewpoint it also drew on Palestinians' feelings of poor self-image—a people "despised and oppressed, without honor, rights and self-worth, and dependent on Israel for jobs, limited in their movements, and now cut off from each other by an Israeli concrete and barbed wire wall."[17]

Intifada II was marked by greater Palestinian use of lethal weaponry, including mortars and missiles, and the emergence of suicide bombers. The latter are called *shaheed* ("martyr") because they willingly strap explosives around themselves and blow themselves up in public places, all for the liberation of Palestine. This suicide bombing campaign, developed mainly by the militant Palestinian organizations Hamas and Islamic Jihad, seriously destabilized Israeli society. On the Israeli side, demolition of homes suspected of harboring militants (now discontinued), periodic military incursions and targeting of Palestinian leaders for missile strikes, along with the frequent closure of borders, have had a devastating effect on the Palestinian society and economy.

In May 2003, President Bush for the first time publicly stated his commitment to the establishment of a Palestinian state alongside Israel. His view was codified in his "road map to peace," which would require commitments and concessions by both sides. The Palestinians would halt suicide bombings and other attacks on Israelis, and in return Israel would stop new settlement construction in the occupied West Bank, release Palestinian prisoners and withdraw its forces.

However the Bush administration, already preoccupied with Iraq, did not put its full support behind that "road map to peace" and bring it to fruition. After Israel began targeting Hamas leaders and other Palestinian militants for assassination, killing Hamas spiritual leader Shaykh Ahmad Yasin and his successor in missile strikes, the Bush administration described the action as "unhelpful." However the U.S. subsequently vetoed a UN Security Council resolution which would have condemned them as violations of international law and the Geneva Convention governing the rights of peoples under occupation.

Israel's construction of a "security fence" that will eventually stretch for 370 miles along the border with the West Bank has created an additional obstacle on the road map to peace. It was described by Israeli officials as a necessary barrier to infiltration by suicide bombers and other attacks on its territory by Palestinian militants. But the net effect will be to isolate Palestinians from their farms, olive groves, even schools and hospitals, separating village from village as it sliced through Palestinian territory. Suits filed with the World court to halt its completion were unsuccessful, as Israeli lawyers argued that it was essential to national security. However the Israeli cabinet, under prodding by the Supreme Court, approved in February 2005 an altered route that would incorporate 7 percent of the West Bank into its territory as opposed to the 16 percent envisaged in the original (2003) route. Even so, the fence has already created Palestinian enclaves separated from one another and surrounded by Jewish settlements linked by exclusive highways "off limits" to Palestinians.

One of the few bright spots in this dismal conflict was the evacuation of Israeli military forces and Jewish settlers from the Gaza Strip in late 2005. Despite outcries from the settler movement and a sort of "color war" within Israel between proponents of evacuation (blue t-shirts) and opponents wearing orange ones, the settler removal was accomplished without violence. Along with Gaza four small West Bank settlements were returned to Palestine control, the Gaza border with Egypt opened, and border control turned over to Egyptian troops. For the first time in 38 years, Gaza's people could inhale the fresh air of freedom. However, that would not last, as that small enclave—the most densely populated piece of land in the world—turned into a a vast jail for 1.5 million people after Hamas took control of it following its 2006 legislative elections.

The Israeli withdrawal from Gaza and removal of all Jewish settlements there has left its economy in shambles. By 2006 per capita income in Gaza had dropped by one-third, to $600, and despite foreign aid of $1 billion, highest per capita in the world, the poverty rate had doubled.

Sharon's success in accomplishing the peaceful withdrawal of the settlers from Gaza and his formation of the centrist party Kadima suggested that he would follow in Rabin's footsteps and fashion a solution to the conflict acceptable to both Israelis and Palestinians. Unfortunately he suffered severe strokes in December 2005 and January 2006, and at this writing he remains in a coma.

The second important development was the 2006 Palestinian elections for a new parliament. Unexpected by most observers, Hamas won 76 seats to 43 for the late Yassir Arafat's Fatah, which had dominated Palestinian politics for half a century in various guises. The rise of Hamas, an organization whose charter commits to non-recognition and the eventual destruction of the Jewish state, placed Israel and the United States as its principal sponsor in an awkward position. Initially, the Israeli government transferred $55 million in customs duties and tax payments to the Palestine National Authority as it had done in past years. It stopped the transfers after Hamas came to power in March, 2006. This had a catastrophic effect on the Palestinian economy. Other outside funding also stopped, consisting of $290 million from UNRWA, $227 million from the United States, $197 million from the European Union, and $249 million from other European country donors.

The contest for power between Hamas and the Fatah government of President Mahmoud Abbas took another twist in mid-2007 when Hamas activists seized control of Gaza. This action effectively separated the two parts of the already-truncated Palestinian state-in-process. In addition to the hardships already imposed on Palestinians by the cutoff in funding, some 6,000 of them who had left Gaza for Egypt for medical care or education were stranded at the Rafah border crossing. It had been closed by Fatah after the Hamas takeover in Gaza. Eventually Israel resumed its transfer of funds, as a humanitarian gesture, and some foreign aid from the European Union and the United States resumed in October 2007, fifteen months after it stopped. The resumption coincided with the takeover of the West Bank government by Fatah.

However, all assistance stopped once again when Israel started a major military offensive against Gaza on December 27, 2008 with the claimed aim of stopping the firing of rockets into its territory. The 22 day deadly and destructive assault—there was almost no Palestinian resistance—left about 1,400 Palestinians dead (mostly civilians) and 13 Israeli dead. According to a UN report, the military campaign, which lasted until January 18, destroyed or damaged more than 50,000 homes, 800 industrial properties, 200 schools, 39 mosques and two churches. As a result of the destruction, some 50,000 Gazans became homeless and 400,000 where left without running water.

Israel defended this vast and destructive campaign as the appropriate response to the thousands of rockets fired against its civilian population from Gaza (some 12,000 rockets and mortars between 2000 and 2008, with close to 3,000 in 2008). In spite of this claim of legitimate defense, many international organizations and human rights groups have called for an investigation of probable war crimes committed by the Israeli army and its commanders. The accusations were based on witness and expert accounts of facts, and on the unlawful use of some weapons, such as phosphorus bombs. Also, a group of Israeli soldiers who took part in the assault declared in a report in July 2009 that the Israeli army has committed widespread abuses against Palestinian civilians under "permissive" rules of engagement.[18]

By August 2009, rocket firing incidents had drastically diminished for a variety of reasons, including the fear of another Israeli onslaught, the discrediting of Hamas in the mind of Palestinians because of the devastation is has brought on them, the tightening of the blockade of Gaza by the Israeli army, and the birth of a resistance movement to Hamas, known as Junud Ansar Allah (Soldiers of the Companions of God), which claimed that Hamas was not implementing Islamic rule in Gaza and needed to be replaced by, On August 15–16, an assault by Hamas forces on the group led to many deaths, including the group's leader Abdul-Latif Moussa.

By the summer of 2009, Hamas rule in Gaza has thus been shaken by the tightened Israeli security measures and the winter offensive, as well as the rapidly deteriorating social and economic conditions throughout the strip. These developments and others have pushed Hamas and the government of Mahmoud Abbas to open talks for an eventual government of national unity, which could take advantage of the American-led push for new peace settlement negotiations with Israel.

## THE U.S. AT WAR

Since September 11, 2001, the U.S. has been in a state of warfare centered in Mahan's "land island" of the Middle East and ranging from outright war (in Iraq) to an unclear state of conflict against adversaries whom the Bush administration collectively terms "terrorists." On September 11 members of this shadowy group, all from various Middle East Arab countries, hijacked American commercial airliners and flew them into the World Trade Center in New York and the Pentagon in Washington D.C., causing significant loss of life and enormous property damage. The management of this and later terrorist actions elsewhere has been traced to an individual and the terrorist network which he founded, organized and still leads, albeit from hiding. His name, Osama Bin Laden, and the organization he leads, Al-Qaeda ("The Base," in Arabic) were unknown to nearly all Americans before September 11. The two today have not only become familiar to Americans but are associated with terrorist violence throughout the world.

Bin Laden is a member of a wealthy Saudi Arabian family originally from the Hadhramaut, in southern Yemen. His father made a fortune as a contractor, much of it in the service of the Saudi royal family. For unclear reasons Osama broke with his family instead of continuing in its various businesses, and joined the *mujahideen* ("freedom fighters") opposing the Soviet invasion of Afghanistan. Out of that experience grew Al-Qaeda, a network of terrorists seeking to overthrow governments they perceived to be repressive and corrupt, and in the case of the United States working to destroy Islam.

Thus far Al-Qaeda has not successfully replicated September 11, in this country, but it is associated with violent actions elsewhere, notably Spain, Britain, Algeria, Mauritania, and Morocco. The belief that Bin Laden is based somewhere in Afghanistan (or tribal Pakistan) led the U.S. and NATO forces to launch war against the then-ruling group in Afghanistan, the Taliban, which are presumably associated with Al-Qaeda. The war continues as of this writing, with 17,000 new American troops committed by President Barak Obama. However, the Taliban challenge became even deadlier by the summer of 2000 as more U.S. and European troops were killed. By mid-August 2009, the U.S. casualties totalled 763.

# AT WAR IN IRAQ

As noted earlier in this essay, the United States engaged in military action in the Middle East for the first time on a major scale with the 1991 Gulf War. The sequence of events since that war, and particularly the conviction held by the second Bush administration that Saddam Hussain was developing weapons of mass destruction (chemical, nuclear and biological) provided the necessary justification for a U.S. invasion to overthrow the Iraqi leader. In retrospect this invasion is likely to have been the greatest blunder in the history of American foreign policy. The administration proceeded despite warnings from numerous reliable sources that the weapons did not exist, an invasion would be counterproductive and would be better served by diplomacy or UN action. There was a total lack of long-range planning for a Saddam-less future for Iraq. Disregarding all these warnings, the invasion was launched in 2003. In a textbook example of effective military technology, the country was invaded and occupied in a very short time. The only delays were caused by sandstorms. Expectations were that with Saddam's overthrow, Iraq would quickly right itself and become a model democracy in the heart of the Arab world.

Iraq is far from reaching this goal. In the absence of a strongman on the Saddam Hussein model who would restore order and establish firm central authority under his leadership, the continued presence of U.S. military forces and long-established divisions among the various groups comprising Iraqi society remain serious obstacles to national unity. In fact, by the end of 2006 the level of sectarian violence and attacks against and the occupation forces reached such a high level that the worst was feared. In that context, President Bush announced on January 10, 2007 a controversial decision to send more than 20,000 additional troops to quell the invigorated insurgency and sectarian killings. His decision went against what most of his top civilian and military advisers had recommended. In the long run, the "surge", along with several other factors, helped diminish violence, but did not resolve the political tensions in Iraq, which threaten to undo the precarious stability.

Bush's successor, President Barak Obama, announced in February 2009 that all U.S. combat brigades will be out of Iraq by August 2010 and all U.S. troops by the end of 2011. In the meantime, U.S. troops started retreating into military bases, leaving most of the security work to the Iraqi security personnel. However, on August 17, 2009, the Iraqi government announced that it may organize a national referendum on the U.S. troop withdrawal which people may wish to happen earlier than planned by President Obama, in spite of yet another spike in violence in the summer of 2009.

# NOTES

1. Charles C. Mann, *1491: New Revelations of the Americas Before Columbus* (New York: Knopf, 2005), pp. 176–177.
2. President Bush stated recently that "I'm surely not going to jutify war based on God. Nevertheless I pray that I will be as good a messenger of His Will as possible." Quoted in Ali A. Allawi, *The Occupation of Iraq* . . . (New Haven: Yale University Press, 2007, p. 9.
3. Terence O'Donnell, *Garden of the Brave in War* (New York: Ticknor and Fields, 1980), p. 19, states that in visits to remote Iranian villages, he was told by informants that the Arabs never washed, went around naked, and ate lizards.
4. After the Gulf War and the failed Shi'a uprising against the regime, some thousands of Shi'as and Kurds were massacred and buried in mass graves that were unearthed after the 2003 U.S. invasion (Allawi, *op.cit.*, pp. 141–144).
5. *Ibid.*, quoted on p. 20.
6. Stephen R. Grummon, *The Iran-Iraq War: Islam Embattled,* The Washington Papers/92, Vol. X (New York: Praeger, 1982), p. 10.
7. *The Christian Science Monitor* (September 23, 1987).
8. Mahjoob Zweiri, "Iran's Presence in Iraq: New Realties?", Iranian Studies Unit, Center for Strategic Studies-University of Jordan, 2007. Online at www.jcss.org/UploadPolling/246.pdf
9. Gen. Stanley Maude, quoted in Anthony Shadid, *Night Draws Near: Iraq's People in the Shadow of America's War* (New York: Henry Holt, 2005), p. 388.
10. *Ibid.*, p. 396.
11. Adam LeBor, *City of Oranges* . . . (New York: W.W. Norton, 2007) provides a vivid portrait of Jaffa, "the Bride of Palestine" and the harmonious coexistence there of Jewish and Arab communities before 1948. The Shamouli oranges grown there were famed the world over for their sweet juicy flavor.
12. Quoted in Sari Nusseibeh, *Once Upon a Country: A Palestinian Life* (New York: Farrar, Straus & Giroux, 2007, p. 28.
13. Constantine Zurayk, *The Meaning of Disaster,* Beirut, 1956. p. 2.
14. Martin Buber, *A Land of Two Peoples,* (The University of Chicago Press, 2005), p. 199.
15. Mohammed Shadid, *The United States and the Palestinians,* (New York: St. Martin Press, 1981), p. 195.
16. David Shipler, *New York Times Week in Review,* June 1, 2003.
17. Avner Falk, *Fratricide in the Holy Land: A Psychoanalytic View of the Arab-Israeli Conflict* (Madison: University of Wisconsin Press, 2004).
18. "Israel Soldiers Speak Out On Gaza," BBC news online, July 15, 2009. URL http://news.bbc.co.uk/2/hi/middle_east/8149464.stm

# The Middle East: Heartland of Islam

## ISLAM IN FERMENT

"The world no barrier to God,
He is visible in all that exists,
Remove yourself from yourself and Him,
Let Him speak to you as to Moses, from
    the burning bush"

Mehmed Esad Dede[1]

**A**s a nation, the United States has long been involved in the Middle East, the "heartland" of Islam and origin of the religion of the majority of its peoples, namely Islam. The first recognition of America's independence outside of Europe was granted by an Islamic ruler, the Sultan of Morocco, and the formation of the U.S. Navy resulted from trade interference and conflicts with the corsairs of the Muslim North African regencies of Algiers, Tunis and Tripoli. Missionaries from various denominations were sent by their churches to found schools and hospitals for their fellow-Christians living under Ottoman Islamic rule throughout the 19th century, and one American, a teacher, became a martyr in Iran during the struggles of Iranians to limit the power of their rulers under a constitution. American pilgrims journeyed to Palestine and its capital city Jerusalem in large numbers before and after the Civil War, and among other authors Mark Twain based his book *Innocents Abroad* on his travels there, selling half a million copies "right along with the Bible."[2]

However, interest in saving Christian souls and finding their Christian roots in the region was not usually accompanied by a similar effort by Americans to gain an understanding of the religion or culture of their hosts.[3] The United States played little or no part in the political restructuring of the region after the defeat and demise of the Ottoman empire after World War I, and the generation that came of age in World War II was similarly uninformed. Young American GIs on their way to victory or death in Italy passed through North Africa in significant numbers. They observed these one-time corsair powers as hot, dusty places where men in robes like bedsheets, turbans or red fezzes on their heads, sat around small tables in fly-blown cafes drinking tea in small glasses. These men spoke a strange guttural language accompanied by much waving of hands and shouting.

This naïve stereotype was supplemented periodically by an action that seemed strange to us as visitors, due to its repetition. Five times a day, what would be heard the *azan*, the Islamic call to prayer. It is universally observed, if not acted upon, but five times a day the same message booms from the throats of the *muezzins*, professional "prayer-callers," often supplemented by loudspeakers or megaphones. The message is simple: "God is Great! I testify that there is no God but God! I testify that Muhammad is the Messenger of God!" It is a rallying cry and order not only to the majority of Middle Easterners but to nearly half the world's population, believers in God, God's Holy Book, and God's Messenger or Prophet of Islam.

(United Nations Photo (UN143185))

The Middle East did not make a real impact on the American consciousness until 1979, when the followers of the Ayatollah Khomeini seized the U.S. Embassy in Teheran and held its occupants hostage for more than a year. The extent to which fundamentalist Shi'a Muslims would follow Khomeini (image on placards) was little recognized before this event.

## ISLAMIC ORIGINS

Islam, the third and youngest of the world's three great monotheistic religions after Judaism and Christianity, means "submission" or "surrender" in Arabic, its basic language. It developed among a particular people, the Arabs, living as many of them do today on the Arabian Peninsula. Fourteen centuries ago they were mostly illiterate, and more importantly they lacked any formal religion except for belief in natural powers such as the wind and rain. They were also outsiders, not subject to any higher authority other than that of the chiefs of the various tribes they belonged to.

All this would change in the seventh century A.D., when a merchant named Muhammad had an incredible religious experience. He lived in the small but important trading city of Mecca,

# THE QUR'AN: THE HOLY BOOK OF ISLAM

Muslims believe that the Qur'an is the literal Word of God and that Muhammad was chosen to receive God's Word through the Angel Gabriel as a *rasul* (messenger). But the Qur'an does not cancel out the Bible and Torah, which preceded it. The Qur'an is viewed, rather, as providing a corrective set of revelations for these previous revelations from God, which Muslims believe have been distorted or not followed correctly. To carry out God's Word, as set down in the Qur'an, requires a constant effort to create the ideal Islamic society, one "that is imbued with Islamic ideals and reflects as perfectly as possible the presence of God in His creation."*

The Qur'an was revealed to Muhammad over the 22-year period of his ministry (A.D. 610–632). The revelations were of varying lengths and were originally meant to be committed to memory and recited on various occasions, in particular the daily prayers. Even today, correct Qur'anic practice requires memorization and recitation; during the fasting month of Ramadan, one section per day should be recited aloud.

In its original form, the Qur'an was either committed to memory by Muhammad's listeners or written down by one or more literate scribes, depending upon who was present at the revelation. The scribes used whatever materials were at hand: "paper, leather, parchment, stones, wooden tablets, the shoulder-blades of oxen or the breasts of men."** The first authoritative version was compiled in the time of the third caliph, Uthman, presumably on parchment. Since then, the Holy Book has been translated into many other languages as Islam has spread to include non-Arab peoples.

All translations stem from Uthman's text. It was organized into 114 *suras* (chapters), with the longest at the beginning and the shortest at the end. (The actual order of the revelations was probably the reverse, since the longer ones came mostly during Muhammad's period in Medina, when he was trying to establish guidelines for the community.)***

Many of the revelations provide specific guides to conduct or social relationships:

*When ye have performed the act of worship, remember Allah sitting, standing and reclining. . . . Worship at fixed times hath been enjoined on the believers. . . .*

(*Sura IV*, 103)

*Establish worship at the going down of the sun until the dark of night, and at dawn. Lo! The recital of the Qur'an at dawn is ever witnessed.*

(*Sura XVII*, 78–79)

*Make contracts with your slaves and spend of your own wealth that God has given you upon them. . . .*

(*Sura XXIV*, 33)

*If you fear that you will be dishonest in regard to these orphan girls, then you may marry from among them one, two, three or four. But if you fear you will not be able to do justice among them, marry only one.*

(*Sura IV*, 3)

Much of the content of the Qur'an is related to the ethical and moral. It is an Arab Qur'an, given to Arabs "in clear Arabic tongue" (*Sura XLI*, 44) and characterized by a quality of style and language that is essentially untranslatable. Muslim children, regardless of where they live, learn it in Arabic, and only then may they read it in their own language, and then always accompanied by the original Arabic version. Recitals of selections from the Qur'an are a feature of births, marriages, funerals, festivals, and other special events and are extraordinarily effective, whether or not the listener understands Arabic.****

* Peter Awn, "Faith and Practice," in Marjorie Kelly, ed., *Islam: The Religious and Political Life of a World Community* (New York: Praeger, 1984), pp. 2–7.
** *The Qur'an, The First American Version*, Translation and Commentary by T.B. Irving (Brattleboro, VT: Amana Books, 1985), Introduction, XXVII.
*** On this topic, see Fazlur Rahman, *Major Themes of the Qur'an* (Chicago: Bibliotheca Islamica, 1980), *passim.*
**** "The old preacher sat with his waxen hands in his lap and uttered the first Surah, full of the soft warm coloring of a familiar understanding. . . . His listeners followed the notation of the verses with care and rapture, gradually seeking their way together . . . like a school of fish following a leader, out into the deep sea." Lawrence Durrell, *Mountolive* (London: Faber and Faber, 1958), p. 265.

in southwest Arabia, and was well-respected as a mediator in disputes. In fact his nickname was al-Amin:, "the Just." It was his practice from time to time to retire to a cave in the hills outside Mecca to meditate. One evening while he was meditating there he received the first of many revelations from God, given him by the Angel Gabriel. These revelations form the basis for the new faith which he preached and propagated among his people. At first the revelations were given orally, but after his death they were written down in book form as the Qur'an, the Holy Book of Islam.

During Muhammad's lifetime, the various revelations he received were used to guide his followers along the path of God. The Arabs followed traditional religions in Muhammad's time, worshipping many gods. Muhammad taught belief in one God—Allah—and in the Word of God sent down to him as messenger. For this reason, Muhammad is considered the Prophet of Islam.

Muhammad's received revelations plus his own teachings issued to instruct his followers make up the formal religious system known as Islam. The word *Islam* is Arabic and has been translated variously as "submission," or "surrender" (i.e., to God's will). Those who receive and accept the Word of God as transmitted to Muhammad and set down in the Qur'an are called Muslims.

The basic sources of Islam are the Qur'an, the *hadith* and *sunnah* (sayings and deeds of Muhammad), the consensus of the community (*ijma'*), and inference or understanding by analogy (*qiyas*). The Qur'an, as the Word of God revealed to Muhammad, is the primary source, and as such it is considered divine, eternal and immutable. Its 114 Suras (chapters) were revealed to Muhammad over a 22-year period and were not set down in book form until long after his death. They were put together by scribes in the period of the Caliph Uthman, and this text is still considered the original version.

Issues and problems not specifically addressed in the Qur'an are dealt with in the collected sayings and decisions of Muhammad. Since many of them derive from oral reports and were not collected until centuries later, inevitably what the Prophet said or did may have errors. It was not until the late ninth century A.D. that an authoritative collection, the Six Books, was completed.

The third source, consensus, was used initially in the selection of caliphs as noted on page 20. Increasingly, and especially for Shi'a Muslims, consensus has come to mean decisions or opinions rendered by religious authorities.

The fourth source, inference by analogy, is used rarely and only when no clear examples are found in the Qur'an or the hadith and there is no agreement or consensus on an issue. It is similar to the use of precedent in Anglo-Saxon legal tradition.

Islam is essentially a simple faith. Five basic duties are required of the believer; they are often called the Five Pillars because they are the foundations of the House of Islam. They are:

1. The confession of faith (*shahada*): "I testify that there is no God but God, and Muhammad is the Messenger of God."
2. Prayer (*salat*), required five times daily, facing in the direction of Mecca, the holy city.
3. Alms giving (*zakat*), a tax or gift of not less than 2½ percent of one's income, to poor.
4. Fasting (*sawm*) during the daylight hours in the month of Ramadan, the month of Muhammad's first revelations.
5. Pilgrimage (*haj*), required at least once in one's lifetime, to the House of God in Mecca, for those who can.

It is apparent from the above description that Islam has many points in common with Judaism and Christianity. All three are monotheistic religions, having a fundamental belief in one God. Muslims believe that Muhammad was the "seal of the Prophets," the last messenger and recipient of revelations. But they also believe that God revealed Himself to other inspired prophets, from Abraham, Moses, and other Old Testament (Hebrew Bible) figures down through history, including Jesus Christ. However, Muslims part company with Christians over the divinity of Jesus as the Son of God; the Resurrection of Jesus; and the tripartite division into Father, Son, and Holy Ghost or Spirit.

Although Muhammad is in no way regarded as divine by Muslims, his life is considered a model for their own lives. His *hadith* ("teachings" or "sayings") that were used to supplement the Qur'an revelations (or to deal with specific situations when no revelation was forthcoming) have served as guides to Muslim conduct since the early days of Islam. The Qur'an, the hadith and the sunnah together provide an Islamic code of conduct for the believers.

The importance of Muhammad's role in Islam cannot be overemphasized. Among Muslims, his name is used frequently in conversation or written communication, always followed

by "Peace Be Unto Him" (PBUH). A death sentence imposed on the writer Salman Rushdie by Iran's revolutionary leader Ayatollah Khomeini resulted from an unflattering portrait of Muhammad in Rushdie's novel *The Satanic Verses* (1988). And an Israeli woman's depiction of Muhammad as a pig writing in the Qur'an, on a poster displayed in Hebron, roused a storm of protest throughout the Muslim world. Because the pig is considered an unclean animal by both Muslims and Jews, she was arrested by Israeli authorities and sentenced to prison for "harming religious sensibilities."[4]

The Five Pillars are not only required to be observed by Muslims, they are also specified in the Qur'an, even as to how they should be performed. The Confession of Faith (*Shahada*) is all that is required of a non-Muslim to become a convert. The ritual of prayer expands on the confession of faith, and its opening prayer comes directly from the first *Sura* ("chapter") of the Holy Book. Thereafter at each session the believers follow a set of ritual kneelings (*rak'a*) and prostrations until the head has touched the floor. After each prayer the following creed is recited: "Peace be on thee, O Prophet! And the mercy of God and his blessings. Peace be on us and the righteous servants of God! I bear witness that none deserves to be worshipped but God, and I bear witness that Muhammad is His servant and apostle."

Almsgiving (*zakat*), the third Pillar of Islam, is enjoined upon the believer in the same Sura as that of prayer (Sura 31.2-5) Since God is the owner of all things, it is each Muslim's obligation to manage money and resources according to His will. This explains why Islam forbids the charging of interest and usury. However almsgiving by the wealthy for the benefit of the poor and needy may take the form of a permanent charitable donation (*waqf*) or endowment for the upkeep of a public institution such as a mosque, school, library or hospital. In general it should consist of not less than 2.5 percent of one's income.

Fasting (*sawm*), the fourth Pillar of Islam, is obligatory for Muslims in Ramadan, the ninth month of the Islamic calendar (see Box). God's first revelation to Muhammad was given on the 27th of that month, which is called *Leilat el-Qadr* ("Night of Power"). Sura 97 of the Qur'an explains: "The Night of Power is better than a thousand months. Therein come down the angels and the Spirit, by God's permission . . ."

It is a thirty-day fasting period, which begins, and ends, when a white thread cannot be distinguished from a black one. During the daylight hours Muslims must abstain from eating, drinking, smoking, sexual intercourse, even taking medicines. The end of the day's fast is called the *Iftar*, and at that time dinner may be served. The great value of the Ramadan fast is the discipline it imposes on the believers, helping them become more conscious of their dependence on God and more aware of the needs, the hunger and thirst of the poor.

Pilgrimage (*Haj*), the fifth Pillar, is incumbent on each Muslim at least once in his/her life, depending on health and financial circumstances. Those who cannot afford the journey will often borrow from others or go into debt in order to do so. The pilgrimage may be made at any time; this is called *Omra* (small version of the full Haj). The greater pilgrimage however takes place yearly on the first ten days of Dhu al-Hijrah, the pilgrimage month, and is sponsored and managed by the government of Saudi Arabia in its role as Guardian of the Holy Places (of Mecca and Medina). In past years, travel there was

---

**THE ISLAMIC CALENDAR**

The Islamic calendar is a lunar calendar. It has 354 days in all, divided into 7 months of 30 days, 4 months of 29 days, and 1 month of 28 days. The first year of the calendar, A.H. 1 (Anno Hegira, the year of Muhammad's "emigration" to Medina to escape persecution in Mecca), corresponds to A.D. 622.

In the Islamic calendar, the months rotate with the moon, coming at different times from year to year. It takes an Islamic month 33 years to make the complete circuit of the seasons. The fasting month of Ramadan moves with the seasons and is most difficult for Muslims when it takes place in high summer.

long and arduous, but today's pilgrims travel by jet and are escorted to Mecca from Jiddah airport in chartered buses, trucks and cars. Upon arrival they put on seamless white robes, and follow a series of prescribed rituals, circling seven times around the Ka'ba, kissing the Black Stone embedded in it, drinking water from the well of Zam Zam which supposedly nourished Hagar after Abraham cast her out and she wandered in the desert with her son Ishmael (Isaac's half-brother, in Biblical lore). Seven times they walk between the hills of Safa and Marwah, then on to Mina, where they symbolically throw stones to drive out Satan. A final seven-fold circumnavigation of the Ka'ba completes the pilgrimage ritual, and those who have taken part are known thereafter as *Hajjis*.

## ISLAMIC DIVISIONS: SUNNIS AND SHI'A

The great majority (90 percent) of Muslims are called Sunnis, because they follow the Sunna, observe the Five Pillars, and practice the rituals of the faith. They also interpret as correct the history of Islam as it developed after Muhammad's death, under a line of successors termed *caliphs* ("agents" or "deputies") who held spiritual and political authority over the Islamic community. However, a minority, while accepting the precepts and rituals of the faith, reject this historical process as contrary to what Muhammad intended for the community of believers. These Muslims are called Shi'a (commonly, but incorrectly, Shiites). The split between Sunnis and Shi'a dates back to Muhammad's death in A.D. 632.

Muhammad left no instructions as to a successor. Since he had said that there would be no more revelations after him, a majority of his followers favored the election of a caliph who would hold the community together and carry on his work. But a minority felt that Muhammad had intended to name his closest male blood relative, Ali, as his successor. Supporters of Ali declared that the succession to Muhammad was a divine right inherited by his direct descendants. Hence they are known as *Shi'at* ("Partisans of") Ali.

Initially the majority of the Islamic community, the *umma*, passed over Ali and by consensus elected Abu Bakr, Muhammad's father-in-law and the first convert after his wife Khadija, as Caliph. The next two caliphs were elected in the same manner, with Ali finally chosen as the fourth caliph after his predecessors had been killed by dissident Muslims. (In addition to the Sunni-Shi'a split, there were other deep divisions within the umma arising from traditional Arab tribal and family rivalries). Ali himself was murdered in A.D. 661, and a rival family, the Umayyads, took over the office and moved Islam's capital from Mecca to Damascus, Syria.

Subsequently Ali's partisans put their support behind Husayn, his younger son, as the rightful caliph. However he and his family were ambushed by the army of the Umayyad caliph in A.D. 680 near the town of Karbala (Iraq), and his head sent to the caliph as proof of his death.

Husayn's murder widened the Sunni-Shi'a split, which has continued to the present day and is visible in the political conflicts raging in Iraq. Lacking a symbolic figure to turn to for leadership, Shi'a recognize a line of either seven or twelve Imams, descendants of Ali and Husayn, as their spiritual leaders. The Imams were not recognized as such by Sunni caliphs and were frequently persecuted, as were their followers. As a result the Shi'a developed the practice of *taqiya* ("dissimulation" or "concealment"). Outwardly they obeyed whatever religious or secular ruler was in power, but inwardly they continued to believe in the divine right of the Imams to rule the Islamic world and to anticipate the return of the last (12th) Imam from hiding as the *Mahdi* ("the Awaited One") to announce the Day of Judgment.

With the exception of Iran, the Shi'a remained a minority in the Islamic world and did not acquire political power. But in the early sixteenth century A.D. the leader of a religious brotherhood there, the Safavis, claimed descent from Ali and declared war on the Ottomans, who ruled most of the Middle East at that time. In order to justify his war he made an agreement with Shi'a religious leaders—they would recognize him as head of state in return for his commitment to recognize Shi'a Islam as the official religion in Iran. Since then Iran has been a Shi'a nation both in population and in political power. The U.S. invasion and occupation of Iraq in 2003 provided a similar opportunity for its Shi'a majority, who had been marginalized under Saddam Hussein's regime but now play a leading role in the process of rebuilding that country.

## SHI'A MUSLIMS AND MARTYRDOM

The murder of Husayn, far more than that of his father Ali, provided the Shi'a community with a martyr figure. This is due to the circumstances surrounding Husayn's death—the lingering image of Muhammad's grandson, with a small band of followers, surrounded in the waterless desert, to be cut down by the vastly superior forces of Yazid, has exerted a powerful influence on Shi'a. As a result, Shi'a often identify themselves with Husayn, a heroic martyr fighting against hopeless odds. For example, an important factor in the success of Iran in repelling the invasion of Iraqi forces in the bitter 1980–1988 Iran–Iraq War was the Basijis, teenage volunteers

---

### 'ASHURA

A special Shi'a Muslim festival not observed by Sunnis commemorates the 10 days of 'Ashura, the anniversary of the death of Husayn. Shi'a Muslims mark the occasion with a series of ritual dramas that may be compared to the Christian Passion Play, except that they may be performed at other times during the year. Particularly in Iran, the ritual, called Ta'ziya is presented by strolling troupes of actors who travel from village to village to dramatize the story with songs, poetry, and sword dances. Ta'ziya also takes place in street parades in cities, featuring penitents who lash themselves with whips or slash their bodies with sharp blades. Freya Stark, the great English travel writer, describes one such procession in her book *Baghdad Sketches*:

> All is represented, every incident on the fateful day of Karbala, and the procession stops at intervals to act one episode or another. One can hear it coming from far away by the thud of beaters beating their naked chests, a mighty sound like the beating of carpets, or see the blood pour down the backs of those who acquire merit with flails made of chains with which they lacerate their shoulders; and finally the slain body comes, headless, carried under a bloodstained sheet through wailing crowds.

led into battle by chanters, in the firm belief that death at the hands of the Sunni Iraqi enemy was a holy action worthy of martyrdom.

# ISLAM AND EUROPE: CHANGING ROLES

The early centuries of Islam were marked by many brilliant achievements. An extensive network of trade routes linked the cities of the Islamic world. It was a high-fashion world in which the rich wore silks from Damascus ("damask" fabric), slept on fine sheets from Mosul ("muslin"), sat on couches of Morocco leather, and carried swords and daggers of Toledo steel. Islamic merchants developed many institutions and practices used in modern economic systems, such as banks, letters of credit, checks and receipts, and bookkeeping. Islamic agriculture, based on sophisticated irrigation systems developed in the arid Middle East, brought to Spain, in particular, a number of previously unknown food crops that include oranges, lemons, eggplant, radishes, and sugar. The very names of these foods are Arabic in origin, as are a great number of words in modern Spanish. Islamic civilization literally "flowered" in Cordoba, capital of Islamic Spain, and Baghdad, the Umayyad

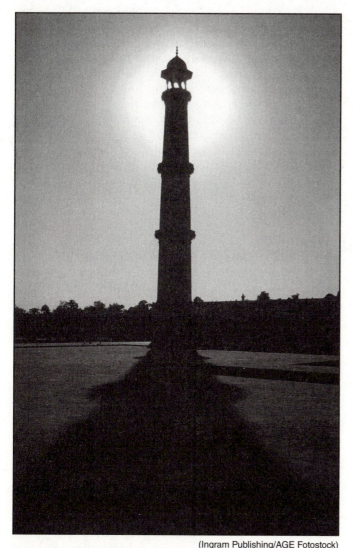

(Ingram Publishing/AGE Fotostock)
Minaret of a mosque silhouetted by the sun.

caliphate's capital and center of Middle Eastern Islam. Both capitals were filled with bookstores, gardens, palaces, fine residences and markets filled with exotic silks and other goods from China, India and elsewhere, at a time when Europe was medieval, dark and gloomy. It was said of Cordoba that "three things there are there that delight the eye; first is the mosque, then the bridge over the Guadalqivir; but the third and greatest of these is knowledge."[5]

Islamic medical technology reached a level of excellence in diagnosis and treatment unequaled in Europe until the nineteenth century. Muslim mathematics gave Europeans Arabic numerals and the concept of zero. Muslim navigators made possible Columbus's voyages, through their knowledge of seamanship and inventions such as the sextant and the compass. Their libraries were the most extensive in existence at that time.

The level of achievements of Islamic civilization from roughly 750 to 1200 was far superior to that of Europe. The first Europeans to come in direct contact with Islamic society were Crusader knights, Christians who invaded the Middle East in order to recapture Jerusalem from its Muslim rulers. The Crusaders marveled at what they saw, even though they were the sworn enemies of Islam. This Christian occupation of the Holy Land, while short-lived (1099–1187), contributed significantly to the mutual hostility that has marked Christian–Muslim relations throughout their coexistence. (A retired German diplomat who became a Muslim in 1980 expressed the hope of a future positive impact of Islam on the West: "the de-Christianization of Europe-not of the United States-has reached a point where this religion no longer has a chance of bringing about the moral revolution necessary for saving the West from itself . . . Only a partial Islamization of the West could turn the driving wheel sufficiently, steering the West away from its present course towards decline and fall." However, he adds, the "Message of Islam cannot be transmitted in the West as long as Muslims play hide and seek with the issues of "democracy" and "human rights", including the rights of women.")[6]

The hostile relationship between Muslims and Christians resulting from the Crusades intensified with the rise to power in the Islamic world of the Ottomas. In 1453 A.D. they captured Constantinople (modern Istanbul), capital of the East Roman or Byzantine empire. Soon Ottoman power extended across all of southeastern Europe. With the conquest of Egypt in 1517 the Ottomans captured the last caliph, who had taken refuge there after the seizure of Baghdad by the Mongols. He was "persuaded" to give up his title in return for security, and the Ottoman sultan became the caliph.

The success of their armies and a belief that God had given Muslims, and particularly Ottomans, a superior way of life gave the Ottomans a feeling of superiority over their Christian European adversaries. Indeed this superiority lasted for several centuries. But gradually the roles were reversed. Militarily the Ottoman armies lost more and more battles, particularly to the expanding Russian power, and with defeat came the humiliation of being forced to sign peace treaties which cost them territory. Another shock came with the discovery that European cities had developed modern technology. They had electric lights, paved streets, telephone and telegraph lines, and other conveniences none of which existed in Ottoman/Middle Eastern cities.

(© Clark Brennan/Alamy)

Egyptian Woman in traditional hijab walks with her daughter.

Since that time the Ottoman empire has disappeared, its former Middle Eastern provinces being replaced by Islamic entities such as Syria, Lebanon, Jordan and Iraq that began their modern existence as dependencies of Christian European countries. Other Middle Eastern Islamic states—Iran, Turkey and Egypt for example—have survived but in a different form politically from what they were before the Christian-Ottoman roles were reversed.

This change in status has caused much soul-searching in the Islamic community, particularly after the terrorist attacks of 9/11 in the United States. Some Islamic groups, such as Hamas in occupied Palestine and Osama Bin Laden's Al-Qaeda, argue that only through violence and the destruction of Israel and of non-representative Islamic regimes, especially those (i.e. Saudi Arabia) that have allowed non-Muslim forces to invade or use sacred Islamic territory, can the equation be balanced. A much larger but less articulate group favors accommodation with the West while holding fast to their faith, while a third, represented by the Wahhabi establishment in Saudi Arabia and possibly the clerical regime in Iran, argues for a return to the simple faith and rigid practice of the original Islam of Muhammad's day.

Today Muslims the world over, and particularly in the Middle East due to its centrality in international conflict, are engaged in a struggle to define an effective framework for their faith, one that will enable them to play a meaningful role in world society. The diversity of Islamic state governments, the clash between tolerant and repressive regimes, are among some of the factors causing Islam's disunity. As a result the views of scholars and religious leaders vary sharply. Hassan al-Turabi, a leading Sudanese scholar-politician, argues that the gates to *ijtihad* (interpretation leading to innovation) are always open; government must be based on consultation and consensus-building

rather than authoritarian rule. Islam has no church as such, he says, and women have equal rights and responsibilities with the faith. At the other end of the spectrum are the religious leaders of Saudi Arabia, who not only share in government but dictate social and cultural rules. (Thus far in 2007 some 102 persons, including three women, have been beheaded for their crimes under shari'a law). Such actions partly prescribed by the law as veiling, wearing headscarfs, and replacement of civil law codes by shari'a, continue to generate much controversy in the lands of Islam.

## ISLAMIC RADICALISM

For a majority of Muslims the challenge today is how to achieve political success and economic and social progress comparable to that of the West without sacrificing their commitment to the faith. In the absence of an Islamic Reformation, advocates of modernization and conservatives struggle for control in a number of Middle Eastern states, notably Iran, Turkey, Algeria and to a lesser extent Lebanon. Elsewhere regimes with varying degrees of authoritarianism remain in control but are increasingly challenged by a vocal opposition. On several occasions, in particular the Taliban in Afghanistan and the National Islamic Front in Sudan, such groups have been on the verge of seizing political control; indeed the Taliban did so before the U.S. invasion of their country. However, a revamped religious party managed to win elections and has been ruling the country by democratic means for a few years now.

It should also be noted that interaction between the West and the Islamic Middle East in recent years has produced two or three generations of Western-educated, Western-oriented academic, professional and intellectual leaders. Even the structure of the Middle East's Islamic regimes is modeled on Western institutions. Bernard Lewis reminds us that the Islamic Republic of Iran—the prototype for putative Islamic regimes—has an elected Assembly and a written Constitution, "for which there is no precedent in the Islamic past." Modern secularist Muslims and conservatives alike view Islam as the best alternative to both communism and Western free-market capitalism. During the period of the last shah's rule, a prominent Iranian philosopher, Ali Shari'ati, coined the term "Westoxication" to describe the Muslim infatuation with the West, usually to the detriment of Islam. Islamic conservatives, rejecting this idea, would remove all elements of Western culture, even principles of law, ethics, politics and Western democratic practice, from Islamic societies, returning to the basic principles of the faith as the sole guiding force in society.

Muslims today, in the Middle East as elsewhere, are searching for ways to reassert their Islamic identity while reconciling a traditional Islamic way of life with the demands of the contemporary world. The commonality of the faith, its overarching cultural and social norms, is easily grasped and appeals to Muslims irrespective of their different backgrounds. One positive result of the conservative movement is that it enables Muslims to take pride in their heritage. They no longer have to defend or apologize for their beliefs or practices. Islam, regardless of what often seems to be a bad press, has not only matured but also stands as a valid, legitimate institution, one that can be respected by adherents and non-adherents alike.

## THE CONCEPT OF JIHAD

Jihad, often described as a "Sixth Pillar" of the House of Islam, may be defined as "sacred struggle" or "striving". The aim is to better the self and the Muslim community according to the tenets of the faith. This is called the "Great Jihad" because it is the most important and the most constant struggle all Muslims are to engage in all their life in Dar al-Islam ("House of Islam" or Muslim land). The "Small Jihad" refers to the struggle against the enemies of the faith and of the Muslim community in Dar el-Harb ("House of War" or non-Muslim land). It can be done by both violent and non-violent means. Also, it must only be a response to a threat or attack, and cannot be aggressive.

In recent decades, many Muslim radicals have altered and extended the meaning of such Jihad and have committed atrocities in its name both in their own countries and outside.

Another definition of *jihad*, the striving of the individual for justice, is perhaps the most controversial. Islam teaches that if rulers—whether elected or appointed over some Islamic territory—become unjust, their subjects should bear the injustices with fortitude; God will, in due course, reward their patience. Some Muslims interpret this injunction to mean that they should strive to help the leaders to see the error of their ways—by whatever action deemed necessary. Centuries ago, a secret society, the Hashishin ("Assassins"; so named because they reportedly were users of hashish), carried out many assassinations of prominent officials and rulers, claiming that God had inspired them to rid Islamic society of tyrants. Since Islam emphasizes the direct relationship of people to God—and therefore people's responsibility to do right in the eyes of God and to struggle to help other believers follow the same, correct path—it becomes most dangerous when individuals feel that they do not need to subject themselves to the collective will but rather, to impose their own concepts of justice on others.

Unfortunately, Jihad has become the province, indeed the raison d'etre, of militant Islamist organizations such as Al-Qaeda and its various spin-off groups. Conversely the founder of the Muslim Brotherhood, Hassan al-Banna, emphasized peaceful change as necessary to reform corrupt or repressive governments. There is some evidence that the Brotherhood's opposition to repressive measures by the Egyptian government has led it to adopt a stronger stance toward Islamism in its program. In October 2007 its leaders announced a draft plan for future action which included a call for the establishment in Egypt of a "Civic Islamic State." It would establish a Majlis al-Ulalama (Council of Islamic Scholars) chosen by religious leaders rather than elected, with power to veto any laws passed by Parliament that were not compatible with Islamic law. Al-Qaeda, in contrast, seeks the overthrow of these governments by violence, considering them unrepresentative and therefore un-Islamic.

Ayatollah Khomeini's opposition to the Shah as an unjust ruler, as expressed in his writings and sermons, was crucial to the success of the 1979 revolution. This opposition underscored the need for collective resistance to unjust authority. It can be argued that its export of revolutionary policy to other Middle Eastern Islamic countries in its early years as an Islamic republic was a form of jihad. But in recent years, the concept and the policy have been hijacked by Al-Qaeda and its terrorist network. Members have developed their own set of rules, according to which one can kill civilians in a "legitimate act" in

(S.M. Amin/Saudi Aramco World/PADIA)

One of the Five Pillars of Islam, or five basic duties of Muslims, is to go on a pilgrimage to Mecca in Saudi Arabia once in their lifetime. There they circle seven times around the Black Box (the Ka'ba, pictured above), kiss the Black Stone, drink from the well of Zam Zam, and perform other sacred rites.

defense of the Muslim land and the Muslims against domestic and foreign enemies. This kind of rationalization or justification of the killing of innocent victims, young and old, has also been used by others, as noted by history professor John O. Voll, of Georgetown University: "Whether you are talking about leftist radicals here in the 1960s, or the apologies for civilian collateral damage in Iraq that you get from the Pentagon, the argument is that if the action is just, the collateral damage is justifiable."[7]

## ISLAM IN THE TWENTY-FIRST CENTURY

The brief period of rule by the Taliban in Afghanistan, with its rigid interpretation of Islam based on Wahhabi principles, might suggest that extremist Islamic fundamentalist movements elsewhere in the Middle East can succeed by using similar tactics. Certainly the ideal of an Islamic community replicating that of the original one founded by Muhammad remains valid. However, the unique nature of the Taliban itself, and the special conditions that made its success possible, do not exist in North Africa or the rest of the Middle East. The Taliban's membership was recruited from Afghan refugee camps in Pakistan or remote villages within Afghanistan. Members, nearly all of them illiterate, were given only the rudiments of Qur'anic instruction, given by semiliterate mullahs, in so-called religious schools (madrasas) set up on a temporary basis in the camps or towns controlled by the organization. When an individual had completed this "education," he became talib ("student"—hence the name Taliban which is the plural of Talib) and were sent to take part in a jihad in Afghanistan intended to restore law and order. Almost without exception Taliban members had no exposure to the larger world and thus were totally inexperienced in state-building. Eventually they were totally isolated from other Islamic states, recognition of their sovereignty withdrawn, and with the U.S-led NATO invasion they became a defeated, albeit still viable, opposition group in this fractured country.

As the millennium moves on, some seventeen centuries after the Prophet Muhammad (PBUH) announced his vision of a community of believers united in faith in One God, in prayer and in justice, Muslims everywhere are struggling to come to terms with a globalized world and to determine where and how their faith fits into this world. Long before there were separate nations with borders to cross or defend, nomadic peoples moved easily across the Middle East, giving visible substance to Ibn Khaldun's thesis that civilizations rise and fall according to a predictable pattern. Islam created one of those civilizations, and it may do so again. But increasingly in the region, borders are no longer barriers. They were formed artificially as nation-states, and they are crossed easily today, not so much by military forces as by technology, in the form of the Internet, satellite TV, cellular phones and the like.

In Europe particularly the 20-million Muslim community spread across many countries have struggled with problems of integrating themselves into European society while preserving their Islamic identity and values. Their difficulty was highlighted in 2005 by the infamous "cartoon crisis." On September 30 of that year a Danish newspaper, Jyllands-Posten, published 12 cartoon caricatures of the Prophet Muhammad. One showed him wearing a turban shaped as a bomb with a burning fuse. Another had him wearing a bushy grey beard and holding a sword, his eyes covered by a black rectangle, while a third pictured him in the desert, a middle-aged prophet walking in front of a donkey.

Aside from being in execrable taste and offensive to the values of a worldwide community, the cartoons seemed and were presented more as examples of European press freedom than as provocations. However, months after their publication they aroused a firestorm of protest, not only in Europe but more intensely in a number of Islamic countries. Danish and other European embassies in Syria and Lebanon, and elsewhere, were attacked and burned, and Muslim leaders in the Middle East called for a boycott of Danish goods.

This event underscores the vast difference between the Islamic past and the present uncertainty of its peoples. It also marks a line between those who would preserve (or restore) this idealized past and others for whom the religion is only one element in the world in which they must live and work today.

A Western-educated Muslim researcher notes that she would rather be considered 'orthodox' than 'moderate.' As she says, "moderate implies that Muslims who are more orthodox are somehow backward and violent. To be a 'moderate' Muslim is to be a 'good' malleable Muslim in the eyes of Western society."[8] However, Western standards of democratization and human rights as essential to social progress continue to raise difficulties for Muslims as they struggle to preserve their faith yet adapt it to changing world conditions. Recent polls suggest that the majority praise democracy as the best of all political systems, yet also insist that Shari'a (Islamic law) be central to their lives. Many Muslims point to Turkey as an example as a viable, secular state with an Islamic government. But a significant minority argue that state and society function best when united under Islam as a universal ethical and legal system. We tend to call this minority "Islamists" and may disagree with them or their methods, but they are one of many voices crying out for necessary reforms in the religion founded centuries ago but still not fully adapted to this era.

## NOTES

1. R. Hrair Dekmejian, *Islam in Revolution* (Syracuse, NY: Syracuse University Press, 1985), p. 99.

2. Michael B. Oren, *Power, Faith and Fantasy* (New York: W.W. Norton, 2007, pp. 241–244.

3. One of the few exceptions was the first George Bush (1796–1859) who taught Oriental languages in what is now New York University and in 1831 published the first biography of the Prophet Muhammad (PBUH) Ted Widmer, "Reconsideration," *New York Times Book Review*, July 22, 2007.

4. Orhan Pamuk, Turkey's Nobel Prize winner in literature, writes of his delight in childhood in eating hot dogs, salami and sausage sandwiches from street vendors in Istanbul, although he was forbidden to do so by his mother because the meat was "from unknown parts of unknown animals." "Forbidden Fare," *The New Yorker*, July 9–16, 2007, pp. 48–50.

5. Details on this period of "high Islamic civilization" when Muslims, Christians and Jews lived in harmony, are given in Zachary Karabell, *Peace Be Upon You: The Story of Muslim, Christian, and Jewish Coexistence* (New York: Alfred A. Knopf, 2008).

6. Murad Hofmann, "Islam in the West," Notes on Facebook, Dr. Murad Hofmann, January 21, 2010, online at www.facebook.com/notes/dr-murad-hofmann/islam-in-the-west-dr-murad-hofmann/263100673772; and Murad Hoffman, "Living Islam—Not just performing it," Notes on Facebook, April 25, 2010, online at www.facebook.com/note.php?note_id=386650048772. Dr. Hoffman who served as ambassador to Algeria and Morocco has published ten books on Islam, including *Islam: The Alternative* (1997) and *Journey to Islam: Diary of a German Diplomat 1951–2000* (2001).

7. John O. Voll, quoted in Michael Moss and Souad Mekhennet, "Permission: The Guidebook For Taking a Life," *New York Times,* June 10, 2007.

8. Asma Khalid, "Why I Am Not a Moderate Muslim," *The Christian Science Monitor,* April 23, 2007. See "Four Views on Islam and the State," a compendium, *The Christian Science Monitor,* August 30, 2007.

# Algeria (Peoples' Democratic Republic of Algeria)

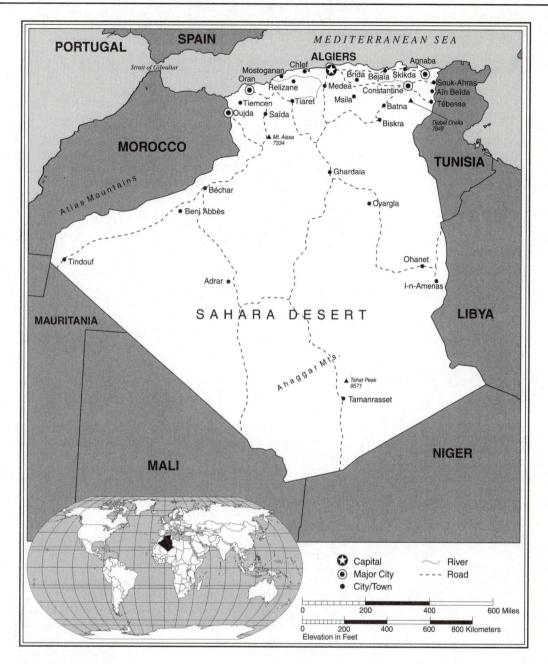

# Algeria Statistics

## GEOGRAPHY

*Area in Square Miles (Kilometers):*
919,352 (2,381,740) (about 3½ times the size of Texas)
*Capital (Population):* Algiers (3,705,000)
*Environmental Concerns:* soil erosion; desertification; water pollution; inadequate potable water
*Geographical Features:* mostly high plateau and desert; some mountains; narrow, discontinuous coastal plain

*Climate:* arid to semiarid; mild, wet winters and hot, dry summers on coastal plain; less rain and cold winters on high plateau; considerable temperature variation in desert

## PEOPLE
### Population

*Total:* 34,178,188
*Annual Growth Rate:* 1.196%
*Rural/Urban Population Ratio:* 35/65

*Major Languages:* Arabic; Berber dialects; French
*Ethnic Makeup:* 99% Arab-Berber; less than 1% European
*Religions:* 99% Sunni Muslim (Islam is the state religion); 1% Christian, and Jewish

### Health

*Life Expectancy at Birth:* 72.35 years (male); 75.77 years (female)

27

*Infant Mortality Rate (Ratio):* 27.73/1,000 live births

### Education

*Adult Literacy Rate:* 79.6%
*Compulsory (Ages):* 6–15

## COMMUNICATION

*Telephones:* 3,068,000 plus 27,563,000 cell phones
*Daily Newspaper Circulation:* 52 per 1,000 people
*Televisions:* 71 per 1,000 people
*Internet Users:* 3,500,000 (2007)

## TRANSPORTATION

*Highways in Miles (Kilometers):* 68,010 (109,452)
*Railroads in Miles (Kilometers):* 2,963 (4,772)
*Usable Airfields:* 142
*Motor Vehicles in Use:* 3,700,000

## GOVERNMENT

*Type:* republic

*Independence Date:* July 5, 1962 (from France)
*Head of State/Government:* President Abdelaziz Bouteflika; Prime Minister Ahmed Ouyahia
*Political Parties:* National Liberation Front has regained its dominant position with most seats in parliament since the election of 2007. It is part of a pro-government coalition made of the National Democratic Rally (RND) and the Movement of Society of Peace (MSP), moderate Islamist. Another Islamist party is also represented in Parliament, Islah (Reform). Other significant parties are the two Berber-based Rally for Democracy and Culture (RCD) and the Front of Socialist Forces (FFS), along with the small communist Workers Party.
*Suffrage:* universal at 18

## MILITARY

*Military Expenditures (% of GDP):* 3.3%
*Current Disputes:* disputed southeastern border with Libya; Algeria supports

Polisario Front which seeks to establish an independent Western Sahara, currently occupied by Morocco

## ECONOMY

*Currency ($U.S. Equivalent):* 72 Algerian dinars = $1
*Per Capita Income/GDP:* $5,000/$171.3 billion
*GDP Growth Rate:* 3%
*Inflation Rate:* 3%
*Unemployment Rate:* 12.9%
*Labor Force:* 9,440,000
*Natural Resources:* petroleum; natural gas; iron ore; phosphates; uranium; lead; zinc
*Agriculture:* wheat; barley, oats; grapes; olives; citrus fruits; sheep; cattle
*Industry:* petroleum; natural gas; light industries; mining; electrical; petrochemicals; food processing
*Exports:* $75.06 billion (primary partners United States, Italy, Spain, Canada, France)
*Imports:* $36.87 billion (primary partners France, China, Italy, Spain, United States)

# Algeria Country Report

The modern state of Algeria occupies the central part of North Africa, which includes Morocco, Tunisia, and Libya; this region is also called the *Maghrib* (which means in Arabic "where the sun sets"). Algeria is called in Arabic *al-Jaza'ir,* "the islands," because of the rocky islets along this part of the Mediterranean coast. Its capital is Algiers, *al-Jaza'ir* in Arabic, the same as the country's name.

The official name of the state is the Democratic and Popular Republic of Algeria. It is the second-largest country in Africa (after Sudan). The overall population density is low, but the population is concentrated in the northern third of the country. The vast stretches of the Algerian Sahara are largely unpopulated. The country had an extremely high birth rate prior to 1988, but government-sponsored family-planning programs have significantly reduced the rate.

## GEOGRAPHY

Algeria's geography is a formidable obstacle to broad economic and social development. About 80 percent of the land is uncultivable desert, and only 12 percent is arable without irrigation. Most of the population live in a narrow coastal plain and in a fertile, hilly inland region called the Tell (Arabic for "hillock"). The Saharan provinces have only 3 percent of the population but comprise more than half the land area.

The mineral resources that made possible Algeria's transformation in two decades from a land devastated by a bloody war of independence to one of the developing world's success stories are all located in the Sahara. Economic growth, however, has been uneven, generally affecting the rural and lower-class urban populations unfavorably. The large-scale exodus of rural families into the cities, with consequent neglect of agriculture, has resulted in a vast increase in urban slums. Economic disparities were a major cause of riots in 1988, that led to political reforms and the dismantling of the socialist system responsible for Algerian development since independence.

Algeria is unique among newly independent Middle Eastern and North African countries in that it gained its independence through full-fledged independence war. For more than 130 years (1830–1962), it was colonized by France and became a French department (similar to a U.S. state such as Hawaii). The country was settled by large numbers of Europeans, who became the politically dominant group in the population although they were a minority. The modern Algerian nation is the product of the interaction of native Muslim Algerians with the European settlers, who also considered Algeria their home.

In addition to its vast Saharan territory, Algeria is broken up into discontinuous regions by a number of rugged mountain ranges. The Mediterranean coastline is narrow and backed throughout its length by mountains, notably the imposing Atlas range, which is a continuation of the Moroccan Atlas; it is a complex system of deep valleys, high plateaux, and peaks rising up to 6,000 feet. In south central Algeria is the most impressive range in the country, the Aurès, a great mountain block.

The original inhabitants of the entire North African region were Berbers, a people of unknown origin grouped into various tribes. Because most Berbers became Arabized over the centuries that followed the Arabo-Islamic invasions of the 7th and 11th centuries AD, actual Berber speakers account for only 25 to 30 percent of the population. The majority live in the eastern Kabylia region and the Aures (Chaouia), with a small, compact group in the five cities of the Mzab, in the Algerian Sahara. Another group, the Tuareg, a nomadic Berber people are spread across southern Algeria, Mali, and Niger. In the past, they were literally "lords of the desert," patrolling the caravan routes on their swift camels and collecting tolls for safe passage as guides for caravaneers. They were a colorful sight in their tents with their indigo robes (which tinted their skin blue, hence the name for them, the "Blue Men"). But Saharan droughts, motorized transport, and the development of the oil industry have largely destroyed their traditional role and lifestyle.

The Arabs, who brought Islam to North Africa in the seventh century A.D., converted the Algerian Berbers after a fierce resistance. The Arabs brought their language as a unifying feature, and religion linked the Algerians with the larger Islamic world. Today, most follow Sunni Islam, but a significant minority, about 100,000, are *kharijit* (outsiders), a group whose ancestors constituted the first dissenters in Islam. They refer to themselves as *Ibadis,* and live in five "holy cities" clustered in a Saharan valley where centuries ago they took refuge from Sunni rulers of northern Algeria. Their valley, the Mzab, has always maintained religious autonomy from Algerian central governments. The much larger Berber population of Kabylia has also resisted central authority, whether Islamic or French, throughout Algerian history. One of many pressures on the government today is that of an organized Kabyle movement, which seeks greater autonomy for the region and an emphasis on Berber language in schools, along with the revitalization of Kabyle culture.

## HISTORY

### The Corsair Regency

The foundations of the modern Algerian state were laid in the sixteenth century, with the establishment of the Regency of Algiers, an outlying province of the Ottoman Empire. Algiers in particular, due to its natural harbor, was developed for use by the Ottomans as a naval base for wars against European fleets in the Mediterranean. The Algerian coast was the farthest westward extent of Ottoman power. Consequently, Algiers and Oran, the two major ports, were exposed to constant threats of attack by Spanish and other European fleets. They could not easily be supported, or governed directly, by the Ottomans.

The regency was established by two Albanian-born Muslim sea captains, Baba Aruj and Khayr al-Din (called Barbarossa by his European opponents because of his flaming red beard). The brothers obtained commissions from the Ottoman sultan for expeditions against the Spanish. They made their principal base at Algiers, then a small port, which Khayr al-Din expanded into a powerful fortress and naval base. His government consisted of a garrison of

Ottoman soldiers sent by the sultan to keep order, along with a naval force.

Corsairing or piracy (the choice of term depended upon one's viewpoint) was a common practice in the Mediterranean, but the rise to power of the Algerine corsairs converted it into a more or less respectable profession.[1] The cities of Tetuan, Tunis (Tunisia), Salé (Morocco), and Tripoli (Libya) also had corsair fleets, but the Algerian corsairs were so effective against European shipping that for 300 years (1500–1800), European rulers called them the "scourge of the Mediterranean." One factor in their success was their ability to attract outstanding sea captains from various European countries. Renegades from Italy, Greece, Holland, France, and Britain joined the Algerian fleet, converted to Islam, and took Muslim names as a symbol of their new status. Some rose to high rank.

The corsair states (also known as the Barbary States), particularly Algiers and Tripoli, were a major factor in the establishment of U.S. naval power and by extension American foreign policy. Prior to independence American merchant vessels traveled under the protection of the Union Jack, England having paid regular tribute in return for exemption of its ships from corsair capture. This protective cover was no longer valid after 1782, and the United States found itself paying huge sums for the return of its ships and crews where possible. The very notion of tribute, then as now, was anathema to American policymakers, and in 1804 President Jefferson ordered and Congress approved, the construction of 6 naval frigates, the first units in the U.S. Navy, to patrol the Mediterranean and protect American merchant shipping there.

Government in Algiers passed through several stages and eventually became a system of deys. The deys were elected by the Divan, a council of the captains of the Ottoman garrison. Deys were elected for life, but most of them never fulfilled their tenure due to constant intrigue, military coups, and assassinations. Yet the system provided considerable stability, security for the population, and wealth and prestige for the regency. These factors probably account for its durability; the line of deys governed uninterruptedly from the late 1600s to 1830.

Outside of Algiers and its hinterland, authority was delegated to local chiefs and religious leaders, who were responsible for tax collection and remittances to the dey's treasury. The chiefs were kept in line with generous subsidies. It was a system well adapted to the fragmented society of Algeria and one that enabled a small military group to rule a large territory at relatively little cost.[2]

### The French Conquest

In 1827, the dey of Algiers, enraged at the French government's refusal to pay an old debt incurred during Napoleon's wars, struck the French consul on the shoulder with a fly-whisk in the course of a meeting. The king of France, Charles X, demanded an apology for the "insult" to his representative. None was forthcoming, so the French blockaded the port of Algiers in retaliation. But the dey continued to keep silent. In 1830, a French army landed on the coast west of the city, marched overland, and entered it with almost no resistance. The dey surrendered and went into exile.[3]

The French, who had been looking for an excuse to expand their interests in North Africa, now were not sure what to do with Algiers. The overthrow of the despotic Charles X in favor of a constitutional monarchy in France confused the situation even further. But the Algerians considered the French worse than the Turks, who were at least fellow Muslims. In the 1830s, they rallied behind their first national leader, Emir Abd al-Qadir. It took the French forces some 40 years to control the rest of the country.

Abd al-Qadir was the son of a prominent religious leader and, more important, a descendant of the Prophet Muhammad. Abd al-Qadir had unusual qualities of leadership, military skill, and courage. From 1830 to 1847, he carried on guerrilla warfare against a French army of more than 100,000 men with such success that at one point the French signed a formal treaty recognizing him as head of an Algerian nation in the interior. Abd al-Qadir described his strategy in a prophetic letter to the king of France:

> France will march forward, and we shall retire. But France will find it necessary to retire, and we shall return. We shall weary and harry you, and our climate will do the rest.[4]

In order to defeat Abd al-Qadir, the French commander used "total war" tactics, burning villages, destroying crops, killing livestock, and levying fines on peoples who continued to support the emir. These measures, called "pacification" by France, finally succeeded.

> The crimes associated with this "pacification" campaign reached their peak in 1845, when hundreds of people were burned alive or asphyxiated in caves where they sought refuge from the advancing French troops that were conducting large scale razzia (systematic raids on villages). The raiding French troops burned, destroyed, or stole property, food,

and animal stocks; they also raped women and killed villagers in great numbers. The violent acts committed at that time against the indigenous population, and which today would constitute internationally recognized crimes, were documented in several witness accounts and reports such as the one issued by a royal commission in 1883.

We tormented, at the slightest suspicion and without due process, people whose guilt still remains more than uncertain [. . .]. We massacred people who carried passes, cut the throats, on a simple suspicion, of entire populations which proved later to be innocent. . . . [Many innocent people were tried just because] they exposed themselves to our furor. Judges were available to condemn them and civilized people to have them executed. . . . In a word, our barbarism was worse than that of the barbarians we came to civilize, and we complain that we have not succeeded with them! (Cited in Pierre Nora, Les Français d'Algérie, 88).[5]

In 1847, Abd al-Qadir surrendered to French authorities. He was imprisoned for several years, in violation of a solemn commitment, and was then released by Emperor Napoleon III. He spent the rest of his life in exile.

## DEVELOPMENT

Algeria ranks eighth in the world in natural gas reserves and fifteenth in oil reserves. It is the world's fourth largest exporter of liquefied natural gas (LNG). Hydrocarbons provide 80 percent of national revenues in 2008, 36.7 percent of GDP and 97.7 percent of export earnings.

Although he did not succeed in his quest, Abd al-Qadir is venerated as the first Algerian nationalist, able by his leadership and Islamic prestige to unite warring groups in a struggle for independence from foreign control. Abd al-Qadir's green and white flag was raised again by the Algerian nationalists during the second war of independence (1954–1962), and it is the flag of the republic today.

### Algérie Française

After the defeat of Abd al-Qadir, the French gradually brought all of present-day Algerian territory under their control.

The Kabyles, living in the rugged mountain region east of Algiers, were the last to submit. They rebelled in 1871 after a series of decrees by the French government had made all Algerian Muslims subjects but not citizens, giving them a status inferior to French and other European settlers.

The Kabyle rebellion had terrible results, not only for the Kabyles but for all Algerian Muslims. More than a million acres of Muslim lands were confiscated by French authorities and sold to European settlers. A special code of laws was enacted to treat Algerian Muslims differently from Europeans, with severe fines and sentences for such "infractions" as insulting a European.

In 1871, Algeria legally became a French department. But in terms of exploitation of natives by settlers, it may as well have remained a colony. One author notes that "the desire to make a settlement colony out of an already populated area led to a policy of driving the indigenous people out of the best arable lands."[6] Land confiscation was only part of the exploitation of Algeria by the colons (French settlers). They developed a modern Algerian agriculture integrated into the French economy, providing France with much of its wine, citrus, olives, and vegetables. Colons owned 30 percent of the arable land and 90 percent of the best farmland. Special taxes were imposed on the Algerian Muslims; the colons were exempted from paying most taxes.

The political structure of Algeria was even more favorable to the European minority. The colons were well represented in the French National Assembly, and their representatives made sure that any reforms or laws intended to improve the living conditions or rights of the Algerian Muslim population would be blocked.

In fairness to the colons, it must be pointed out that many of them had come to Algeria as poor immigrants and worked hard to improve their lot and to develop the country. By 1930, the centenary of the French conquest, many colon families had lived in Algiers for two generations or more. Colons had drained malarial swamps south of Algiers and developed the Mitidja, the country's most fertile region. A fine road and rail system linked all parts of the country, and French public schools served all cities and towns. Algiers even had its own university, a branch of the Sorbonne. It is not surprising that to the colons, Algeria was their country, "Algérie Française." Throughout Algeria they rebaptized Algerian cities with names like Orléansville and Philippeville, with paved French streets, cafes, bakeries, and little squares with flower gardens and benches where old men in berets dozed in the hot sun.

Jules Cambon, governor general of Algeria in the 1890s, once described the country as having "only a dust of people left here." What he meant was that the ruthless treatment of the Algerians by the French during the pacification had deprived them of their natural leaders. A group of leaders developed slowly in Algeria, but it was made up largely of evolués—persons who had received French educations, spoke French better than Arabic, and accepted French citizenship as the price of status.[7]

Other Algerians, several hundred thousand of them, served in the French Army in the two world wars. Many of them became aware of the political rights that they were supposed to have but did not. Still others, religious leaders and teachers, were influenced by the Arab nationalist movement for independence from foreign control in Egypt and other parts of the Middle East.

Until the 1940s, the majority of the evolués and other Algerian leaders did not want independence. They wanted full assimilation with France and Muslim equality with the colons. Ferhat Abbas, a French-trained pharmacist who was the spokesman for the evolués, said in 1936 that he did not believe that there was such a thing as an Algerian nation separate from France.

Abbas and his associates changed their minds after World War II. In 1943, they had presented to the French government a manifesto demanding full political and legal equality for Muslims with the colons. It was blocked by colon leaders, who feared that they would be drowned in a Muslim sea. On May 8, 1945, the date of the Allied victory over Nazi Germany, a parade of Muslims celebrating the event but also demanding equality led to violence in the city of Sétif. Several colons were killed; in retaliation, army troops and groups of colon vigilantes swept through Muslim neighborhoods, burning houses and slaughtering 45 thousand Muslims. From then on, Muslim leaders believed that independence through armed struggle was the only choice left to them.

### The War for Independence

November 1 is an important holiday in France. It is called Toussaint (All Saints' Day). On that day, French people remember and honor all the many saints in the pantheon of French Catholicism. It is a day devoted to reflection and staying at home.

In the years after the Sétif massacre, there had been scattered outbreaks of violence in Algeria, some of them created by the Secret Organization (OS), which had developed an extensive network of

Agriculture is important in raising the living standards of Algeria. Farmers harvest forage peas, which will be used for animal feed.

cells in preparation for armed insurrection. In 1952, French police accidentally uncovered the network and jailed most of its leaders. One of them, a former French Army sergeant named Ahmed Ben Bella, subsequently escaped and went to Cairo, Egypt.

As the day of Toussaint 1954 neared, Algeria seemed calm. But appearances were deceptive. Earlier in the year, nine former members of the OS had laid plans in secret for armed revolution. They divided Algeria into six *wilayas* (departments), each with a military commander. They also planned a series of coordinated attacks for the early morning hours of November 1, when the French population would be asleep and the police preparing for a holiday. Bombs exploded at French Army barracks, police stations, storage warehouses, telephone offices, and government buildings. The revolutionaries circulated leaflets in the name of the National Liberation Front (FLN), warning the French that they had acted to liberate Algeria from the colonialist yoke and calling on Algerian Muslims to join in the struggle.

There were very few casualties as a result of the Toussaint attacks; for some time the French did not realize that they had a revolution on their hands. But as violence continued, regular army troops were sent to Algeria to help the hard-pressed police and the colons. Eventually there were 400,000 French troops in Algeria, as opposed to just 6,000 guerrillas. But the French consistently refused to consider the situation in Algeria a war. They called it a "police action." Others called it the "war without a name."[8] Despite their great numerical superiority, they were unable to defeat the FLN.

The French tried various tactics. They divided the country into small sectors, with permanent garrisons for each sector. They organized mobile units to track down the guerrillas in caves and hideouts. About 2 million villagers were moved into barbed-wire "regroupment camps," with a complete dislocation of their way of life, in order to deny the guerrillas the support of the population.

The war was settled not by military action but by political negotiations. The French people and government, worn down by the effects of World War II and their involvement in Indochina, grew sick of the slaughter, homemade bombs exploding in public places (in France as well as Algeria), and the brutality of the army in dealing with guerrilla prisoners. A French newspaper editor expressed the general feeling: "Algeria is ruining the spring. This land of sun and earth has never been so near us. It invades our hearts and torments our minds."[9]

The colons and a number of senior French Army officers were the last to give up their dream of an Algeria that would be forever French. Together the colons and the army forced a change in the French government. General Charles de Gaulle, the French wartime resistance hero, returned to power after a dozen years in retirement. But de Gaulle, a realist, had no intention of keeping Algeria forever French. He began secret negotiations with FLN leaders for Algerian independence.

By 1961 the battlefield had extended into metropolitan France, with bombs set off in cafés and other public places, killing hundreds of people. On its side, the French military routinely used torture and gang-style executions without trial to crush

the rebellion. Some 3,000 of those arrested simply disappeared.[10] Clashes between FLN fighters and those of its Algerian rivals caused further disruptions. In October, the shooting of Paris police officers led to the deaths of several hundred Algerians by the police during a peaceful protest march (an error not revealed by the French government until its archives for the period were opened in 1999). The "Paris massacre" of October 17, 1961 was allegedly ordered by the chief of the Paris police, Maurice Papon. The police attacked a peaceful demonstration of 30,000 supporters of Algeria's independence. Between 100 and 200 people were killed, many of them thrown into the Seine river after being badly beaten by the police. In 1997, Papon was tried and found guilty of complicity in the arrests of 1,690 Jews in Bordeaux and in their subsequent internment and deportation to internment camps from 1942 to 1944. He was also known for having participated in the extensive torture of Algerians during the French occupation of their country.

Subsequently, colon and dissident military leaders united in a last effort to keep Algeria French. They staged an uprising against de Gaulle in Algiers, seizing government buildings and demanding his removal from office. But the bulk of the French Army remained loyal to him.

An attempted assassination of the French president in 1962 was unsuccessful. The colon–military alliance, calling itself the Secret Army Organization (OAS), then launched a savage campaign of violence against the Muslim population, gunning down people or shooting them at random on streets and in public markets. The OAS expected that the FLN would

The rapid growth in the population of Algeria, coupled with urban migration, created a serious housing shortage, but the government has started an ambitious plan to solve the housing crisis and to embellish the city.

break the cease-fire in order to protect its own people. But it did not.

## THE AGONY OF INDEPENDENCE

With the collapse of the OAS campaign against the Algerians and the independence negotiations engaged by France with the FLN in early 1962, the way was clear for Algeria to become an independent modern state. This became a reality on July 2, 1962, after a referendum of the population the day before resulted in 75 percent approving independence. The referendum itself was called for by the agreement (Accords d'Evian) negotiated by the French government and the FLN and signed on March 18, 1962. However, Independence Day is celebrated on July 5th to coincide with the French invasion 132 years earlier.

Few modern nations have become self-governing with so many handicaps. Several hundred thousand people—French, Algerian Muslims, men, women, and children—were casualties of the conflict. Panicked colons and their families left the country; most of them went to France, a land they knew only as visitors. Nearly all of the skilled workers, managers, landowners, and professionals in all fields were French, and they had done little to train Algerian counterparts. Algeria's oil and gas resources were developed by the French. Commercial production and exports began in 1958 and continued through the war for independence; they were not affected, since the Sahara was

governed under a separate military administration. The oil fields were turned over to Algeria after independence but continued to be managed by French technicians until 1970, when the industry was nationalized.

The new Algerian government was also affected by factional rivalries among its leaders. The FLN revolutionaries had to invent a new system, one that would bring dignity and hope to people dehumanized by 130 years of French occupation and eight years of savage war.

The first to emerge from intraparty struggle to lead the country was Ahmed Ben Bella, who had spent much of the war in French prisons but had great prestige as the political brains behind the FLN. Ben Bella laid the groundwork for an Algerian political system centered on the FLN as a single legal political party, and in September 1963, he was elected president. Ben Bella introduced a system of *autogestion* (workers' self-management), by which tenant farmers took over the management of farms abandoned by their colon owners and restored them to production as cooperatives. Autogestion became the basis for Algerian socialism— the foundation of development for decades.

Ben Bella did little else for Algeria, and he alienated most of his former associates with his ambitions for personal power. In June 1965, he was overthrown by the defense minister, Colonel Houari Boume-dienne. Ben Bella was placed under house arrest for 15 years; he was pardoned and exiled in 1980. While in exile, he founded

the Movement for Democracy in Algeria (MDA), a moderate Islamist party. In 1990, he returned to Algeria and announced he would lead his party as a broad-based opposition movement in the framework of the multiparty system. However, neither he nor his party gathered any substantial support in a political environment of over 60 parties, most born after the end, in 1989, of the one-party system which Ben Bella himself established in 1963.

Boumedienne declared that the coup was a "corrective revolution, intended to reestablish authentic socialism and put an end to internal divisions and personal rule."[11] The government was reorganized under a Council of the Revolution, all military men, headed by Boumedienne, who subsequently became president of the republic. A National Charter (an ideological blueprint), approved by voters in 1976, defined Algeria as a socialist state with Islam as the state religion, basic citizens' rights guaranteed, and leadership by the FLN as the only legal political party. A National Popular Assembly was responsible for legislation.

In theory, the Algerian president had no more constitutional powers than the U.S. president. However, in practice, Boumedienne was the ruler of the state, being president, prime minister, and commander of the armed forces rolled into one. In November 1978, he became ill from a rare blood disease; he died in December. For a time, it appeared that factional rivalries would again split the FLN, especially as Boumedienne had named neither a vice-president nor a prime minister, nor had he suggested a successor.

The Algeria of 1978 was a very different country from that of 1962. The scars of war had mostly healed. The FLN closed ranks and named Colonel Chadli Bendjedid to succeed Boumedienne as president for a five-year term. In 1984, Bendjedid was reelected. But the process of ordered socialist development was abruptly and forcibly interrupted in October 1988. A new generation of Algerians, who had come of age long after the war for independence, took to the streets, protesting high prices, lack of jobs, inept leadership, a bloated bureaucracy, and other grievances.

The riots stimulated the institution of political pluralism and the dismantlement of the single-party system. President Bendjedid initially declared a state of emergency; and for the first time since independence, the army was called in to restore order. Some 500 people were killed in the rioting, most of them jobless youths. But the president moved swiftly to mobilize the country in the wake of the violence. In a national referendum, voters approved changes in the governing system to allow political parties to form outside the FLN. Another constitutional change, also effective in 1989, made the cabinet and prime minister responsible to the National Assembly.

The president retained his popularity during the upheaval and was reelected for a third term, winning 81 percent of the votes. A number of new parties were formed in 1989 representing a variety of political and social positions. Among them was the Islamic Front of Salvation (known by its French acronym FIS) which advocated the establishment of an Islamic regime governed by the Shari'a laws, and The Front of Socialist Forces (FFS), founded many years earlier by exiled war of independence leader Hocine Ait Ahmed, and resurfacing with a manifesto urging Algerians to support "the irreversible process of democracy."

For its part, the government sought to revitalize the FLN as a genuine mass party. Recruitment of new members was extended to rural areas. Electoral laws were amended in a way that may help the FLN in electoral contests, notably by giving more weight to the rural districts.

## THE ECONOMY

Beyond the Maghreb region, France is Algeria's first economic partner, with more than 20 percent of all Algerian exports and imports exchanged with that country. Also, some 2 million Algerians live in France. However, relations between the two have not always been cordial. Tensions have arisen as a result of France's support for Morocco on the Western Sahara; unbalanced trade relations in favor of France; the often decried treatment of Algerian emigrants in France, where there is a prevalent negative attitude toward people of North African descent; France's indirect support of a Berber autonomist movement in Algeria; and France's refusal to apologize for the brutal colonization of Algeria. This last issue has stood in the way of a planned treaty of friendship between the two countries. However, these sensitive issues did not prevent normalcy in the relations. In 2008, Algeria agreed to be part of a plan of French President Nicholas Sarkozy to establish a Union for the Mediterranean, a projects-based type of union whose real goals and means remain unclear.

Since assuming leadership, President Bouteflika has tried to counterbalance Algeria's relations with Europe with those with the United States, China, and Russia. Since September 11, 2001, relations with the United States dramatically improved, especially in the area of security, notably because of Algeria's long fight against armed Islamist groups. Also, American investments in Algerian hydrocarbons increased substantially in the last decade. However, in spite of this rapprochement, Algerians do not wholeheartedly and openly embrace the United States due to the latter's unconditional support of Israel, invasion of Iraq, and increased involvement in Afghanistan and Pakistan. It is hoped by both sides that the new American administration led by Barack Hussein Obama and its policies will help change that attitude. Algeria's oil and gas resources were developed by the French. Commercial production and exports began in 1958 and continued through the war for independence; they were not affected, since the Sahara was governed under a separate military administration. The oil fields were turned over to Algeria after independence but continued to be managed by French technicians until 1970, when the industry was nationalized.

During President Boumedienne's period in office, Algeria went through an assertive state construction and a development strategy characterized by the mobilization of all natural resources by the state, the nationalization of foreign assets, the centralization of economic decisionmaking through state planning, and the creation of a strong public sector whose core was a heavy industry. The purpose was to create a self-sustained socialist economy. However, persistent economic difficulties caused by a combination of a failing development strategy, lower oil prices and global oversupply led the Bendjedid government to gradually scrap the socialist orientation and engage in restructuring the industrial sector whose growth was financed by oil revenue and international borrowing.

After a number of years of negative economic growth, the government initiated an austerity program in 1994. The program was approved by the International Monetary Fund. In 1995, the IMF loaned $1.8 billion to cover government borrowing up to 60 percent under the approved austerity program to make the required "structural adjustment." In exchange for the IMF assistance (debt rescheduling and financing assistance), Algeria had to execute a structural adjustment program which included the devaluation of its currency by more than 40 percent, the lifting of subsidies on basic consumption items, the tightening of money and credit policies, the liberalization of foreign trade, the lowering of the budget deficit, and the privatization of failing public enterprises. While some of these measure helped stop the economic decline, they contributed to the worsening of the socioeconomic conditions of the masses due to wide-scale layoffs and reduced or eliminated subsidies, and currency devaluation.

The agricultural sector employs 14 percent of the labor force and accounts for 8.1 percent of gross domestic product. But inasmuch as Algeria must import 70 percent of its food, better agricultural production is essential to overall economic development. Overall agricultural production growth has averaged 5 percent annually since 1990 (5.9 percent in 2007). The autogestion system introduced as a stop-gap measure after independence and enshrined later in FLN economic practice, when it seemed to work, was totally abandoned. In 1988, some 3,500 state farms were converted to collective farms, with individuals holding title to lands.

The key features of Bouteflika's economic reform program, one designed to attract foreign investment, include banking reforms, reduction of the huge government bureaucracy, and privatization of state-owned enterprises. The telecommunications industry was privatized in 2000 and the government-owned cement and steel industries in 2002.

**FREEDOM**

Algeria's constitution, issued in 1976 and amended 4 times, defines the country as a multiparty republic. However, it specifies that no political association may be formed on the basis of religious, linguistic, race, gender, or regional characteristics. The gradual restoration of parliamentary life was expedited with the 2002 election for a National Popular Assembly and the election of two-thirds of the new 144 member upper house, the Council of the Nation; the remaining third was appointed by the president. The Freedom House 2009 Report indicates that "Algerian parliamentary elections are more democratic than those in many other Arab states." Bouteflika was re-elected president in April 2004 by an 83 percent majority, and in April 2009 for a third term after a constitutional amendment ended term limit. In these two elections, military leaders declared their strict neutrality, in effect leaving politics to the politicians and reflecting the will of the people. The independent press remains vibrant in spite of an increase in government restrictions through anti-defamation and security laws. The state of emergency instituted in the early 1990s has not been lifted yet in spite of improved security conditions.

Privatization of state-owned enterprises is a key feature of the government's plan to attract foreign investment; however, the privatization process has been going very slowly. A first attempt to privatize the banking system was shelved in 2009 due to the global financial crisis and some domestic issues.

Since 2002, the government launched two ambitious investment programs to upgrade the infrastructure, to stimulate the development of non-hydrocarbon sectors, and to create jobs. A $7 billion investment plan for economic revival between 2002 and 2004 was complemented by an additional $145 billion Program for the Support of Economic Growth (2005–09). Most of the investment went into housing and infrastructure, including the East-West Highway linking Algeria to east Morocco and Tunisia, desalination stations, some non-hydrocarbon industries and tourism.

The economy has grown at an average rate of 5 percent in recent years, with most macroeconomic indicators on an upward trend. Inflation has remained under control and unemployment has steadily decreased. High oil prices in 2007 and 2008 have helped improve the fiscal and external balances, build up massive foreign exchange reserves ($150 billion by the end of 2008), and pay most of the external debt, bringing it down to less than $4 billion in 2008 from $35 billion just a few years earlier. However, these positive aggregate indices seem to have emboldened the government in 2009 to reverse its foreign investment policy by tightening the rule and imposing substantial limits on foreign investors. Also, these positive economic signs have clashed with worsening socioeconomic conditions for most Algerians. The benefits of economic recovery and substantial hydrocarbon revenues have not yet brought about better living conditions for most people.

## THE CHALLENGE OF RADICAL ISLAMISTS

The failure of successive Algerian governments to resolve severe economic problems, plus the lack of representative political institutions nurtured within the ruling FLN, brought about the rise of religion-based opposition groups which took advantage of the 1988 riots by mobilizing the masses for a radical political change. The Islamic Front of Salvation claimed 3 million adherents among the then 25 million Algerians.

FIS candidates won 55 percent of urban mayoral and council seats in the 1990 municipal elections. The FLN conversely managed to hold on to power largely in the rural areas.

In accordance with President Bendjedid's commitment to multiparty democracy, the first stage of multiparty parliamentary elections took place on December 26, 1991, with FIS candidates winning 188 out of

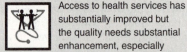

## HEALTH/WELFARE

Access to health services has substantially improved but the quality needs substantial enhancement, especially in efficiency and delivery, and in the oversight of the expanding private medical sector. According to the World Bank, the problems include the prevalence of chronic and infectious diseases and inadequate preventive care for women. In the social assistance/welfare areas, there are problems in targeting and monitoring systems and insurance systems. Although housing availability has been improving, substantial shortages remain. Potable water supply remains a serious problem throughout the country.

231 contested seats. But before the second stage could take place, the army stepped in. FIS leaders were arrested, and the elections were postponed indefinitely. President Bendjedid was pushed by the army to resign on January 17, 1992. Mohammed Boudiaf, one of the nine historic chiefs of the Revolution, returned from years of exile in Morocco to become head of the Higher Council of State, set up by military leaders after the aborted elections and resignation of President Bendjedid. FIS headquarters was closed and the party declared illegal by a court in Algiers. Local councils and provincial assemblies formed by the FIS after the elections were dissolved and replaced by "executive delegations" appointed by the Higher Council.

Subsequently, Boudiaf named a 60-member Consultative Council to work with the various political factions to reach a consensus on reforms. However, the refusal of such leaders as former president Ben Bella and Socialist Forces Front (FFS) leader Hocine Ait Ahmed to participate limited its effectiveness. On June 29, 1992, Boudiaf was assassinated, reportedly by a member of his own presidential guard.

With Boudiaf gone, Algeria's generals turned to their own ranks for new leadership. In 1994, General Liamine Zeroual, who had retired from the military, was named head of state by the Higher Council. Zeroual pledged that elections for president would be held in November 1995 as a first step toward the restoration of parliamentary government. The top FIS leaders, Abbas Madani and Ali Belhaj, who had been given 12-year jail sentences for "endangering state security" were released but had their sentences commuted to house arrest, on the assumption that in return for dialogue, they would call a halt to the spiraling violence.

However, the dialogue proved inconclusive, and Zeroual declared that the presidential elections would be held on schedule. Earlier, leaders of the FIS, FFS, FLN, and several smaller parties had met in Rome, Italy, under the sponsorship of Sant-Egidio, a Catholic service agency, and announced a "Rome Platform." It called for the restoration of FIS political rights in return for an end to violence, multiparty democracy, and exclusion of the military from government. The Algerian "personality" was defined in the Contract as Islamic, Arab, and Berber.

Military leaders rejected the Rome Platform due to the FIS's participation. However, the November 1995 presidential election was held as scheduled, and Zeroual won handily, as expected, garnering 61 percent of the votes. But the fact that the election was held at all, despite a boycott call by several party leaders and threats of violence from the Armed Islamic Group (GIA), was impressive.[12]

## THE KILLING FIELDS OF THE 1990s

Algeria's modern history has been well described as one of excesses. Thus "the colonial period was unusually harsh, the war for independence particularly costly . . . . the insistence on one-party rule initially unwavering and the projects for industrialization overly ambitious," as specialists on the country have noted.[13] Extremes of violence are nothing new in Algerian life. But in addition to horrifying violence, the real tragedy of the conflict has been to pit "an inflexible regime and a fanatical opposition" against "innocent victims doomed by their secular lifestyle or their piety."[14]

Shortly before the 1995 election, Ahmed Ben Bella, Algeria's first president and the leader of the Movement for a Democratic Algeria, wrote a thoughtful analysis of the "dialogue at Rome" in which he had participated and that produced the National Contract. He noted: "A mad escalation of violence is the hallmark of everyday life. Nobody is safe: journalists, intellectuals, women, children and old people are all equally threatened. Yet the use of force, the recourse to violence, will not allow any of the protagonists to solve the problem to their advantage, and the solution must be a political one." The dialogue at Rome, he added, "was meant to lead to a consensus that would bring together everyone—including the regime in power—within the framework of the current Constitution, which stipulates political pluralism, democracy, respect for all human rights and freedoms."[15]

The conflict between the armed wing of the FIS, the Armed Islamic Group (GIA), and the military regime reached a level of violence in the period after the 1995 "election" that left no room for compromise. The GIA targeted not only the army and police but also writers, journalists, government officials and other public figures, professional women, even doctors and dentists. Ironically, one of its victims was the head of the Algerian League for Human Rights, which had protested the detention without trial of some 9,000 FIS members in roofless prisons deep in the Sahara, under unbelievably harsh conditions.

The GIA widened its circle of violence in the rest of the decade before it died out by the end of the 1990s. In addition to Algerians it carried out attacks on foreigners, killing tourists as well as long-term foreign residents. Rural villages were easy targets, since they had neither police nor army protection. Entire village populations were massacred in a manner eerily reminiscent of the war for independence. The army and security forces did their share of killings, often arresting people and holding them indefinitely without charges. In 2003 the international organization Human Rights Watch reported that in addition to 120,000 deaths, some 7,000 persons had simply disappeared, never to be seen again by their families.

---

## ACHIEVEMENTS

Algeria's recent economic achievements include the end of a steep economic decline, the substantial improvement of aggregate indices and the return of foreign investors. The external debt was slashed to less than $4 billion by the end of 2008 from a high of $35 billion in the mid-1990s and $16.5 billion just two years ago. As a result of increased income from high oil prices in 2006–2008, the country's foreign exchange reserves reached $140 billion. Budget deficits were replaced by surpluses and inflation was reduced to 3 percent from a high of 30 percent in the 1990s. Also, the unemployment rate was reduced to 12 percent by 2009 from a high of 35 percent a decade ago; however, among the youth it remains substantially high.

---

Through referenda, President Bouteflika enacted two amnesty programs (2000 and 2005) that allowed Islamic militants who did not commit blood crimes to give up the fight and surrender their weapons without being prosecuted. The Islamic Army of Salvation (AIS), one of the largest armed groups, was first to take advantage of the new law. Thousands of fighters accepted the amnesty deal and hundreds more were freed from jail while several exiled leaders returned to the country. The Salafist Group

for Preaching and Combat (GSPC), a small ultra-conservative faction which rejected the amnesty deal, sought radical change through violence and occasionally attacks military and civilian targets. In a probable survival effort, it officially declared in January 2007 that it had become part of al-Qaeda and renamed itself al-Qaeda in the Islamic Land of the Maghreb. Since then, it has claimed several terrorist actions which killed scores of civilians and security personnel in Algeria, Morocco, Tunisia, and Mauritania.

## WHAT PRICE DIALOGUE?

In June 1997, following Zeroual's accession to the presidency, elections to the 380-member Assembly took place, the first national election since the one aborted in 1992. A newly formed party to support Zeroual, the National Democratic Rally, won 115 seats. Along with the FLN's 64 seats, the results gave the regime a slim majority. Two moderate Islamist parties (so called because they rejected violence) also participated in the elections. The Movement obtained 69 seats; and Ennahdah won 34 seats, giving at least a semblance of opposition in the Assembly. The 1997 local and municipal elections continued the trend as government-backed candidates won the majority of seats.

In fall 1999, Zeroual resigned and scheduled open presidential elections for April. His resignation appears to have been caused by the army's opposition to his dialogue attempt with the radical groups for the purpose of restoring peace and security. Among the seven candidates who hoped to replace him was former foreign minister Abdelaziz Bouteflika, who had lived in the Gulf for many years. Subsequently all the other candidates withdrew, citing irregularities in the election process. But the election went off as scheduled, and Bouteflika was declared the winner, with 74 percent of the vote.

Bouteflika's good intentions and early success became mired in 2000 and 2001 in a power struggle with military leaders. However, the popular approval of his 1999 amnesty program which was geared toward establishing lasting peace and security, strengthened his legitimacy and power position. However, the ills from which the country was suffering were numerous and quite challenging to the new leader.

In 2001, riots in Kabylia have compounded Bouteflika's difficulties. Berber militants of that region have chafed since independence against Arab cultural domination, and have fought to preserve their culture and language. The death of a young

Berber while in the custody of the gendarmerie (rural paramilitary police) sparked riots during April and May 2001. Rioters clashed with gendarmerie in Bejaia and Tizi Ouzou, the regional capitals, after heavy-handed police actions had killed some 80 persons.

Under continued pressure from Berber militants, the government officially recognized the Berber culture as a fundamental component of Algerian identity, and agreed to make the Berber language (Tamazight) a national language, next to Arabic, but refused to make it an official one. Earlier, under Zeroual, a High Council for the Amazigh language was created, with a role to promote the Berber language and oversee its teaching in schools.

The Kabyle challenge, which primarily had the hallmarks of an ethnocultural conflict, dealt in fact with a host of problems from which most of the country's population suffers, including housing shortages, high unemployment among the youth, the repressive and unresponsive government, injustice, and lack of accountability of high office holders. In the 15-point list of demands presented by the Berberist militants, only one dealt with the language issue. What is worth noting also, is that the movement was led by informal village associations, known as "arch" rather than the Berber based political parties (FFS and the Rally for Culture and Democracy, RCD) which were shunned because of their disconnection from their constituencies and their ineffectiveness in a political system that leaves little room for the impact of opposition parties.[16]

In the May 2007 parliamentary elections, the FLN won a majority of seats, but the results were tainted by the fact that only 35.51 percent of the electorate participated. This lack of interest suggests that most Algerians have lost faith in the political process, parties and leaders, who have failed to address their pressing problems. Reports of recent visitors indicate that the main concerns for most Algerians today are the cost of living, housing and security. President Bouteflika promised just that when he ran for a third presidential term and won in April 2009. However, since 2007, security, which had improved in previous years, started to deteriorate as the al-Qaeda in the Land of Islamic Maghreb (AQIM, former GSPC) increased its attacks and started resorting to suicide bombing, something that was not used even in the worst years of violence of the 1990s. Most attacks targeted security personnel and foreign workers, but many Algerian civilians were also killed. The standards of living seem to worsen for the masses as the cost of living increased and incomes did not, in spite of the substantial hydrocarbon export earnings. By the end of 2009, Algeria appears to have the means to weather these various challenges, but it also runs the risk of another major social explosion if significant and well designed economic and political reforms are not quickly put in place.

## FOREIGN POLICY

During the first decade of independence, Algeria's foreign policy was strongly nationalistic and anti-Western. Having won their independence from a colonial power, the Algerians were vocally hostile toward the United States and its allies, calling them enemies of popular liberation and ruthless imperialist powers. Algeria supported revolutionary movements all over the world, providing funds, arms, and training. The Palestine Liberation Organization, rebels against Portuguese colonial rule in Mozambique, Muslim guerrillas fighting the Christian Ethiopian government in Eritrea—all benefited from active Algerian support.

The government broke diplomatic relations with the United States in 1967, due to American support for Israel, and did not restore them for a decade. In the mid-1970s, Algeria moderated its anti-Western stance in favor of nonalignment and good relations with both East and West. Relations improved thereafter to such a point that Algerian mediators were instrumental in resolving the 1979–1980 American hostage crisis in Iran.

In the 1980s, internal economic and political problems and changed global circumstances led to a further pragmatic shift in Algeria's foreign policy. Strategic, economic, and political interests became more important than ideological commitment to Third World causes. Political liberalization further increased the constraints, and Algerian foreign policy came to reflect the actions of a state accountable to its citizens and their perspectives, as evidenced by the dramatic reversal of the government's position on the Iraqi invasion of Kuwait in 1990.

Thanks to President Bouteflika, Algeria has regained a prominent place in the Organization of African Unity (OAU), mainly in the areas on conflict resolution and economic development. He assumed the presidency of the OAU for one year after Algeria hosted its 1999 summit, and successfully mediated a peace agreement between Ethiopia and Eritrea. When the OAU changed into the African Union in 2001, Algeria started playing an active role in the New African Partnership for Africa's Development (NEPAD). In July, 2009, Algeria hosted the second African cultural festival—the first was held in 1968.

Algeria has been little active in the Arab League, mainly regarding support to the Palestinian cause. At the time of the Iraqi inva-

## Timeline: PAST

**1518–1520**
Establishment of the Regency of Algiers

**1827–1830**
The French conquest, triggered by the "fly-whisk incident"

**1847**
The defeat of Abd al-Qadir by French forces

**1871**
Algeria becomes an overseas department of France

**1936**
The Blum-Viollette Plan, for Muslim rights, is annulled by colon opposition

**1943**
Ferhat Abbas issues the Manifesto of the Algerian People

**1954–1962**
War of independence ending with Algerian independence

**1965**
Ben Bella is overthrown by Boumedienne

**1976**
The National Charter commits Algeria to revolutionary socialist development

**1978**
President Boumedienne dies

**1980s**
Land reform is resumed with the breakup of 200 large farms into smaller units; Arabization campaign

**1990s**
The first multiparty elections are annulled by the army when the FIS was poised to win them; President Bendjedid is pushed to resign; the FIS was banned and its leaders imprisoned; the Islamists started a ten-year armed rebellion

**1999**
Abdelaziz Bouteflika elected by voters as new president. His first action was to propose an amnesty program inviting the armed Islamists to surrender and not be persecuted. The plan was popularly approved via referendum.

**2001**
Berber Spring, many demonstrators killed in clashes between security forces and Berber militants in Kabylie region after the death of a teenager in gendarmerie custody.

**2002**
Berber language is recognized as national language; Multiparty parliamentary elections and establishment of the upper house of parliament, the Council of the Nation; a second amnesty program for the Islamist rebels is enacted; President Bouteflika is elected for a second term

**2003**
A powerful earthquake east of Algiers kills over 2,000 people; FIS leaders Madani and Belhadj released

## PRESENT

**2007**
The GSPCS renamed itself the al-Qaeda in the Land of Islamic Maghreb; Parliamentary elections with the lowest voter turnout ever (35 percent) but pro-government parties retain absolute majority

**2008**
Constitutional amendment by parliament deletes presidential term limit

**2009**
President Bouteflika elected for a third term

sion of Kuwait in August 1990, an offensive of the Western coalition, the government was pushed by popular mobilization in favor of Iraq to abandon its initial neutral position.

Algeria's relations with its neighbors were strained after independence, but stabilized after two decades, except with Morocco. Relations between the two countries have mostly been marked by suspicion and hostility. The two clashed briefly in 1963 over ownership of the Tindouf region in south west Algeria, which Morocco invaded and occupied briefly. Algeria also supported the Western Saharan nationalist movement fighting for independence from Spain, and later against Moroccan occupation. Algeria provided bases, sanctuary, funds, and weapons to the Polisario Front, the military wing of the movement. Algeria and many other countries recognized the self-declared Sahrawi Arab Democratic Republic in 1980 and sponsored SADR membership in the Organization for African Unity (OAU). Furthermore, the two countries' border has been closed since 1994 following Morocco's imposition of a visa requirement on Algerians after a terrorist attack killed two Spanish tourists in Marrakech; Morocco accused Algeria of being behind the attack. In 1989, a treaty established an economic and political Arab Maghrib Union (UMA) between Algeria, Libya, Mauritania, Morocco, and Tunisia. However, due to remaining differences between Morocco and Algeria, the Union is still just a project on paper.

Beyond the Maghreb region, France is Algeria's first economic partner, with more than 20 percent of all Algerian exports and imports exchanged with that country. Also, some 2 million Algerians live in France. However, relations between the two have not always been cordial. Tensions have arisen as a result of France's support for Morocco on the Western Sahara; unbalanced trade relations in favor of France; the often decried treatment of Algerian emigrants in France, where there is a prevalent negative attitude toward people of North African descent; France's indirect support of a Berber autonomist movement in Algeria; and France's refusal to apologize for the brutal colonization of Algeria. This last issue has stood in the way of a planned treaty of friendship between the two countries. However, these sensitive issues did not prevent normalcy in the relations. In 2008, Algeria agreed to be part of a plan of French President Nicholas Sarkozy to establish a Union for the Mediterranean, a projects-based type of union whose real goals and means remain unclear.

Since assuming leadership, President Bouteflika has tried to counterbalance Algeria's relations with Europe with those with the United States, China, and Russia. Since September 11, 2001, relations with the United States dramatically improved, especially in the area of security, notably because of Algeria's long fight against armed Islamist groups. Also, American investments in Algerian hydrocarbons increased substantially in the last decade. However, in spite of this rapprochement, Algerians do not wholeheartedly and openly embrace the United States due to the latter's unconditional support of Israel, invasion of Iraq, and increased involvement in Afghanistan and Pakistan. It is hoped by both sides that the new American administration led by Barack Hussein Obama and its policies will help change that attitude.

Relations with Europe and the United States have substantially changed by the end of the 1990s. Economic liberalization at home and a moderate foreign policy have effected this shift. Algeria's importance to the West came to be based on that country's energy resources, increasing global demand for them, as well as a common fight against radical Islamism.

## NOTES

1. See William Spencer, *Algiers in the Age of the Corsairs* (Norman, OK: University of Oklahoma Press, 1976), Centers of Civilization Series. "The corsair, if brought to justice in maritime courts, identified himself as *corsale* or *Korsan,* never as fugitive or criminal; his occupation was as clearly identifiable as that of tanner, goldsmith, potter or tailor," p. 47.

2. Raphael Danziger, *Abd al-Qadir and the Algerians* (New York: Holmes and Meier, 1977), notes that Turkish intrigue kept the tribes in a state of near-constant tribal warfare, thereby preventing them from forming dangerous coalitions, p. 24.

3. The usual explanation for the quick collapse of the regency after 300 years is that its forces were prepared for naval warfare but not for attack by land. Danziger, *Abd al-Qadir and the Algerians,* Op. Cit., pp. 36–38.

4. Quoted in Harold D. Nelson, *Algeria, A Country Study* (Washington, D.C.: American University, Foreign Area Studies, 1979), p. 31.

5. Azzedine Layachi, "French Genocide in Algeria," *Encyclopedia of Genocide and Crimes Against Humanity,* (Macmillan Reference USA, 2005).

6. Marnia Lazreg, *The Emergence of Classes in Algeria* (Boulder, CO: Westview Press, 1976), p. 53.

7. For Algerian Muslims to become French citizens meant giving up their religion, for all practical purposes, since Islam recognizes only Islamic law and to be a French citizen means accepting French laws. Fewer than 3,000 Algerians became French citizens during the period of French rule. Nelson, *op. cit.,* pp. 34–35.

8. John E. Talbott, *The War Without a Name: France in Algeria, 1954–1962* (New York: Alfred A. Knopf, 1980).

9. Georges Suffert, in *Esprit,* 25 (1957), p. 819.

10. The opening of French historical archives in 1999 and recent interviews with leading French generals in Algiers at the time, such as Jacques Massu, have reopened the debate in France about the conduct of the war. In December 2000, members of the French Communist Party, which had backed the FLN, urged the formation of a special commission to investigate charges of torture and provide compensation for the victims' families. Retired general Paul Aussarress was fined $6,500 in 2001 for his 1999 book, *Algeria Special Forces 1955–1957,* in which he admitted the torture and execution of many Algerians and the disappearance of some 3,000 suspects while in custody; he was charged with "trying to justify war."

11. Nelson, *op. cit.,* p. 68.

12. Robert Mortimer, "Algeria: The Dialectic of Elections and Violence," *Current History* (May 1997), p. 232.

13. Frank Ruddy, who was assigned to Tindouf by the United Nations as a member of the observer group monitoring the referendum in the Western Sahara, comments on the town's national-history museum, "the one cultural attraction." However, "most of its space is devoted to especially grisly photos of terrible things the French did to Algerians during the Algerian war of independence." *The World & I* (August 1997), p. 138.

14. "One last chance for Algeria," *The Independent* (UK) (March 16, 1995). www .independent.co.uk/opinion/leading-article-one-last-chance-for-algeria-1611394.html

15. Ahmed Ben Bella, "A Time for Peace in Algeria," *The World Today* Vol. 51, No 11 (November 1995), p. 209.

16. For more on the Berber challenge in Kabylie, see Azzedine Layachi, "The Berbers in Algeria: Politicization of Ethnicity and Ethnicization of Politics," in Maya Shatzmiller, ed., *Nationalism and Minority Identities in Islamic Societies,* (McGill University Press, 2005): 193–228.

# Bahrain (State of Bahrain)

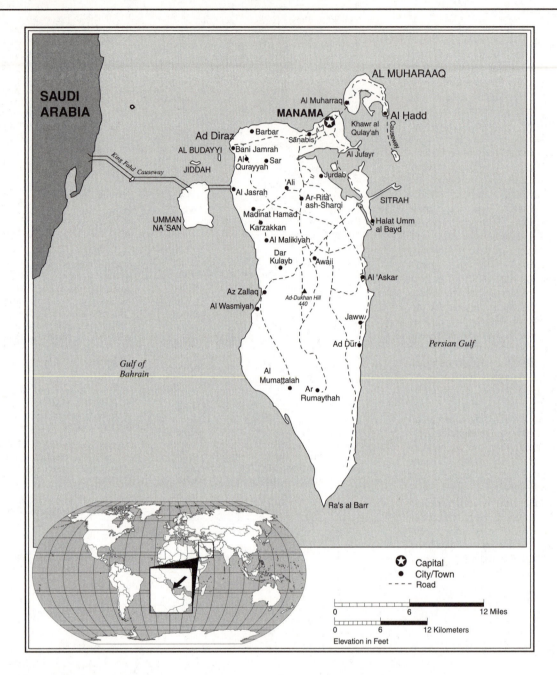

# Bahrain Statistics

## GEOGRAPHY

*Area in Square Miles (Kilometers):* 266 (688) (about 3 $\frac{1}{2}$ times the size of Washington, D.C.)

*Capital (Population):* Manama (166,200)

*Environmental Concerns:* desertification; coastal degradation resulting from oil spills and discharges from ships and industry; no natural freshwater

*Geographical Features:* mostly low desert plain, rising gently to low central escarpment

*Climate:* hot and humid summers; temperate winters

## PEOPLE

### Population

*Total:* 738,004 (235,108 non-nationals)

*Annual Growth Rate:* 1.243%

*Rural/Urban Population Ratio:* 9/91

*Major Languages:* Arabic; English widely used; Farsi, Urdu

*Ethnic Makeup:* 63% Bahraini; 19% Asian; 10% other Arab; 8% Iranian

*Religions:* 70% Shi'a Muslim; 15% Sunni Muslim; 15% Bahai, Christian, and others

## Health

*Life Expectancy at Birth:* 72 years (male),
78 years (female)
*Infant Mortality Rate (Ratio):* 14.76/1,000
live births

## Education

*Adult Literacy Rate:* 89%
*Compulsory (Ages):* 6–17; free

## COMMUNICATION

*Telephones:* 220,000 main lines
*Daily Newspaper Circulation:* 128 per
1,000 people
*Televisions:* 442 per 1,000 people
*Internet Users:* 402,900 (2000)

## TRANSPORTATION

*Highways in Miles (Kilometers):* 1,927
(3,103)
*Railroads in Miles (Kilometers):* none
*Usable Airfields:* 3
*Motor Vehicles in Use:* 172,000

## GOVERNMENT

*Type:* Hereditary monarchy as per 2002
Constitution
*Independence Date:* August 15, 1971
(from the United Kingdom)
*Head of State/Government:* King
Hamad bin Isa al-Khalifa; Prime
Minister Shaykh Salman bin Hamad
al-Khalifa
*Political Parties:* none formally approved,
but "political societies" were legalized
under a 2005 royal decree
*Suffrage:* none formalized

## MILITARY

*Military Expenditures (% of GDP):*
4.5%
*Current Disputes:* none; dispute with
Qatar resolved in 2001

## ECONOMY

*Currency ($U.S. Equivalent):* 0.377
dinar = $1 (fixed rate)

*Per Capita Income/GDP:* $25,300/$17.7
billion
*GDP Growth Rate:* 7.6%
*Inflation Rate:* 3.5%
*Unemployment Rate:* 15%
*Labor Force:* 370,000 (4,470
non-nationals)
*Natural Resources:* oil; associated and
non-associated natural gas; fish
*Agriculture:* fruits; vegetables; poultry;
dairy products; shrimp; fish
*Industry:* petroleum processing and
refining; aluminum smelting; offshore
banking; ship repairing; tourism
*Exports:* $12.62 billion (primary
partners India, United States, Saudi
Arabia)
*Imports:* $9 billion (primary partners
Saudi Arabia, Japan, Germany)

## SUGGESTED WEB SITES

http://lcweb2.loc.gov/frd/cs/
bhtoc.html
www.usembassy.com.bh

# Bahrain Country Report

**B**ahrain is the smallest Arab state. It is also
the only Arab island state, consisting of an
archipelago of 33 islands, just five of them
inhabited. The largest island, also named
Bahrain (from the Arabic *bahrayn,* or "two
seas"), has an area of 216 square miles.

Although it is separated from the Arabian mainland, Bahrain is not far away; it
is just 15 miles from Qatar and the same
distance from Saudi Arabia. A causeway
linking Bahrain with mainland Saudi Arabia opened in 1986, technically ending its
insular status. Improvements to the causeway in 2001 link the country even closer to
its larger neighbor, as Saudis pour across
the border to enjoy the movies, bars, and
shopping boutiques of the freer Bahraini
society.

Bahrain is unusual among the Persian
Gulf states in that it started to diversify
its economy early. Oil was discovered
there in 1932. Its head start in the exportation of oil enabled the government to build
up an industrial base over a long period
and to develop a large, indigenous, skilled
labor force.

## HISTORY

Excavations by archaeologists indicate that
roughly 5,000 years ago, Bahrain was the
legendary *Dilmun,* "home of the gods" and
the land of immortality in the Mesopotamian Epic of Gilgamesh. It had a fully
urbanized society and was the center of a
far-flung trade network between Mesopotamia, Oman, the Arabian Gulf, and the
Indus Valley cities farther east.

### DEVELOPMENT

Bahrain's economy continues
to develop and diversify. GDP
continued steady in the early
years of the new millennium,
reaching 7.6 percent in 2006–2007. In
addition to a revived offshore banking industry
it has the largest concentration of Islamic
(non-interest charging) banks in the region.

During the centuries of Islamic rule in
the Middle East, Bahrain (it was renamed
by Arab geographers) became wealthy from
the pearl-fishing industry. By the fourteenth
century A.D., it had 300 villages. Bahraini
merchants grew rich from profits on their
large, lustrous, high-quality pearls. Bahraini sea captains and pearl merchants built
lofty palaces and other stately buildings on
the islands.

The Portuguese were the first Europeans
to land on Bahrain, which they seized in the
early sixteenth century as one of a string of
fortresses along the coast to protect their
monopoly over the spice trade. They ruled
by the sword in Bahrain for nearly a century
before they were ousted by Iranian invaders. The Iranians, in turn, were defeated
by the al-Khalifas, a clan of the powerful
Anaizas. In 1782, the clan leader, Shaykh
Ahmad al-Khalifa, established control over
Bahrain and founded the dynasty that rules
the state today. (The al-Khalifas belong to
the same clan as the al-Sabahs, the rulers
of Kuwait, and are distantly related to the
Saudi Arabian royal family.)

### A British Protectorate

In the 1800s, Bahrain came under British protection in the same way as other Gulf states.
The ruler Shaykh Isa, whose reign was one of
the world's longest (1869–1932), signed an
agreement making Britain responsible for
Bahrain's defense and foreign policy. He
also agreed not to give any concessions for
oil exploration without British approval.
The agreement was important because
the British were already developing oil
fields in Iran. Control of oil in another
area would give them an added source of
fuel for the new weaponry of tanks and
oil-powered warships of World War I.
The early development of Bahrain's oil
fields and the guidance of British political
advisers helped prepare the country for
independence.

## INDEPENDENCE

Bahrain became fully independent in 1971. The British encouraged Bahrain to join with Qatar and seven small British-protected Gulf states, the Trucial States, in a federation. However, Bahrain and Qatar felt that they were more advanced economically, politically, and socially than were the Trucial States and therefore did not need to federate.

A mild threat to Bahrain's independence came from Iran. In 1970, Shah Mohammed Reza Pahlavi of Iran claimed Bahrain, on the basis of Iran's sixteenth-century occupation, plus the fact that a large number of Bahrainis were descended from Iranian emigrants. The United Nations discussed the issue and recommended that Bahrain be given its independence, on the grounds that

### FREEDOM

Reinstatement of the suspended 1973 constitution and the National Action Charter issued by decree marked King Hamad's moves to restore parliament after years of absolute royal rule. In 2005 the ruler also ended the 25-year state of emergency which had effectively suspended civil rights. Although political parties are still proscribed, in 2006 elections were held for the lower house of Parliament. Al-Wifaq, the Shi'a–dominated "political opposition society," won the majority of seats. The Charter also gives women the right to vote and run for public office. A number did so, but none were elected. Subsequently the ruling emir appointed seven women as cabinet ministers.

"the people of Bahrain wish to gain recognition of their identity in a fully independent and sovereign state."[1] The shah accepted the resolution, and Iran made no further claims on Bahrain during his lifetime.

The gradual development of democracy in Bahrain reached a peak after independence. Shaykh Khalifa (now called emir) approved a new Constitution and a law establishing an elected National Assembly of 30 members. The Assembly met for the first time in 1973, but it was dissolved by the emir only two years later.

### What Had Happened?

Bahrain is an example of a problem common in the Middle East: the conflict between traditional authority and democracy. Fuad Khuri describes the problem as one of a "tribally controlled government that rules by historical right, opposed to a community-based urban population seeking to participate in government through elections. The first believes and acts as if government is an earned right, the other seeks to modify government and subject it to a public vote."[2]

Governmental authority in Bahrain is defined as hereditary in the al-Khalifa family, according to the 1973 Constitution. The succession passes from the ruling emir to his eldest son. Since Bahrain has no tradition of representative government or political parties, the National Assembly was set up to broaden the political process without going through the lengthy period of conditioning necessary to establish a multiparty system. Members were expected to debate laws prepared by the Council of Ministers and to assist with budget preparation. But as things turned out, Assembly members spent their time arguing with one another or criticizing the ruler instead of dealing with issues. When the emir dissolved the Assembly, he said that it was preventing the government from doing what it was supposed to do.

Since that time, government in Bahrain has reverted to its traditional patriarchal-authority structure. However, Shi'a demands for reinstatement of the Assembly, a multiparty system with national elections, and greater representation for Shi'as in government have been met in part through changes in the governing structure. In 1993, the emir appointed a 30-member *Majlis al-Shura* (Consultative Council), composed of business and industry leaders along with members of the ruling family.

King Hamad, who changed his title as part of the country's move toward constitutional monarchy, has taken several long steps in that direction in recent years. In 2000 the Shura Council was enlarged to 40 members, including women and representatives of the large Shi'a community. The King

(United Nations Photo/Ian Steele (UN152807))

Students and their teacher at a nursery school near Manama. Bahrain may be the first of the Gulf states to get out of the oil business, due to its dwindling reserves. Other income-generating industries are being explored, and the diversification of the economy, along with political stability, make Bahrain a stable regional business center. The need for an effective educational system to supply an informed labor force is paramount.

appointed also, for the first time, non-Muslims to the Consultative Council, including a Christian—and a Jewish businessman. The king also issued a "National Action Charter" which was endorsed in a referendum by 80 percent of voters. It provides for release of political prisoners, abolition of state security courts, and the annulment of a 1974 law which permitted imprisonment without trial or the right of appeal for persons charged with "political" crimes.

The region-wide anger over the U.S. invasion of Iraq and its continued support for Israel in its dealing with the Palestinians, reached Bahrain in 2005 as people staged the largest protest demonstration in memory. Earlier in the year, demands by opposition movement's bloggers to use the Internet website to demand a new constitution, separation of powers, and greater political liberties resulted in arrests of several bloggers. The ministry of information then issued an edict requiring all websites to be registered with the government. One of them, Bahrain Online, had posted a UN report of governmental discrimination of the Shi'a majority.

In 2002, Bahrain held its first local and parliamentary elections in almost 30 years and allowed for the first time women to vote and be candidates. No woman was elected, but in April 2004, Nada Haffadh, who was made health minister, was the first woman to head a ministry. The Shi'a opposition also made political headway when, in the 2006 parliamentary elections, it won 40 percent of the vote, making it possible for a Shi'a Muslim, Jawad bin Salem al-Oraied, to become deputy prime minister. However, in spite of these political reforms, opposition to the monarchy has remained quite active.

In December 2008, many people were arrested for allegedly planning to detonate bombs during national celebrations. To mend fences for such unrelenting opposition, the monarch pardoned in April 2009 more than 170 prisoners accused of threatening national security—35 of them were accused of trying to overthrow the monarchy itself.

This was not the first development of this nature since the 1979 Revolution in Iran caused much concern in Bahrain. The new Iranian government revived then old territorial claims, and a Teheran-based Islamic

Front for the Liberation of Bahrain called on Shi'a Muslims in Bahrain to overthrow the Sunni regime of the emir. In 1981, the government arrested a group of Shi'a Bahrainis and others, charging them with a plot (backed by Iran) against the state. The plotters had expected support from the Shi'a population, but this did not materialize. After seeing the results of the Iranian Revolution, few Bahraini Shi'a Muslims wanted the Iranian form of Islamic government. In 1982, 73 defendants were given prison sentences ranging from seven years to life.

Until the 1990s, the Shi'a community was politically inactive, and as a result, 100 Shi'a activists were pardoned by the emir and allowed to return from exile. However, the increase in opposition activities (especially Islamist) against Middle Eastern regimes elsewhere has caused serious concern in the island country. Between 1994 and 1999, a low-level campaign of antigovernment violence claimed 30 lives and resulted in a number of sabotage incidents. In 1996, eight opposition leaders were arrested; they included Shaykh Abdul-Ameer al-Jamri, allegedly the head of the opposition movement. In July 1999, he was given a 10-year jail sentence and fined $14.5 million for having spied for an unnamed foreign power, for inciting unrest, and for continuing to agitate illegally for political reform. But he was released the day after his sentencing, partly due to his ill health, but also due to criticisms from the United States and other countries of Bahrain's failure to respect his civil and legal rights. The government also released some 320 other detainees. As indicated by these events, the pattern of repression followed by some accommodation of the opposition continues through the late 2000s. However, it is important to note that the opposition to monarchy and its policies has not been limited to Shi'a groups.

The main Shi'a political group Al Wefaq has not been alone in making demands for serious and sustained political, social and economic reforms. It is often joined also by Sunni groups. "Shiite and Sunni groups have successfully teamed up . . . in pressing Bahrain to release information on its management of public companies" and to enact comprehensive reforms. However, the Sunni groups do not push for the power sharing demand of their Shi'a counterparts. The latter also want "an end to what they say are government efforts to grant nationality to foreign Sunnis, which would dilute Shiite numbers. They also want more low-income housing."[3]

## FOREIGN RELATIONS

United States interest in Bahrain dates back over a century (see Health/Welfare Box). American missionaries subsequently founded a number of schools, including the

Bahrain-American School, which still exists. In recent years, Bahrain has become a key factor in U.S. Middle Eastern policy, due to its strategic location in the Persian Gulf. During the Iran–Iraq War, Bahrain's British-built naval base was a staging point for U.S. convoy escort vessels in the Gulf. Then, in the aftermath of the 1991 Gulf War, Bahrain became a "front-line state" in the American containment strategy toward Iraq. It is the permanent headquarters for the new U.S. Fifth Fleet, under a mutual defense agreement, with some 1,000 American military and naval personnel stationed there. Following the September 11, 2001 terrorist attacks in the United States, Bahrain supported the international coalition against terrorism and granted use of its base for U.S. air strikes in Afghanistan.

Bahrain's only serious foreign-policy problem since its independence has involved neighboring Qatar. In 1992, the Qatari ruler unilaterally extended Qatar's territorial waters to include the islands of Hawar and Fishat al-Duble, which had been controlled by Bahrain since the 1930s, when both countries were British protectorates. Bahrain in turn demanded that Qatar recognize Bahrain's sovereignty over the al-Zeyara coastal strip, which adjoins Bahraini territorial waters. After considerable wrangling, the two countries agreed to take their dispute to the International Court of Justice (ICJ). In 2001, the ICJ confirmed Qatari sovereignty over Zabarah and Janan Islands. Bahrain was awarded sovereignty over Hawar and Qit'at Jaradeh Islands. The boundary between their maritime zones is to be drawn in accordance with the Court's decision.

In 1981, concern over threats from its more powerful neighbors led Bahrain to join with other Gulf states in forming the Gulf Cooperation Council, a regional mutual-defense organization. The other members are Kuwait, Oman, Qatar, Saudi Arabia, and the United Arab Emirates. In 2001, the members signed a formal defense pact, sponsored by the United States. The pact expanded the rapid-deployment force of 5,000 soldiers to 22,000, with members contributing troops in accordance with the size of their armed forces. The United States agreed to provide a $70 million early warning system to identify any chemical or biological weapons used by belligerent forces in an attack on GCC member states. In 2004 Bahrain and the United States signed a Free Trade Agreement and in January 2008, President George W. Bush made the first visit by a sitting president to Bahrain, whereas King Hamad visited Washington the following March.

## AN OIL-LESS ECONOMY?

Bahrain was an early entrant in the oil business and may be the first Gulf state to face an oil-less future. Current production

## ACHIEVEMENTS

In 2002 a female lawyer, Dr. Mariam bint Hassan Al-Khalifa, was appointed president of Bahrain University, the first to hold such a position in the Arab world. And in 2003 Bahrain's economy was named as the freest in the Arab Middle East by the Heritage Foundation.

from its own oil fields is 42,000 barrels per day. The Bahrain Petroleum Company (Bapco) controls all aspects of production, refining, and export. However, Bapco must import 70,000 b/d from Saudi Arabia to keep its refinery operating efficiently.

In the past, Bahrain's economic development was characterized by conservative management. This policy changed radically with the accession of the current ruler. A January 2001 decree allows foreign companies to buy and own property, particularly for non-oil investment projects. (Oil currently accounts for 80 percent of exports and 60 percent of revenues.)

The slow decline in oil production in recent years has been balanced by expansion of the liquefied natural gas (LNG) sector. Current production is 170 million cubic feet per day. But with 9 billion cubic feet of proven reserves, production of LNG will long outlast oil production.

Aluminium Bahrain (ALBA), which accounts for 60 percent of Bahrain's non-oil exports, expanded its production in 2001 to become the world's largest aluminium smelter, with an annual output of 750,000 tons. Some 450,000 of this is exported. A seawater-desalination plant was completed in 1999. It uses waste heat from the smelter to provide potable water for local needs.

## INTERNATIONAL FINANCE

During the Lebanese Civil War, Bahrain encouraged the establishment of "Offshore Banking Units" in order to replace Lebanon as a regional finance center. OBUs are set up to attract deposits from governments or large financial organizations such as the World Bank as well as to make loans for development projects. OBUs are "offshore" in the sense that a Bahraini cannot open a checking account or borrow money. However, OBUs bring funds into Bahrain without interfering with local growth or undercutting local banks.

The drop in world oil prices in the 1980s and the Iraqi occupation of Kuwait seriously disrupted the OBU system, and a number of offshore banks were closed. Increased oil production and higher world prices have revitalized the system, both for

offshore and on-shore banks. In 2001, BNP Paribas, the sixth largest bank in the world, relocated its Middle East operations office to Bahrain, as did Turkey's Islamic Bank, an emerging giant in the Islamic banking system.

Bahrain's economic recovery has been enhanced by the Systems Development Council, a government body set up in 2000 to oversee development. The Bahrain Stock Exchange, opened in 1992, has revised its regulations to require foreign firms to employ 60 percent local labor, which strengthens Bahrainis' participation in the development of the emirate.

## THE FUTURE

One key to Bahrain's future may be found in a Qur'anic verse *(Sura XIII, II):*

> *Lo! Allah changeth not the condition of a people until they first change what is in their hearts.*

For a brief time after independence, the state experimented with representative government. But the hurly-burly of politics, with its factional rivalries, trade-offs, and compromises found in many Western democratic systems, did not suit the Bahraini temperament or experience. Democracy takes time to mature. Emile Nakhleh reminds us that "any serious attempt to democratize the regime will ultimately set tribal legitimacy and popular sovereignty on a collision course."[4]

The emir demonstrated his commitment to gradual democratization in 2000, issuing an edict, confirmed in a national referendum, that defines Bahrain as a constitutional monarchy ruled by a king. Municipal council elections were held in 2002, followed by those for a restored national parliament. Both male and female voters participated. But as noted earlier, these small steps toward representative government were felt to be inadequate by the large Shi'a population.

Bahrain today is sufficiently modernized and internationally active that the comment of an English expatriate banker, "it was first (among Arab states) to become gently westernized" seems appropriate. Traditionally a free, open place for vacationers, with high-rise buildings rising almost overnight from man-made peninsulas, Bahrain has tailors and shoemakers working cross-legged in open storefronts, nightclubs and bars on nearly every street, and heavy traffic. The latest western import is a Formula One speed race, the Bahrain Grand Prix, now in its fourth year. As an Italian racing driver observed, "in Bahrain what is cool is that they have good ideas, and they just build them, day by day."[5]

## NOTES

1. UN Security Council *Resolution 287,* 1970. Quoted from Emile Nakhleh, *Bahrain* (Lexington, KY: Lexington Books, 1976), p. 9.

2. Fuad I. Khuri, *Tribe and State in Bahrain* (Chicago: University of Chicago Press, 1981), p. 219.

3. Reuter, "Polls 'Unlikely' to Heal Bahraini Sectarian," Kuwait Times, July 15, 2010. The title refers to the upcoming parliamentary elections (end of 2010) which are not expected to change much in the configuration of representation and in power sharing. Online at www.kuwaittimes.net/read_news.php?newsid=ODM4NTM1NDg2. Retrieved on July 27, 2010.

4. Nakhleh, *Bahrain,* op. cit., p. 11.

5. Quoted in Austin Considine, "Built for Speed: Race Weekend in an Arab Kingdom," *The New York Times,* August 5, 2007.

# Egypt (Arab Republic of Egypt)

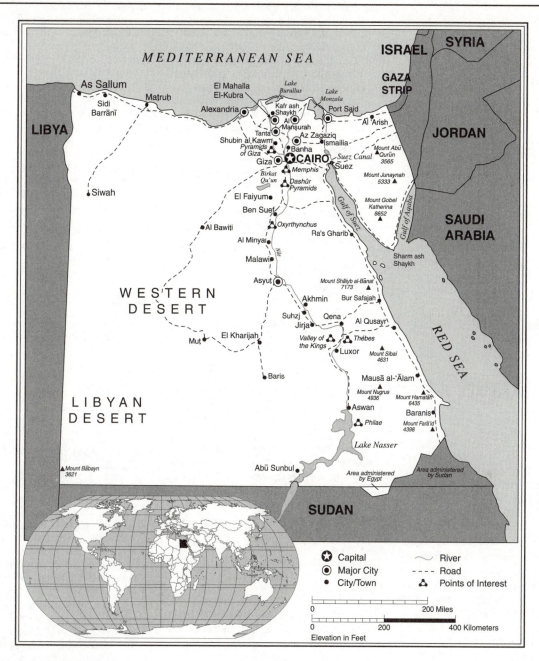

# Egypt Statistics

## GEOGRAPHY

*Area in Square Miles (Kilometers):*
386,258 (1,001,258) (about 3 times the size of New Mexico)
*Capital (Population):* Cairo (6,800,000)
*Environmental Concerns:* loss of agricultural land; increasing soil salinization; desertification; oil pollution threatening coral reefs and marine habitats; other water pollution; rapid population growth overstraining the Nile and natural resources

*Geographical Features:* a vast desert plateau interrupted by the Nile Valley and Delta
*Climate:* desert; dry, hot summers; moderate winters

## PEOPLE
### Population
*Total:* 83,082,869
*Annual Growth Rate:* 1.64%
*Rural/Urban Population Ratio:* 57/43
*Major Languages:* Arabic; English widely used by educated classes

*Ethnic Makeup:* 99.6% Eastern Hamitic (Egyptian, Bedouin, Arab, Nubian); 0.4% others
*Religions:* 90% Muslim (mostly Sunni); 9% Coptic Christian and others

## Health

*Life Expectancy at Birth:* 69 years (male), 74 years (female)
*Infant Mortality Rate (Ratio):* 27.26/1,000 live births

## Education

*Adult Literacy Rate:* 71.4%
*Compulsory (Ages):* for 5 years between 6 and 13

## COMMUNICATION

*Telephones:* 12,600,000 main lines
*Daily Newspaper Circulation:* 43 per 1,000 people
*Televisions:* 110 per 1,000 people
*Internet Users:* 11,414,000

## TRANSPORTATION

*Highways in Miles (Kilometers):* 46,490 (74,820)
*Railroads in Miles (Kilometers):* 17,550 (28,243)
*Usable Airfields:* 85
*Motor Vehicles in Use:* 3,200,000

## GOVERNMENT

*Type:* presidential republic
*Independence Date:* July 23, 1952, for the republic; February 28, 1922, marking the end of British rule

*Head of State/Government:* President Mohammed Hosni Mubarak; Prime Minister Ahmad Nazif
*Political Parties:* National Democratic Party (NDP), majority Party; approved opposition parties include New Wafd, National Progressive Unionist Group (Tagammu), Socialist Liberal Party. The Muslim Brotherhood is prohibited from functioning as a political party but its members take part in elections running as independents.
*Suffrage:* universal and compulsory at 18

## MILITARY

*Military Expenditures (% of GDP):* 3.4%
*Current Disputes:* Sudan continues to claim the Egyptian-administered Hala'ib Triangle, a small territory north of The 22nd parallel of latitude. It was originally included in British-controlled Sudan in the 1899 treaty defining the Egyptian-Sudanese border.

## ECONOMY

*Currency:* 5.4 Egyptian pounds = $1
*Per Capita Income/GDP:* $5,400/$162.2 billion

*GDP Growth Rate:* 7.2%
*Inflation Rate:* 18.3%
*Unemployment Rate:* 8.4%
*Labor Force:* 24,600,000 (note: a substantial number of Egyptian workers, especially skilled ones, are employed in nearby Arab countries)
*Natural Resources:* petroleum; natural gas; iron ore; phosphates; manganese; limestone; gypsum; talc; asbestos; lead; zinc
*Agriculture:* cotton; sugarcane; rice; corn; wheat; beans; fruits; vegetables; livestock; fish
*Industry:* textiles; food processing; tourism; chemicals; petroleum; construction; cement; metals
*Exports:* $29.85 billion (primary partners Italy, United States, Spain, Syria, Saudi Arabia)
*Imports:* $56.62 billion (primary partners US, China, Italy, Germany, Saudi Arabia)

## SUGGESTED WEB SITES

www.sis.gov.eg/En/Default.aspx
www.egyptdailynews.com/

# Egypt Country Report

The Arab Republic of Egypt is located at the extreme northeastern corner of Africa, with part of its territory—the Sinai Peninsula—serving as a land bridge to Southwest Asia. The country's total land area is approximately 386,000 square miles. However, 96 percent of this is uninhabitable desert. Except for a few scattered oases, the only settled and cultivable area is a narrow strip along the Nile River. The vast majority of Egypt's population is concentrated in this strip, resulting in high population density. Migration from rural areas to cities has intensified urban density; Cairo's population is currently 6.8 million, with millions more in the greater metropolitan area. It is a city that is literally "bursting at the seams."

Egypt today identifies itself as an Arab nation and is a founding member of the League of Arab States (which has its headquarters in Cairo). But its "Arab" identity is relatively new. It was first defined by the late president Gamal Abdel Nasser, who as a schoolboy became aware of his "Arabness" in response to British imperialism and particularly Britain's establishment of a national home for Jews in Arab Palestine. But Egypt's incredibly long history as a distinct society has given its people a

separate Egyptian identity and a sense of superiority over other peoples, notably desert people such as the Arabs of old.[1] Also, its development under British tutelage gave the country a headstart over other Arab countries or societies. Despite its people's overall low level of adult literacy, Egypt has more highly skilled professionals than do other Arab countries.

## HISTORY

Although Egypt is a modern state in terms of independence from foreign control, it has a distinct national identity and a rich culture that dates back thousands of years. The modern Egyptians take great pride in their brilliant past; this sense of the past gives them patience and a certain fatalism that enable them to withstand misfortunes that would crush most peoples.

The Egyptian peasants, the *fellahin,* are as stoic and enduring as the water buffaloes they use to do their plowing. Since the time of the pharaohs, Egypt has been invaded many times, and it was under foreign control for most of its history. When Nasser, the first president of the new Egyptian republic, came to power in 1954, he said that he was the first native Egyptian to rule the country in nearly 3,000 years.

**DEVELOPMENT**

Egypt's GDP growth rate, which held steady at 4–5 percent in the 90s, was affected by external events, notably the 9/11 terrorist attacks in the U.S. and the 2003 invasion of Iraq. The tourist industry, which generates 20 percent of revenues, saw a downturn but rebounded strongly in the early 2000s. However multiple bomb-blasts at the Sharm El-Shaikh Red Sea resort and in Cairo in 2004–2005, the first in 7 years, posed a new threat to the industry. The Sharm El-Shaikh attack in particular killed 88 people and injured 119, mostly Egyptians but some foreigners. The tourism industry recovered from that by 2007; however, in 2009, the number of tourists dropped by 18 percent due to the global economic recession and terrorist threats looming in the region. This year, the government started wide-scale efforts to remedy the slump.

It is often said that Egypt is the "gift of the Nile." The mighty river, flowing north to the Mediterranean with an enormous annual spate that deposited rich silt along its banks, attracted nomadic peoples

(© Kirk Treakle/Alamy)

The pyramids at Giza are among the most famous momentos of Egypt's past.

to settle there as early as 6000 B.C. They developed a productive agriculture based on the river's seasonal floods. They lived in plastered mud huts in small, compact villages. Their villages were not too different from those one sees today in parts of the Nile Delta.

Each village had its "headman," the head of some family more prosperous or industrious (or both) than the others. The arrival of other nomadic desert peoples gradually brought about the evolution of an organized system of government. Since the Egyptian villagers did not have nearby mountains or wild forests to retreat into, they were easily governable.

The institution of kingship was well established in Egypt by 2000 B.C., and in the time of Ramses II (1300–1233 B.C.), Egyptian monarchs extended their power over a large part of the Middle East. All Egyptian rulers were called pharaohs, although there was no hereditary system of descent and many different dynasties ruled during the country's first 2,000 years of existence. The pharaohs had their capital at Thebes, but they built other important cities on the banks of the Nile. Recent research by Egyptologists indicate that the ancient Egyptians had an amazingly accurate knowledge of astronomy. The Pyramids of Giza, for example, were built so as to be aligned with true north. Lacking modern instruments, their builders apparently used two stars, Thaban and Draconis, in the Big Dipper, for their alignment, with a point equidistant from them to mark their approximation of true north. Only centuries later was the North Star identified

as such. Recent excavations at the Great Pyramid of Giza indicate that some 2,500 years ago Egyptian builders used concrete technology in their work, mixing lime, sand and clay to form concrete blocks for both the outer and inner casings of this and other massive structures. The archaeological evidence suggests that concrete blocks, rather than the much heavier limestone ones, would have enabled the builders to work much faster and thus speeded up construction.

Another important discovery, in November 1999, was that of inscriptions on the walls of *Wadi Hoi* ("Valley of Terror") that may well be the world's oldest written language, predating the cuneiform letters developed by the Sumerians in Mesopotamia.

In the first century B.C., Egypt became part of the Roman Empire. The city of Alexandria, founded by Alexander the Great, became a center of Greek and Roman learning and culture. Later, it became a center of Christianity. The Egyptian Coptic Church was one of the earliest organized churches. The Copts, direct descendants of the early Egyptians, are the principal minority group in Egypt today. (The name Copt comes from *aigyptos,* Greek for "Egyptian.") The Copts welcomed the Arab invaders who brought Islam to Egypt, preferring them to their oppressive Byzantine Christian rulers. Muslim rulers over the centuries usually protected the Copts as "Peoples of the Book," leaving authority over them to their religious leaders, in return for allegiance and payment of a small tax. But in recent years, the rise of Islamic radicalism has made life more difficult for Egypt's Coptic

minority. Coptic-Muslim friction declined significantly in the 1990s, but the 10 million Copts continue to complain of petty discrimination (such as university admission) and political disenfranchisement. To its credit, the government has eased building restrictions on new churches and allowed broadcasting of Christian services on state TV. Recently it restored property expropriated by the Nasser regime in 1950s to Coptic Church ownership and in 2002 declared Christmas a national holiday.

## THE INFLUENCE OF ISLAM

Islam was the major formative influence in the development of modern Egyptian society. Islamic armies from Arabia invaded Egypt in the seventh century A.D. Large numbers of nomadic Arabs followed, settling the Nile Valley until, over time, they became the majority in the population. Egypt was under the rule of the caliphs ("successors" of the Prophet Muhammad) until the tenth century, when a Shi'a group broke away and formed a separate government. The leaders of this group also called themselves caliphs. To show their independence, they founded a new capital in the desert south of Alexandria. The name they chose for their new capital was prophetic: *al-Qahira*—"the Victorious"—the modern city of Cairo.

In the sixteenth century, Egypt became a province of the Ottoman Empire. It was then under the rule of the Mamluks, originally slaves or prisoners of war who converted to Islam. Many Mamluk leaders had been freed and then acquired their own slaves. They formed a military aristocracy, constantly fighting with one another for land and power. The Ottomans found it simpler to leave Egypt under Mamluk control, merely requiring periodic tribute and taxes.

## EGYPT ENTERS
## THE MODERN WORLD

At the end of the eighteenth century, rivalry between Britain and France for control of trade in the Mediterranean and the sea routes to India involved Egypt. The French general Napoleon Bonaparte led an expedition to Egypt in 1798. However, the British, in cooperation with Ottoman forces, drove the French from Egypt. A confused struggle for power followed. The victor was Muhammad Ali, an Albanian officer in the Ottoman garrison of Cairo. In 1805, the Ottoman sultan appointed him governor of Egypt.

Although he was not an Egyptian, Muhammad Ali had a vision of Egypt under his rule as a rich and powerful country. He began by forming a new army consisting

(© Glowimages/Getty Images)

The Egyptian Museum, situated at Tahrir Square in Cairo, Egypt, was built during the reign of Khedive Abbass Helmi II in 1897 and opened in 1902.

of native Egyptians instead of mercenaries or slave-soldiers. This army was trained by European advisers and gave a good account of itself in campaigns, performing better than the regular Ottoman armies.[2] His successor, Ismail, went a step further by hiring some 50 demobilized veterans of the American Civil War, both Yankees and rebels, who brought discipline and military experience to the training of Egyptian recruits. These mercenaries remained in Egypt after the end of the campaigns of Ismail and his successors in the Middle East, and when they died they were buried in the long-forgotten and neglected American cemetery in a corner of Cairo.

Muhammad Ali set up an organized, efficient tax-collection system. He suppressed the Mamluks and confiscated all the lands that they had seized from Egyptian peasants over the years, lifting a heavy tax burden from peasant backs. He took personal charge of all Egypt's exports. Cotton, a new crop, became the major Egyptian export and was known the world over for its high quality. Dams and irrigation canals were dug to improve cultivation and expand arable land. Although Muhammad

Ali grew rich in the process of carrying out these policies, he was concerned for the welfare of the peasantry. He once said, "One must guide this people as one guides children; to leave them to their own devices would be to render them subject to all the disorders from which I have saved them."[3]

Muhammad Ali's successors were named *khedives* ("viceroys"), in that they ruled Egypt in theory on behalf of their superior, the sultan. In practice, they acted as independent rulers. Under the khedives, Egypt was again drawn into European power politics, with unfortunate results. Khedive Ismail, the most ambitious of Muhammad Ali's descendants, was determined to make Egypt the equal of Western European countries. His major project was the Suez Canal, built by a European company, with Egyptian labor, and opened in 1869. The Italian composer Verdi was invited to compose the opera *Aida* for its inauguration. He refused to do so at first, saying that Egypt was a country whose civilization he did not admire. Eventually he was persuaded (with the help of the then-princely bonus of $20,000!) and set to music the ancient Egyptian legend of imperialism and grand passion. Verdi's task was

eased by the fact that Auguste Mariette, the preeminent Egyptologist of the period, wrote the libretto and designed sets and costumes with absolute fidelity to pharaonic times.

However, the expense of this and other grandiose projects bankrupted the country. Ismail was forced to sell Egypt's shares in the Suez Canal Company—to the British government!—and his successors were forced to accept British control over Egyptian finances. In 1882, a revolt of army officers threatened to overthrow the khedive. The British intervened and established a de facto protectorate, keeping the khedive in office in order to avoid conflict with the Ottomans.

## EGYPTIAN NATIONALISM

The British protectorate lasted from 1882 to 1956. An Egyptian nationalist movement gradually developed in the early 1900s, inspired by the teachings of religious leaders and Western-educated officials in the khedives' government. They advocated a revival of Islam and its strengthening to enable Egypt and other Islamic lands to resist European control.

During World War I, Egypt was a major base for British campaigns against the Ottoman Empire. The British formally declared their protectorate over Egypt in order to "defend" the country, since legally it was still an Ottoman province. The British worked with Arab nationalist leaders against the Turks and promised to help them form an independent Arab state after the war. Egyptian nationalists were active in the Arab cause and wanted independence from Britain.

At the end of World War I, Egyptian nationalist leaders created the *Wafd* party (Arabic for "delegation"). In 1918, the Wafd presented demands to the British for the complete independence of Egypt. The British rejected the demands, saying that Egypt was not ready for self-government. The Wafd then turned to violence, organizing boycotts, strikes, and terrorist attacks on British soldiers and on Egyptians accused of cooperating with the British.

Under pressure, the British finally abolished the protectorate in 1922. But they retained control over Egyptian foreign policy, defense, and communications as well as the protection of minorities and foreign residents and of Sudan, which had been part of Egypt since the 1880s. Thus, Egypt's "independence" was a hollow shell.

Egypt did eventually regain control over internal affairs. The government was set up as a constitutional monarchy under a new king, Fuad. Political parties were allowed, and in elections for a Parliament in 1923, the Wafd emerged as the dominant party. But neither Fuad nor the son who succeeded him, Farouk, trusted Wafd leaders. They feared that the Wafd was working to establish a republic. For their part, the Wafd leaders did not believe that the rulers were seriously interested in the good of the country.

## THE EGYPTIAN REVOLUTION

During the years of the monarchy, the Egyptian Army gradually developed a corps of professional officers, most of them from lower- or middle-class Egyptian backgrounds. They were strongly patriotic and resented what they perceived to be British cultural snobbery as well as Britain's continual influence over Egyptian affairs.

The training school for these young officers was the Egyptian Military Academy, founded in 1936. Among them was Gamal Abdel Nasser, the eldest son of a village postal clerk. Nasser and his fellow officers were already active in anti-British demonstrations by the time they entered the academy. During World War II, the British, fearing a German takeover of

Egypt, reinstated the protectorate. Egypt became the main British military base in the Middle East. This action galvanized the officers into forming a revolutionary movement. Nasser said at the time that it roused in him the seeds of revolt. "It made [us] realize that there is a dignity to be retrieved and defended."[4]

When Jewish leaders in Palestine created Israel in May 1948, Egypt, along with other nearby Arab countries, sent troops to destroy the new state. Nasser and several of his fellow officers were sent to the front. The Egyptian Army was defeated; Nasser himself was trapped with his unit, was wounded, and was rescued only by an armistice. Even more shocking to the young officers was the evident corruption and weakness of their own government. The weapons that they received were inferior and often defective, battle orders were inaccurate, and their superiors proved to be incompetent in strategy and tactics.

Nasser and his fellow officers attributed their defeat not to their own weaknesses but to their government's failures. When they returned to Egypt, they were determined to overthrow the monarchy. They formed a secret organization, the Free Officers. It was not the only organization dedicated to the overthrow of the monarchy, but it was the most disciplined and had the general support of the army.

On July 23, 1952, the Free Officers launched their revolution. It came six months after "Black Saturday," the burning of Cairo by mobs protesting the continued presence of British troops in Egypt. The Free Officers persuaded King Farouk to abdicate, and they declared Egypt a republic. A nine-member Revolutionary Command Council (RCC) was established to govern the country.

## EGYPT UNDER NASSER

In his self-analytical book *The Philosophy of the Revolution*, Nasser wrote, "I always imagine that in this region in which we live there is a role wandering aimlessly about in search of an actor to play it."[5] Nasser saw himself as playing that role. Previously, he had operated behind the scenes, but always as the leader to whom the other Free Officers looked up to. By 1954, Nasser had emerged as Egypt's leader. When the monarchy was formally abolished in 1954, he became president, prime minister, and head of the RCC.

Nasser came to power determined to restore dignity and stature to Egypt, to eliminate foreign control, and to make his country the leader of a united Arab world. It was an ambitious set of goals, and Nasser was only partly successful in attaining

them. But in his struggles to achieve these goals, he brought considerable prestige to Egypt. The country became a leader of the "Third World" of Africa and Asia, developing nations newly freed from foreign control.

Nasser was successful in removing the last vestiges of British rule from Egypt. British troops were withdrawn from the Suez Canal Zone, and Nasser nationalized the canal in 1956, taking over the management from the private foreign company that had operated it since 1869. That action made the British furious, since the British government had a majority interest in the company. The British worked out a secret plan with the French and the Israelis, neither of whom liked Nasser, to invade Egypt and overthrow him. British and French paratroopers seized the canal in October 1956, but the United States and the Soviet Union, in an unusual display of cooperation, forced them to withdraw. It was the first of several occasions when Nasser turned military defeat into political victory. It was also one of the few times when Nasser and the United States were on the same side of an issue.

Between 1956 and 1967, Nasser developed a close alliance with the Soviet Union—at least, it seemed that way to the United States. Nasser's pet economic project was the building of a dam at Aswan, on the upper Nile, to regulate the annual flow of river water and thus enable Egypt to reclaim new land and develop its agriculture. He requested aid from the United States through the World Bank to finance the project, but he was turned down, largely due to his publicly expressed hostility toward Israel. Again Nasser turned defeat into a victory of sorts. The Soviet Union agreed to finance the dam, which was completed in 1971, and subsequently to equip and train the Egyptian Army. Thousands of Soviet advisers poured into Egypt, and it seemed to U.S. and Israeli leaders that Egypt had become a dependency of the Soviet Union.

The lowest point in Nasser's career came in June 1967. Israel invaded Egypt and defeated its Soviet-trained army, along with those of Jordan and Syria, and occupied the Sinai Peninsula in a lightning six-day war. The Israelis were restrained from marching on Cairo only by a United Nations cease-fire. Nasser took personal responsibility for the defeat. He announced his resignation, but the Egyptian people refused to accept it. The public outcry was so great that he agreed to continue in office. One observer wrote, "The irony was that Nasser had led the country to defeat, but Egypt without Nasser was unthinkable."[6]

Nasser had little success in his efforts to unify the Arab world. One attempt, for example, was a union of Egypt and Syria, which lasted barely three years (1958–1961). Egyptian forces were sent to support a new republican government in Yemen after the overthrow of that country's autocratic ruler, but they became bogged down in a civil war there and had to be withdrawn. Other efforts to unify the Arab world also failed. Arab leaders respected Nasser but were unwilling to play second fiddle to him in a single Arab state. In 1967, after the defeat, Nasser lashed out bitterly at the other Arab leaders. He said, "You issue statements, but we have to fight. If you want to liberate [Palestine] then get in line in front of us."[7]

Inside Egypt, the results of Nasser's 18-year rule were also mixed. Although he talked about developing representative government, Nasser distrusted political parties and remembered the destructive rivalries under the monarchy that had kept Egypt divided and weak. The Wafd and all other political parties were declared illegal. Nasser set up his own political organization to replace them, called the Arab Socialist Union (ASU). It was a mass party, but it had no real power. Nasser and a few close associates ran the government and controlled the ASU. The associates took their orders directly from Nasser; they called him *El-Rais*—"The President."

As he grew older, Nasser, plagued by health problems, became more dictatorial, secretive, and suspicious. He tolerated no opposition and ensured tight control over Egypt with a large police force and a secret service that monitored activities in every village and town.

Nasser died in 1970. Ironically, his death came on the heels of a major policy success: the arranging of a truce between the Palestine Liberation Organization and the government of Jordan. Despite his health problems, Nasser had seemed indestructible, and his death came as a shock. Millions of Egyptians followed his funeral cortege through the streets of Cairo, weeping and wailing over the loss of their beloved Rais.

## ANWAR AL-SADAT

Nasser was succeeded by his vice-president, Anwar al-Sadat, in accordance with constitutional procedure. Sadat was one of the original Free Officers and had worked with Nasser since their early days at the Military Academy. In the Nasser years, Sadat had come to be regarded as a lightweight, always ready to do whatever was asked of him.

Many Egyptians did not even know what Sadat looked like, but when he became president, it did not take long for the Egyptian people to learn. Sadat introduced a "revolution of rectification," which he said was needed to correct the errors of his predecessor.[8] These included too much dependence on the Soviet Union, too much government interference in the economy, and failure to develop an effective Arab policy against Israel. He was a master of timing, taking bold action at unexpected times to advance Egypt's international and regional prestige. Thus, in 1972 he abruptly ordered the 15,000 Soviet advisers in Egypt to leave the country, despite the fact that they were training his army and supplying all his military equipment. His purpose was to reduce Egypt's dependence on one foreign power, and as he had calculated, the United States now came to his aid.

A year later, in October 1973, Egyptian forces crossed the Suez Canal in a surprise attack and broke through Israeli defense lines in occupied Sinai. The attack was coordinated with Syrian forces invading Israel from the east, through the Golan Heights. The Israelis were driven back with heavy casualties on both fronts, and although they eventually regrouped and won back most of the lost ground, Sadat felt he had won a moral and psychological victory. After the war, Egyptians believed that they had held their own with the Israelis and had demonstrated Arab ability to handle the sophisticated weaponry of modern warfare.

Anwar al-Sadat's most spectacular action took place in 1977. It seemed to him that the Arab–Israeli conflict was at a stalemate. Neither side would budge from its position, and the Egyptian people were angry at having so little to show for the 1973 success. In November, he addressed a hushed meeting of the People's Assembly and said, "Israel will be astonished when it hears me saying . . . that I am ready to go to their own house, to the Knesset itself, to talk to them."[9] And he did so, becoming for a second time the "Hero of the Crossing,"[10] but this time to the very citadel of Egypt's enemy.

Sadat's successes in foreign policy, culminating in the 1979 peace treaty with Israel, gave him great prestige internationally. Receipt of the Nobel Peace Prize, jointly with Israeli prime minister Menachem Begin, confirmed his status as a peacemaker. His pipe-smoking affability and sartorial elegance endeared him to U.S. policymakers.

The view that more and more Egyptians held of their world-famous leader was less flattering. Religious leaders and

conservative Muslims objected to Sadat's luxurious style of living. The poor resented having to pay more for basic necessities. The educated classes were angry about Sadat's claim that the political system had become more open and democratic when, in fact, it had not. The Arab Socialist Union was abolished and several new political parties were allowed to organize. But the ASU's top leaders merely formed their own party, the National Democratic Party, headed by Sadat. For all practical purposes, Egypt under Sadat was even more of a single-party state under an authoritarian leader than it had been in Nasser's time.

Sadat's economic policies also worked to his disadvantage. In 1974, he announced a new program for postwar recovery, *Infitah* ("Opening"). It would be an open-door policy, bringing an end to Nasser's state-run socialist system. Foreign investors would be encouraged to invest in Egypt, and foreign experts would bring their technological knowledge to help develop industries. Infitah, properly applied, would bring an economic miracle to Egypt.

Rather than spur economic growth, however, Infitah made fortunes for just a few, leaving the great majority of Egyptians no better off than before. Chief among those who profited were members of the Sadat family. Corruption among the small ruling class, many of its members newly rich contractors, aroused anger on the part of the Egyptian people. In 1977, the economy was in such bad shape that the government increased bread prices. Riots broke out, and Sadat was forced to cancel the increase.

On October 6, 1981, President Sadat and government leaders were reviewing an armed-forces parade in Cairo to mark the eighth anniversary of the Crossing. Suddenly, a volley of shots rang out from one of the trucks in the parade. Sadat fell, mortally wounded. The assassins, most of them young military men, were immediately arrested. They belonged to *Al Takfir Wal Hijra* ("Repentance and Flight from Sin"), a secret group that advocated the reestablishment of a pure Islamic society in Egypt—by violence, if necessary. Their leader declared that the killing of Sadat was an essential first step in this process.

Islamic radicalism developed rapidly in the Middle East after the 1979 Iranian Revolution. The success of that revolution was a spur to Egyptian Islamists. They accused Sadat of favoring Western capitalism through his Infitah policy, of making peace with the "enemy of Islam" (Israel), and of not being a good Muslim. At their trial, Sadat's assassins said that they had acted to rid Egypt of an unjust ruler, a proper action under the laws of Islam.

## HEALTH/WELFARE

Women's rights in Egypt have improved in recent years. A 1999 law banned female circumcision and a 2001 Family Law allows them to file for divorce. However the over-crowded court system and continuation of male patriarchal dominance of families makes female divorce very difficult to obtain. Technology has added to the problem in that text-messaging facilitates husbands in divorce action cases. Egypt's Grand Mufti in 2008 ordered online training of imams to provide rulings acceptable under Islamic law.[11]

Encouraged by a fatwa (Islamic religious ruling) on its lawfulness under Shari'a law given by a scholar at Al-Azhar University, Egypt's In Vitro Fertilization Center in Cairo became, in October 2005, the first in the Arab world to conduct stemcell research.

Sadat may have contributed to his early death (he was 63) by a series of actions taken earlier in the year. About 1,600 people were arrested in September 1981 in a massive crackdown on religious unrest. They included not only religious leaders but also journalists, lawyers, intellectuals, provincial governors, and leaders of the country's small but growing opposition parties. Many of them were not connected with any radical Islamic organization. It seemed to most Egyptians that Sadat had overreacted, and at that point, he lost the support of the people. In contrast to Nasser's funeral, few tears were shed at Sadat's. His funeral was attended mostly by foreign dignitaries. One of them said that Sadat had been buried without the people and without the army. In October 2006 Sadat's nephew Talaat was given a one-year jail sentence and stripped of his parliamentary immunity on charges he blamed the military for negligence in his uncle's death.[12]

## MUBARAK IN POWER

Vice-President Hosni Mubarak, former Air Force commander and designer of Egypt's 1973 success against Israel, succeeded Sadat without incident. Mubarak dealt firmly with the Islamists at the beginning of his regime. He was given emergency powers and approved death sentences for five of Sadat's assassins in 1982. But he moved cautiously in other areas of national life, in an effort to disassociate himself from some of Sadat's more unpopular policies. The economic policy of Infitah, which had led to widespread graft and corruption, was abandoned; stiff sentences were

handed out to a number of entrepreneurs including Sadat's brother-in-law and several associates of the late president.

Mubarak also began rebuilding bridges with other Arab states that had been damaged by the peace treaty with Israel. Egypt was readmitted to membership in the Islamic Conference, the Islamic Development Bank, the Arab League, and other Arab regional organizations. In 1990, the Arab League headquarters was moved from Tunis back to Cairo, its original location. Egypt backed Iraq with arms and advisers in its war with Iran, but Mubarak broke with Saddam Hussein after the invasion of Kuwait, accusing the Iraqi leader of perfidy. Some 35,000 Egyptian troops served with the U.S.-led coalition during the Gulf War; and as a result of these efforts, the country regained its central role in Arab politics.

Despite the peace treaty, relations with Israel continued to be difficult. One bone of contention was removed in 1989 with the return of the Israeli-held enclave of Taba, in the Sinai Peninsula, to Egyptian control. It had been operated as an Israeli beach resort.

The return of Taba strengthened the government's claim that the 10-year-old peace treaty had been valuable overall in advancing Egypt's interests. The sequence of agreements between the Palestine Liberation Organization and Israel for a sovereign Palestinian entity, along with Israel's improved relations with its other Arab neighbors, contributed to a substantial thaw in the Egyptian "cold peace" with its former enemy. In March 1995, a delegation from Israel's Knesset arrived in Cairo, the first such parliamentary group to visit Egypt since the peace treaty.

But relations worsened after the election in 1996 of Benjamin Netanyahu as head of a new Israeli government. Egypt had strongly supported the Oslo accords for a Palestinian state, and it had set up a free zone for transit of Palestinian products in 1995. The Egyptian view that Netanyahu was not adhering to the accords led to a "war of words" between the two countries. Israeli tourists were discouraged from visiting Egypt or received hostile treatment when visiting Egyptian monuments, and almost no Egyptians opted for visits to Israel. The newspaper *Al-Ahram* even stopped carrying cartoons by a popular Israeli-American cartoonist because he had served in the Israeli Army. The two governments cooperated briefly in the return of a small Bedouin tribe, the Azazma, to its Egyptian home area in the Sinai. The tribe had fled into Israel following a dispute with another tribe that turned into open conflict.

The election of Ehud Barak as Israel's new prime minister was well received

in Eygpt, notably due to his resumption of peace negotiations with the then-Palestinian leader Yassir Arafat. However, the breakdown of those negotiations and Barak's defeat by Ariel Sharon in the 2000 Israeli elections re-established the "deep freeze" between the two countries. In 2004 President Mubarak declared Sharon incapable of making peace. However Israel's withdrawal from the Gaza Strip in 2005 helped improve Sharon's image in Egypt as peacemaker rather than butcher. One result was a prisoner swap. Mubarak released an Israeli Arab convicted of espionage in Egypt in return for 6 Egyptian students who had been studying in Israel.

### Internal Politics

Although Mubarak's unostentatious lifestyle and firm leadership encouraged confidence among the Egyptian regime, the system that he inherited from his predecessors remained largely impervious to change. The first free multiparty national elections held since the 1952 Revolution took place in 1984—although they were not entirely free, because a law requiring political parties to win at least 8 percent of the popular vote limited party participation. Mubarak was reelected easily for a full six-year term (he was the only candidate), and his ruling National Democratic Party won 73 percent of seats in the Assembly. The New Wafd Party was the only party able to meet the 8 percent requirement.

New elections for the Assembly in 1987 indicated how far Egypt's embryonic democracy had progressed under Mubarak. This time, four opposition parties presented candidates. Although the National Democratic Party's plurality was still a hefty 69.6 percent, 17 percent of the electorate voted for opposition candidates. The New Wafd increased its percentage of the popular vote to 10.9 percent, and a number of Muslim Brotherhood members were elected as independents. The National Progressive Unionist Group, the most leftist of the parties, failed to win a seat.

Mubarak was re-elected for a fourth six-year term in 1999, receiving 94 percent of the vote, as 79 percent of the country's 24 million voters cast their ballots. Again, he was the only candidate. But in February 2005 he announced that henceforth Egypt's presidential elections would be multi-party, with other candidates allowed to run for the office.

In September Mubarak was re-elected for his fifth term in office against token opposition. (His main opponent, Ayman Nour, had been jailed earlier on charges seen generally to be politically motivated.) Elections followed in three stages for the 444-seat National Assembly (Parliament). The NDP won 311 seats, while its main opponent, the Muslim Brotherhood, although disallowed as a political party and its members required to run as independents, won 88.

## FREEDOM

The Islamist challenge to Egypt's secular government has caused the erosion of many rights and freedoms enshrined in the country's Constitution. A state of emergency issued in 1981 is still in effect; it was renewed in 2001 for a 3-year period and in 2008 for an additional 2 year period. In June 2003 the Peoples' Assembly approved establishment of a National Council for Human Rights that would monitor violations or misuse of government authority.

## AT WAR WITH ISLAMISM

Egypt's seemingly intractable social problems—high unemployment, an inadequate job market flooded annually by new additions to the labor force, chronic budgetary deficits, and a bloated and inefficient bureaucracy, to name a few—have played into the hands of the Islamists, those who would build a new Egyptian state based on the laws of Islam. Although they form part of a larger movement in the Islamic world, one that would replace existing secular regimes with regimes that adhere completely to spiritual law and custom (*Shari'a*), Egypt's Islamists do not harbor universal goals. Their aim is to replace the Mubarak regime with a purely "Islamic" one, faithful to the laws and principles of the religion and dominated by religious leaders.

Egypt's Islamists formed numerous groups, such as al-Gamaa al-Islamiya, the Vanguard of Islam and Islamic Jihad, itself an outgrowth of al-Takfir wal-Hijra, which was responsible for the assassination of Anwar Sadat. Ironically, Sadat had formed Al-Gamaa to counter leftist political groups. However, it differs from its parent organization, the Muslim Brotherhood, in advocating the overthrow of the government by violence. During his first term, Mubarak kept a tight lid on violence. But in the 1990s, the increasing strength of the Islamists and their popularity with the large number of educated but unemployed youth led to an increase in violence which caused instability and insecurity in the country.

Violence was initially aimed at government security forces, but starting in 1992, the radicals' strategy shifted to vulnerable targets such as foreign tourists and the Coptic Christian minority. A number of Copts were killed and many Copt business owners were forced to pay "protection money" to al-Gamaa in order to continue in operation. Subsequently the Copts' situation improved somewhat, as stringent security measures were put in place to contain the Islamist violence. Gun battles in 1999 between Muslim and Copt villagers in southern Egypt resulted in 200 Christian deaths and the arrests of a number of Muslims as well as Copts. Some 96 Muslims were charged with violence before a state-security court, but only four were convicted, and to short jail terms. However, Muslim–Coptic relations remained unstable. Early in 2002, two Coptic weekly newspapers were shut down after the Superior Press Council, a quasi-government body, filed a lawsuit charging them with "offending Egyptians and undermining national unity."

Islamic Jihad, the major Islamist organization subsequently shifted its strategy and objectives in order to evade the repression of the Mubarak government. Many of its members joined the fighters in Afghanistan who were resisting the Soviet occupation of that country. After the Soviet withdrawal in 1989, some 300 of them remained, joining the Taliban force that eventually won control of 90 percent of Afghanistan. In that capacity, they became associated with Osama bin Laden and his al-Qaeda international terror network. Two of their leaders, Dr. Ayman al-Zawahiri (a surgeon) and Muhammad Atif, are believed to have planned the September 11, 2001, terrorist bombings in the United States. However, Islamic Jihad's chief aim is the overthrow of the Mubarak government and its replacement by an Islamic one. Its hostility to the United States stems from American support for that government and for the U.S. alliance with Israel against the Palestinians.

In targeting tourism in their campaign to overthrow the regime, the Islamists have attacked tourist buses. Four tourists were killed in the lobby of a plush Cairo hotel in 1993. In November 1997, 64 tourists were gunned down in a grisly massacre at the Temple of Hatshepsut near Luxor, in the Valley of the Kings, one of Egypt's prize tourist attractions. Aftershocks from the terrorist attacks on the United States have decimated the tourist industry, which is Egypt's largest source of income ($4.3 billion in 2000, with 5.4 million visitors in that year). Egyptair, the national airline, lost $56 million in October 2001 alone; and cancellations of package tours, foreign-airline bookings, and hotel reservations led to a 45 percent drop in tourist revenues.

One important reason for the rise in political violence stems from the government's ineptness in resolving social crises. After a disastrous earthquake in October 1992, Islamist groups were the first to provide aid to the victims, distributing $1,000 to each family made homeless, while the cumbersome, multilayered government bureaucracy took weeks to respond. Similarly, al-Gamaa established a network of Islamic schools, hospitals, clinics, daycare centers, and even small industries in poor districts such as Cairo's Imbaba quarter.

The Mubarak government's response to rising violence has been one of extreme repression. The state of emergency that was established after Anwar Sadat's assassination in 1981 has been renewed regularly, most recently in 2008 for a two-year extension. Some 770 members of the Vanguard of Islam were tried and convicted of subversion in 1993. The crackdown left Egypt almost free from violence for several years. But in 1996, eighteen Greek tourists were murdered in April, and the State Security Court sentenced five Islamists to death for killing police and civilians in a murderous rampage.

An unfortunate result of government repression of the militants is that Egypt, traditionally an open, tolerant, and largely nonviolent society, has taken on many of the features of an authoritarian state. Human rights are routinely suspended, the prime offenders being officers of the dreaded State Security Investigation (SSI). Indefinite detention without charges is a common practice, and torture is used extensively to extract "confessions" from suspects or their relatives. All of al-Gamaa's leaders are either in prison, in exile, or dead; and with 20,000 suspected Islamists also jailed, the government could claim with some justification that it had broken the back of the 1990s insurgency. Its confidence was enhanced in March 1999 when al-Gamaa said that it would no longer engage in violence. Two previous cease-fire offers had been spurned, but this newest offer resulted in the release of several hundred Islamists to "test its validity."

Due to the extremism of methods employed by both sides, the conflict between the regime and the Islamists has begun to polarize Egyptian society. The Islamists, in struggling to overthrow the regime and replace it with a legitimately Islamic one (in their view) have at times attacked intellectuals, journalists, writers and others who oppose them. The novelist Farag Foda, who strongly criticized Egypt's "creeping Islamization" in his works, was killed outside of his Cairo home in the early 1990s, and Haguib Mahfouz, the Arab world's only Nobel laureate in literature, was critically wounded in 1994 by al-Gamaa gunman.

In 1995, the regime imposed further restrictions on Egypt's normally free-wheeling press and journalistic bodies. A law imposed fines of up to $3,000 and five-year jail sentences for articles "harmful to the state." The long arm of the law reached into the educational establishment as well. A university professor and noted Quranic scholar was charged with apostasy by clerics at Al-Azhar University, on the grounds that he had argued in his writings that the Qur'an should be interpreted in its historical/linguistic context alongside its identification as the Word of God. The charge came under the Islamic principle of *hisba,* according to which a Muslim can demand a court decision to stop the behavior or actions of others deemed contrary to Islam and harmful to society. He was found guilty and ordered to divorce his wife, since a Muslim woman may not be married to an apostate. A 1996 law prohibited the use of *hisba* in the courts, but the damage had been done; the professor and his wife were forced into exile to preserve their marriage.

The government's posture toward its citizens has changed little since emergency laws went into effect. However, a small but significant step toward reawakening the country's moribund political system was taken in September 2005 with an open presidential election. The incumbent was opposed by 9 candidates, the most prominent being Ayman Nour, leader of the Al Ghad ("Tomorrow") opposition party. Mubarak was re-elected but won "only" 88.6 percent of the popular vote. However voting irregularities charged by opposition leaders led to a further crackdown. In December Ayman Nour was given a 5-year forced labor sentence for what U.S. officials later described as false charges. He had finished second to Mubarak in the popular vote.

Elections for the Shura, the upper house of the National Assembly, in June 2007 re-emphasized the flawed nature of Egypt's political system. (The Shura lacks law-making powers but members have parliamentary immunity and other perquisites that make membership attractive, particularly to business owners and wealthy investors.)

Despite government claims that the election marked a "great leap forward" for public participation, obstacles such as limited access to polling places, stuffed ballot boxes, voter intimidation and the pre-election arrest of some 800 Muslim Brotherhood members kept the turnout low. One Muslim Brotherhood leader noted sadly,

"the regime is incapable of honest political competition. Its aim is to marginalize the Brotherhood and prevent us from moving forward toward successful reforms and change through legal and constructive means." [13]

Government repression and arrests of hundreds of its activists along with those of Kifaya (which wishes to remove President Mubarak), and more recently a number of opposition editors for articles critical of the regime, has forced the Muslim Brotherhood to rethink its position in terms of "forceful negativism." In October 2007 its leaders issued a draft platform, according to which a Majlis of Ulama (Council of Islamic Scholars), selected by the membership rather than in a popular election, would have veto power over legislation passed by the National Assembly (Parliament) that it considered incompatible with Islamic law. Under its terms Egypt would be no longer a republic but a "Civic Islamic State." [14]

In a further effort to blunt the opposition, Mubarak in February 2006 abruptly postponed local council elections scheduled for April, canceling a promise he had made during the presidential campaign to promote greater democracy. While these councils have little actual power, a constitutional change in 2005 gave them control over nomination of candidates for president in 2011, when Mubarak is prohibited from running or serving.

However, it is important to note that the Muslim Brothers managed, in the 2005 parliamentary elections, to win 88 seats as independent candidates (they are not recognized as a party). With a control of 20 percent of parliament seats, the Brotherhood has refashioned itself as a mainstream reform party that promotes freedom of speech, "the independence of unions and professional organizations, transparency of government transactions, a crackdown on corruption and freedom for political prisoners." [15] The movement does not call for Islamic-oriented social change (e.g., mandatory veils for women, alcohol ban), but focuses on comprehensive political reforms that would eventually change the nature of the system in the long run.

## A STRUGGLING ECONOMY

Egypt's economy rests upon a narrow and unstable base, due to rapid demographic growth and limited arable land and because political factors have adversely influenced national development. The country has a relatively high level of education and is a net exporter of skilled labor to other Arab countries. But the over-production of university graduates has

produced a bloated and inefficient bureaucracy, as the government is required to provide a position for every graduate who cannot find other employment.

Agriculture is the most important sector of the economy, accounting for about one third of national income. The major crops are long-staple cotton and sugarcane. Egyptian agriculture since time immemorial has been based on irrigation from the Nile River. In recent years, greater control of irrigation water through the Aswan High Dam, expansion of land devoted to cotton production, and improved planting methods have begun to show positive results.

A new High Dam at Aswan, completed in 1971 upstream from the original one built in 1906, resulted from a political decision by the Nasser government to seek foreign financing for its program of expansion of cultivable land and generation of electricity for industrialization. When Western lending institutions refused to finance the dam, also for political reasons, Nasser turned to the Soviet Union for help. By 1974, just three years after its completion, revenues had exceeded construction costs. The dam made possible the electrification of all of Egypt's villages as well as a fishing industry at Lake Nasser, its reservoir. It proved valuable in providing the agricultural sector with irrigation water during the prolonged 1980–1988 drought, although at sharply reduced levels. However, the increased costs of land reclamation and loss of the sardine fishing grounds along the Mediterranean coast have made the dam a mixed blessing for Egypt.

Egypt was self-sufficient in foodstuffs as recently as the 1970s but now must import 60 percent of its food. Such factors as rapid population growth, rural-to-urban migration with consequent loss of agricultural labor, and Sadat's open-door policy for imports combined to produce this negative food balance. Subsidies for basic commodities, which cost the government nearly $2 billion a year, are an important cause of inflation, since they keep the budget continuously in deficit. Fearing a recurrence of the 1977 Bread Riots, the government kept prices in check. However, inflation, which had dropped to 8 percent in 1995 due to International Monetary Fund stabilization policies required for loans, rose to 37 percent in 1999 as the new free-market policy produced a tidal wave of imports. As a result, the foreign trade deficit increased drastically.

After having been just 5.4 percent in 2005, the inflation rate increased drastically in 2008 as a result of rising international commodity prices. This created a serious crisis as people could not afford the highly inflated prices of food. At a time, in 2008, bread even became scarce and the "bread crisis" set in. This condition prompted the government to increase food subsidies, as well as the number of beneficiaries (18 million more people), cut customs duties on imported food, such as wheat and poultry, and ban the export of rice. In 2009, the inflation rate was down to around 10 percent.

Egypt has important oil and natural-gas deposits, and new discoveries continue to strengthen this sector of the economy. Oil reserves increased to 3.3 billion barrels in 2001, due to new fields being brought on stream in the Western Desert. Proven natural-gas reserves are 51 trillion cubic feet, sufficient to meet domestic needs for 30 years at current rates of consumption.

A 2001 agreement with Jordan would guarantee Jordan's purchase of Egyptian natural-gas supplies, contingent on completion of the pipeline under the Red Sea from Al-Arish to Aqaba. But an earlier agreement with Israel, Egypt's closest and potentially most lucrative gas market, has been put on hold due to the renewed Palestinian–Israeli conflict. Under the agreement, Egypt would have provided $300 million a year in gas, meeting 15 percent of Israel's electric-power needs.

Egypt also derives revenues from Suez Canal tolls and user fees, from tourism, and from remittances from Egyptian workers abroad, mostly working in Saudi Arabia and other oil-producing Gulf states. The flow of remittances from the approximately 4 million expatriate workers was reduced and then all but cut off with the Iraqi invasion of Kuwait. Egyptians fled from both countries in panic, arriving

home as penniless refugees. With unemployment already at 20 percent and housing in short supply, the government faced an enormous assimilation problem apart from its loss of revenue. The United States helped by agreeing to write off $4.5 billion in Egyptian military debts. However, the imprisonment and unduly harsh sentence of dissident presidential candidate Ayman Nour led the U.S. in January 2006 to suspend a projected trade and tariff elimination agreement between the two countries.

One encouraging sign of brighter days ahead is the expansion of local manufacturing industries, in line with government efforts to reduce dependence upon imported goods. A 10-year tax exemption plus remission of customs duties on imported machinery have encouraged a number of new business ventures, notably in the clothing industry.

Unfortunately one of the few enterprises affecting Egypt's poor directly was literally "dumped" in January 2003 when the government stopped renewing licenses to the Zabbaleen, a 60,000-member Coptic community that traditionally collects a third of Cairo's 10,000 daily tons of garbage and trash. Furthermore, due to the Swine Flu epidemic, the government decided in April 2009 to exterminate all pigs in Egypt, which consumed part of the garbage collection. This decision not only made things worse for the Zabbaleen, but it also worsened the garbage collection crisis in cities like Cairo. Future collections of all garbage and trash are to be made by foreign companies under contract. The new system would have certain advantages over the Zabbaleen system, mainly in terms of sanitation, but the economic impact on them will be severe. Over the years the Zabbaleen have used profits from trash collection to fund neighborhood improvements, schools and jobs for a great number of women.

In 1987, Mubarak gained some foreign help for Egypt's cash-strapped economy when agreement was reached with the International Monetary Fund for a standby credit of $325 million over 18 months to allow the country to meet its balance-of-payments deficit. The Club of Paris, a group of public and private banks from various industrialized countries, then rescheduled $12 billion in Egyptian external debts over a 10-year period.

Expanded foreign aid and changes in government agricultural policy required by the World Bank for new loans helped spur economic recovery in the 1990s, especially in agriculture. Production records were set in 1996 in wheat, corn, and rice, meeting 50 percent of domestic needs. The cotton harvest for that year was 350,000 tons,

with 50,000 tons exported. However, a new agricultural law passed in 1992 but not implemented until 1997 ended land rents, allowing landlords to set their own leases and in effect reclaim their properties taken over by the government during the Nasser era. The purpose is to provide an incentive for tenant farmers to grow export crops such as cotton and rice. But as a result, Egypt's 900,000 tenant farmers have faced the loss of lands held on long-term leases for several generations.

However, these economic successes must be balanced against Egypt's chronic social problems and the lack of an effective representative political system. The head of the Muslim Brotherhood made the astute observation in a 1993 speech that "the threat is not in the extremist movement. It is in the absence of democratic institutions." Until such institutions are firmly in place, with access to education, full employment, broad political participation, civil rights, and the benefits of growth spread evenly across all levels of society, unrest and efforts to Islamize the government by force are likely to continue.

By 2000, the government's harsh repression had seriously weakened the Islamist movement, albeit at a heavy cost. Some 1,200 police officers and militants had been killed during the 1990s, and 16,000 persons remained jailed without charges on suspicion of membership in Islamic Jihad or other organizations. However, public disaffection continues to grow and to involve increasing numbers of non-Islamists.

Egypt's own difficulties with the Islamists caused some reluctance on its part when support for the U.S.–led international coalition against terrorism formed after the September 11, 2001, bombings of the World Trade Center in New York City and the Pentagon near Washington, D.C. The reluctance stemmed in part from public anger over continued American support for Israel against the Palestinians and the suffering of Iraq's fellow Arabs under the 11-year sanctions imposed on that country.

In March 2004 the government reached agreement with Israel to set up a number of Qualifying Industrial Zones (Q.I.Z.) in an effort to boost its flagging economy. Egyptian manufacturers, notably textiles, will be able to export goods duty-free to the U.S. provided that 35 percent of goods exported were locally produced and a percentage reserved for Israeli products. Egypt's total exports to the U.S. of $3.3 billion included $336 million in textiles and clothing. The Q.I.Z.s will add significantly to this total.

In 2007, Egypt signed a Free Trade Agreement with the EU which covers trade in industrial products, including processed agricultural products. In the same year, a Free Trade Agreement between Egypt and Turkey came into effect and has contributed to increased commercial exchanges between the two countries.

## NOTES

1. Leila Ahmed, in *A Border Passage* (New York: Farrar, Strauss & Giroux, 1999), deals at length with Egyptian vs. Arab identity from the perspective of growing up in British-controlled Egypt.

2. An English observer said, "In arms and firing they are nearly as perfect as European troops." Afaf L. Marsot, *Egypt in the Reign of Muhammad Ali* (Cambridge, England: Cambridge University Press, 1984), p. 132.

3. *Ibid.,* p. 161.

4. Quoted in P. J. Vatikiotis, *Nasser and His Generation* (New York: St. Martin's Press, 1978), p. 35.

5. Gamal Abdel Nasser, *The Philosophy of the Revolution* (Cairo: Ministry of National Guidance, 1954), p. 52.

6. Derek Hopwood, *Egypt: Politics and Society 1945–1981* (London: George Allen and Unwin, 1982), p. 77.

7. Quoted in Panayiotis J. Vatikiotis, *Nasser and His Generation,* op. cit., p. 245.

8. Hopwood, *Egypt: Politics and Society,* op. cit., p. 106.

9. David Hirst and Irene Beeson, *Sadat* (London: Faber and Faber, 1981), p. 255.

10. "Banners slung across the broad thoroughfares of central Cairo acclaimed The Hero of the Crossing (of the October 1973 War)." *Ibid.,* pp. 17–18.

11. With a high unemployment rate and a high number people under age 15, most young graduates must struggle to find a job, let alone get married. To do so a man must provide shelter, jewelry and gifts for his bride and proof to her family that he can support her and their future children.

## Timeline: PAST

**2500–671 B.C.**
Period of the pharaohs

**671–30 B.C.**
The Persian conquest, followed by Macedonians and rule by Ptolemies

**30 B.C.**
Egypt becomes a Roman province

**A.D. 641**
Invading Arabs bring Islam

**969**
The founding of Cairo

**1517–1800**
Egypt becomes an Ottoman province

**1798-1831**
Napoleon's invasion, followed by the rise to power of Muhammad Ali

**1869**
The Suez Canal opens to traffic

**1882**
The United Kingdom establishes a protectorate

**1952**
The Free Officers overthrow the monarchy and establish Egypt as a republic

**1956**
Nationalization of the Suez Canal

**1958–1961**
Union with Syria into the United Arab Republic

**1967**
The Six-Day War with Israel ends in Israel's occupation of the Gaza Strip and the Sinai Peninsula

**1970**
Gamal Abdel Nasser dies; Anwar Sadat succeeds as head of Egypt

**1979**
A peace treaty is signed at Camp David between Egypt and Israel

**1980s**
Sadat is assassinated; he is succeeded by Hosni Mubarak; a crackdown on Islamic fundamentalists

**1990s**
The government employs strong measures in its battle with the Islamists

## PRESENT

**2000s**
Deep social and economic problems persist

In 2005, constitutional amendment allowed multiple candidates for presidential elections

Marriages must also be registered with the government. Increasingly young couples are entering into "temporary (*urfi*) marriages," essentially common-law partnerships, involving witnesses, consent of the guardian of the bride, and public declaration that they meet Islamic standards. Some 3 million such arrangements are registered with notaries public, but given Egypt's economic instability there is probably three times this number in the country.

12. Reported by Jano Charbel and Michael Slackman in *The New York Times,* November 1, 2006. Sadat's nephew had also charged the government with secretly releasing his uncle's chief assassin.

13. Mohammed Habib, quoted in Dan Murphy, "Egypt Vote Shows Unease with Democracy," *The Christian Science Monitor,* June 12, 2007.

14. Mohammed Elmenshawy, "The Muslim Brotherhood Shows Its True Colors," *The Christian Science Monitor,* October 12, 2007.

15. Daniel Williams, "Egypt's Muslim Brotherhood May Be Model for Islam's Political Adaptation," *Washington Post,* February 3, 2006.

# Iran (Islamic Republic of Iran)

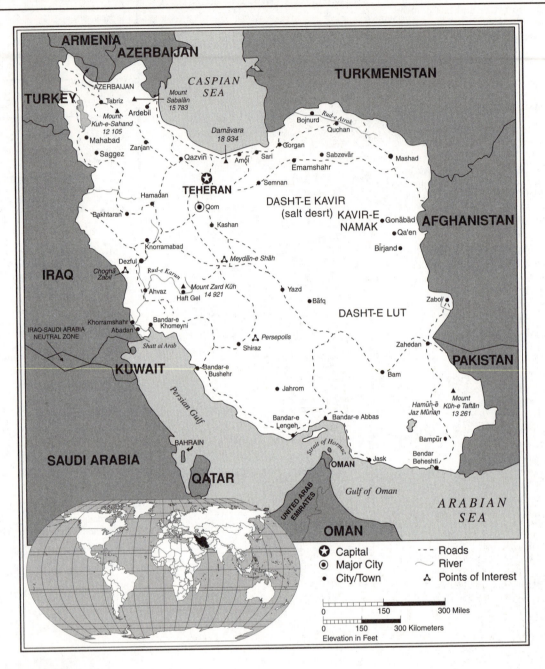

# Iran Statistics

## GEOGRAPHY

*Area* in *Square Miles (Kilometers):*
636,294 (1,648,000) (about the size of Alaska)

*Capital (Population):* Teheran (7,797,520)

*Environmental Concerns:* air and water pollution; deforestation; overgrazing; desertification; oil pollution; insufficient potable water

*Geographical Features:* a rugged, mountainous rim; a high central basin with deserts and mountains; discontinuous plains along both coasts

*Climate:* mostly arid or semiarid; subtropical along Caspian Sea coast

## PEOPLE

### Population

*Total:* 66,429,284
*Annual Growth Rate:* 0.883%
*Rural/Urban Population Ratio:* 68/32

*Major Languages:* Farsi (Persian); Turkic, Kurdish, Luri

*Ethnic Makeup:* 51% Persian; 24% Azeri; 8% Gilaki and Mazandarani; 7% Kurd; 10% others

*Religions:* Muslim 98% (Shia 89%, Sunni 9%), 2% Zoroastrian, Jewish, Christian, and Bahai.

### Health

*Life Expectancy at Birth:* 69 years (male), 72 years (female)

54

*Infant Mortality Rate (Ratio):* 35/1,000
live births

## Education

*Adult Literacy Rate:* 77%
*Compulsory (Ages):* 6–10; free

## COMMUNICATION

*Telephones:* 24,000,000 main lines
*Daily Newspaper Circulation:* 20 per
1,000 people
*Televisions:* 117 per 1,000
*Internet Service Providers:* 8 (2000)

## TRANSPORTATION

*Highways in Miles (Kilometers):* 86,924
(140,200)
*Railroads in Miles (Kilometers):* 3,472
(5,600)
*Usable Airfields:* 305
*Motor Vehicles in Use:* 8,920,000

## GOVERNMENT

*Type:* theocratic republic
*Independence Date:* April 1, 1979
(Islamic Republic of Iran proclaimed)

*Head of State/Government:* Supreme
Guide Ayatollah Ali Hoseini-
Khamenei; President Mahmoud
Ahmadinejad
*Political Parties:* none formally
approved, but "political societies"
may submit candidates for Majlis
elections. They include: Islamic
Society of Engineers; Combatant
Clergy Association; Islamic Iran
Participation Front, National
Confidence Party; Executives of
Construction

## MILITARY

*Military Expenditures (% of GDP):*
2.5%
*Current Disputes:* maritime boundary
with Iraq in Shatt al-Arab not formally
demarcated, and prisoner exchange not
complete. Iran's occupation of Greater
and Lesser Tunbs Islands disputed by
United Arab Emirates; Iran disagrees
with Azerbaijan, Russia, Kazakhstan
and Turkmenistan over sharing of
Caspian Sea waters.

## ECONOMY

*Currency ($U.S.Equivalent):* 9,966
rials = $1
*Per Capita Income/GDP:* $12,800/$335.2
billion
*GDP Growth Rate:* 6.5%
*Inflation Rate:* 25.6%
*Unemployment Rate:* 12.5%
*Labor Force:* 24,360,000 (shortage of
skilled labor)
*Natural Resources:* petroleum; natural
gas; coal; chromium; copper; iron ore;
lead; manganese; zinc; sulfur
*Agriculture:* grains; sugar beets; fruits;
nuts; cotton; dairy products; wool;
caviar
*Industry:* petroleum; petrochemicals;
textiles; cement and other construction
materials; food processing; metal
fabrication; armaments
*Exports:* $98.42 billion (primary partners
China, Japan, India)
*Imports:* $67.25 billion (primary partners
Germany, United Arab Emirates, China,
South Korea)

# Iran Country Report

Iran is in many respects a subcontinent, ranging in elevation from Mount De-mavend (18,386 feet) to the Caspian Sea, which is below sea level. Most of Iran consists of a high plateau ringed by mountains. Much of the plateau is covered with uninhabitable salt flats and deserts—the Dasht-i-Kavir and Dasht-i-Lut, the latter being one of the most desolate and inhospitable regions in the world. The climate is equally forbidding. The so-called Wind of 120 Days blows throughout the summer in eastern Iran, bringing dust and extremely high temperatures.

Most of the country receives little or no rainfall. Settlement and population density are directly related to the availability of water. The most densely populated region is along the Caspian Sea coast, which has an annual rainfall of 80 inches. The provinces of Azerbaijan in the northwest and Khuzestan along the Iraqi border, and the urban areas around Iran's capital, Teheran, are also heavily populated.

Water is so important to the Iranian economy that all water resources were nationalized in 1967. Lack of rainfall caused the development of a sophisticated system of underground conduits, *qanats,* to carry water across the plateau from a water source, usually at the base of a mountain.

Many qanats were built thousands of years ago and are still in operation. They make existence possible for much of Iran's rural population.

Until the twentieth century, the population was overwhelmingly rural; but due to rural–urban migration, the urban population has increased steadily. Nearly all of this migration has been to Teheran, whose metropolitan area now has a population of nearly 8 million, as compared to 200,000 in 1900. Yet the rural population has also increased. This fact has had important political consequences for Iran, when it was a monarchy as well as an Islamic republic. Attachment to the land and family solidarity have preserved the strong rural element in Iranian society as a force for conservatism and loyalty to religious leaders, who then are able to influence whatever regime is in power. Indeed, the rural population strongly supported the first Islamic regime and contributed much of the volunteer manpower recruited to defend the country after the invasion by Iraqi forces in 1980.

## ETHNIC AND RELIGIOUS DIVERSITY

Due to Iran's geographic diversity, the population is divided into a large number of separate and often conflicting ethnic groups.

Ethnic Iranians constitute the majority. The Iranians (or *Persians,* from Parsa, the province where they first settled) are an Indo-European people whose original home was probably in Central Asia. They moved into Iran around 1100 B.C. and gradually dominated the entire region, establishing the world's first empire (in the sense of rule over various unrelated peoples in a large territory). Although its rulers failed to conquer Greece and thereby extend their empire into Europe, such achievements as their imperial system of government, the Persian language (Farsi), the monumental architecture of their capital at Persepolis, and their distinct cultural/historical heritage provide modern Iranians with pride in their ancient past and a national identity, unbroken to the present day.

The largest ethnic minority group is the Azeri (or Azerbaijani) Turks. The Azeris live in northwestern Iran. Their ethnic origin dates back to the ancient Persian Empire, when Azerbaijan was known as Atropene. The migration of Turkish peoples into this region in the eleventh and twelfth centuries A.D. encouraged the spread of the Turkish language and of Islam. These were reinforced by centuries of Ottoman rule, although Persian remained the written and literary language of the people.

Shi'a Islam Prayer meeting outdoors at Teheran University. Iranian society has a considerable level of cultural conformity. Shi'a Islam is the dominant religion of Iran, and observance of this form of Islam permeates society.

Turkish dynasties originating in Azerbaijan controlled Iran for several centuries and were responsible for much of premodern Islamic Iran's political power and cultural achievements. In the late nineteenth and early twentieth centuries, Azeris were in the forefront of the constitutional movement to limit the absolute power of Iranian monarchs. They formed the core of the first Iranian Parliament. The Azeris have consistently fought for regional autonomy from the central Iranian government in the modern period and refer to their province as "Azadistan, Land of Freedom."

The Kurds are another large ethnic minority. Iran's Kurd population is concentrated in the Zagros Mountains along the Turkish and Iraqi borders. The Kurds are Sunni Muslims, as distinct from the Shi'a majority. The Iranian Kurds share a common language, culture, social organization, and ethnic identity with Kurds in Iraq, Turkey, and Syria. Kurds are strongly independent mountain people who lack a politically recognized homeland and who have been unable to unite to form one. The Kurds of Iran formed their own Kurdish Republic, with Soviet backing, after World War II. But the withdrawal of Soviet troops, under international pressure, caused its collapse. Since then, Iranian Kurdish leaders have devoted their efforts toward greater regional autonomy. Kurdish opposition to the central Iranian government was muted during the rule of the

Pahlavi dynasty (1925–1979), but it broke into the open after the establishment of the Islamic republic. The Kurds feared that they would be oppressed under the Shi'a Muslim government headed by Ayatollah Khomeini and boycotted the national referendum approving the republic. Central-government authority over the Kurds was restored in 1985. In 1992, Iraqi Kurdish leaders made an agreement with the Iranian government for deliveries of fuel and spare parts for their beleaguered enclave; in return, they pledged that the enclave would not be used by the People's Mujahideen or any other antigovernment group for military actions against Iran.

The Arabs are another important minority group (Iran and Turkey are the only two Islamic countries in this region of the world with a non-Arab majority). The Arabs live in Khuzestan Province, along the Iraqi border. The Baluchi, also Sunni Muslims, are located in southeast Iran and are related to Baluchi groups in Afghanistan and Pakistan. They are semi-nomadic and have traditionally opposed any form of central-government control. The Baluchi were the first minority to oppose openly the fundamentalist Shi'a policies of the Khomeini government. Non-Islamic minorities include Jews, Zoroastrians, and Armenians and other Christians. Altogether they make up 1 percent of the population. They are represented in the *Majlis* (Parliament) by two Armenian deputies and one each for

Zoroastrians and Jews. Zoroastrians, about 30,000 in all, follow the ancient Persian religion preached by the prophet Zoroaster 2,500 years ago. Zoroaster defined life as a constant struggle between good (*Ahura Mazda,* "light") and evil (*Ahriman,* "darkness"). Zoroastrianism was the official religion of Iran during the pre-Islamic Sassanid empire. Its priests formed a privileged class, charged with responsibility for tending the sacred fire, which was (and still is) kept burning in the fire temples that are centers of faith and worship. Zoroastrians also traditionally buried their dead atop "towers of silence" rather than pollute the ground. Their religiously based customs and traditions have carried over into modern Iranian life. Thus Nowruz ("New Year"), the beginning of spring, the most important and popular of Iranian festivals, is Zoroastrian in origin, as is the solar calendar introduced by Reza Shah to replace the Arabic lunar one.

The Armenians, another small minority, are also protected under Article 13 of the republic's Constitution. Formerly, Armenians were important middlemen and traders in Iran. Armenian hairstylists were very popular before the Revolution, but the republic's strict Islamic code on male–female contacts forced them, as men, out of business. Armenian butcher shops are also required to post signs saying "Minority Religion" because they sell pork.

The Bahais, a splinter movement from Islam founded by an Iranian mystic called the *Bab* ("Door," i.e., to wisdom) and organized by a teacher named Baha'Ullah in the nineteenth century, are the largest non-Muslim minority group. Although Baha'Ullah taught the principles of universal love, peace, harmony, and brotherhood, his proclamations of equality of the sexes, ethnic unity, the oneness of all religions, and a universal rather than a Muslim God aroused the hostility of Shi'a religious leaders. Bahais in Iran were protected from Shi'a hostility during the Qajar and Pahlavi monarchy periods. But with the overthrow of Mohammed Reza Pahlavi, the religious leaders of the Islamic Republic undertook a campaign of persecution and mistreatment described by outside observers as "the genocide of a non-combatant people."[1]

Since 1979 over 200 Bahais have been executed and hundreds more jailed for various "offenses against Islam." Some 10,000 Bahais employed by the Shah's government were summarily terminated after the Revolution. The Bahai Institute of Higher Education, established as an alternative, was shut down in 1998 for a short period. Bahai marriages are not recognized by the authorities and they are prohibited from owning property. The Bab's house in Shiraz, where the faith was founded in 1844, was razed along with other important Bahai sites in 2001.

Despite inflammatory rhetoric from Iran's present president about "wiping Israel off the map" and denying that the Holocaust ever took place, the Jewish minority is recognized as such in the constitution and is free in its observance of Jewish law and custom. Jews have lived there for more than two millennia, and although two-thirds have emigrated since the 1979 revolution, about 25,000 remain. In general they take no part in politics, although there is one Jewish deputy in the Majlis. However the anti-Israeli stance of the regime led to the arrest and trial in 1999 of 13 Jews from Shiraz and Isfahan on charges of espionage. Despite widespread criticism from Jewish groups abroad as well as the international community, ten of the accused were given 13-year prison sentences, with three acquitted. The Iranian Supreme Court in 2001 denied an appeal for clemency from defense lawyers. Eventually the ten were pardoned and continue living in the country. As the Jewish deputy in the Majlis observed, "the Jewish community was probably one of the first minority groups to join in with the revolution and gave many martyrs (to the cause)."[2]

## CULTURAL CONFORMITY

Despite the separatist tendencies in Iranian society caused by the existence of these various ethnic groups and religious divisions, there is considerable cultural conformity. Most Iranians, regardless of background, display distinctly Iranian values, customs, and traditions. Unifying features include the Farsi language, Islam as the overall religion, the appeal (since the sixteenth century) of Shi'a Islam as an Iranian nationalistic force, and a sense of nationhood derived from Iran's long history and cultural continuity.

### DEVELOPMENT

As the world's fourth largest oil exporter and holder of 11 percent of global oil reserves, Iran depends heavily on this product for revenue. In 2008 the country earned $28 billion, down from $44.6 in 2006 due to a sharp drop in oil prices and the recession in the United States and Europe. Current production is 3.9 million barrels per day (bpd). However domestic consumption is 1.7 million bpd. The government spends $20 to $25 billion a year in subsidies in order to keep prices low for gasoline (35 cents a gallon!), electricity and other energy needs for the population. Due to delays in developing new fields and lack of refining capacity it must import 170,000 bpd to keep its car-oriented people happy. Also the sanctions imposed by the UN for its nuclear energy development have resulted in a serious shortage of foreign technical help.

Iranians at all levels have a strongly developed sense of class structure. It is a three-tier structure, consisting of upper, middle, and lower classes. However, some scholars distinguish two lower classes: the urban wage earner, and the landed or landless peasant. The basic socioeconomic unit in this class structure is the patriarchal family, which functions in Iranian society as a tree trunk does in relation to its branches. The patriarch of each family is not only disciplinarian and decision maker but also guardian of the family honor and inheritance.

The patriarchal structure, in terms of the larger society, has defined certain behavioral norms. These include the seclusion of women, ceremonial politeness *(ta'aruf),* hierarchical authoritarianism with domination by superiors over subordinates, and the importance of face *(aberu)*—maintaining "an appropriate bearing and appearance commensurate with one's social status."[3] Under the republic, these norms have been increasingly Islamized as religious leaders have asserted the primacy of Shi'a Islam in all aspects of Iranian life.

## HISTORY

Modern Iran occupies a much smaller territory than that of its predecessors. The Persian Empire (sixth–fourth centuries B.C.) included Egypt, the Arab Near East, Afghanistan, and much of Central Asia, prior to its overthrow by Alexander of Macedon. The Parthian and Sassanid monarchies were major rivals of Rome. Under the latter rulers (A.D. 226–651), Zoroastrianism became the state religion. The Sassanid administrative system, which divided its territory into provinces under a single central authority, was taken over intact by invading Arab armies bringing Islam to the land.

The establishment of Islam brought significant changes into Iranian life. Arab armies defeated the Sassanid forces at the Battle of Qadisiya (A.D. 637) and the later Battle of Nihavand (A.D. 641), which resulted in the death of the last Sassanid king and the fall of his empire. The Arabs gradually established control over all the former Sassanid territories, converting the inhabitants to Islam as they went. But the well-established Iranian cultural and social system provided refinements for Islam that were lacking in its early existence as a purely Arab religion. The Iranian converts to Islam converted the religion from a particularistic Arab faith to a universal faith. Iranian Islamic mystics, called Sufis from the plain wool robes they wore, added their special concept of the search for God (*gnosis,* or esoteric knowledge) to the barebones Arab faith, placing a distinct Persian mark on Islam. In addition to their enormous contributions to scientific, medical and technical knowledge, Persian geographers, astronomers, philosophers, scholars, even poets, provided a Persian legacy to Islam that endures to this day.

Shi'a Muslims, currently the vast majority of the Iranian population and represented in nearly all ethnic groups, were in the minority in Iran during the formative centuries of Islam. Only one of the Twelve Shi'a Imams—the eighth, Reza—actually lived in Iran. (His tomb at Meshed is now the holiest shrine in Iran.) *Taqiya* ("dissimulation" or "concealment")—the Shi'a practice of hiding one's beliefs to escape Sunni persecution—added to the difficulties of the Shi'a in forming an organized community.

In the sixteenth century, the Safavids, who claimed to be descendants of the Prophet Muhammad, established control over Iran with the help of Turkish tribes. The first Safavid ruler, Shah Ismail, proclaimed Shiism as the official religion of his state and invited all Shi'as to move to Iran, where they would be protected. Shi'a domination of the country dates from this period. Shi'a Muslims converged on Iran from other parts of the Islamic world and became a majority in the population.

The Safavid rulers were bitter rivals of the Sunni Ottoman sultans and fought a number of wars with them. The conflict was religious as well as territorial. The Ottoman sultan assumed the title of caliph of Islam in the sixteenth century after the conquest of Egypt, where the descendants of the last Abbasid caliph of Baghdad had taken refuge. As caliph, the sultan claimed the right to speak for, and rule, all Muslims. The Safavids rejected this claim and called on Shi'a Muslims to struggle against him. In more recent years, the Khomeini government issued a similar call to Iranians to carry on war against the Sunni rulers of Iraq, indicating that Shi'a willingness to struggle and, if necessary, incur martyrdom was still very much alive in Iran.

## King of Kings

The Qajars, a new dynasty of Turkish tribal origin, came to power after a bloody struggle at the end of the eighteenth century. They made Teheran their capital. Most of Iran's current borders were defined in the nineteenth century by treaties with foreign powers—Britain (on behalf of India), Russia, and the Ottoman Empire. Due to Iran's military weaknesses, the agreements favored the outside powers and the country lost much of its original territory.

Despite Iran's weakness in relation to foreign powers, the Qajar rulers sought to revive the ancient glories of the monarchy at home. They assumed the old Persian title *Shahinshah,* "King of Kings." At his coronation, each ruler sat on the Peacock Throne, the gilded, jewel-encrusted treasure brought to Iran by Nadir Shah, conqueror of northern India and founder of the short-lived Iranian Afshar dynasty. They assumed other grandiose titles, such as "Shadow of God on Earth" and "Asylum of the Universe." A shah once told an English visitor, "Your King, then, appears to be no more than a first magistrate. I, on the other hand, can elevate or degrade all the high nobles and officers you see around me!"[4]

Qajar pomp and grandeur were more illusion than reality, as was shown in a recent exhibit of Qajar art. Thus portraits of Fath Ali Shah, the second Qajar ruler, show him receiving the bows of European envoys, in poses meant to duplicate those of the great Sassanid rulers of the pre-Islamic Iranian past. Unfortunately, Iran's grandeur had passed. Its strategic location between British-ruled India and the Russian Empire that extended across Central Asia guaranteed that it would become a pawn in the contest for control, usually referred to as the "Great Game." Under these difficult circumstances, Qajar rulers survived mainly by manipulating

tribal leaders and other groups against one another with the tacit support of the mullahs (religious leaders).

Nasr al-Din Shah, Iran's ruler for most of the nineteenth century, was responsible for a large number of concessions to European bankers, promoters, and private companies. His purpose was to demonstrate to European powers that Iran was becoming a modern state and to find new revenues without having to levy new taxes, which would have aroused more dangerous opposition. The various concessions helped to modernize Iran, but they bankrupted the treasury in the process. The shah realized that the establishment of a trained professional army would not only defend Iran's territory but would also demonstrate to the European powers that the country was indeed "modern." To that end he reached agreement with the Russian Czar to send officers from the Cossacks, a traditionally warlike tribe in Russia, to train the core of such an army. This unit subsequently became known as the Cossack Brigade, Iran's only elite military force.

In the mid-nineteenth century, the shah was encouraged by European envoys to turn his attention to education as a means of creating a modern society. In 1851, he opened the Polytechnic College, with European instructors, to teach military science and technical subjects. The graduates of this college, along with other Iranians who had been sent to Europe for their education and a few members of aristocratic families, became the nucleus of a small but influential intellectual elite. Along with their training in military subjects, they acquired European ideas of nationalism and progress. They were "government men" in the sense that they worked for and belonged to the shah's government.

But they also came to believe that the Iranian people needed to unite into a nation, with representative government and a European-style educational system, in order to become a part of the modern world. The views of these intéllectuals put them at odds with the shah, who cared nothing for representative government or civil rights, only for tax collection. The intellectuals also found themselves at odds with the mullahs, who controlled the educational system and feared any interference with their superstitious, illiterate subjects.

The intellectuals and mullahs both felt that the shah was giving away Iran's assets and resources to foreigners. For a long time the intellectuals were the only group to complain; the illiterate Iranian masses could not be expected to protest against actions they knew nothing about. But in 1890, the shah gave a 50-year concession

to a Briton named Talbot for a monopoly over the export and distribution of tobacco. Faced with higher prices for the tobacco they grew themselves, Iranians staged a general strike and boycott, and the shah was forced to cancel the concession. A similar pattern of protests that evolved into mass opposition to arbitrary rule marked the Constitutional Revolution of 1905, the 1979 revolution that overthrew Shah Mohammed Reza Pahlavi, and most recently the present contest between "reformers" advocating a more liberal Islamic government and the Khomeini regime.

By the end of the nineteenth century, the people were roused to action, the mullahs had turned against the ruler, and the intellectuals were demanding a constitution that would limit his powers. One of the intellectuals wrote, "It is self-evident that in the future no nation—Islamic or non-Islamic—will continue to exist without constitutional law. . . . The various ethnic groups that live in Iran will not become one people until the law upholds their right to freedom of expression and the opportunity for [modern] education."[5] One century and two revolutions later, Iran is still struggling to put this formula into operation.

According to Roy Mottahedeh, "the bazaar and the mosque are the two lungs of public life in Iran."[6] The bazaar, like the Greek agora and the Roman forum, is the place where things are bought, deals are consummated, and political issues are aired for public consideration or protest. The mosque is the bastion of religious opinion; its preachers can, and do, mobilize the faithful to action through thundering denunciations of rulers and government officials. Mosque and bazaar came together in 1905 to bring about the first Iranian Revolution, a forerunner, at least in pattern, of the 1979 revolt. Two sugar merchants were bastinadoed (a punishment, still used in Iran, in which the soles of the feet are beaten with a cane) because they refused to lower their prices; they complained that high import prices set by the government gave them no choice. The bazaar then closed down in protest. With commercial activity at a standstill, the shah agreed to establish a "house of justice" and to promulgate a constitution. But six months later, he still had done nothing. Then a mullah was arrested and killed for criticizing the ruler in a Friday sermon. Further protests were met with mass arrests and then gunfire; "a river of blood now divided the court from the country."[7]

In 1906, nearly all of the religious leaders left Teheran for the sanctuary of Qum, Iran's principal theological-studies center. The bazaar closed down again, a general strike paralyzed the country, and thousands of Iranians took refuge in the British Embassy in Teheran. With the city paralyzed, the shah gave in. He granted a Constitution that provided for an elected Majlis, the first limitation on royal power in Iran in its history. Four more shahs would occupy the throne, two of them as absolute rulers, but the 1906 Constitution and the elected Legislature survived as brakes on absolutism until the 1979 Revolution. In this sense, the Islamic Republic is the legitimate heir to the constitutional movement.

## The Pahlavi Dynasty

Iran was in chaos at the end of World War I. British and Russian troops partitioned the country, and after the collapse of Russian power due to the Bolshevik Revolution, the British dictated a treaty with the shah that would have made Iran a British protectorate. Azeris and Kurds talked openly of independence; and a Communist group, the Jangalis, organized a "Soviet Republic" of Gilan along the Caspian coast.

The only organized force in Iran at this time was the Cossack Brigade. Its commander was Reza Khan, a villager from an obscure family who had risen through the ranks on sheer ability. In 1921, he seized power in a bloodless coup, but he did not overthrow the shah. The shah appointed him prime minister and then left the country for a comfortable exile in Europe, never to return.

Turkey, Iran's neighbor, had just become a republic, and many Iranians felt that Iran should follow the same line. But the religious leaders wanted to keep the monarchy, fearing that a republican system would weaken their authority over the illiterate masses. The religious leaders convinced Prime Minister Reza that Iran was not ready for a republic. In 1925, Reza was crowned as shah, with an amendment to the Constitution that defined the monarchy as belonging to Reza Shah and his male descendants in succession. Since he had no family background to draw upon, Reza chose a new name for his dynasty: Pahlavi. It was a symbolic name, derived from an ancient province and language of the Persian Empire.

Reza Shah was one of the most powerful and effective monarchs in Iran's long history. He brought all ethnic groups under the control of the central government and established a well-equipped standing army to enforce his decrees. He did not tamper with the Constitution; instead, he approved all candidates for the Majlis and outlawed political parties, so that the political system was entirely responsible to him alone.

## Reza Shah's New Order

Reza Shah wanted to build a "new order" for Iranian society, and he wanted to build it in a hurry. He was a great admirer of Mustafa Kemal Ataturk, founder of the Turkish Republic. Like Ataturk, Reza Shah believed that the religious leaders were an obstacle to modernization, due to their control over the masses. He set out to break their power through a series of reforms. Lands held in religious trust were leased to the state, depriving the religious leaders of income. A new secular code of laws took away their control, since the secular code would replace Islamic law. Other decrees prohibited the wearing of veils by women and the fez, the traditional brimless Muslim hat, by men. When religious leaders objected, Reza Shah had them jailed; on one occasion, he went into a mosque, dragged the local mullah out in the street, and horse whipped him for criticizing the ruler during a Friday sermon.

In 1935, a huge crowd went to the shrine of Imam Reza, the eighth Shi'a Imam, in Meshad, to hear a parade of mullahs criticize the shah's ruthless reform policies. Reza Shah ringed the shrine with troops. When the crowd refused to disperse, they opened fire, killing a hundred people. It was the first and last demonstration organized by the mullahs during Reza Shah's reign. Only one religious leader, a young scholar named Ruhollah al-Musavi al-Khomeini, consistently dared to criticize the shah, and he was dismissed as being an impractical teacher.

Iran declared its neutrality during the early years of World War II. But Reza Shah was sympathetic to Germany; he had many memories of British interference in Iran. He allowed German technicians and advisers to remain in the country, and he refused to allow war supplies to be shipped across Iran to the Soviet Union. In 1941, British and Soviet armies simultaneously occupied Iran. Reza Shah abdicated in favor of his son, Crown Prince Mohammed, and was taken into exile on a British warship. He never saw his country again.

## Mohammed Reza Pahlavi

When the new shah came to the throne, few suspected that he would rule longer than his father and hold even more power. Mohammed Reza Pahlavi was young (22) and inexperienced, and he found himself ruling a land occupied by British and Soviet troops and threatened by Soviet-sponsored separatist movements in Azerbaijan and Kurdistan. Although these movements were put down, with U.S. help, a major challenge to the shah developed in 1951–1953.

A dispute over oil royalties between the government and the Anglo-Iranian Oil Company (AIOC) aroused intense national feeling in Iran. Mohammed Mossadegh, an author, a prominent nationalist politician, and member of parliament, was elected on April 28, 1951 by the Majlis as prime minister by a vote of 79 to 12. The Shah had no choice then but to appoint Mossadegh to the post mainly because of his rising popularity and power and also due to the popular resentment against the oil deal with the British. Mossadegh moved quickly on May 1, 1951 to nationalize the AIOC and cancel its oil concession. The AIOC responded by closing down the industry, and all foreign technicians left the country. The Iranian economy was not affected at first, and Mossadegh's success in standing up to the company, which most Iranians considered an agent of foreign imperialism, won him enormous popularity.

Mossadegh served as prime minister from 1951 to 1953, a difficult time for Iran due to loss of oil revenues and internal political wrangling. He was passionately opposed to foreign intervention in Iran and interference with its economy and politics. He was the architect of the nationalization of Iran's oil industry which had been controlled by the British since 1913 through the Anglo-Iranian Oil Company (AIOC), which later became British Petroleum (BP). Mossadegh, who was passionately opposed to foreign intervention in Iran and interference with its economy and politics, was the architect of the nationalization of Iran's oil industry which has been controlled by the British control since 1913 through the Anglo-Iranian Oil Company (AIOC), which later became British Petroleum (BP). The British government was very concerned by these developments and sought, with the help of the United States, to reverse this loss. The Cold War confrontation between the United States and the Soviet Union was then at its height, and the Dwight Eisenhower administration feared that Mossadegh's policies would lead to a Communist takeover of Iran.

Both the British government, under Winston Churchill, and the United States started making plans to overthrow the prime minister and sought the cooperation of the shah.

The effect of the nationalization and the departure of the British oil technicians led the entire Iranian oil production into a steep decline: The oil production went from 241.4 million barrels in 1950 to 10.6 million in 1952. Displeased by the turn of events, the shah tried to replace Mossadegh, but the popular reaction was so great (street protests, strikes, and refusal of the army to intervene), ended with the shah fleeing the country to end up in exile in Italy.

The British/U.S. plan to oust Mossadegh was put into motion and on August 19, 1953, the prime minister was overthrown by a coup organized by the CIA in collusion with the British MI6. The coup was code-named by the CIA "Operation Ajax." After his arrest by the army, Mossadegh was tried, jailed for three years, and then placed under house arrest until his death in March 1967. On August 19, 1953, the shah returned to his country and gradually gathered all authority in his hands and developed the vast internal security network that eliminated parliamentary opposition.

By the 1960s, the shah felt that he was ready to lead Iran to greatness. In 1962, he announced the Shah–People Revolution, also known as the White Revolution. It had these basic points: land reform, public ownership of industries, nationalization of forests, voting rights for women, workers' profit sharing, and a literacy corps to implement compulsory education in rural areas. The plan drew immediate opposition from landowners and religious leaders. But only one spoke out forcefully against the shah: Ayatollah Ruhollah Khomeini, by then the most distinguished of Iran's religious scholars. "I have repeatedly pointed out that the government has evil intentions and is opposed to the ordinances of Islam," he said in a public sermon. His message was short and definite: The shah is selling out the country; the shah must go.

Khomeini continued to criticize the shah, and in June 1963, he was arrested. Demonstrations broke out in various cities. The shah sent the army into the streets, and again a river of blood divided ruler from country. Khomeini was released, re-arrested, and finally exiled to Iraq. For the next 15 years, he continued attacking the shah in sermons, pamphlets, and broadsides smuggled into Iran through the "bazaar network" of merchants and village religious leaders. Some had more effect than others. In 1971, when the shah planned an elaborate coronation at the ancient Persian capital of Persepolis to celebrate 2,500 years of monarchy, Khomeini declared, "Islam is fundamentally opposed to the whole notion of monarchy. The title of King of Kings . . . is the most hated of all titles in the sight of God. . . . Are the people of Iran to have a festival for those whose behavior has been a scandal throughout history and who are a cause of crime and oppression . . . in the present age?"[8]

Yet until 1978, the possibility of revolution in Iran seemed to be remote. The shah controlled all the instruments of power. His secret service, SAVAK, had informers everywhere. The mere usage of a word such as "oppressive" to describe the weather was enough to get a person arrested. Whole families disappeared into the shah's jails and were never heard from again.

The public face of the regime, however, seemed to indicate that Iran was on its way to wealth, prosperity, and international importance. The shah announced a 400 percent increase in the price of Iranian oil in 1973 and declared that the country would soon become a "Great Civilization." Money poured into Iran, billions of dollars more each year. The army was modernized with the most sophisticated U.S. equipment available. A new class of people, the "petro-bourgeoisie," became rich at the expense of other classes. Instead of the concessions given to foreign business firms by penniless Qajar shahs, the twentieth-century shah became the dispenser of opportunities to business people and bankers to develop Iran's great civilization with Iranian money—an army of specialists imported from abroad.

## FREEDOM

Iran's Constitution calls its political system a "religious democracy," leaving the term ambiguous. Under a sort of checks and balances, the Supreme Legal Guide (see below) appoints a Council of Constitutional Guardians (CCG) which approves (or rejects) candidates for the Majlis or other public offices in advance of elections. Another constitutional body, the Assembly of Experts, supervises national elections including that for the president. It may (at least in theory) replace the Supreme Legal Guide if it is determined that he is acting contrary to the constitution. A third body (unelected), The Expediency Council, functions as a brake on overuse of power or authoritarianism on the part of the CCG or the Assembly of Experts.

In 1976, the shah seemed at the pinnacle of his power. His major adversary, Khomeini, had been expelled from Iraq and was now far away in Paris. U.S. president Jimmy Carter visited Iran in 1977 and declared, "Under your leadership (the country) is an island of stability in one of the more troubled areas of the world." Yet just a month later, 30,000 demonstrators marched on the city of Qum, protesting an unsigned newspaper article (reputed to have been written by the shah) that had attacked Khomeini as being anti-Iranian. The police fired on the demonstration, and a massacre followed.

Gradually, a cycle of violence developed. Massacre followed massacre in city after city. In spite of the shah's efforts to modernize his country, it seemed to more and more Iranians that he was trying to undermine the basic values of their society by striking at the religious leaders. Increasingly, marchers in the streets were heard to shout, "Death to the shah!"

Even though the shah held absolute power, he seemed less and less able or willing to use his power to crush the opposition. It was as if he were paralyzed. He wrote in his last book, "A sovereign may not save his throne by shedding his countrymen's blood. . . . A sovereign is not a dictator. He cannot break the alliance that exists between him and his people."[9] The shah vacillated as the opposition intensified. His regime was simply not capable of self-reform nor of accepting the logical consequences of liberalization, of free elections, a return to constitutional monarchy, and the emergence of legitimate dissent.[10]

## THE ISLAMIC REPUBLIC

The shah and his family left Iran for good in January 1979. Ayatollah Ruhollah Khomeini returned from exile practically on his heels, welcomed by millions who had fought and bled for his return. The shah's Great Civilization lay in ruins. Like a transplant, it had been an attempt to impose a foreign model of life on the Iranian community, a surgical attachment that had been rejected.

In April 1979, Khomeini announced the establishment of the Islamic Republic of Iran. He called it the first true republic in Islam since the original community of believers was formed by Muhammad. Khomeini said that religious leaders would assume active leadership, serve in the Majlis, even fight Iran's battles as "warrior mullahs." A "Council of Guardians" was set up to interpret laws and ensure that they were in conformity with the sacred law of Islam.

Khomeini, as the first Supreme Guide, embodied the values and objectives of the republic. Because he saw himself in that role, he consistently sought to remain above factional politics yet to be accessible to all groups and render impartial decisions. But the demands of the war with Iraq, the country's international isolation, conflicts between Islamic radicals and advocates of secularization, and other divisions forced the aging Ayatollah into a day-to-day policy-making role. It was a role that he was not well prepared for, given his limited experience beyond the confines of Islamic scholarship.

A major responsibility of the Council of Guardians was to designate—with the Ayatollah's approval—a successor to Khomeini as Supreme Legal Guide. In 1985, the Council chose Ayatollah Hossein Ali Montazeri, a former student and close associate of the patriarch. Montazeri, although politically inexperienced and lacking Khomeini's charisma, had directed the exportation of Iranian Islamic doctrine to other Islamic states after the Revolution, with some success. This responsibility had identified him abroad as the architect of Iranian-sponsored terrorist acts such as the taking of hostages in Lebanon. But during his brief tenure as Khomeini's designated successor, he helped make changes in prison administration, revamped court procedures to humanize the legal system and reduce prisoner mistreatment, and urged a greater role for opposition groups in political life. However, Montazeri resigned in March 1989 after publishing an open letter, which aroused Khomeini's ire, criticizing the mistakes made by Iranian leaders during the Revolution's first decade. He remained one of the most vocal critics of the government and its policies until he died on December 20, 2009.

The Islamic Republic staggered from crisis to crisis in its initial years. Abol Hassan Bani-Sadr, a French-educated intellectual who had been Khomeini's right-hand man in Paris, was elected president in 1980 by 75 percent of the popular vote. But it was one of the few post revolutionary actions that united a majority of Iranians. Although the United States, as the shah's supporter and rescuer in his hour of exile, was proclaimed the "Great Satan" and thus helped to maintain Iran's revolutionary fervor, the prolonged crisis over the holding of American Embassy hostages by guards who would take orders from no one but Khomeini embarrassed Iran and damaged its credibility more than any gains made from tweaking the nose of a superpower. The hostages were held for over a year and the crisis damaged the credibility of President Carter so much that it as to cost him the 1980 presidential election.

Historically, revolutions often seem to end by devouring those who carry them out. A great variety of Iranian social groups had united to overthrow the shah. They had different views of the future; an "Islamic republic" meant different things to different groups. The Revolution first devoured all those associated with the shah, in a reign of terror intended to compensate for 15 years of repression. Islamic tribunals executed thousands of people—political leaders, intellectuals, and military commanders.

The major opposition to Khomeini and his fellow religious leaders came from the radical group Mujahideen-i-Khalq. The group favored an Islamic socialist republic and was opposed to too much influence on government by religious leaders. However, the Majlis was dominated by the religious leaders, many of whom had no experience in government and knew little of politics beyond the village level. As the conflict between these groups sharpened, bombings and assassinations occurred almost daily.

The instability and apparently endless violence during 1980–1981 suggested to the outside world that the Khomeini government was on the point of collapse. Iraqi president Saddam Hussain thought so, and in September 1980, he ordered his army to invade Iran—a decision that proved to be a costly mistake. President Bani-Sadr was dismissed by Khomeini after an open split developed between him and religious leaders over the conduct of the war; he escaped to France subsequently and has remained out of politics. In his absence the Mujahideen continued their assaults against the regime, and in 1981 carried out a series of bomb attacks on government leaders. One in particular killed more than 70 of them, and the present Supreme Legal Guide, Ali Khamenei, lost an arm in another attack.

The Khomeini regime showed considerable resilience in dealing with its adversaries. In 1983, Mujahideen leaders were hunted down and killed or imprisoned. Their organization had been the vanguard in the Iranian Revolution, but their Marxist, atheist views caused them to be viewed by the clerical regime as an enemy. The Mujahdeen leader, Massoud Rajavi, escaped to France, where he was given asylum. While there he organized the National Council of Resistance as the Mujahideen's political and PR arm. However the French government expelled him in 1986, in a move to improve relations with Iran. Rajavi then found refuge in Iraq, where he was welcomed by Khomeini's old adversary Saddam Hussein. Saddam found him a useful ally, and provided the Mujahideen with money, weapons and bases along the border from whence to launch raids and intelligence-gathering activities into Iran.

Toward the end of the war the Mujahideen took advantage of Iraqi successes to seize several towns inside Iran, freeing political prisoners and executing minor officials, such as prison wardens, without trial. But the organization had little internal support in the country. Its Marxist views were not shared by the majority of people, and Mujahideen claims of 90,000 executions and more than 150,000 political prisoners held by the regime were believed to be wildly exaggerated.

## HEALTH/WELFARE

Drugs and heroin cross-border smuggling from Afghanistan have become a major problem in Iran, costing the country some $800 million a year. Over 3,000 border guards have been killed by smugglers since 1999 and an average of a dozen police die monthly in urban shoot outs with dope dealers. It was estimated that Iran had 1.3 million addicts in 2000, and that number is rising. In 2003 it was estimated that there were 200,000 street children in Teheran alone, many of them addicts and abandoned by their families.

The U.S. invasion and occupation of Iraq in 2003 set up an awkward situation both for the Mujahideen and for U.S. forces. Although it continued to be labeled as a terrorist organization by the U.S. State Department, its opposition to the Iranian regime indicated to U.S. policy makers that it might serve as a useful ally in the event of a future confrontation.

In 2003 an amnesty offer to the Mujahideen from the Khatami government was accepted by 250 members, out of a total of 3,500. They returned to Iran under guarantees of safe conduct by the Red Cross and were reunited with their families, most of whom never expected to see them again.

Otherwise Iran continues to view the organization as its enemy. In 1990, Rajavi's brother was killed by unknown gunmen in Geneva, Switzerland. In August 1991, Shahpour Bakhtiar, the last prime minister under the monarchy, was murdered under similar circumstances in Paris, where he had been living in exile.

The other main focus of opposition was the Tudeh (Masses) Party. Although considered a Communist party, its origins lay in the Iranian constitutional movement of 1905–1907, and it had always been more nationalistic than Soviet-oriented. The shah banned the Tudeh after an assassination attempt on him in 1949, but it revived during the Mossadegh period of 1951–1953. After the shah returned from exile in 1953, the Tudeh was again banned and went underground. Many of its leaders fled to the Soviet Union. After the 1979 Revolution, the Tudeh again came out into the open and collaborated with the Khomeini regime. It was tolerated by the religious leaders for its nationalism, which made its Marxism acceptable. Being militarily weak at that time, the regime also wished to remain on good terms with its Soviet neighbor. However, the rapprochement was brief. In 1984, top Tudeh leaders were arrested in a series of surprise raids and were given long prison terms.

## DOMESTIC POLITICAL DYNAMICS

What may be described as the "surreal world" of Iranian politics is largely the result of institutions grafted onto the structure of the pre-revolutionary government by clerical leaders. The clerical regime preserved that structure, which consisted of the Majlis, cabinet of ministers, civil service and the armed forces. SAVAK was replaced by a similar and equally repressive security and intelligence called SAVAM. Then a parallel structure of government was formed under the authority and leadership of the Supreme Legal Guide, responsible only to him as the final repository of Islamic law.

The parallel structure consists of the 12-member unelected CCG, the 88-member Assembly of Experts appointed for 8-year terms, and the 31-member Expediency Council appointed by the Supreme Legal Guide with the concurrence of the CCG. Clerical dominance of the system is underscored by the requirement that all members of the Assembly must be clerical leaders and their candidacy approved by the CCG prior to an election. Similarly half the members of the CCG must come from the ranks of the clerics.

The Expediency Council, currently headed by former President Ali Akbar Hashimi Rafsanjani, was set up to resolve disputes over legislation between the Majlis and the CCG and to verify whether laws passed by the Majlis are compatible with Islamic law. The Supreme Legal Guide also controls the judiciary, the Radio-TV Ministry, the chiefs of the armed forces, the Revolutionary Guard and SAVAM and the police. In the light of the present conflict over reform, pitting advocates of more openness in the system against those determined at all cost to preserve the Islamic republic as it stands, this parallel structure represents a formidable obstacle.

The Revolution that overturned one of the most ruthless authoritarian regimes in history has been in effect long enough to provide some clues to its future direction. One clue is the continuity of internal politics. Despite wreaking savage vengeance on persons associated with the shah's regime, Khomeini and his fellow mullahs preserved most of the Pahlavi institutions of government. The Majlis, civil service, secret police, and armed forces were continued as before, with minor modification to conform to strict Islamic practice. The main addition was a parallel structure of

revolutionary courts, paramilitary Revolutionary Guards (Pasdaran), workers' and peasants' councils, plus the Council of Guardians as the watchdog over legislation.

An important change between the monarchy and the republic concerns the matter of appropriate dress. Decrees issued by Khomeini required women to wear the enveloping chador and *hijab* (headscarf) in public. Painted nails or too much hair showing would often lead to arrests or fines, sometimes jail. The decrees were enforced by Revolutionary Guards and *komitehs* ("morals squads") patrolling city streets and urban neighborhoods. Also, the robe and turban worn by Ayatollah Khomeini and his fellow clerics were decreed as correct fashion, preferred over the "Mr. Engineer" business suit and tie of the shah's time. The necktie in particular was considered a symbol of Western decadence and derided as a "donkey's tail" by the country's new leaders.

In recent years the dress code and other restrictions on personal or public behavior have ranged between extremes, from relative laxity during Khatami's two presidencies to harsh crackdowns under Ahmadinejad's. Despite the presence in the country of Nobel Peace laureate Shirin Ebadi, the organization that she co-founded to monitor women's rights has become the object of governmental repression. Two distinguished Iranian-American scholars sympathetic to the regime were arrested while visiting Iran and detained for long periods before their release after protests from their U.S. institutions and the academic international world. Thus the present social crackdown, it would seem, has less to do with a particular Iranian government than with the effort of Iran's clerical leaders to forge a new national identity, blending Shi'a Islam with revolutionary teachings and ideology.

The 1985 presidential election in Iran continued the secular trend. The ruling Islamic Republican Party (since dissolved) nominated President Ali Khamenei for a second term, against token opposition. A pre-election problem emerged when Mehdi Bazargan, the republic's first prime minister, announced his candidacy as head of the then-opposition Freedom Movement. The CCG disqualified him on grounds that as an opponent of the war with Iraq his election would damage national solidarity. Khamenei won re-election handily, and on Khomeini's death in 1989 succeeded him as Supreme Legal Guide.

Relations with other countries have varied between cooperation and hostility, perhaps the only constant being Iran's determination to play an important regional role. Iranian negotiators helped privately

to arrange the release of Western hostages in Lebanon in 1990–91. In 2005 the government reopened the case of an Iranian-Canadian journalist killed while in custody in 2003. Her death had seriously affected relations with Canada.

In 1989 Iran was further estranged from Western countries after Khomeini issued a *fatwa* sentencing the Anglo-Pakistani writer Salman Rushdie to death for his novel *The Satanic Verses*. The fatwa stated that the novel was blasphemous because it vilified the Prophet Muhammad. In addition to a storm of support for Khomeini in the Islamic world, a number of prominent Western leaders and writers such as Jimmy Carter, Roald Dahl, Stephen Spender, and John Le Carre said that the sentence was appropriate given Rushdie's apparent opportunism and awareness that the book would offend believers.[11] Britain broke diplomatic relations with Iran. They were restored after the Iranian government supposedly suspended the decree. However in June 2007, the issue was reopened after Britain's award of knighthood to Rushdie.

The regime has had difficulties in ensuring popular support and making use of its majority in the fractious Majlis to carry out necessary economic reforms. In the 1992 Majlis elections, two political groups presented candidates: the Society of Radical Clergy (*Ruhaniyat,* loosely but incorrectly translated as "moderates") and the Combatant Religious Leaders (*Ruhaniyoun,* "hard-liners"). All candidates had to be approved by the Council of Constitutional Guardians (CCG).

Recent elections for the Majlis reflect the surreal political world in which Iranians live and vote. In the 1992 elections two groups presented candidates vetted by the CCG, the Society of Radical Clergy and the Combatant Religious Leaders. An outsider would have been hard-pressed to distinguish between them. In the 1996 elections, the distinction between Ruhaniyat and Ruhaniyoun became even more blurred, reflecting the arcane nature of Iranian politics. The former, renamed the Conservative Combatant Clergy Society, was now opposed by the Servants of Iran's Construction, a coalition of centrist supporters of then–president Rafsanjani. The Freedom Movement was outlawed in 2001 by the CCG and 30 of its members arrested.

In the 2000 and 2005 Majlis elections the electorate was increasingly divided into groups, roughly but inaccurately, described as "reformist" and "conservative" (hardline or fundamentalist). A coalition of "reformist" groups, the Islamic Iran Participation Front, dominated the 2000 election. In 2005 a new group, the

National Trust, replaced it as the majority in the Majlis. One difference between these two groups is that "reformists" support a more open, civil, Western-type society and "conservatives" advocate a rigid Islamic system as Khomeini defined it. From the former's viewpoint Khatami's first election marked the success of the reformist program, bringing Iran into the family of democratic countries, while Ahmadinejad's election and the furor over Iran's nuclear program has restored the conservative viewpoint, replacing to some extent these divisions by a sense of national unity and rejection of foreign interference in its internal affairs.

The dominance of the conservative trend was confirmed and consolidated after the March14/April 25, 2008 two-round parliamentary elections in which around 4,500 candidates nationwide ran for 290 seats. Close to 2,000 candidates (mostly independent and reformists) were barred from running by the Guardian Council's Supervisory and Executive Election Boards. On the first round, 125 seats were captured by the conservatives and only 23 by the reformists. After the second round of voting on April 25, 2008, the conservatives had won a total of 132 seats, the reformists 31 and 40 seats went to independents. To many observers, given the fact that many reformists and independents were barred from running, the 2008 parliamentary elections were no more than a contest between conservatives who supported President Ahmadinejad and those who were critical of his performance both at home and in foreign policy.

## IRAN AFTER KHOMEINI

In June 1989, Ayatollah Ruhollah Khomeini died of a heart attack in a Teheran hospital. He was 86 years old and had struggled all his life against the authoritarianism of two shahs.

The Imam left behind a society entirely reshaped by his uncompromising Islamic ideals and principles. Every aspect of social life in republican Iran is governed by these principles, from prohibition of the production and use of alcohol and drugs to a strict dress code for women outside the home, compulsory school prayers, emphasis on theological studies in education, and required fasting during Ramadan. One positive result of this Islamization program has been a renewed awareness among Iranians of their cultural identity and pride in their heritage.

Khomeini also bequeathed many problems to his country. The most immediate problem concerned the succession to him as Supreme Legal Guide.

A separate body of senior religious leaders and jurists, the Assembly of Experts, resolved the succession question by electing President Khamenei as Supreme Guide. However, the choice emphasized Khomeini's unique status as both political and spiritual leader. As a *Hojatulislam* (a lower-ranking cleric), Khamenei lacked the credentials to replace the Ayatollah. But he was an appropriate choice, having served as a part of the governing team. Also, he was the most available religious leader. He had completed two terms as president and was ineligible for reelection.

## THE PRESIDENCY

The chief executive's powers in the Iranian system were greatly strengthened by a constitutional amendment abolishing the office of prime minister, approved by voters in a July 1989 referendum. Elections to replace Ali Khamenei as president were won handily by Rafsanjani Ali Akbar Hashemi with 95 percent of the 14.1 million votes cast.

Rafsanjani's first cabinet consisted mostly of technocrats, suggesting some relaxation of the policy of exporting the Revolution and supporting revolutionary Islamic groups outside the country. At home, there was also a slight relaxation of the strict enforcement of Islamic codes of behavior enforced by the morals squads and security police. But the easing was temporary. In 1992, the new Supreme Guide issued an edict ordering these codes enforced. A similar edict was issued for arts and culture, and the minister of culture and Islamic guidance was forced to resign after clerical leaders charged him with being "too permissive" in allowing concerts and films of a "non-Islamic" nature to be presented to the public. (His name: Mohammed Khatami.)

Rafsanjani was reelected in 1993, but by a much smaller margin of the electorate, 63 percent. The decline in his popularity was due mainly to his failure to improve the economy, but also for continuation of the strict Islamic dress and behavior codes. When his term ended, he kept his seat in the Majlis. In the February 2000 Majlis elections, he finished 29th in the contest for Teheran's 30 seats, barely avoiding a run-off. However, Ayatollah Khamenei appointed him chairman of the powerful Expediency Council, which serves as the final advisory body to the Supreme Legal Guide in political and legislative matters. In this capacity, he continued to play an important role in Iran's evolving political process.

In May 1997, Iranian voters went to the polls to elect a new president. Four candidates had been cleared and approved

by the CCG: a prominent judge; a former intelligence-agency director; Majlis speaker Ali Akbar Nalegh-Nouri; and Mohammed Khatami, the former minister of culture and Islamic guidance who had been out of office for five years and was not well known to the public. However, Khatami, a moderate, emerged as the winner in a startling upset, with 69 percent of the votes. Support for the new president came from women and the large number of Iranians under age 25, who grew up under the republic but were deeply dissatisfied with economic hardships and Islamic restrictions on their personal freedom. On June 8, 2001, Mohammed Khatami was reelected handily for a second term as Iran's president, garnering 77 percent of the 28.2 million votes cast.

The June 2005 election for president produced further surprises. Out of over 1,000 candidates for the office only eight were approved by the Guardian Council. The favorite and front-runner, former president Rafsanjani, campaigned on the basis of liberalizing the economy and normalizing relations with the U.S. His chief rival, the former minister of science, was favored by the youth population for his platform emphasizing intellectual freedom and cultural diversity. However the unexpected winner was former Tehran mayor Ahmad Ahmadinejad. On August 3, 2005, he became Iran's sixth president after winning 62% of the runoff election votes. His main support came from the conservative coalition known as the Alliance of Builders of Islamic Iran. He had previously served as provincial governor and mayor.

A man of humble origins (his father was a blacksmith) and a "success story" in U.S. terms, Ahmadinejad was elected largely due to campaign promises to deal vigorously with public corruption, economic problems, and the disparity between rich and poor. He almost immediately took center stage with inflammatory statements indicating that Israel should be wiped off the map and that the Holocaust had never existed. However, his policies at home and abroad reflect the return to "conservative" values and patterns of behavior. He also articulates Iran's determination to pursue nuclear energy, which brought a sense of unity to this fractured nation. He stated many times that "Iran has the right to peaceful nuclear technology and scientific progress."

In the summer of 2008, Supreme Leader Ali Khamenei indirectly indicated his support for a second five year presidential term for Ahmadinejad. In the elections of June 12, 2009, according to official results, Ahmadinejad won 62.63% of the vote while Mir-Hossein Mousavi, who came in second, won 33.75%. Supporters of the latter rejected the results and denounced them as based on widespread electoral fraud. Several street protests took place—which met a strong police response—but in the end, the Supreme Leader confirmed the results and Ahmadinejad was sworn in on August 5, 2009.

## FOREIGN POLICY

The end of the war with Iraq left a number of issues unresolved. A formal peace treaty ending the 1980s war with Iraq and an agreement on navigation rights in the Shatt al-Arab have yet to be signed. However relations between the two neighbor countries have improved significantly since the overthrow of Saddam Hussein, whose regime was the principal backer of the Mujahidin-I-Khalq.

In July 1996, Total of France was given a concession to develop newly discovered oil fields near Sirri Island in the Gulf. The concession had been granted previously to the U.S. Conoco Oil Company, but Conoco withdrew under pressure from the Clinton administration to comply with sanctions regulations.

The conviction of four Iranians in a German court in 1997 for the 1992 assassinations of Iranian Kurd opposition leaders in Berlin temporarily halted the increase in European–Iranian contacts. More than 100,000 people marched in Teheran to protest the decision, and the European Union suspended the "dialogue" with Iran on sanctions pertaining to Iran's nuclear development program. But the Iranian market remains too attractive to Europe in terms of investment. Foreign investment hit a record $10.2 billion in 2007, up from $4.2 billion in 2005 and $2 million in 1994.

The long and often hostile relationship with Russia, dating back to the years of gradual acquisition of Iranian territory by advancing Russian armies and settlers in the 1800s, entered a new phase in the new millennium with a joint agreement for training of Iranian officers at Russian bases. However the international furor over Iran's nuclear program led Russia in 2007 to suspend completion work on the German-built nuclear reactor at Bushehr, on grounds that the last two payments due for Russian technical help had not been made.

Iran's relations with the United States remained glacially frozen, at least on the official level. For more than two decades, the only official connections had been through the Swiss Embassy in Teheran and the Pakistan Embassy in Washington, D.C. However, an indirect channel through the U.S.–Iran Claims Tribunal set up in the

Hague has been quite successful. It was set up to adjudicate claims by U.S. firms for work contracted and equipment delivered to the shah's regime but not paid for due to the Revolution. The tribunal is also responsible for examining Iranian claims against U.S. companies. To date it has awarded $6 billion to U.S. claimants and $4 billion to Iranian claimants. In 2006 the first lawsuit from the Iranian side, on behalf of a Cyprus-based Iranian businessman was filed. The suit alleged a bungled terrorism action by U.S. customs agents. A Tehran court awarded him $500 million. According to its terms the United States would either pay him direct or present to the court a list of its assets in Iran for seizure in compensation. These included the former U.S. embassy, valued at $120 million. While it was highly unlikely that the businessman would become the owner of the embassy, further steps in the claims process, including the release of Iranian assets still held in American banks, would go a long way toward restoring relations. The United States has transferred $8 billion in Iranian frozen assets to the Bank of England and another $3.6 billion to the Federal Reserve.

Although Iranians continue to view the American people favorably, the clerical regime and its hard-line supporters insist that the U.S. government is the cause of their failure to establish a sound economy, and an obstacle to improved relations with the outside world. In November 2001, the 22nd anniversary of the occupation of the U.S. Embassy in Teheran and the holding of 52 Americans as hostages for 444 days, the embassy building was reopened as a museum, with an exhibit of alleged "crimes against the Iranian people" committed by America. One exhibit showed photos of the U.S. helicopters that had crashed in the desert on a failed rescue mission.

### ACHIEVEMENTS

The Imam Khomeini Relief Foundation (Komiteh Emdad) is one of the world's great success stories as a charity organization. Founded prior to the revolution to serve jailed anti-Shah demonstrators, it has evolved into a significant provider of needs for Iran's poor and disadvantaged population. Of the 5 million poor Iranian people, Komiteh Emdad, helps 92 percent by providing such services as job creation, bank loans, low-cost housing, free health care and homes for orphans. In 2007 families were scheduled to take up residence in some 350 low-cost residential units in Tehran. Komiteh Emdad even operates a shelter for battered women and drug addicts.

Prior to the election of a new Iranian president in 1997, the U.S.–Iranian relationship became truly ice-bound. The Clinton administration imposed a trade embargo in 1995, calling the country a major sponsor of international terrorism. Congress then passed a bill penalizing companies that invest $40 million or more in Iran's oil and gas industry. The ban would apply equally to U.S. and foreign companies.

As might have been expected, the bill aroused a storm of protest in Europe. It was viewed as unwarranted interference in the internal affairs of European countries, and the European Union denounced it as a violation of the principles of international free trade. It was patently unenforceable outside U.S. borders, and in May 1998, the administration approved a waiver to allow the consortium formed to exploit the former Conoco concession.

## THE DOOR OPENS—SLIGHTLY

President Khatami's reelection prompted a reassessment of U.S. policy toward Iran. Former secretary of state Madeleine Albright acknowledged some "mistakes of the past" shortly after the February 2000 Majlis elections. They included the overthrow of Mossadegh, U.S. support for Iraq in the war with Iran, and alignment with the shah's regime despite its brutal suppression of dissent.

There remains a considerable reservoir of good will among ordinary Iranians toward the U.S. After the southeastern city of Bam, with its ancient citadel, was leveled by a massive earthquake with some 45,000 casualties, the U.S. sent a medical disaster team along with volunteers from many humanitarian agencies. Another crack opened in the door when Iran agreed to participate in an international conference of NGOs on reconstruction in Iraq. However a conference in Tehran in December 2005 convened by Ahmadinejad on the "myth" of the Holocaust was criticized strongly by Iranian scholars both in and outside the country, as an exercise in propaganda and not helpful to regional peace.

U.S.-Iranian relations entered a more hopeful phase with the election of Barak Hussein Obama to the Presidency. In a videotaped message to Iran made on March 20, 2009, President Obama called for better relations between the two countries and indicated that his government was committed to diplomacy, mutual respect, and to doing away with any mistrust and misunderstanding that exist between the two countries. President Obama ended the prohibition on direct contacts with Iranian diplomats. The first such contact happened in The Hague on March 31, 2009 between Presidential Envoy Richard C. Holbrooke and Iran's deputy foreign minister Mohammad Mehdi Akhondzadeh, on the sidelines of a conference on Afghanistan. However, disagreement over Iran's nuclear program remains the biggest hurdle in the normalization of relations between the two countries.

Iran's foreign policy in recent years has been essentially regional. In 2001, it signed an agreement with Saudi Arabia for joint efforts to combat terrorism and drug trafficking. Iran's relations with the newly independent Islamic republics of Central Asia expanded rapidly in the late 1990s, both in diplomatic relations and exchanges of trade. However, a dispute with Azerbaijan over oil exploration rights in the Caspian Sea—which holds an estimated 200 billion barrels of offshore oil and 600 billion cubic meters of natural gas—came to a head in July 2001, when an Iranian warship halted exploration in the offshore Alov field by Azerbaijani research vessels.

The dispute over this field reflects the larger issue of Caspian Sea boundaries. After the collapse of the Soviet Union in 1991, the five countries bordering the Caspian—Iran, Azerbaijan, Kazakhstan, Russia, and Turkmenistan—signed an agreement that gave Iran 12 percent of shoreline but left open the issue of oil and gas development. With exploration under way, Iran is demanding control of 20 percent, including the Alov field, which lies 60 miles north of its current territorial waters.

In a related dispute, Iran has objected strenuously to the U.S.–sponsored plan for a pipeline to carry Azerbaijani oil from Baku to the Turkish port of Ceyhan (Adana) on the Mediterranean, thus bypassing Iranian territory. For its part, the Azerbaijan government accused Iran of funding new mosques and paying their prayer leaders to support pro-Iranian subversive activities.

After the September 11, 2001, terrorist attacks in the United States, the Iranian government condemned the action and the killing of civilians. In a mosque sermon, Expediency Council president Rafsanjani stated that "despite all our differences we are willing to join the U.S.–international coalition against terrorism under the umbrella of the United Nations, if America does not impose its own view." Iran closed its border with Afghanistan to Afghan refugees, although it allowed private relief organizations to continue making food deliveries to that war-ravaged country.

An important element in Iran's willingness to cooperate with the United States against the Afghanistan-based al-Qaeda network and its leader, Osama bin Laden, stemmed from drug smuggling. The

Taliban regime that controlled 90 percent of that country until its overthrow in late 2001 had encouraged drug cultivation as a means of income and turned a blind eye to smuggling, much of it through Iran. Since 1996, some 3,000 Iranian border guards have been killed by smugglers, and easy access to drugs has resulted in a large number of Iranian addicts.

But any further thawing of U.S.-Iranian relations was quickly refrozen when Bush included Iran in his "axis of evil" covering countries supposedly sponsoring terrorism. The charge was made more explicit in August 2003 when Bush administration officials claimed that Iran was close to achieving a nuclear weapons capability based on its underground enrichment plant near the town of Natanz. Iranian officials insist that extraction of newly-discovered uranium resources near the town of Natanz, along with the heavy water plant at Arak, both serve its intention to develop peaceful uses for nuclear energy. Adding to the confusion that surrounds Iran's nuclear program was the report by United States Intelligence agencies that the country had halted the enrichment program in 2003, thus undermining President Bush's claim that the program represented a serious threat.

The disclosure of Iran's 20-year development of this energy source and implications that it could lead to nuclear weaponry has embroiled the country in a seemingly endless confrontation with the United States and other members of the UN Security Council (see Conflict Essay). As a signatory to the Nuclear Non-Proliferation Treaty (NPT) and a member of the International Atomic Energy Agency (IAEA) of the United Nations, the country is required to disclose its program and to invite IAEA inspectors to examine its facilities. Iran suspended its enrichment program to comply with these requirements, and inspectors proceeded to examine the Natanz enrichment plant. However the country insisted it had the right to develop nuclear energy for peaceful uses on its own soil. IAEA inspectors have been barred periodically from visits to Natanz, although in June 2007 the facility was reopened for them. An earlier ban had been imposed in January after the Security Council had imposed sanctions in response to Iran's ignoring its deadline to halt enrichment.

In January, Iran reported it's activation of 3,000 centrifuges as a preliminary step toward enrichment. The UN sanctions carry a 60-day enrichment limit. They also freeze Iranian bank assets. These assets are owned separately by the Revolutionary Guard, and prohibit the country from weapons sales abroad. In the long run, continued expansion of its nuclear

program would cost Iran heavily, notably in its aging oil industry sector. Iran's defiant rejection of sanctions, along with the support of China and Russia. (Iran's main customers) suggest that it is unlikely to abandon the program or comply fully with IAEA restrictions and international pressure.

The nuclear issue ironically united all Iranians in a new-found pride. "We will definitely not stop our nuclear activities; it is our red line"—so read the lettering on a banner carried in a demonstration in Tehran.[12] This new unity also has made it more problematic for the U.S. to seek regime change as a prelude to normalization of relations. In February 2006 Secretary of State Condoleezza Rice requested funding from Congress of $75 million to support "pro-democracy forces" within the country. But as observers pointed out, such forces only exist outside Iran and consist mainly of discredited groups such as the Iraq-based Peoples' Majahideen.

## THE INTERNAL CONTEST

During the short-lived openness of Iran's 1997 version of "Prague Spring," civic and press freedom flourished, with many new newspapers and magazines appearing on the streets. *Society,* a new magazine, even dared to publish articles mildly critical of the regime and photographs of unveiled women on its front pages. Another harbinger of change was the impressive victory of Khatami supporters in the local and municipal elections, the first since the 1979 Revolution. They won the great majority of the 200,000 seats on town and city councils, including 15 seats on the influential Teheran City Council. The 2003 municipal elections brought similar results, with reform candidates garnering the majority of seats.

The contest intensified between the moderate reformists and the hard-liners who want to hold on to the Islamic structure as laid out by Khomeini and implemented by his successor. In February 1998, the popular mayor of Teheran, Gholarn Hossein Karbaschi, was arrested and charged with corruption in office. He had won popular favor with his beautification and cleanup program for the capital and had been active in Khatami's election campaign. During his trial, the embattled mayor described it as "politically motivated on the part of enemies of reform and openness." Nonetheless, he received a two-year sentence; however, in January 2000, Khamenei pardoned him in another of the unexpected twists that give Iranian politics its unique flavor.

Since the much contested presidential election of June 2009, criticism has become more open and street protest against the government and its policies continue to increase in frequency, intensity, and violence. One of the biggest clashes happened in the last week of December 2009 as thousands of protesters poured into the streets of Teheran calling for the dismissal of Ahmadinejad and Iran's Supreme Leader. The demonstrations of Sunday, December 28, ended with the worst bloodshed since the first major post election unrest the previous summer. Several people were killed and hundreds were arrested. Among the dead was Seyed Ali Mousavi, the nephew of the opposition leader Mir Hossein Mousavi. A few days later, on December 31, tens of thousands of pro-regime hard-liners demonstrated in support of Iran's religious leadership. It is certain that when that leadership decided in June 2009 to maintain Ahmadinejad in power in spite of the questionable electoral process, it did not expect such a lasting and intensifying backlash which put the entire governing establishment at risk.

## THE ECONOMY

Iran's bright economic prospects during the 1970s were largely dampened by the 1979 Revolution. Petroleum output was sharply reduced, and the war with Iraq crippled industry as well as oil exports. Ayatollah Khomeini warned Iranians to prepare for a decade of grim austerity before economic recovery would be sufficient to meet domestic needs. After the cease-fire with Iraq, Khomeini enlarged upon his warning, saying that the world would be watching to see if the Revolution would be destroyed by postwar economic difficulties.

Iran had a remarkable turnaround since the end of the war with Iraq, despite the U.S.–imposed trade restrictions. The country's foreign debts were paid off by 1990. Since then, however, loans for new development projects and purchase of equipment, including a nuclear reactor for peaceful uses set up by Russian technicians in 1998, along with reduced oil revenues, have generated a foreign debt fluctuating between $20 and $30 billion. It stood at $21 billion in 2008.

Iran was self-sufficient in food until 1970. The White Revolution redistributed a considerable amount of land, most of it from estates that Reza Shah had confiscated from their previous owners. But the new owners, most of them former tenant farmers, lacked the capital, equipment, and technical knowledge needed for productive agriculture. The revolutionary period caused another upheaval in agriculture, as farmers abandoned their lands to take part in the struggle, and fighting between government forces and

(UN Human Rights Council/A. Hollmann (UNHCR16049_11.1986))
Refugee school children in a make shift school in Iran. Iran's future will be in the hands of the young and how well they are educated.

ethnic groups disrupted production. Production dropped 3.5 percent in 1979–1980, the first full year of the Islamic Republic of Iran, and continued to drop at the same rate through 1982. The war with Iraq caused another upheaval. Rural youths, traditionally Khomeini's strongest supporters, flocked to join the army, most of them as *basijis,* "volunteers," advancing ahead of regular troops in human wave tactics that wore down the Iraqis but caused enormous Iranian casualties, and as a consequence decimating the able-bodied rural population.[13]

These difficulties, plus large-scale rural–urban migration, have hampered development of the agricultural sector, which accounts for 20 percent of gross domestic product. Formerly self-sufficient

in food, Iran is now the world's biggest wheat importer. In the non-oil sector, Iran is the world's major producer of pistachio nuts. (Former president Rafsanjani is himself a pistachio farmer in his home province of Rafsanjan, the center of production.) Caviar exports from Iran's Caspian Sea waters, formerly significant, have been reduced due to too much fishing and pollution from on-shore development. The country is also the number-one world producer of saffron; unfortunately, much of the crop is stolen by poachers and smuggled into Europe, where it sells for up to $272 per pound!

Petroleum is Iran's major resource and the key to economic development. Oil was discovered there in 1908, making the

Iranian oil industry the oldest in the Middle East. Until 1951, the Anglo-Iranian Oil Company produced, refined, and distributed all Iranian oil. After the 1951–1953 nationalization period, when the industry was closed down, a consortium of foreign oil companies—British, French, and American—replaced the AIOC. In 1973, the industry was again nationalized and was operated by the state-run National Iranian Oil Company.

After the Revolution, political difficulties affected oil production, as the United States and its allies boycotted Iran due to the hostage crisis. Other customers balked at the high prices ($37.50 per barrel in 1980, as compared to $17.00 per barrel a year earlier). The war with Iraq was a further blow to the industry. Japan, Iran's biggest customer, stopped purchases entirely in 1981–1982. War damage to the important Kharg Island terminal reduced Iran's export capacity by a third, and the Abadan refinery was severely crippled. Periodic Iraqi raids on other Iranian oil terminals in more distant places such as Lavan and Qeshm, reachable by longer-range aircraft, seriously decreased Iran's export output.

Domestic subsidies, notably to keep gasoline prices at 35 cents to the gallon and delays in developing new fields due to lack of foreign investment, are having a serious adverse effect on the oil industry. Iran does have important natural gas reserves, but a preliminary contract with Shell and Reposo (of Spain) to develop South Pars, the world's largest gas field, has been suspended due to political uncertainties. (Under the country's buyback contracts with foreign companies, contracts have strict time limits, the companies are not allowed to control reserves during extraction, and they do not benefit from extra profits when global energy prices rise).

In addition to its oil and gas reserves, Iran has important bauxite deposits, and in 1994, it reported the discovery of 400 million tons of phosphate rock to add to its mineral resources. It is now the world's sixth-largest exporter of sulfur. However, oil and gas remain the mainstays of the economy. Oil reserves are 88 billion barrels; with new gas discoveries each year, the country sits astride 70 percent of the world's reserves.

Iran's great natural resources, large population, and strong sense of its international importance have fueled its drive to become a major industrial power. The country is self-sufficient in cement, steel, petrochemicals, and hydrocarbons (as well as sugar—Iranians are heavy users). Production of electricity meets domestic needs. The nuclear power plant at Bushire, begun by German engineers, is now in the last stages of completion after numerous construction delays, with the work being done by some 3,700 Russian technicians, and should be operative in 2010. It could meet 20 percent of energy needs.

Since the breakup of the Soviet Union into independent states, Iran has been active in developing economic relations with the mainly Islamic republics of Central Asia. A rail link from the port of Bandar Abbas to Turkmenistan was completed in 1996, giving that landlocked country access to the outside world by a watery "Silk Road" to India and the Far East.

Aside from the hydrocarbons industry much of Iran's economy is controlled by the state, either directly or through the network of *bazaaris* (urban merchants and business owners) and semi-public foundations called *bonyads*. The support of the bazaaris was essential to the Revolution, while the bonyads were set up after 1979 ostensibly to administer properties confiscated by the republic from the monarchy. They are accountable only to the Supreme Legal Guide and control the bulk of the non-oil economy. A foreign investment law was passed by the Majlis in 2002 and approved by the CCG in hopes of spurring foreign investment, particularly through purchases of equipment and parts for Iran's aging industries. But international concern over the country's nuclear program continues to deter such investment. In 2005 European countries that held $18 billion in loan guarantees against Iran agreed with the United States to withhold such guarantees to any companies linked with the nuclear program.

A major obstacle to international pressure on Iran to abandon its nuclear program or change clerical control stems from the economic and political power exercised by the Islamic Revolutionary Guard Corps (IRGC also known as the Army of the Guardians of the Islamic Revolution). Created after the 1979 revolution because the loyalty of the army was suspect, the regime is unusual in having parallel military institutions, an army to defend its territorial integrity and a guard corps to protect "the revolution and its achievements." Like the Roman pretorian guard, the IRGC plays a role in politics, being responsible for elections management as well as the social behavior of the Iranian people. Economically the corps controls or is connected with over 100 business enterprises ranging from defense industries to smuggling. Its engineering section, *Khatam al-Anbiyeh* (Seal of the Prophets) employs 40,000 workers and currently holds contracts worth $7 billion. Since the contested re-election of Ahmadinejad in June 2009, the power of the IRGC (known also as Pasdaran) seems to have increased substantially. In exchange for a tremendous economic clout, the organization has become an even greater supporter of the regime and has been helping in the crack down against the reformist opposition. "The Guard's expanded economic role is mirrored by a greater role in politics and security since the disputed presidential election in June."[14]

## A REVOLUTION FROM WITHIN?

Two decades after the Revolution that brought the first Islamic republic into existence, a debate is still under way to determine how "Islamic" Iranian society should be. The debate is between those Iranians who advocate strict adherence to Islamic law and those who would open up the society to diverse social behavior and norms. "A crisis of authority raises fundamental questions about the respective roles of religion and politics. By having united the two, the regime now has to face antagonisms directed at the clerics for the failure to deliver on lofty promises . . . Voices of protest have been heard not only from disadvantaged religious minorities and women, but also from some of those who believe in an Islamic order but do not want to see the continuation of rule by the clerics."[15]

Politically, the Islamic Republic of Iran is a unique institution. Its population is sharply divided between "hard-liners" and "reformers," terms that do little to explain Iran's political complexities. The former, generally speaking, are those who would preserve at all costs the theocratic rule and Islamic values bequeathed to the republic by its founders. The latter seek to reshape Iran as a more open society, committed to justice and the rule of law and with personal freedom and rights guaranteed. The imbalance between the "two Irans" became apparent since Khatami's first term, which was marred by the murders of leading writers and intellectuals, and by several violent confrontations of university students with security police, the former being at the forefront of resistance to hard-liners. More recent demonstrations generated scenes reminiscent of the last days of the monarchy before the Revolution.

However, the re-election of Ahmadinejad to the presidency in 2009 and the increasing inhibition of the reformist call, dashed the hope to move Iranian society away from the strict Islamic interpretation of social and political behavior of the clerical regime, toward a more open society receptive to ideas and influences from the outside world, yet without compromising its Islamic nature.

Several times in the last decade new newspapers deemed critical of these policies were closed almost before they began publication, and their reporters and editors arrested. A group of Iranian journalists attending a conference in 2000 in Berlin on human rights were given jail sentences on their return. At one point, it was estimated that Iran had more journalists in prison than any other country in the world.

The hard-liners also used public floggings as a visible method of slowing the clock of political and social change. In August 2001, 13 young men were given 80 lashes each for "offenses against public order," notably use of alcohol or being seen in public with women to whom they were not related. The head of the judiciary defended the floggings as necessary to combat un-Islamic behavior and rising rates of crime and drug use.

With a firm control over the levers of power, the regime has been able to repress the reform movement effectively during Khatami's first term. During the second term, a reform bill was passed in June 2003 by the Majlis which would strip the CCG of its power to veto candidates for public office. However, and as expected, the CCG, which can veto legislation, rejected the bill.

The 2004 and 2008 Majlis elections and especially the 2008 presidential vote brought to a head the evolving conflict between hard-liners committed to all-out support of the clerical regime and moderates advocating a democratic and somewhat secular society with fewer limits on personal freedoms (e.g., expression, dress codes, and mixing of genders). Prior to both Majlis elections the CCG had disqualified thousands of candidates on the grounds that their "speech and behavior" were disloyal to Islam and to the revolution. In 2004, following a strong protest, the CCG reinstated 200 candidates but refused to do so for the remainder. To no one's surprise the hard-liners won a huge majority of seats in both parliamentary elections and in the presidential vote which was widely contested from the start. All three electoral results seemed to reinforce what one opposition leader called the "dictatorship of the mullahs."

A brief "honeymoon" of reformist and conservative elements brought about by the nuclear issue ended abruptly in 2007 with a nationwide crackdown by the regime on its perceived opponents. Some 150,000 persons were arrested and detained briefly for "inappropriate dress" and other marks of social misbehavior. The crackdown was certainly facilitated by disclosure of the Bush administration's offer of $75 million in funds to support "pro-democracy" activities. But at base it seems intended more

## Timeline: PAST

**551–331 B.C.**
The Persian Empire under Cyrus the Great and his successors includes most of ancient Near East and Egypt

**A.D. 226–641**
The Sassanid Empire establishes Zoroastrianism as the state religion

**637–641**
Islamic conquest at the Battles of Qadisiya and Nihavard

**1520–1730**
The Safavid shahs develop national unity based on Shi'a Islam as the state religion

**1905–1907**
The constitutional movement limits the power of the shah by the Constitution and Legislature

**1925**
The accession of Reza Shah, establishing the Pahlavi Dynasty

**1941**
The abdication of Reza Shah under Anglo Soviet pressure; he is succeeded by Crown Prince Mohammed Reza Pahlavi

**1951–1953**
The oil industry is nationalized under the leadership of Prime Minister Mossadegh

**1962**
The shah introduces the White Revolution

**1979–1980**
Revolution overthrows the shah; Iran becomes an Islamic republic headed by the Ayatollah Khomeini

**1980s**
The Iran–Iraq war; Khomeini dies

**1990s**
Iran's economy begins to recover; foreign relations improve; debate over how Islamic the Islamic Republic should be

## PRESENT

**2000s**
Former Tehran mayor Ahmadinejad unexpectedly wins 2005 presidential election; Iran's secret nuclear energy development program exposed, bringing country into conflict with the IAEA and by extension the UN Security Council

Ahmadinejad was reelecte to a second term with 62.63% of the vote according to official results. However, his rival Mir-Hossein Mousavi, who came in second, rejected the results and inspired a wide movement of protest against the government that ran well into the 31st anniversary of the Iranian Revolution in February 2010.

to forestall serious social unrest, notably among youth, due to the regime's failure to meet national social and economic needs. Newspapers and news agencies have been closed, student and women

leaders arrested, and universities purged of "liberal" academics, on a level painfully reminiscent of the early days of the revolution. However, undaunted students protested Ahmadinejad's appearance at the University of Tehran in October following his well-publicized talk at Columbia University in September 2007, shouting "Dictator!" and clashing with police and Basij religious militia, as further evidence of public dissatisfaction.

Today, this public dissatisfaction is not limited to the issue of basic freedoms and democracy; it is also prompted by the economic difficulties Iran has been experiencing in recent years. The country has not been able to raise its oil production back to the pre-Revolution level of 6 million barrels a day. It now produces around 4 million barrels and exports only a little over half of that due to increased domestic consumption (the population doubled since 1979). Oil and gas income provide most of the country's income. The GDP growth rate reached 7.8 percent in 2007 due to rising oil prices, but, despite an estimated $85 billion in income that year, in 2008 it declined to 4.5 percent due to the heavy domestic subsidies and to the structural nature of the economy (inflexibility and rising monopolistic control by the Revolutionary Guards). Moreover, inflation rose to around 28 percent, housing prices also increased sharply, food imports reached a record level, and the growth rate of agricultural value added and manufacturing declined. In this context, and due also to the absence of domestic private investment and a decline in foreign investment, unemployment remained high (close to 13 percent in 2008).[16]

These domestic economic difficulties, combined with the international sanctions that were imposed on the country, will continue to be the source of discontent and instability in the near future, along with the political crisis generated by the last presidential election.

## NOTES

1. A 1991 memo from Ayatollah Khamenei ordered that Bahais should be expelled and prevented from attaining "positions of influence," and denied employment and access to education. The memo is in sharp contrast to UN General Assembly *Resolution 52/142,* which calls on Iran to "emancipate" its Bahai population.

2. Quoted by Scott Peterson, *Christian Science Monitor,* April 27, 2007. A Jewish charity hospital, Sapir, housed wounded demonstrators during the 1979 revolution and refused to hand them over to the Shah's police. Later the hospital received a letter of thanks from Ayatollah Khomeini and a $27,000 donation for its work.

3. Golamreza Fazel, "Persians," in Richard V. Weekes, ed., *Muslim People: A World Ethnographic Survey,* (Westport, 2nd Edition, Connecticut: Greenwood Press, 1984), p. 610. "Face-saving is in fact one of the components of *Ta'aruf,* along with assertive masculinity (*gheyrat*).

4. John Malcom, *History of Persia,* (London: John Murray, 1829), Vol. II, p. 303.

5. Behzad Yaghmaian, *Social Change in Iran* (Albany, NY: State University of New York Press, 2001), p. 127.

6. Roy Mottahedeh, *The Mantle of the Prophet* (New York: Simon & Schuster, 1985), p. 52.

7. *Ibid.,* p. 34.

8. Imam Khomeini, *Islam and Revolution,* translated by Hamid Algar, tr. (Berkeley, CA: Mizan Press, 1981), p. 175.

9. Mohammed Reza Pahlavi, Shah of Iran, *Answer to History* (New York: Stein and Day, 1980), pp. 152–153.

10. Sepehr Zabih, *Iran's Revolutionary Upheaval: An Interpretive Essay* (San Francisco, CA: Alchemy Books, 1979), pp. 46–49.

11. Rachel Donadio, "Fighting Words on Sir Salman," *New York Times Book Review,* July 15, 2007. 12. Online at www.nytimes.com/2007/07/15/books/review/15donadio.html. Retrieved on July 26, 2010.

12. Scott-Peterson, "Iran rebuffs US over nuclear plans," *The Christian Science Monitor,* March 14, 2005. Online at www.csmonitor.com/2005/0314/p01s03-wome.html. Retrieved on January 18, 2010.

13. "Wearing red headbands and inspired by professional chanters before battle, their heads were filled with thoughts of death and martyrdom and going to Paradise." V. S. Naipaul, "After the Revolution," *The New Yorker* (May 26, 1997), p. 46.

14. Thomas Erdbrink, "Elite Revolutionary Guard's expanding role in Iran may limit U.S. options," *Washington Post,* January 10, 2010; A10. Retrieved on January 18, 2010.

15. Farhad Kazemi, "The precarious revolution: Unchanging institutions and the fate of reform in Iran," *Journal of International Affairs* vol. 57, no. 1, Fall 2003, p. 81.

16. Fariborz Ghadar, "Iran at the Crossroads," Center for Strategic and International Studies, July 10, 2009. Online at http://csis.org/publication/iran-crossroads. Retrieved on January 22, 2010.

# Iraq (Republic of Iraq)

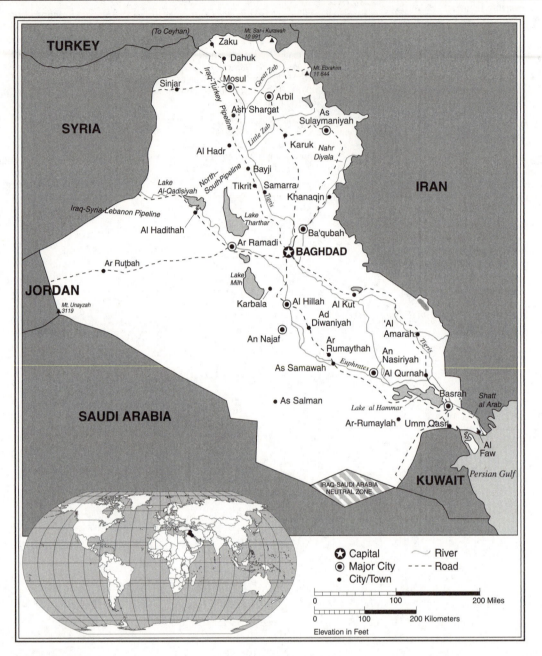

# Iraq Statistics

## GEOGRAPHY

*Area in Square Miles (Kilometers):*
168,710 (437,072) (about twice the size of Idaho)

*Capital (Population):* Baghdad (3,842,000)

*Environmental Concerns:* draining of marshes near An Nasiriyah has affected wetlands and destroyed ecosystems with heavy impact on wildlife; inadequacy of potable water; air and water pollution in cities; soil degradation due to excess salinity and erosion; desertification

*Geographical Features:* the "land of the two rivers" (Tigris and Euphrates) covers a variety of terrains and landscapes, from mountainous Kurdistan in the north south to well-watered and agriculturally productive plains in the center and around Baghdad. West of the rivers is desert. In the deep south are the 3,000-square-mile marshes mostly drained by Saddam Hussein but today about 40 percent restored. The rivers eventually flow into the Shatt al-Arab, a broad estuary linking the country with the Persian/Arab Gulf.

*Climate:* dry and extremely hot, with very short winters, except in northern mountains which have cold winters with much snow and temperate summers

## PEOPLE

### Population

*Total:* 29,671,605
*Annual Growth Rate:* 2.449%
*Rural/Urban Population Ratio:* 25/75
*Major Languages:* Arabic (Iraqi dialect), Kurdish; English widely used
*Ethnic Makeup:* 75% Arab; 20% Kurdish; 5% Turkoman, and others
*Religions:* 60% Shi'a Muslim; 35% Sunni Muslim; 5% others (Christian, Yazidi, Sabaean)

### Health

*Life Expectancy at Birth:* 68 years (male), 71 years (female)
*Infant Mortality Rate (Ratio):* 43.16/1,000 live births

### Education

*Adult Literacy Rate:* 40.4% (males 55.9%, females 24%) (*Note:* Iraq had a much higher rate prior to Saddam's wars. War disruption and UN sanctions have lowered the literacy rate significantly. In the 1970s Iraq had the highest level in the Arab world.
*Compulsory (Ages):* 6–12 free under the Ba'thist regime. UN sanctions effectively nullified the requirement; by 2003 25% of school-age population had dropped out to work to supplement family resources

## COMMUNICATION

*Telephones:* 1.082 million main lines in use

*Daily Newspaper Circulation:* n/a (same reason)
*Televisions:* n/a (same reason)
*Internet Users:* 300,000 (2008)

## TRANSPORTATION

*Highways in Miles (Kilometers):* 27,900 (44,900)
*Railroads in Miles (Kilometers):* 1,262 (2,032)
*Usable Airfields:* 109
*Motor Vehicles in Use:* 1,040,000

## GOVERNMENT

*Type:* Presently under U.S. military occupation with some efforts to establish a system of representative government. To date these have included a constitution and 275-member National Assembly (Parliament) both established in 2005.
*Independence Date:* October 3, 1932, from Britain; July 14, 1958, as republic after the overthrow of the monarchy
*Political Parties:* United Iraqi Alliance (Shi'a), The Iraqi List (Sunni-Shi'a), Kurdish Alliance List, largest Parties; others are Assembly of Independent Democrats (Sunni-Shi'a), National Democratic Party (Sunni), National Rafidain List (Christian)
*Suffrage:* universal at 18

## MILITARY

*Military Expenditures (% of GDP):* 8.6%
*Current Disputes:* Active involvement of Al-Qaeda members and extremist militants from outside the country have created a full-blown internal insurgency. Turkey's conflict with Kurdish PKK based in Iraqi Kurdistan has caused frequent border closures. Iran also supports Iraqi Shi'as with weapons and training.

## ECONOMY

*Currency ($U.S. Equivalent):* 1,466 dinars = $1
*Per Capita Income/GDP:* $2,900/$70 billion
*GDP Growth Rate:* 4.3%
*Inflation Rate:* 64.8%
*Unemployment:* 25–30%
*Labor Force:* 8.175 million
*Natural Resources:* petroleum; natural gas; phosphates; sulfur; lead; gypsum; iron ore
*Agriculture:* wheat; barley; rice; vegetables; dates; cotton; sheep; cattle
*Industry:* petroleum; chemicals; textiles; construction materials; food processing
*Exports:* $38 billion, exclusively crude oil (primary partners United States, Italy, Spain)
*Imports:* $55.4 billion (primary partners Turkey, Syria, United States)

# Iraq Country Report

Today's Republic of Iraq is a contemporary state in a very ancient land. Western archaeologists called it Mesopotamia, meaning "the land between the rivers" (i.e. the Tigris and the Euphrates, as described above). Its fertility encouraged human settlement and agriculture from an early date. The oldest farming community yet discovered anywhere was unearthed in 1989 near Nineveh, capital of the Assyrian Empire; it dates back to 9000 B.C. Other settlements grew in time into small but important cities with local governments, their economies based on trade and crafts production in addition to agriculture. The process of using a written alphabet with characters rather than symbols probably originated here. In 1999, President Saddam Hussein announced an international festival for the year 2000 to mark the 5,000th anniversary of this Mesopotamian invention (although recent archaeological discoveries in Egypt suggest that writing may have developed there even earlier).

Present-day Iraq (*Iraq* is an Arabic word meaning "cliff" or, less glamorously, "mud bank") occupies a much larger territory than the original Mesopotamia. Iraqi territory also includes a Neutral Zone on the border with Saudi Arabia. Iraq's other borders are with Turkey, Syria, Jordan, Kuwait, and Iran. These borders were established by the British on behalf of the newly formed Iraqi government, which they controlled after World War I. Disagreement with Kuwait over oil production and allocation from their shared Rumaila field was a factor in Iraq's 1990 invasion of Kuwait.

In 1994, Iraq accepted the border demarcated under United Nations *Resolutions 687, 773,* and *883,* formally relinquishing its claims to Kuwait and the islands of Bubiyan and Warbah. The new border, realigned northward by an international commission, removed 1,870 feet from Iraqi jurisdiction.

Iraq's other border in question, disputed with Iran, is in the Shatt al-Arab (Arab Delta), a broad, navigable estuary extending from the confluence of the Tigris and Euphrates Rivers down to the Persian Gulf. During the years of the British mandate and early independence, Iraq claimed ownership from the west to east banks. Iran's claim extended from its own (east) bank to mid-channel. Iraq recognized the Iranian claim in a 1975 agreement; in return, Iran withdrew support from Kurds in northern

71

Iraq who were seeking autonomy. The unilateral abrogation of this agreement by Saddam Hussain was one factor in the 1980–1988 Iran–Iraq War.

## History

The "land between the rivers" has had many occupiers in its long history as a settled area, and it has seen many kingdoms and empires rise and fall. Over the centuries many peoples—Sumerians, Babylonians, Assyrians, Persians, Arabs and others added layer upon layer to the mix of Mesopotamian civilization. The world's first cities probably began there, as did agriculture, the growing of food crops, made possible by an ingenious irrigation system developed by Sumerian "engineers" to bring Tigris-Euphrates water from those rivers to their fields. Since theirs was essentially an agricultural society, the Sumerians developed a system of recording land ownership and grain sales on clay tablets, in what is generally considered the world's first written alphabet. Their transactions were recorded in cube-shaped letters called cuneiform, rather than the picture-words (hieroglyphs) used in ancient Egypt which were much more cumbersome.

The Sumerians seem to have disappeared as a people around 2,200 B.C.E., absorbed into other more powerful peoples, though there is some evidence that their descendants may still be found in the marshlands of southern Iraq, where they survived as "people of the reeds" until the 1990s, when their habitat was largely destroyed by the government, partly for land reclamation but also to pursue Shi'a rebels who had taken refuge there.

Successor Mesopotamian peoples also contributed much to our modern world. The Babylonian king Hammurabi developed the first code of laws; there are 282 of them in all, inscribed on steles (pillars) placed at strategic points in his kingdom to warn people what they should or should not do, and the consequences thereof. A later Babylonian king, Nebuchadnezzar, built the world's first capital city, at Babylon. Its Hanging Gardens, a series of overhanging terraces planted with flowers and trees and watered by hidden waterwheels, was considered one of the Seven Wonders of the ancient world. The king had constructed it to please his queen, who came from far-off mountains and pined for her homeland.

Other contributions have come down to us from this ancient land. The first political system, based on sovereign city-states, began there. Each Mesopotamian city was built around a central sacred space, the earthly home of a god. His shrine was the *ziggurat*, a stepped pyramid reaching many stories toward the sky and from whence he could descend to earth when needed.

One would think that the modern Iraqis would take great pride in their storied heritage. But unlike the Iranians and the Chinese, whose history goes back as far and who have an innate sense of their grandeur as peoples, until recently this glorious past was largely forgotten, unimportant except to archaeologists, most of them foreigners. Gertrude Bell, Leonard Woolley and many others spent years literally digging up Ur, Babylon, Nineveh and other ancient Mesopotamian cities, collecting priceless artifacts which were kept on display in the National Museum in Baghdad. One of the first horror stories of the overthrow of Saddam Hussain by coalition forces in 2003 was the looting of the museum. Thus far some 3,411 priceless artifacts have been recovered or returned. Fortunately the loss was scaled down by the museum director as being less serious than had been expected and the building itself restored.

Although occupying peoples and their rulers have made Mesopotamia a place of many-layered civilizations, the most important influence in Iraqi social and cultural life today comes from the conquest of the region by Islamic Arabs. In A.D. 637, an Arab army defeated the Persians, who were then rulers of Iraq, near the village of Qadisiya, not far from modern Baghdad, a victory of great symbolic importance for Iraqis today. Arab peoples settled the region and intermarried with the local population, producing the contemporary Iraqi–Arab population.

The most important element in the shaping of Iraq's people historically was that of Islam. As noted, the religion was brought by invaders from Arabia, themselves newly-converted under the leadership of Prophet Muhammad. Arab tribal families followed the military advance, at first keeping separate from the native population but then intermarrying, as garrison bases grew into cities. The resultant tribal mix has always defined Iraqi character and Iraq's Arab identity.

The transfer of the political capital of Islam from Mecca to Damascus (Syria) and then Baghdad marked Iraq's evolution from a distant occupied territory to the center of power in the Islamic caliphate. From very early days it figured strongly in Islam's history. The tombs of Ali, Muhammad's son-in-law, fourth caliph and putative successor to the Prophet for Shi'a Muslims, and his son Hussein, martyred in a contest for leadership with his rival the Damascus-based Caliph Yazid, are both in Iraq, the first in Najaf and the second in Karbala (See essay Middle East: Heartland of Islam).

In the period of the Abbasid caliphs (A.D. 750–1258), Iraq was the center of a vast Islamic empire stretching from Morocco on the west to the plains of India. Caliph al-Mansur laid out a new capital for the world of Islam, some 60 miles from the ruins of Babylon. He named his new capital Baghdad, possibly derived from a Persian word for "garden," and, according to legend, laid bricks for its foundations with his own hand. During his time in power Saddam Hussein undertook the rebuilding of Babylon as his conscious link with Hammurabi and the Babylonian emperor Nebuchadnezzar, carrying bricks to the site which he inscribed "Saddam Hussein, son of Nebuchadnezzar, to the glory of Iraq."

Baghdad was a round city, built in concentric circles, each one walled, with the caliph's green-domed palace and mosque at the center. It was the world's first planned city, in the sense of having been laid out in a definite urban configuration and design. Under the caliphs, Baghdad became a center of science, medicine, philosophy, law, and the arts, at a time when London and Paris were mud-and-wattle villages. The city became wealthy from the goods brought by ships from Africa, Asia, and the Far East, since it was easily reachable by shallow-draught boats from the Gulf and the Indian Ocean moving up the Tigris to its harbor.

In the thirteenth century A.D. the Mongols, a group of tribes in Central Asia near the Chinese border, were united under the leadership of Genghis Khan and swept across the Middle East, conquering the Islamic lands as far as Egypt as well as present-day Russia. A Mongol army led by Genghis Khan's son Hulagu captured Baghdad in 1258. The city was not destroyed as completely as other Islamic cities but it suffered extensive damage.

That year also marked the end of the Abbasid Caliphate. The ruling caliph was seized and executed by the non-Muslim, shaman-worshipping Mongols. A more serious result of the Mongol invasion was their destruction of the ancient irrigation system that had made agriculture not only possible but also extremely productive. However, after their invasion and occupation the Mongols were converted to Islam, settled down and became peaceful farmers and herdsmen, as their descendants are today.

After the fall of Baghdad, Iraq came under the rule of various local princes and dynasties. In the sixteenth century, it was included in the expanding territory of the Safavid Empire of Iran. The Safavid shah championed the cause of Shi'a Islam; as a result, the Ottoman sultan, who was Sunni, sent forces to recover the area from his hated Shi'a foe. Possession of Iraq went back and forth between the two powers, but the Ottomans eventually established control until the twentieth century.

Iraq was administered as three separate provinces under appointed Ottoman governors. The governors paid for their appointments and were interested only in recovering their losses. The result was heavy taxation and indifference to social and economic needs. The one exception was the province of Baghdad. It was governed by a man whom today we would call an enlightened administrator. This governor, Midhat Pasha, set up a provincial newspaper, hospitals, schools, munitions factories, and a fleet of barges to carry produce down river to ports on the Gulf. His administration also ensured public security and an equitable taxation system. Midhat Pasha later became the grand vizier (prime minister) of the Ottoman Empire and was the architect of the 1876 Constitution, which limited the powers of the sultan.

## The British Mandate

World War I found England and France at war with Germany and the Ottoman Empire. British forces occupied Iraq, which they rechristened Mesopotamia, early in the war. British leaders had worked with Arab leaders in the Ottoman Empire to launch a revolt against the sultan; in return, they promised to help the Arabs form an independent Arab state once the Ottomans had been defeated. A number of prominent Iraqi officers who were serving in the Ottoman Army then joined the British and helped them in the Iraqi campaign.

The British promise, however, was not kept. The British had made other commitments, notably to their French allies, to divide the Arab provinces of the Ottoman Empire into British and French "zones of influence." An independent Arab state in those provinces was not in the cards.

The most that the British (and the French) would do was to organize protectorates, called mandates, over the Arab provinces, promising to help the population become self-governing within a specified period of time. The arrangement was approved by the new League of Nations in 1920. Iraq then became a British mandate, with Faisal ibn Hussein as its king, but with British advisers appointed to manage its affairs. (Faisal had been ruler of the short-lived Arab kingdom of Syria set up after the war, but he was expelled when the French occupied Damascus and established their mandate.)

The British kept their promise with the mandate. They worked out a Constitution for Iraq in 1925 that established a constitutional monarchy with an elected Legislature and a system of checks and balances. Political parties were allowed, although most of them were groupings around prominent personalities and had no platform other than independence from Britain. In 1932, the mandate formally ended, and Iraq became an independent kingdom under Faisal. It also joined the League of Nations, as the first Middle Eastern country to do so. Although its sovereignty was limited in certain areas, especially in British control of military bases and management of foreign policy, by that time Iraq had reached the goal of Arab nationalists of a sovereign state.

## The Iraqi Monarchy: 1932–1958

The new kingdom cast adrift on perilous international waters was far from being a unified nation. It was more of a patchwork of warring and competing groups. The Muslim population was divided into Sunni and Shi'a, as it is today, with the Sunnis forming a minority but controlling the government and business and dominating urban life. The Shi'as, although a majority, were mostly rural peasants and farmers, many of them migrants to the cities, where they formed a large underclass.

The country also had large Christian and Jewish communities, the latter tracing its origins back several thousand years to the exile of Jews from Palestine to Babylonia after the conquest of Jerusalem by Nebuchadnezzar. The Assyrians formed the largest Christian group. Formerly residents in Ottoman Turkey, they supported the British as "our smallest ally" in World War I and, as a result, were allowed to resettle in Iraq after the establishment of the Turkish Republic. The British protected them, recruiting Assyrians as guards for military and air bases and the British-controlled police force. "To the Iraqis, the swaggering Assyrian Levies with their slouch hats and red or white hackles . . . became the symbols of British domination."[1]

However, when they pushed their luck to the point of demanding autonomy in 1933, the British-trained Iraqi Army moved against them, destroying villages and massacring their Assyrian inhabitants.[2] Many fled into exile, forming large communities (particularly in Detroit and San Diego). A small minority remained in Iraq, but most of them have now left, due to the country's economic difficulties.

The new Iraqi state also included other non-Muslim communities, such as the Yazidis (called "devil-worshippers," from their religious practice) and the Sabaeans, descended from the ancient Babylonians. Until recently, and particularly under Saddam Hussein's regime, they were protected and allowed to practice their faith under their own religious leaders as they had in Ottoman times. But one of the many adverse developments of the post-invasion insurgency is that of attacks against these minorities. In August 2007, a suicide bombing at their principal shrine near Sheikhan killed some 500 Yazidis. By late 2007, some 70,000, 15 percent of their population, had fled the country.[3]

King Faisal I was the single stabilizing influence in Iraqi politics, so his untimely death in 1933 was critical. His son and successor, Ghazi, was more interested in racing cars than anything else and was killed at the wheel of one in 1939. Ghazi's infant son succeeded him as King Faisal II, while Ghazi's first cousin became regent until the new ruler came of age.

In a statement just before his death, King Faisal prophetically observed, "with my heart filled with sadness, I have to say that it is my belief that there is no Iraqi people inside Iraq . . . there are only diverse groups with no national sentiments. . . . They easily accept rumours and are prone to chaos, prepared always to revolt against any government."[4] During Faisal II's minority the regent, Abd al-Ilah, ruled through a coalition of landowners, tribal leaders, merchants and intellectuals, almost all members of the Sunni minority. An Iraqi once described the government as a pack of cards. You must shuffle them often, he said, because the same faces keep turning up.[5]

## THE REVOLUTION OF 1958

To their credit, the king's ministers kept the country's three broad social divisions—the Kurdish north, the Sunni Arab center, and the Shi'a Arab south—in relative balance and harmony. Oil revenues were channeled into large-scale development projects. The formation of a modern school system with a Western-model curriculum, along with adult literacy programs, establishment of a national army, and opportunities for its officers to attend British military academies such as Sandhurst, gave Iraq a head start toward self-government, well ahead of other Arab States. Education was promoted strongly, and the literacy rate was the highest in the Arab world. The press was free, and, though it had a small and ingrown political elite, there was much participation in legislative elections. Despite its legitimate Arab credentials as one of the successor states fashioned by the British after World War I, however, a new generation of pan-Arab nationalist Iraqis viewed the royal regime as a continuation of foreign rule, first Turkish and then British.

Resentment crystallized in the Iraqi Army. On July 14, 1958, a group of young officers overthrew the monarchy in a swift, predawn coup. The king, regent, and royal family were killed. Iraq's new leaders proclaimed a republic that would be reformed,

Mokhtars from Abu Ghrayek, one of 15 subdistricts of the Babel Governate, listen to a speaker on the basics of democracy and the selection process that will allow for delegates to select 20 members from their communities to a new district council in 2003.

free, and democratic, united with the rest of the Arab world and opposed to all foreign ideologies.

The republic passed through many different stages, with periodic coups, changes in leadership, and political shifts, most of them violent. Continuing sectarian and ethnic hatreds, maneuvering of political factions, ideological differences, and lack of opportunities for legitimate opposition to express itself without violence have created a constant sense of insecurity among Iraqi leaders. A similar paranoia affected Iraq's relations with its neighbors. The competition for influence in the Arab world and the Persian/Arab Gulf and other factors combined to keep the leadership constantly on edge.

This pattern of political instability showed itself in the coups and attempted coups of the 1960s. The republic's first two leaders were overthrown after a few years. Several more violent shifts in the Iraqi government took place before the Ba'th Party seized control in 1968. Since that time, the party has dealt ruthlessly with internal opposition. A 1978 decree outlawed all political activity outside the Ba'th for members of the armed forces. Many Shi'a clergy were executed in 1978–1979 for leading antigovernment demonstrations after the Iranian Revolution; and following his rise to the presidency, Saddam Hussain purged a number of members of the Revolutionary Command Council (RCC), on charges that they were part of a plot to overthrow the regime.

## THE BA'TH PARTY IN POWER

The Ba'th Party in Iraq began as a branch of the Syrian Ba'th founded in the 1940s by two Syrian intellectuals: Michel Aflaq, a Christian teacher, and Salah al-Din Bitar, a Sunni Muslim. Like its Syrian parent, the Iraqi Ba'th was dedicated to the goals of Arab unity, freedom, and socialism. However, infighting among Syrian Ba'th leaders in the 1960s led to the expulsion of Aflaq and Bitar. Aflaq went to Iraq, where he was accepted as the party's true leader. Eventually, he moved to Paris, where he died in 1989. His body was brought back to Iraq for burial, giving the Iraqi Ba'th a strong claim to legitimacy in its struggle with the Syrian Ba'th for hegemony in the movement for Arab unity.

Prior to the 2003 U.S. invasion and overthrow of Saddam Hussein the country was governed by a Provisional Constitution issued by the Revolutionary Command Council of the Ba'th, the party's decision-making body. It defined Iraq, without elaboration, as a sovereign peoples' democratic republic. Other clauses provided for a National Assembly responsible only for ratification of Ba'th-issued laws and RCC decisions.

The Iraqi Communist Party, founded in the 1930s, survived inter-party conflict during the monarchy and gained a pre-eminent position after the 1958 coup, being the only one with a strong central organization. It was banned in 1978 and went underground,

continuing to oppose Saddam Hussein on a sub rosa basis. The party was declared illegal in 1980. After his overthrow, its secretary-general, Hamid Majid Moussa, was appointed as a member of the Iraq Governing Council set up by U.S. authorities to prepare for a transfer of power.

An abortive coup in 1973, which pitted a civilian faction of the Ba'th against the military leadership headed by President Ahmad Hasan al-Bakr, stirred party leaders to attempt to broaden their base of popular support. They reached agreement with the Iraqi Communist Party to set up a Progressive National Patriotic Front. Other organizations and groups joined the Front later. Although the Iraqi Communist Party had cooperated with the Ba'th on several occasions, the agreement marked its first legal recognition as a party. However, distrust between the two organizations deepened as Ba'th leaders struggled to mobilize the masses. The Communists withdrew from the Front in 1979 and refused to participate in parliamentary elections. Their party was declared illegal in 1980.

## SADDAM HUSSEIN

As in many other countries coming out of colonialism, Iraq's politics since it became a state had a need for a strong leader, one who could unite (or subdue) its diverse and conflicting factions. Saddam Hussein performed these functions until his execution. He was born in 1937 in the small town of Tikrit, on the Tigris halfway between Baghdad and Mosul. Tikrit's chief claim to fame, until the twentieth century, was that it was the birthplace of Salah Eddine (Saladin), hero of the Islamic world in the Middle Ages against the Crusaders. (Saddam Hussein had, at times, identified himself with Salah Eddine as another great Tikriti. His family belonged to the Begat clan of the Al Bu Nasser tribe, settled around Tikrit. They lived in a nearby village and farmed some 12 acres of land. According to accounts, Saddam was a bully and street fighter from early childhood. He spent little time in school and was hired out from time to time as a shepherd. As a teenager he left home for Baghdad, lived with an uncle, and joined the Ba'th Party. He played a very minor role in the Ba'th's attempted assassination in 1959 of Abd al-Karim Qassem, leader of the 1958 Revolution, and escaped to Egypt in disguise. He returned to Iraq after Qassem's overthrow and execution and gradually worked his way up through the ranks of the Ba'th. Eventually he became vice-chairman, and then chairman, of the Revolutionary Command Council, the party's ruling body. As chairman, he automatically became president of Iraq under the 1970 Constitution. As there are no constitutional provisions limiting the terms of office for the position, the National Assembly named him president-for-life in 1990.

## DEVELOPMENT

The Security Council formally ended sanctions on Iraq in May 2003. Aside from their devastating impact on the population, the 13-year sanctions had severely limited oil production and led to the deterioration of oil refinery installations, industries and service systems. Oil production was 3.5 million barrels per day (bpd) before 1991, but it dropped significantly during the sanctions period (despite the oil-for-food program) and stopped entirely during the 2003 U.S. invasion. In 2009, production reached 2.42 million bpd, but has been frequently interrupted by sabotage of pipelines and refineries. A relative decrease in violence and improved security conditions helped resume economic activity, especially in the retail and construction sectors.

Saddam Hussein came to office with none of the attributes needed for a leader and statesman. The 1980–1988 war with Iran was a severe test for him and the Ba'th (see essay The Middle East: Theater of Conflict). A series of Iraqi defeats, with heavy casualties, after initial successes, suggested that military leaders might organize a coup against him. However, the recapture of the Fao Peninsula and other strips of territory seized by Iran shifted the conflict in Iraq's favor, and Saddam not only stayed in power but also was able to build a semblance of national unity. Thereafter, Saddam combined ruthlessness toward (real or imagined) opponents of his regime with a sort of "father of his country" image, taking part in family events, visiting farms, etc., always in the appropriate dress besides his trademark beret. Posters of him sprouted with ever-increasing frequency on public buildings, in banks, schools, and on larger-than-life highway billboards. His numerous presidential palaces, most of them occupying choice real estate, reminded the Iraqis of his power on a daily basis as they walked, drove, or did business.

The end of the war with Iran and Saddam Hussein's popularity as the heroic defender of the Iraqi Arab nation against the Shi'a Iranian enemy prompted a certain lifting of Ba'thist repression and authoritarian rule. Emergency wartime regulations in force since 1980 were relaxed in 1989, and an amnesty was announced for all political exiles except "agents of Iran."

In July 1990, the RCC and the Arab Ba'th Regional Command, the party's governing body, approved a draft constitution to replace the 1970 provisional one. The new Constitution "legalized" the formation of political parties other than the Ba'th, as long as they conformed to Ba'thist principles. It also established freedom of the press and other civil rights, although again in conformity with Ba'thism.

The 1990 Iraqi occupation of Kuwait and the ensuing Gulf War halted even these small steps toward representative government. The draft Constitution remained in suspension; it was neither issued unilaterally by the regime nor submitted to voters in a referendum. In the 1990s the regime implemented a law in the provisional constitution to allow elections for local and municipal councils. Candidates were required to be members of the Ba'th, or if they weren't, to run as independents. The councils were given the authority under a 1995 law to administer programs in health, education, and economic development in their respective localities.

To further his goal of establishing Iraq as a major regional power, he allegedly engaged in a large scale project of building weapons of mass destruction (WMD), mainly nuclear, chemical, and biological. However, after the U.S. invasion in 2003, no trace of such weapons were ever found even though their presumed existence was the key official justification given by the Bush administration for such invasion.

The plan to invade Iraq and overthrow Saddam was "justified" by his presumed possession of Weapons of Mass Destruction, according to Bush administration policymakers, although the evidence was ambiguous at best and intelligence analysts had indicated in their reports that what was left of the program had been uncovered by UN inspectors.

## THE KURDS

The Kurds, the largest non-Arab minority in Iraq today, form a relatively compact society in the northern mountains. Formerly the Ottoman province (*vilayet*) of Mosul, the territory was occupied by British troops after World War I and included in the mandate over Iraq by the League of Nations, despite angry protests by the Turks demanding its inclusion in the new Republic of Turkey. The Kurds living there demanded self-rule periodically during the monarchy; for a few months after World War II, they formed their own republic in Kurdish areas straddling the Iraq–Iran and Iraq–Turkey borders.

In the 1960s, the Kurds rebelled against the Iraqi government, which had refused to

meet their three demands (self-government in Kurdistan, use of Kurdish in schools, and a greater share in oil revenues). The government sent an army to the mountains but was unable to defeat the Kurds, masters of guerrilla warfare. Conflict continued intermittently into the 1970s. Although the 1970 Constitution named Arabs and Kurds as the two nationalities in the Iraqi state and established autonomy for Kurdistan, the Iraqi government had no real intention of honoring its pledges to the Kurds.

A major Iraqi offensive in 1974 had considerable success against the Kurdish *Pesh Merga* ("Resistance"), even capturing several mountain strongholds. At that point, the shah of Iran began to supply arms to the Pesh Merga and kept the Iraq–Iran border open as sanctuary for the guerrillas.

In 1975, a number of factors caused the shah to change his mind. He signed an agreement with Saddam Hussain, redefining the Iran–Iraq border to give Iran control over half of the Shatt al-Arab. In return, the shah agreed to halt support for the Kurds. The northern border was closed and, without Iranian support, Kurdish resistance collapsed. A similar fate befell the Assyrian community. Entire villages were destroyed, and the surviving population was resettled farther south as Saddam Hussein pressed to preserve Sunni Arab minority authority.

In 1986, Iran resumed support for the Pesh Merga, to use its warriors as an auxiliary force against the Iraqis. Kurdish forces carried out a number of raids into northern Iraq.

However, with the end of the war with Iran in 1988, the Iraqi Army turned on the Kurds in a savage and deliberate campaign of genocide. Operation *Anfal* ("spoils," in Arabic) involved the launching of chemical attacks on such villages as Halabja and the forced deportation of Kurdish villagers from their mountains to detention centers in the flatlands. Some 4,000 Kurdish villages were destroyed, and 5,000 Kurds, mostly old men, women and children were killed in a cyanide gas attack on the border town of Halabya.[6]

A second exodus of Kurdish refugees took place in 1991, after uprisings of Kurdish rebels in northern Iraq were brutally suppressed by the Iraqi Army, which had remained loyal to Saddam Hussein. The United States and its allies sent troops and aircraft to the Iraqi–Turkish border and barred Iraq from using its own air space north of the 36th Parallel, the main area of Kurdish settlement. Several hundred thousand refugees subsequently returned to their homes and villages.

Under this umbrella of air protection and the exclusion of Iraqi forces from the Kurdish region, the Iraqi Kurds moved toward self-rule in their region. The two main factions—the Kurdish Democratic Party (KDP), led by Massoud al-Barzani, and the Patriotic Union of Kurdistan (PUK) of Jalal al-Talabani—agreed to the formation of a joint Parliament elected by the Kurdish population. This new Parliament, which was divided equally between KDP and PUK members, approved a law defining a federal relationship with Iraq, providing for internal autonomy for the Kurdish region. Kurdish was confirmed as the official language, and a Kurdish university was established.

But the tragedy of the Kurds has always been their inability to unite unless there is an external threat. With the Iraqi regime effectively removed from Kurdistan, the traditional cleavages and inner conflicts of Kurdish society came to the surface. A new Kurdish Parliament was scheduled to be elected in September 1995. However, clashes between the two factions broke into open conflict before the elections could take place. By 1996, the PUK controlled two thirds of the region, including the major cities of Irbil and Sulaymaniyah. Barzani's KDP, although it controlled only one third, held an economic advantage over its rival because of its control over the main source of Kurdish revenues. The lion's share of these revenues came from trade (and smuggling) across the Turkish border.

The bell rang for another tragic hour in Iraqi Kurdistan in September 1996. Barzani's KDP struck a deal with Saddam Hussain to help him unseat the rival PUK; and KDP forces, backed by 30,000 to 40,000 Iraqi troops with tanks and artillery, swept down on Irbil and Sulaymaniyah to drive the PUK from its strongholds. The KDP success was brief; the PUK withdrew into the mountains to regroup and then launched a counteroffensive, which recovered all its lost territories, except Irbil, by mid-October. Saddam Hussain withdrew his forces after a blunt warning from the United States, but not before rounding up opposition dissidents who had remained there after the Gulf War and were supported by the U.S. Central Intelligence Agency to form the anti-Saddam Iraqi National Congress (INC).

Operation Provide Comfort, which was set up after the Gulf War to give the Kurds in northern Iraq a "safe haven" under U.S. and British air protection, enabled the Kurdish region to develop institutions of self-government and preserve its culture while remaining part of the Iraqi state. In 2001 reconciliation between the KDP and PUK ended nearly a decade of party conflict. The establishment of an elected parliament, a school system and bureaucracy with Kurdish as the primary language of instruction and government documents, a university and police force, and an economy based in part on oil revenues from northern Iraqi fields all underscore the emergence of an autonomous Iraqi Kurdistan.

Despite periodic Turkish cross-border strikes against PKK militants operating from bases in Iraqi Kurdistan, the region remains almost the only stable one in Iraq. Protected by the "no-fly zone" north of the 36th parallel patrolled by U.S. and British aircraft and its well-armed *pesh merga,* it has become essentially autonomous. Kurdish leader Jalal Talabani has served two terms as Iraq's president, and Kurdish parties are well-represented in the Iraqi parliament. It remains the only region with its own self-propelled economy, and in 2007 its government signed agreements valued at $1 billion with foreign oil companies for oil exploration and construction of two refineries.

## THE OPPOSITION

Saddam Hussain's ruthless repression of opposition, made possible by his control of security services, the brutality of his sons and his legion of spies and informers, made sure that no organized group of opponents would emerge to challenge his rule. Those who could do so left the country for exile. But the Iraqi defeat in the Gulf War, followed by the Kurdish and Shi'a popular uprisings—although they were unsuccessful—suggested that

Saddam might be overthrown from abroad. The success of Iraq's Kurds in establishing de facto autonomy under UN–U.S. protection also encouraged the opposition, as did the continuing UN–imposed limitations on Iraqi sovereignty. In June 1992, representatives of some 30 opposition groups met in Vienna, Austria, to form the Iraqi National Congress.

Composed of various opposition groups, the INC described its purpose as the overthrow of Saddam Hussain and the Ba'th Party and their replacement by a secular Islamic regime. The state would be governed under a constitution providing specific guarantees of human rights, protection of minorities, and a multiparty political system. The United States then began funneling funds through its Central Intelligence Agency to the INC, while other CIA operatives worked with its rival anti-Saddam organization, the Iraq National Accord (INA), based in Jordan. In 1994, a team of CIA officers went to Iraqi Kurdistan to establish a base for the INC as the starting point for a coup against the Iraqi dictator.

However, the conflict between Kurdish rival groups described above encouraged the Iraqi Army to invade their territory. The CIA/INC base was overrun. Those of its members not arrested or executed by the Iraqis were evacuated to the United States after the 1996 presidential election. A similar fate befell the INA, which was potentially more dangerous to Saddam because it was centered in units that formed the core of his support, the Republican Guards and the Security Service (the dreaded *Mukhabarat*). In June 1996, the officers involved were arrested, tortured, and executed as they prepared to stage their coup.[7]

## OTHER COMMUNITIES

The Shi'a community, which forms approximately two-thirds of the total population of Iraq, has been ruled by the Sunni minority since independence. Shi'as have been consistently underrepresented in successive Ba'thist governments and are the most economically deprived component of the population. However, they remained loyal to the regime (or at least quiescent) during the war with Iran. In a belated attempt to undo decades of deprivation and assure their continued loyalty, the government invested large sums in the rehabilitation of Shi'a areas in southern Iraq after the war ended. Roads were built, and sacred Shi'a shrines were repaired.

Long-held Shi'a grievances against Ba'thist rule erupted in a violent uprising after Iraq's defeat in the Gulf War. The uprising was crushed, however, as Iraqi troops remained loyal to Saddam Hussain. Some 600 troops were killed in an Alamo-type siege of the sacred shrines, which were badly damaged. A few rebels escaped into the almost impenetrable marshlands of southern Iraq. But their expectations of U.S. support proved illusory. The Clinton administration feared that Iran would intervene on behalf of the Iraqi Shi'as. U.S. helicopters did nothing except to overfly Iraqi gunships as they strafed columns of fleeing refugees. In a half-hearted policy, the Clinton administration eventually declared a no-fly zone south of the 32nd Parallel, off limits to Iraqi aircraft. But by then, the uprising had been crushed.

The rebels' retreat into the marshlands served as an excuse for the Iraqi regime to bring another distinctive community—the Marsh Arabs—under centralized government control. This community, believed by some to be descended from the original inhabitants of southern Iraq and by others to be descended from slaves, has practiced for centuries a unique way of life based on fishing and hunting in the marshes, living in papyrus-and-mud houses and traveling in reed boats through the maze of unmarked channels of their watery region. Prior to 1990, they numbered about 750,000. The late intrepid English explorer Sir Wilfred Thesiger (died 2003) lived with them in the 1950s and chronicled their lifestyle in his eloquent book *The Marsh Arabs*. Tragically this lifestyle was the victim of perhaps Saddam Hussain's most ruthless and repressive actions toward his people in his decades in power. In 1991 he sent troops and artillery ferried by helicopters into the marshes in pursuit of Shi'a rebels who had fled there after their failed uprising.

### HEALTH/WELFARE

Manpower losses in two wars plus violence since the 2003 U.S. occupation have resulted in a surplus of women; they make up approximately 60 percent of the population today. However the UN sanctions and lack of hospital care and obstetrics training have adversely affected women, particularly pregnant mothers. In 2003, the most recent year of accurate measurements of mortality, some 370 out of 100,000 women died in childbirth. Infant mortality rates of 47 per 1,000 live births are also high. But of more concern for Iraq's future is the large number of malnourished children caused by the sanctions and the resultant lack of access to potable water and health services of nearly 50 percent of the population. The seven-year war has worsened these conditions as tens of thousands were killed, more were wounded and millions were displaced by the violence.

After destroying a number of villages and removing much of the population for resettlement elsewhere, Saddam Hussein followed the military campaign with a vast reclamation project. It involved construction of a "third river," a canal between the Tigris and the Euphrates Rivers which would draw water from both rivers through a network of small dams, levees, and diked ponds to irrigate new land being brought under cultivation. A body of 6,000 workers drawn from surplus Iraqi labor, working around the clock, completed the project in 3 months in 1993. And a decade later 93–95 percent of the 3,000-square mile marshes, larger than the state of Maryland, lay bone-dry and almost uninhabited.[8]

## THE ECONOMY

Since independence Iraq's economy has been based on oil production and exports. The country also has large natural-gas reserves as well as phosphate rock, sulfur, lead, gypsum, and iron ore. Ancient Mesopotamia was probably the first area in the world to develop agriculture, using the fertile soil nourished by the Tigris and Euphrates Rivers. Until recently, Iraq was the world's largest exporter of dates. However, by 1999 the UN embargo and the longest drought in a century had brought food production to a near standstill. An estimated 70 percent of wheat and barley crops, mainstays of agriculture, were lost, and government officials described the situation as a "food catastrophe" comparable to the collapse of the health-care system. The Ba'th economic policies emphasized state control of the economy while the party was in power, under the Ba'thist rubric of guided socialism. In 1987, the regime began a major economic restructuring program. More than 600 state organizations were abolished, and young technocrats replaced many senior ministers. In 1988, the government began selling off state-run industries, reserving only heavy industry and hydrocarbons for state operation. Light industries such as breweries and dairy plants would henceforth be run by the private sector.

The oil industry was developed by the British during the mandate but was nationalized in the early 1970s. Nationalization and price increases after 1973 helped to accelerate economic growth. The bulk of Iraqi oil shipments are exported via pipelines across Turkey and Syria. During the war with Iran, the Turkish pipeline proved essential to Iraq's economic survival, since the one across Syrian territory was closed and Iraq's own refineries and ports were put out of commission by Iranian attacks. Turkey closed this pipeline during

the 1990–1991 Gulf crisis, a decision that proved a severe strain for the Iraqi economy (not to mention a huge sacrifice for coalition-member Turkey).

Iraq has proven oil reserves of some 100 billion barrels, the fifth largest in the world, and new discoveries continue to augment the total. Oil output was cut to 2 million barrels per day in 1986–1987, in accordance with quotas set by the Organization of Petroleum Exporting Countries, but was increased to 4.5 million b/d in 1989 as the country sought to recover economically from war damage.

The economic impact of the eight-year Iran–Iraq War was heavy, causing delays in interest payments on foreign loans, defaults to some foreign contractors, and postponement of major development projects except for dams, deemed vital to agricultural production. The war also was a heavy drain on Iraqi finances; arms purchases between 1981 and 1985 cost the government $23.9 billion. By 1986, the external debt was $12 billion. By 1988, the debt burden had gone up to nearly $60 billion, although half this total had been given by the Arab Gulf states as war aid and was unlikely ever to be repaid.

Iraq's economic recovery after the war with Iran, despite heavy external debts, suggested rapid growth in the 1990. Even in 1988, Iraq's GDP of $50 billion was the highest in the Arab world, after Saudi Arabia's. With a well-developed infrastructure and a highly trained workforce, Iraq appeared ready to move upward into the ranks of the developed nations.

## THE UN EMBARGO

Iraq's invasion and occupation of Kuwait and the resulting Gulf War ended these optimistic prospects. Bombing raids destroyed much of Iraq's infrastructure, knocking out electricity grids, bridges, and sewage and water-purification systems and refurbishing of industries, oil refineries and installations in particular. UN resolutions imposing sanctions on the country after the Gulf War added to its economic distress.

The UN embargo that was imposed on Iraq after the Gulf War to force compliance with resolutions ordering the country to dismantle its weapons program has not only brought development to a halt but has also caused untold suffering for the Iraqi population. The resolutions in question were *Resolution 687*, which required the destruction of all missile, chemical, and nuclear facilities; *Resolution 713*, which established a permanent UN monitoring system for all missile test sites and nuclear installations; and *Resolution 986*, which allowed Iraq to sell 700,000 barrels of oil

An Iraqi child looks through the gate of her house in central Baghdad.

per day for six months, in return for its compliance with the first two resolutions. Of the $1.6 billion raised through oil sales, $300 million would be paid into a UN reparations fund for Kuwait. Another $300 million would be put aside to finance the UN monitoring system as well as providing aid for the Kurdish population. The remainder would revert to Iraq to be used for purchases of food and medical supplies.

Saddam Hussain initially refused to be bound by *Resolution 986,* calling it an infringement of Iraq's national sovereignty. But in 1996, he agreed to its terms. By then, the Iraqi people were nearly destitute, suffering from extreme shortages of food and medicines. The United Nations estimated that 750,000 Iraqi children were "severely malnourished." Half a million had died, and the monthly death toll from malnutrition-related illnesses was averaging 5,750, the majority of them children under age five, due to lack of basic medicines and hospital equipment.

Despite disagreement within the Security Council over the scope, effectiveness and moral legitimacy of the sanctions, they were kept in force in 6-month increments

up until the U.S. invasion and overthrow of the Iraqi regime, the last renewal being in December 2002. However concern in many countries about their devastating effect on the population and the economy led the Arab states and others who had been Iraq's trading partners to bypass or simply ignore them. By 2001, 20 countries had resumed regular air service to Baghdad International Airport, much of it in humanitarian supplies. They included Turkey, Egypt and Syria, all former members of the Desert Storm coalition. A free-trade agreement with Syria in January 2001 would triple the annual trade volume of the two countries, to $1 billion, and additional contracts with Jordan, Lebanon and the UAE would generate $4.7 billion in Iraqi exports. Unfortunately the "oil-for-food" program, rather than bringing material benefits to the people, resulted in huge profits for the companies involved. In what one writer called "the many streams that fed the river of graft to Hussein," some 4,758 companies in the program paid over $1.8 billion in illegal contributions, most of it in kickbacks on aid contracts or surcharges on oil purchases. By mid-2007 there were between 126,000 and

180,000 such contractors working for various companies. The Iraqi insurgency has not spared them. Some 234 Americans in this category have been killed since 2003. The most contentious among these private contractors are those providing security services. Most of them are not Americans—a large contingent of the 20,000–30.000 personnel are supplied by a private firm in Uganda—the company most in disfavor among Iraqis is Blackwater USA, a private company detailed under Pentagon contracts to provide armed guards for military convoys and protection of visiting dignitaries. Blackwater's workers are presently immune from Iraqi law, but after 17 Iraqi bystanders were killed by its guards at a Baghdad crossroads on September 16, 2007, the Iraqi government demanded curtailment of its operations in the country by March, 2008. However, in February 2010 all private security guards linked to Blackwater Worldwide were asked to leave the country within seven days. The U.S. government also decided not to renew its contract for the protection of diplomats. Blackwater withdrew its personnel and changed its name Xe Services.

## GLORIOUS LEADER, VANQUISHED SURVIVOR

During his two-plus decades in power Saddam Hussain held complete sway over this people, his authority buttressed by a loyal army, his specially-trained Revolutionary Guards, an efficient security service and a huge corps of informers covering practically every street corner in Iraq. Internally his control over the Ba'th Party was enhanced by the Tikritis, his relatives and other Sunni loyalists from Tikrit. The impact of sanctions fell heaviest on the middle class, which had become the best-educated and collectively most prosperous in the Arab world. The combination of Saddam Hussain's disastrous foreign policy ventures and the destabilization that has followed the U.S. occupation has largely ruined this class. It comprises the majority of the 2 million Iraqis who have fled the country.

Saddam Hussain's central role as ruler of Iraq was underscored during his years in power by his extreme visibility. In addition to his numerous palaces, gigantic statues and posters of him in cities, on highway billboards, and before banks and other public buildings served as constant reminders of the Glorious Leader. In Baghdad, victory arches and a statue of him were erected on the first anniversary of the U.S. air strikes. Saddam called it a "great victory," similar to the "defence" of the homeland after the 1991 Gulf War.

In spite of his absolute power, Saddam's rule was not entirely free from attempted coups. An army coup by officers from the Dalaimi clan, traditional rivals of his Tikriti clan, was thwarted with considerable difficulty in June 1995. Saddam's skill in evading the direct impact of sanctions on his lifestyle and playing off more powerful countries against each other for Iraq's benefit was more than equaled by his internal actions. Those who survived arrest, torture and incarceration in his infamous prisons, many of them skilled professionals, usually fled into exile. The assassination of Grand Ayatollah Sadiq al-Badr, spiritual head of the Shi'a community in Iraq, was a grim warning that anyone who spoke out against the Iraqi leader or questioned his decisions would suffer the same fate.

Until early 2003 it seemed that the Glorious Leader would survive UN sanctions, U.S. air attacks and international isolation and maintain his grip on power. Internal opposition was ruthlessly suppressed. The murder of the spiritual leader of the Shi'a community served as a warning of what future dissidents might expect. As a result the only organized opposition to the regime operated outside the country. It was the Iraqi National Congress, headed by Ahmad Chalabi. In 1999 Congress appropriated $97 million for its activities. Little of this money was actually spent. However, under the Bush administration the Pentagon began paying the organization $340,000 per month. The payments were described as part of an "intelligence collection program" authorized by Congress under the Iraq Liberation Act. Unfortunately most INC reports were either falsified or incorrect. As a "favorite Iraqi" of the U.S. Defense Department, Chalabi returned to Iraq after many years in exile, most of it in Jordan. After the January 2005 elections he was considered briefly as a possible prime minister. As a secular Shiite Arab he enjoys some support within the Shi'a community, but his association with the U.S. has proven more handicap than asset.

The other organized opposition group outside the country, the Supreme Council for Islamic Revolution in Iraq (SCIRI), was formed in 1982 in Iran. It was essentially an umbrella group for various Saddam opponents, most of them Shi'a. SCIRI's original goal was to establish an Islamic regime in Iraq similar to Khomeini's in Iran. Its military wing, the Badr Brigade, fought with Iranian forces against Iraq in the later stages of that war.

Following the September 11, 2001, terrorist bombings in the United States, Saddam denounced the action and the killing of innocent civilians. However, there were huge public demonstrations in Baghdad, presumably government-sponsored, to protest continued U.S. and British air raids on Iraqi territory and the U.S. military campaign in Afghanistan. Protesters carried banners that read "Down With American Terrorism Against Islam." Subsequently, in January 2002 President George Bush included Iraq in his "axis of evil" of countries sponsoring terrorism and accused it of violating the 1972 treaty banning bacteriological, chemical, and other weapons of mass destruction. (Iraq is a signatory to the treaty.)

## THE U.S. INVASION AND ITS IMPACT

The invasion of March 2003 and overthrow of Saddam Hussein by U.S. and British forces is dealt with as a conflict issue elsewhere in this book (see essay Middle East: Theater of Conflict). But its impact on the Iraqi people as they struggle to put years of authoritarian rule behind them and construct a viable system of government, one based on law and human rights and buttressed by constitutional protections has been, and continues to be extremely difficult especially given the destructive impact of the invasion and of the resistance that followed it.

From its beginnings as an artificial nation–state patched together by outsiders, Iraq has always lacked the essential ingredients for successful nationhood. It was traditionally fragmented into many different groups with different and often opposed identities. Iraqi society was and to a great extent still is tribal, ethnic, religious, linguistic, urban and rural. Saddam Hussein was able to override these differences by sheer force or personality and absolute power. Amid a host of negative contributions, he must be credited for forcing these disparate elements into an Iraqi unitary state.

What lies ahead for this battered nation? The abrupt removal of Saddam Hussein and the collapse of his regime left a huge political vacuum in Iraq. What seems to have escaped by U.S. policymakers was the deplorable condition of the Iraqi economy. This fact alone militated against any possibility of an on-going weapons program there. The years of UN sanctions and U.S. bombings had destroyed most of its infrastructure. Roads, electricity, the water system and health care had dropped to a primitive level. The sudden collapse of the regime also set off an orgy of looting, revenge killings and destruction of the remaining essential services and facilities. By 2010 civilian deaths had reached more than 100,000; the country became divided into areas of "turf" contested by various groups, tribal and ethnic militias and the like, with Sunnis attacking Shi'as and vice versa and an overall insurgency aimed at the expulsion of U.S. forces but little else. As columnist Thomas L. Friedman observed prophetically, "there's no middle ground left in Iraq."[9]

Following President Bush's April 2003 announcement that the war had ended, Coalition forces set out to eliminate the top Ba'th leadership. Those captured or killed included Saddam's two sons, Uday and Qusay, killed in a gunfight after an anonymous tip. In December 2003 Saddam Hussein was trapped in an underground hideout in Adwar, near Tikrit. After inordinate delays Saddam was brought to trial and sentenced to death for a specific crime, the massacre of 148 Shi'a men and boys in the village of Dujail. On December 30, 2006, he was hanged in a cell in the former headquarters of the military intelligence service[10]

In 2008 and 2009 U.S. casualties continued to mount but the brunt of the violence has been directed at ordinary Iraqis and the police, security services, and all who seem in any way connected with or supported the U.S. forces. It has been a vicious cycle—the more American troops

attempted to curb the violence, the more they alienated the Iraqi people.[11]

Meanwhile Iraq's children are trickling back to their reopened schools, business improves, the sanctions are lifted and a sense of normalcy is slowly returning. Some have argued that the Iraq of the future may already have a role model in the Kurdish region, with its institutions well in place. In September 2003 a 25-member Governing Council took office with the U.S. Coalition administrator's approval. Its members were drawn from the Shi'a, Sunni and Kurdish populations, the Turkomans, the Communist Party, clerics and women. On September 10 Hoshyar Zebari, a Kurdish Council member, took his seat in the Council of Ministers of the Arab League as Iraq's representative. His opening statement may well portend the Iraqi future: "the new Iraq will be based on diversity, democracy, constitutional law and respect for human rights. It will stand firm against terrorism, from which it is now suffering." In light of this statement, the land between the rivers may well become the role model for Arab Middle Eastern democracy that George Bush insists it will.

## THREE ELECTIONS

In 2005 Iraq took the first of what would be many halting steps toward becoming a multi-party state with representative government to replace the diverse aggregation of ethnic, social, political, tribal and other groups that have characterized the land in much of its history. The first election, January, elected a 275-member Transitional National Assembly. While the Sunni population largely boycotted the proceedings, some 8.4 million valid votes were cast, half from the 4 provinces of Baghdad, Sulaimaniya, Basra and Erbil. The United Iraqi Alliance, a Shi'a coalition, won 48 percent of the popular vote to 26 percent for the Kurdistan Alliance and 14 percent for the Iraqi List, a Sunni-Shi'a coalition headed by interim prime minister Ayad Allawi. The successful Alliance candidates included the ever-resourceful Ahmed Chalabi.

Iraq's second vote was the national referendum to approve the new national constitution. To win their support, Sunnis were promised the right to propose constitutional amendments during the first 4 months of the Transitional National Assembly, which took office in January 2005.

On December 15, 2005, Iraq held its first free multi-party parliamentary election in half a century. Voters would choose from some 6,650 candidates belonging to 307 parties, most of them belonging to larger political alliances. Despite threats

of violence 70 percent of the country's 15 million eligible voters cast their ballots. The election was organized differently from the Transitional one, as voters chose candidates according to provinces and districts. The election pattern also guaranteed 15 percent of seats to women and 13 percent to Sunnis.

This election's results were more or less expected. The United Iraqi Alliance, a Shi'a coalition, won 128 seats, with the two Sunni Alliance blocs taking 55 and the Kurdish Alliance List 53. In March, 2006, Shi'a lawmakers exercised their constitutional rights as a parliamentary majority by re-electing Jaafari as prime minister by a one-vote margin. Unfortunately the same disagreements and factional rivalries, along with the insurgency, that have hampered nation-building in the past, continue to hamper nation-building in the present. Jaafari was forced to resign due to these difficulties and criticism of his leadership. Nouri Kamel al-Maliki, the secretary-general of the Islamic Dawa Party, was named prime minister on April 22, 2006, with a term expiring in 2010.

On January 31, 2009 elections were held to replace the local councils in fourteen of the eighteen governorates (provinces) where 444 seats were contested. The 14,431 candidates came from over 400 secular and religious parties, and included 3,912 women. The State of Law Coalition, which was led by the Islamic Dawa Party of Prime Minister Nouri al-Maliki, dominated this contest, winning the largest number of seats, mostly in Shi'a south. The State of Law Coalition is a secular alliance dominated by the Dawa Party but also includes some small Sunni, Christian, and Kurdish parties.

The second parliamentary elections since the 2003 foreign invasion were held on 7 March 2010. The aim was to elect the 325 members of the Council of Representatives of Iraq, which in turn would choose the prime minister and president. The results were almost immediately contested by the incumbent prime minister, al-Maliki, as it appeared that the alliance Iraqi National Movement, led by former Interim Prime Minister Ayad Allawi, had won 91 seats, forming thereby the largest group in parliament, followed by Maliki's State of Law Coalition with 89 seats. The National Iraqi Alliance won 70 seats and Kurdistan Alliance 43. Prime Minister Maliki contested the results alleging electoral fraud. However, on May 14, the Independent High Electoral Commission (IHEC) decided that, after the recounting of 11,298 ballot boxes, as requested by Maliki, there was no sign of fraud and thus initial results were valid. It seemed that Maliki wanted

**Timeline: PAST**

**1520–1920**
Border province of the Ottoman Empire

**1920–1932**
British mandate

**1932**
Independent kingdom under Faisal I

**1958**
The monarchy is overthrown by military officers

**1968**
The Ba'th Party seizes power

**1975**
The Algiers Agreement between the shah of Iran and Hussain ends Kurdish insurrection

**1980s**
Iran–Iraq War; diplomatic relations are restored with the United States after a 17-year break

**1990s**
Iraq invades and occupies Kuwait, leading to the brief but intense Gulf War; Saddam Hussein retains power

**PRESENT**

**2000s**
The U.S. forces invade and topple Saddam Hussein in 2003; Saddam tried and executed in 2006; civilian government and constitution approved by voters in 2005; very violent insurgency and counter-insurgency destabilizes the country and delays recovery. Normalcy seems to slowly return by 2010 and the the United States prepares to withdraw more than 50,000 of its troops (out of 120,000) by September.

not only another term as prime minister but also 50% of the seats for his alliance.

This deadlock created a crisis which prevented the formation of a new government for months. By early July 2010, there was still no deal among the main parliamentary groups at a time when the United States continued to prepare for the withdrawal of troops, which would leave 50,000 by August 31 (down from over 112,000 in 2010 and 165,000 following the "surge" ordered by President Bush). The remaining troops will continue to engage in combat operations renamed "stability operations," in the sense that they will only help hunt down remaining fighters and help the Iraqi forces build security across the country. The current plan calls for the withdrawal of all remaining troops by the end of 2011. However, no one believes that all American military presence will be withdrawn in the foreseeable future. Some observers say that when a new Iraqi government is formed, it is likely that negotiations will decide the shape and form of a long-term U.S. military presence in Iraq.[12]

Iraq faces many challenges today as it tries to return to normalcy. Political violence has diminished but not ended. Much of Iraq's infrastructure and economy need to be rebuilt and people's confidence in their future and their leaders need a serious boost. However, the political deadlock does not seem to help. Maliki has been trying to remain in control by working out an alliance with other Shiite blocs in parliament. If he succeeds, a Shiite-dominated government will antagonize not only the Sunnis, but also the seculars and, probably, the Kurds if they do not get more concessions on local autonomy. It would also not sit well with Iraq's Arab neighbors.

## NOTES

1. Khaldun S. Husry, "The Assyrian Affair of 1933 (I)," *International Journal of Middle East Studies,* Vol. 5, No. 2 (April, 1974), p. 166. The Assyrians are also called Chaldeans.

2. *Ibid.*

3. Damien Cave and James Glanz, "Toll Rises Above 500 in Iraq Bombings," *New York Times,* August 22, 2007. Online at www.nytimes.com/2007/08/22/world/middleeast/22iraq.html

4. Ali Allawi, *The Occupation of Iraq: Winning the War, Losing the Peace,* (New Haven: Yale University Press, 2007), p.17. The statement appeared originally in a book written (in Arabic) by the Iraqi historian Abd al-Razzaq al-Hassani.

5. Quoted in Wendell L. Willkie, "One World," *Life Magazine,* April 26, 1943, p. 75.

6. "Anafal" is the Arabic name of the 8th sura (chapter) of the Qur'an and appeared as a revelation to Muhammad after the battle of Badr, the first victory of the Muslims over their Meccan enemies. It was viewed by them (and by Saddam) as proof that God and right were on their side. See Human Rights Watch, *Iraq's Crime of Genocide: The Anfal Campaign Against the Kurds* (New Haven, CT: Yale University Press, 1995), p. 4. The campaign would have never come to light but it was fully documented when 18 tons of Iraqi government documents were captured by Kurdish pesh mergas during the uprising that followed the Gulf War.

7. The INA was "managed" from Jordan by a special CIA team. After the coup had been thwarted—the regime had advance warning through penetration of the CIS's satellite technology communications system—the team received a message: "We have arrested all your people. You might as well pack up and go home." The CIA team did just that. Andrew Cockburn and Peter Cockburn, *Out of the Ashes: The Resurrection of Saddam Hussein* (New York: HarperCollins, 1999), p. 229.

8. In June 2003 heavy spring rains and snow melt in the Turkish highlands where the rivers begin led occupation forces to join with the remaining marsh Arabs (the Ma'adan) to open floodgates and levees to allow water to flow back into the marshes. An international scientific team has been formed to resurrect the marshes and it may be that in this case nature can heal herself with human help!

9. Thomas L. Friedman, "Ten Months or Ten Years," *The New York Times,* October 29, 2006. As a participant in the "repair process" observed, "the Iraqi political class that inherited the mantle of the state from the Ba'thist regime was manifestly culpable in presiding over the deterioration of conditions. There was no national vision . . . just a series of deals to push forward the political process." Ali Allawi, *The Occupation of Iraq,* Op. Cit., p. 460.

10. The legality of the execution was seen as questionable and negative by the Arab world, and as essentially an example of victors' justice. In Iraq itself the Kurds argued that Saddam's summary execution would leave Anfal and other atrocities not liable to legal exposure.

11. Christian Parenti, "Two Sides: Scenes from a Nasty Brutish War," *The Nation,* February 27, 2004, p. 14. Online at www.alternet.org/story/17986/?page=entire

12. Tim Arango, "War in Iraq Defies U.S. Timetable for End of Combat," *New York Times,* July 2, 2010. Online at www.nytimes.com/2010/07/03/world/middleeast/03iraq.html?_r=1&ref=middleeast

# Israel (State of Israel)

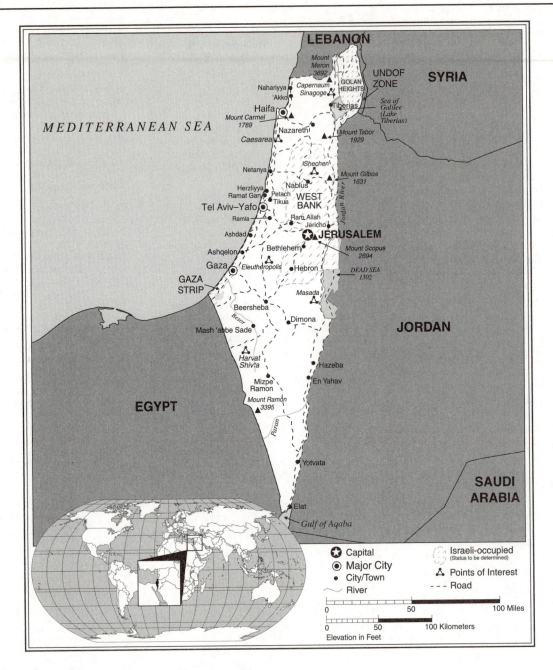

# Israel Statistics

## GEOGRAPHY

*Area in Square Miles (Kilometers):* 8,017
(20,770) (about the size of New Jersey)

*Capital (Population):* Tel Aviv (356,000)
recognized by most countries;
Jerusalem (591,000) claimed as
the capital but not internationally
recognized

*Environmental Concerns:* limited arable
land and fresh water; desertification;
air and groundwater pollution;
fertilizers; pesticides

*Geographical Features:* desert in south;
low coastal plain; central mountains;
Jordan Rift Valley

*Climate:* hot and dry in southern Negev
Desert area

## PEOPLE

### Population

*Total:* 7,353,985 (includes 187,000 Jewish
settlers in the occupied West Bank,
20,000 settlers in the Israeli-annexed
Golan Heights, and approximately
177,000 in East Jerusalem

*Annual Growth Rate:* 1.628%
*Rural/Urban Population Ratio:* 9/91
*Major Languages:* Hebrew; English; Arabic
*Ethnic Makeup:* Jews 76.4%, non-Jews (mostly Arabs) 23.6%
*Religions:* Jewish 76.4%, Muslim 16%, Druze 1.6%, Christian 2.1%, unspecified 3.9%

### Health

*Life Expectancy at Birth:* 80.86 years (male); 81 years (female)
*Infant Mortality Rate:* 4.1/1,000
*Physicians Available (Ratio):* 1/206 people

### Education

*Adult Literacy Rate:* 97.1%
*Compulsory (Ages):* 5–16; free

### COMMUNICATION

*Telephones:* 3,100,000 main lines
*Cellular Phones:* 9,500,000
*Internet Users:* 2.106 million

### TRANSPORTATION

*Highways in Miles (Kilometers):* 9,603 (15,464)

*Railroads in Miles (Kilometers):* 590 (949)
*Usable Airfields:* 47
*Motor Vehicles in Use:* 1,544,000

### GOVERNMENT

*Type:* republic
*Independence Date:* May 14, 1948 (from a League of Nations mandate under British administration)
*Head of State/Government:* President (ceremonial), Shimon Peres; Prime Minister Benjamin Netanyahu, Deputy Prime Minister Dan Meridor
*Political Parties:* Kadima (centrist), majority party but rules in coalition with Labor Alignment, Likud Bloc, SHAS, Yisrael Beitenu. Parties outside the coalition include Democratic Front for Peace and Equality (Hadash), Meretz-Yahad, National Religious Party (NRP), United Arab List
*Suffrage:* universal at 18

### MILITARY

*Military Expenditures (% of GDP):* 7.3%
*Current Disputes:* Evacuation of settlers and military forces from the Gaza Strip in November 2005 ended one phase of the Israeli-Palestinian conflict. Dispute with Syria over Israeli occupation and annexation of the Golan Heights

is unresolved but inactive. Israel has officially relinquished sovereignty over 4 West Bank towns but remains in occupation.

### ECONOMY

*Currency ($U.S. Equivalent):* 4.456 shekels = $1
*Per Capita Income/GDP:* $26,200/$166.3 billion
*GDP Growth Rate:* 4.5%
*Inflation Rate:* 0.1%
*Unemployment Rate:* 8.3%
*Labor Force:* 2,600,000
*Natural Resources:* copper; phosphates; bromide; potash; clay; sand; timber; manganese; natural gas; oil
*Agriculture:* citrus fruits; vegetables; cotton; beef; poultry; dairy products
*Industry:* food processing; diamond cutting; textiles and apparel; chemicals; high-technology projects; wood and paper; others
*Exports:* $42.86 billion (primary partners United States, Benelux, Hong Kong)
*Imports:* $47.8 billion (primary partners United States, Benelux, Germany)

### SUGGESTED WEB SITE

http://lcweb2.loc.gov/frd/cs/iltoc.html

# Israel Country Report

**I**srael is a small state about the size of New Jersey with a population of a little over 7 million people. The country occupies a larger land area than it held at the time of its creation in 1948, due to expansion wars with its neighbors. In the 1967 war, it took control of Egypt's Sinai peninsula and Gaza strip, Syria's Golan Heights, and Jordan's West Bank and East Jerusalem. Sinai was returned to Egypt following a 1979 peace agreement, while the Jordanian territory, which was ceded by Jordan to the Palestinians, has become an occupied territory with a nominal Palestinian control, except for the many Jewish settlements established there since 1967.

Israeli forces occupied a nine mile-wide, self-declared "security zone" along the Lebanese border from 1982 until 2000, when they were withdrawn due to increasing pressure from Lebanese forces in the south. In 1994, Israel signed a peace treaty with Jordan. Among its provisions, their common border was demarcated, and

areas in the Galilee were returned to Jordan. Peace treaties with Israel's other two Arab neighbors, Syria and Lebanon, have yet to be signed.

Although it is small, Israel has a complex geography, with a number of distinct regions. The northern region, Galilee, is a continuation of the Lebanese mountains, but at a lower altitude. The Galilee uplands drop steeply on three sides: to the Jordan Valley on the east; to a narrow coastal plain on the west; and southward to the Valley of Esdraelon, a broad inland valley from the Mediterranean to the Jordan River, which is fertile and well irrigated and has become important to Israeli agriculture.

Another upland plateau extends south from Esdraelon for about 90 miles. This area contains the ancient Jewish heartland—Judea and Samaria to Israelis, the West Bank to Palestinians—which is supposed to serve as the core of the self-governing Palestinian state as defined in the 1993 Oslo Agreement. This plateau gradually levels off into

semidesert, the barren wilderness of Judea. The wilderness merges imperceptibly into the Negev, a desert region that comprises 60 percent of the land area but has only about 12 percent of the population.

### TERRITORIAL CHANGES

The return of the Gaza Strip, captured from Egypt in the 1967 Six-Day War, to Palestinian control in 2005 leaves three territories held by Israel which were not part of the Jewish state approved in the 1947 UN partition plan for Palestine. They are the West Bank (of the Jordan River), East Jerusalem and the Golan Heights which was annexed unilaterally by Israel in 1981. Since the 1973 Yom Kippur War, the United Nations has maintained a small observer force in the demilitarized zone between Syrian and Israeli territory on the Golan. Syria's nonrecognition of Israel and Israel's insistence that the Golan Heights are essential to its security have made resolution of

Israelis regard Jerusalem as the political and spiritual capital of Israel. East Jerusalem was annexed from Jordan after the 1967 Six-Day War, and returning this part of the city to Jordan is not considered by Israel.

the dispute all but impossible. In January 2000, Syrian and Israeli negotiators met in Shepherdstown, West Virginia, under U.S. sponsorship, but they were unable to reconcile their conflicting claims to the territory. In 2006–07 Israel reportedly eased cross-border passage by Druze family members, especially wives, to allow them into Syrian territory for family reunions. Monitoring by a UN peacekeeping force has helped keep the border quiet. However an Israeli strike on an alleged Syrian nuclear facility in September 2007 underscores the vast gulf between the two neighbors on territorial and other issues.

The 1993 Oslo Agreement and the 1998 Wye Agreement, signed by then-prime minister Binyamin Netanyahu and the late Yassir Arafat, leader of the Palestine Liberation Organization (PLO), set guidelines for the gradual transfer of Gaza and the West Bank (excluding the Jewish settlements) to Palestinian self-rule. The Wye Agreement specified that 15 percent of the West Bank would be transferred by February 2000. In September 1999, Israel transferred 7 percent (160 square miles) of West Bank land to Palestinian control. An additional 5 percent was transferred in January 2000. The following summer, the new Israeli prime minister, Ehud Barak, met with Arafat at the presidential retreat in Camp David, Maryland, under U.S. sponsorship, and offered to turn over 94 percent of the West Bank for inclusion in the new Palestinian state. The Palestine National Authority (PNA) would be given administrative rule over the Dome of the Rock, excluding the Wailing Wall, as well as the non-Jewish quarters of East Jerusalem. However, Arafat rejected the offer because it did not recognize the "right of return" of Palestinian refugees to their former homes with appropriate compensation and also because Barak, at the last minute, reneged on interim steps that were necessary for the Palestinians to trust that Israel will live up to the deal.[1]

The issue of East Jerusalem—the "Old City" sacred to three faiths but revered especially by Jews as their spiritual, emotional, and political capital—remains a difficult one to resolve. From 1949 to 1967, it was under Jordanian control, with Jews prohibited from visiting the Wailing Wall and other sites important in the history of Judaism. Almost the only contact between the divided sectors of east and west was at the Mandelbaum Gate. In the 1967 Six-Day War, Israeli forces captured the Old City in fierce fighting. Since then its holy sites, sacred to Muslims, Christians, and Jews, have been opened to denominational and religious use. The Israeli government and its people are united in regarding Jerusalem as their eternal and political capital, although it is recognized as such by very few countries. Israel's reported annexation of East Jerusalem (the Old City) and purchase of homes by prospective Jewish settlers there have yet to be recognized by the international community. The 40th anniversary celebration of its capture by Israeli forces in 2007 was boycotted by all European ambassadors as well as the U.S.

ambassador to emphasize the point. In any case the higher birth rate among the Arab population, 3 percent to a bare 1 percent Jewish, and a steady outflow of Jews due to lack of job opportunities and crowded housing, make Jerusalem's justification as the country's eternal capital unrealistic. In the past, Jerusalem's status as Israel's undivided capital was considered non-negotiable by both the population and the government.

## THE POPULATION

The great majority of the Israeli population are Jewish. Judaism is the state religion; Hebrew, the ancient liturgical language revived and modernized in the twentieth century, is the official language, although English is widely used. Language and religion, along with shared historical traditions, a rich ancient culture, and a commitment to the survival of the Jewish state, have fostered a strong sense of national unity among the Israeli people. They are extremely patriotic, and these feelings are increased because of insecurity in a region that is generally hostile to Israel. Most Israelis believe that their neighbors are determined to destroy their state, and this belief has helped to develop a "siege mentality" among them.

Except for a small population of Jews that remained in the region (the village of Peki'in in Galilee is said to be the only one with an unbroken Jewish presence over the past 2,000 years), Jews dispersed throughout the world after Jerusalem's conquest by Roman legions in A.D. 70. Those who settled in Europe are called Ashkenazis (from Ashkenaz, Genesis 10:3). Most of them settled in France and Germany, and later in Central/Eastern Europe. Other Jewish communities found refuge in Spain, where they later prospered under Islamic rule for seven centuries (A.D. 711–1492). Such Jewish intellectual leaders as Moses Ben Maimon (Maimonides) rendered important services to Muslim rulers, and their role in trans-Mediterranean trade was so valuable that their Hispano–Moorish commercial language, Ladino, became the lingua franca of Christian–Islamic economic relations.

The Reconquista (Reconquest) of all Spain by the crusading army of Christian rulers Ferdinand of Leon and Isabella of Castile brought misfortune and tragedy to both Jews and Muslims. Both groups were ordered to convert or face expulsion. Jews who chose to convert were called Conversos, or less flatteringly *marranos* (lit. "pigs"), and many of them came under suspicion by the Spanish Inquisition for preserving and practicing their Jewish faith in secret. In 1511 A.D. the Spanish

king, Philip II, issued an "Edict of Expulsion" ordering all Muslims and Jews to leave Spain. As a result the remaining Jews left their Spanish homeland, settling either in Muslim North Africa, where they were assured safety and protection. As a result of this second Diaspora they became known collectively as Sephardim (from Sepharah, Obadiah 1:20).

The diversity among incoming Jews, particularly the Sephardic communities, was so great during the early years of independence that the government developed a special orientation program of Hebrew language and culture, called Ulpan (which is still in use), to help with their assimilation.

The election of Moshe Katsav, originally from Yazd (Iran), as Israel's president in 2000, and of Moroccan-born Amir Peretz as head of Histadrut and then leader of Labor Alignment, has brought a new-found sense of pride to the Sephardic community which was, for a long time, living in the shadows of the Ashkenazis which have controlled Israel since its creation.

Another difference among Israelis has to do with religious practice. The Hasidim, or Orthodox Jews, strictly observe the rules and social practices of Judaism and live in their own separate neighborhoods within cities. Reform Jews, by far the majority, are Jewish in their traditions, history, and faith, but they modify their religious practices to conform to the demands of modern life and thought. Both the Orthodox and Reform Jews have chief rabbis who sit on the Supreme Rabbinical Council, the principal interpretive body for Judaism.

Small groups of Jews of ancient origins, the Samaritans, have lived for centuries in Palestine in two locations, Holon (near Tel Aviv) and Nablus (in the West Bank). They are descended from one of the ancient Jewish tribes, one that broke away from the mainstream Jerusalem-based community over the location of Abraham's putative sacrifice of Isaac to God. (They believe that it took place on Mt. Gerizim rather than Mt. Moriah.) After the 1948 war for the creation of Israel, they were separated; the Holon community became part of Israel, while the Nablus Samaritans came under Jordanian rule. The 1967 Six-Day War reunited them, and since then they have served as intermediaries between their Palestinian neighbors and the Israeli authorities, being acceptable to both. The Samaritan community currently has just over 600 members. Most of them speak Arabic as well as Hebrew and are at home in both cultures.

Relations between the majority Reform Jews in Israel and the much smaller Orthodox community were marked by occasional incidents of friction but overall

coexistence until the rise to power of Menachem Begin's Likud Bloc. Begin's own political party, Herut, always emphasized the country's biblical heritage in its platform. But during Begin's period in office, the small religious parties that represent the Orthodox acquired political power because they were essential to the coalition government. The higher birth rate among haredim and other factors, such as exemption from military service for students enrolled in *yeshivas* (religious schools), gives them political clout to supplement the respect accorded them by Reform Jews due to their strict observance of Judaic law and custom. Their importance in Israel's fractious politics was amply demonstrated in the January 2003 Knesset elections. The Likud Party won the majority of seats with 38, but in order to govern the country it had to accept a coalition with Shinui and Shas, the ultra-Orthodox parties, which won 30.

Differences in historical experiences have also divided the Ashkenazis. Most lived in Central/Eastern Europe, sometimes isolated from other Jews as well as from their Christian neighbors. At one time, "They were closed off in a gigantic ghetto called the Pale of Settlement, destitute, deprived of all political rights, living in the twilight of a slowly disintegrating medieval world."[2] However, by the nineteenth century, Jews in Western Europe had become politically tolerated and relatively well-off, and, due to the Enlightenment, found most occupations and professions open to them. These "emancipated" Jews played a crucial role in the Zionist movement, but the actual return to Palestine and settlement was largely the work of Ashkenazis from Central/Eastern Europe. The former Soviet Union, which had a Jewish population of 3.5 million, nearly all in Russia itself, was among the first countries to recognize the new state of Israel. However, Soviet diplomatic representation was suspended from 1967 to 1991. U.S. restrictions on the entry of Soviet Jews caused the majority of them to emigrate to Israel. By 1992, some 350,000 had arrived in Israel. The majority were highly educated and professionally trained, but they were often unable to find suitable jobs and placed an added strain on housing and social services in Israel. One reason for the Israeli request to the United States for $10 billion in loan guarantees, which was held up by the George H. Bush administration and partially released by its successor, the Clinton administration, was to obtain funds for housing Soviet immigrants. Disillusionment with their experiences and lack of professional opportunities in Israel led the immigrants to form their own political party, Yisrael Ba'Aliya, to press for better conditions. The party joined the Binjamin

(© Neil Beer/Getty Images)

The Wailing Wall, a focal point of Jewish worship, is all that remains of the ancient Jewish temple destroyed by Roman legions led by Titus in A.D. 70. The Wailing Wall stands as a place of pilgrimage for devout Jews throughout the world.

Netanyahu coalition after the Knesset (Parliament) elections and shifted to support for Ehud Barak after he became prime minister. Its leader, Natan Sharansky, was named minister of interior in return for his party's support. His appointment put him in direct conflict with Shas, which had previously controlled that ministry. Yisrael Ba' Aliya was also promised $65 million for jobs and housing for Soviet emigrants.

The *Aliyah* ("going up" in Hebrew, i.e., to Israel) policy has resulted in the migration of many formerly isolated Jewish communities to Israel. The first group to arrive were from Yemen, where they had lived in scattered villages, working as craftsmen and using Aramaic in their liturgy. Some 90 percent of them were airlifted directly to Israel. Although Yemen closed its borders in the 1960s, most of the remaining Jews were allowed to emigrate, leaving about 300 members of this oldest of diaspora communities.

Since the 1980s nearly 100,000 Ethiopian Jews have migrated to Israel. They have been reasonably well absorbed into the larger Israeli community with one exception, that of the Falash Mura. The ancestors of this group supposedly converted to Christianity centuries ago, probably through coercion as was the case with the Conversos of Spain. Like the Conversos, however, they continued to practice their Jewish faith privately and more recently in public. Fears that this rather impoverished community would impose additional burdens on Israeli social services led the government in 2003 to require that only those Falashas who could document Jewish ancestry on the maternal side would be allowed into Israel. Some 15–20,000 of them were believed to meet the requirement.

Up until now Israel has limited Falasha immigration to 300 per month. But in January 2005 as the result of a civil action suit an accelerated immigration process for them was approved. As of June 2005, 600 Falash per month were granted admission with the immigration process completed in 2007. The 17,000 plus Falasha were granted citizenship under the law of return plus rabbinical verification of their jewish lineage.

Israel has two important non-Jewish minorities, totaling about 1.5 million—about 24 percent of the population. The larger group consists of Muslim and some Christian Arabs who stayed after Israel achieved statehood. This Arab population was ruled under military administration from 1948 until 1966, when restrictions were lifted and the Arabs became citizens. However they are still prohibited from serving in the armed forces and do not have priority with Israeli Jews in education, housing and jobs. The Christian Arab population, originally much larger but now forming at most 3 percent, has experienced similar treatment, and events such as the 2002 siege of the Bethlehem Church of the Nativity by Israeli forces due to the presence there of Palestinian militants has encouraged many to migrate.

Efforts by Israeli Arabs to gain economic and social equality with Jews has concentrated on improving their political representation. The first Arab political party was formed in 1988 and won one seat in the Knesset. In 1996, the party won four seats. In 1999, 95 percent of the Arab electorate voted for Barak; they were a major factor in his victory over Netanyahu.

Thus far, political representation in the Knesset has not been accompanied by social and economic equality for Israel's Arabs. The Barak government took several small steps in that direction in the new century. El Al, the Israeli airline, hired its first Arab flight attendant and appointed its first Arab ambassador in the foreign service, and in 2007 the Olmert government appointed its first Arab Muslim cabinet minister.

The resumption of the Palestinian Intifada in 2000, after Ariel Sharon's visit to the Dome of the Rock and its Islamic holy places to emphasize Israel's sovereignty over its entire territory, led to a demonstration by Israeli Arabs to show their sympathy with the Palestinian cause. It was broken up by police, with 13 Arabs killed.

In the past, Israel's Arab population has been concerned primarily with such issues as underfunding for its schools and municipal services. This concern has changed, as it has become more active politically. Early in 2007 a number of Israeli Arab intellectuals issued a "Future Vision" position paper which among other concerns demanded that Israel declare itself a "state for all its citizens." As one of the signatories observed, "a state for all its citizens" means that the country should cease to be a *Jewish* state. But to Israeli Jews this is the reason for being of the state, "you're challenging its very foundations."[3] Acceptance of Israeli Arab demands for equal social and political rights as outlined in the Vision paper would eventually alter the very nature of the Jewish state by making it in actuality one for all citizens.

Another non-Jewish minority is the Druze, who are also found in mountain enclaves in Lebanon and Syria. They form a majority of the population in the Golan Heights, occupied by Israeli forces in the 1967 Six-Day War and annexed in 1981. They practice a form of Islam that split off from the main body of the religion in the tenth century. Most Druze have remained loyal to the Israeli state. In return, they have been given full citizenship, are guaranteed freedom to practice their faith under their religious leaders, and may serve in the armed forces.

At present about 70,000 Druze live in Israel in 16 large villages in the Galilee and near Haifa. Another 16,000 Druze live in the Israeli-annexed Golan Heights, where they are physically separated from their families on the Syrian side by the

UN demilitarized zone. These Druze have rejected Israeli citizenship. When Israel annexed the Golan Heights unilaterally in 1981, they reacted with a six-month-long general strike; it ended only when the government agreed not to force citizenship on the Druze. In 1997, on the 15th anniversary of the strike, the villagers showed their continued defiance of Israeli rule by flying the Syrian flag over their schools. Despite their relative freedom, the Druze in Israel, like the Israeli Arabs, experience discrimination in educational and work opportunities.

There are two other small minority groups in Israel, both Sunni Muslims. The Circassians, descendants of warriors from the Caucasus brought in centuries ago to help Muslim armies drive the Christian Crusaders from Palestine, have been completely integrated into Israeli society. The second minority group, the Bedouins, formerly roamed the barren uplands of Judea and the Negev Desert. Until recently they followed their traditional nomadic lifestyle unhindered. But economic hardship, along with lack of water supplies, has led increasing numbers to move onto state lands, which cover much of the Negev. Like rural migrants in many countries they settle down, building shanty villages (which are considered illegal under Israeli housing laws). By 2003 there were 46 such "unrecognized villages," with a population of 70,000.

Other Bedouin communities, which had been removed from the Sinai Peninsula when it was returned to Egypt in 1979 and resettled in Gaza, were again evacuated in 2005 prior to its return to Palestinian control. As Israeli citizens the government said it was obligated to do so for them. They will join other semi-nomadic Bedouin in the Negev, near the Dead Sea. Commenting prophetically on their second removal from their homes, Sheik Abed Shtawi, a spokesman for the group, said: "This is a hard situation for us. But I see my future as a Bedouin and an Israeli citizen."[4]

# HISTORY

The land occupied by the modern State of Israel has been a crossroads for conquering armies and repository for many civilizations in history. It is part of biblical history and an important component of the Judeo-Christian heritage. The ruins of Megiddo, near Haifa, are believed by scholars to be the site of Armageddon, described in *Revelations* as the final clash between good and evil resulting in the end of the world.

Jews believe that Israel is the modern fulfillment of the biblical covenant between God and a wanderer named Abraham (Abram) that granted him a homeland in a particular place. Jews have held fast to this covenant during the centuries of their exile in foreign lands. Each of these periods of exile is called a *diaspora* ("dispersion"). The most important one, in terms of modern Israel, took place in the first century A.D. Abraham's descendants through Isaac had called the land given to them in covenant Judea and Samaria; and when it became part of the expanding Roman Empire, it was known as the province of Judea. Initially the Romans preferred to rule the unruly Jews indirectly through appointed governors. The best-known of them, Herod, "bought" his appointment from Rome and then elevated his status to that of King. Aside from ruling Judea and Samaria at the time of Jesus, he made noteworthy contributions to its people, including renovation of the Temple.

After Herod's death Rome imposed direct rule over the province by appointed governors called *procurators,* the best-known being Pontius Pilate. In 69–70 A.D., the Jews rebelled. The forces of Roman general (later emperor) Titus then besieged Jerusalem. The city fell in A.D. 70, and Roman legions sacked and destroyed much of it. (A portion of the Temple Wall remains standing to this day. It is called the Wailing Wall because Jews come there to pray and mourn the loss of the original central shrine to their faith.)

From then until the twentieth century, most Jews were dispersed, living among other peoples and subject to foreign rulers. Periodically persecuted and often mistrusted, they coexisted with the populations around them, in part by preserving their ancient rituals and customs but also due to the restrictions imposed on them by their non-Jewish rulers.

## Zionism

The organized movement to establish a national home for dispersed Jews in Palestine is known as Zionism. This secular movement that was born in Europe considered several other options for the new state, including Argentina and Uganda. As a political movement, its main aim was to establish, by Jewish settlement, a homeland where dispersed Jews may gather, escape persecution, and create a modern state. As a political movement, it differs sharply from spiritual Zionism, the age-old dream of "the return." Most Orthodox Jews and traditionalists opposed *any* movement to establish a Jewish state in the holy land; they believed that it is blasphemy to do so, for only God can perform the miracle of restoring the Promised Land. The reality of the establishment of the Jewish state by force of arms, with a secular political system backed by strong Jewish nationalism, has created what one author calls "an unprecedented Jewish dialogue with power, an attempt to historicize the Jewish experience as a narrative of liberation by armed Jews."[5] On May 15, the anniversary of Israel's independence, many Haredim display a black flag rather than the Israeli one, marking their belief that Zionism has usurped the role of the Messiah and prevented His return.

Zionism as a political movement began in the late nineteenth century. Its founder was Theodore Herzl, a Jewish journalist from Vienna, Austria. Herzl had grown up in the Jewish Enlightenment period. He was bitterly disillusioned by the wave of Jewish persecution that swept over Central/Eastern Europe after the murder of the liberal Russian czar, Alexander II, in 1881. He was even more disillusioned by the trial of a French Army officer, Alfred Dreyfus, for treason. Dreyfus, who was Jewish, was convicted after a trumped-up trial brought public protests that he was part of an anti-government Jewish conspiracy.

Herzl concluded from these events that the only hope for the long-suffering Jews, especially those from Central/Eastern Europe, was to live together, separate from non-Jews. In his book *The Jewish State,* he wrote: "We have sincerely tried everywhere to merge with the national communities in which we live, seeking only to preserve the faith of our fathers. It is not permitted to us."[6]

Herzl had attended the Dreyfus trial as a journalist. Concerned about growing anti-Semitism in Western Europe, he organized a conference of European Jewish leaders in 1897 in Basel, Switzerland. The conference ended with the ringing declaration that "the aim of Zionism is to create a Jewish homeland in Palestine secured by public law." Herzl wrote in an appendage: "In Basel I have founded the Jewish state."[7]

The Zionist movement planned to buy land in Palestine, which it declared "a land without people" but the Ottoman governor, Sultan Abdul-Hamid II refused to allow that for internal and external political reasons. A number of Jews were able to do so privately by purchases from absentee owners. Also a substantial number of East European Jews escaping pogroms in Russia and Poland made their way to Palestine in the last years of the 19th century. Many of them arrived as penniless immigrants, and in order to survive they grouped together in communal agricultural farms called *Kibbutzim.* The first one established on the Sea of Galilee, Degania, was founded in 1909. Through the years the founding principles of Degania and its successors—the sacredness of work, the Jewish right to the soil of Palestine, and the right of displaced Jews to return there—defined the character of the future Jewish state.

## DEVELOPMENT

By international standards, Israel is a "developed" country with a per capita income, GDP, and other economic levels comparable to those of Europe. The Palestinian intifada and the collapse of the Internet brought a brief recession which adversely affected tourism and the developing high-tech industry. But despite political turmoil, a 34-day inconclusive war with Hezbollah in neighboring Lebanon, and other destabilizing factors, the economy rebounded strongly in 2006–2007. After a brief slow-down caused by the global financial crisis of 2008–2009, which brought down the GDP growth rate from 4 percent to 0.5 percent in 2009, the economy seemed to rebound by early 2010. Unfortunately, the rising tide of prosperity does not yet lift every Israeli boat. Families living below the poverty level ($7/day) now comprise 20 percent of the population due to uneven distribution of income.

## The Balfour Declaration

Although the Zionist movement attracted many Jewish supporters, it had no influence with European governments, nor with the Ottoman government. The Zionists had difficulty raising money to finance land purchases in Palestine and to pay for travel of emigrants.

It appeared in the early 1900s that the Zionists would never reach their goal. But World War I gave them a new opportunity. The Ottoman Empire was defeated, and British troops occupied Palestine. Many British officials favored the Zionist cause, among them Winston Churchill. During his term as colonial secretary after World War I, he organized the 1921 Cairo Conference, which among other issues confirmed the League of Nations' assignment of Palestine to Britain as a mandate.

As a result, the name Palestine came into common usage for the territory. It is probably derived from Philistine, from the original tribal inhabitants (who are also called Canaanites), but this covenanted land had been ruled by many other peoples and their rulers for centuries, due to its location as a strategic corridor between Asia and Africa. After it became part of the Ottoman Empire, along with Lebanon it was divided into *vilayets* (provinces), those of Beirut and Acre respectively; Jerusalem was administered

separately as a *sanjak* (subprovince). The majority of the population were small farmers living in compact villages and rarely traveling elsewhere. Most were Muslims, but there was a substantial minority of Christians. Leadership, such as it was, was held by a small urban elite, the principal families being the Husseinis and Nashashibis.

During World War I, a specific commitment of Great Britain to the Zionist cause came in the form of a 1917 letter from Foreign Secretary Arthur James Balfour to Lord Rothschild, a prominent statesman and a Zionist sympathizer. The latter's qualified endorsement favoring a Jewish national home in Palestine included also a commitment to guarantee the rights of the indigenous population. The Balfour Declaration was taken by the Zionists as official British support for their cause and an authorization for them to begin building in Palestine a national home for dispersed Jews. Weizmann, a British Zionist, and his colleagues established the Jewish Agency to organize the return. Great Britain's obligation under the mandate was to prepare Palestine's inhabitants for eventual self-government. British officials assigned to Palestine tended to favor Jewish interests over those of the native population. This was due in part to their Judeo–Christian heritage, but also to the active support of Jews in Britain during the war. In addition to Weizmann's contribution, the Jewish Legion, a volunteer group, had fought with British forces against the Turks.

Britain's "view with favor" toward Zionism weighed heavily in the application of mandate requirements to Palestine. Jews were allowed to emigrate, buy land, develop agriculture, and establish banks, schools, and small industries. The Jewish Agency established a school system, while former members of the dispersed Jewish Legion regrouped into what became Haganah, the defense force for the Jewish community.

Compounding the difficulties of adjustment of two different peoples to the same land was the fact that most Zionist leaders had never been to Palestine. They envisaged it as an empty land waiting for development by industrious Jews.

Palestinian Arabs were opposed to the mandate, to the Balfour Declaration, and to Jewish immigration. They turned to violence on several occasions, against the British and the growing Jewish population. In 1936, Arab leaders called a general strike to protest Jewish immigration, which led to a full-scale Arab rebellion. The British tried to steer a middle ground between the two communities. But they were unwilling (or unable) either to accept Arab demands for restrictions on Jewish immigration and land purchases or Zionist demands for a Jewish

majority in Palestine. British policy reports and White Papers during the mandate wavered back and forth. In 1937, the Peel Commission, set up after the Arab revolt, recommended a halt to further Jewish immigration, and subsequently the 1939 "White Paper" stated that the mandate should be replaced by a self-governing Arab state with rights assured for the Jewish minority.

One important difference between the Palestinian Arab and Jewish communities was in their organization. The Jews were organized under the Jewish Agency, which operated as a "state within a state" in Palestine. Jews in Europe and the United States also contributed substantially to the agency's finances and made arrangements for immigration. The Palestinian Arabs, in contrast, were led by heads of urban families who often quarreled with one another. The Palestinian Arab cause also did not have outside Arab support; leaders of neighboring Arab states were weak and still under British or French control.

A unique feature of Zionism that helped strengthen the Jewish pioneers in Palestine in their struggle to establish their claim to the land were the kibbutzim. They were collective-ownership communities with self-contained, communal-living arrangements; members shared labor, income, and expenses. Leaders of the new Jewish state, such as Ben Gurion, Shimon Peres, Moshe Dayan and Yitzhak Rabin, came out of the Kibbutz movement, and for years its members dominated the Knesset and the armed forces.

Unfortunately, for a variety of reasons, the movement has lost much of its reason for being in recent years. By 2007 two-thirds of the country's kibbutzes had been privatized or closed their doors entirely, Those that remain, however, fill a small niche in the Israeli economy, employing some 30,000 workers in various enterprises with an output of $7.4 billion.[8]

## FREEDOM

Israel is a multi-party democracy with a unicameral legislature (the Knesset), an independent legal system capped by a Supreme Court, press freedom and other civil rights, and open elections. It has no written constitution but is governed by a set of Basic Laws. These include the Law of Return, which guarantees the right of Diaspora Jews to return and be granted citizenship. However, these rights have not been made available to the Israeli Arab minority, which is disadvantaged in access to higher education, government jobs, housing and other benefits.

Adolf Hitler's policy of genocide (total extermination) of Jews in Europe, developed during World War II, gave a special urgency to Jewish settlement in Palestine. American Zionist leaders condemned the 1939 British White Paper and called for unrestricted Jewish immigration into Palestine and the establishment of an independent, democratic Jewish state. After World War II, the British, still committed to the White Paper, blocked Palestine harbors and turned back desperate Jewish refugees from Europe. Supplies of smuggled weapons enabled Haganah to fend off attacks by Palestinian Arabs, while Jewish terrorist groups such as the Stern Gang and Irgun Zvai Leumi carried out acts of murder and sabotage against British troops and installations, the most sensational being the bombing of the King David Hotel in Jerusalem, headquarters of the British military command and administration.

## PARTITION AND INDEPENDENCE

In 1947, the British decided that the Palestine mandate was unworkable. They asked the United Nations to come up with a solution to the problem of "one land, two peoples." A UN Special Commission on Palestine (UNSCOP) recommended partition of Palestine into two states—one Arab, one Jewish—with an economic union between them. A minority of UNSCOP members recommended a federated Arab–Jewish state, with an elected legislature and minority rights for Jews. The majority report was approved by the UN General Assembly on November 29, 1947, by a 33–13 vote, after intensive lobbying by the Zionists. The partition would establish a Jewish state, with 56 percent of the land, and a Palestinian Arab state, with 44 percent. The population at that time was 60 percent Arab and 40 percent Jewish. Due to its special associations for Jews, Muslims, and Christians, Jerusalem would become an international city administered by the United Nations.

The Jewish delegation, led by Abba Eban and David Ben-Gurion, accepted the UN partition plan but the Palestinian leaders, backed by few newly independent Arab states, rejected the plan outright. On May 14, 1948, in keeping with Britain's commitment to end its mandate, the last British soldiers left Palestine. Ben-Gurion promptly announced the "birth of the new Jewish State of Israel." On May 15, the United States and the Soviet Union recognized the new state, even as the armies of five Arab states converged on it to "push the Jews into the sea."

## CREATION OF ISRAEL AND THE PALESTINIANS

Some 700,000 to 800,000 Palestinians fled Israel during the 1948 War. After the 1967 Six-Day War, an additional 380,000 Palestinians became refugees in Jordan. Israeli occupation of the West Bank brought a million Palestinians under military control.

The unifying factor among all Palestinians is the recovery of the homeland. Abu Iyad, a top Palestine Liberation Organization leader, once said, ". . . our dream . . . [is] the reunification of Palestine in a secular and democratic state shared by Jews, Christians and Muslims rooted in this common land. . . . There is no doubting the irrepressible will of the Palestinian people to pursue their struggle . . . and one day, we will have a country."[9]

Those Israelis born in Palestine—now in their third generation—call themselves *Sabras,* after the prickly pear cactus of the Negev. The work of Sabras and of a generation of immigrants has created a highly urbanized society, sophisticated industries, and a productive agriculture. Much of the success of Israel's development has resulted from large contributions from Jews abroad, from U.S. aid, from reparations from West Germany for Nazi war crimes against Jews, and from bond issues. Yet the efforts of Israelis themselves should not be understated.

## ISRAELI POLITICS

Israel is unique among Middle Eastern states in having been a multiparty democracy since its establishment as a state. It does not have a written constitution, mainly because secular and Orthodox communities cannot agree on its provisions. The Orthodox community, for example, argues that it already has its constitution, in the Bible and Torah. For the Orthodox, a constitution would be something imported from a foreign country such as a Canada or Sweden, not a document that truly belonged to Israel.

In place of a constitution, the Israeli state is governed by a series of Basic Laws. They include the Law of Return, by which all Jews who move to Israel are automatically granted citizenship. In addition, a series of seven Basic Laws established the Knesset, the national army (Israel Defense Forces), the office of president, the legal system, and so on. Two new Basic Laws issued in 1992 provide for direct election of the prime minister and for the recognition of human dignity and rights before the power of the state.

Power in the Israeli political system rests in the unicameral Knesset. It has 120 members who are elected for four-year terms under a system of proportional representation from party lists. The prime minister and cabinet are responsible to the Knesset, which must approve all policy actions.

From time to time Israeli politics has been disfigured by undemocratic or corrupt practice. The 1997 Bar-On affair, "Israel's Watergate" for a time threatened to bring about a no-confidence vote in the Knesset against then-Prime Minister Netanyahu. Charges of sexual misconduct and obstruction of justice against President Katsav in 2007 caused his resignation before the end of his term. In 2009 and 2010 Ehud Olmert, the former Prime Minister and former mayor of Jerusalem, faced charges in three cases of corruption while holding public office.[10] Also, he was indicted for bribery, fraud, breach of trust, and income tax evasion. Similar charges have brought about the resignation of top police officials, and the chief of the Israel Defense Forces resigned to take personal responsibility for its failure to defeat Hezbollah in the 34-day war.

### HEALTH/WELFARE

The continued upsurge in the Israeli economy has not brought uniform benefits to all sectors of the population, despite a growth rate averaging 5 percent and significant foreign investment. The 2003–2005 Netanyahu reform package cut social programs drastically. As a result Israeli Arabs and Orthodox Jews, which have high birth rates and low participation in the work force, now constitute the bulk of the 20 percent of the population living below the poverty level.

Ben-Gurion's Labor Party controlled the government for the first three decades of independence. However, the party seldom had a clear majority in the Knesset. As a result, it was forced to join in coalitions with various small parties. Israeli political parties are numerous. Many of them have merged with other parties over the years or have broken away to form separate parties. The Labor Party itself is a merger of three Socialist labor organizations. The two oldest parties are Agudath Israel World Organization (founded in 1912), which is concerned with issues facing Jews outside of Israel as well as within, and the Israeli Communist Party (Rakah, founded in 1919).

The Labor Party's control of Israeli politics began to weaken seriously after the October 1973 War. Public confidence was shaken by the initial Israeli defeat, heavy casualties, and evidence of Israel's unpreparedness. Austerity measures imposed to deal with inflation increased Labor's unpopularity. In the 1977 elections, the opposition, the Likud bloc, won more seats than Labor but fell short of a majority in the Knesset. The new prime minister, Menachem Begin, was forced to make concessions to smaller parties in order to form a governing coalition.

However, the Israeli invasion of Lebanon in 1982 weakened the coalition. It seemed to many Israelis that for the first time in its existence, the state had violated its own precept that wars should be defensive and waged only to protect Israeli land. The ethical and moral implications of Israel's occupation, and in particular the massacre by Lebanese Christian militiamen of Palestinians in refugee camps in Beirut who were supposedly under Israeli military protection, led to the formation in 1982 of Peace Now, an organization of Israelis who mounted large-scale demonstrations against the war and are committed to peace between Israel and its Arab neighbors.

Begin resigned in 1983, giving no reason but clearly distressed not only by the difficulties in Lebanon but also by the death of his wife. He remained in seclusion for the rest of his life. He died in 1992.

## RECENT INTERNAL POLITICS

The Labor Party won the majority of seats in the Knesset in the 1984 elections—but not a clear one. As a result, the two major blocs reached agreement on a "government of national unity," the first in Israel's history. The arrangement established alternating two-year terms for each party's leader as prime minister. Shimon Peres (Labor) held the office from 1984 to 1986 and Yitzhak Shamir (Likud) from 1986 to 1988.

In the 1988 elections, certain fundamental differences between Labor and Likud emerged. By this time the first Palestinian *intifada* ("uprising") was in full swing. It would not only change the relationship between Israelis and Palestinians forever but would also alter the norms of Israeli politics. Labor and Likud differed over methods of handling the uprising, but they differed even more strongly in their views of long-term settlement policies toward the Palestinians. Labor's policy was to "trade land for peace," with some sort of self-governing status for the occupied territories and peace treaties with the Arab neighbors guaranteeing Israel's "right to exist." Likud would give away none of the sacred land; it could not be bartered for peace.

The election results underscored equally deep divisions in the population. Neither party won a clear majority of seats in the Knesset; Likud took 40 seats, Labor 39. Four minority ultra-religious parties gained the balance of power, with 15 percent of the popular vote and 18 seats. Their new-found political power encouraged the religious parties to press for greater control on the part of Orthodox Jewry over Israeli life. However, a proposed bill to amend the Law of Return to allow only Orthodox rabbis to determine "who is a Jew" for citizenship purposes aroused a storm of protest among Jews living abroad who are mostly Reform or Conservative and would be barred from citizenship. In February 2002, the Israeli Supreme Court ruled that both movements would be listed as Jews in the official census registry. For Reform and Conservative Jews living in Israel, it was a major step toward official recognition.

The 1992 Knesset election ended 15 years of Likud dominance. Labor returned to power, winning a majority of seats. However, the splintered, multiparty Israeli electoral system denied it an absolute majority. Concessions to minority parties enabled Labor to establish a functioning government, and party leader Yitzhak Rabin was named prime minister. With the support of these minority parties, notably Shas, an ultra-religious, non-Zionist party of mostly Sephardic Jews, and the left-wing Meretz Party, the Rabin government could count on 63 votes in the Knesset. This majority ensured support for the government's policies, including the 1993 Oslo agreements with the Palestinians.

## JEWISH AND ARAB EXTREMISTS

The deep divisions in Israeli society regarding future relations with the Palestinian population in the occupied territories (for many Israelis, these lands are Judea and Samaria, part of the ancestral Jewish homeland) were underscored by the uncovering in the 1980s of a Jewish underground organization that had attacked Palestinian leaders in violent attempts to keep the territories forever Jewish. The group had plotted secretly to blow up the sacred Islamic shrines atop the Dome of the Rock. A number of the plotters were given life sentences by a military court. But the outcry of support from right-wing groups in the population was such that their sentences were later commuted by then-president Chaim Herzog.

A more virulent form of anti-Arab, anti-Palestinian violence emerged in 1984 with the founding of Kach, a political party that advocated expulsion of all Arabs from Israel. Its founder, Brooklyn, New York—born Rabbi Meir Kahane, was elected to the Knesset in 1984, giving him parliamentary immunity, and he began organizing anti-Arab demonstrations. The Knesset subsequently passed a law prohibiting any political party advocating racism in any form from participation in national elections. On that basis, the Israeli Supreme Court barred Kach and its founder from participating in the 1988 elections. Kahane was murdered by an Egyptian-American while in New York for a speaking engagement. His son Binyamin formed a successor party, *Kahane Chai* ("Kahane Lives"), based in the West Bank Jewish settlement of Tapuah. Both Kach and Kahane Chai were labeled terrorist groups by the U.S. Department of State. They were also outlawed in Israel after a member, Baruch Goldstein, murdered 29 Muslims in a mosque in Hebron. In September 2000, Binyamin Kahane and his wife were killed in an ambush while driving their children to school, in another blow to the struggling Palestinian–Israeli peace negotiations.

Palestinian extremism evolved in the 1990s largely as a result of Palestinian anger and disillusionment over the peace agreement with Israel, which was seen as accommodation on the part of Palestinian leaders, notably Yassir Arafat, with Israel rather than negotiations to establish a Palestinian state. A number of militant Palestinian organizations, including the PLO itself, have taken up arms against Israel over the years, the most effective one being *Hamas* (Arabic acronym for The Movement of Islamic Resistance). Hamas began as a spin-off from the Cairo-based Muslim Brotherhood (see Egypt Country Report). After the establishment of the Palestine National Authority (PNA) under Arafat, it served mainly as a social service agency. It became politicized after the lack of success of the intifada in achieving Palestinian self-rule. In 1992 Hamas attacks on Israelis led Israel to deport 415 activists to Lebanon. The Lebanese government refused to admit them, and consequently they languished for some months in a hillside in southern Lebanon, until ordered released by the UN Security Council under *Resolution 799*—one of the very few accepted by Israel.

Subsequently, Hamas entered the political sphere of the Occupied Territories, and in 2006 it came to power in the new Palestinian parliament from its political base in Gaza (see Conflict Essay for further details).

### Israel and America

Israel's relationship with the United States has been close since the establishment of the Jewish state, in large part due to the large American Jewish population and its unstinting support. This friendship has been severely tested on two occasions. During the 1967 Six-Day War, the *Liberty,* a slow-moving, lightly armed U.S. Navy ship working with the U.S. National Security Agency to monitor the conflict, was attacked by Israeli aircraft and torpedo boats off the Mediterranean coast. Thirty-four American sailors were killed, and 171 wounded. Israeli statements that the attack was a "mistake" were accepted at face value by the Lyndon Johnson administration, which was concerned with maintaining good relations with Israel at that time of war. However, more recent information from the National Security Agency and other archives suggest that it was deliberate.

A second major strain on U.S.–Israeli relations was the Pollard affair. It involved an American Jew, Jonathan Jay Pollard, who was convicted of spying on his own country for Israel. Pollard's reports on U.S. National Security Agency intelligence-collecting methods and his duplication of military satellite photographs seriously compromised U.S. security. They also damaged Israel's image in the American Jewish community.

In the years following Pollard's incarceration, many efforts have been made by Israeli and American Jewish organizations to have his sentence commuted. As yet, successive U.S. presidents have not done so. But these two negative events have not altered the "special relationship" between Israel and its major ally. The country remains the recipient of the largest amount of U.S. aid worldwide. With very few interruptions, the notable one being President Eisenhower's intervention in the 1956 Suez War, the United States has consistently supported Israel's foreign policy. The acclaimed "road map to peace" between the Israelis and the Palestinians issued by President George Bush in 2003 requires that Israel take certain steps toward the establishment of a Palestinian state. While the "road map" has largely disappeared or been overtaken by recent events, pressure from the Bush administration was to some extent responsible for Israel's withdrawal from Gaza and its cession of certain West Bank towns to Palestinian authority.

In early 2010, President Barak Obama, while reconfirming America's staunch support for Israel, exhibited overt exasperation regarding Israel's refusal to halt building settlements on Palestinian land and for going ahead with a planned housing project in East Jerusalem even though the policy gets in the way of the peace process he wanted to resume. He even declared that peace between Israel and the Palestinians has become a "vital national security interest of the United States," in the sense that procrastination in that area jeopardizes the lives of American troops and vital U.S. interest in the region.[11]

## Contentious Issues of Religion and Citizenship

The puzzling question of "Who is a Jew?" became a major issue separating Orthodox and Reform and Conservative Jewry in 1998 and 1999. A bill introduced in the Knesset in 1997 by the three religious parties would ban Reform and Conservative Jews from serving on religious councils. The action was rejected by the Israeli Supreme Court, and in January 1998, the first non-Orthodox representatives took their seats on the Haifa Council.

In December 1998, the Court ruled that the system of exemptions from military service for yeshiva students (those enrolled in religious-study programs) was illegal because it was not anchored in law. The court ordered the Knesset to pass legislation dealing with the issue. Ehud Barak had pledged the end of the draft-deferral system during his campaign for the prime ministership. But after his election, he approved changing the system rather than eliminating it. Under the changes, yeshiva students would be exempt from service from ages 18 to 23. They would be allowed a "year of deliberation" thereafter; they could go to trade school or get jobs. At age 24, if they decided to leave the yeshiva, they would be required to do four months' service, either national or military, in a special unit.

Despite Barak's backtracking on the draft-deferral issue, other issues continued to divide Orthodox from secular Jews. Shas, flexing its political muscle after joining Barak's coalition, gained control of the Labor Ministry and promptly enforced a 1953 law that banned employment of Jewish teenagers on the Sabbath. As a result, a McDonald's franchise in Jerusalem was hit with $20,000 in fines.

The *haredim* (Orthodox) community holds itself apart from Reform and Conservative Parties on a number of issues, notably use of roads on the Sabbath, attendance at movies, and other activities. Until recently only Orthodox rabbis could perform marriages and approve divorces. In effect this allowed them alone to decide who was, and who was not, a Jew. Under a government ruling in 2001 the Interior Ministry would be responsible for recognizing and registering civil marriages involving Jews performed at consulates abroad. And in a further broadening of the Jewish identity issue, the Israeli Supreme Court ruled in March 2005, by a 7–4 vote, that non-Orthodox conversions to Judaism must

be recognized as legitimate by the state regardless of where they were, and are, performed. The case that triggered this decision was a civil action suit by some 14 converts in this category, one of them a Colombian who had emigrated to Israel in 1991 but was not able to convert there since he was non-Orthodox. He then went to Buenos Aires, where he converted to Reform Judaism in 1997. Upon returning to Israel, however, his conversion was not recognized, leading to the civil suit. The court's decision would set a precedent for some 250,000 Israelis whose religious status is currently "undefined" and will further limit Orthodox control of religious affairs. One of many recent court cases involving authority on conversion is to be decided in May 2010 by the High Court of Justice. The case stems from a petition filed by a convert to Judaism and her husband against the Rabbinate (state's official body in charge of religious matters) and "four city rabbis who . . . refused to grant marriage licenses to Israelis who converted to Judaism in Orthodox religious courts."[12]

Other issues separating the two communities include closing of roads near haredim neighborhoods on the Sabbath, and the government's refusal to recognize non-Orthodox Conservative, Reform, and Reconstruction Judaism as legitimately Jewish, for fear of offending the Orthodox community.

Rejection by Hamas of Israel's right to exist on "sacred Arab territory" as specified in its charter is matched to a large extent in Israel by the disagreement between the secular Jewish majority and the Orthodox minority over the nature of the state. After two millennia of marginalization as a people and the horrors of Auschwitz, the new Israel was expected to be in Ben Gurion's words, "a self-sufficient people, master of its own fate." But since its inception the state has been balanced precariously between secularism and a God-given covenant to ownership of a sacred homeland. A civil suit in 2004 brought before the Supreme Court by a group of Jewish and Arab intellectuals asks that both populations be defined officially as "Israeli." If and when the court issues its verdict, the result would be to replace religious affiliation ("Jewishness") by citizenship.

In September 2000 then-Prime Minister Barak proposed adding 3 basic laws to the canon as part of his "civil-social agenda." They covered due process of law, freedom of expression, and the public's right to education and housing. For various reasons they were never passed into law, and the Sharon government, dependent upon Orthodox support in the ruling coalition, made no effort to re-introduce them for consideration.

## THE INTIFADA

The Palestinian intifada in the West Bank and Gaza Strip, which began in December 1987, came as a rude shock to Israel. Coming as it did barely $2\frac{1}{2}$ years after the trauma of the Lebanon War, the uprising found the Israeli public as well as its citizen army unprepared. The military recall of middle-aged reservists and dispatch of new draftees to face stone-throwing Palestinian children created severe moral and psychological problems for many soldiers.

Military authorities devised a number of methods to deal with the uprising. They included deportation of suspected terrorists, demolition of houses, wholesale arrests, and detention of Palestinians without charges for indefinite periods. In February 2006 the government officially halted the practice of demolishing homes suspected of harboring Palestinian militants, after military leaders determined that demolitions were ineffective as deterrents. According to B'Tselem, the Israeli human rights organization, some 2,500 houses have been demolished since 1967. However, growing international criticism of the policy of "breaking the bones" of demonstrators (particularly children) developed by then-defense minister Yitzhak Rabin brought a change in tactics, with the use of rubber or plastic dum-dum bullets, whose effect is less lethal except at close range.

The government also tried to break the Palestinian resistance through arbitrary higher taxes, arguing that this was necessary to compensate for revenues lost due to refusal of Palestinians to pay taxes, a slowdown in business, and lowered exports to the territories. A value added tax (VAT) imposed on olive presses just prior to the processing of the West Bank's major crop was a particular hardship. Along with the brutality of its troops, the tax-collection methods drove Palestinians and Israelis further apart, making the prospect of any amicable relationship questionable.

The opening of emigration to Israel for Soviet Jews added an economic dimension to the intifada. Increased expropriation of land on the West Bank for new immigrant families, along with the expansion of Jewish settlements there, added to Palestinian resentment. Many Palestinians felt that because the new immigrants were unable to find professional employment, they were taking menial jobs ordinarily reserved for Palestinian workers in Israel.

In October 1990, the most serious incident since the start of the intifada occurred in Jerusalem. Palestinians stoned a Jewish group, the Temple Mount Faithful, who had come to lay a symbolic cornerstone for a new Jewish Temple near the Dome of the Rock. Israeli security forces then opened fire, killing some 20 Palestinians and injuring more than 100. The UN Security Council approved a resolution condemning Israel for excessive response (one of many that the Israeli state has ignored over the years). Israel appointed an official commission to investigate the killings. The commission exonerated the security forces, saying that they had acted in self-defense.

## Shamir's Election Plan

In May 1989, responding to threats by Labor to withdraw from the coalition and precipitate new elections, the government approved a plan drafted by Defense Minister Rabin for elections in the West Bank and Gaza as a prelude to "self-government." Under the plan, the Palestinians would elect one representative from each of 10 electoral districts to an Interim Council. The Council would then negotiate with Israeli representatives for autonomy for the West Bank and Gaza, as defined in the 1979 Camp David treaty. Negotiations on the final status of the territories would begin within three years of the signing of the autonomy agreement.

The implementation of the Rabin plan would have forced Israelis to decide between the Zionist ideal of "Eretz Israel" (the entire West Bank, along with the coast from Lebanon to Egypt, as the Jewish homeland) and the trading of "land for peace" with another nation struggling for its independence. The success of the intifada lay in demonstrating for Israelis the limits to the use of force against a population under occupation. It also served as a pointed reminder to Israelis that "incorporating the occupied territories would commit Israel to the perpetual use of its military to control and repress, not 'Arab refugees' but the whole Palestinian population living in these lands."

## THE PEACE AGREEMENT

Prior to September 1993, there were few indications that a momentous breakthrough in Palestinian–Israeli relations was about to take place. The new Labor government had cracked down on the Palestinians in the occupied territories harder than had its predecessor in six years of the intifada. In addition to mass arrests and deportations of persons allegedly associated with Hamas, the government sealed off the territories, not only from Israel itself but also from one another. With 120,000 Palestinians barred from their jobs in Israel, poverty, hunger, and unemployment became visible facts of life in the West Bank and the Gaza Strip.

However, what 11 rounds of peace talks, five wars, and 40 years of friction had failed to achieve was accomplished swiftly that September, with the signing of a peace and mutual-recognition accord between Israel and its long-time enemy. The accord was worked out in secret by Israeli and PLO negotiators in Norway and under Norwegian Foreign Ministry sponsorship. It provided for mutual recognition, transfer of authority over the Gaza Strip and the West Bank city of Jericho (but not the entire West Bank) to an elected Palestinian council that would supervise the establishment of Palestinian rule, withdrawal of Israeli forces and their replacement by a Palestinian police force, and a Palestinian state to be formed after a transitional period.

### ACHIEVEMENTS

In 2005 Israeli scientist Robert Aumann and U.S. Professor Thomas Schilling shared the Nobel Prize in Economics for their work on game theory. This theory explains the choices competitors make in situations that require strategic thinking. Aumann's model was the Oslo Accords between Israeli and Palestinian negotiators, in which he applied the theory to make "irrational" behavior understandable and rational. On the home front, Israel's success in attracting foreign investment in its booming economy was marked by U.S. millionaire investor Warren Buffett's acquisition of Iscar Metalworks, a world leader in precision metal-cutting tool production, and Donald Trump's development of as 70-story luxury residential building near Tel Aviv.

Opposition to the accord from within both societies was to be expected, given the intractable nature of Palestinian–Israeli differences—two peoples claiming the same land. Implementation of the Oslo agreements has been hampered from the start by groups opposed to any form of Palestinian–Israeli accommodation. On the Israeli side, some settler groups formed vigilante posses for defense, even setting up a "tent city" in Jerusalem to protest any giveaway of sacred Jewish land. Palestinian gunmen and suicide bombers responded with attacks on Jews, sometimes in alleyways or on lonely stretches of road outside the cities, but also in public places. One of the bloodiest incidents in this tragic vendetta was the killing of 29 Muslim worshippers in a mosque in Hebron by an American emigrant, an Orthodox Jew, during their Friday service.

Labor's return to power in 1992 suggested that, despite this virulent opposition, the peace process would go forward under its own momentum. The new government, headed by Rabin as prime minister and Peres as foreign minister, began to implement the disengagement of Israeli forces and the transfer of power over the territories to Yassir Arafat's Palestine National Authority (PNA). The Gaza Strip, Jericho, and several West Bank towns were turned over to PNA control. Israel's seeming commitment to the peace process at that time helped to improve relations with its Arab neighbors. The Arab boycott of Israeli goods and companies was lifted. In 1994, the country signed a formal peace treaty with Jordan and opened trade offices in several Gulf states.

## RABIN'S DEATH AND ITS CONSEQUENCES

The second stage in transfer of authority over the West Bank had barely begun when Rabin was assassinated by an Orthodox Jew while speaking at a Peace Now rally in Jerusalem on November 4, 1995. The assassination climaxed months of increasingly ugly anti-Rabin rhetoric orchestrated by Orthodox rabbis, settlers, and right-wing groups who charged the prime minister with giving away sacred Jewish land while gaining little in return. The assassin, Yigal Amir, stated in court that God had made him act, since the agreement with the Palestinians contradicted sacred Jewish religious principles. He stated: "According to *halacha* [Judaic tradition] a Jew who like Rabin gives over his people and his land to the enemy must be killed. My whole life I have been studying the *halacha* and I have all the data."[13]

Rabin's assassination marked a watershed in Israeli political life; for the first time an Israeli leader had been struck down by one of his own people. Amir's action was condemned abroad. Most secular Israelis regard it as a terrible and useless tragedy, and Israeli society as a whole has yet to come to terms with the murder of its most respected statesman. Unfortunately, many Orthodox Jews subscribed to Amir's stated belief that he had acted rightly to preserve the sacred homeland. Rabin's widow, Leah, continued to call Amir a traitor to his country until her own death in 2001, and she traveled throughout the world to promote the cause of Israeli–Palestinian coexistence. In August 2001, however, President Katsav pardoned Amir's co-conspirator Margalit Has-Sheft, who had been serving a nine-month jail term for complicity in the assassination. Amir's brother and others associated with his plot remain in prison, but the pardon re-exposed the deep fault lines in Israeli society that had emerged with Rabin's death.

After Rabin's death, Peres was confirmed as his successor by a 111–9 Knesset vote. However, he was defeated in the 1996 elections by the new Likud leader, Benjamin Netanyahu. It was Israel's first direct election for prime minister. Peres had hurt his cause by undertaking the ill-advised "Operation Grapes of Wrath" into Lebanon, which resulted in the deaths of many Lebanese civilians. The vote was close, a razor-thin margin of 50.3 percent for Netanyahu to 49.6 percent for Peres. However, Likud failed to win a majority of seats in the Knesset and was forced into another coalition with the religious parties. Labor actually won more seats than Likud (34 to 32), but support from Shas and the National Religious Party (20 seats) and the Russian-immigrant Yisrael Ba'Aliya party gave Netanyahu a narrow majority in the Knesset.

Netanyahu's victory, by a scant 16,000 votes, foreshadowed what would prove to be a near-total deadlock in the peace process. The deadlock was also marked by a deep and angry division within the Israeli society. Divisions have always been present in Jewish society, in the Diaspora as well as in modern Israel. God Himself described them as a "stiff-necked People" (in Exodus) and this cultural trait, honed over centuries, has certainly helped them to survive and preserve their separate identity as a people. But in the modern world it has set Haredim against Reform and Conservative Jewry, culminating in the murder of Yitzhak Rabin.

In contrast to the vision of Israel's founders of Jewish immigrants from many countries and cultures unified into a model democracy, Israeli society as it exists today would be better described as a land of contentious tribes, traceable back to Abraham's expulsion of Hagar and her son Ishmael (ancestor of the Arabs) in favor of Isaac and his descendants. In addition to not honoring the Oslo agreements, Netanyahu encouraged increased Jewish settlements in the West Bank and Gaza. He used his office to cultivate various groups and parties at the expense of other groups, changing sides when it suited him. A Labor Party official observed before the 1999 election that Israeli elections are more anthropology than politics; the nation does not have a democratic "pendulum" that swings voters away from a leader en masse when his policies seem to be failing.

Elections for the office of prime minister were scheduled for 2000, but Netanyahu advanced them by a year to preempt increasing opposition to his policies. However, his principal rival, retired general Ehud Barak, defeated him handily in the election, and Netanyahu gave up his seat in the Knesset and retired to private life. After the fall of Barak's government in late 2000, Netanyahu expressed the desire to return to politics. Barak's successor, Ariel Sharon made him Foreign Minister and then Finance Minister. In March he recaptured the office of Prime Minister.

Barak was forced to form a coalition of several parties in order to retain support for his peace initiatives with the Palestinians. In return for Shas's support, the party was granted four ministerial portfolios, including that of the powerful Interior Ministry. Shas leaders then demanded more concessions; they included $36 million to bail out its bankrupt religious-schools system, as well as debt relief and tax exemptions for the party's social services. When these demands were rejected, Shas pulled out of the coalition. (Earlier, its leader, Rabbi Aryeh Deri, had been convicted of fraud, bribery, and misuse of public power while he was a cabinet minister. He was given a three-year jail sentence).

Although the president's office in Israel is largely ceremonial, it has usually been held by a distinguished former leader and serves as a symbol of national unity. The last two presidents have been forced to resign due to their misuse of public power; Weizman for accepting unreported cash gifts and Katsav for sexual misconduct and obstruction of justice.

Ariel Sharon's well-publicized visit on September 28, 2000, to the Dome of the Rock not only set off a new Palestinian intifada; it also had a direct impact on the muddled Israeli political system. The collapse of Barak's coalition left him in the awkward position of negotiating a settlement with the Palestinians without the support of the Knesset or of his own people, particularly the latter, since the negotiations involved territorial concessions. With Netanyahu not being able to run because he was not a member of the Knesset at that time, Barak faced an uphill battle against former Defense Minister Ariel Sharon who won with a huge margin on February 6, 2001.

The new prime minister took office amid foreboding on the part of many Israelis, as well as by the country's Arab neighbors and the world at large. Noting Sharon's record, which includes masterminding the 1982 invasion of Lebanon and ultimate responsibility for the slaughter of Palestinians by Israel's Christian allies in Lebanese refugee camps, one author suggested that his election "looked like appointing the village pyromaniac to head its fire brigade."[14] In 2001, survivors of the families killed at the camps filed suit against him in a Belgian court, under the new international statute allowing for prosecution of national leaders for war crimes and genocide.

Sharon's first year in office coincided with the renewal of the Palestinian intifada, which has brought Israel and the Palestinians into a head-on conflict verging on total war. The accelerated cycle of violence was marked by new tactics on both sides—relentless suicide bombings by Palestinians, mostly against Israeli civilians, and use of massive retaliation by Israeli tanks, missiles, and helicopter gunships. The first Israeli government official was killed in November, and since then Israel embarked on a policy of targeting Palestinians suspected of leading the violence. The death toll and the destruction had traumatic impact on the two societies.

By 2004 the violence had not only reached unprecedented levels but was increasingly dividing government from people. There was even opposition within the military. In January a military court sentenced five "refuseniks" to one-year jail terms for refusing to serve in the West Bank. Earlier, 27 Air Force pilots had refused to attack civilian areas there; they were joined by reservists from the elite Sayeret Matkal unit of the IDF. On the official side, several former heads of Shin Bet, the Israeli security service, publicly denounced the government's repressive measures. Some government officials spoke openly of the need for unilateral withdrawal from the occupied territories.

The personal hostility between Sharon and the late Yassir Arafat did little to move the peace process forward. In December 2001 Sharon declared that Arafat was "irrelevant" and Israeli forces blockaded his Ramallah headquarters. For the rest of his life Arafat remained essentially under house arrest. In September 2004, with Israel permission (under U.S. and European pressure) he was airlifted to a French military hospital. He died there on November 11, probably of a stroke brought on by a blood disorder, disseminated intravascular coagulation (D.I.C.) which had never been controlled. However, some people suspected that he was poisoned.

With Arafat's death Sharon was able to proceed with a policy of staged withdrawal from the occupied territories, beginning with the Gaza Strip. Withdrawal was completed in 2005 despite a furious outcry from the settler population there. Next the "old warrior" broke with Likud to form his own party, Kadima. After Sharon's re-election as prime minister and the dominance of his new party, expectations rose that withdrawal would be extended to the West Bank. But in the high noon of

his success, Sharon was felled by a heart attack, followed by a second, that have left him immobile and in a coma ever since.

Sharon was succeeded, on a temporary basis, pending new elections, by his deputy Ehud Olmert, and his protégé Tzvi Lipni was elevated to foreign minister. What has become in essence a new generation of untried leaders, lacking the prestige or grand effectiveness of their predecessors, is now in charge in Israel.

Following parliamentary elections in March 2006, in which Olmert's Kadima party won the largest number of seats, though not a majority, (Sharon was declared permanently incapacitated on April 14, 2006), the Interim prime minister formed a new coalition government and was approved on May 4 by the Knesset as Prime Minister. Olmert's tenure in office was marred by problems, including charges of corruption going back to when he was mayor of Jerusalem and a disastrous war against Hezbollah in Lebanon. As for the corruption charges, Olmert's trial began in 2009 and continued in 2010.

## The 2006 War with Hezbollah

The decision to invade Lebanon on July 14, 2006 came after persistent Hezbollah rocket attacks on Northern Israel and incursion into the Israeli side of the border fence, killing three soldiers and abducting two others. Israel's aim in what became known as the "Hezbollah War" or "the Second Lebanon War," was to put an end to the rocket attacks by destroying much of Hezbollah's military capability. Hezbollah, through its rocket attacks, sought the return of all remaining Lebanese territory (Shebaa Farms) still controlled by Israel and the release of all Lebanese prisoners. Olmert's government responded with the widescale bombardments, a ground invasion, and an air and naval blockade on Lebanon. In the 34-day war, Hezbollah engaged the Israeli ground forces while still firing rockets into Israel. The Israeli casualties included 118 Israeli soldiers and 43 Israeli civilians dead; while around 1,000 Lebanese—mostly civilians—died along with 500 Hezbollah fighters. Around some 300,000 Israeli and 1 million Lebanese civilians were temporarily displaced by the conflict and most of Lebanon's infrastructure—electricity and water plants, roads and bridges—were heavily damaged by Israel's bombs.

While the war ended with a stalemate, Hezbollah claimed victory based on its ability to not only survive the Israeli air and ground assault, but also to inflict significant damage on the Israeli Defense Forces. In the end, and while Hezbollah's political stature in Lebanon and in the

whole region increased tremendously, the Olmert government and its high military officers were fiercely criticized for having rushed into war and for causing harm to so many Lebanese civilians. The political fallout in Israel further discredited the Olmert leadership.

## The Offensive on Gaza

Less than two years after the failed invasion of Lebanon, Israel engaged in yet another military offensive, code named "Operation Cast Lead," with far worse consequences. On December 27, 2008, it started a major military offensive against Gaza with the aim of stopping the firing of Palestinian rockets into its territory. The 22 day deadly and destructive assault, which faced almost no Palestinian resistance, caused the death of 1,400 Palestinians (mostly civilians) and 13 Israelis. The offensive, which lasted until January 18, 2009, caused major material damage, including the destruction of thousands of homes, hundreds of industrial properties, 200 schools, 39 mosques and two churches. The already precarious living condition of the Palestinians in Gaza turned into an instant humanitarian crisis as people were deprived of basic living necessities such as clean water, food, and various services. In spite of its claim of legitimate defense, Israel was widely criticized for this particularly violent offensive and a UN investigation began into probable war crimes committed by the Israeli army. According to the report of a fact finding mission led by South African judge Richard J. Goldstone, the Israeli army unlawfully used some weapons such as phosphorus bombs and killed unarmed civilians.[15] A group of Israeli soldiers who took part in the assault declared in a report in July 2009 that their army had committed widespread abuses against Palestinian civilians.[16] Following the offensive, a tightening of Israel's blockade on Gaza contributed to rapidly deteriorating social and economic conditions throughout the strip.

## THE ECONOMY

In terms of national income and economic and industrial development, Israel is ahead of a number of Middle Eastern states that have greater natural resources. Agriculture is highly developed; Israeli engineers and hydrologists have been very successful in developing new irrigation and planting methods that not only "make the desert bloom" but also are exported to other countries under the country's technical-aid program.

In Israel water usage is as much a political problem as it is economic. The

187,000 Jewish settlers in the West Bank use 76 gallons of water per day per capita, leaving the much larger Palestinian population 18.5 gallons daily, below WHO minimum health and sanitation standards. The Dead Sea, a vital water resource not only for Israel but also for Jordan, has shrunk from 50 miles wide in 1950 to 30 miles today, with its water level dropping 3 feet yearly. Israel's diversion of the Jordan River, its main recharge source, into a national water carrier pipeline in 2004, has lowered Dead Sea water input from 160 billion gallons annually to 16 billion, insufficient to maintain it at its present size. Hydrologists agree that given the influence of the agricultural lobby in Israel and demands of the settler population the Dead Sea's prospects for recovery are bleak. Even the tourist industry has been affected. Elegant resorts like Ein Gedi, formerly located at waterside, are now a mile inland. It is an crisis compounded by urban congestion and high pollution levels. Unfortunately, the higher priority placed on security and national defense has left these long-term economic issues unresolved.

The cutting and export of diamonds and other gemstones is a small but important industry. Since 1996, exports of rough diamonds from the Ramat Gan diamond exchange have increased 80 percent, from $5.2 billion to $9.8 billion. The aircraft industry is the largest industrial sector but it has fallen on hard times. The national airline, El Al, which began its existence with the founding of the state, was restructured as a public enterprise in 1982 by the Begin government. It continued to lose money, in part due to high operating costs and unique security arrangements. A $600 million upgrade in equipment enabled the company to expand its flights, and in 1998, it showed a modest $25 million profit. In 2001, the high-speed wireless companies BreezeCom and Floware merged to form a single company capitalized at $330 million.

In January 2001, Israel signed an agreement with Egypt to import $3 billion in natural gas annually until 2012. Despite angry Egyptian criticism of Israel's policies toward the Palestinians, Egypt remained committed to the sale, which began in June 2003.

An added boost for the Israeli economy was the discovery recently of large natural-gas deposits offshore near the Gaza Strip. Development of these resources will help meet Israel's chronic freshwater shortages by providing energy for desalination plants near Tel Aviv.

The Israel-based Solel Solar Systems currently produces 50 kilowatts annually of solar power, meeting 80 percent of the country's power needs in hotels, hospitals, and other public buildings. Thus far, it is the only solar power system in the world that generates electricity from conventional turbines.

In 2001, Israel successfully tested its Arrow II ABM missile which can intercept and destroy an incoming enemy missile. Although Israel's nuclear capability remains a closely-guarded secret, its stockpile is estimated to contain between 200 and 500 neutron bombs and small nuclear bombs. Also, the Israeli Navy has 3 missile-equipped submarines.

## Timeline: PAST

**1897**
The Zionist movement is organized by Theodor Herzel

**1917**
The Balfour Declaration

**1922–1948**
British mandate over Palestine

**1947–1948**
A UN partition plan is accepted by the Jewish community; following British withdrawal, the State of Israel is proclaimed

**1949**
Armistices are signed with certain Arab states, through U.S. mediation

**1967**
The Six-Day War; Israeli occupation of East Jerusalem, the Gaza Strip, and the Sinai Peninsula

**1973**
Yom Kippur War

**1979**
Peace treaty with Egypt

**1980s**
The Israeli invasion of Lebanon

**1990s**
Israeli–Palestinian efforts toward peace; violence escalates on both sides in response; Prime Minister Yitzhak Rabin is assassinated

## PRESENT

**2000s**
Arafat's death and Sharon's incapacity have left Palestinian-Israeli peace prospects suspended. Although Israel has withdrawn from Gaza, border controls and frequent incursions plus the "security Wall" woven around Palestinian land limits Palestinian economic development and social unity. The 34-day war in 2006 between the IDF and Hezbollah in Lebanon, ending in stalemate, has seriously undermined Israeli confidence in the future of the state

The Israeli economy has been strengthened through the success of its high-technology companies, many of which are subsidiaries of U.S. firms like Net Manage and Geotek Communications. Its cadre of army-trained computer experts and skilled Russian emigrés made the country second to the United States in the number of start-up companies in the 1990s.

After the Israeli economy started picking up following a crisis in the early 1980s, the intifada, with its consequent loss of confidence on the part of foreign investors, led to a major recession in 2002. Exports dropped by 10 percent and both inflation and unemployment rates rose dramatically. In April 2003 Finance Minister Binyamin Netanyahu introduced a program of drastic measures to reduce the budget deficit and stabilize the economy. They included a wage freeze for public employees, higher pension premiums and dismissal of several thousand workers.

In 2004, under Netanyahu's economic reform program, the Knesset approved a major reform of capital markets which required banks to sell their provident and mutual funds and reduce their insurance company holdings by 10 percent. The reform package aimed also to privatize Bank Leumi, the country's largest.

The 2008–09 global financial crisis affected the Israeli economy only marginality—a brief recession. This was due past liberalization reforms and a prudent fiscal policy. As a result, the banking system proved resilient and the economy began recovering quickly. Israel's GDP grew by 0.5% in 2009, down 4% in 2008, but is expected to expand in 2010. The effect of global economic crisis was mostly a reduced demand in the United States and EU for Israel's exports (45% of the GDP). Just like other countries, the Israeli Government responded with a set of emergency policies, including a monetary stimulus package and a reduction of interest rates. The latter were increased in the summer of 2009 due to inflationary pressure at a time when the economy began to recover.

### Politics Trumps Economics

Israel's per capita income is near $30,000 a year, which is higher than, or close to, that of many developed countries, and life expectancy, 80 years, is among the highest in the world. The country has come out almost unaffected by the 2008–2009 global financial crisis, and the prospects for resuming a healthy growth rate are good. Contrary to the positive condition and outlook of the economy, the political atmosphere in early 2010 appeared gloomy and worrisome in Israel. Many Israelis are worried about several things. In an article about the celebration of Israel's 62nd year of existence, Ethan Bronner wrote that while there is nothing unusual about the celebration, "there is something about the mood this year that feels darker than usual. It has a bipartisan quality to it. Both left and right are troubled."[17]

Many important, non-economic, issues are making many Israeli worry these days. There are the usual disputes among the political elite over procedural and substantive issues, some of which are about peace and security with the Palestinians and the Arab neighbors. There is what is perceived as Iran's intention to develop nuclear weapons and to use them to destroy Israel. There is also the Palestinian problem itself, which is an existential issue to both societies which have not been able escape the stalemate in which they find themselves nowadays. There is yet another cause of distress: America appears to have lost patience with their government's persistence in building illegal settlements on occupied Palestinian land and avoidance of negotiations with the Palestinians for a permanent solution. The urgency of such negotiations was expressed by President Barak Obama when he stated in early 2010 that the Israeli-Palestinian problem constitutes a security threat to the United States; the statement came in the wake of Prime Minister Netanyahu's refusal to halt the construction of a housing project in the Palestinian part of Jerusalem. This change of tone was felt in Israel as an earthquake in the otherwise solid bilateral relations. Moreover, there is the moral and political backlash of Israel's 2008 offensive against Gaza which damaged Israel's prestige in the West and elsewhere. All of these issue and events seem to put pressure on the government of Netanyahu to do something to alleviate the malaise;

that may include resuming negotiations with the Palestinians, halting indefinitely the building of new Jewish housing in East Jerusalem and the West Bank, and doing something to dispel the effects of the incriminating Goldstone report on the Gaza offensive.

## NOTES

1. Sasha Polakow-Suransky, "Who Killed Camp David? Middle East Negotiator Dennis Ross Says There's Plenty Of Blame To Go Around," *The American Prospect,* September 19, 2004, online at www.prospect.org/cs/articles?article=who_killed_camp_david. Consulted on April 22, 2010.

2. Dan V. Segre, *A Crisis of Identity: Israel and Zionism* (Oxford, England: Oxford University Press, 1980), p. 25.

3. Quoted in Ilene Prusher, "An Israeli Arab's Troubles Mirror Woes of Dual Identity," *Christian Science Monitor,* April 26, 2007. Due to these stresses Bishara resigned from the Knesset in April and left the country. As yet he has not returned. As Palestinian journalist Mamoun al-Huseini noted, "His case summarizes the huge rift between the Israeli vision and the reality, between its vision of solving the Arab-Israeli conflict and the Arab minority's demand for national, social, and political rights."

4. Quoted in Laura King, "Israel evacuates Bedouins from Gaza village," *Los Angeles Times,* August 30, 2005. Online at www.staugustine.com/stories/083005/wor_3293472.shtml. Consulted on April 22, 2010.

5. Yaron Ezrahi, *Rubber Bullets: Power and Conscience in Modern Israel* (New York: Farrar, Straus & Giroux, 1997), p. 269.

6. Theodor Herzl, *The Jewish State,* (Minneapolis, MN: Filiquarian Publishing, LLC., 2006), p. 8.

7. The text is in "Documents on Palestine," in *The Middle East and North Africa* (London: Europa Publications, 1984), p. 58.

8. Yossi Katz, quoted in "Kibbutz: Collectivist Vision Dims in Modern Era," *Christian Science Monitor,* March 1, 2007.

9. Abu Iyad with Eric Rouleau, *My Home, My Land: A Narrative of the Palestinian Struggle,* Linda Butler Koseoglu, tr. (New York: New York Times Books, 1981), pp. 225–226.

10. Liel Kyzer, "Olmert denies charges against him in double-billing affair," Haaretz, March 20, 2010. Online at www.haaretz.com/hasen/spages/1159147.html. Consulted on April 30, 2010. See also "Olmert denies bribery allegations," Reuter, April 15, 2010. Online at www.reuters.com/article/idUSTRE63E43R20100415. Consulted on May 1, 2010.

11. Mark Landler and Helene Cooper, "Obama Speech Signals a U.S. Shift on Middle East," *New York Times,* April 14, 2010. Online at www.nytimes.com/2010/04/15/world/middleeast/15mideast.html. Consulted on May 1, 2010.

12. Jonah Mandel, "Rabbinate Torn Between State, Halacha," *The Jerusalem Post,* April 26, 2010. Online at www.jpost.com/Home/Article.aspx?id=173934. Consulted on May 1, 2010.

13. Yigal Amir, quoted in Amos Elon, *A Blood-Dimmed Tide: Dispatches from the Middle East* (New York: Columbia University Press, 1998, p. 306.

14. Avishai Margalit, "The Middle East: Snakes & Ladders," *The New York Review of Books,* May 17, 2001. Online at www.nybooks.com/articles/archives/2001/may/17/the-middle-east-snakes-ladders/?pagination=false. Consulted on May 1, 2010.

15. Richard J. Goldstone, "Human Rights In Palestine and Other Occupied Arab Territories, Report of the United Nations Fact Finding Mission on the Gaza Conflict." Online at www2.ohchr.org/english/bodies/hrcouncil/specialsession/9/docs/UNFFMGC_Report.pdf

16. "Israel Soldiers Speak Out On Gaza," BBC, July 15, 2009. Online at http://news.bbc.co.uk/2/hi/middle_east/8149464.stm. Consulted on August 10, 2009.

17. Ethan Bronner, "Mood Is Dark as Israel Marks 62nd Year as a Nation," *New York Times,* April 19, 2010. Online at www.nytimes.com/2010/04/20/world/middleeast/20israel.html. Consulted on April 21, 2010.

# Jordan (Hashimite Kingdom of Jordan)

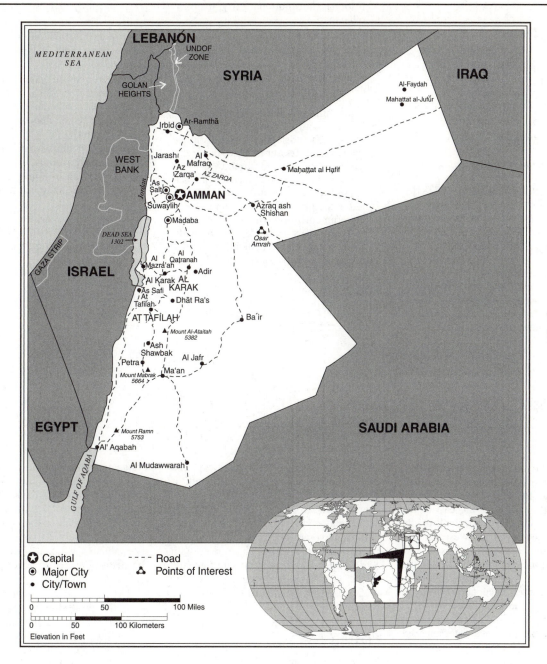

# Jordan Statistics

## GEOGRAPHY

*Area in Square Miles (Kilometers):* 35,000 (92,300) about the size of Indiana
*Capital (Population):* Amman (483,000)
*Environmental Concerns:* limited natural freshwater reserves; deforestation; overgrazing; soil erosion; desertification
*Geographical Features:* mostly desert plateau in the east; a highland area in the west; the Great Rift Valley separates the east and west banks of the Jordan River
*Climate:* mostly arid desert; a rainy season in the west

## PEOPLE

### Population

*Total:* 6,407,085
*Annual Growth Rate:* 2.159%
*Rural/Urban Population Ratio:* 28/72

*Major Languages:* Arabic; English widely understood
*Ethnic Makeup:* 98% Arab; 1% Circassian; 1% Armenian
*Religions:* 92% Sunni Muslim; 8% Christian and others

### Health

*Life Expectancy at Birth:* 78 years (male); 81 years (female)
*Infant Mortality Rate (Ratio):* 17.03/1,000 live births

### Education

*Adult Literacy Rate:* 91.3%
*Compulsory (Ages):* 6–16; free

## COMMUNICATION

*Telephones:* 503,000 main lines
*Daily Newspaper Circulation:* 62 per
  1,000 people
*Televisions:* 176 per 1,000
*Internet Users:* 1.5 million (2008)

## TRANSPORTATION

*Highways in Miles (Kilometers):* 4,968
  (8,000)
*Railroads in Miles (Kilometers):* 507 (816)
*Usable Airfields:* 18
*Motor Vehicles in Use:* 265,000

## GOVERNMENT

*Type:* constitutional monarchy
*Independence Date:* May 25, 1946 (from
  League of Nations mandate)
*Head of State/Government:* King Abdullah
  II; Prime Minister Marouf al-Bakhit

*Political Parties:* Al-Umma (Nation)
  Party; Jordanian Democratic Popular
  Unity Party; Islamic Action Front;
  National Constitutional Party; many
  others
*Suffrage:* universal at 18

## MILITARY

*Military Expenditures (% of GDP):* 8.6%
*Current Disputes:* Jordan has accepted
  some million Iraqis fleeing the war
  in that country although it generally
  recognizes and supports its constituted
  government. Closer at hand, the
  deteriorating situation in the West
  Bank and the Hamas takeover in Gaza
  caused Jordan to restore financial
  aid to the Fatah-led Palestinian
  government-in-process in 2007. And
  in 2005 a 30-year border dispute with
  Syria was resolved with a land swap
  along with the present border.

## ECONOMY

*Currency ($U.S. Equivalent):* 0.709
  dinar = $1 (fixed rate)

*Per Capita Income/GDP:* $4,900/$28.89
  billion
*GDP Growth Rate:* 3.1%
*Unemployment Rate:* officially 15%; more
  likely 25%–30%
*Labor Force:* 1.667 million
*Natural Resources:* phosphates; potash;
  shale oil
*Agriculture:* wheat; barley; fruits;
  tomatoes; olives; livestock
*Industry:* phosphate mining; petroleum
  refining; cement; potash; light
  manufacturing
*Exports:* $6.989 billion (primary partners
  India, United States, Iraq)
*Imports:* $12.31 billion (primary
  partners Germany, Saudi Arabia,
  China)

## SUGGESTED WEB SITES

http://lcweb2.loc.gov/frd/cs/
  jotoc.html
www.odci.gov/cia/publications/
  factbook/index.html

# Jordan Country Report

The Hashimite Kingdom of Jordan (previously called Transjordan) is a small country which formerly consisted of two regions: the East Bank (lying east of the Jordan River) and the West Bank of the Jordan. Israel occupied the West Bank in June 1967. In 1988, King Hussein formally severed the relationship, leaving the West Bank to the Palestinians even though it was under Israeli occupation. Between 1948 and 1967, Jordanian-occupied territory also included the old city of Jerusalem (East Jerusalem), which was later annexed by Israel.

Modern Jordan is the result of historical forces and events that shaped the Middle East in the twentieth century. It used to be known as the land east of the Jordan River, a region of diverse peoples, some nomadic, others sedentary farmers and herders. Jordan's current neighbors are Iraq, Syria, Saudi Arabia, and Israel. Their joint borders were all established by the British after World War I, when Britain and France divided the territories of the defeated Ottoman Empire between them.

The Jordan-Israel Peace Treaty of 1994 has resulted in a redrafting of borders.

Israel returned 340 square miles captured in 1967 in the Arava Valley and south of the Galilee to Jordanian control. However, Israeli *kibbutzim* (communal farm settlements) will be allowed to continue cultivating some 750 acres in the territory under a 25-year lease. The border with Syria, which had been in dispute since the 1970s, was formally demarcated in 2005 with exchanges of land on both sides of the present border.

## HISTORY

The territory of modern Jordan was ruled by outside powers until it became an independent country in the twentieth century. Under the Ottoman Empire, it was part of the province of Syria. The Ottoman authorities in Syria occasionally sent military patrols across the Jordan River to "show the flag" and collect taxes, but otherwise they left the people of the area to manage their own affairs.[1]

This tranquil existence ended with World War I. The Ottomans were defeated and their provinces were divided into protectorates, called mandates, set up by the League of Nations and assigned to Britain and/or

France to administer and prepare for eventual self-government. The British received a mandate over Palestine and extended its territory to include Transjordan east of the River Jordan. Due to their commitment to help Jews dispersed throughout the world to establish a national home in Palestine, the British decided to govern Transjordan as a separate mandate.

The terms of the mandate system required the protecting power to appoint a native ruler. During the war, the British worked with Sharif Husayn to organize an Arab revolt against the Ottomans. Hussein bin Ali, Sharif of Mecca, who ruled over the northern Hejaz region of the Arabian Peninsula, was promised in 1916, by the British, a homeland for the Arabs if he helped foment an Arab revolt against the Ottomans. The revolt, which was led by two of the Sharif's sons, Faisal and Abdullah, did not succeed. After World War I, Faisal was crowned, in 1918, by the Syrian National Congress as King of Syria. However, after France obtained, in 1920, a League of Nations mandate over Syria, he was expelled by its forces, and in August 1921, the British made him king of Iraq. When Faisal's brother, Abdullah, decided to enter

(© The McGraw-Hill Companies/Barry (Barker, photographer))

Exterior of the eroded façade of sandstone ruins in Petra, Jordan

Transjordan with his troops with the plan to wrestle Syria back from the French, the British, who feared a conflict with France over Syria and maybe Palestine, decided to make Abdullah governor of Transjordan as a separate entity from the Palestine mandate. The incidental Hashemite Kingdom of Jordan was thus born. He later negotiated with the British Transjordan's independence and on May 25, 1946, the independent Hashemite Kingdom of Transjordan (renamed Jordan in 1949) was proclaimed.

## EMIR ABDULLAH

Through his father, Abdullah traced his lineage back to the Hashim family of Mecca, the clan to which the Prophet Muhammad belonged. This ancestry gave him a great deal of prestige in the Arab world, particularly among the nomads of Transjordan. Abdullah used the connection assiduously to build a solid base of support among his kinspeople.

Abdullah's new country was a peaceful, quiet place, consisting entirely of what is today the East Bank of the Jordan River,

with vaguely defined borders across the desert. The population was about 400,000, mostly peasants and nomads; the capital, Amman, was little more than a large village spread over some Roman ruins.

During the period of the mandate (1921–1946), Abdullah was advised by resident British officials. The British helped him draft a constitution in 1928, and Transjordan became independent in everything except financial policy and foreign relations. But Emir Abdullah and his advisers ran the country like a private club. In traditional Arab desert fashion, Abdullah held a public meeting outside his palace every Friday; anyone who wished could come and present a complaint or petition to the emir.

Abdullah did not trust political parties or institutions such as a parliament, but he agreed to issue the 1928 Constitution as a step toward eventual self-government. He also laid the basis for a regular army. A British Army officer, John Bagot Glubb, was appointed in 1930 to train the Transjordanian Frontier Force to curb Bedouin raiding across the country's borders. Under

Glubb's command, this frontier force eventually became the Arab Legion; during Emir Abdullah's last years, it played a vital role not only in defending the kingdom against the forces of the new State of Israel but also in enlarging Jordanian territory by the capture of the West Bank and East Jerusalem.[2]

When Jordan gained independence in 1946, it was not vastly different from the tranquil emirate of the 1920s. However, events beyond its borders soon overwhelmed it, like the dust storm rolling in from the desert that sweeps everything before it. The conflict between the Arab and Jewish communities in neighboring Palestine had become so intense and unmanageable that the British decided to terminate their mandate. They turned the problem over to the United Nations. In November 1947, the UN General Assembly voted to partition Palestine into separate Arab and Jewish states, with Jerusalem to be an international city under UN administration.

The partition plan was not accepted by the Palestine Arabs, and as British forces evacuated Palestine in 1947–1948, they prepared to fight the Jews for possession of all of Palestine. The State of Israel was proclaimed in 1948. Armies of the neighboring Arab states, including Jordan, immediately invaded Palestine. But they were poorly armed and trained. Only the Jordanian Arab Legion performed well. The Legion's forces seized the West Bank, originally part of the territory allotted to a projected Palestinian Arab state by the United Nations. The Legion also occupied the Old City of Jerusalem (East Jerusalem). Subsequently, Abdullah annexed both territories.

## DEVELOPMENT

Continued budgetary deficits, the interruption of trade with Iraq, the global economic slowdown, and a sharp fall in foreign assistance in 2009, have hampered economic growth and the alleviation of highs rates of poverty (over 14%) and unemployment (13%). Recent reforms have included the liberalization of trade, the privatization of state-owned companies, and the elimination of fuel subsidies. These reforms have generated some economic growth, attracted foreign investment and created some jobs. However, more needs to be done. One plan is to develop nuclear power generation in order to diminish dependency on costly foreign oil and gas.

Jordan became a vastly different state. Its population tripled with the addition of half a million West Bank Arabs and half a million Arab refugees from Israel. Abdullah still did not trust the democratic process, but he realized that he would have to take firm action to strengthen Jordan and to help the dispossessed Palestinians who now found themselves reluctantly included in his kingdom. He approved a new Constitution, one that provided for a bicameral Legislature, with an appointed Senate and an elected House of Representatives. He appointed prominent Palestinians to his cabinet. A number of Palestinians were appointed to the Senate; others were elected to the House of Representatives.

On July 20, 1951, King Abdullah was assassinated as he entered the Al Aqsa Mosque in East Jerusalem for Friday prayers. His grandson Hussein was at his side and narrowly escaped death. Abdullah's murderer, who was killed immediately by royal guards, was a Palestinian. Many Palestinians felt that Abdullah had betrayed them by annexing the West Bank and because he was thought to have carried on secret peace negotiations with the Israelis (recent evidence suggests that he did so). In his *Memoirs,* King Abdullah

wrote, "The paralysis of the Arabs lies in their present moral character. They are obsessed with tradition and concerned only with profit and the display of oratorical patriotism."[3]

Abdullah dealt with the Zionists because he despaired of Arab leadership. Ironically, Abdullah's proposal to Britain in 1938 for a unified Arab-Jewish Palestine linked with Jordan, if it had been accepted, would have avoided five wars and hundreds of thousands of casualties. Yet this same proposal forms the basis for discussion of the Palestinian-Israeli settlement in recent years.[4]

## KING HUSSEIN

Abdullah's son Crown Prince Talal succeeded to the throne. He suffered from mental illness (probably schizophrenia) and had spent most of his life in mental hospitals. When his condition worsened, advisers convinced him to abdicate in favor of his eldest son, Hussein.

At the time of his death from cancer in February 1999, Hussein had ruled Jordan for 46 years, since 1953—the longest reign of any Middle Eastern monarch and one of the longest in the world in the twentieth century. To a great extent he *was* Jordan, developing a small desert territory with no previous national identity into a modern state.

During his long reign, Hussein faced and overcame many crises and challenges to his rule. These crises stemmed mainly from Jordan's involvement in the larger Arab-Israeli conflict. Elections for the Jordanian Parliament in 1956 resulted in the election of a majority of West Bank Palestinian candidates. Controversy developed as these representatives pressed the king to declare his all-out support for the Palestinian cause. At one point, the rumor spread that he had been killed. Hussein immediately jumped into a jeep and rode out to the main Arab Legion base at Zerqa, near Amman. He then presented himself to the troops to prove that he was still alive and in command.[5]

The "Zerqa incident" illustrated Hussein's fine sense of timing, undertaking bold actions designed to throw real or potential enemies off balance. It also emphasized the importance of army support for the monarchy. The majority of the Arab Legion's soldiers came from Bedouin tribes, and for them, loyalty to the crown has always been automatic and unfailing.

Other challenges followed. Syrian fighters tried to shoot down King Hussein's plane in 1958, and Communists and Palestinian leaders plotted his overthrow.

The June 1967 Six-Day War produced another crisis in Jordan. Israeli forces

## FREEDOM

The National Charter guarantees full civil and other rights to all Jordanians. In practice, however, press freedom, political activity, and other rights are often circumscribed. In 2002, Queen Noor roused a storm of criticism with a decree giving Jordanian women the same rights as men in passing their nationality on to their children. The Bedouins, traditionally the monarchy's strongest supporters, objected that the decree would give citizenship to stateless Palestinians born to Palestinian-Jordanian mothers, making Palestinians the majority of Jordan's citizens. However, a few days later, the government amended the decree so that there will be no automatic right of naturalization. Beyond this problem, Freedom House finds that "Jordanian women enjoy equal rights with respect to their entitlement to health care, education, political participation, and employment."

occupied 10 percent of Jordanian territory, including half of its best agricultural lands. The Jordanian Army suffered 6,000 casualties, most of them in a desperate struggle to hold the Old City of Jerusalem against Israeli attack. Nearly 300,000 more Palestinian refugees from the West Bank fled into Jordan. To complicate things further, guerrillas from the Palestine Liberation Organization, formerly based in the West Bank, made Jordan its new base for the continued struggle against Israel. Its leaders talked openly of removing the monarchy.

By 1970, Hussein and the PLO were headed toward open confrontation. The guerrillas had the sympathy of the population, and successes in one or two minor clashes with Israeli troops had made them arrogant. They swaggered through the streets of Amman, directing traffic at intersections and stopping pedestrians to examine their identity papers. Army officers complained to King Hussein that the PLO was really running the country. The king became convinced that unless he moved against the guerrillas, his throne would be in danger. He declared martial law and ordered the army to move against them.

The ensuing war lasted until July 1971, but in the PLO annals, it is usually referred to as "Black September," because of its starting date and because it ended in disaster for the guerrillas. Their bases were dismantled, and most of the guerrillas were driven from Jordan. The majority went to Lebanon, where they reorganized. In time they became as powerful there as they had been in Jordan.

For the remainder of his reign, there were no serious internal threats to King

Hussein's rule. Jordan shared in the general economic boom in the Arab world that developed as a result of the enormous price increases in oil after the 1973 Arab-Israeli War and the oil embargo on the supporters of Israel during that war. As a consequence, Hussein was able to turn his attention to the development of his country. Like his grandfather, he did not entirely trust political parties or elected legislatures, and he was leery of the Palestinians' intentions toward him. He was also convinced that Jordan, rather than the PLO, should be the natural representative of the Palestinians. But he realized that in order to represent them effectively and to build the kind of Jordanian state that he could safely hand over to his successors, he would need to develop popular support in addition to that of the army. Accordingly, Hussein set up a National Consultative Council in 1978, in what he called an interim step toward democracy. The Council had a majority of Palestinians (those living on the East Bank) as members.

Hussein's unilateral separation of Jordan from the West Bank has had important implications for internal politics in the kingdom. It enabled the king to proceed with political reforms without the need to involve the Palestinian population there. The timetable was accelerated by nationwide protests in 1989 over price increases for basic commodities. The protests turned swiftly to violence, resulting in the most serious riots in national history. Prime Minister Zaid Rifai was dismissed; he was held personally responsible for the increases and for the country's severe financial problems, although these were due equally to external factors. King Hussein appointed a caretaker government, headed by his cousin, to oversee the transitional period before national elections for the long-promised lower chamber of the Legislature.

In 1990, the king and leaders of the major opposition organization, the Jordanian National Democratic Alliance (JANDA), signed a historic National Charter, which provides for a multiparty political system. Elections were set under the Charter for an 80-member House of Representatives. Nine seats would be reserved for Christians and three for Circassians, an ethnic Muslim minority originally from the Caucasus.

In 1992, Hussein ended martial law, which had been in effect since 1970. Henceforth, security crimes such as espionage would be dealt with by state civilian-security courts. New laws also undergirded constitutional rights such as a free press, free speech, and the right of public assembly.

With political parties legalized, 20 were licensed by the Interior Ministry to take part in Jordan's first national parliamentary election since 1956. The election was scheduled for November 1993. However, the September 13 accord between Israel and the PLO raised questions about the process. Many people in Jordan committed to democratization feared that the election would become a battle between supporters and opponents of the accord, since half the Jordanian population are of Palestinian descent. As a result, the government placed strict limits on campaigning. Political rallies were banned; the ban was rescinded by the courts several weeks before the election. Hussein also suspended the

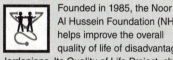
Parliament elected in 1990 and an amendment was added to the election law stipulating that voting would be "one person, one vote" rather than by party lists.

Despite these forebodings, the election went off on schedule, with few hitches. The results were an affirmation of Hussein's policy of gradual democratization. Pro-monarchy candidates won 54 of the 80 seats in the House of Representatives to 16 for the Islamic Action Front, the political arm of the Muslim Brotherhood. The remaining seats were spread among minor parties and independents. Voter turnout was 68 percent, far higher than in the 1990 election. The electorate also surprised by choosing the first woman member, Toujan Faisal, a feminist and television personality who, in the earlier campaign had been charged with apostasy by the Muslim Brotherhood.

Elections for the House of Representatives took place in November 1997, with pro-government candidates winning 62 of the 80 seats. The remainder were won by Islamic Action Front candidates and independents. However the restrictive press

law, along with widespread disillusionment over the lack of positive benefits from the peace treaty with Israel and the increasing gap between rich and poor Jordanians, resulted in a turnout of barely 50 percent of Jordan's registered voters.

The next parliamentary elections took place in 2003 (delayed from 2001 due to international and regional tensions). They were preceded by changes in the electoral laws which added six seats for women, lowered the voting age to 18 from 19, resized electoral districts and raised their number from 20 to 45. The ethnic representation quotas for Circassians, Chechens, and Christians were maintained. The contest for 110 seats in the Chamber of Deputies was boycotted by several parties due to disagreement with the new electoral rules, which were said to strengthen tribal allies of the royal family. Aside from the Islamic Action Front, most other candidates ran as independents and won 80 percent of the seats, while the religious group obtained 14.5 percent. The 55 members of the Senate were appointed by the king.

The 2007 elections fetched similar results with independents winning most seats (98), the Islamists 6 (down from 17 in 2003) and women 6. Nader al-Dahabi, a Western-educated technocrat, was appointed by the king as prime minister, replacing Marouf al-Bakhit who had the office since 2005. His main mandate was to improve the economy, which meant, among other things, improving living standards, stimulating investments, and streamlining the government's tasks. However, for allegedly failing to accomplish much in these areas, al-Bakhit and his cabinet were replaced in December 2009 by a new government led by Samir Rifai, a U.S. educated technocrat and a former advisor to the monarch.

## FOREIGN POLICY

During the 40-year cycle of hostilities between Israel and its Arab neighbors, there were periodic secret negotiations involving Jordanian and Israeli negotiators, including at times King Hussein himself, as Jordan sought to mend fences with its next-door neighbor. But in 1991 and 1992, Jordan became actively involved in the "peace process" initiated by the United States to resolve the vital issue of Palestinian self-government. As these negotiations proceeded, opponents of the process in Jordan did their best to derail them. Islamic Action Front members of the lower house of Parliament called for a vote of no-confidence in the government (but not in Hussein's leadership) for "treachery to Jordan and the Arab nation." However, the motion failed; most

Jordanians supported the peace talks, and a majority of members of the House disagreed with the motion and voted against it.

Peace with Israel became a reality in October 1994, with Jordan the second Arab nation to sign a formal treaty with the Israeli state. Subsequently, the normalization of relations moved ahead with lightning speed. In July 1995, the Senate voted to annul the last anti-Israel laws still on the books. Embassies opened in Amman and Tel Aviv under duly accredited ambassadors.

The treaty produced some positive results. However, its anticipated benefits and its spin-off in terms of U.S. aid and renewed close relations were negated largely by the breakdown of the Oslo and subsequent agreements for Palestinian statehood. The late king Hussein worked tirelessly to mediate the conflict. Working within the framework of the Jordan-Israel peace treaty, King Abdullah II has closed down the Amman office of Hamas, the militant nationalist Palestinian organization presently in control of the Gaza Strip. However the hardships imposed on the Palestinian people by the cutoff in Israeli and international aid has led Abdullah to modify his position.

The Jordanian people have yet to follow up the peace treaty with cultural and social interchanges. Journalists who attended a workshop with their Israeli counterparts in Haifa in September 1999 were even expelled from the Jordan Press Association. They were reinstated only after issuing a public statement that "we still view Israel to be a conquest state and hold that it is impossible to conduct policies of normalization with her."[6]

In 2006, rumors ran in the region that Jordan was considering a federal or confederal arrangement with an independent Palestinian state as the most feasible solution to the problem. However, in an interview given on July 1, 2007, King Abdullah indicated "We reject the formula of confederation and federation and we believe that proposing this issue at this specific period is a conspiracy against both Palestine and Jordan."[7] Jordan fears that any such arrangement before a final settlement of the Palestinian-Israeli conflict would play into the hands of the Israeli hardliners who believe that pushing all West Bank Arabs into Jordan is the best solution.

The peace agreement has to some extent isolated Jordan from other Arab countries. Iraq, its major trading partner, broke relations after the Jordanian government allowed the Iraq National Accord, an umbrella opposition group working to overthrow Saddam Hussein, to set up an office in Amman.

Inter-Arab solidarity was restored after the breakdown of the Palestinian-Israeli peace negotiations in 2000–2001. Saudi Arabia resumed oil shipments to Jordan after an eight-year break, caused by Jordan's alignment with Iraq, its principal supplier and trade partner. Kuwait also agreed to provide Jordan with 30 million barrels per day of oil; and in 2001, with the border open, regular deliveries of Iraqi oil were resumed.

The late King Hussein's cordial relations with successive U.S. administrations have continued to generate positive results for the country under his successor. In October 2001, the U.S. Senate approved the free-trade agreement with Jordan negotiated by the Bill Clinton administration and supported by that of George W. Bush. Although it had been in the works long before the September 11, 2001, terrorist attacks on the United States, it offered an added incentive for Jordan to join the international coalition against terrorism. In November, King Abdullah offered troops in support of the offensive against Osama bin Laden and his al Qaeda network.

## ACHIEVEMENTS

Following the 2003 parliamentary election and cabinet selection, King Abdullah appointed Taghreed Hikmat, a lawyer and activist for women's rights, as the country's first female judge. Another of ex-Queen Noor's Quality of Life projects, the Village Business Incubator project in Umm Qasr, is the first of its kind in a rural area targeted particularly to help village women. Over a 15-year period the QLF has trained 1,500 persons from 22 countries to launch similar self-help projects.

A "speedy solution" to the conflict may well be too late to spare Jordan from Islamic extremism. U.S. diplomat Francis Foley was murdered in 2003, allegedly by members of Takfir al-Hijra, an affiliate of Osama Bin Laden's Al-Qaeda. In November 2005 coordinated bomb attacks on three Amman hotels frequented by foreigners killed 67 persons and injured 150. The attacks were attributed to al Qaeda, whose leader in the Iraqi insurgency, Abu Musab al-Zarqawi, is a Jordanian. (The connection was exposed when one of the four bombers, a female, was captured when her explosives belt failed to ignite). Some 100,000 Jordanians marched in a demonstration in support of the king, shouting their opposition to al Qaeda. The government also issued strict anti-terrorism regulations.

## THE ECONOMY

Jordan is rich in phosphates. Reserves are estimated at 2 billion tons, and new deposits are constantly being reported. Phosphate rock is one of the country's main exports, along with potash, which is mined on the Jordanian side of the Dead Sea.

The mainstay of the economy is agriculture. The most productive agricultural area is the Jordan Valley. A series of dams and canals from the Jordan and Yarmuk Rivers has increased arable land in the valley by 264,000 acres and has made possible the production of high-value vegetable crops for export to nearby countries.

During the years of Israeli occupation of the West Bank, Jordan was estimated to have been deprived of 80 percent of its citrus crops and 45 percent of its vegetable croplands. It also lost access to an area that had provided 30 percent of its export market, as Israeli goods replaced Jordanian ones and the shekel became the medium of exchange there. The peace treaty guaranteed Jordan 7.5 billion cubic feet of water annually from the Jordan and Yarmuk Rivers, but to date the country has received less than half the agreed-on amount.

Jordan's economy has traditionally depended on outside aid and remittances from its large expatriate skilled labor force to make ends meet. A consequence of the Gulf War was the mass return from Kuwait of some 350,000 Jordanian and Palestinian workers. Despite the loss in remittances and the added burden on its economy, Jordan welcomed them. However, their return to Jordan complicated the country's efforts to meet the requirements of a 1989 agreement with the International Monetary Fund for austerity measures as a prerequisite for further aid. The government reduced subsidies, but the resulting increase in bread prices led to riots throughout the country. The subsidies were restored but were again reduced in 1991, this time with basic commodities (including bread) sold at fixed low prices under a rationing system. Later price increases that were required to meet budgetary deficits in 1996 and 1998 met with little public protest, as the population settled down stoically to face a stagnating economy. One opposition leader remarked, "I don't want us to end up as an economic colony of the United States and Israel, enslaved as cheap labor."[8]

Jordan has backed strongly the development of a Palestinian state governed by the Palestine National Authority. Initially, the Jordanian government set up a preferential tax and customs exemption system for 25 Palestinian export products. A transit agreement reached in 1996 allows Palestinian exporters direct access to Aqaba port.

King Hussein's death and the accession to the throne of Abdullah rather than Crown Prince Hassan, the late king's brother, has caused concern over Jordan's political future. But a greater concern is that of the country's economic progress. As the result of the high birth rate—75 percent of the population are under age 29, with those age 15 to 29 accounting for 34.4 percent—there are not enough jobs. Unemployment for this age group is about 30 percent. A UN-financed Jordan Human Development Report 2000 found that Jordan's youth "are not well-equipped to meet the challenges of a globalizing world."

In addition to the free-trade pact, the United States has helped Jordan to set up a number of free-trade zones. A $300 million supplemental aid package for Jordan was approved by the U.S. Congress in 1999,

## Timeline: PAST

**1921**
Establishment of the British mandate of Transjordan

**1928**
The first Constitution is approved by the British-sponsored Legislative Council

**1946**
Treaty of London; the British give Jordan independence and Abdullah assumes the title of emir

**1948**
The Arab Legion occupies the Old City of Jerusalem and the West Bank during the first Arab-Israeli War

**1967**
Jordanian forces are defeated by Israel in the Six-Day War; Israelis occupy the West Bank and Old Jerusalem

**1970–1971**
"Black September"; war between army and PLO guerrillas ends with expulsion of the PLO from Jordan

**1990s**
Politically, economically, and socially, Jordan was one of the primary losers in the Gulf crisis; Jordan signs a peace treaty with Israel; King Hussein dies and is succeeded by his son Abdullah

## PRESENT

**2000s**
Jordan signs Free Trade Agreement with the United States in 2000; the Aqaba Special Economic Zone opens in 2001; on November 9, 2005, suicide bombers kill 60 people in three U.S.-based hotels in Amman; Pope Benedict XVI visits Jordan in May 2009.

and the country currently ranks fourth in the Middle East in U.S. aid appropriations (after Israel, Egypt, and Turkey). Also, Jordan joined the World Trade Organization in 2000 and in 2001 started participation in the European Free Trade Association.

King Hussein died in February 1999, and in accordance with his purported dying wish Abdullah, his son by an earlier marriage, succeeded him. It had been expected that Prince Hamza, his son by his fourth wife Queen Noor, would succeed him. Upon his accession Abdullah named Hamza, his half-brother, as crown prince. But in late November 2005 the king relieved him of his duties, saying that his job as heir to the throne impeded his ability to undertake more responsibilities.

Despite his youth and political inexperience, Abdullah's early actions indicated a much greater awareness of, and concern for, Jordan's economic problems than his late father, at least during his last years on the throne. Like the caliphs of old, King Abdullah went out in public in disguise, accompanied only by his driver, to learn about these problems first-hand. "There are sightings all over the place," he told an interviewer. "The bureaucrats are terrified. It's great"—as he changes into a wig, plastic glasses, false beard, and cane, before visiting the Finance Ministry.[9] He has inspected the free-trade zones incognito to hear complaints about fiscal mismanagement. Abdullah envisions Jordan as a "Middle Eastern Singapore," a model for development. "We can be symbols," he says, "for someone in Yemen who might say 'I don't want my country to be like it is today. I want it to be like the Jordanian or the Bahraini model, modern and progressive.'"[10]

In addition to a liberalized economy, the king launched in 2005 his new "national agenda." "It would," he said, "lead the country into a new age where there is more press freedom, health insurance for all, an independent judiciary, a more politically active public, political pluralism and . . . empowered women and youth."[11] One component of the agenda would be an electoral law giving Palestinians resident in Jordan greater representation in Parliament. Earlier, the number of seats in the legislature was increased from 80 to 120 in 2003. In the parliamentary elections for that year, the parties supporting the monarchy won half the seats. They included six women, resulting from Abdullah's new quota system intended to provide greater population balance and diversity. Elections in November 2007 were intended supposedly to mark a watershed in Jordan's move toward more democratic government. But developments

elsewhere, notably the Hamas takeover of Gaza, have slowed progress. Prior to the election the government canceled plans to amend the electoral law. It also banned former lawmaker Toujan al-Faisal from running again, due to her 2002 conviction for "harming state dignity." Government restrictions limited the number of candidates from the Islamic Action Front. Only 22 members entered the election, half the number who ran in 2003. Its Secretary-general commented, "the government insists on no reform, no political change, no democracy, because they are looking at what happened to Hamas."[12]

The king also took an active role internationally in promoting for both Muslims and non-Muslims his moderate vision of Islam. In February 2006 he spoke to a gathering of U.S. clergy leaders emphasizing the linkages between Christianity, Judaism and Islam, and rejected the idea of a "clash of civilizations" which preoccupies many Westerners as well as some jihadists. "Our greatest challenge," he said, "comes from violent extremists. . . . Extremism is a political movement under religious cover. Its adherents want nothing more than to pit us against each other, denying all that we have in common."[13] To survive and evolve peaceful in the region, Jordan and its monarchy has to carefully tread through the dangers of an unstable region and a constraining global economy. Being located between Israel, Iraq, Syria, and Saudi Arabia, it learned that it cannot afford to antagonize anyone, nor appear to take sides in a conflict, even if the domestic pressure to do so is strong. It also seems willing to be responsive to its domestic constituencies but not at the expense of the monarchy's survival.

## NOTES

1. The Ottomans paid subsidies to nomadic tribes to guard the route of pilgrims headed south for Mecca. Peter Gubser, *Jordan: Crossroads of Middle Eastern Events* (Boulder, CO: Westview Press, 1983).

2. Years later, Glubb wrote, "In its twenty-eight years of life it had never been contemplated that the Arab Legion would fight an independent war." Quoted in Harold D. Nelson, ed., *Jordan, A Country Study* (Washington, D.C.: American University, Foreign Area Studies, 1979), p. 201.

3. King Abdullah of Jordan, *My Memoirs Completed,* Harold W. Glidden, trans. (London: Longman, 1951, 1978), preface, xxvi.

4. The text of the proposal is in King Abdullah, *My Memoirs Completed,* Op. cit., pp. 89–90. See also, Avi Shlaim, *Collusion Across The Jordan: King Abdullah, The Zionist Movement And The Partition Of Palestine,* (New York: Columbia University Press, July 1988).

5. Naseer Aruri, *Jordan: A Study in Political Development (1925–1965)* (The Hague, Netherlands: Martinus Nijhoff, 1967), p. 159.

6. Helen Schary Motro, "Israel the Invisible?" *The Christian Science Monitor,* (January 12, 2000). Online at www.csmonitor.com/2000/0112/p9s2.html. Consulted on August 1, 2010.

7. King Abdulla, quoted in "Jordanian king Abdullah Rejects Confederation with Palestinians," *Kuwait Times Newspaper,* July 2, 2007. Online at www.kuwaittimes.net/read_news.php?newsid=MTk4NTg4NTg2Mw==. Consulted on July 9, 2010.

8. Laith Shbeilat, quoted in William A. Orme, "Neighbors Rally to Jordan, Easing Financial Fears," The New York Times (February 19, 1999). Online at www.nytimes.com. Consulted on August 1, 2010.

9. Jeffrey Goldberg, "Learning to Be a King," *The New Times Magazine* (February 8, 2000).

10. *Ibid.*

11. Quoted in "Caught In the Middle, As Usual," The Economist, November 11, 2005. Online at www.economist.com/node/5136462. Consulted on August 1, 2010.

12. Zaki Bani Rsheid, quoted in Thanassis Cambanis, "Jordan, Fearing Islamists, Tightens Grip on Elections," The New York Times, November 11, 2007. Online at www.nytimes.com. Consulted on August 1, 2010.

13. Banerjee, "Jordan's Leader Calls for Unity Among Religions," The New York Times, February 2, 2006. The king's speech was the first by a Muslim head-of-state before a mainly evangelical Christian audience at a National Prayer Breakfast gathering. Online at www.nytimes.com. Consulted on August 1, 2010.

# Kuwait (State of Kuwait)

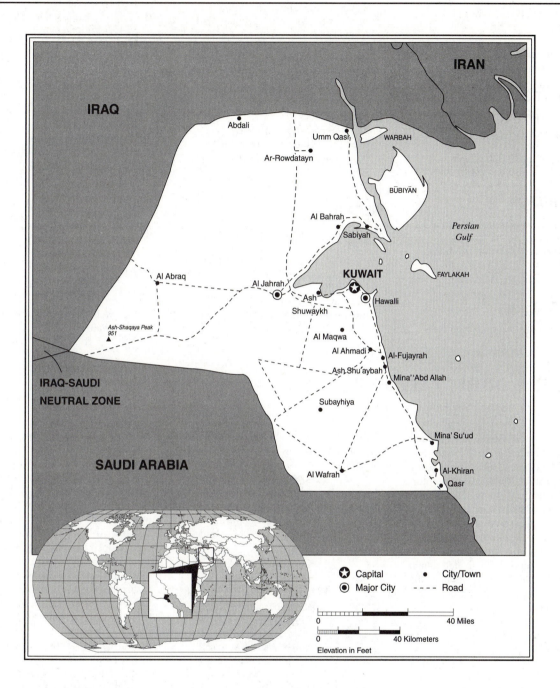

IRAN

IRAQ

Abdali

Umm Qash

WARBAH

Ar-Rowdatayn

BŪBIYĀN

Al Bahrah

Sabiyah

Persian
Gulf

Al Abraq

KUWAIT

FAYLAKAH

Al Jahrah

Ash
Shuwaykh

Hawalli

Ash-Shaqaya Peak
951

Al Maqwa

Al Ahmadi

Al-Fujayrah

Ash Shu'aybah

Mina''Abd Allah

IRAQ-SAUDI
NEUTRAL ZONE

Subayhiya

Mina' Su'ud

SAUDI ARABIA

Al Wafrah

Al-Khiran

Qasr

★ Capital     • City/Town
◉ Major City    --- Road

0              40 Miles

0            40 Kilometers

Elevation in Feet

# Kuwait Statistics

## GEOGRAPHY

*Area in Square Miles (Kilometers):* 6,880
(17,818) (about the size of New Jersey)
*Capital (Population):* Kuwait (277,000)
*Environmental Concerns:* limited natural
freshwater reserves; air and water
pollution; desertification
*Geographical Features:* flat to slightly
undulating desert plain

*Climate:* intensely hot and dry summers;
short, cool winters

## PEOPLE

### Population

*Total:* 2,789,132 (includes 1,169,911
non-nationals)
*Annual Growth Rate:* 3.50% (note:
a large number of both Kuwaiti and

expatriate workers returned after the
Gulf War, partly accounting for the
increase)
*Rural/Urban Population Ratio:* 3/97
*Major Languages:* Arabic; English
*Ethnic Makeup:* 45% Kuwaiti; 35% other
Arab; 9% South Asian; 4% Iranian; 7%
others
*Religions:* 85% Muslim; 15% Christian,
Hindu, Parsi, and others

# GLOBAL STUDIES

### Health

*Life Expectancy at Birth*: 76.2 years (male), 79.18 years (female) Infant Mortality Rate (Ratio): 9.47/1,000 live births

### Education

*Adult Literacy Rate:* 93.3%
*Compulsory (Ages):* 6–14; free

## COMMUNICATION

*Telephones:* 541,000 main lines
*Daily Newspaper Circulation:* 401 per 1,000 people
*Televisions:* 390 per 1,000 people
*Internet Users:* 1 million (2008)

## TRANSPORTATION

*Highways in Miles (Kilometers):* 3,572 (5,749)
*Railroads in Miles (Kilometers):* none
*Usable Airfields:* 7
*Motor Vehicles in Use:* 700,000

## GOVERNMENT

*Type:* nominal constitutional monarchy

*Independence Date:* June 19, 1961 (from the United Kingdom)
*Head of State/Government:* Emir Shaykh Sabah Ahmad al-Sabah; Prime Minister Shaykh Nasir Muhammad Ahmad al-Sabah
*Political Parties:* none legal, but various political groups or blocs may present candidates for seats in the National Assembly. The largest bloc in the present Assembly is the Islamic (Sunni Muslim) bloc.
*Suffrage*: universal for citizens over 21, excluding male members of the military and security forces

## MILITARY

*Military Expenditures (% of GDP):* 5.3%
*Current Disputes:* none. In 1994 Iraq formally accepted the UN-demarcated border between the two-countries and ended its claims to Kuwait and the offshore islands of Bubiyan and Warbah.

## ECONOMY

*Currency ($U.S. Equivalent):* 0.302 dinars = $1 (fixed rate)
*Per Capita Income/GDP:* $54,000/ $145.7 billion
*GDP Growth Rate:* −1.7%
*Inflation Rate:* 3%
*Unemployment Rate:* 2.2%
*Labor Force*: 2.04 million (80% non-Kuwaiti)
*Natural Resources:* petroleum; fish; shrimp; natural gas
*Agriculture:* fish
*Industry:* petroleum; petrochemicals; desalination; food processing; construction materials; salt; construction
*Exports:* $56.06 billion (primary partners Japan, United States, Korea)
*Imports:* $19.12 billion (primary partners United States, Japan, Germany)

## SUGGESTED WEB SITES

http://lcweb2.loc.gov/frd/cs/kwtoc.html
http://kuwait-info.org

# Kuwait Country Report

The State of Kuwait consists of a wedge-shaped, largely desert territory located near the head of the Persian Gulf and just southwest of the Shatt al-Arab. Kuwaiti territory includes the islands of Bubiyan and Failaka in the Gulf, both of them periodically claimed by Iraq. Kuwait also shares a Neutral Zone, consisting mainly of oil fields, which it administers jointly with Iraq and Saudi Arabia; oil production is supposedly divided equally among them. The Iraqi accusation that Kuwait was taking more than its share was one of the points of contention that led to Iraq's invasion of Kuwait in 1990.

Kuwait's location has given the country great strategic importance in the modern rivalries of regional powers and their outside supporters. The country played a major role in the Iran-Iraq War, supporting Iraq financially and serving as a conduit for U.S. naval intervention through the reflagging of Kuwaiti tankers. The Iraqi invasion reversed roles, with Iraq the aggressor and Kuwait both the victim and the target of U.S.-led military action of the brief Gulf War in 1991.

## HISTORY

Kuwait was inhabited entirely by nomadic peoples until the early 1700s. Then a number of clans of the large Anaiza tribal confederation settled along the Gulf in the current area of Kuwait. They built a fort for protection from raids—*Kuwait* means "little fort" in Arabic—and elected a chief to represent them in dealings with the Ottoman Empire, the major power in the Middle East at that time. The ruling family of modern Kuwait, the al-Sabah, traces its rule back to this period.

### DEVELOPMENT

Declining oil revenues resulted in budgetary deficits, which reached $6 billion in 1998 and 1999. With the Assembly dissolved, the emir issued some 60 decrees, intended to begin to privatize the economy and reduce expenditures by 20%. In 2001, 35% of ownership in the Kuwait Cement Company was turned over to private management.

Kuwait prospered under the al-Sabahs. Its well-protected natural harbor became headquarters for a pearl-fishing fleet of 800 dhows (boats). The town (also called Kuwait) became a port of call for British ships bound for India.

In the late 1700s and early 1800s, Kuwait was threatened by the Wahhabis, orthodox Muslims from central Arabia. Arab piracy also adversely affected Kuwait's prosperity. Kuwait's rulers paid tribute to the Ottoman sultan in return for protection against the Wahhabis. However, they began to fear that the Turks would occupy Kuwait, and they turned to the British. In 1899, Shaykh Mubarak, who reigned from 1896 to 1915, signed an agreement with Britain for protection. In return, he agreed to accept British political advisers and not to have dealings with other foreign governments. In this way, Kuwait became a self-governing state under British protection.

During the 1890s, Kuwait gave refuge to Ibn Saud, a leader from central Arabia whose family had been defeated by its rivals. Ibn Saud left Kuwait in 1902, traveled in secret to Riyadh, the rivals' headquarters, and seized the city in a surprise raid. Kuwait thus indirectly had a hand in the founding of its neighbor state, Saudi Arabia.

## INDEPENDENCE

Kuwait continued its peaceful ways under the paternalist rule of the al-Sabahs until the 1950s. When production increased rapidly, the small pearl-fishing port became a booming modern city. In 1961, Britain and

Refugees at camp near Iraq/Jordan border who left Kuwait after Iraqi invasion.

(S.M. Amin/Saudi Aramco World/PADIA (SA3670041))

Kuwait jointly terminated the 1899 agreement, and Kuwait became fully independent under the al-Sabahs.

A threat to the country's independence developed almost immediately, as Iraq refused to recognize Kuwait's new status and claimed the territory on the grounds that it had once been part of the Iraqi Ottoman province of Basra. Iraq was also interested in controlling Kuwaiti oil resources. The ruling emir asked Britain for help, and British troops rushed back to Kuwait. The Arab League agreed also that several of its members would send troops to defend Kuwait—and, incidentally, to ensure that the country would not revert to its previous protectorate status. The Arab contingents were withdrawn in 1963. A revolution had overthrown the Iraqi government earlier in the year, and the new government recognized Kuwait's independence. However, the Ba'th Party's concentration of power in Saddam Hussein's hands in the 1970s led to periodic Iraqi pressure on Kuwait, culminating in the 1990 invasion and occupation. After the expulsion of Iraqi forces, Kuwait requested a realignment of its northern border. In 1992, the United Nations Boundary Commission approved the request, moving the border approximately 1,880 feet

northward. The change gave Kuwait full possession of the Rumaila oil fields and a portion of the Iraqi Umm Qasr naval base. Kuwait had argued that the existing border deprived it of its own resources and access to its territorial waters as specified in the 1963 agreement. Some 3,600 UN observers were assigned to patrol the new border. Kuwaiti workers dug a 130-mile trench, paid for by private donations, as a further protection for the emirate. Iraq's 1994 acceptance of the UN border demarcated between the two states officially resolved the issue, although before his overthrow by U.S. forces Iraqi president Saddam Hussein had his army conduct training exercises and maneuvers near the border.

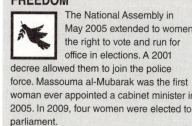

**FREEDOM**

The National Assembly in May 2005 extended to women the right to vote and run for office in elections. A 2001 decree allowed them to join the police force. Massouma al-Mubarak was the first woman ever appointed a cabinet minister in 2005. In 2009, four women were elected to parliament.

## REPRESENTATIVE GOVERNMENT

Kuwait differs from other patriarchally ruled Arabian Peninsula states in having a Constitution that provides for an elected National Assembly. Its 50 members are elected for four-year terms.

Friction developed between the Assembly and the ruling family soon after independence. Assembly members criticized Shaykh Abdullah and his relatives, as well as the cabinet, for corruption, press censorship, refusal to allow political parties, and insufficient attention to public services. Since all members of the ruling family were on the government payroll, there was some justification for the criticism.

Abdullah died in 1965, but his successor, Shaykh al-Sabah, accepted the criticism as valid. Elections were held in 1971 for a new Assembly.

Unfortunately for democracy in Kuwait, the new Assembly paid more attention to criticism of the government than to law making. In 1976, it was suspended by Shaykh al-Sabah. He died the following year, but his successor, Shaykh Jabir, reaffirmed the ruling family's commitment to the democratic process. A new Assembly was formed in 1981, with different members. The majority were traditional patriarchs loyal to the rulers, along with technical experts in various fields, such as industry, agriculture, and engineering. However, the new Assembly fared little better than its predecessor in balancing freedom of expression with responsible leadership. The ruler suspended it, along with the Constitution, in 1986.

Pressures to reinstate the Assembly have increased in recent years. Just prior to the Iraqi invasion, the ruler had convened a 75-member National Council to assess the "parliamentary experiment." The process was halted during the Iraqi occupation; but, after the Iraqi withdrawal and the return to Kuwait of the ruling family, the emir pledged to hold elections for a new Assembly in October 1992. The vote was limited to males over age 21 who could trace their residence in Kuwait back to 1920 or earlier. Under these rules, some 82,000 voters would elect two candidates from each of 25 constituencies to the 50-member Assembly.

The emir kept his pledge, and on October 5, 1992, the election took place as scheduled. More than half of the seats were won by critics of the government. They had campaigned on a platform of demands for government accountability and broadening of the franchise to include women. In the next Assembly election, in 1996, pro-government candidates won the majority of seats. But to appease his critics, the emir appointed a new cabinet with nine non-Sabah family members as ministers.

## HEALTH/WELFARE

The 1.4 million foreign workers in Kuwait have had little protection under law until very recently. In November 2000, a large number of unemployed or underemployed Egyptians, the largest component of the expatriate labor force, rioted over bad working conditions and exploitation by sponsors who charge up to $3,000 for residency and work permits. The government agreed to review labor laws to limit payments to sponsors by mutual agreement.

The emir suspended the Assembly in May 1999, after opposition deputies had paralyzed government action by endless criticism of government ministers who were presenting their programs for legislative concurrence. However, he approved elections for a new Assembly to take place in July. During the suspension period he issued a decree giving women the right to vote and run for public office in 2003. (Under Kuwaiti law only native citizens or those

naturalized for 30 years or more have the franchise; women are excluded along with the police and members of the armed services.) When the new Assembly (all-male) took office, its members refused to approve the decree as required by Kuwaiti law.

Subsequently women undertook organized efforts to gain voting rights, appealing both to the Assembly and the courts. During the July 2003 Assembly election they even set up mock polling booths and cast ballots. Several of their appeals were rejected by the conservative-dominated legislature in close votes. But in May 2005 the Assembly approved the measure by a 35–23 vote. In part to mollify conservative legislators an addendum was attached to the right-to-vote bill that would require women voters and candidates for public office to abide by Shari'a Islamic law.

The Assembly's improvement as a responsible legislative body was illustrated in the leadership crisis of early 2006. Following the death of ruling emir Shaykh Jaber al-Sabah after 29 years of rule, his ailing successor, Shaykh Saad, was deposed by pressure from the legislators and replaced by his brother Shaykh Ahmad al-Sabah as the new emir. Ahmad named another brother as Crown Prince and a nephew as prime minister, breaking a long tradition that had alternated the top posts in the government between the Sabah family and the Salems, the other branch of the ruling family in Kuwait.

Elections for a new National Assembly in 2006 showed the relatively even balance between the country's political blocs or groups. The largest number of seats, 17, was won by members of the Sunni-dominated Islamic Bloc. They were followed by the Popular Bloc, with 9, and the National Action Bloc, with 8. The remaining seats went to independents with no bloc affiliation.

## VULNERABILITY

Kuwait's location and its relatively open society make the country vulnerable to external subversion. In the early 1970s, the rulers were the target of criticism and threats from other Arab states because they did not publicly support the Palestinian cause. For years afterward, Kuwait provided large-scale financial aid not only to the Palestine Liberation Organization, but also to Arab states such as Syria and Jordan that were directly involved in the struggle with Israel because of their common borders.

A new vulnerability surfaced with the Iranian Revolution of 1979, which overthrew the shah. Kuwait has a large Shi'a Muslim population, while its rulers are Sunni. Kuwait's support for Iraq and the

development of closer links with Saudi Arabia (and indirectly the United States) angered Iran's new rulers. Kuwaiti oil installations were bombed by Iranian jets in 1981, and in 1983 truck bombs severely damaged the U.S. and French Embassies in Kuwait City. The underground organization Islamic Jihad claimed responsibility for the attacks and threatened more if Kuwait did not stop its support of Iraq. Kuwaiti police arrested 17 persons; they were later jailed for complicity in the bombings. Since Islamic Jihad claimed links to Iran, the Kuwaiti government suspected an Iranian hand behind the violence and deported 600 Iranian workers.

Tensions with Iran intensified in the mid-1980s, as Iranian jets and missile-powered patrol boats attacked Kuwaiti tankers in the Gulf and pro-Iranian terrorists carried out a series of hijackings. A 1988 hijacking caused international concern when a Kuwaiti Airways 747 jet with several members of the royal family aboard was seized and its passengers held for 16 days while being shuttled from airport to airport. The hijackers demanded the release of the 17 truck bombers as the price for the hostages' freedom. The Kuwaiti government refused to negotiate; after the hostages were released through mediation by other Arab states, it passed a law making hijacking punishable by death.

Fear of Iran led Kuwait to join the newly formed Gulf Cooperation Council in 1981. The country also began making large purchases of weapons for defense, balancing U.S. with Soviet equipment. Its arms buildup made it the world's third-highest defense spender, at $3.1 billion, an average of $2,901 per capita.

During the Iran–Iraq War, Kuwait loaned 13 tankers to the United States. They were reflagged and given U.S. naval escort protection to transit the Gulf. After the United States assumed a major role in the region due to the Iraqi invasion and the resulting Gulf War, Kuwait signed a 10-year mutual-defense pact, the first formal agreement of its kind for the Gulf states.

## ACHIEVEMENTS

In addition to their recent success in gaining the right to vote and to be elected to parliament, women have done well in the non-political arena. The first all-female national soccer tournament was held in April 2000 and there are regular leagues throughout the emirate. A woman heads the Kuwaiti Economists Association, and others have enjoyed success as journalists, newspaper columnists, university lecturers and doctors.

## THE IRAQI OCCUPATION AND AFTERMATH

The seven months of Iraqi occupation (August 1990–February 1991) had a devastating effect on Kuwait. Some 5,000 Kuwaitis were killed, and the entire population was held hostage to Iraqi demands. Oil production stopped entirely. Iraqi forces opened hundreds of oil storage tanks as a defense measure, pouring millions of gallons of oil into the sea, thus creating a serious environmental hazard. (As they retreated, the Iraqis also set 800 oil wells on fire, destroying production capabilities and posing enormous technical and environmental problems. These conflagrations were not extinguished for nearly a year.) In Kuwait City, basic water, electricity, and other services were cut off; public buildings were damaged; shops and homes were vandalized; and more than 3,000 gold bars, the backing for the Kuwaiti currency, were taken to Iraq.

Some 605 Kuwaitis, out of thousands taken to Iraq, are still unaccounted for. Most of them are civilians, including 120 students, whose "crime" was noncooperation with the Iraqi occupation forces. The U.S. invasion and occupation of Iraq in 2003 offered new hope that some of them were still alive, and the Kuwait government offered $1 million for information on their whereabouts. However, in May an informant led U.S. forces to an abandoned military camp near Habbaniya where some 600 Kuwaiti prisoners were supposedly buried. According to the informant, they were brought to Baghdad in October 1991, blindfolded, lined up in horseshoe formation, killed by machine gun fire, hauled to the site in trucks and buried there.

In 2001, the UN Repatriations Commission, set up to compensate Kuwaitis and others for losses sustained during the occupation, approved payment of more than $360 million for this purpose. As a result, 230 Kuwait-based companies are to share $174 million in payment for their claims against Iraq.

Iraqi maneuvers near the Kuwait border and the incursion of Iraqi forces into UN-protected Kurdistan led the United States in 1996 to invoke the mutual-defense pact by sending an additional 5,000 ground troops to Kuwait to take part in a new attack on Iraq. The Kuwaiti government, which had not been consulted, agreed to accept only 3,500. But the contest of wills between the Clinton administration and Saddam Hussein over Iraq's secret weapons program, and the resulting fears of Kuwaitis of an Iraqi missile attack on the emirate led it to allow the stationing of 10,000 U.S. troops on its territory, along with Patriot missiles and fighter aircraft. After the September 11, 2001, terrorist attacks in the United States, Kuwait joined with other Gulf Cooperation Council member states in supporting the international coalition against terrorism.

After decades of hostility toward Israel and strong support for the Palestinian cause, Kuwait's leaders begun to rethink national policy toward the Israeli state in the light of Israel's evacuation of the Gaza Strip. The Kuwaiti newspaper *Al-Seyassa*, a voice of government opinion, published an op-ed column in October 2005 urging the termination of the country's long-standing trade embargo on Israel. Whether this would lead to further action remains doubtful, but the mere prospect of future normalization of relations with the Zionist state marked a milestone in itself.

## THE PEOPLE

Until the economic recession in the region, the country had a high rate of immigration. As a result, there are more non-Kuwaitis than Kuwaitis in the population, though dislocation resulting from the Iraqi occupation has changed the balance. Today, approximately 45 percent of the population are native Kuwaitis.

About one third of the total population, both citizens and noncitizens, are Shi'a Muslims. After the 1979 Revolution in Iran, they were blamed for much of the unrest in the country; Shi'a terrorists were charged with the 1983 truck bombings of embassies in Kuwait City. The improvement in Kuwait-Iran relations that followed the end of the Iran-Iraq War lessened this Shi'a anti-government activity, and Shi'a and Sunni residents suffered equally under the Iraqi occupation.

The insurgency against U.S. forces occupying Iraq and the U.S.-installed temporary government there spilled over into Kuwait early in 2005. Gun battles between Islamic militants and security forces in January killed 12 of the militants, who were said to be members of three cells of al Qaeda according to the Interior Ministry. The government also allocated 5.5 million dinars toward a campaign to promote moderate Islam in opposition to Islamic extremists, and closed down two websites belonging to a radical preacher, one being Amer Khleif al-Enezi, who was killed subsequently in a gun battle with police.

Before the Gulf War, the largest non-native population group was Palestinian. Although denied citizenship, the Palestinians were generally better educated and more industrious than the native Kuwaitis. Palestinians formed the nucleus of opposition to the ruling family, and a number of them collaborated with the Iraqi occupation forces. After the war, more than 600 Palestinians were tried and sentenced to prison terms for collaboration. Some 300,000 Palestinians abruptly left for Jordan. However, their management skills were not entirely missed, as their places were filled by Lebanese or Western expatriates. Low-level jobs also filled rapidly with the arrival of workers from less-developed countries. But their low pay and

## Timeline: PAST

**1756**
Establishment of the al-Sabah family as the rulers of Kuwait

**1899**
Agreement with Great Britain making Kuwait a protectorate

**1961–1963**
Independence, followed by Iraqi claim and British/Arab League intervention

**1971**
Elections for a new National Assembly

**1976**
The ruler suspends the Assembly on the grounds that it is a handicap to effective government

**1980s**
Bombings by Islamic Jihad; massive deportation of Iranians after public buildings and oil installations are sabotaged; the government places the tanker fleet under U.S. protection by reflagging ships and providing naval escorts in the Gulf

**1990s**
Iraqi forces occupy Kuwait; Kuwait is liberated in the Gulf War; tension between the government and the Assembly; tensions rise between Kuwaitis and foreign workers

## PRESENT

**2003**
Thousands of US troops use Kuwait territory to invade Iraq; parliamentary elections, won mostly by Islamist and pro-government candidates

**2005**
Parliament approves law allowing women to vote and run for parliament

**2006**
Emir, Sheikh Jaber dies and Sheikh Sabah al-Ahmad is sworn in as new monarch; parliamentary elections. Women run and vote for the fist time for legislature

**2008**
Early parliamentary elections after the Emir dissolves parliament

**2009**
Emir dissolves parliament again to avoid corruption probe by parliament. New parliamentary elections in which four women were elected

lack of fringe benefits triggered riots in April 2000 over a government plan to levy annual payments, up to $155, on foreign workers in return for their inclusion in the national health service.

## THE ECONOMY

Kuwait's only abundant resource is petroleum. Less than 1 percent of the land can be cultivated, and there is almost no fresh water. Drinking water comes from sea water converted to fresh water by huge desalination plants.

Kuwait's oil reserves of 94 billion barrels are the world's third largest, comprising 10 percent of global reserves. According to a 1996 study by the International Monetary Fund, the oil industry—and, with it, the economy—has recovered "impressively" from the effects of the Iraqi occupation. Oil production in 1997 reached 2 million barrels per day. The 1995–2000 Five-Year Plan approved by the Assembly projected a balanced budget by the end of the plan, largely through privatization of state enterprises, increased oil and non-oil revenues, and expansion of petrochemical industries.

Kuwait's economic recovery following the Iraqi occupation was hampered not only by the damage to its oil industry but also by an overstaffed public sector, huge welfare subsidies, and other factors. Despite some opposition in the Assembly, mainly on procedural grounds, the government went ahead with the reforms.

As a result, the Kuwaiti economy has rebounded to such an extent that, in 1996, Kuwait became the first Gulf state to receive an "A" rating from the International Banking Credit Association, an organization that evaluates countries on the basis of short- and long-term risks. In 2005 Kuwait's 950,000 citizens earned $45 billion in revenues.

In addition to restoring its oil fields to full production, by 2001 nearly all the land mines left by the retreating Iraqis had been cleared from Kuwait's vast stretches of desert. An enormous oil slick from oil-well destruction that had threatened to pollute the water supply (which comes from desalinization) was also cleared up.

# Lebanon (Lebanese Republic)

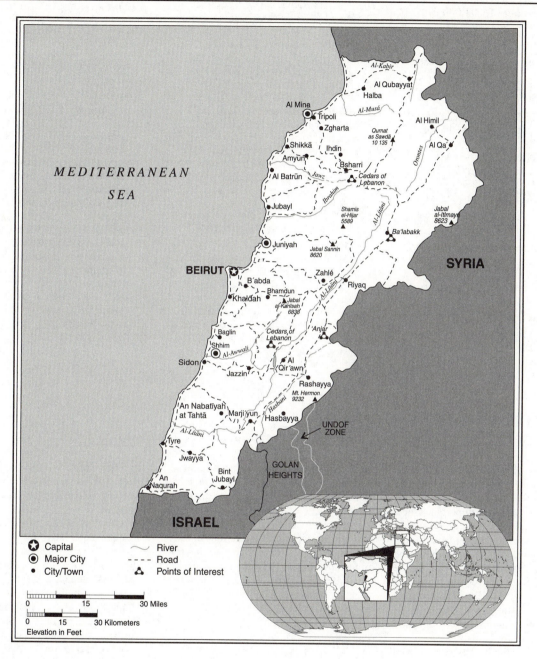

**Capital** ✪  |  **River** ～
**Major City** ◉  |  **Road** - - -
**City/Town** •  |  **Points of Interest** ▲

0    15    30 Miles
0    15    30 Kilometers
Elevation in Feet

# Lebanon Statistics

## GEOGRAPHY

*Area in Square Miles (Kilometers):* 4,015 (10,452) (smaller than Connecticut)
*Capital (Population):* Beirut (1,826,000)
*Environmental Concerns:* deforestation; soil erosion; air and water pollution
*Geographical Features:* a narrow coastal plain; the Biqa' Valley separates Lebanon and the Anti-Lebanon Mountains

*Climate:* Mediterranean (hot, humid summers; cool, damp winters); heavy winter snows in mountains

## PEOPLE

### Population

*Total:* 4,125,247
*Annual Growth Rate:* 0.621%
*Rural/Urban Population Ratio:* 12/88

*Major Languages:* Arabic; French; English
*Ethnic Makeup:* 90% Arab; 10% Armenian and other
*Religions:* 17 sects recognized—Muslims 59% (Shia, Sunni, Ismaili, Alawite, also Druze), Christian 39% (Maronite, Melkite Catholic, Armenian Orthodox, Syrian Catholic, Armenian Catholic, Greek Orthodox, Greek Catholic) 2% Protestant

**Health**

*Life Expectancy at Birth:* 73.28 years
(male); 76.36 years (female)
*Infant Mortality Rate:* 16.4/1,000 live
births

**Education**

*Adult Literacy Rate:* 87.4%

## COMMUNICATION

*Telephones:* 714,000 (2008) main lines
*Daily Newspaper Circulation:* 172 per
1,000 people
*Televisions:* 291 per 1,000 people
*Internet Users:* 2.19 million (2008)

## TRANSPORTATION

*Highways in Miles (Kilometers):* 4,380
(7,300)
*Railroads in Miles (Kilometers):* 138
(222)
*Usable Airfields:* 8
*Motor Vehicles in Use:* 1,183,000

## GOVERNMENT

*Type:* republic

*Independence Date:* November 22, 1943
(from League of Nations mandate
under French administration)
*Head of State/Government:* President
Emile Lahoud; Prime Minister Fouad
Siniora
*Political Parties:* normally based on
religious confessions as above; the
new National Assembly elected in
2005 is divided into larger power
blocs, two-thirds Christian, Sunni
Muslim and Druze, one-third Shi'a
Muslim (including Hizbullah and
Amal)
*Suffrage:* compulsory for males at 21;
authorized for women at 21 with
elementary-school education

## MILITARY

*Military Expenditures (% of GDP):*
3.1%
*Current Disputes:* Disagreement with
Israel over ownership of Shab'a
Farms in Israeli-occupied Golan
Heights, presently dormant; although
Syrian forces are withdrawn, Syrian
intervention continues; all-out conflict
between Lebanese army and Islamic

militants based in Palestinian refugee
camps developed in 2007

## ECONOMY

*Currency ($U.S. Equivalent):* 1,507
pounds = $1
*Per Capita Income/GDP:*
$5,500/$33.04 billion
*GDP Growth Rate:* 7%
*Inflation Rate:* 4.8%
*Unemployment Rate:* 20%
*Labor Force:* 1,500,000 (plus an
estimated 1,000,000 foreign
workers)
*Natural Resources:* limestone; iron ore;
salt; water; arable land
*Agriculture:* fruits; vegetables; olives;
tobacco; hemp (hashish); sheep;
goats
*Industry:* banking; food processing;
jewelry; cement; textiles; mineral
and chemical products; wood and
furniture products; oil refining; metal
fabricating
*Exports:* $1.88 billion (primary partners
Syria, UAE, Switzerland)
*Imports:* NA (primary partners Italy,
Spain, France)

# Lebanon Country Report

The Lebanese Republic is located at the
eastern end of the Mediterranean Sea. The
coastal plain, which contains the capital,
Beirut and all the other important cities,
is narrow, rising just a few miles east of
Beirut to a rugged mountain range, Mount
Lebanon. Beyond Mount Lebanon is the
Biqa', a broad, fertile valley that is the
country's main wheat-growing region. At
the eastern edge of the Biqa', the land rises
again abruptly to the snow-capped Anti-
Lebanon Range, which separates Lebanon
from Syria.

Lebanon's geography has always been
important strategically. Many invaders
passed through it over the centuries on their
conquests—Egyptians, Assyrians, Persians,
Crusaders, Arabs, and Turks. However,
they were seldom able to gain control of
Mount Lebanon. For this reason, the mountain served as a refuge for ethnic and religious minorities, and it became in time the
nucleus of the modern Lebanese state.

Lebanon's Mediterranean ports have
traditionally served as an outlet for goods
from the region's interior, notably Syria.
Lebanese merchants have profited for centuries by being middlemen for this trade.
However, its strategic location and its role

as a commercial entrepôt have hampered
Lebanon's unification as a nation in the
twentieth century. Unification and the
establishment of a national identity have
also been blocked by religious divisions
and territorial rivalries by various clans. A
Lebanese scholar described the country's
political system as "a feudal hierarchy with
fluctuating political influence, as powerful
families asserted themselves to acquire
power and prominence."[1]

## HISTORY

In ancient times, Lebanon was known as
Phoenicia. The Phoenicians were great
traders who traveled throughout the Mediterranean and probably out into the Atlantic
Ocean as far north as Cornwall in England,
in search of tin, copper, and iron ore, which
were valued in the ancient world for their
many uses. Phoenician merchants established trading posts, some of which eventually grew into great cities.

No central government was ever
established in Phoenicia itself. Phoenician towns like Byblos, Tyre, Sidon, and
Tripoli were independent states, often
in conflict or rivalry over trade with one

another. This city-state rivalry has always
been a feature of Lebanese life and is
another reason for the lack of a national
unity.

Lebanon began to develop a definite
identity much later, in the seventh century
A.D. when a Christian group, the Maronites,
took refuge in Mount Lebanon after they
were threatened with persecution by the
government of the East Roman or Byzantine
Empire because of theological disagreements over the nature of Christ. The Muslim
Arabs brought Islam to coastal Lebanon at
about the same time, but they were unable
to dislodge or convert the Maronites. Mount
Lebanon's sanctuary tradition attracted
other minority groups, Muslim as well
as Christian. Shi'a Muslim communities
moved there in the ninth and tenth centuries
to escape persecution from Sunni Muslims,
the Islamic majority. In the eleventh century,
the Druze, adherents of an offshoot of Islam
who followed the teachings of an Egyptian
mystic and also faced persecution from
Sunni Muslims, established themselves in
the southern part of Mount Lebanon. These
communities were originally quite separate.
In the modern period of Lebanese history,
however, they have tended to overlap, a fact,

David Gordon says, "that makes both for unity and in troubled times for a dangerous struggle for turf."[2]

Lebanon acquired a distinct political identity under certain powerful families in the sixteenth and seventeenth centuries. The Ottoman Turks conquered it along with the rest of the Middle East, but they were content to leave local governance in the hands of these families in return for tribute. The most prominent was the Ma'an family, who were Druze. Their greatest leader, Fakhr al-Din (1586–1635), established an independent principality that included all of present-day Lebanon, Israel, and part of Syria. It was during al-Din's rule that French religious orders were allowed to establish missions in the country, which facilitated later European intervention in Lebanon.

The Ma'ans were succeeded by the Shihabs, who were Maronites. Their descendants continue to hold important positions in the country, underscoring the durability of the extended-family system, which still dominates Lebanese politics. They also allied the Maronite Church with the Roman Catholic Church, an action that had great consequences in the twentieth century, when the Maronites came to view Lebanon as a "Christian island in a Muslim sea," preserving the unique Lebanese identity only through Western support.

European countries began to intervene directly in Lebanon in the nineteenth century, due to conflict between the Maronite and Druze communities. Mount Lebanon was occupied by Egyptian armies of the Ottoman khedive (viceroy) of Egypt, Muhammad Ali, in the 1830s. Egyptian development of Beirut and other coastal ports for trade purposes, particularly exports of Lebanese silk (still an important cash crop) at the expense of Mount Lebanon, and heavy taxes imposed by the khedive's overseers led to peasant uprisings in 1840 and 1857. By then the Ottomans had reestablished their authority with European help. However, the European powers refused to allow the sultan to change Mount Lebanon's special status as an autonomous province. Ottoman governors resorted to intrigues with Maronite and Druze leaders, playing one against the other. The result was a Maronite-Druze civil war, which broke out in 1860. The cause was insignificant— "an affray between two boys, the shooting of a partridge or the collision of two pack animals," asserts one author; but whatever the spark, the two communities were ready for a fight.[3]

Although the Maronite fighters greatly outnumbered the Druze, the latter had better leadership. The Druze massacred 12,000 Christians and drove 100,000 from their homes during a four-week period. At that point, the European powers intervened to protect their coreligionists. French troops landed in Beirut and moved on to occupy Damascus. France and England forced the Ottoman sultan to establish Mount Lebanon as a self-governing province headed by a Christian governor. The province did not include Beirut. Although many Lebanese emigrated during this period because Mount Lebanon was small, rather poor, and provided few job opportunities, those who stayed (particularly the Maronites) prospered. Self-government enabled them to develop a system of small, individually owned farms and to break their former dependence on absentee landowners.

### The French Mandate

After the defeat of the Ottomans in World War I, Lebanon fell under a French mandate. The French had originally intended the country to be included in their mandate over Syria; but in 1920, due to pressure from Maronite leaders, they separated the two mandates. "New" Lebanon was much larger than the old Maronite-Druze territory up on Mount Lebanon. The new "Greater Lebanon" included the coast— in short, the area of the current Lebanese state. The Maronites found themselves linked not only with the Druze but also with both Sunni and Shi'a Muslims. The Maronites already distrusted the Druze, out of bitter experience. Their distrust was caused by fear of a Muslim majority and fear that Muslims, being mostly Arabs, would work to incorporate Lebanon into Syria after independence.

---

### DEVELOPMENT

The end of the civil war and a reform program pursued vigorously by the late Prime Minister Rafik Hariri restored much of Lebanon's infrastructure in the 1990s, including the renovation of war-ravaged central Beirut. GDP growth reached 8 percent in 1994. However Hariri's murder, the withdrawal of Syrian military forces and with them low-wage Syrian workers, internal conflict between pro-Syrian and anti-Syrian groups in the government, and the 34-day war between Israel and the Lebanese Hezbullah, have combined to devastate the economy. Unemployment has risen, along with the budget deficit and the public debt which was estimated to be $50 billion in 2010.

---

France gave Lebanon its independence in 1943, but French troops stayed on until 1946, when they were withdrawn due to British and American pressure on France.

The French made some contributions to Lebanese development during the mandate, such as the nucleus of a modern army, development of ports, roads, and airports, and an excellent educational system dominated by the Université de St. Joseph, a training ground for many Lebanese leaders. The French language and culture served until recently as one of the few things unifying the various sects and providing them with a sense of national identity.

## THE LEBANESE REPUBLIC

The major shortcoming of the mandate was the French failure to develop a broad-based political system with representatives from the major religious groups. The French very pointedly favored the Maronites. The Constitution, originally issued in 1926, established a republican system under an elected president and a Legislature. Members would be elected on the basis of six Christians to five Muslims. The president would be elected for a six-year term and could not serve concurrently. (The one exception was Bishara al-Khuri [1943–1952], who served during and after the transition period to independence. The Constitution was amended to allow him to do so.) By French-Maronite agreement, the custom was established whereby the Lebanese president would always be chosen from the Maronite community.

In 1943, an oral agreement, known as National Pact, was made between Bishara al-Khuri, head of the Maronite community, and Riad al-Sulh, his Muslim Sunni counterpart. The Pact, as important to Lebanese politics as the Constitution, included two important provisions: first, the Lebanese Christians would not enter into alliances with foreign (i.e., Christian) countries and the Muslims would not attempt to merge Lebanon with the Muslim Arab world; and second, the six-to-five formula for representation in the Assembly would apply to all public offices. The pact has never been put in writing, but in view of the delicate balance of sects in Lebanon, it has been considered by Lebanese leaders, particularly the Maronites, as the only alternative to anarchy.

## THE 1958 CRISIS

In July 1958, a major political crisis almost led to the collapse of the precarious balance between Maronite Christians and Muslims. It was mostly caused by external development, including the 1956 Suez Canal crisis which opposed Egypt to Israel and Western powers. Tensions between Lebanon and Egypt developed when Camille Chamoun, Lebanon's pro-Western Christian president, did not break diplomatic relations with France and Great Britain which had attacked Egypt after Nasser nationalized the Suez Canal. Furthermore, when Egypt and Syria became the United Arab Republic (UAR) in 1958, Lebanon's Sunni Prime Minister Rachid Karami supported the Union, just as he supported Nasser, Egypt's president, in the 1956 crisis. The Lebanese Muslim population called on the government to join the UAR while the Christians rejected the idea and supported close ties with Western powers.

According to some accounts, a Muslim rebellion, armed with weapons from UAR through Syria, tried to overthrow the government; this led President Chamoun to seek the assistance of the United Nations against what he termed a UAR interference in Lebanon. Growing internal instability, and the overthrow of Iraq's pro-Western government on July 14, worried the Christian Lebanese to the point that President Chamoun called on the United States to help. Fearing the spread of Communism, U.S. president Dwight Eisenhower decided on July 15 to send 14,000 troops (from the U.S. Mediterranean fleet) to Lebanon to end the crisis and prop-up the government of Chamoun which was facing internal challenge and external threat from the new Syria and Egypt union. After succeeding in quelling the rebellion, the U.S. forces withdrew on October 25, 1958. President Chamoun resigned as president; he was replaced by Fuad Chehab, and Prime Minister Karami who then formed a national reconciliation government, marking the formal end of the 1958 crisis.

Despite periodic political crises and frequent changes of government due to shifting alliances of leaders, Lebanon functioned quite well during its first two decades of independence. The large extended family, although an obstacle to broad nation building, served as an essential support base for its members, providing services that would otherwise have to have been drawn from government sources. These services included education, employment, bank loans, investment capital, and old-age security. Powerful families of different religious groups competed for power and influence but also coexisted, having had "the long experience with each other and with the rules and practices that make coexistence possible."[4] The freewheeling Lebanese economy was another important factor in Lebanon's relative stability. Per capita annual income rose from $235 in 1950 to $1,070 in 1974, putting Lebanon on par with some of the oil-producing Arab states, although the country does not have oil.

The private sector was largely responsible for national prosperity. A real-estate boom developed, and many fortunes were made in land speculation and construction. Tourism was another important source of revenues. Many banks and foreign business firms established their headquarters in Beirut because of its excellent communications with the outside world, its educated, multilingual labor force, and the absence of government restrictions.

## THE 1975–1990 CIVIL WAR

The titles of books on Lebanon in recent years have often contained adjectives such as "fractured," "fragmented," and "precarious." These provide a generally accurate description of the country's situation as a result of the Civil War of 1975–1990. There is not one single cause of the war since many factors built up during the year to create an explosive situation by 1975.

The causes of the bloody and destructive civil war may be traced back to several events starting in the Ottoman era and including modern era developments such as the effects of the establishment of Israel and the ensuing flight of hundreds of thousands of Palestinian refugees into Lebanon; the effects of the Cold War; the 1958 crisis; and the inter-communal tensions of the mid-1970s. The substantial inflow of Palestinian refugees directly affected the precarious demographic balance as they ended up making up 10 percent of the population and caused Lebanon to become directly involved in external tensions and wars. The first group, which fled there after the 1948 Arab-Israeli war, consisted mostly of urban educated people who gravitated around Beirut and were absorbed quickly into the population. Many of them became successful in banking, commerce, journalism, and teaching at the American University of Beirut. A second Palestinian group arrived as destitute refugees after the 1967 Six-Day War. They have been housed ever since in refugee camps run by the United Nations Relief and Works Agency. The Lebanese government provides them with identity cards but no passports. For all practical purposes, they are stateless persons.

Neither group was a threat to Lebanese internal stability until 1970, although Lebanon backed the Palestine Liberation Organization cause and did not interfere with guerrilla raids from its territory into Israel. After the PLO was expelled from Jordan, the organization made its headquarters in Beirut. This new militant Palestinian presence in Beirut created a double set of problems for the Lebanese. Palestinian raids into Israel brought Israeli retaliation, which caused more Lebanese than Palestinian casualties. Yet the Lebanese government could not control the Palestinians. To many Lebanese, especially the Maronites, their government seemed to be a prisoner in its own land.

In April 1975, a bus carrying Palestinians returning from a political rally was ambushed near Beirut by the Kata'ib, members of the Maronite Phalange Party. The incident triggered the Lebanese Civil War of 1975–1990. The war officially ended with a peace agreement arranged by the Arab League. But the bus incident also brought to a head conflicts derived from the opposing goals of various Lebanese groups. The Palestinians' goal was to use Lebanon as a springboard for the liberation of Palestine. The Maronites' goal was to drive the Palestinians out of Lebanon and preserve their privileged status. Sunni Muslim leaders sought to reshape the National Pact to allow for equal political participation with the Christians. Shi'a leaders were determined to get a better break for the Shi'a community, generally the poorest and least represented in the Lebanese government.[5] The Druze, also interested in greater representation in the system and traditionally hostile to the Maronites, are disliked and distrusted by all of the other groups.

The Lebanese Civil War was a war where sides changed frequently and battles raged from street to street in Beirut. It caused the almost total destruction of the country and the death of an estimated 200,000 people. The conflict was substantially exacerbated by the involvement of Syria, Israel, the United States and the Palestine Liberation Organization (PLO). The Syrian forces moved in quickly in June 1976 in response to President Suleiman Frangieh's demand for Syria's assistance, which Syria did supply but to the Christian groups which were on the verge of collapse. Syria also had its own economic and strategic interests to protect by intervening. An Arab League mediation brought about a short break in the fighting and mandated Syria to keep 40,000 troops in Lebanon to stabilize the country. However, as some areas were controlled by the Syrian forces—which were contested later by Christian militia in bloody exchanges—the conflict moved to the south where Palestinian forces opposed a force named the South Lebanon Army (SLA) in fierce fighting. The complexity of the situation was described in graphic terms by a Christian religious leader:

> The battle is between the Palestinians and the Lebanese. No! It is between the Palestinians and the Christians. No! It is between Christians and Muslims. No! It is between Leftists and Rightists. No! It is between Israel and the

Palestinians on Lebanese soil. No! It is between international imperialism and Zionism on the one hand, and Lebanon and neighboring states on the other.[6]

## FREEDOM

The 1943 National Pact, an unwritten agreement based on a handshake between leaders of the Maronite and Sunni Muslim leaders, defined Lebanon as a "confessional democracy" with political representation based on religious affiliation. (There are seventeen religious bodies represented in the population). The Pact specified that the president be a Maronite, the prime minister a Sunni Muslim, the foreign minister a Druze, and the Speaker of the Chamber of Deputies (Parliament) a Shi'a Muslim. In recent years this demographic balance has changed significantly with the growth of the Muslim population. The 1989 Taif Accord that "officially" ended the civil war reflected the change, setting a 6-5 ratio for Muslim and Christian deputies in the Chamber.

## THE ISRAELI INVASION

The immediate result of the Civil War was to divide Lebanon into separate territories, each controlled by a different faction. The Lebanese government, for all practical purposes, could not control its own territory. Israeli forces, in an effort to protect northern Israeli settlements from constant shelling by the Palestinians, established control over southern Lebanon. The Lebanese-Israeli border, ironically, became a sort of "good fence" open to Lebanese civilians for medical treatment in Israeli hospitals.

In March 1978, PLO guerrillas landed on the Israeli coast near Haifa, hijacked a bus, and drove it toward Tel Aviv. The hijackers were overpowered in a shoot out with Israeli troops, but 35 passengers were killed along with the guerrillas. Israeli forces invaded southern Lebanon in retaliation and occupied the region for two months, eventually withdrawing after the United Nations, in an effort to separate Palestinians from Israelis, set up a 6,000-member "Interim Force" in Lebanon, made up of units from various countries, in the south.

Although the Lebanese themselves often refer to UNFIL "United Nothings," the UN units deployed along the border have kept the peace, especially after the withdrawal of Israeli forces from Lebanese territory. UNIFIL's 2,000-member force

was increased to 13,300 after the 2006 Israeli-Hezbullah war. UNIFIL's mandate to preserve peace has been respected by both sides.

The Lebanese factions themselves continued to tear the country apart until 1990. Political assassinations of rival leaders were frequent. Many Lebanese settlements became ghost towns; they were fought over so much that their residents abandoned them. Some 300,000 Lebanese from the Israeli-occupied south fled to northern cities as refugees. In addition to the thousands of casualties, a psychological trauma settled over Lebanese youth, the "Kalashnikov generation" that knew little more than violence, crime, and the blind hatred of religious feuds.

## HEALTH/WELFARE

The withdrawal of Israeli forces from southern Lebanon left Hizbullah as the sole on-site agency for reconstruction of that war-torn region. In late 2000, teams of fighters-turned-humanitarian-workers cleaned village streets, set up potable water dispensers, sent mosquito-spraying trucks into the villages, and established and equipped mobile health clinics. Schools were reopened, and the former Israeli hospital at Bint Jbail, the regional capital, is now managed completely by Hizbullah doctors and nurses.

The Israeli invasion of Lebanon in June 1982 was intended as a final solution to the Palestinian problem. It did not quite work out that way. The Israeli Army surrounded Beirut and succeeded with U.S. intervention in forcing the evacuation of PLO guerrillas from Lebanon. Some of the Lebanese factions were happy to see them go, particularly the Maronites and the Shi'a community in the south. But they soon discovered that they had exchanged one foe for another. The burden of war, as always, fell heaviest on the civilian population. A Beirut newspaper estimated almost 50,000 civilian casualties in the first two months of the invasion. Also, the Lebanese discovered that they were not entirely free of the Palestinian presence. The largest number of PLO guerrillas either went to Syria and then returned secretly to Lebanon or retreated into the Biqa' Valley to take up new positions under Syrian Army protection.

Israeli control over Beirut enabled the Christians to take savage revenge against the remaining Palestinians. In September 1983, Christian Phalange militiamen

entered the refugee camps of Sabra and Shatila in West Beirut and massacred hundreds of people, mostly women and children. The massacre led to an official Israeli inquiry and censure of Israeli government and military leaders for indirect responsibility. The Christian-dominated Lebanese government's own inquiry failed to fix responsibility on the Phalange.

The 1982 Israeli invasion brought a change in government; the Phalange leader, Bashir Gemayel, was elected to head a "government of national salvation." However his ruthlessness in his career had enabled him to compile an impressive list of enemies. He was killed by a bomb explosion at Phalange headquarters before he could take office. Gemayel was succeeded by his older brother, Amin. The new president was persuaded by U.S. negotiators to sign a troop-withdrawal agreement with Israel. However, the agreement was not supported by leaders of the other Lebanese communities, and in March 1984, Gemayel unilaterally repudiated it. The Israelis then began working their way out of the "Lebanese quagmire" on their own, and in June 1985, the last Israeli units left Lebanon. However, they maintained control of a "security zone" along the border for necessary reprisals for attacks by PLO or Shi'a guerrillas.

The Israelis left behind a country that had become almost ungovernable. Gemayel's effort to restructure the national army along nonsectarian lines came to nothing, since the army was not strong enough to disband the various militias. The growing power of the Shi'a Muslims, particularly the Shi'a organization Amal, presented a new challenge to the Christian leadership, while the return of the Palestinians brought bloody battles between Shi'a and PLO guerrillas. As the battles raged, cease-fire followed cease-fire and conference followed conference, but without noticeable success.

The Israeli withdrawal left the Syrians as the major power brokers in Lebanon. In 1985, Syrian president Hafez al-Assad masterminded a comprehensive peace and reform agreement with Elie Hobeika, the commander of the Christian Falange militia. Hobeika was later ousted by one of his rivals and went into exile in Syria; his departure made the agreement worthless. He returned to Lebanon at the end of the Civil War and held several ministerial portfolios. In January 2002, however, he was killed in a car-bomb blast.

## SYRIA INTERVENES

The collapse of peace efforts led Syria to send 7,000 heavily armed commandos into west Beirut in 1987 to restore law and order. They did restore a semblance of order to that part of the capital and opened checkpoints into east Beirut. But the Syrians were unable, or perhaps unwilling, to challenge the powerful Hizbullah faction, which controlled the city's southern suburbs.

Aside from Hizbullah, Syria's major problem in knitting Lebanon together under its tutelage was with the Maronite community. With President Gemayel's six-year term scheduled to end in September 1988, the Syrians lobbied hard for a candidate of their choice. (Under the Lebanese parliamentary system, the president is elected by the Chamber of Deputies.) Unfortunately, due to the Civil War, only 72 of the 99 deputies elected in 1972, when the last elections had been held, were still in office. They rejected Syria's candidate, former president Suleiman Franjieh (1970–1976), because of his identification with the conflict and his ties with the Assad regime. When the Chamber failed to agree on an acceptable candidate, the office became vacant. Gemayel's last act before leaving office was to appoint General Michel Aoun, the commander of Christian troops in the Lebanese Army, to head an interim government. But the Muslim-dominated civilian government of Prime Minister Salim al-Hoss contested the appointment, declaring that it remained the legitimate government of the country.

## BREAKDOWN OF A SOCIETY

The assassination in 1987 of Prime Minister Rachid Karami graphically underlined the mindless rejection of law and order of the various Lebanese factions. The only show of Lebanese unity in many years occurred at the funeral of former president Camille Chamoun, dead of a heart attack at age 87. Chamoun's last public statement, made the day before his death, was particularly fitting to this fractured land. "The nation is headed toward total bankruptcy and famine," he warned. The statement brought to mind the prophetic observations of a historian, written in 1966: "Lebanon is too conspicuous and successful an example of political democracy and economic liberalism to be tolerated in a region that has turned its back on both systems."[7]

The death of the Mufti (the chief religious leader of the Sunni Muslim community) in a car-bomb attack in 1989 confirmed Chamoun's gloomy prediction. The Mufti had consistently called for reconciliation and nonviolent coexistence between Christian and Muslim communities. The political situation remained equally chaotic. Rene Moawwad, a respected Christian

lawyer, was elected by the Chamber to fill the presidential vacancy. However, he was murdered after barely 17 days in office. The Chamber then elected Elias Hrawi, a Christian politician from the Maronite stronghold of Zahle, as president. General Aoun contested the election, declaring himself the legitimate president of Lebanon, and holed up in the presidential palace in east Beirut, defended strongly by his Maronite militiamen.

But the Maronite community was as fragmented as the larger Lebanese community. Aoun's chief Christian rival, Samir Geagea, rejected his authority, and early in 1990, a renewed outbreak of fighting between their militias left east Beirut in shambles, with more than 3,000 casualties. After another shaky cease-fire had been reached, Syrian Army units supporting the regular Lebanese Army surrounded the Christian section. Aoun's palace became an embattled enclave, with supplies available only by running the Syrian blockade or from humanitarian relief organizations.

Aoun's support base eroded significantly in the spring, when his rival recognized the Hrawi government as legitimate and endorsed the Taif Accord.[8] In October, Hrawi formally requested Syrian military aid for the Lebanese Army. After an all-out assault on the presidential palace by joint Syrian-Lebanese forces, the general surrendered, taking refuge in the French Embassy and then going into exile.

Aoun's departure enabled the Hrawi government to begin taking the next step toward rebuilding a united Lebanon. This involved disarming the militias. The continued presence of Syrian forces was a major asset to the reconstituted Lebanese Army as it undertook this delicate process.

Following the reestablishment of central-government authority, a new transitional Council of Ministers (cabinet) was appointed by President Hrawi in 1992. Its responsibilities were to stabilize the economy and prepare for elections for a new Chamber of Deputies. In preparation for the elections the Chamber was enlarged from 108 to 128 seats.

The first national elections since the start of the Civil War were held in 1992. Due in part to a boycott by Christian parties, which had demanded Syrian withdrawal as their price for participation, Shi'a candidates won 30 seats. Shi'a Amal leader Nabih Berri was elected speaker; Rafiq Hariri, a Sunni Muslim and millionaire (who had made his fortune as a contractor in Saudi Arabia) was named prime minister.

In any case, the growing demographic imbalance of Muslims and Christians

indicated that, in the not too distant future, Lebanon would no longer be "a Christian island in a Muslim sea." By 1997, Christians numbered at most 30 percent of the population (composed of 800,000 Maronites, 400,000 Greek Orthodox, 300,000 Greek Catholics or Melkites, and 75,000 Armenians). Half a million Christians had left the country during the Civil War, along with top leaders such as Michel Aoun, Amin Gemayel, and Raymond Edde, in exile in Paris.

Changes in the election laws in the 1990s reshaped the Lebanese political configuration. The former governorates were incorporated into 14 constituencies, and the number of seats in the Chamber of Deputies (Parliament) per constituency increased from six to sixteen. Another change allowed government officials to run for president while still in office. As a result, Gen. Emile Lahoud, the army chief of staff, ran and was elected in October 1998 for a six-year term. Lahoud came under fire in 2005 during the "Independence Intifada" that led to Syria's withdrawal from Lebanon. However a constitutional amendment narrowly approved by the legislature would extend his term for an additional three years.

As army chief of staff, Lahoud, a Maronite, had been responsible for disarming the country's numerous militias. By 1993, the one remaining armed organization was Hizbullah. Its members were allowed to keep their weapons in order to deal with Israeli forces in the "security zone" along the border and with their allies, the South Lebanon Army (SLA). With weapons and training supplied by Iran and Syria, Hizbullah developed into a formidable fighting force. In 1998, its fighters succeeded in overrunning the main SLA base at Jezzin. The impending defeat of its Lebanese ally and the endless "war of attrition" with Hizbullah led to a complete withdrawal of Israeli forces from the self-proclaimed "security zone," inside the Lebanese border, in May 2000. Israeli prime minister Ehud Barak had originally set July 2000 for the withdrawal, but he accelerated the process for policy reasons. On May 24, the last Israeli soldiers pulled out of the zone, ending a 22-year occupation.

The Israeli withdrawal resulted in jubilant celebrations throughout Lebanon. The government declared May 24 a national holiday, National Resistance Day, as crowds danced in the streets.

The absence of formal demarcation of the 198-mile Lebanese-Syrian border continued to cause problems for the two countries. It was drawn up by French military cartographers in the 1920s to separate the two mandates. In 2007 an anti-Syrian

Lebanese group reported that Syria still occupies 177 square miles of productive agricultural land on the Lebanese side of the border despite the 2005 withdrawal of Syrian forces from the country.

The other area of border contention is Shab'a Farms, a 15.6 square mile area that was originally Lebanese territory but had been awarded to Syria by the League of Nations in 1920, after the establishment of the Syrian and Lebanese mandates. For that reason, the United Nations had excluded it from Israel's "security zone."

Along with guerrilla warfare, Hizbullah engaged in a "propaganda war" with Israel through its satellite-television station, *Al-Manar* ("The Beacon"). Its programs were greatly expanded after the Israeli withdrawal from Lebanon and the revived Palestinian intifada. Its broadcasts in Hebrew to Israelis and in Arabic to the Palestinians, with video images of clashes and casualties, helped to strengthen the resolve of the Palestinians against the Israelis.

## LEBANON AND THE WORLD

Aside from its vulnerability to international and inter-Arab rivalries because of internal conflicts, Lebanon drew world attention in the 1980s for its involvement in hostage taking. Lebanese militias such as Hizbullah, and shadowy organizations like the Islamic Jihad, Revolutionary Justice, and Islamic Jihad for the Liberation of Palestine kidnapped foreigners in Beirut. The conditions set for their release were rarely specific, and the refusal of the U.S. and other Western governments to "deal with terrorists" left them languishing in unknown prisons for years.

Release negotiations were pursued by then UN secretary-general Javier Pérez de Cuéllar. The hostages, mostly British and American, were freed individually or in small groups. They included Terry Waite, an envoy of the archbishop of Canterbury originally sent to negotiate the hostages' release (he was charged mistakenly with espionage). Several had been professors at the American University of Beirut or Beirut College for Women, and the last to be released was Terry Anderson, a well-known *New York Times* correspondent.

Since then, Lebanese–American relations have remained stable. However, the September 11 terrorist bombings in the United States and President George W. Bush's effort to form an international antiterrorism coalition placed the Lebanese government in an awkward position because Lebanon was accused of sheltering "terrorist organizations," including Hizbullah, since it had been responsible for the 1983 destruction of the American

(U.S. Department of State)
Secretary of State Hillary Clinton and Lebanese Defense Minister Elias Murr at the U.S. State Department on April 8, 2009

Embassy in Beirut and a truck-bomb onslaught on a U.S. Marine barracks that killed 241 Americans. Despite Hizbullah's newfound respectability as a social-service organization and political party represented in the Chamber of Deputies, the government feared that its past actions might motivate the United States to seek retribution by including Lebanon in its antiterrorism campaign. A Bush administration request to the Lebanese government to freeze Hizbullah assets as a "terrorist organization" was rejected.

## SYRIA LEAVES LEBANON

The assassination of ex-prime minister Rafik Hariri by a remote-control bomb that blew up his motorcade in Beirut, killing him and 18 associates, was the catalyst in increasing Lebanese resentment to the point of bringing about a withdrawal of Syrian forces from the country. Syria disclaimed any connection with the murder, but UN investigators determined quite conclusively in 2005 that both pro-Syrian Lebanese police and Syrian intelligence agents were directly involved. Hariri had resigned in October, 2004, under Syrian pressure, and had begun to form an opposition coalition to win control of the Chamber of Deputies in the 2005 elections and form a new government independent of Syrian control.

Hariri's assassination triggered widespread demonstrations demanding Syrian troop withdrawal. The resulting "Cedar Revolution" (an indirect reference to the Lebanese national flag) briefly united all Lebanese fractions in a nonviolent campaign demanding an end to the Syrian occupation. The UN Security Council weighed in with *Resolution 1559,* which called for the complete withdrawal of Syrian forces. With the exception of Shab'a Farms and the area mentioned above along the border, Syrian forces have left the country to

its own devices in patching itself together from a fractured state. The Syrian withdrawal has its negative side. In addition to Syrian funds brought in to pay for its occupation forces, the departure of Syrian construction and service workers has been financially and socially damaging. Low-paying jobs such as that of garbage collection remain unfilled, and Beirut itself remains an unfinished restoration project, its skyline dominated by idly swinging cranes.

However, political normalcy still eluded Lebanon after the Syrian withdrawal. In 2007, Hezbollah-led opposition increased pressure for institutional reform, starting with the resignation of the government. As parliament failed to elect a new president, incumbent president Emile Lahoud stepped down in November and Prime Minister Fouad Siniora decided to temporarily assume the presidency. It was not until May 2008 that parliament finally elected army chief Michel Suleiman as president. He reappointed Siniora as prime minister; he managed to form a new national unity government in July. In October, Lebanon established diplomatic relations with Syria for the first time since the independence of both countries in the 1940s. In the June 2009 parliamentary elections, a pro-Western alliance led by Saad Hariri won 71 of 128 seats and the alliance led by Hezbollah won 57. Hariri was appointed prime minister and formed, in November, a government of national unity.

While the peaceful political reconciliations were happening, sporadic violence continued to rock Lebanon. From May to September 2007, clashes between Islamist militants and the Lebanese army led to the siege of the Palestinian refugee camp Nahr al-Bared, which ended with more than 300 people dead and 40,000 residents displaced. In May 2008, clashes between Hezbollah and pro-government factions killed more than 80 people and stimulated fears of the return of civil war. In spite of this, in December 2009, the government agreed to allow Hezbollah to keep its military arsenal because of its role as resistance and its commitment to "liberate Lebanese territory."

## THE ECONOMY

In the mid-1970s, the Lebanese economy began declining steadily. The Civil War and the resulting instability caused most banks and financial institutions to move out of Lebanon to more secure locations, notably Jordan, Bahrain, and Kuwait. Aside from the cost in human lives, the Israeli raids and the 1982 invasion severely damaged the economy. The cost of the invasion in terms of damages was estimated at $1.9 billion. Remittances from

Lebanese emigrants abroad dropped significantly. The Lebanese currency, once valued at 4.74 pounds to $1, had dropped in value to 3,000 to $1 by 1992, although rebounding to LL 1,502 to $1 by 2010.

Yet by a strange irony of fate, some elements of the economy continued to display robust health. Most middle-class Lebanese had funds invested abroad, largely in U.S. dollar accounts, and thus were protected from economic disaster.

The expansion of the Civil War in 1989–1990 and the intervention of Syrian troops tested the survival techniques of the Lebanese people as never before. But they adjusted to the new "Battle of Beirut" with great inventiveness. A newspaper advertisement announced: "Civilian fortifications, 24-hour delivery service. Sandbags and barrels, full or empty." With the Syrian-Christian artillery exchanges concentrated at night, most residents fled the city then, returning after the muezzin's first call for morning prayers had in effect silenced the guns, to shop, to stock up on fuel smuggled ashore from small tankers, or to sample the luxury goods that in some mysterious way had appeared on store shelves.

The long, drawn-out civil conflict badly affected Lebanese agriculture, the mainstay of the economy. Both the coastal strip and the Biqa' Valley are extremely fertile, and in normal times produce crop surpluses for export. Lebanese fruit, particularly apples (the most important cash crop) and grapes, is in great demand throughout the Arab world. But these crops are no longer exported in quantity. Israeli destruction of crops, the flight of most of the farm labor force, and the blockade by Israeli troops of truck traffic from rural areas into Beirut had a devastating effect on production.

Lebanon has no oil resources, but one of its main sources of revenue came from transit fees for oil shipments across its territory. Another important source was cannabis (the opium poppy), which was cultivated extensively in the Biqa' region. Production is illegal, and after the "golden years" of the civil war, when processed heroin flooded U.S. and European markets, crops were bulldozed annually. In 1994 the UN Development Program (UNDP) declared the Biqa' drug free. Unfortunately some $300 million in UNDP funds to develop alternative crops did not materialize, along with the political crisis, deteriorating economic prospects and battles between the army and Palestinian militants have encouraged farmers to return to marijuana cultivation. With each poppy field yielding 15 kilograms (33 pounds) and generating

some $10,000 in return for minimum effort (a little seed, a little water), many Biqa' farmers have no incentive to plant other crops.

Armed with $458 million in aid from the World Bank, the European Union, and the Paris-based Mediterranean Development Agency, Hariri had launched a major economic reform drive in February 2001. He laid off 500 employees from the bloated public sector, and privatized the state-owned electricity company as a start toward further privatization. The cabinet also agreed to shut down the state-owned TeleLiban, saving $33 million a year. Elimination of the sugar subsidy will save another $40 million annually.

According to a 2010 World Bank country report, most of Lebanon's income (60 percent of GDP) came in the form of financial transfers and capital inflows from abroad, including investment capital and

remittances. The reasons for this massive inflow of capital include a sound banking system based on secrecy which proved able to withstand not only the internal turmoil, but also the global financial crisis of the late 2000s.[9] However, most of the capital has not been invested in productive activities and has thus not helped create much needed new jobs. The political instability of 2008 and 2009 (inability to form a government) has undermined economic reform efforts. In spite of a high growth rate in 2009 (around 8 percent), major structural changes need to be made in order to help the economy fully recover, lower the substantial budget deficit and public debt, improve the productive sector and create more jobs for a population yearning for a stable and peaceful life.

## Timeline: PAST

**9th–11th centuries**
Establishment of Mount Lebanon as a sanctuary for religious communities

**1860–1864**
The first Civil War, between Maronites and Druze, ending in foreign military intervention

**1920–1946**
French mandate

**1958**
Internal crisis and the first U.S. military intervention

**1975–1990**
Civil war, halted temporarily by an Arab League-sponsored cease-fire and peacekeeping force of Syrian troops but resumed shortly thereafter

**1980s**
Israeli occupation of Beirut; Syrian troops reoccupy Beirut; foreigners are seized in a new outbreak of hostage taking; the economy nears collapse

**1990s**
The withdrawal of Israeli forces from Lebanon; all foreign hostages are released; Lebanon begins rebuilding

## PRESENT

**2000s**
Hezbollah's presence in Lebanon causes tension with the United States after 9/11; Israel invades Lebanon and engages in a 34 day war with Hezbollah; following parliamentary elections, army chief Michel Suleiman become president of Lebanon in 2008

## NOTES

1. Abdo Baaklini, *Legislative and Political Development: Lebanon 1842–1972* (Durham, NC: Duke University Press, 1976), pp. 32–34.

2. David C. Gordon, *The Republic of Lebanon: Nation in Jeopardy* (Boulder, CO: Westview Press, 1983), p. 4.

3. Samir Khlaf, *Lebanon's Predicament* (New York: Columbia University Press, 1987), p. 69.

4. Gordon, *The Republic of Lebanon,* op. cit., p. 25. See also Baaklini, *Legislative and Political Development,* op. cit., pp. 200–202, for a description of the coexistence process as used by Sabri Hamadeh, for many years as head of parliament between 1927 and 1972.

5. Shi'a religious leader Imam Musa al-Sadr's political organization was named Harakat al-Mahrumin ("Movement of the Disinherited") when it was founded in 1969–1970. See Marius Deeb, *The Lebanese Civil War* (New York: Praeger, 1980), pp. 69–70.

6. Gordon, *The Republic of Lebanon,* op. cit., p. 110.

7. Charles Issawi, "Economic Development and Political Liberalism in Lebanon," in Leonard Binder, ed., *Politics in Lebanon* (New York: John Wiley, 1966), pp. 80–81.

8. The Taif Accord, signed under Arab League auspices in Taif, Saudi Arabia, changed the power-sharing arrangement in the Lebanese government from a 6:5 Christian-Muslim ratio to one of equal representation in the government. The powers of the president were also reduced.

9. The World Bank, "Country Brief: Lebanon," April 2010. Online at http://go.worldbank.org/I59TTVC2M0. Consulted on July 14, 2010.

# Libya (Socialist People's Libyan Arab Jamahiriyya)

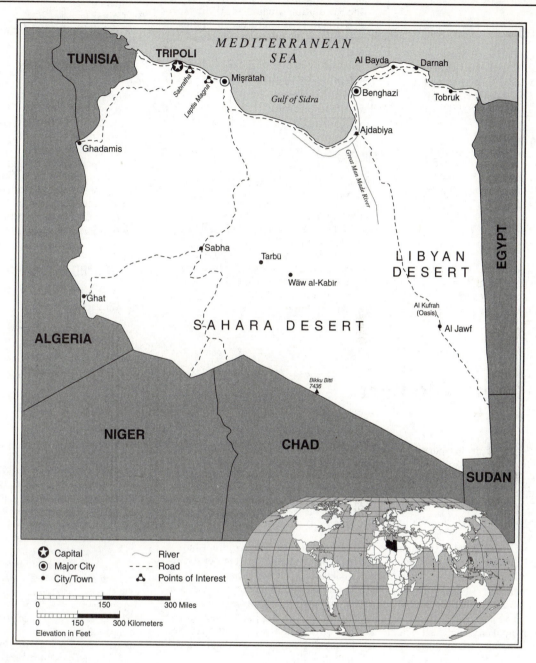

# Libya Statistics

## GEOGRAPHY

*Area in Square Miles (Kilometers):*
679,147 (1,759,450) (about the size of Alaska)

*Capital (Population):* Tripoli (1,509,890)

*Environmental Concerns:* desertification; very limited freshwater resources

*Geographical Features:* mostly barren, flat to undulating plains, plateaus, depressions

*Climate:* Mediterranean along the coast; dry, extreme desert in the interior

## PEOPLE

### Population

*Total:* 6,310,434 (includes 166,510 non-nationals)

*Annual Growth Rate:* 2.17%

*Rural/Urban Population Ratio:* 22/78

*Major Languages:* Arabic; English; Italian

*Ethnic Makeup:* 97% Berber and Arab; 3% others

*Religions:* 97% Sunni Muslim; 3% others

### Health

*Life Expectancy at Birth:* 74.98 years (male); 79.65 years (female)

*Infant Mortality Rate:* 21.05/1,000 live births

## Education

*Adult Literacy Rate:* 86.3%
*Compulsory (Ages):* 6–15

## COMMUNICATION

*Telephones:* 1,033,000 main lines
*Daily Newspaper Circulation:* 15 per 1,000 people
*Televisions:* 146 per 1,000 people
*Internet Service Providers:* 5 (2009)

## TRANSPORTATION

*Highways in Miles (Kilometers):* 35,551 (57,214)
*Railroads in Miles (Kilometers):* none
*Usable Airfields:* 137
*Motor Vehicles in Use:* 904,000

## GOVERNMENT

*Type:* officially a *Jamahiriyya* ("state belonging to the people") with government authority exercised by a General Peoples' Congress

*Independence Date:* December 24, 1951 (from Italy)
*Head of State/Government:* Leader of the Revolution Muammar al-Minyar al-Qadhafi ("Brother Leader") holds no official title but is de facto head of state. Al-Baghdadi Ali al-Mahmudi, General Secretary of the GPC, holds a position comparable to that of Prime Minister.

*Political Parties:* none
*Suffrage:* universal at 18

## MILITARY

*Military Expenditures (% of GDP):* 3.9%
*Current Disputes:* Libya claims 32,000 square kilometers of land in southeastern Algeria and 25,000 square kilometers in the Tommo region of Niger, both claims resulting from the 1899 treaty establishing France's West African colonies. Both claims are presently dormant.

## ECONOMY

*Currency ($U.S. Equivalent):* 1.211 dinars = $1
*Per Capita Income/GDP:* $14,400 (PPP)/$100.1 billion
*GDP Growth Rate:* 6.3%
*Inflation Rate:* 10.4%
*Unemployment Rate:* 30%
*Labor Force:* 1,640,000
*Natural Resources:* petroleum; natural gas; gypsum
*Agriculture:* wheat; barley; olives; dates; citrus fruits; vegetables; peanuts; beef; eggs
*Industry:* petroleum; food processing; textiles; handicrafts; cement
*Exports:* $60.26 billion (primary partners Italy, Germany, France)
*Imports:* $25.31 billion (primary partners Italy, Germany, China)

## SUGGESTED WEB SITES

www.lcweb4.loc.gov/frd/cs/lytoc.html
www.libyaonline.com/

# Libya Country Report

The Socialist People's Libyan Arab Jamahiriyya (Republic), commonly known as Libya, is the fourth largest Arab country. It consists of three geographical regions: Tripolitania, Cyrenaica, and the Fezzan. Most of the population lives in Tripolitania, the northwestern part of the country, where Tripoli, the capital and major port, is located. Cyrenaica, in the east along the Egyptian border, has a narrow coastline backed by a high plateau (2,400-feet elevation) called the Jabal al-Akhdar ("Green Mountain"). It contains Libya's other principal city, Benghazi. The two regions are separated by the Sirte, an extension of the Sahara Desert that reaches almost to the Mediterranean Sea. Most of Libya's oil fields are in the Sirte.

The Fezzan occupies the central part of the country. It is entirely desert, except for a string of widely scattered oases. Its borders are with Chad, Algeria, Niger, and Sudan. The border with Chad, established during French colonial rule in sub-Saharan Africa, was disputed more than once by Libya. The matter was settled through international mediation, with the border formally demarcated in 1994. Libya also claims areas in northern Niger and southeastern Algeria left over from the colonial period, when they formed part of the

French West African empire. In the Libyan view, these areas should have been transferred to its control under the peace treaty that established the Libyan state.

## HISTORY

Until modern times, Libya did not have a separate identity, either national or territorial. It always formed a part of some other territorial unit and in most cases was controlled by outsiders. However, control was usually limited to the coastal areas. The Berbers of the interior were little affected by the passing of conquerors and the rise and fall of civilizations.

Libya's culture and social structure have been influenced more by the Muslim Arabs than by any other invaders. The Arabs brought Islam to Libya in the early seventh century. Arab groups settled in the region and intermarried with the Berber population to such an extent that the Libyans became one of the most thoroughly Arabized peoples in the region.

Coastal Libya, around Tripoli, was an outlying province of the Ottoman Empire for several centuries. Like its urban neighbors Tunis and Algiers, Tripoli had a fleet of corsairs in the Mediterranean. When the United States became a Mediterranean

## DEVELOPMENT

Restoration of full diplomatic relations with the United States and the end of sanctions now permits American firms, particularly oil companies, to invest in Libya's renewed economic development. Similarly European countries, notably those that are heavy purchasers of Libyan oil, have become active investors in the country's infrastructure. Italy's export credit agency agreed to write off $230 million in Libyan debts in exchange for investments by Italian companies. The Bush administration in 2007 allocated $1.15 million in aid to the Libyan economy in "normalizing" relations.

trading country, the corsairs of Tripoli included American ships among their targets. The USS *Philadelphia* was sent to Tripoli to "teach the corsairs a lesson" in 1804, but it got stuck on a sandbar and was captured. Navy Lieutenant Stephen Decatur led a commando raid into Tripoli harbor and blew up the ship, inspiring the words to what would become the official U.S. Marine hymn: "From the halls of Montezuma to the shores of Tripoli. . . ." Ironically the Marines never reached

Mourzouk Erg camel caravan, Sahara Desert, Libya

(© PIXFOLIO/Alamy Images)

territories in North and West Africa, the Sanusi became warrior-monks and fought the invaders.

## Italy Conquers Libya

The Italian conquest of Libya began in 1911. The Italians needed colonies, not only for prestige but also for the resettlement of poor and landless peasants from Italy's crowded southern provinces. The Italians expected an easy victory against a weak Ottoman garrison; Libya would become the "Fourth Shore" of a new Roman Empire from shore to shore along the Mediterranean. But the Italians found Libya a tougher land to subdue than they had expected. Italian forces were pinned to Tripoli and a few other points on the coast by the Ottoman garrison and the fierce Sanusi warrior-monks.

The Italians were given a second chance after World War I. The government of swaggering dictator Benito Mussolini sent an army to occupy Tripolitania. When the Italians moved on Cyrenaica, the Grand Sanusi crossed the Egyptian border into exile under British protection. The Italians found Cyrenaica much more difficult to control than Tripolitania. It is ideal guerrilla country, from the caves of Jabal al-Akhdar to the stony plains and dry, hidden *wadis* (river beds) of the south. It took nine years (1923–1932) for Italy to overcome all of Libya, despite Italy's vast superiority in troops and weapons. Sanusi guerrilla bands harried the Italians, cutting supply lines, ambushing patrols, and attacking convoys. Their leader, Shaykh Omar Mukhtar, became Libya's first national hero.

The Italians finally overcame the Sanusi by the use of methods that do not shock us today but seemed unbelievably brutal at the time. Cyrenaica was made into a huge concentration camp, with a barbed-wire fence along the Egyptian border. Nomadic peoples were herded into these camps, guarded by soldiers to prevent them from aiding the Sanusi. Sanusi prisoners were pushed out of airplanes, wells were plugged to deny water to the people, and flocks were slaughtered. In 1931, Omar Mukhtar was captured, court-martialed, and hanged in public. The resistance ended with his death.

The Italians did not have long to cultivate their Fourth Shore. During the 1930s, they poured millions of lire into the colony. A paved highway from the Egyptian to the Tunisian border along the coast was completed in 1937; in World War II, it became a handy invasion route for the British. A system of state-subsidized farms was set up for immigrant Italian peasants. Each was given free transportation, a house, seed, fertilizers, a mule, and a pair of shoes as

Tripoli, although a land campaign led by the itinerant American soldier of fortune William Eaton, who had been hired by a dispossessed member of the ruling dynasty to recover his throne, reached only Darna, well east of the capital in 1805.

This ruling dynasty, founded by an ex-Ottoman officer named Ahmad Karamanli, controlled Tripoli and its coastline from the 18th century on. Its corsair fleet was allied with the Ottoman navy. In 1815, at the end of the Napoleonic Wars, British and French naval forces defeated the Tripolitan corsairs and forced the Karamanli ruler of that time to end payment of tribute. Lacking its main source of revenue, his population rebelled. By 1835 France had seized control of Algiers and Tunis, the other main corsair states. To forestall further territorial losses, the Ottoman sultan, Tripoli's nominal ruler, sent forces to occupy the city and, for the first time, place it under direct Ottoman rule.

## The Sanusiya Movement

At various stages in Islam's long history, new groups or movements have appeared committed to purifying or reforming Islamic society and taking it back to its original form of a simple community of believers led by just rulers. Several of these movements, such as the Wahhabis of Saudi Arabia, were important in the founding of modern Islamic states. The movement called the Sanusiya was formed in the nineteenth century and later became an important factor in the formation of modern Libya.

The founder, the Grand Sanusi, was a religious teacher from Algeria. He left Algeria after the French conquest and settled in northern Cyrenaica. The Grand Sanusi's teachings attracted many followers. He also attracted the attention of the Ottoman authorities, who distrusted his advocacy of a strong united Islamic world in which Ottomans and Arabs would be partners. In 1895, to escape from the Ottomans, the Grand Sanusi's son and successor moved Sanusiya headquarters to Kufra, a remote oasis in the Sahara.

The Sanusiya began as a peaceful movement interested only in bringing new converts to Islam and founding a network of *zawiyas* ("lodges") for contemplation and monastic life throughout the desert. But when European countries began to seize inducements to come to Libya. By 1940, the Italian population had reached 110,000, and about 495,000 acres of land had been converted into productive farms, vineyards, and olive groves.[1]

## Independent Libya

Libya was a major battleground during World War II, as British, German, and Italian armies rolled back and forth across the desert. The British defeated the Germans and occupied northern Libya, while a French army occupied the Fezzan. The United States later built an important air base, Wheelus Field, near Tripoli. Thus the three major Allied powers all had an interest in Libya's future, but they could not agree on what to do with occupied Libya.

Italy wanted Libya back. France wished to keep the Fezzan as a buffer for its African colonies, while Britain preferred self-government for Cyrenaica under the Grand Sanusi, who had become staunchly pro-British during his exile in Egypt. The Soviet Union favored a Soviet trusteeship over Libya, which would provide the Soviet Union with a convenient outlet in the Mediterranean. The United States waffled but finally settled on independence, which would at least keep the Soviet tentacles from enveloping Libya.

Due to lack of agreement, the Libyan "problem" was referred to the United Nations General Assembly. Popular demonstrations in Libya in support of independence impressed a number of the newer UN members; in 1951, the General Assembly approved a resolution for an independent Libyan state, a kingdom under the Grand Sanusi, Idris.

In 2009, Italy agreed to pay Libya $5 billion as compensation for its 30-year occupation of the country (1911–1943). During a visit to Italy in June 2009, Qaddhafi with Italian Prime Minister Silvio Berlusconi signed a memorandum that pledged the disbursement of the compensation over a 20 year period and agreed on construction projects in Libya and student grants and pensions for Libyan soldiers who served with the Italians during World War II. In exchange for the deal, Libya agreed to help stem illegal African emigration from its shores and to give Italian business companies priority in contracts, especially in the area of infrastructure.

## THE KINGDOM OF LIBYA

Libya has been governed under two political systems since independence: a constitutional monarchy (1951–1969); and a Socialist republic (1969– ), which has no constitution because all power "belongs" to the people. Qadhafi's Libyan Arab Jamahiriyya has lasted more than twice as long as its monarchical predecessor, and its aggressive forays into foreign affairs are significantly different from foreign policy under King Idris.

At independence, Libya was an artificial union of the three provinces. The Libyan people had little sense of national identity or unity. Loyalty was to one's family, clan, village, and, in a general sense, to the higher authority represented by a tribal confederation. The only other loyalty linking Libyans was the Islamic religion. The tides of war and conquest that had washed over them for centuries had had little effect on their strong, traditional attachment to Islam.[2]

Political differences also divided the three provinces. Tripolitanians talked openly of abolishing the monarchy. Cyrenaica was the home and power base of King Idris; the king's principal supporters were the Sanusiya and certain important families. The distances and poor communication links between the provinces contributed to the impression that they should be separate countries. Leaders could not even agree on the choice between Tripoli and Benghazi for the capital. For his part, the king distrusted both cities as being corrupt and overly influenced by foreigners. He had his administrative capital in Baida, in the Jabal al-Akhdar.

Libya at the start of independence was an extremely poor country. Per capita income in 1951 was about $30 per year; in 1960, it was about $100 per year. Approximately 5 percent of the land was marginally usable for agriculture, and only 1 percent could be cultivated on a permanent basis. Most economists considered Libya to be a hopeless case, almost totally dependent on foreign aid for survival.

Despite its meager resources and lack of political experience, Libya was valuable to the United States and Britain in the 1950s and 1960s because of its strategic location. The United States negotiated a long-term lease on Wheelus Field in 1954, as a vital link in the chain of U.S. bases built around the southern perimeter of the Soviet Union due to the Cold War. In return, U.S. aid of $42 million sweetened the pot, and Wheelus became the single largest employer of Libyan labor. The British had two air bases and maintained a garrison in Tobruk.

Political development in the kingdom was minimal. King Idris knew little about parliamentary democracy, and he distrusted political parties. The 1951 Constitution provided for an elected Legislature, but a dispute between the king and the Tripolitanian National Congress, one of several Tripolitanian parties, led to the outlawing of all political parties. Elections were held every four years, but only property-owning adult males could vote (women were granted the vote in 1963). The same legislators were reelected regularly. In the absence of political activity, the king was the glue that held Libya together.

## THE 1969 REVOLUTION

At dawn on September 1, 1969, a group of young, unknown army officers abruptly carried out a military coup in Libya. King Idris, who had gone to Turkey for medical treatment, was deposed, and a "Libyan Arab Republic" was proclaimed by the officers. These men, whose names were not known to the outside world until weeks after the coup, were led by Captain Muammar al-Qadhafi. He went on Benghazi radio to announce to a startled Libyan population: "People of Libya . . . your armed forces have undertaken the overthrow of the reactionary and corrupt regime. . . . From now on Libya is a free, sovereign republic, ascending with God's help to exalted heights."[3]

Qadhafi's new regime made a sharp change in policy from that of its predecessor. Wheelus Field and the British air bases were evacuated and returned to Libyan control. Libya took an active part in Arab affairs and supported Arab unity, to the extent of working to undermine other Arab leaders whom Qadhafi considered undemocratic or unfriendly to his regime.[4]

## REGIONAL POLICY

Qadhafi's efforts to unite Libya with other Arab states have not been successful. A 1984 agreement for a federal union with Morocco, which provided for separate sovereignty but a federated Assembly and unified foreign policies, was abrogated unilaterally by the late King Hassan II, after Qadhafi had charged him with "Arab treason" for meeting with Israeli leader Shimon Peres. Undeterred, Qadhafi tried again in 1987 with neighboring Algeria, receiving a medal from President Chadli Bendjedid but no other encouragement.

Although distrustful of the mercurial Libyan leader, other North African heads of state have continued to work with him on the basis that it is safer to have Qadhafi inside the circle than isolated outside. Tunisia restored diplomatic relations in 1987, and Qadhafi agreed to compensate the Tunisian government for lost wages of Tunisian workers expelled from Libya during the 1985 economic recession. Qadhafi also accepted International Court of Justice arbitration over Libya's dispute with Tunisia over oil rights in the Gulf of Gabes. But Qadhafi continued to be unpredictable in his Arab policy. In 2007, for example, he refused to attend the Arab summit meeting, saying that other Arab countries were now serving American "imperial" interests. He added that Libya had now turned its back on the Arabs and become an African nation.

Libya's "re-formation" as an African nation was underscored by an open-ended invitation to sub-Saharan African leaders to send their workers to work in the country. By 2000, nearly a million had arrived, most of them from Nigeria, Chad, and Ghana. Economic problems in sub-Saharan Africa caused thousands more to use Libya as an escape route for Europe, many of them also fleeing from civil war in Côte d' Ivoire and Sierra Leone. The flood of migrants generated tension between them and Libyan natives; the latter viewed the migrants as agents of social misbehavior ranging from prostitution to drug usage and AIDS. In August 2000, the Libyan government deported several thousand African workers. They were hauled to the Niger border in trucks and dumped across the border. Qadhafi had announced earlier that a "United States of Africa" would come into existence in March 2001 under Libyan sponsorship. But for once the Libyan people did not agree with him; "We are native Arabs, not Africans," they told their leader.

## SOCIAL REVOLUTION

Qadhafi's desert upbringing and Islamic education gave him a strong, puritanical moral code. In addition to closing foreign bases and expropriating properties of Italians and Jews, he moved forcefully against symbols of foreign influence. The Italian cathedral in Tripoli became a mosque, street signs were converted to Arabic, nightclubs were closed, and the production and sale of alcohol were prohibited.

But Qadhafi's revolution went far beyond changing names. In a three-volume work entitled *The Green Book,* he described his vision of the appropriate political system for Libya. Political parties would not be allowed, nor would constitutions, legislatures, even an organized court system. All of these institutions, according to Qadhafi, eventually become corrupt and unrepresentative. Instead, "people's committees" would run the government, business, industry, and even the universities. Libyan embassies abroad were renamed "people's bureaus" and were run by junior officers. (The takeover of the London bureau in 1984 led to counterdemonstrations by Libyan students and the killing of a British police officer by gunfire from inside the bureau. The Libyan bureau in Washington, D.C., was closed by the U.S. Federal Bureau of Investigation and

the staff deported on charges of espionage and terrorism against Libyans in the United States.) The country was renamed the Socialist People's Libyan Arab Jamahiriyya, and titles of government officials were eliminated. Qadhafi became "Leader of the Revolution," and each government department was headed by the secretary of a particular people's committee.

Qadhafi developed a so-called Third International Theory, based on the belief that neither capitalism nor communism could solve the world's problems. What was needed, he said, was a "middle way" that would harness the driving forces of human history—religion and nationalism—to interact with each other to revitalize humankind. Islam would be the source of that middle way, because "it provides for the realization of justice and equity, it does not allow the rich to exploit the poor."[5]

## THE ECONOMY

Modern Libya's economy is based almost entirely on oil exports. Concessions were granted to various foreign companies to explore for oil in 1955, and the first oil strikes were made in 1957. Within a decade, Libya had become the world's fourth-largest exporter of crude oil. During the 1960s, pipelines were built from the oil fields to new export terminals on the Mediterranean coast. The lightness and low sulfur content of Libyan crude oil make it highly desirable to industrialized countries, and, with the exception of the United States, differences in political viewpoint have had little effect on Libyan oil sales abroad.

After the 1969 Revolution, Libya became a leader in the drive by oil-producing countries to gain control over their petroleum industries. The process began in 1971, when the new Libyan government took over the interests of British Petroleum in Libya. The Libyan method of nationalization proceeded against individual companies rather than to take on the "oil giants" all at once. It took more than a decade before the last company, Exxon, capitulated. However, the companies' $2 billion in assets were left in limbo in 1986, when the administration of U.S. president Ronald Reagan imposed a ban on all trade with Libya to protest Libya's involvement in international terrorism. Sanctions were continued under Reagan's successors until 2004, when the United States, the last holdout, lifted them in acknowledgement of Libya's improved international respectability. Among other actions the country has closed down its unconventional weapons program and permitted Libyan agents allegedly involved in the 1988 Lockerbie, Scotland airline bombing to be tried in a neutral court.

Libya's oil reserves are estimated at 36 billion barrels, along with 51.3 billion cubic feet of proven natural gas reserves total, third highest in Africa behind Algeria and Nigeria, with unproven reserves estimated to be as much as twice that amount. The low sulfur content of Libyan oil and its proximity to the Mediterranean coast, which keeps transport costs low, have made its oil highly marketable. With oil production reaching a record 1.4 million barrels per day, Libya has been able to build a strong petrochemical industry. The Marsa Brega petrochemical complex is one of the world's largest producers of urea.

Until recently, industrial-development successes based on oil revenues enabled Libyans to enjoy an ever-improving standard of living, and funding priorities were shifted from industry to agricultural development in the budget. But a combination of factors—mismanagement, lack of a cadre of skilled Libyan workers, absenteeism, low motivation of the workforce, and a significant drop in revenues (from $22 billion in 1980 to $7 billion in 1988)—cast doubts on the effectiveness of Qadhafi's *Green Book* socialist policies.

In 1988, the leader began closing the book. As production incentives, controls on both imports and exports were eliminated, and profit sharing for employees of small businesses was encouraged. In 1990, the General People's Congress (GPC), Libya's equivalent of a parliament, began a restructuring of government, adding new secretariats (ministries) to help expand economic development and diversify the economy.

## FREEDOM

Qadhafi in *The Green Book* argues that representative democratic government is a fraud; all citizens of a country must participate in state-building. Under his system, governance is entrusted to a 3000-member General Peoples' Congress (GPC), which is responsible for implementing Brother Leader's legislative guidelines. At a secondary level the GPC directs the activities of some 3,000 committees, each headed by a leader who is a GPC member. These committees in turn are responsible to the GPC concerning various developmental matters such as health, finance, budget, education, family planning, etc. In recent years bans on studying English, listening to Western music, use of alcohol and other restrictions on social life imposed by the Sanusi and continued under Qadhafi's puritanical desert lifestyle have been lifted. But the more familiar form of representative government found elsewhere is far in the future for Libya.

In January 2000, Qadhafi marched into a GPC meeting waving a copy of the annual budget. He tore up the copy and ordered most of the secretariats abolished. Their powers would be transferred to "provincial cells" outside of Tripoli. Only five government functions—finance, defense, foreign affairs, information, and African unity—would remain under central-government control. In October of that year, Qadhafi ordered further cuts, continuing his direct management of national affairs. For the first time he named a prime minister, Mubarak al-Shamekh, to head the stripped-down government. The secretariat for information was abolished, and the heads of the justice and finance secretariats summarily dismissed. The head of the National Oil Company (NOC), Libya's longest-serving government official, was transferred to a new post; Qadhafi had criticized the NOC for mismanagement of the oil industry and lack of vision.

Libya also started developing its considerable uranium resources. A 1985 agreement with the Soviet Union provided the components for an 880-megawatt nuclear-power station in the Sirte region. Libya has enough uranium to meet its foreseeable domestic needs. The German-built chemical-weapons plant at Rabta, described by Libyans as a pharmaceutical complex but confirmed as to its real function by visiting scientists, was destroyed in a mysterious fire in the 1980s. A Russian-built nuclear reactor at Tajoora, 30 miles from Tripoli, suffered a similar fate, not from fire but due to faulty ventilation and high levels of radiation. But the Libyans have pressed on. An underground complex at Mount Tarhuna, south of Tripoli, was completed in 1998 and closed subsequently to international inspection. Libya claims that it is part of the Great Man-Made River (GMR) project and thus not subject to such inspections.

The GMR, a vast $30 billion complex of pipelines to draw water from underground Saharan aquifers, was begun in 1983. A component of Qadhafi's vision of a self-sufficient sovereign Libya, its goals were to expand irrigation in the fertile coastal agricultural area and improve the potable water supply in Libyan cities. It was planned in five stages. As of 2006–07 it was in full operation, with one set of pipelines serving the Jefara agricultural plain through Jebel Nafusah, a network of lines serving Tripoli from three aquifers deep in the Sahara, and separate lines serving Benghazi and Tobruk. The GMR may never bring economic benefits sufficient to offset its cost, but aside from providing potable water to Libya's cities it has helped build national unity and given

Libyans a strong sense of national pride. The Guinness World Records 2008 book has acknowledged this as the world's largest irrigation project.

In addition to its heavy dependence on oil revenues, another obstacle to economic development in Libya is derived from an unbalanced labor force. One author observed, "Foreigners do all the work. Moroccans clean houses, Sudanese grow vegetables, Egyptians fix cars and drive trucks. Iraqis run the power stations and American and European technicians keep the equipment and systems humming. All the Libyans do is show up for makework government jobs."[6] Difficult climatic conditions and little arable land severely limit agricultural production; the country must import 75 percent of its food.

## AN UNCERTAIN FUTURE

The revolutionary regime has been more successful than the monarchy was in making the wealth from oil revenues available to ordinary Libyans. Per capita income, which was $2,170 the year after the revolution, had risen to $10,900 by 1980. U.S sanctions and the drop in global oil prices have resulted in sharp reductions; per capita income was $8,900 in 2001 and $6,700 in 2005. In 2009, it reached $14,400 due to the increase in oil prices.

This influx of wealth changed the lives of the people in a very short period of time. Semi-nomadic tribes such as the Qadadfas of the Sirte (Qadhafi's kin) have been provided with permanent homes, for example. Extensive social-welfare programs, such as free medical care, free education, and low-cost housing, have greatly enhanced the lives of many Libyans. However, this wealth has yet to be spread evenly across

**HEALTH/WELFARE**

Shortages of adequately educated Libyans remains a major obstacle to national development. A recent survey of government managers found that only 3–5 percent had had leadership training. As a starting point in dealing with educational inadequacy the government approved in October 2006 a project with One Laptop Per Child, a U.S. firm, to provide wireless laptop computers to all Libyan school children by June 2008. In return for its $250 million investment Libya will receive 1.2 million computers, one server per school, technical advisers, satellite internet service and other infrastructure elements for the school system. However, Libya reneged later on paying for most of the computers.

society. The economic downturn of the 1990s produced a thriving black market, along with price gouging and corruption in the public sector. In 1996, Libya organized "purification committees," mostly staffed by young army officers, to monitor and report instances of black-market and other illegal activities.

Until recently, opposition to Qadhafi was confined almost entirely to exiles abroad, centered on former associates living in Cairo, Egypt, who had broken with the Libyan leader for reasons either personal or related to economic mismanagement. But economic downturns and dissatisfaction with the leader's wildly unsuccessful foreign-policy ventures increased popular discontent at home. In 1983, Qadhafi had introduced two domestic policies that also generated widespread resentment: He called for the drafting of women into the armed services, and he recommended that all children be educated at home until age 10. The 200 basic "people's congresses," set up in 1977 to recommend policy to the national General People's Congress (which in theory is responsible for national policy), objected strongly to both proposals. Qadhafi then created 2,000 more people's congresses, presumably to dilute the opposition, but withdrew the proposals. In effect, suggested one observer, *The Green Book* theory had begun to work, and Qadhafi didn't like it.

Qadhafi's principal support base rests on the armed forces and the "revolutionary committees," formed of youths whose responsibility is to guard against infractions of *The Green Book* rules. "Brother Colonel" also relies upon a small group of collaborators from the early days of the Revolution, and his own relatives and members of the Qadadfa form part of the inner power structure. This structure is highly informal, and it may explain why Qadhafi is able to disappear from public view from time to time, as he did after the United States conducted an air raid on Tripoli in 1986, and emerge having lost none of his popularity and charismatic appeal.

In recent years, disaffection within the army has led to a number of attempts to overthrow Qadhafi. The most serious coup attempt took place in 1984, when army units allied with the opposition based in Cairo and headed by several of Qadhafi's former associates, attacked the central barracks in Tripoli where he usually resides. The attackers were defeated in a bloody gun battle. A previously unknown opposition group based in Geneva, Switzerland, claimed in 1996 that its agents had poisoned the camel's milk that Qadhafi drinks while eating dates on his desert journeys, but proof of this claim is lacking.

## INTERNAL CHANGES

Qadhafi has a talent for the unexpected that has made him an effective survivor. In 1988, he ordered the release of all political prisoners and personally drove a bulldozer through the main gate of Tripoli's prison to inaugurate "Freedom Day." Exiled opponents of the regime were invited to return under a promise of amnesty, and a number did so.

In June of that year, the GPC approved a "Charter of Human Rights" as an addendum to *The Green Book*. The charter outlaws the death penalty, bans mistreatment of prisoners, and guarantees every accused person the right to a fair trial. It also permits formation of labor unions, confirms the right to education and suitable employment for all Libyan citizens, and places Libya on record as prohibiting production of nuclear and chemical weapons. In March 1995, the country's last prison was destroyed and its inmates freed in application of the charter's guarantees of civil liberty.

With political reform unlikely given Qadhafi's hold on the levers of power and his general popularity, the most likely changes in Libyan life and prospects appear to be socioeconomic. Apart from its educational deficiencies mentioned above, the country still lacks an effective legal system, hospitals and clinics, broad-based leadership and other components of successful state-building. In an effort to move in this direction, the government in 2007 announced layoffs for 400,000 workers, nearly all of them employed by the state. The reduction will save some $3 billion in salaries. Dismissed employees would be guaranteed $40,000 in individual loans, to be used in starting a business or working in the almost-nonexistent private sector.

One important problem that remains a challenge today is the large influx of African migrant laborers who flocked into Libya following an open invitation by Qadhafi as a helpful gesture toward some African countries with ailing economies. The number of African migrant workers, many illegally in the country, reached close to two million in recent years. A repatriation program was put in place to reduce their number and stop some of them from attempting to reach Europe's southern shores.

## THE WAR WITH CHAD

Libyan forces occupied the Aouzou Strip in northern Chad in 1973, claiming it as an integral part of the Libyan state. Occupation gave Libya access also to the reportedly rich uranium resources of the region. In subsequent years, Qadhafi played upon political rivalries in Chad to extend the occupation into a de facto one of annexation of most of its poverty-stricken neighbor.

But in late 1986 and early 1987, Chadian leaders patched up their differences and turned on the Libyans. In a series of spectacular raids on entrenched Libyan forces, the highly mobile Chadians, traveling mostly in Toyota trucks, routed the Libyans and drove them out of northern Chad. Chadian forces then moved into the Aouzou Strip and even attacked nearby air bases inside Libya. The defeats, with casualties of some 3,000 Libyans and loss of huge quantities of Soviet-supplied military equipment, exposed the weaknesses of the overequipped, undertrained, and poorly motivated Libyan Army.

### ACHIEVEMENTS

The Great Man-Made River (GMR) called by Qadhafi the world's eighth wonder, is in the third stage of completion as noted above. In addition to the network of pipes, each one 13 feet in diameter, excess water pumped will be stored in the Kufra basin, which has a capacity for 5000 cubic meters. The water flow to Tripoli and Benghazi is presently 200 million cubic feet per day, sufficient to meet the needs of residents of both cities.

In 1989, after admitting his mistake, Qadhafi signed a cease-fire with then-Chadian leader Hissène Habré and agreed to submit the dispute over ownership of Aouzou to the International Court of Justice (ICJ). The ICJ affirmed Chadian sovereignty in 1994 on the basis of a 1955 agreement arranged by France as the occupying power there. Libyan forces withdrew from Aouzou in May, and since then the two countries have enjoyed a peaceful relationship. In 1998, the border was opened completely, in line with Qadhafi's policy of "strengthening neighborly relations."

## FOREIGN POLICY

Libya's relations with the United States have remained hostile since the 1969 Revolution, which not only overthrew King Idris but also resulted in the closing of the important Wheelus Field air base. In 1986, U.S. war planes bombed Tripoli and Benghazi in retaliation for the bombing of a disco in Berlin, Germany, which killed two U.S. servicemen and injured 238 others. The retaliatory U.S. air attack on Libya killed 55 Libyan civilians, including Qadhafi's adopted daughter.

Libya resumed its old role of "pariah state" in 1992 by refusing to extradite two officers of its intelligence service suspected of complicity in the 1988 bombing of a Pan American jumbo jet over Lockerbie, Scotland. The United States, France, and Britain had demanded the officers' extradition and introduced a resolution to that effect in the UN Security Council; in the event of noncompliance on Libya's part, sanctions would be imposed on the country. *Resolution 748* passed by a 10-to-zero vote, with five abstentions. A concurrent ruling by the ICJ ordered Libya to turn over the suspects or explain in writing why it was not obligated to do so.

Qadhafi, however, refused to comply with *Resolution 748*. He argued that the suspects should be tried (if at all) in a neutral country, since they could not be given a fair trial either in Britain or the United States.

The Security Council responded by imposing partial sanctions on Libya. Despite the partial embargo, Libya's leader continued to reject compliance with the resolution. As a result, the Security Council in 1993 passed *Resolution 883,* imposing much stiffer sanctions on the country. The new sanctions banned all shipments of spare parts and equipment sales and froze Libyan foreign bank deposits. International flights to Libya were prohibited. The only area of the economy not affected was that of oil exports, since Britain and other Western European countries are dependent on low-sulfur Libyan crude for their economies.

The tug-of-war between the United Nations and its recalcitrant member went on for six years. In March 1998, the United Nations set a 60-day deadline for compliance. Subsequently Qadhafi reversed his stance and agreed to turn over the suspects to be tried in a neutral court under Scottish law. The two were then flown to the Netherlands, where they were tried. In 2000, one of the suspects was acquitted. The other, former Libyan intelligence agent Abdel Basset al-Megrahi, was found guilty in 2001 and sentenced to life imprisonment. However several Scottish judges involved in the trial recently declared that prosecution and conviction were flawed by flimsy or fabricated evidence. This would have been grounds for a new trial. Megrahi was freed by the Scottish government on August 20, 2009 on compassionate grounds because he had only a few months to live due to terminal prostate cancer. In exchange for his freedom, Megrahi agreed to forego the appeal he had planned, but on September 18 he released 300 pages of evidence that challenged the prosecution case against him.

In 2003 the Libyan leader agreed to compensate the families of the victims. Each of the 270 families would receive between $5 million and $10 million under a $2.7 billion settlement. The agreement resulted in the end of sanctions on the country and paved the way for the full restoration of diplomatic relations between Libya and the United States.

## PROSPECTS

The tide of fundamentalism sweeping across the Islamic world and challenging secular regimes has largely spared Libya thus far, although there were occasional clashes between fundamentalists and police in the 1980s, and in 1992, some 500 fundamentalists were jailed briefly. However, the bloody civil uprisings against the regimes in neighboring Algeria and Egypt caused Qadhafi in 1994 to reemphasize Libya's Islamic nature. New laws passed by the General People's Congress would apply Islamic law (Shari'a) and punishments in such areas as marriage and divorce, wills and inheritance, crimes of theft and violence (where the Islamic punishment is cutting off a hand), and for apostasy. Libya's tribal-based society and Qadhafi's own interpretation of Islamic law to support women's rights and to deal with other social issues continue to serve as obstacles to Islamic radicalism.

Resolution of the Lockerbie issue and other positive steps taken by Qadhafi have gained Libya international respectability. A more recent incident involved the sentencing by a Libyan court of Bulgarian nurses and a Palestinian doctor (later given Bulgarian citizenship) on charges of infecting children in a hospital in Benghazi with H.I.V. The court first sentenced them to death, but after an international outcry plus credible evidence that unsanitary conditions in the hospital were responsible for the outbreak the sentences were commuted to life imprisonment. Eventually after further international pressure, including warnings by Britain and France, Libya's largest oil recipients, and continued U.S. sanctions, the nurses and doctor were released to Bulgaria, under the terms of a 1984 treaty which allows citizens of one country convicted of crimes in the other to serve out their sentences in their home country. The pot was further "sweetened" by payments of some $460 million to the victims' families from an unspecified international fund.

Despite his continued hostility toward Israel, Qadhafi has sought to cultivate an image of international respectability in recent years. He has emphasized in particular Libya's role in African unity. With support from other African states, Libya was elected to the chairmanship of the UN Commission on Human Rights (UNCHR) in 2003.

In September 2007 Qadhafi's African policy took another major step forward when the Libyan leader agreed to mediate in Sudan's Darfur conflict. Wearing a brown shirt patterned in green patches in the shape of Africa, he met with UN Secretary-General Ban Ki-Moon in his desert tent in Sirte, his desert home, and agreed to host Darfur peace talks in Tripoli on October 27. The Libyan Minister for African Affairs struck the tone for the forthcoming talks: "We have three-quarters of a million Darfuris working in Libya, and our security is united with Sudan and Darfur."[7] In 2009, Qadhafi was elected president of the African Union, a one-year term.

On September 7, 1999, the Libyan leader celebrated his 30th year in power with a parade of thousands of footsoldiers, along with long-range missiles and tanks, through the streets of Tripoli. Libyan jets, many of them piloted by women, flew overhead.

Qadhafi's excellent health and commitment to the rather unrealistic ideas of the *Green Book* make forecasting Libya's political future dubious at best. His eldest son, Sayf, recently formed an Economic Development Board charged with developing the private sector. Another son, El-Saadi, made an official visit to Japan in 2001. But lacking either monarchical or dictatorial strongman traditions, it seems likely that the structure of authority established in 1969 will continue for the foreseeable future. "It is all him, because there are no institutions in Libya to share his power or challenge his behavior."[8]

The lifting of UN sanctions on the country resulted from Qadhafi's acceptance of international jurisdiction in the Lockerbie case. As a result, relations with Europe have been normalized. The moribund tourist industry is also beginning to show signs of life, offering desert oases, splendid beaches and well-preserved Roman ruins to prospective visitors. In December 2003 Qadhafi again confounded his critics by agreeing to discontinue Libya's nuclear weapons development program and open its facilities to international inspection. The country also signed the Nuclear Non-Proliferation Treaty. In March 2004 the Libyan leader ordered 3,300 chemical bombs destroyed and agreed to halt further production.

## NOTES

1. "[I]rrigation, colonization and hard work have wrought marvels. Everywhere you see plantations forced out of the sandy, wretched soil." A. H. Broderick, *North Africa* (London: Oxford University Press, 1943), p. 27.

2. Religious leaders issued a *fatwa* ("binding legal decision") stating that a vote against independence would be a vote against religion. Omar el Fathaly, et al., *Political Development and Bureaucracy in Libya* (Lexington, KY: Lexington Books, 1977).

---

**Timeline: PAST**

**1835**
Tripoli becomes an Ottoman province with the Sanusiya controlling the interior

**1932**
Libya becomes an Italian colony, Italy's "Fourth Shore"

**1951**
An independent kingdom is set up by the UN under King Idris

**1969**
The Revolution overthrows Idris; the Libyan Arab Republic is established

**1973–1976**
Qadhafi decrees a cultural and social revolution with government by people's committees

**1980s**
A campaign to eliminate Libyan opponents abroad; the United States imposes economic sanctions in response to suspected Libya-terrorist ties; U.S. planes attack targets in Tripoli and Benghazi; Libyan troops are driven from Chad, including the Aouzou Strip

**1990s**
Libya's relations with its neighbors improve; the UN votes to impose sanctions on Libya for terrorist acts; Qadhafi comes to an agreement with the UN regarding the trial of the PanAm/Lockerbie bombing suspects

In 1999, Libya agrees and hands over two suspects in the Lockerbie bombing to be tried in the Netherlands.

**2000s**
One of the suspects tried was acquitted and the other, Abdel Basset al-Megrahi, was found guilty and sentenced to life imprisonment

In 2003, Libya agreed to compensate the families of the victims. The agreement ended the sanctions on the country

In 2009, al-Megrahi was freed from jail on humanitarian grounds because he was dying of cancer

3. See *Middle East Journal,* vol. 24, no. 2 (Spring 1970), Documents Section.

4. John Wright, *Libya: A Modern History* (Baltimore, MD: Johns Hopkins University Press, 1982), pp. 124–126. Qadhafi's idol was former Egyptian president Nasser, a leader in the movement for unity and freedom among the Arabs. While he was in school in Sebha, in the Fezzan, he listened to Radio Cairo's Voice of the Arabs and was later expelled from school as a militant organizer of demonstrations.

5. *The London Times* (June 6, 1973).

6. Khidr Hamza, with Jeff Stein, *Saddam's Bombmaker* (New York: Scribner's, 2000), p. 289. The author was head of the Iraqi nuclear-weapons program before defecting to Libya and eventually the United States.

7. Quoted by Warren Hoge, *The New York Times,* Sept. 8, 2007.

8. Attia Essawy, quoted in Michael Slackman, "A Leader Beyond Reproach Limits the Possibilities for Political Change," *New York Times,* March 19, 2009.

# Mauritania (Islamic Republic of Mauritania)

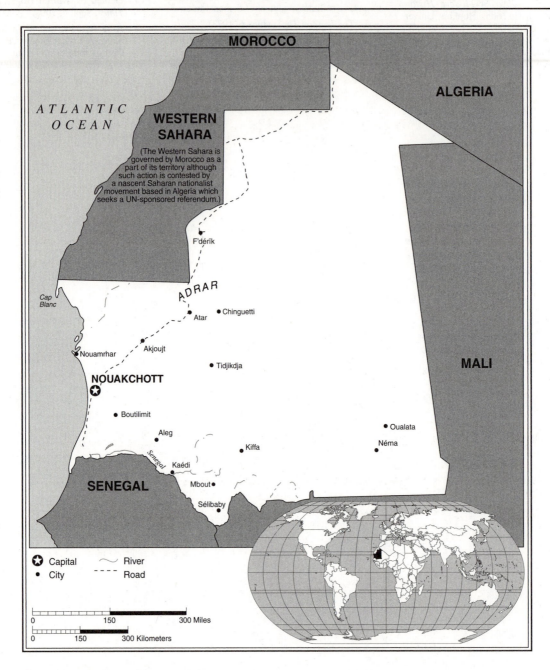

# Mauritania Statistics

## GEOGRAPHY

*Area in Square Miles (Kilometers):*
398,000 (1,030,700) (about 3 times the size of New Mexico)
*Capital (Population):* Nouakchott (743,500)
*Environmental Concerns:* overgrazing; deforestation; soil erosion; desertification; very limited natural freshwater resources; overfishing

*Geographical Features:* mostly barren, flat plains of the Sahara; some central hills
*Climate:* desert

## PEOPLE

### Population

*Total:* 3,129,486
*Annual Growth Rate:* 2.39%
*Rural/Urban Population Ratio:* 44/56

*Major Languages:* Hasanixa; Soninke; Arabic; Pular; Wolof
*Ethnic Makeup:* 40% mixed Maur/black; perhaps 30% Maur; 30% black
*Religion:* 99.84% Muslim, 0.16% Christians

### Health

*Life Expectancy at Birth:* 58 years (male); 62 years (female)
*Infant Mortality:* 63.4/1,000 live births

*Physicians Available:* 1/11,085 people
*HIV/AIDS Rate in Adults:* 0.8%

### Education

*Adult Literacy Rate:* 51.2%
*Compulsory (Ages):* 6–12

## COMMUNICATION

*Telephones:* 71,400 main lines
*Internet Users:* 30,000 (2002)

## TRANSPORTATION

*Highways in Miles (Kilometers):* 4,560
   (7,600)
*Railroads in Miles (Kilometers):* 422 (704)
*Usable Airfields:* 26
*Motor Vehicles in Use:* 150,000

## GOVERNMENT

*Type:* republic
*Independence Date:* November 28, 1960
   (from France)

*Head of State/Government:* President
   Mohamed Ould Abdel Aziz; Prime
   Minister Moulaye Ould Mohamed
   Laghdaf
*Political:* Union for the Republic, Popular
   Alliance for Progress; National Front
   for the Defense of Democracy; Rally
   of Democratic Forces; National Rally
   for Reform and Development, others
*Suffrage:* universal at 18

## MILITARY

*Military Expenditures (% of GDP):* 5.5%
*Current Disputes:* ethnic tensions and
   growing threats from Al-Qaeda in the
   Islamic Maghreb.

## ECONOMY

*Currency ($ U.S. equivalent):* 262
   ouguiyas = $1
*Per Capita Income/GDP:* $2,100/
   $6.32 billion

*GDP Growth Rate:* 3.5%
*Inflation Rate:* 7.3%
*Unemployment Rate:* 30%
*Labor Force by Occupation:* 50%
   agriculture; 40% services; 10%
   industry
*Population Below Poverty Line:* 50%
*Natural Resources:* iron ore; gypsum;
   fish; copper; phosphates; oil
*Agriculture:* millet; sorghum; dates; root
   crops; cattle and sheep; fish products
*Industry:* iron-ore and gypsum mining;
   fish processing
*Exports:* $1.395 billion (primary partners
   China, France, Spain, Italy)
*Imports:* $1.475 billion (primary partners
   France, China, Netherlands, Spain)

## SUGGESTED WEB SITES

www.cia.gov/cia/publications/factbook/
   geos/mr.html
http://news.bbc.co.uk/2/hi/middle_east/
   country_profiles/791083.stm

# Mauritania Country Report

Since the adoption of its current Constitution in 1991, Mauritania has legally been a multiparty democracy, but in practice, power remains in the hands of the chief executive and has changed hands in recent years by way of military coups.

President Mohamed Ould Abdel Aziz, a General, came to power in August 2008 by overthrowing the elected president Sidi Ould Cheikh Abdallahi. In July 2009, General Ould Abdel Aziz was made president through elections in which he won 52% of the votes while his main rival, parliament speaker Messaoud Ould Boulkheir, received only 16%. Sidi Ould Cheikh Abdallahi, the ousted president had won the 2006 elections with 52.85% and promised important political and economic changes. The coup that overthrew him was the second since 2005 when President Ould Taya, who ruled Mauritania for a decade since 1984, was ousted in August 2005 by Colonel Ely Ould Mohamed Vall while he was attending the funeral of Saudi King

Fahd. Upon assuming power, Colonel Ely Ould Mohamed Vall promised democratic elections within a year which would return power to civilians. On June 26, 2006, a referendum approved by 97% a new constitution which limited the presidency to two 5-year terms, and on November 19 and December 3 of the same year parliamentary and municipal elections were held, to be followed by presidential elections in 2007. These elections were won by Sidi Ould Cheikh Abdallahi, who within two years would be ousted by yet another military coup led by Abel Aziz. This was the 11th coups or attempted coups since independence from France in 1960.

## POVERTY AND THE ETHNIC DIVIDE

For decades, Mauritania has grown progressively drier. Today, about 75 percent of the country is covered by sand. Less than

1 percent of the land is suitable for cultivation, 10 percent for grazing. To make matters worse, the surviving arable and pastoral areas have been plagued by grasshoppers and locusts.

In the face of natural disaster, people have moved. Since the mid-1960s, the percentage of urban dwellers has swelled, from less than 10 percent to over 40 percent, while the nomadic population during the same period has dropped, from more than 80 percent to perhaps 20 percent. In Nouakchott, the capital city, vast shantytowns now house a quarter of the population. As the capital has grown, from a few thousand to 743,500 in a single generation, its poverty—and that of the country as a whole—has become more obvious. People seek new ways to make a living away from the land, but there are few jobs. The best hope for lifting up the economy may lie in offshore oil exploration. A prospecting report in 2002 attracted the interest of major international oil companies and by 2009, the country had 100 million barrels of proven reserves and produced a little over 30,000 barrels a day.

Mauritania's faltering economy has coincided with an increase in racial and ethnic tensions. Since independence, the government has been dominated by the Maurs (or Moors), who speak Hasaniya Arabic. This community has historically been divided between the aristocrats and commoners, of Arab and Berber origin, and the

## DEVELOPMENT

Mauritania's coastal waters are among the richest in the world. During the 1980s, the local fishing industry grew at an average annual rate of more than 10%. Many now believe that the annual catch has reached the upper levels of its sustainable potential.

## FREEDOM

The Mauritanian government is especially sensitive to continuing allegations of the existence of chattel slavery in the country. While slavery is outlawed, there is credible evidence of its continued existence. In 1998, five members of a local advocacy group SOS–Esclaves (Slaves) were sentenced to 13 months' imprisonment for "activities within a non-authorized organization."

Haratine, who were black African slaves who assimilated Maurish culture but remain socially segregated. Including the Haratine, the Maurs account for perhaps 60 percent of the population (the government has refused to release comprehensive data from the last two censuses).

The other half of Mauritania's population is composed of the "blacks," who mostly speak Pulaar, Soninke, or Wolof. Like the Maurs, all these groups are Muslim. Mauritania's rulers have stressed Islam as a source of national unity. The country proclaimed itself an Islamic republic at independence, and since 1980 the Shari'a—the Islamic penal codes—has been the law of the land.

Islamic brotherhood has not been able to overcome the divisions between the northern Maurs and southern blacks. One major source of friction has been the official Arabization effort, which is opposed by most southerners. In recent years, the country's desertification has created new sources of tension. As their pastures turned to sand, many of the Maurish nomads who did not find refuge in the urban areas moved southward. There, with state support, they began in the 1980s to deprive southerners of their land.

## HEALTH/WELFARE

There have been some modest improvements in the areas of health and education since the country's independence, but conditions remain poor. Mauritania has received low marks regarding its efforts in human development.

Oppression of blacks has been met with resistance from the underground Front for the Liberation of Africans in Mauritania (FLAM). Black grievances were also linked to an unsuccessful coup attempt in 1987. In 1989, interethnic hostility exploded when a border dispute with Senegal led to race riots that left several hundred "Senegalese" dead in Nouakchott. In response, the "Moorish" trading community in Senegal became the target of reprisals. Mauritania claimed that 10,000 Maurs were killed, but other sources put the number at about 70. Following this bloodshed, more than 100,000 refugees were repatriated across both sides of the border. Mass deportations of "Mauritanians of Senegalese origin"

have fueled charges that the Nouakchott regime is trying to eliminate its non-Maurish population.

## ACHIEVEMENTS

There is a current project to restore ancient Mauritanian cities, such as Chinguette, which are located on traditional routes from North Africa to Sudan. These centers of trade and Islamic learning were points of origin for the pilgrimage to Mecca and were well known in the Middle East.

Tensions between Mauritania and Senegal were eased in June 2000 by the newly elected Senegalese president Abdoulaye Wade. This helped to reduce cross-border raids by deported Mauritanians. Genuine peace, however, will require greater reform within Mauritania itself and provision for the return of refugees.

In recent years, the government sent out conflicting signals. Although the government has legalized some opposition parties, it has also continued to pursue its Arabization program and has clamped down on genuine dissent. Maur militias have been armed, and the army has been expanded with assistance from Arab countries.

The expansion of the army may be helpful in not only dissipating old internal tensions, but in dealing with the new serious threat posed by the al-Qaeda in the Islamic Maghreb which is said to have been behind several armed attack in Mauritania in recent years. Already in 2005, a major armed attack was led by the Salafist Group for Call and Combat (GSPC), a radical Algerian Islamist group which changed into the al-Qaeda subsidiary in 2007. In that attack again a military post, 15 soldiers were killed. In 2008 the killing of four French tourists was also attributed to al-Qaeda, just like the attack against the Israeli embassy in the capital, Nouakchott, and the killing of twelve Mauritanian soldiers in the same year.

Attacks by forces alleged to belong to al-Qaeda continued through the end of the 2000s and also in 2010. In July 2010, a joint military raid was carried out by Mauritanian and French forces against elements of that group who were holding a French hostage. The attack, which took place in northern Mali aimed particularly to rescue the French hostage Michel Germaneuaa.

Mauritania faces several challenges as it tries to find some stability and resume development. These challenges include serious economic security threats coming from the North Africa affiliate of al-Qaeda and weak political legitimacy of the institutions and the rulers of the country. While it may count on the French and American assistance in the area of security, Mauritania is alone responsible in putting its own house in order and in being responsive to the fundamental needs of its people.

## Timeline: PAST

**1035–1055**
The Almoravids spread Islam in the Western Sahara areas through conquest

**1920**
The Mauritanian area becomes a French colony

**1960**
Mauritania becomes independent under President Moktar Ould Daddah

**1978**
A military coup brings Khouma Ould Haidalla and the Military Committee for National Recovery to power

**1979**
The Algiers Agreement: Mauritania makes peace with Polisario and abandons claims to Western Sahara

**1980**
Slavery is formally abolished

**1990s**
Multiparty elections are boycotted by the opposition; tensions continue between Mauritania and Senegal; Mauritania establishes full diplomatic relations with Israel

## PRESENT

**2000s**
Desertification takes its toll on the environment and the economy; Senegal and Mauritania seek better relations; President Taya is ousted by a military coup; his successor Cheikh Abdallahi is also ousted.

**2007**
Parliament outlaws slavery. It was still practiced in spite of a 1981 ban.

**2009**
Military strongman Abdel Aziz is elected president; Al-Qaeda in the Islamic Maghreb commits several deadly attacks against security forces.

# Morocco (Kingdom of Morocco)

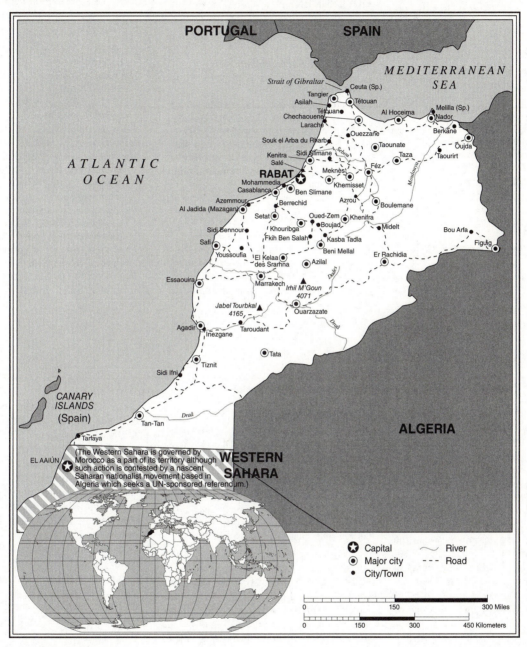

# Morocco Statistics

## GEOGRAPHY

*Area in Square Miles (Kilometers):* 277,131 (446,550) about the size of California
*Capital (Population):* Rabat (2,000,000)
*Environmental Concerns:* land degradation; desertification; soil erosion; overgrazing; contamination of water supplies; oil pollution of coastal waters
*Geographical Features:* the northern coast and interior are mountainous, with large areas of bordering plateaux, intermontane valleys, and rich coastal plains; south, southeast is desert
*Climate:* varies from Mediterranean to desert

## PEOPLE

### Population

*Total:* 34,859,364
*Annual Growth Rate:* 1.479%
*Rural/Urban Population Ratio:* 44/56
*Major Languages:* Arabic; Tamazight (spoken Berber Language with 3 main dialects): Tashelheit (south), Tarifit (north) and Tamazight (central). French widely used and understood
*Ethnic Makeup:* 99.1% Arab-Berber; 0.2% Jewish; 0.7% other; 1% non-Moroccan and Jewish
*Religions:* 99% Sunni Muslim; 1% Christian and Jewish

**Health**

*Life Expectancy at Birth:* 69.42 years
(male), 74.3 years (female)
*Infant Mortality Rate (Ratio):* 36.88/1,000
live births

**Education**

*Adult Literacy Rate:* 52.3%
*Compulsory (Ages):* 7–13

## COMMUNICATION

*Telephones:* 2,394,00 main lines
*Daily Newspaper Circulation:* 13 per
1,000 people
*Televisions:* 167 per 1,000 people
*Internet Service Providers:* 8 (2009)

## TRANSPORTATION

*Highways in Miles (Kilometers):* 37,649
(60,626)
*Railroads in Miles (Kilometers):* 1,184
(1,907)

*Usable Airfields:* 69
*Motor Vehicles in Use:* 1,950,000

## GOVERNMENT

*Type:* constitutional monarchy
*Independence Date:* March 2, 1956 (from
France)
*Head of State/Government:* King
Muhammad VI; Prime Minister Abbas
El Fassi
*Political Parties:* Istiqlal (Independence)
Party; Justice and Development Party;
Popular Movement; National Rally
of Independents; Socialist Union of
Popular Forces; Constitutional Union;
Party of Progress and Socialism; others
*Suffrage:* universal at 18

## MILITARY

*Military Expenditures (% of GDP):* 5%
*Current Disputes:* final resolution on the
status of Western Sahara remains to be
worked out; from time to time Morocco
demands the retrocession of Ceuta and

Melilla, cities located physically within
its territory but considered extensions of
mainland Spain (plazas de soberaniá by
the Spanish government)

## ECONOMY

*Currency ($U.S. Equivalent):* 7.72
dirhams = $1
*Per Capita Income/GDP (PPP):* $4,000/
$86.39 billion
*GDP Growth Rate:* 5.9%
*Inflation Rate:* 3.9%
*Unemployment Rate:* 10%
*Labor Force:* 11,500,000
*Natural Resources:* phosphates; iron ore;
manganese; lead; zinc; fish; salt
*Agriculture:* barley; wheat; citrus fruits;
wine; vegetables; olives; livestock
*Industry:* phosphate mining and
processing; food processing; leather
goods; textiles; construction; tourism
*Exports:* $20.6 billion (primary partners
France, Spain, Brazil)
*Imports:* $39.16 billion (primary partners
France, Spain, Italy)

# Morocco Country Report

The Kingdom of Morocco is the western-most country in North Africa. Morocco's population is the second largest (after Egypt) of the Arab states. The country annexed progressively since 1975 the Western Sahara (formerly two Spanish colonies, Rio de Oro and Saguia al-Hamra), but the final status of that territory is yet to be decided either by way of a referendum or through negotiations between the independence movement led by the Polisario Front (Popular Front for the Liberation of Saguia el-Hamra and Rio de Oro) and Morocco. Since it annexed it, Morocco has been ruling the Western Sahara as one of its provinces.

Two other territories physically within Morocco remain outside Moroccan control. They are the cities of Ceuta and Melilla, both located on rocky peninsulas that jut out into the Mediterranean Sea. They have been held by Spain since the fifteenth century. (Spain also owns several small islands off the coast in Moroccan territorial waters in the Mediterranean.) Spain's support for Morocco's admission to the European Union (EU) as an associate member has eased tensions between them over the enclaves. An additional reason is the tacit acquiescence to Morocco's annexation of the Western Sahara. Another reason is the growing economic ties between the two countries.

## DEVELOPMENT

Morocco has important reserves of phosphate rock. It also has exportable supplies of certain rare metal, such as antimony. Unfortunately it lacks oil resources. An oil strike in the Sahara in 2000 proved abortive. Abundant rainfall has improved agricultural production; GDP growth presently averages 5 percent annually.

In 1986 a Spanish law excluding Moroccan Muslim residents from Spanish citizenship led to protests among them. The Moroccan government did not pursue the protests, and in 1988 the question of citizenship became moot when the Spanish Cortes (Parliament) passed a law formally incorporating Ceuta and Melilla into Spain as overseas territories.

In recent years the two cities have been all but overwhelmed by migrants, most of them undocumented, from sub-Sahara Africa seeking to cross into Europe, where they hope to find jobs and a better life than is available in their own countries of origin. Some 15,000 attempted the hazardous crossing in 2004 as compared with 350 in all in the previous 6-year period. A mass breakthrough in October, which resulted in many casualties as the migrants scaled the razor-wire fences around the enclaves, led

the Spanish government to send military units to guard the borders. On its side, the Moroccan government stepped up efforts to block illegal migration through its territory and break up the criminal networks bringing the migrants northward. Thousands of sub-Sahara illegal migrants have been captured, interned in the desert, and then deported. The UN and human rights groups, notably Doctors Without Borders, criticized the deportations. In a response in October 2005, large-scale demonstrations took place in Rabat, with marchers carrying signs that read "we are all Africans; Morocco cannot become Europe's immigration policeman."[1]

Although Morocco is better off than many of its African neighbors which provide the bulk of would-be immigrants, its growing youth population and lack of jobs continue to encourage Moroccans particularly in the lower age groups to attempt the risky sea crossing into Europe in search of employment. This was due partly to the closure of Ceuta and Melilla.

Morocco is a rugged land, dominated by several massive mountain ranges. The Rif Range, averaging 7,000 feet in elevation, runs parallel to the Mediterranean, isolating the northern region from the rest of the country. The Atlas Mountains dominate the interior of Morocco. The Middle Atlas begins south of the Rif, separated by operated as independent units. Moroccan rulers made periodic military expeditions into Berber territory to collect tribute and if possible to secure full obedience. When the ruler was strong, the Berbers paid up and submitted; when he was weak, they ignored him. At times Berber leaders might invade "government territory," capturing cities and replacing one ruler with another more to their liking. When they were not fighting with urban rulers, different Berber groups fought among themselves; as a result, the system did little to foster Moroccan national unity.

## HISTORY

Morocco has a rich cultural history, with many of its ancient monuments more or less intact. It has been governed by some form of monarchy for close to a thousand years, although royal authority was frequently limited or contested by rivals. The current ruling dynasty, the Alawis, assumed power in the 1600s. One reason for their long rule is the fact that they descend from the Prophet Muhammad. Thus, Moroccans have had a real sense of Islamic traditions and history through their rulers.

The first identifiable Moroccan "state" was established by a descendant of Muhammad named Idris, in the late eighth century. Idris had taken refuge in the far west of the Islamic world to escape war in the east. Because of his piety, learning, and descent from Muhammad, he was accepted by a number of Berber groups as their spiritual and political leader. His son and successor, Idris II, founded the first Moroccan capital, Fez. Father and son established the principle whereby descent from the Prophet was an important qualification for political power as well as social status in Morocco.

The Idris ruled over only a small portion of the current Moroccan territory, and, after the death of Idris II, their "nation" lapsed into decentralized family rule. But in the eleventh and twelfth centuries, two Berber confederations developed that brought imperial grandeur to Morocco. These were the Almoravids and the Almohads. Under their rule, North Africa developed a political structure separate from that of the eastern Islamic world.

The Almoravids began as camel-riding nomads from the Western Sahara who were inspired by a religious teacher to carry out a reform movement to revive the true faith of Islam. (The word *Almoravid* comes from the Arabic *al-Murabitun,* "men of the ribat," rather like the crusading religious orders of Christianity in the Middle Ages.) Fired by religious zeal, the Almoravids conquered all of Morocco and parts of western Algeria.

A second "imperial" dynasty, the Almohads, succeeded the Almoravids and

Morocco has a rich history. The Karawiyyin Mosque at Fez was founded in the ninth century A.D. It is the seat on one of Africa's oldest universities.

the Taza Gap (the traditional gateway for invaders from the east), and extends from northeast to southwest to join the High Atlas, a snow capped range containing North Africa's highest peak. A third range, the Anti-Atlas, walls off the desert from the rest of Morocco. These ranges and the general inaccessibility of the country have isolated Morocco throughout most of its history, not only from outside invaders but internally as well, because of the geographical separation of peoples.

Moroccan geography explains the country's dual population structure. A significant number are Berber, descendants of the region's original inhabitants, who were called *Barbari* by the Romans when they arrived in North Africa, due to their lack

of a written language (i.e. Latin) and their ignorance of Roman culture and laws. The Berbers were, until recently, grouped into tribes, often taking the name of a common ancestor, such as the Ait ("Sons of") 'Atta of southern Morocco.[2] Invading Arabs converted them to Islam in the eighth century but made few other changes in Berber life.

When the Arabs invaded their land, a large number of Berbers withdrew into mountain areas. They accepted Islam but held stubbornly to their basic independence. Much of Morocco's past history consisted of efforts by various rulers, both Berber and Arab, to control Berber territory. The result was a kind of balance-of-power political system. The rulers had their power bases in the cities, while the rural groups improved on their performance. They were the first, and probably the last, to unite all of North Africa and Islamic Spain under one government. Almohad monuments, such as the Qutubiya tower, the best-known landmark of Marrakesh, and the Tower of Hassan in Rabat, still stand as reminders of their power and the high level of the Almohads' architectural achievements.

The same fragmentation, conflicts, and Berber/Arab rivalries that had undermined their predecessors brought down the Almohads in the late thirteenth century. From then on, dynasty succeeded dynasty in power. An interesting point about this cyclical pattern is that despite the lack of political unity, a distinctive Moroccan style and culture developed. Each dynasty contributed something to this culture, in architecture, crafts, literature, and music. The interchange between Morocco and Islamic Spain was constant and fruitful. Poets, musicians, artisans, architects, and others traveled regularly between Spanish and Moroccan cities. One can visit the city of Fez today and be instantly transported back into the Hispano-Moorish way of life of the Middle Ages.

## Mulay Ismail

The Alawis came to power and established their rule partly by force, but also as a result of their descent from the Prophet Muhammad. This link enabled them to win the support of both Arab and Berber populations. The real founder of the dynasty was Mulay Ismail, one of the longest-reigning and most powerful monarchs in Morocco's history.

Mulay Ismail unified the population. The great majority of the Berber groups accepted him as their sovereign. The sultan built watchtowers and posted permanent garrisons in Berber territories to make sure they continued to do so. He brought public security to Morocco also; it was said that in his time, a Jew or an unveiled woman could travel safely anywhere in the land, which was not the case in most parts of North Africa, the Middle East, and Europe.

Mulay Ismail was a contemporary of Louis XIV, and the reports of his envoys to the French court at Versailles convinced him that he should build a capital like it. He chose Meknes, not far from Fez. The work was half finished when he died of old age. The slaves and prisoners working on this "Moroccan Versailles" threw down their shovels and ran away. The enormous unfinished walls and arched Bab al-Mansur ("Gate of the Victorious") still stand today as reminders of Mulay Ismail's dream.

Mulay Ismail had many wives and left behind 500 sons but no instructions as to which one should succeed him. His eventual successor, Sultan Muhammad II, was the first foreign sovereign to recognize U.S. independence (in 1777). However the removal of British naval protection for U.S. merchant shipping after the Revolution led to attacks by corsairs from Morocco and other North African states. In 1784 the brig *Betsy* was seized by Moroccan corsairs and its crew taken hostage. The sultan had allowed this to happen because of delays in Congress in signing a formal peace treaty. In 1786, "armed with Innocence and the Olive Branch," Thomas Jefferson, John Adams and Benjamin Franklin collectively negotiated the first U.S. treaty with a foreign power, admittedly sweetened by a $20,000 "gift" to the sultan. Under its terms the United States was allowed to set up a consulate (or legation) in Tangier, and although it is now a museum it remains the only national landmark abroad.[3] The oldest property owned by the U.S. government abroad is the American Consulate in Tangier; a consul was assigned there in 1791.

## The French Protectorate

In the 1800s and early 1900s, Morocco became increasingly vulnerable to outside pressures. The French, who were established in neighboring Algeria and Tunisia, wanted to complete their conquests. The nineteenth-century sultans were less and less able to control the mountain Berbers and were forced to make constant expeditions into the "land of dissidence," at great expense to the treasury. They began borrowing money from European bankers, not only to pay their bills but also to finance arms purchases and the development of ports, railroads, and industries to create a modern economy and prove to the European powers that Morocco could manage its own affairs. Nothing worked; by 1900, Morocco was so far in debt that the French took over the management of its finances.

## FREEDOM

In spite of a very low 37 percent voter turnout, the 2007 parliamentary elections were cited by observers as free and fair, with a balance of seats among various parties. King Muhammad VI's "National Action Plan" raised the legal marriage age for women to 18 and gave other rights to them. In 2003 the king proposed revisions to the 1957 *Mudawanna* (Family Law) which were approved by the Chamber. Women now have the right to file for divorce, share equally in family property, and travel without prior consent from male family members.

In 1904, France, Britain, Spain, and Germany signed secret agreements partitioning the country. The French would be given the largest part of the country, while Spain would receive the northern third as a protectorate plus some territory in the Western Sahara. In return, the French and Spanish agreed to respect Britain's claim to Egypt and Germany's claim to East African territory.

The ax fell on Morocco in 1912. French workers building the new port of Casablanca were killed by Moroccans. Mobs attacked foreigners in Fez, and the sultan's troops could not control them. French troops marched to Fez from Algeria to restore order. The sultan, Mulay Hafidh (Hafiz), was forced to sign the Treaty of Fez, establishing a French protectorate over southern Morocco. The sultan believed that he had betrayed his country and died shortly thereafter, supposedly of a broken heart. Spain then occupied the northern third of the country, and Tangier, the traditional residence of foreign consuls, became an international city ruled by several European powers.

The French protectorate over Morocco covered barely 45 years (1912–1956). But in that brief period, the French introduced significant changes into Moroccan life. For the first time, southern Morocco was brought entirely under central government control, although the "pacification" of the Berbers was not complete until 1934. French troops also intervened in the Spanish Zone to help put down a rebellion in the Rif led by Abd al-Krim, a *Qadi* ("religious judge") and leader of the powerful Ait Waryaghar tribe.

The organization of the protectorate was largely the work of the first French resident-general, Marshal Louis Lyautey. His goal was to develop the country and modernize the sultan's government while preserving Moroccan traditions and culture. He preferred the Berbers to the Arabs and set up a separate administration under Berber-speaking French officers for Berber areas.[4]

Lyautey's successors were less respectful of Moroccan traditions. The sultan, supposedly an independent ruler, became a figurehead. French *colons* (settlers) flocked to Morocco to buy land at rock-bottom prices and develop vineyards, citrus groves, and orchards. Modern cities sprang up around the perimeters of Rabat, Fez, Marrakesh, and other cities. In rural areas, particularly in the Atlas Mountains, the French worked with powerful local chiefs (*qaids*). Certain qaids used the arrangement to become enormously wealthy. One qaid, al-Glawi, as he was called, strutted about like a rooster in his territory and often said that he was the real sultan of Morocco.[5]

## Morocco's Independence Struggle

The movement for independence in Morocco developed slowly. The only symbol of national unity was the sultan, Muhammad ibn Yusuf. But he seemed ineffectual to most young Moroccans, particularly those educated in French schools, who began to question the right of France to rule a people against their will.

The hopes of these young Moroccans had a boost during World War II. The Western Allies, Great Britain and the United States, had gone on record in favor of the right of subject peoples to self-determination after the war. When U.S. president Franklin D. Roosevelt and British prime minister Winston Churchill came to Casablanca for an important wartime conference, the sultan was convinced to meet them privately and get a commitment for Morocco's independence. The leaders promised their support.

However, Roosevelt died before the end of the war, and Churchill was defeated for reelection. The French were not under any pressure after the war to end the protectorate. When a group of Moroccan nationalists formed the Istiqlal ("Independence") Party and demanded the end of French rule, most of them were arrested. A few leaders escaped to the Spanish Zone or to Tangier, where they could operate freely. For several years, Istiqlal headquarters was the home of the principal of the American School at Tangier, an ardent supporter of Moroccan nationalism.

With the Istiqlal dispersed, the sultan represented the last hope for national unity and resistance. Until then, he had gone along with the French; but in the early 1950s, he began to oppose them openly. The French began to look for a way to remove him from office and install a more cooperative ruler. In 1953, he was forced into exile and an elderly uncle was named to replace him.

The sultan's departure had the opposite effect from what was intended. In exile, he became a symbol for Moroccan resistance to the protectorate. A Moroccan Army of Liberation began battling French troops in rural regions. Although the French could probably have contained the rebellion in Morocco, they were under great pressure in neighboring Algeria and Tunisia, where resistance movements were also under way. In 1955, the French abruptly capitulated. Sultan Muhammad ibn Yusuf returned to his palace in Rabat in triumph, and the elderly uncle retired to potter about his garden in Tangier.

## INDEPENDENCE

Morocco became independent on March 2, 1956. (The Spanish protectorate ended in April, and Tangier came under Moroccan control in October, although it kept its free-port status and special banking and currency privileges for several more years.) It began its existence as a sovereign state with a number of assets—a popular ruler, an established government, and a modern system of roads, schools, hospitals, and some industries inherited from the protectorate. Against these assets were the liabilities of age-old Arab-Berber and inter-Berber conflicts, little experience with political parties or democratic institutions, and an economy dominated by Europeans.

The sultan's goal was to establish a constitutional monarchy. His first action was to give himself a new title, King Muhammad V, symbolizing the end of the old autocratic rule of his predecessors. Because of their collaboration with colonial France, the power of caids and pasha was severely curtailed; "they were compromised by their association with the French, and returned to the land to make way for nationalist cadres, many . . . not from the regions they were assigned to administer."[6]

Muhammad V did not live long enough to reach his goal. He died unexpectedly in 1961 and was succeeded by his eldest son, Crown Prince Hassan. Hassan II ruled until his death in 1999. While he fulfilled his father's promise immediately with a Constitution, in most other ways Hassan II set his own stamp on Morocco.

The Constitution provided for an elected legislature and a multiparty political system. In addition to the Istiqlal, a number of other parties were organized, including one representing the monarchy. But the results of the French failure to develop a satisfactory party system soon became apparent. In spite its plurality—almost unique in the Arab world at that time—the party system could not challenge the powerful monarch who was both at the center and above the political system.

In 1965, riots broke out in Casablanca. The immediate cause was labor and student unrest, but other reasons include the authoritarian rule and the overall bad socioeconomic conditions, especially in the slums of Casablanca. The riots were harshly repressed, leaving many people dead. The king declared a state of emergency, dismissed the legislature, and assumed full powers under the Constitution.

For the next dozen years, Hassan II ruled as an absolute monarch. He continued to insist that his goal was a parliamentary system, a "government of national union." But he depended on a small group of cronies, members of prominent merchant families, the large Alawi family, or powerful Berber leaders as a more reliable group than the fractious political parties. The dominance of "the king's men" led to growing dissatisfaction and the perception that the king had sold out to special interests. Gradually, unrest spread to the army, previously loyal to its commander-in-chief. In 1971, during a diplomatic reception, cadets from the main military academy invaded the royal palace near Rabat. A number of foreign diplomats were killed and the king held prisoner briefly before loyal troops could crush the rebellion. The next year, an attempt by airforce pilots to shoot down the king's plane failed. The two escapes helped confirm in Hassan's mind his invincibility under the protection of Allah.

But they also prompted him to reinstate the parliamentary system. A new Constitution issued in 1972 defined Morocco "as a democratic and social constitutional monarchy in which Islam is the established religion."[8] However, the king retained the constitutional powers that, along with those derived from his spiritual role as "Commander of the Faithful" and lineal descendant of Muhammad, undergirded his authority.

## HEALTH/WELFARE

In October 2000, the International Labor Organization (ILO) ranked Morocco as the 3rd-highest country in the world, after China and India, in the exploitation of child labor. Moroccan children as young as 5, all girls, are employed in the carpet industry. In addition to Moroccan and other African illegal immigrants to Europe, the Spanish government tries to control illegal immigration through a new program of recruitment of Moroccan women to leave their families for short-term work on Spanish farms. However, in 2008, due to economic crisis, Spain offered Moroccan workers, along with other non-EU foreigners, a financial incentive to leave. Many of those who remained are now either unemployed or underemployed.

## INTERNAL POLITICS

Morocco's de facto annexation of the Western Sahara has had important implications for national development due to the territory's size, underpopulation, and mineral resources, particularly shale oil and phosphates. But the annexation has been equally important to political unity. The "Green March" of 350,000 unarmed Moroccans into Spanish territory in 1975 to dramatize Morocco's claim was organized by the king and supported by all segments of the population and the opposition parties. In 1977, opposition leaders agreed to serve under the king in a

(Courtesy of Azzedine Layachi)

Artisan Cooperative in Fez, Morocco

the government for many reasons, including the king's refusal to give the opposition the so-called three ministries of sovereignty (Interior, Foreign Affairs, and Justice) which have always been led by people chosen by the king himself.

King Hassan resolved the crisis by appointing then-USFP leader Abdellatif Filali as the new prime minister, thus bringing the opposition into the government. The king continued with this method of political reconciliation by appointing the new head of the USFP, Abderrahmane Youssoufi, to the position after the latter's return from political exile in 1998.

A referendum in 1996 approved several amendments to the constitution. One in particular replaced the unicameral legislature by a bicameral one. The upper house (Chamber of Counselors) has 270 seats, elected indirectly by municipal councils, professional associations, and labor syndicates for 9-year terms. The lower house (Chamber of Representatives) has 325 seats, 295 elected by popular vote for 5-year terms, with 30 seats reserved for women. The first lower house election was held in 2002; the last one was held in 2007.

The 2002 elections underlined the broad spectrum of Moroccan politics. The Socialist Union of Popular Forces (USFP) won 50 seats, the venerable Istiqlal 48, the National Rally of Independents (RNI) 41 and the Popular Movement 27. The relatively new Islamist party, Party of Justice and Development (PJD) won 42 seats, becoming thereby the third party in the country.

In the September 7, 2007 parliamentary elections the Istiqlal won the largest number of seats (52) while the PJD increased its representation to 46, lower than expected. The USFP ran fifth with 38 seats after the Popular Movement (41) and the RNI (39). The voter turnout was the lowest ever, at 37 percent, and as usual there were claims of electoral fraud, vote buying, and manipulation of the results by the state and the monarchy in order to block the rise of a single party and more importantly, to prevent the Islamists from gaining the upper hand in the rough-and-tumble game of Moroccan politics.

In the June 12, 2009 municipal elections, in which some 30 parties competed for 27,795 seats, the new pro-monarchy Authenticity and Modernity Party (PAM), won the highest number (6,015) at the expense of the established parties Istiqlal and USFP. The Islamist party PJD came in sixth. It is important to note that, thanks to a new quota of 12 percent of the seats reserved for women, 3,406 women were elected, a far cry from only 127 in 2003.

"government of national unity." The first elections in 12 years were held for a new Legislature.

In the 1984 parliamentary elections, the pro-monarchist Constitutional Union (CU) party won a majority of seats in the Chamber of Representatives. A new party, the National Rally of Independents (RNI), formed by members with no party affiliations, emerged as the chief rival to the CU.

New elections were scheduled for 1989 but were postponed three times; the king said that extra time was needed for the economic-stabilization program to show results and generate public confidence. The elections finally took place in two stages in 1993: the first for election of party candidates, and the second for trade-union and professional-association candidates. The final tally showed 195 seats for center-right (royalist) candidates, to 120 for the Democratic-bloc opposition. As a result, coalition government became necessary. However, the two leading opposition parties—the Socialist Union of Popular Forces (USFP) and the Istiqlal—refused to participate, claiming election irregularities. These two parties and five others formed in 1992 an alliance named the "Koutla" which means alliance in Arabic. Opposition from members of this alliance and other parties, blocked legislative action until 1994. The Koutla block walked out of the legislature and announced a boycott of

## FOREIGN RELATIONS

During his long reign, King Hassan II served effectively in mediating the long-running Arab-Israeli conflict. He took an active part in the negotiations for the 1979 Egyptian-Israeli peace treaty and for the treaty between Israel and Jordan in 1994. For these services he came to be viewed by the United States and by European powers as an impartial mediator. However, his absolute rule and suppression of human rights at home caused difficulties with Europe. The European Union suspended $145 million in aid in 1992; it was restored only after Hassan had released long-time political prisoners and pardoned 150 alleged Islamist militants. In 1995, Morocco became the second African country, after Tunisia, to be granted associate status in the EU.

Thus far, Morocco's only venture in "imperial politics" has been in the Western Sahara. This California-size desert territory, formerly a Spanish protectorate and then a colony after 1912, was never a part of the modern Moroccan state. Its only connection is historical—it was the headquarters and starting point for the Almoravid dynasty, camel-riding nomads who ruled western North Africa and southern Spain in the eleventh century. But the presence of so much empty land, along with millions of tons of phosphate rock and potential oil fields, encouraged the king to secure the territory. In October 1975 the king organized a "Green March" of 350,000 Moroccans into the Spanish Sahara "to recover sacred Moroccan territory. As a result, Spain agreed in 1976 to cede two thirds of it to Morocco and one third to Mauritania. After the overthrow of the Mauritanian government by a military coup in 1978, its new leaders abandoned their share and signed a peace agreement with the Polisario.

Since then Morocco's control has been challenged by Polisario. The latter's goal is a sovereign state, the Sahrawi Arab Democratic Republic (S.A.D.R.) It has been recognized as such by a number of African countries. However the territory remains under Moroccan control; it has been defined as the country's newest province. As a frontier province, over the past three decades thousands of Moroccan settlers have moved there, encouraged by free land, farm equipment, subsidized housing and other inducements.

Conflict between the Moroccan army and Polisario forces operating from Algerian bases with Algerian support for their cause continued throughout the 1980s. It eventually led the Moroccan army to construct a 350-mile "Sand Wall" around the province's land border. Meanwhile some 150,000 Sahrawis became refugees in camps in southern Algeria.

The dispute eventually came before the UN in 1991. The Security Council, prodded by Algeria, called for voter registration for a referendum to determine the future of the territory. The two parties agreed to a cease-fire, and a UN Observer Force, MINURSO, was established to monitor the cease-fire and supervise voter registration. Due largely to Morocco's intransigence, the referendum has yet to be held, despite efforts at mediation by ex-U.S. Secretary of State James Baker and others.

The "glacial chill" between Morocco and the Polisario thawed a bit in 2005, when the latter released 404 Moroccan prisoners in a "humanitarian gesture." But with the demographic balance tipped in its favor by large-scale Moroccan settlement, it seemed that nothing short of strong international pressure would make Morocco give up the annexed territory or accept the holding of the referendum called for by the United Nations through a myriad of resolutions.

King Hassan II unilaterally named the territory Morocco's newest province, and by 2001 Moroccan settlers formed a majority in the population of 244,593. In December 2001, French president Jacques Chirac made an official visit to Morocco and saluted the country for the development of its "southern provinces." Earlier, the United Nations had appointed former U.S. secretary of state James Baker as mediator between Morocco and the Polisario. After several failed attempts at mediation, Baker submitted a plan for postponement of the referendum until 2006. In the interim, the Sahrawis would elect an autonomous governing body, with its powers limited to local and provincial affairs. The voting list would include all residents. Because of the large-scale Moroccan settler movement into the territory with government inducements any future referendum is unlikely to result in a vote for independence. Moroccan and Polisario negotiators continue to meet under UN auspices from time to time, most recently in August 2009 in Duernstein, Austria. The meeting, which was facilitated by Christopher Ross, the new UN Special Envoy, was inconclusive but the conflicting parties agreed to meet again. The Moroccans have been pushing for local autonomy for Western Sahara, but Polisario's representatives held firmly to a referendum which would include the Sahrawis in Algerian refugee camps.

## THE ECONOMY

Morocco has two thirds of the world's known reserves of phosphate rock and is the top exporter of phosphates. The major thrust in industrial development is in phosphate-related industries. Access to deposits was one reason for Morocco's annexation of the Western Sahara, although to date there has been little extraction there due to the political conflict. The downturn in demand and falling prices in the global phosphates market brought on a debt crisis in the late 1980s. Increased phosphate demand globally and improved crop production following the end of several drought years have strengthened the economy.

The country also has important but undeveloped iron-ore deposits and a small but significant production of rare metals such as mercury, antimony, nickel, and lead. In the past, a major obstacle to development was the lack of oil resources. In 2001, the French oil company TotalFinaElf and Kerr-McGee of Texas were granted parallel concessions of 44,000 square miles offshore in Western Saharan waters near Dakhla. However, in 2002, following a request by the Security Council, the United Nation's top legal officer determined that oil prospecting by foreign companies in disregard of the interests of the people of Western Sahara would violate international legal principles dealing with non-self-governing territories.

Although recurring droughts have hampered improvement of the agricultural sector, it still accounts for 20 percent of gross domestic product and employs 40 percent of the labor force. Production varies widely from year to year, due to fluctuating rainfall. In 2007 droughts caused the worst production in recent history and led to a steep decline of Morocco's GDP growth rate from 7.9% in 2006 to 3% in 2007. However, things turned out better in 2008 and 2009 thanks to better rain conditions and some reforms.

The fisheries sector is equally important to the economy; they account for 16 percent of exports; annual production is approximately 1 million tons. The agreement with the European Union for associate status has been very beneficial to the industry. Morocco received $500 million in 1999–2001 from European countries in return for fishing rights for their vessels in Moroccan territorial waters.

But the economic outlook and social prospects remain bleak for most people. Although the birth rate has been sharply reduced, job prospects are limited for the large number of young Moroccans entering the labor force each year. The "suicide bombers," who attacked a Jewish community center, a hotel, foreign consulates and other structures in Casablanca in May 2003, killing some 41 persons, were said to belong to the radical Islamist organization al-Sirat al-Mustakim (Righteous Path), believed to be linked with al Qaeda. However, the fact that they came mostly from the impoverished slum area of the city suggests that they acted out of frustration with the problems that face Morocco's youth today, namely unemployment, poverty and lack of opportunities in the workplace. As one observer noted of those arrested (only 12 were suicide bombers), little distinguished them from the group of young men idling in the streets or hawking designer sunglasses at intersections around town.

## PROSPECTS

King Hassan II died in July 1999. The monarch had ruled his country for 38 years—the second-longest reign in the Middle East. Like King Hussein of Jordan, Hassan became identified with his country to such a degree that "Hassan was Morocco, and Morocco was Hassan." But unlike Jordan's ruler, Hassan combined religious with secular authority. Among his many titles was that of "Commander of the Faithful," and the affection felt for him by most Moroccans, particularly women and youth, was amply visible during his state funeral. His frequent reminders to the nation in speeches and broadcasts that "I am the person entrusted by God to lead you" clearly identified him in the public mind not only as their religious leader but also as head of the family.

The king's eldest son, Crown Prince Muhammad, succeeded him without incident as Muhammad VI. Morocco's new ruler began his reign with public commitments to reform human-rights protections and an effort to atone for some aspects of Hassan's autocratic rule. One of his first actions was the dismissal of Interior Minister Driss Basri, the acknowledged "power behind the throne." He had been considered largely responsible for the "Years of Lead" during Hassan's rule, when human rights were routinely violated and opposition political leaders jailed on various pretexts by the police, army and security services.

Mohammad VI also publicly admitted the existence of the Tazmamat "death camp" and other camps in the Sahara, where rebel army officers and political prisoners were held, often for years and without trial or access to their families. (The family of General Oufkir, leader of the 1972 attempted coup who was later executed, were among those held, but they managed to escape after 20 years in jail.)[7] The new king also committed $3.8 million in compensation to the families of those who had been imprisoned.

The expansion of what has been variously described as "Islamism", "Islamic fundamentalism" and "Islamic radicalism" in the Muslim world has not escaped Morocco entirely. Hassan II kept the movement on a tight rein during his years in power. He outlawed the main Islamist movement Adl wa Ihsan ("Justice and Charity") and locked its leader away in a mental institution. After his accession Muhammad VI established the Equity and Reconciliation Commission, headed by human rights activist Driss Benezkri, to investigate rights violations during the Years of Lead. By April 2005, when it was disbanded, the Commission had investigated 22,000 cases and compensated the families involved on behalf of the victims. Unfortunately because it had been established as only an investigative body, it could not prosecute defendants. Any such action would have to be taken through the judiciary.

Mohammed VI also issued in 2000 a "National Action Plan" which included women's rights, a free press, and other elements lacking in the country's social structure. But actions attributed to Islamists, such as the Casablanca bombings, provoked a heavy reaction particularly in the security services. Independent publications such as *Le Journal,* the most popular French-language magazine, and newspapers were closed. The head of the Moroccan Association for Human Rights was arrested and beaten, and riot police broke up demonstrations protesting the restrictions, arresting 800 persons. A police officer noted that "we don't want the chaos of a second intifada," a reference to the Palestinian uprising against Israel.

The king's major social reform effort to date is the Family Code of Laws known as the Mudawana, approved by the Chamber of Representatives in 2003. Among other provisions it makes wives equal to their husbands in ownership of property and allows them to initiate divorce proceedings. In a separate action, Muhammad VI appointed the first female Royal Counselor, and reserved 30 seats for women in parliament.

Reform in Morocco continues to face numerous obstacles, nonetheless. A 2005 Report by Reporters Without Borders indicated that 80 percent of the country's journalists did not feel free to write about many issues, despite the protection presumably afforded by the Action Plan. One indicated in the Report that "while the practice of freedom is clear, the legal guarantee is not there. I would not necessarily say that we are in a process of democratization. I would say we are in a process."[8]

Protests in Berber areas, notably the Rif, led the king in July 2001 to establish a Royal Amazigh Language and Culture Institute. Its goals are to standardize the language, teach it in schools, and develop media programs devoted to cultural preservation. The important carpet industry, mostly represented by women, is being expanded through technology and global marketing. A Berber *(Amazigh)* satellite TV channel was launched in 2007 and the important Moroccan tourism industry reoriented to emphasize Amazigh dance, restoration of Berber *qasbas* (fortresses) and other elements in traditional Berber culture.[9]

## Timeline: PAST

**788–790**
The foundations of the Moroccan nation are established by Idris I and II, with the capital at Fez

**1062–1147**
The Almoravid and Almohad dynasties, Morocco's "imperial period"

**1672**
The current ruling dynasty, the Alawi, establishes its authority under Mulay Ismail

**1912**
Morocco is occupied and placed under French and Spanish protectorates

**1956**
Independence under King Muhammad V

**1961**
The accession of King Hassan II

**1975**
The Green March into the Western Sahara dramatizes Morocco's claim to the area

**1980s**
Bread riots; agreement with Libya for a federal union; the king unilaterally abrogates the 1984 treaty of union with Libya

**1990s**
Elections establish parliamentary government; King Hassan dies and is succeeded by King Muhammad VI

## PRESENT

**2000s**
King Muhammad VI works to improve human rights; the economic picture brightens; parliamentary elections in 2007; two deadly terrorist attacks, one of them killed 41 persons; inconclusive direct negotiation series between Morocco and the Polisario Front in Manhasset, New York, on the fate of Western Sahara.

## NOTES

1. Sue Miller, "Migration Station," *Christian Science Monitor,* June 26, 2003.

2. See David M. Hart, *Dadda 'Atta and His Forty Grandsons* (Cambridge, England: Menas Press, 1981), pp. 8–11. Dadda 'Atta was a historical figure, a minor saint or marabout.

3. Michael B. Oren, *Power, Faith and Fantasy: America and The Middle East Since 1776* (New York: W.W. Norton, 2007, p. 28).

4. See David Woolman, *Rebels in the Rif: Abd 'al Krim and the Rif Rebellion* (Palo Alto, CA: Stanford University Press, 1968). On the Ait Waryaghar, see David M. Hart, *The Ait Waryaghar of the Moroccan Rif: An Ethnography and a History* (Tucson, AZ: University of Arizona Press, 1976). Abd 'al Krim had annihilated a Spanish army and set up a Republic of the Rif (1921–1926).

5. For a detailed description of protectorate tribal administration, see Robin Bidwell, *Morocco Under Colonial Rule* (London: Frank Cass, 1973). For more on Lyautey's colonial tenure in Morocco, see Moshe Gershovich, "Collaboration and "Pacification": French Conquest, Moroccan Combatants, and the Transformation of the Middle Atlas," *Comparative Studies of South Asia, Africa and the Middle East* 24.1 (2004) 139–146. It is online at http://muse .jhu.edu/journals/comparative_studies_ of_south_asia_africa_and_the_middle_ east/v024/24.1gershovich.html

6. Mark Tessler, "Morocco: Institutional Pluralism and Monarchical Dominance," in W. I. Zartman, ed., *Political Elites in North Africa* (New York: Longman, 1982), p. 44.

7. See Malika Oufkir, with Michele Fitoussi, *Stolen Lives: Twenty Years in a Desert Jail* (New York: Hyperion Books, 1999). Another prisoner, Ahmed Marzouki, recently published his memoir of life there. Entitled *Cell 10,* it has sold widely in Morocco.

8. Geoff Pingree and Lisa Abend, "Morocco moves gradually to address past repression." *The Christian Science Monitor,* September 23, 2005.

9. Shaina Adams and Brahim El Guabli, "The Amazigh People of Morocco," *Fellowship,* Vol. 73, No.7–9, Fall 2007, pp. 21–24.

# Oman (Sultanate of Oman)

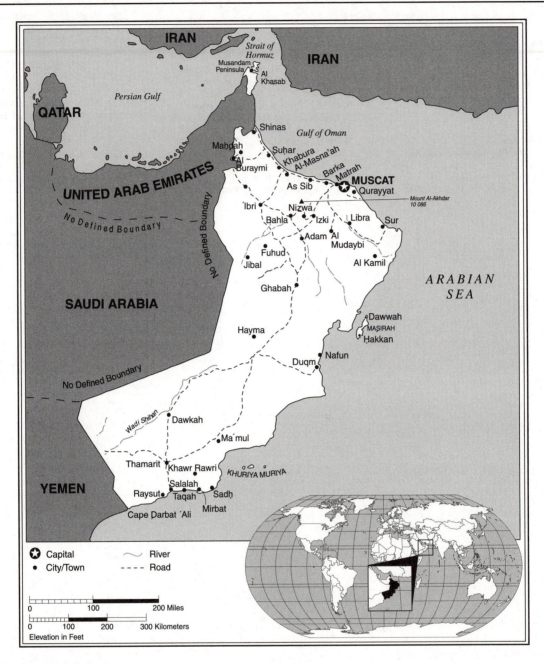

**Capital** ⭐
**City/Town** ●
**River** ～
**Road** ---

0  100  200 Miles
0  100  200  300 Kilometers
Elevation in Feet

# Oman Statistics

## GEOGRAPHY

*Area in Square Miles (Kilometers):* 192,314
  (309,500) (about the size of Kansas)
*Capital (Population):* Muscat (400,000)
*Environmental Concerns:* rising soil salinity; beach pollution from oil spills;
  very limited freshwater
*Geographical Features:* central desert plain;
  rugged mountains in the north and south
*Climate:* coast, hot and humid; interior,
  hot and dry

## PEOPLE

### Population

*Total:* 2,967,717 (includes 577,293
  non-nationals)
*Annual Growth Rate:* 1.99%
*Rural/Urban Population Ratio:* 22/78
*Major Languages:* Arabic; English;
  various South Asian languages
*Ethnic Makeup:* almost entirely Arab;
  small Baluchi, South Asian, and
  African groups

*Religions:* 75% Ibadi Muslim; remainder
  Sunni Muslim, Shi'a Muslim, some
  Hindu

### Health

*Life Expectancy at Birth:* 72 years (male);
  76 years (female)
*Infant Mortality Rate:* 16/1,000 live
  births

### Education

*Adult Literacy Rate:* 75.8%

140

## COMMUNICATION

*Telephones:* 274,200 main lines
*Daily Newspaper Circulation:* 31 per 1,000 people
*Televisions:* 711 per 1,000 people
*Internet users:* 465,000 (2008)

## TRANSPORTATION

*Highways in Miles (Kilometers):* 26,284 (42,300)
*Railroads in Miles (Kilometers):* none
*Usable Airfields:* 143
*Motor Vehicles in Use:* 347,000

## GOVERNMENT

*Type:* limited constitutional monarchy (under 1996 Basic Law, which defines the succession and provides for a prime minister)
*Independence Date:* 1650 (expulsion of the Portuguese)

*Head of State/Government:* Sultan and Prime Minister Qaboos ibn Said Al Said is both head of state and head of government
*Political Parties:* none allowed, but the Basic Law provides for a bicameral legislature to be elected by popular vote
*Suffrage:* universal at 21

## MILITARY

*Military Expenditures (% of GDP):* 11.4%
*Current Disputes:* boundary with United Arab Emirates defined bilaterally in 2002. Other boundaries, with UAE Emirates Ras al-Khaymah and Sharjah, which separate the Musandam Peninsula from Oman proper, are administrative and not treaty-defined

## ECONOMY

*Currency ($U.S. Equivalent):* 0.3845 rials = $1

*Per Capita Income/GDP:* $14,100/ $52.95 billion
*GDP Growth Rate:* 2.7%
*Inflation Rate:* 3%
*Unemployment Rate:* 15%
*Labor Force:* 968,800
*Natural Resources:* petroleum; copper; asbestos; marble; limestone; chromium; gypsum; natural gas
*Agriculture:* dates; limes; bananas; alfalfa; vegetables; camels; cattle; fish
*Industry:* crude-oil production and refining; natural-gas production; construction; cement; copper
*Exports:* $29.34 billion (primary partners China, South Korea, Japan)
*Imports:* $18.41 billion (primary partners United Arab Emirates, Japan, United Kingdom)

## SUGGESTED WEB SITES

http://lcweb2.loc.gov/frd/cs/omtoc.htm
www.oman.org/

# Oman Country Report

The Sultanate of Oman was, at least until about 1970, one of the least-known countries in the world. Yet it is a very old country with a long history of contact with the outside world. Merchants from Oman had a near monopoly on the trade in frankincense and myrrh. Oman-built, shallow-draught, broad-beamed ships called dhows crisscrossed the Indian Ocean, trading with India and the Far East.

In the twentieth century, Oman became important to the outside world for two primary reasons: it began producing oil in the 1960s; and it has a strategic location on the Strait of Hormuz, the passageway for supertankers carrying Middle Eastern oil to the industrialized countries. Eighty percent of Japan's oil needs passes through Hormuz, as does 60 percent of Western Europe's. A Swiss journalist called the Omanis "sentinels of the Gulf" because they watch over this vital traffic.

## GEOGRAPHY

Oman is the third-largest country in the Arabian Peninsula after Yemen and Saudi Arabia. However, the population is small, and large areas of land are uninhabited or sparsely populated. The geographical diversity—rugged mountains, vast gravelly plains, and deserts—limits large-scale settlement. The bulk of the population is centered in the Batinah coastal plain, which stretches from the United Arab Emirates border south to the capital, Muscat. Formerly this area was devoted to fishing and agriculture; but with the rapid development of Oman under the current sultan, it has become heavily industrialized, with extensive commerce. The ancient system of *falaj*—underground irrigation channels that run for miles, bringing water downhill by gravity flow—has made farming possible, although the agricultural sector is often adversely affected by prolonged drought. Oman's southern Dhofar Province is more fertile and productive than the rest of the country, due to monsoon rains. In addition to citrus and other tropical fruits, Oman is the major world source of frankincense and gum from a small tree that grows wild and has been prized since ancient times.

Behind Oman's coast is the Jabal al-Akhdar ("Green Mountain"), a spine of rugged mountains with peaks over 10,000 feet. The mountains form several disconnected chains, interspersed with deep, narrow valleys where village houses hang like eagles' nests from the mountaintops, above terraced gardens and palm groves.

## DEVELOPMENT

Vision Oman 2020, the sultan's blueprint for long-term growth, sets among its objectives increasing economic diversity to reduce dependence on oil, developing a competitive private sector producing manufactured goods for export, and Omanization of the labor force. With some half-million young Omanis entering the workplace yearly the government has had to reduce significantly the number of non-nationals, especially skilled workers, employed in its development projects.

Most of Oman's oil wells are located in the interior of the country. The interior is a broad, hilly plain dotted with oasis villages, each one a fortress with thick walls to keep out desert raiders. The stony plain eventually becomes the Rub al-Khali ("Empty Quarter"), the great uninhabited desert of southeastern Arabia.

Omani territory includes the Musandam Peninsula, at the northeastern tip of Arabia projecting into the Strait of Hormuz. The peninsula and the neighboring Midha oasis are physically separated from the rest of Oman by U.A.E. territory. In

(© Brinda A. Toprani)

Traditional Omani Boat

1995, the Omani border with Yemen was formally demarcated in accordance with a UN-sponsored 1992 agreement. The oasis of Buraimi, on the Oman/Saudi Arabia/U.A.E. border, is currently under U.A.E. control, although it is claimed by both Saudi Arabia and Yemen. The surrounding desert hinterland is shared by the three states and remains undefined.

## HISTORY

As was the case elsewhere in Arabia, the early social structure of Oman consisted of a number of tribal groups. Many of them were and still are nomadic (Bedouin), while others became settled farmers and herders centuries ago. The groups spent much of their time feuding with one another. Occasionally, several would join in an alliance against others, but none of them recognized any higher authority than their leaders.

In the seventh century A.D., the Omanis converted to Islam and developed their own form of Islam called Ibadhia, a name derived from the name of Abdullah ibn Ibadh at-Tamimi, one of its early theologians. The Ibadhi (or Ibadi) movement is a Muslim sect that is distinct from Sunni and Shia Islam with whom it has several doctrinal differ-

ences. It is believed that it grew in the seventh century out of a movement known as the Khawarij or Kharijites (the outsiders), which constituted the first opposition to ever form in Islam. Ibadites constitute more than 75% of the Omani population and are found also in Algeria, Tunisia, Libya and the Zanzibar region of Tanzania.

### FREEDOM

In 1996 Sultan Qaboos issued a Basic Law that provides for an appointed Council of State (including a few women members) and a Majlis al-Shura, also appointed, which may draft legislation on social issues for his approval. If approved, the draft then becomes law. Unlike in other Gulf states, most Omani women are educated, and many play an active part in national life. In 2004, the Sultan appointed Oman's first female minister with portfolio.

The Ibadi peoples elect their own leader, called an Imam. The Ibadi Imams do not have to be descendants of the prophet Muhammad, as do the Imams in the main body of Shi'a Muslims. The Ibadi community believes that anyone, regardless of

background, can be elected Imam, as long as the individual is pious, just, and capable. If no one is available who meets those requirements, the office may remain vacant.[1]

Ibadi Imams ruled interior Oman with the support of family leaders until the eighteenth century. Well before then, however, coastal Oman was being opened up to foreign powers. The Portuguese captured Muscat in the 1500s for use as a stopping place for their ships on the trade route to India. (An Omani served as navigator to Portuguese admiral Vasco da Gama in his voyage across the Indian Ocean to India.) They built two great forts guarding the entrance to Muscat harbor, forts that still stand, giving the town its picturesque appearance. The Portuguese were finally driven out in 1650. Since that time, Oman has not been ruled directly by any foreign power.

The current ruling dynasty in Oman is the Al Bu Said Dynasty. It has been in power since 1749, when a chief named Ahmad ibn Said defeated an Iranian invasion and established his authority over most of Oman. But, for most of the period, Oman actually had two rulers—a sultan ruling in Muscat and an Imam ruling in the interior at the same time.

The most successful Omani sultan before the twentieth century was Said ibn Sultan

(1804–1856). He added Dhofar Province and Zanzibar, on the East African coast, to Omani territory. He signed a treaty with the British that stated, "the friendship between our two states shall remain unshook to the end of time." The sultan also signed a friendship treaty with the United States in 1833; in 1836, to the surprise of the New York Port authorities, an Omani ship docked in New York harbor. Its captain said that the sultan had sent him to get to know the Americans whom he had heard so much about and to arrange trade contacts. Just under 170 years later, some 100 "cultural ambassadors" from Oman, including indigo dyers, shipwrights, bagpipers and sword dancers, arrived in Washington DC to participate in the 39th annual Smithsonian Folklife Festival, representing the first Arab country to do so.[2]

## HEALTH/WELFARE

In the last 35 years, the combination of improved health services, effective government-sponsored family planning programs, and the use of mobile health teams that travel to remote areas not served by hospitals or clinics, has reduced infant mortality rates by 14 folds (a world record), reaching 16 per 1,000 live births in 2009. Life expectancy increased to 74 years, up from 60 years in the 1970s.

After Said's death, a number of ethnic, tribal, and religious differences re-asserted themselves, and Oman lost its importance in regional affairs. Its territory was again restricted to its small corner of southeastern Arabia. The opening of the Suez Canal in 1869 diverted shipping to new Red Sea routes, and ships no longer called at Muscat harbor. Piracy and the slave trade, both of which had provided revenues for the sultan, were prohibited by international law. For the rest of the 1800s and most of the 1900s, Oman sank into isolation, forgotten by the world. Only Britain paid the Omanis any attention, giving the sultan a small subsidy in the event that Oman might be of some future use to it.

In the early twentieth century, the Imams of inner Oman and the sultans ruling in Muscat came to a complete parting of the ways. In 1920, a treaty between the two leaders provided that the sultan would not interfere in the internal affairs of inner Oman. Relations were reasonably smooth until 1951, when Britain recognized the independence of the Sultanate of Muscat-Oman, as it was then called, and withdrew its advisers. Subsequently, the Imam declared inner Oman to be a separate state from the sultanate. A number of Arab states supported the Imam on the grounds that the sultan was a British puppet. Conflict between the Imam and the

sultan dragged on until 1960, when the sultan finally reestablished his authority.

Oman's ruler for nearly four decades in the twentieth century was Sultan Said ibn Taimur (1932–1970). The most interesting aspect of his reign was the way in which he stopped the clock of modernization. Oil was discovered in 1964 in inland Oman; within a few years, wealth from oil royalties began pouring in. However, the sultan was afraid that the new wealth would corrupt his people. He refused to spend money except for the purchase of arms and a few personal luxuries such as an automobile, which he liked to drive on the only paved road in Salalah. He would not allow the building of schools, houses, roads, or hospitals for his people. Before 1970, there were only 16 schools in all of Oman. The sole hospital was the American mission in Muscat, established in the 1800s by Baptist missionaries. All 10 of Oman's qualified doctors worked abroad because the sultan did not trust modern medicine. The few roads were rough caravan tracks; many areas of the country, such as the Musandam Peninsula, were inaccessible.

## ACHIEVEMENTS

A new Iranian-built power plant began operations in 1999 in Oman, meeting domestic needs for electricity. Oman is also self-sufficient in cement and textiles, most of the latter made in factories located in the Rusayl free-trade zone near Muscat. The zone now has more than 60 industries and produces $60 million in finished goods, generating $24 million in exports.

In the entire country, there were only about 1,000 automobiles; to import a car, one had to have the sultan's personal permission. On the darker side, slavery was still a common practice. Women were almost never seen in public and had to be veiled from head to foot if they walked to a neighbor's house to visit. On the slightest pretext, prisoners could be locked up in the old Portuguese fort at Muscat and left to rot.

As the 1960s came to an end, there was increasing unrest in Oman. The opposition centered around Qaboos ibn Said, the sultan's son. Qaboos had been educated in England. When he came home, his father shut him up in a house in Salalah, a town far from Muscat, and refused to give him any responsibilities. He was afraid of his "Western ideas."

On July 23, 1970, supporters of Crown Prince Qaboos overthrew the sultan, and Qaboos succeeded him. Sultan Qaboos ibn Said brought Oman into the twentieth century in a hurry. The old policy of isolation was reversed.

Qaboos also ended a long-running rebellion in Dhofar. His father had considered the province his personal estate, and did nothing to develop it. In 1962, Marxist Omanis backed by the Peoples' Democratic Republic of Yemen (PDRY) next door led a rebellion against Said's rule. The sultan crushed the rebellion in 1975 with the help of troops from Britain and Iran.

## OMANI SOCIETY

Oman today is a land in flux, its society poised between the traditional past and a future governed increasingly by technology. An Omani business executive or industrial chief may wear a Western suit and tie to an appointment, but more than likely he will arrive for his meeting in a *dishdasha* (the traditional full-length robe worn by Gulf Arabs), with either a turban or an embroidered skullcap to complete the outfit. A ceremonial dagger called *khanjar* will certainly hang from his belt or sash. He will have a cellular phone pressed to his right ear and a digital watch on his wrist, courtesy of Oman's extensive trade with Japan. Older Omani women are also in traditional costume, covered head to toe with the enveloping *chador* and their faces (except for the eyes) hidden behind the black *batula,* the eagle-like mask common in the region. But increasingly their daughters and younger sisters opt for Western clothing, with only head scarves to distinguish them as Muslims.

In social, economic, and even political areas of Omani life, Qaboos has brought about changes that have proceeded at a dizzying pace during his three-decade rule. Education, health care, and roads were his three top priorities when he took office. By 2003 Oman had 1,022 schools, 49 hospitals, 199 health clinics and over 20,000 miles of paved highways. Sultan Qaboos University, which opened in 1986 has now thousands of students. Expansion and improvement of the educational system with added emphasis on adult and community programs have led to a steep rise in the literacy rate, currently 75.8 percent.

The sultan has also begun the process of replacing authoritarian rule by representative government. In 1996, his silver-anniversary year, he issued a Basic Law which, among other reforms, sets up a bicameral legislature. Its upper chamber (Majlis al-Dawla) has 58 members appointed by the sultan. The lower house (Majlis al-Shura) has 84 members elected for 4-year terms by popular vote.[3]

## THE ECONOMY

Oman began producing and exporting oil in limited quantities in 1967. The industry was greatly expanded after the accession of Sultan Qaboos. It is managed by a national corporation, Petroleum Development Oman (PDO). Oil production in the 1990s reached 900,000 barrels per day but was reduced to 860,000 bpd in 2000–2001, in accordance with OPEC production cuts. Oman's oil reserves are 5.7 billion barrels. Natural-gas reserves are 29.3 trillion cubic feet. The new liquefied natural gas (LNG) plant at Qalhat produced 6.6 million tons of LNG in 2001. Some 4 million tons were exported to South Korea in 2000; it was the largest single gas-export contract arranged by two state companies.

In its search for ways to supplement its oil income, Oman in 1996 formed a Caspian Sea Consortium with Russia, Kazakhstan, and several U.S. oil companies, which aimed to build a shipper-owned oil export pipeline from Kazakhstan to the Russian Black Sea port of Novorossyisk. In spite of the success of the project after it became operational in 2001, Oman withdrew from the Consortium in 2008 and sold its 7 percent share to Russia. It was apparently frustrated by delays in the expansion of the oil export route. Oman also became the first Gulf country to establish a privately-owned electricity grid. In the industrial sector the Oman Oil Company has undertaken a number of new joint ventures, such as new refineries and a fertilizer plant being developed in conjunction with Indian industrialists. In 2005 the country's second oil refinery came on stream, along with an aluminum smelter at Sohar, on the Batinah coast.

Barely 2 percent of Oman's land is arable. Rainfall averages two to four inches annually except in monsoon-drenched Dhofar, and recent drought has largely dried up the long-established falaj system. The interior oases and Dhofar provide for intensive cultivation of dates. They also produce coconuts and various other fruits. Agriculture provides 35 percent of non-oil exports and employs 12 percent of the labor force.

The fishing industry employs 10 percent of the working population, but obsolete equipment and lack of canning and freezing plants have severely limited the catch in the past. Another problem is the unwillingness of Omani fishermen to move into commercial production; most of them catch just enough fish for their own use. The Oman Fish Company was formed in 1987 to develop fishery resources, financing the purchase by fishermen of aluminum boats powered by outboard motors to replace the seaworthy but slow traditional wooden dhows. A new fish-processing plant at Rusayl, built at a cost of $34 million, and the enlargement of the main fishing harbor at Raysut, generated a 5.6 percent increase in that sector of the economy in 2003.

## FOREIGN RELATIONS

Oman joined with other Arab countries in opening links with Israel after its Oslo agreements with the Palestine Liberation Organization for Palestinian autonomy and the 1994 Jordan-Israel peace treaty. However, the freeze in Arab-Israeli relations ordered by the Arab League caused Oman to cancel the proposed Israeli trade mission in Muscat.

As a member of the Gulf Cooperation Council, Oman has become active in regional affairs, a role emphasized by its strategic location. Its long history of dealings with the United States—a relationship dating back to Andrew Jackson's presidency—has made Oman a partner in U.S. efforts to promote stability in the Gulf region. In 1980, Oman granted American military and naval personnel use of its Masirah Island and other military bases and the right to station troops and equipment there. In turn, the United States has provided new equipment to the Omani armed forces and built base housing for American personnel. During the Iran-Iraq War of 1980–1988, the country provided logistical support for U.S. warships escorting oil tankers in the Gulf to protect them from Iranian attacks, and U.S. jet fighters were based in Oman during the 1991 Gulf War.

After the September 11, 2001, terrorist attacks on the World Trade Center and the Pentagon, Sultan Qaboos took the lead among the Gulf states in supporting the U.S.-led international coalition against terrorism. In October, 20,000 British troops arrived in Muscat to supplement the U.S. forces already there. The United States also reached agreement for a $1.1 billion arms sale to Oman. It included 12 F-16 fighter aircraft, Sidewinder air-to-air missiles, and Harpoon antiship missiles. However the Sultan's close alignment with Britain and the U.S. does not preclude his periodic adoption of an independent foreign policy. He maintained good relations with Iran during the Iran-Iraq war and with Iraq during its occupation of Kuwait and in the postwar UN sanctions period.

## NOTES

1. For more on Ibadhia, see Valerie J. Hoffman, "Ibadi Islam: An Introduction," online at www.uga.edu/islam/ibadis.html. See also Amr Khalifa Ennami, Al-Ibadhiyah, distributed by the Ministry of Awqaf & Religious Affairs of the Sultanate of

Timeline: **PAST**

**1587–1588**
The Portuguese seize Muscat and build massive fortresses to guard the harbor

**1749**
The Al Bu Said Dynasty is established; extends Omani territory

**late 1800s**
The British establish a de facto protectorate; the slave trade is supposedly ended

**1951**
Independence

**1970**
Sultan Said ibn Taimur is deposed by his son, Prince Qaboos

**1975**
With British and Iranian help, Sultan Qaboos ends the Dhofar rebellion

**1980s**
Oman joins the Gulf Cooperation Council; Sultan Qaboos sets up a Consultative Assembly as the first step toward democratization

**1990s**
The sultan focuses on expanding Oman's industrial base; Sultan Qaboos issued in 1996 the Basic Law, a set of reform laws focused on state institutions and citizen rights

**PRESENT**

**2000s**
Sultan continues modest democratization program by establishing universal suffrage and an elected Council of State with advisory powers and inclusion of women. The growing tourism sector welcomed 2 million visitors in 2002; Oman signs in 2006 a free trade agreement with the United States

Oman. An online excerpt is at: www.angelfire.com/ok5/ibadhiyah/history.html. Consulted on August 9, 2010.

2. "Smithsonian Folklife Festival Features Traditions of Oman," Fulbright Focus (Alumni Newsletter), Summer 2005. Online at www.amideast.org/programs_services/exchange_programs/fulbright/Alumni_Newsletter/Fulbright%20Focus%20Summer%202005.pdf Consulted on August 9, 2010.

3. For a critical assessment of the Basic Law, see Nikolaus A. Siegfried, "Legislation and Legitimation in Oman: The Basic Law," Islamic Law and Society, Vol. 7, No. 3 (2000), pp. 359–397. The author argues that the Law is largely symbolic in character and changes nothing to the way power is exercised in Oman.

# Qatar (State of Qatar)

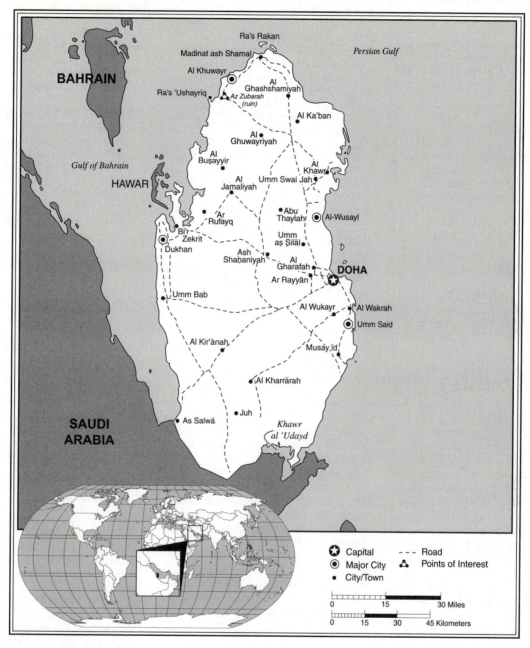

**BAHRAIN**

Persian Gulf

Ra's Rakan

Madinat ash Shamal

Al Khuwayr

Ra's 'Ushayriq

Az Zubarah (ruin)

Al Ghashshamiyah

Al Ka'ban

Al Ghuwayriyah

Gulf of Bahrain

Al Buşayyir

HAWAR

Al Jamaliyah

Al Khawr

Umm Swai Jah

'Ar Rufayq

Abu Thaylah

Al-Wusayl

Bi'r Zekrit

Umm aş Şilāl

Dukhan

Ash Shaḥaniyah

Al Gharafah

DOHA

Ar Rayyān

Umm Bab

Al Wukayr

Al Wakrah

Umm Said

Al Kir'ànah

Musay'īd

Al Kharrārah

As Salwá

Juh

Khawr al 'Udayd

**SAUDI ARABIA**

★ Capital    - - - Road
◉ Major City    ▲ Points of Interest
• City/Town

0   15   30 Miles
0   15   30   45 Kilometers

# Qatar Statistics

## GEOGRAPHY

*Area in Square Miles (Kilometers):*
4,400 (11,400) (about the size of
Connecticut)
*Capital (Population):* Doha (340,000)
*Environmental Concerns:* limited natural
freshwater supplies; increasing
dependence on large-scale desalination
facilities
*Geographical Features:* mostly flat and
barren desert covered with loose sand
and gravel
*Climate:* desert; hot and dry; humid and
sultry summers

## PEOPLE
### Population

*Total:* 840,926
*Annual Growth Rate:* 0.869%
*Rural/Urban Population Ratio:* 8/92
*Major Languages:* Arabic; English widely
used

*Ethnic Makeup:* 40% Arab; 18% Pakistani; 18% Indian; 10% Iranian; 14% others
*Religions:* 95% Muslim; 5% others

## Health

*Life Expectancy at Birth:* 73.78 years (male); 77 years (female)
*Infant Mortality Rate (Ratio):* 12.24/1,000 live births

## Education

*Adult Literacy Rate:* 89%

## COMMUNICATION

*Telephones:* 150,500 main lines
*Daily Newspaper Circulation:* 143 per 1,000 people
*Televisions:* 451 per 1,000 people
*Internet Service Provider:* 1 (2000)

## TRANSPORTATION

*Highways in Miles (Kilometers):* 764 (1,230)

*Railroads in Miles (Kilometers):* none
*Usable Airfields:* 4
*Motor Vehicles in Use:* 183,000

## GOVERNMENT

*Type:* traditional monarchy
*Independence Date:* September 3, 1971 (from the United Kingdom)
*Head of State/Government:* Emir Hamad bin Khalifa al-Thani; Crown Prince Tamim Bin Hamid Al-Thani (heir apparent); Prime Minister Hamad Bin Jasim Bin-Jabir Al-Thani
*Political Parties:* None as such, but the 2003 constitution provides for a Government Council two-thirds elected by universal suffrage and one-third appointed by the ruling emir
*Suffrage:* universal at 18

## MILITARY

*Military Expenditures (% of GDP):* 10%
*Current Disputes:* none; territorial dispute with Bahrain settled in 2001 by the International Court of Justice

## ECONOMY

*Currency ($U.S. Equivalent):* 3.64 rials = $1 (fixed rate)
*Per Capita Income/GDP (PPP):* $121,700/$101.4 billion
*GDP Growth Rate:* 9.5%
*Inflation Rate:* 7.2%
*Labor Force:* 1.202 million
*Unemployment Rate:* 0.5%
*Natural Resources:* petroleum; natural gas; fish
*Agriculture:* fruits; vegetables; poultry; dairy products; beef; fish
*Industry:* crude-oil production and refining; fertilizers; petrochemicals; steel reinforcing bars; cement
*Exports:* $33.25 billion (primary partners Japan, Singapore, South Korea)
*Imports:* $12.36 billion (primary partners France, Japan, United States)

## SUGGESTED WEB SITES

http://lcweb2.loc.gov/frd/cs/ qatoc.html
www.qatar-info.com/

# Qatar Country Report

**Q**atar is a country on the eastern (Gulf) coast of Arabia. It is the second-smallest Middle Eastern state, after Bahrain, but due to its oil wealth and small population, it has an extremely high per capita annual income. Before 1949, when its oil exports began, there were about 20,000 Qataris, all descendants of peoples who had migrated to the coast centuries ago in search of a dependable water supply. Since then, rapid economic growth has attracted workers and residents from other Arab countries and distant Muslim states such as Pakistan. As a result, Qatar has a high number of immigrants, which makes for some tension.

## HISTORY

Although the peninsula has been inhabited since 4000 B.C., little is known of its history before the nineteenth century. At one time, it was ruled by the al-Khalifa family, the current rulers of Bahrain. It became part of the Ottoman Empire formally in 1872, but the Turkish garrison was evacuated during World War I. The Ottomans earlier had recognized Shaykh Qassim al-Thani, head of the important al-Thani family, as emir of Qatar, and the British followed suit when they established a protectorate after the war.

The British treaty with the al-Thanis was similar to ones made with other leaders in Arabia and the Persian Gulf in order to keep other European powers out of the area and to protect their trade and communications links with India. In 1916, the British recognized Shaykh Abdullah al-Thani, grandfather of the current ruler, as ruler of Qatar and promised to protect the territory from outside attack either by the Ottomans or overland by hostile Arabian groups. In return, Shaykhal-Thani agreed not to enter into any relationship with any other foreign government and to accept British political advisers.

### DEVELOPMENT

Qatar's huge gas reserves are among the largest in the world, but are concentrated in a single field. They form the basis for ongoing economic development. New petrochemical and related fertilizer industries are beginning to diversify sources of revenue.

Qatar remained a tranquil British protectorate until the 1950s, when oil exports began. Since then, the country has

developed rapidly, though not to the extent of producing the dizzying change visible in other oil-producing Arab states.

## INDEPENDENCE

Qatar became independent in 1971. The ruler, Shaykh Ahmad al-Thani, took the title of emir. Disagreements within the ruling family led the emir's cousin, Shaykh Khalifa, to seize power in 1972. Khalifa made himself prime minister as well as ruler and initiated a major program of social and economic development, which his cousin had opposed.

Shaykh Khalifa limited the privileges of the ruling family. There were more than 2,000 al-Thanis, and most of them had been paid several thousand dollars a month whether or not they worked. Khalifa reduced their allowances and appointed some nonmembers of the royal family to the Council of Ministers, the state's chief executive body. In 1992, he set up a Consultative Council of 30 members to advise the cabinet on proposed legislation and budgetary matters. Subsequently, the cabinet itself was enlarged, with new ministries of Islamic affairs, finance, economy, and industry and trade. While the majority of cabinet and Consultative Council members belonged to the royal family, the appointment of a number of nonfamily members to both these organizations heralded the "quiet revolution" toward power sharing to which Shaykh Khalifa was committed.

## FOREIGN RELATIONS

Because of its small size, great wealth, and proximity to regional conflicts, Qatar is vulnerable to outside intervention. The government fears especially that the example of the Iranian Shi'a Revolution may inspire its own Shi'a Muslim population. After the discovery of a Shi'a plot to overthrow the government of neighboring Bahrain in 1981, Qatari authorities deported several hundred Shi'a Qataris of Iranian origin. But thus far the government has avoided singling out the Shi'a community for heavy-handed repression, preferring to concentrate its efforts on economic and social progress. On the 10th anniversary of Qatar's independence, the emir said that "economic strength is the strongest guarantee that safeguards the independence of nations, their sovereignty, rights and dignity."[1]

Fears of a possible attack by Iran led the country to sign a bilateral defense agreement with Saudi Arabia in 1982. The Iraqi invasion of Kuwait in 1990, exposed Saudi military weakness, and, as a result, Qatar turned to the United States for its defense. A Qatar official noted, "Saudi Arabia was the protector, but the war showed that the emperor had no clothes."[2] The emir emphasized Qatar's independent stance in foreign policy early in 2007 when he transferred $22 million to Hamas, the militant anti-Israeli organization elected in 2006 to leadership in the Palestinian government, after its funds had been shut off by Israel and the United States. To balance the equation he allowed the Israeli trade mission to Doha to remain open and welcomed Israeli Prime Minister Olmert on the first visit to the Gulf by any Israeli official in decades. However, these new trade ties with Israel were halted after the 2009 Israeli offensive on Gaza.

## FREEDOM

Since he deposed his father, the ruling emir has abolished press censorship, established Al Jazeerah as a service of uncensored news to the Arab world, and appointed younger members of the ruling family to replace his father's advisers and ministers.

The continued U.S./UN sanctions imposed on Iraq after the Gulf War drew increased opposition among Qataris, as the extent of harm to the Iraqi civilian population became more evident. Qatar was the first Gulf state to criticize openly U.S. and British air attacks on Iraq.

However, the expanded U.S. military presence in the Gulf, and the Qatari government's fears of a threat to its territory by a remilitarized Iraq, resulted in 2000 in the establishment in the country of the largest American military base outside the continental United States. The base was placed on full military alert in July 2000, after the attack on the U.S. destroyer *Cole* in Aden (Yemen) harbor. The emir also completed the $1 billion air base at Al-Ubeid, which holds up to 100 fighter aircraft. An attack in November 2001 by a lone gunman on guards at the base was a reminder of the unpopularity of the U.S. military presence in the Gulf region. When he was criticized by Islamist opposition leaders for "Christianizing" the country by making the base available to the United States, the emir responded: "We intend to be essential to the American presence in the Gulf. What do we get in exchange? We don't need to spend a lot of money on defense, we'll be attractive to U.S. businessmen, and we'll get international status and prestige."[3]

## HEALTH/WELFARE

Qatar's first private hospital opened in 1996 and is now fully staffed by Qatari doctors and nurses, who have replaced foreign medical personnel. Among the Arab states, Qatar has an unusually high ratio of physicians to population.

Inasmuch as Iraq was apparently not involved or charged with complicity in the September 11, 2001 terrorist attacks on the United States, the Qatari government felt less constrained about actively participating in the international coalition being formed to combat global terrorism than it had before the attacks. The American military and air bases in Qatar went on full alert for the invasion of Afghanistan, and the troops were reinforced by U.S. special forces and fighter aircraft.

Qatar's main foreign-policy concern has involved the islands of Hawar and Fishat al-Duble, which lie off of its northwest coast. Ownership was disputed with Bahrain, which controlled them under arrangements made in the 1930s, when both countries were British protectorates. In 1992, Qatar unilaterally extended its territorial waters to 12 nautical miles to bring the islands and adjacent seabed under Qatari sovereignty. Bahrain filed a complaint with the International Court

of Justice (the ICJ, or World Court). In 2001, the World Court confirmed Bahraini ownership of the islands and adjacent territorial waters. The Qatari emir had said previously that he would not accept World Court arbitration, but following the Court's decision, he accepted Bahraini sovereignty. Under the terms of the Court's ruling, Qatar was awarded sovereignty over Zabarah and Janan Islands, and the elevation at low tide of Fasht and Dubal. Qatari ships were also guaranteed the right of unobstructed passage through the Bahrain territorial sea. Further evidence of the country's growing influence internationally was its election in 2005 to a 2-year term on the UN Security Council starting in January 2006.

## THE ECONOMY

With oil reserves expected to be used up within 20-plus years at current extraction rates, the Qatari economy has not only diversified but more important, shifted to natural gas. The main source of development is the huge natural gas field at Ras Laffan, the world's third largest. But in February 2007 Exxon Mobil, the foreign partner with the state oil company, cancelled its participation. The project would have produced 154,000 barrels per day (bpd) of diesel fuel from natural gas, but its $7 billion cost was considered too high by the company to be manageable. Earlier Qatar had declared a moratorium on new natural gas projects; the only exception was an Exxon Mobil drilling project in the Barzan field. When completed it will produce 1.5 billion cubic feet of liquefied natural gas (lng) per day for the domestic market.

Depletion of water supplies due to heavy demand and dependence on outdated desalination plants for its fresh water have prompted the country to undertake some innovative food-production projects. One such project, begun in 1988, uses solar energy and seawater to cultivate food crops in sand. As a result of such projects, Qatar produces sufficient food both to meet domestic needs and to export vegetables to neighboring states.

## SOCIETAL CHANGES

Qatar was originally settled by nomadic peoples, and their influence is still strong. Traditional Bedouin values, such as honesty, hospitality, pride, and courage, have carried over into modern times.

Most Qataris belong to the strict puritanical Wahhabi sect of Islam, which is also dominant in Saudi Arabia. They are similar to Saudis in their conservative outlook, and Qatar generally defers to its larger neighbor in foreign policy. There are, however, significant social differences between Qataris and Saudis. Western movies may be shown in Qatar, for example, but not in Saudi Arabia. Furthermore, Qatar does not have religious police or "morals squads" to enforce Islamic conventions, and foreigners may purchase alcoholic beverages legally.

Qatar also differs from its Arab peninsular neighbors and the Arab world in general in permitting free discussion in the media of issues generally suppressed by Arab rulers. Following his accession to the throne, the new emir abolished press censorship and eliminated the Information Ministry from his cabinet. In 1997, his government licensed a new satellite TV network station called Al-Jazeera ("Island," in Arabic), supported by an annual subsidy to meet its operating costs. Despite its freewheeling broadcasting style and frequent criticism of Arab rulers, including its own, the ruling emir does not attempt to censor the station or close it down. As one analyst noted, "its reporters . . . openly challenge the sycophantic tone of the state-media and the mainstream Arab press, both of which play down controversy and dissent."[4] Al-Jazeera has featured interviews with a variety of Islamic and other global leaders, ranging from ex-U.S. Secretary of State Colin Powell and European heads of state to Osama bin Laden. The station's frank approach to controversial issues and frequent criticism of U.S. foreign policy led President Bush in 2005 to declare he would shut it down, if he had the power to do so. In 2006, it launched an English-language station; it also has now a sports channel, a conference channel, a documentary channel and a children's channel.

## ACHIEVEMENTS

Education City, a project set up by the ruling emir's second wife, Shaykha Mozah, has set up satellite on-site campuses of U.S. universities, notably Georgetown and Carnegie-Mellon, in the emirate. Tuition and costs are covered by the government. Although some scholars have questioned the possible undermining of Qatar's Islamic identity by the establishment of these institutions on its soil, supporters of the project feel it will foster greater understanding of the modern world by Qatari students.

The most significant societal change in Qatar involves the position of women. The first school for girls opened there in 1956. But change in women's rights and roles has accelerated in recent years. In 1998, the new emir, who had deposed his father in 1995 while the latter was vacationing in Switzerland, granted women the right to vote and to run for and hold public office.

The wife of emir Hamad bin Khalifa Al Thani, Sheikha Mozah bint Nasser Al Missned, who chairs the Qatar Foundation for Education, Science and Community Development, has been instrumental in advancing women's civil and social rights. She has set up a battered women's shelter, funded non-Muslim places of worship, and provided help and guidance for women in the workplace (Some 30 percent of Qatari women work outside the home, drive their own cars and attend the university). In 2007 she introduced her latest project, Doha Debates, a monthly public forum for women and men to discuss voting rights and obligations for good citizenship. In an interview, she told a reporter, "you cannot build a healthy society without giving your citizens a sense of ownership. We are creating full, well-rounded human beings that will enable Qatar to build up its society."[5]

## INTERNAL POLITICS

Crown Prince Shaykh Hamad bin Khalifa's "palace coup" was bloodless, although several attempts by supporters of the deposed ruler to overthrow his son have been thwarted. In July 1999, Shaykh Hamid al-Thani, the ruling emir's cousin and former chief of police, was arrested and brought back from his hiding place "somewhere abroad" for trial. He was charged with being the leader and organizer of the attempted coups. The ex-emir agreed to return $2 billion in government funds that he had deposited abroad over the years in personal accounts.

In April 2003, a new constitution was approved by referendum; it provides for a 45-member parliament with 30 elected members and the rest selected by the emir. Elections for a unicameral Central Municipal Council of 29 members for Doha were held first in 1999 and subsequently in 2003, two "firsts" for the emirate. Some 221 men and 3 women competed for the 29 seats. One of the women was elected, the first female to hold elective office not only in Qatar but in the entire Gulf region. As a first step toward constitutional government, the Council has consultative powers, although these are limited to improving municipal services.

The "quiet revolution" initiated by the new emir entered a new stage in March 1999, with elections for a Doha Central Municipal Council, the country's first public elections. The Council does not have executive powers, but it is intended as a transitional body between patriarchal rule and the establishment of an elected parliament. All Qataris over age 18 were allowed to vote, including women (who make up 44 percent of registered voters). Six women ran with 221 men for the Council's 29 seats.

## Timeline: PAST

**1916**
Britain recognizes Shaykh Abdullah al-Thani as emir

**1949**
The start of oil production in Qatar

**1971**
An abortive federation with Bahrain and the Trucial States (U.A.E.), followed by independence

**1972**
The ruler is deposed by Shaykh Khalifa

**1990s**
Qatar condemns the Iraqi invasion of Kuwait and expels resident Palestinians; Crown Prince Hamad al-Thani deposes his father and takes over as emir

## PRESENT

**2000s**
World Court favors Bahrain against Qatar in territorial dispute; First Christian church in Qatar since Islam's arrival in 7th century A.D. established to serve the state's 70,000 Egyptian and Indian Christian workers

**2003**
A New constitution is approved by referendum; The emir names his younger son Prince Tamim as crown prince

**2004**
Former Chechen President Zelimkhan Yanderbiyev is killed in an explosion in Doha allegedly by two Russian agents

**2005**
Qatar and the Unites States start a joint $14 billion project to build the world's largest liquefied natural gas plant

**2008**
Qatar and Saudi Arabia agree on final delineation of their common borders

**2009**
Qatar ends trade ties with Israel because of the Gaza offensive

## NOTES

1. Emir Hamad bin Khalifa Al Thani, quoted by Qatar News Agency (November 23, 1981).

2. Douglas Jehl, *The New York Times International* (July 20, 1997).

3. Mary Anne Weaver, "Democracy by Decree," *The New Yorker* (November 20, 2000), p. 57.

4. Fouad Ajami, "What the Muslim World Is Watching," *The New York Times Magazine* (November 18, 2001).

5. Sheikha Mozah quoted in Donna Harman. "Qatar reformed by a modern marriage," *Christian Science Monitor,* March 6, 2007.

# Saudi Arabia (Kingdom of Saudi Arabia)

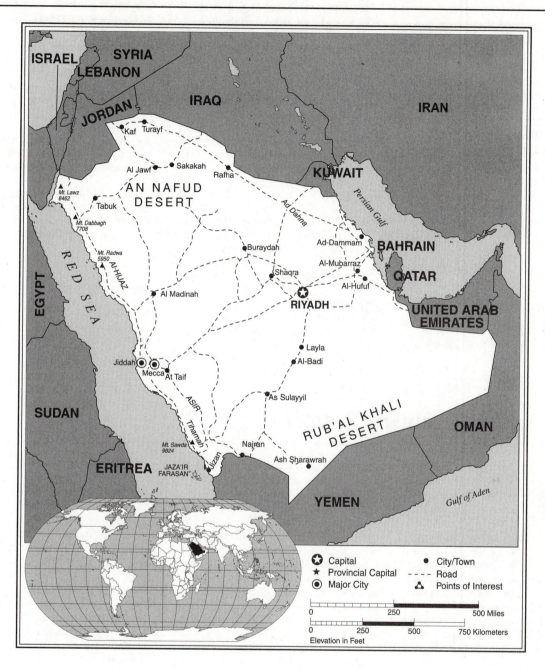

# Saudi Arabia Statistics

## GEOGRAPHY

*Area in Square Miles (Kilometers):* 756,785 (1,960,582) (about 1/5 the size of the United States)

*Capital (Population):* Riyadh (4,087,152)

*Environmental Concerns:* desertification; depletion of underground water resources; coastal pollution from oil spills

*Geographical Features:* mostly uninhabited sandy desert

*Climate:* harsh, dry desert, with great extremes of temperature

## PEOPLE

### Population

*Total:* 28,686,633 (includes 6,000,000 non-nationals)

*Annual Growth Rate:* 1.848%

*Rural/Urban Population Ratio:* 18/82

*Major Languages:* Arabic; English widely used

*Ethnic Makeup:* 90% Arab; 10% Afro-Asian

*Religion:* 100% Muslim

### Health

*Life Expectancy at Birth:* 74 years (male); 78 years (female)

*Infant Mortality Rate (Ratio):* 11.57/1,000 live births

**Education**

*Adult Literacy Rate:* 78.8%

## COMMUNICATION

*Telephones:* 4,500,000, plus 36 million mobile cellular phones
*Daily Newspaper Circulation:* 54 per 1,000 people
*Televisions:* 274 per 1,000 people
*Internet Service Providers:* 21 (2006)

## TRANSPORTATION

*Highways in Miles (Kilometers):* 93,8270 (151,470)
*Railroads in Miles (Kilometers):* 863 (1,392)
*Usable Airfields:* 209
*Motor Vehicles in Use:* 2,800,000

## GOVERNMENT

*Type: Head of State/Government:* King Abdullah Ibn Aziz Al-Saud (he also serves as prime minister); in October 2006 a royal decree established an Allegiance Commission which will lay out the procedure for selection of future kings, to take effect after the death or retirement of the present Crown Prince
*Independence Date:* September 23, 1932 (unification)
*Head of State/Government:* King Abdullah ibn Aziz Al Saud, as of August 2005; he also serves as prime minister
*Political Parties:* none, but elections were held under unspecified guidelines for local and provincial councils in 2005
*Suffrage:* none

## MILITARY

*Military Expenditures (% of GDP):* 13%
*Current Disputes:* the border with Yemen has now been completely demarcated, with a security barrier on the Saudi side at certain points to block infiltration

## ECONOMY

*Currency (U.S. Equivalent):* 3.745 riyals = $1

*Per Capita Income/GDP:* $20,700/ $467.7 billion
*GDP Growth Rate:* 4.2%
*Inflation Rate:* 9.9%
*Labor Force:* 6,922,000 (20 percent are male Saudis)
*Unemployment Rate:* 11.8% (exclusively male Saudis)
*Natural Resources:* petroleum; natural gas; iron ore; gold; copper
*Agriculture:* wheat; barley; tomatoes; melons; dates; citrus fruits; mutton; chickens; eggs; milk
*Industry:* crude-oil production; petroleum refining; basic petrochemicals; cement; construction; fertilizer; plastics
*Exports:* $180.5 billion (primary partners United States, Japan, South Korea)
*Imports:* $86.61 billion (primary partners United States, Japan, Germany)

## SUGGESTED WEB SITES

http://lcweb2.loc.gov/frd/cs/ satoc.html
www.saudinf.com/main/start.htm

# Saudi Arabia Country Report

The Kingdom of Saudi Arabia is the geographical giant of the Arabian Peninsula. It is also a giant in the world economy because of its oil. To many people, the name Saudi Arabia is a synonym for oil wealth. Indeed, its huge oil reserves, large financial surpluses from oil production, and ability to use oil as a source of political power (as in the 1973 embargo) enable the country to play an important role in international as well as regional affairs.

Saudi Arabia's population is small in relation to the country's size and is heavily urbanized. Urban growth has been very rapid, considering that only 1 percent of the land can be used for agriculture and all employment opportunities are in the cities or in the oil-producing regions. The kingdom has relied strongly on foreign workers, skilled as well as unskilled, in its development. The economic dislocation of the Gulf War, along with the political support given to Iraq by Palestinians and the government of Yemen, led to the expulsion of nearly 1 million foreign workers, most of them Palestinians and Yemenis. But due to the unwillingness of most Saudis to take on low-paying work that seems to be below them professionally, the government has had to continue its dependence on foreign

labor. Some 67 percent of government jobs and 95 percent of those in private industry are held by foreigners.

The country has three main geographical regions: the Hejaz, along the Red Sea; the Nejd, a vast interior plateau that comprises the bulk of Saudi territory; and the Eastern Province. The kingdom's largest oases, al-Hasa and Safwa, are located in this third region, along with the major oil fields and industrial centers. The Empty Quarter (al-Rub' al-Khali), an uninhabited desert where rain may not fall for a decade or more, occupies the entire southeastern quadrant of the country.

## THE WAHHABI MOVEMENT

In the eighteenth century, most of the area included in present-day Saudi Arabia was the home of nomads, as it had been for centuries. These peoples had no central government and owed allegiance to no one except their chiefs. They spent much of their time raiding one another's territories in the struggle for survival. Inland Arabia was a great blank area on the map—a vast, empty desert.

The only part of modern Saudi Arabia under any government control in the

eighteenth century was the Hejaz, which includes the Islamic holy cities of Mecca and Medina. It was a province of the Ottoman Empire, the major power in the Middle East at that time.

Saudi Arabia became a state, in the modern sense of the word, in 1932. However, the origins of the Saudi nation go back to the eighteenth century. One of the tribes that roamed the desert beyond Ottoman control was the tribe of Saud. Its leader, Muhammad Ibn Saud, wanted to gain an advantage over his rivals in the constant search for water and good grazing land for animals. He approached a famous religious scholar named Abd al-Wahhab, who lived in an oasis near the current Saudi capital, Riyadh (then a mud-walled village). Abd al-Wahhab promised Allah's blessing to Ibn Saud in his contests with his rivals. In return, the Saudi leader agreed to protect Abd al-Wahhab from threats to his life by opponents of the strict doctrines he taught and preached, and he swore an oath of obedience to these doctrines. The partnership between these two men gave rise to a religious movement called Wahhabism.

In the late 1700s, the puritanical zeal of the Wahhabis led them to declare a "holy war"

The Ka'abah at the center of Great Mosque at Mecca, the holiest of shrines to Muslims. Mecca was the site at which Islam was founded in the seventh century A.D. by the prophet Muhammad. Pilgrims still flock to the Great Mosque to fulfill their Muslim duties as set down by the Five Pillars of Islam.

against the Ottoman Turks, who were then in control of Mecca and Medina, in order to restore these holy cities to the Arabs. In the 1800s, Wahhabis captured the cities. Soon the Wahhabis threatened to undermine Ottoman authority elsewhere. Wahhabi raiders seized Najaf and Karbala in Iraq, centers of Shi'a pilgrimage, and desecrated Shi'a shrines. In Mecca, they removed the headstones from the graves of members of the Prophet's family, because in their belief system, all Muslims are supposed to be buried unmarked.

The Ottoman sultan did not have sufficient forces at hand to deal with the Wahhabi threat, so he called upon his vassal, Muhammad Ali, the khedive (viceroy) of Egypt. Muhammad Ali organized an army equipped with European weapons and trained by European advisers. In a series of hard-fought campaigns, the Egyptian Army defeated the Wahhabis and drove them back into the desert. Inland Arabia reverted to its old patterns of conflict. The Saudis and other rival tribes were Wahhabi in belief and practice, but this religious bond was countered by age-old disputes over water rights, territory, and control over trade routes. In the 1890s, the Saudis' major rivals, the Rashidis, seized Riyadh. The Saudi chief escaped across the desert to Kuwait, a town on the Persian Gulf

that was under British protection. He took along his young son, Abd al-Aziz ibn Saud.

Wahhabism is a strict and puritanical form of Sunni Islam. The Wahhabi code of law, behavior, and conduct is modeled on that of the original Islamic community established in Mecca and Medina by Prophet Muhammad. Although there has been some relaxation of the code due to the country's modernization, it remains the law of Saudi Arabia today. Interpretation of Islamic law is the responsibility of the *ulema* (a body of religious scholars and jurists in Sunni Islam). As a result, Saudi society is more conservative and puritanical than many other Islamic societies, including those of its Persian Gulf neighbors. The Taliban, the Islamic movement that held power in Afghanistan from 1996 to 2001, is thus far the only large-scale movement in Islam to have embraced Wahhabism.

Although Wahhabi social and cultural restrictions are still very much in effect in the country and are enforced stringently by the religious police, modification of these restrictions has slowly become the norm in the new century. This is particularly evident regarding the rights and status of women. In 1990 a group of women from prominent families defied a government ban on female driving and drove their

family cars into downtown Riyadh. The religious authorities promptly issued an edict emphasizing the ban, and the women were jailed briefly and deprived of their passports. As an indicator of changing conditions in the kingdom, the members of the group held a public celebration in 2005 to mark the 15th anniversary of their exploit. They were supported by a leading member of the Majlis al-Shura who argued that such a ban existed neither in the Qur'an nor in Islamic law. A poll in December 2005 indicated that 60 percent of Saudi males agreed that women should have the right to drive. However the poll results were qualified by Crown Prince Sultan bin Abdul-Aziz, who stated that the government had no objections as long as their husbands, fathers and brothers agreed.

Other changes included in 2005 the removal of a ban on forced marriages, prompted by the 50 percent divorce rate. Perhaps the greatest change was the country's first-ever election, held in April 2005 to elect members of municipal councils. In November 2005 a second election was held for members of chamber of commerce boards. Women were not only allowed to vote but to run for seats on the boards, and two were elected to the board in Jiddah; two additional businesswomen were appointed to the board by the Minister of Commerce and Industries who has the authority to appoint one third of the board's members.

The September 11, 2001, terrorist attacks in the United States and the resulting war on terrorism proclaimed by President George W. Bush against Osama bin Laden and his al Qaeda network placed the Saudi government in an awkward position. As a valued ally, it was expected to provide active support for such war. However, a large section of the Saudi population is opposed to U.S. policy in the Middle East because of its support for Israel and its intervention in Iraq and Afghanistan. A number of Wahhabi religious leaders chastised the monarchy due to its close relationship with the West, some of them even urged its overthrow. Although the Saudi government in October 2001 ended its recognition of the Taliban as the legitimate government of Afghanistan, the presence of 5,000 U.S. troops on "sacred Saudi Islamic soil" and bin Laden's popularity as a symbol of Muslim defiance against American "arrogance" in stationing them there forced the monarchy to walk a tightrope in balancing its international obligations with the views of its own people.

Fears that Saudi Arabia would be next on Saddam Hussein's invasion list after Kuwait led to the formation of the coalition of United Nations–sponsored forces that carried out Operation Desert Storm. This action involved stationing of American and other non-Muslim troops in the kingdom. The Saudi leadership was divided on the issue. But at this critical juncture, Bin Baz issued a fatwa. His edict said that in an extreme emergency, it was permissible for an Islamic state to seek help from non-Islamic ones. A later edict ruled that the campaign against Iraq was a *jihad,* further justifying the coalition and buildup of non-Muslim troops on Saudi soil.

## DEVELOPMENT

The Eighth Saudi 5-Year Plan (2005–2009) sets a growth rate of 3.16% annually, with increased diversification of the economy to reduce dependence on oil. With revenues dropping, a high birth rate and high unemployment, there are simply not enough jobs being created for the 100,000 Saudis entering the workforce each year.

## IBN SAUD

Abd al-Aziz al-Rahman Al Sa'ud, or Ibn Saud, grew up in exile in Kuwait, where he brooded and schemed about how to regain the lands of the Saudis.[1] When he reached age 21, in 1902, he decided on a bold stroke to reach his goal. On 5 Shawwal 1319 (January 1902), he led a force of 48 warriors across the desert from Kuwait to Riyadh. They scaled the city walls at night and seized the Rashidi governor's house, and then the fort in a daring dawn raid. The population seems to have accepted the change of masters without incident, while Bedouin tribes roaming in the vicinity came to town to pledge allegiance to Ibn Saud and applaud his exploit.

Over the next three decades, Ibn Saud steadily expanded his territory. He said that his goal was "to recover all the lands of our forefathers."[2] In World War I, he became an ally of the British, fighting the Ottoman Turks in Arabia. In return, the British provided arms for his followers and gave him a monthly allowance. The British continued to back Ibn Saud after the war, and in 1924, he entered Mecca in triumph. His major rival, Sharif Husayn, who had been appointed by the Ottoman government as the "Protector of the Holy Places," fled into exile. (Sharif Husayn was the great-grandfather of King Hussein I of Jordan.)

Ibn Saud's second goal, after recovering his ancestral lands, was to build a modern nation under a central government. He used as his motto the Qur'anic verse, "God changes not what is in a people until they change what is in themselves" *(Sura XIII, 2).* The first step was to gain recognition of Saudi Arabia as an independent state. Britain recognized the country in 1927, and other countries soon followed suit. In 1932, the country took its current name of Saudi Arabia, a union of the three provinces of Hejaz, Nejd, and al-Hasa.

## INDEPENDENCE

Ibn Saud's second step in his "grand design" for the new country was to establish order under a central government. To do this, he began to build settlements and to encourage the nomads to settle down, live in permanent homes, and learn how to grow their own food. Those who settled on the land were given seeds and tools, were enrolled in a sort of national guard, and were paid regular allowances. These former Bedouin warriors became in time the core of the Saudi armed forces.

Ibn Saud also established the country's basic political system. The basis for the system was the Wahhabi interpretation of Islamic law. Ibn Saud insisted that "the laws of the state shall always be in accordance with the Book of Allah and the Sunna (Conduct) of His Messenger and the ways of the Companions."[3] He saw no need for a written constitution, and as yet Saudi Arabia has none. Ibn Saud decreed that the country would be governed as a monarchy, with rulers always chosen from the Saud family. He was unfamiliar with political parties and distrusted them in principle; political organizations were therefore prohibited in the kingdom. Yet Ibn Saud was himself humble in manner, and spartan in his living habits. He remained all his life a man of the people and held every day a public assembly (*majlis*) in Riyadh at which any citizen had the right to ask favors or present petitions. (The custom of holding a daily majlis has been observed by Saudi rulers ever since.) More often than not, petitioners would address Ibn Saud not as Your Majesty but simply as Abd al-Aziz (his given name).

Ibn Saud died in 1953. He had witnessed the beginning of rapid social and economic change in his country due to oil revenues. Yet his successors have presided over a transformation beyond the wildest imaginations of the warriors who had scaled the walls of Riyadh half a century earlier. Riyadh then had a population of 8,000. Today, it has 4 million inhabitants. It is one of the fastest-growing cities in the world.[4]

Ibn Saud was succeeded by his eldest surviving son, Crown Prince Saud. A number of royal princes felt that the second son, Faisal, should have become the new king because of his greater experience in foreign affairs and economic management. Saud's only experience was as governor of Nejd.

Although he was large and corpulent and lacked Ibn Saud's forceful personality, the new king was like his father in a number of ways. He was more comfortable in a desert tent than running a bureaucracy or meeting foreign dignitaries. Also, like his father, he had no idea of the value of money. Ibn Saud would carry a sackful of riyals (the Saudi currency) to the daily majlis and give them away to petitioners. His son, Saud, not only doled out money to petitioners but also gave millions to other members of the royal family. One of his greatest extravagances was a palace surrounded by a bright pink wall.[5]

By 1958, the country was almost bankrupt. The royal family was understandably nervous about a possible coup supported by other Arab states, such as Egypt and Syria, which were openly critical of Saudi Arabia because it was a conservative monarchy. The senior princes issued an ultimatum to Saud: First he would put Faisal in charge of straightening out the kingdom's finances, and, when that had been done, he

(Royal Embassy of Saudi Arabia, Washington, DC (RESA002))

King Faisal was instrumental in bringing Saudia Arabia into the international community and establishing domestic plans that took his country into the twentieth century.

would abdicate. When the financial overhaul was complete, with the kingdom again on a sound footing, Saud abdicated in favor of Faisal.

The transfer of authority from Saud to Faisal illustrates the collective principle of government of the Saudi family monarchy. The sovereign rules in theory but in practice, the inner circle of Saudi senior princes, along with ulema leaders, make all decisions concerning succession, foreign policy, the economy, and other issues. The reasons for a decision must always be guessed; the Saudis never explain them. It is a system that has given Saudi Arabia stability and leadership on occasions when crises have threatened the kingdom.

## FAISAL AND HIS SUCCESSORS

In terms of state-building, the reign of King Faisal (1964–1975) is second in importance only to that of Ibn Saud. One author wrote of King Faisal during his reign, "He is leading the country with gentle insistence from medievalism into the jet age."[6] Faisal's gentle insistence showed itself in many different ways. Encouraged by his wife, Queen Iffat, he introduced education for girls. Before Faisal, the kingdom had had no systematic development plans. In introducing the first five-year development plan, the king said that "our religion requires us to progress and to bear the burden of the highest tradition and best manners."[7]

In foreign affairs, Faisal ended the Yemen Civil War on an honorable basis

for both sides; took an active part in the Islamic world in keeping with his role as Protector of the Holy Places; and, in 1970, founded the Organization of the Islamic Conference, which has given the Islamic states of the world a voice in international affairs. Faisal laid down the basic strategy that his successors have followed, namely, avoidance of direct conflict, mediation of disputes behind the scenes, and use of oil wealth as a political weapon when necessary. The king never understood the American commitment to Israel, any more than his father had. (Ibn Saud had met U.S. president Franklin D. Roosevelt in Egypt during World War II. Roosevelt, motivated by American Jewish leaders to help in the establishment of a Jewish homeland

## FREEDOM

Saudi Arabia's strict adherence to Islamic law not only imposes harsh punishments for many crimes, but also restricts human rights. The country ranks second in the world in executions per million population: 102 in 2008. Shari'a law applies equally to Saudis and non-Saudis; in 2001, 4 Britons were flogged publicly for dealing in alcohol. A new Code of Criminal Procedure took effect in July 2001. But although Saudi judges (qadis) in theory are bound to respect judicial procedure and legal rights (e.g. of lawyers to defend their clients), they often revert to arbitrary decisions and base these purely on Islamic law.

in Palestine, sought to convince Ibn Saud, as head of the only independent Arab state at that time, to moderate Arab opposition to the project.) But Faisal's distrust of communism was equally strong. This distrust led him to continue the ambivalent yet close Saudi alliance with the United States that has continued up to the present.

King Faisal was assassinated in 1975 by a deranged nephew while he was holding the daily majlis. The assassination was another test of the system of rule by consensus in the royal family, and the system held firm. Khalid, Faisal's eldest half-brother, his junior by six years, succeeded him without incident. He ruled until his death in 1982. The next-oldest half-brother, Fahd, succeeded him.

One of the most shocking events in Saudi Arabia since the founding of the kingdom was the seizure of the Great Mosque in Mecca, Islam's holiest shrine, by a group of radical Sunni Muslims in November 1979. The leader of the group declared that one of its members was the *Mahdi* (the "Guided One") who had come to announce the Day of Judgment. The group occupied the mosque for two weeks. The siege was finally overcome by army and national guard units, but with considerable loss of life on both sides. No one knows exactly what the group's purpose was, nor did the event lead to any general expressions of dissatisfaction with the regime. But the incident reflects the very real fear of the Saudi rulers of a coup attempted by ultra-religious Sunni or Shiite groups.

Although the Saudi government remains staunchly conservative, it has before it the example of Iran, where a religion-based movement overthrew a well-established monarchy. The country's Shi'a population is concentrated in al-Hasa province, where the oil fields are mostly located. The government's immediate fear after the Great Mosque seizure was of an outside plot inspired by Iran. Although this never materialized, the event motivated a significant increase in development funding for the Shi'a community.

## THE ECONOMY

Oil was discovered in Saudi Arabia in 1938, but exports did not begin until after World War II. Reserves in 2009 were 264 billion barrels, 26 percent of the world's oil reserves. The oil industry was controlled by Aramco (Arabian-American Oil Company), a consortium of four U.S. oil companies. In 1980, it came under Saudi government control, but Aramco continued to manage marketing and distribution services. The last American president of Aramco retired in 1989 and was succeeded by a Saudi. The company was renamed Saudi Aramco. But after a quarter-century of exclusion of foreign firms from the oil and gas industry, Saudi Arabia opened the gates in June 2001. A consortium of foreign oil companies was granted exploration rights in a desert area the size of Ireland. As a spin-off from the concession, the consortium will develop the existing South Ghawar gas field, and related power, desalination, and petrochemical plants.

The Saudi government continues to pursue economic development and diversification, notably since its accession to membership in the World Trade Organization (WTO) in 2005. It also encourages foreign investment; a new investment law issued in 2000 permits 100% foreign ownership of projects.

King Faisal's reorganization of finances and development plans in the 1960s set the kingdom on an upward course of rapid development. The economy took off after 1973, when the Saudis, along with other Arab oil-producing states, reduced production and imposed an export embargo on Western countries as a gesture of protest against the U.S. and European support to Israel in the 1973 war. After 1973, the price per barrel of Saudi oil continued to increase, to a peak of $34.00 per barrel in 1981. (Prior to the embargo, it was $2.50 per barrel; in 1979, it was $13.30 per barrel.) The outbreak of the Iran-Iraq War in 1980 caused a huge drop in world production. The Saudis took up the slack.

The huge revenues from oil made possible economic development on a scale undreamed of by Ibn Saud and his Bedouin warriors. The old fishing ports of Yanbu, on the Red Sea, and Jubail, on the Persian Gulf, were transformed into new industrial cities, with oil refineries, cement and petrochemical plants, steel mills, and dozens of related industries. Riyadh experienced a building boom; Cadillacs bumped into camels on the streets, and the shops filled up with imported luxury goods. Most Saudis profited from the boom through free education and health care, affordable housing, and guaranteed jobs.

The economic boom also lured many workers from poor countries, attracted by the high wages and benefits available in Saudi Arabia. Most came from such countries as Pakistan, Korea, and the Philippines, but the largest single contingent was from Yemen, next door. However, the bottom dropped out of the Saudi economy in the late 1980s. Oil prices fell, and the kingdom was forced to draw heavily on its cash reserves. Yemen's support for Iraq during the Gulf War led the Saudi government to deport 850,000 Yemeni workers, seriously disrupting the Yemeni economy with the stop of remittances.

## HEALTH/WELFARE

Although Saudi schools are administratively under the Ministry of Education, the curriculum is controlled by the religious authorities. After a disastrous fire at a girls' school in which a number of students died when religious police blocked their escape on grounds they were not fully covered, the government transferred responsibility for female education to the Ministry. Also a nonpartisan advisory group was formed in 2003 to revise the Saudi school curriculum to remove unfavorable references to other religions, and to strengthen instruction in higher education to prepare Saudi youth to better function in a world of globalization and high technology.

Continued low world oil prices in the 1990s had a very bad effect on what was formerly a freewheeling economy. In 1998, the country's oil income dropped 40 percent, to $20 billion; after a two-year surplus, the budget showed a $13 billion deficit. Lowered oil prices accounted only in part for the deficit. Monthly stipends ranging from $4,000 to $130,000 given to the 20,000-plus descendants of Ibn Saud continued to drain the treasury, while free education, health care, and other benefits guaranteed for all Saudis under the Basic Law of Government generated some $170 billion in internal debts. The steady downturn in the economy, along with significant population increase (it doubled in the past two decades) and high unemployment have called these social benefits into question. The age group most affected is that from 15 to 20.

The Saudi economy experienced a 2-year surge in growth in 2003–2004, aided by the highest global oil price increases in two decades, with a $12 billion budget surplus after three years of deficits. The surplus was invested in infrastructure projects, particularly transportation and utilities. The economy's growth rate, after a marked slowdown at the end of the second half of the decade, barely reached 4.2% by December 2009 due to the global economic slowdown, falling oil prices, and tight international credit. However, large income gains made during the 2004–08 period of high oil prices ($147 a barrel by July 2008), helped the Kingdom increase substantially its financial reserves (more than $500 billion by February 2009). These cash reserves helped it weather the impact of the global financial crisis temporarily. The economic crunch set in as a result of the substantial drop in oil income, large stock market losses, weak business

confidence, and tightening lending policies of local banks. To prevent the decline in economic growth from leading to lasting recession, the government enacted a stimulus spending plan that included direct assistance to the banking sector (direct capital injections and rates reduction) and extensive infrastructure projects over the next several years. The government plans to create six new "economic cities" in different regions of the country aimed at spurring development and economic diversification. The diversification efforts will focus on sectors such as power generation, natural gas exploration, petrochemical industries, and telecommunications.

The economic slowdown of the late 2000s directly affected the non-oil sector and private economic activities. The growth of the non-oil private sector was stifled by tight domestic and international monetary lending. The oil sector accounts for some 80% of the state's budget revenues, 45% of the country's GDP, and 90% of its export earnings. This situation continues to make the country vulnerable to any sharp decline in the price of oil. Unemployment remains high as 11.8% of the work force is without a job. The rate is much higher among the youth and even more among women.

King Fahd died in August 2005, ending a decade in which he had been essentially wheelchair-bound and had ceded the responsibility for leadership to his half-brother Abdullah. As the longest-serving Saudi ruler after his father, he had presided over or initiated many significant developments. They included establishment of a formal succession process, mediation to settle the civil war in Lebanon, and perhaps most important, the stationing of U.S. and other non-Muslim troops on sacred Islamic soil as a result of the Iraqi invasion of Kuwait. Ironically this action, although it came about logically out of fears that the Saudi regime was next on Saddam Hussein's list, has generated the creation of al Qaeda, headed by Osama bin Laden., whose aims include the overthrow of the Saudi government and the departure of all Western military personnel from the country.

## A CHANGING KINGDOM

Its size, distance from major Middle Eastern urban centers, and oil wealth historically have insulated Saudi Arabia from the winds of political change. Domestic and foreign policy alike evolve from within the ruling family. Officials who undertake independent policy actions are quickly brought into line (an example being the freewheeling former oil minister Zaki Yamani). The ruling family is also closely aligned with the ulema; Saudi rulers since Ibn Saud's time have held the title "Guardians of the Holy Mosques" (of Mecca and Medina), giving them a preeminent position in the Islamic world. The modern version of the Saudi-Wahhab partnership permits the ruler to appoint the Council of Senior Theologians, whose job it is to ensure Islamic cultural and social "rules" (such as women driving). In return, their presence and prescripts on Islamic behavior serve as an endorsement of the monarchy. But as one Saudi scholar told an interviewer, "the clerics can issue edicts to their hearts' content, answering weighty questions like whether or not a wife can wear jeans in front of her husband. Our clerics' religion has little to do with ethics, only lifestyle. They never do what they should do—denounce tyranny, injustice, corruption."[8]

Pressure to broaden participation in political decision making outside of the royals has increased markedly in recent years. This is due not only to greater contact by educated Saudis with democratic political systems, but also to the vastly increased use of satellite dishes and the Internet. While agreeing in principle to changes, the House of Saud, strongly supported by the religious leaders, has held fast to its patriarchal system.

Given these strictures, it was somewhat surprising in 1991 when the ulema submitted a list of 11 "demands" to King Fahd. The most important one was the formation of a *Majlis al-Shura* (Consultative Council), which would have the power to initiate legislation and advise the government on foreign policy. The king's response, developed in deliberate stages with extensive behind-the-scenes consultation, in typical Saudi style, was to issue in February 1992 an 83-article "Organic Law," comparable in a number of respects to a Western constitution. The law sets out the basic rules for Saudi government.

A significant step in the country's glacial progress toward a more representative political system took place in early 2005 when the first public elections in history were held for members of newly-formed municipal councils. Voters were asked to choose half of some 178 council seats, the remainder being filled by government appointees with only men allowed to participate, voter turnout was small. Even so there were some surprising results. Islamist candidates in Riyadh won all the seats on its council, and in the primarily Shi'a Eastern Province Shi'a candidates also swept the ballot.

Saudi Arabia is defined in the Organic Law as an Arab Islamic sovereign state (Article 5), with Islam the state religion (Article 1), and as a monarchy under the rule of Ibn Saud's descendants. Other articles establish

an independent judiciary under Islamic law (*shari'a*) and define the powers and responsibilities of the ruler.

Aside from some internal pressures, mainly from intellectuals, the main reason for Fahd's decision to broaden the political process was the Gulf War, which exposed the Saudi system to international scrutiny and pointed up the risks of patriarchal government. A major difference between the Saudi Organic Law and Western-style constitutions is the absence of references to political, civil, and social rights. Political parties as such remain illegal; but, in 1993, the first human-rights organization in the country, the Committee for the Defense of Legitimate Rights, was formed by a group of academics, tribal leaders, and government officials. Its members included the second-ranking religious scholar, Shaykh Abdullah al-Jubrien, and the former head of Diwan al-Mazalem, the Saudi equivalent of ombudsman. The Committee's goal was the elimination of oppression and injustice, which is considered an important part of its members' religious duty. But its emergence was perceived as a threat to the ulema. An edict condemned it, stating that there was no need for such an organization in a country ruled by Islamic law.

Satellite television, instant worldwide communications, the Internet, and other features of the contemporary interlinked world certainly threaten the self-imposed isolation of regimes such as Saudi Arabia's. In 2009, 21 licensed Internet service providers were operational in the country. Although Internet usage is controlled through a single central-government authority that may block out websites considered pornographic or politically objectionable, Saudi Arabia's huge youth population (nearly 50 percent are under age 15) has easy access to satellite television and foreign websites, enabling viewers to circumvent such control. The opening of the U.S.-style Faisalah Mall in Riyadh in 2000 provided Saudi young people with the first public meeting-place and entertainment venue in the absence of movie theaters and other mass media centers.

After the 1991 Gulf War the country's large-scale purchases of American arms and particularly the stationing of 5,000 American troops on Saudi soil have been strongly criticized, not only by the Saudi public but also by some Arab leaders and the "Arab street," the barometer of Arab public opinion. This criticism has been ignored by the monarchy. Alignment with the United States as its major ally has been one of the cornerstones of Saudi foreign policy since World War II. However the unqualified U.S. support for Israel and the presence of non-Muslim forces on

sacred Saudi territory have begun to fray the strands holding the alliance together. A truck-bomb attack on the U.S. military base at Khobar, near Riyadh, killed 24 Americans and injured 400 in 1996, and other incidents of sabotage and violence spurred the United States to pullout its forces early in the millennium. (It is worth noting that most of the hijackers who blew up the World Trade Center in 2001 were Saudis).

## ISLAMIC MILITANTS POSE NEW THREATS

The Occupation of the Great Mosque in Mecca by militants in 1979 provided an early impetus to opponents of the monarchy. After the siege ended many of those involved were deported to Afghanistan and took part in the resistance to the Soviet invasion and occupation of that country. After the Soviet withdrawal in 1989, many of these "Arab Afghans" returned to Saudi Arabia and other Middle Eastern Islamic countries. Some even migrated to Europe and Canada, ultimately entering the United States. Most of them were Saudi nationals; they included Osama bin Laden. Although bin Laden was deprived of his Saudi citizenship and deported (to Sudan) in 1994, the nucleus of his organization remained in Saudi Arabia. It presented a serious widespread threat to the monarchy. In 2003 suicide bombers attacked residential districts in Riyadh, killing 9 Americans along with other non-Saudis. Since then Saudi security forces have been engaged in almost-weekly battles with al Qaeda militants organized into cells throughout the country. The government has offered bounties of $267,000 each for some 26 known militants. In September 2005 the U.S. consulate in Dhahran was closed due to extremist threats. Subsequently the Jiddah consulate was attacked, as al Qaeda continued to target Westerners in its effort to cripple the Saudi economy and overthrow the monarchy.

The government also cooperated with U.S. and other intelligence organizations in closing down international banks that had served as fronts for al Qaeda funding, but due to the large number of fighters essentially detached from Saudi society and conditioned to violence, their elimination as threats to the monarchy remained difficult.

As things stand, the government's vulnerability to Al-Qaeda-inspired terrorism stems almost equally from economic imbalance and the need for political reforms. Despite its huge oil resources and a growing petrochemical infrastructure, its economic growth has not kept pace with population expansion and particularly the surge of youth. Unfortunately the heavy hand of Wahhabism, exercised by clerics and their "morals police", continues to block even small steps toward social and political reform. Extreme segregation of the sexes results from this 200-year-old revivalist version of Islam. Its most restrictive component is the judiciary, dominated by ultra-puritanical judges who believe their rulings represent the will of God, along with a body of 700 clerics chosen by other Islamic scholars who define Islamic law (shari'a) as they see fit. Thus the overhaul of the judicial system decided in 2007 will establish three tiers of courts and their division into courts specializing in criminal, commercial, labor and family cases, represents a positive move toward aligning Saudi law with western legal systems and others elsewhere. The reforms moved along since then and in major reshuffling of key government posts in February 2009, King Abdullah appointed a new Head of the Supreme Judicial Council who is less conservative than his predecessor. One of the key aims of the reform is to create a relatively independent judicial system which will function according to written laws and codes rather than the whimsical interpretations of overtly conservative judges.

One unexpected breakthrough in the system has been in literature. Although the clerical establishment opposes modern literature and other components of freewheeling "modern" (i.e. Western) culture, for unknown reasons the ban does not extend to novels. Thus in 2006 some 50 novels by Saudi writers were approved and published. Half of the authors were women. Thus a novel by Rajaa Alsanea, *Girls of Riyadh,* breaks taboos by focusing on the lives of four wealthy women as they navigate the minefield of patriarchal rules governing sex, marriage and social class.

At age 83, King Abdullah's time in office may not run much longer, and there is no guarantee that his successors will continue what is in many respects a significant set of reforms. Of particular interest, his accession has been a sidelining of the clergy's traditional powers. In 2004, for example, the clergy's demand for a ban on the use of cell phones as "spreaders of obscenity" was rejected after foreign businesses in the country threatened to close down their operations. Overhaul of

the educational system in 2006 to make the curriculum more relevant to global technology has been another royal initiative, as is the new King Abdullah University for Science and Technology, the country's first coeducational institution. A number of private foreign-supported universities formerly banned by the clerical leadership were legalized in 2005–2006.

Another Abdullah innovation is an annual "National Dialogue" forum, at which invitees, including prominent Shi'a intellectuals but excluding the Wahhabi clergy, are encouraged to express their views on future leadership and management of the kingdom. While these may be small steps, they suggest that Saudi Arabia may be at a "tipping point" in its evolution as a state.

The monarchy's gradualist approach to political reform took two small steps forward in 2004. The first was the formation of the Saudi Human Rights Association. Its mandate calls for investigation into reported violations of human rights. A second government-sponsored organization, the Council for the National Dialogue, is intended to bring together the various sectors of society for discussion of needed political reform issues.

The Crown Prince has also taken some steps to revitalize the economy. Foreigners are now allowed to own property and new laws were approved in 2001–2002 to encourage foreign investment, particularly in the huge natural gas industry. Changes in the legal system, notably the "Saudization" (replacing foreigner workers with Saudi nationals) of banks and other industries, will in time reduce unemployment as more Saudis can be added to their staffs.

Saudi vulnerability stems from internal weaknesses rather than external threats, as was the case a decade ago when Iraqi forces had seized Kuwait and stood on the borders of the kingdom. King Fahd marked his 20th anniversary on the throne in 2001 in poor health, confined to a wheelchair, and reportedly suffering from Alzheimer's disease. Prior to his death and Abdullah's formal accession as king he had formed in 2000 a family council to manage royal-family affairs for the 7,000 or so princes; in 2001, he directed members to pay their own electricity and phone bills and placed a five-year moratorium on military contracts, another source of graft and kickbacks.

## FOREIGN POLICY

The Iraqi invasion and occupation of Kuwait caused a major shift in Saudi policy, away from mediation in regional conflicts and bankrolling of popular causes (such as the Palestinian) to one of direct

confrontation. For the first time in its history, the Saudi nation felt directly threatened by the actions of an aggressive neighbor. Diplomatic relations were broken with Iraq and subsequently with Jordan and Yemen, due to their support of the Iraqi occupation. Yemeni workers were rounded up and expelled, and harsh restrictions were imposed on Yemeni business owners in the kingdom. Saudi Arabia closed its border with Yemen in January 2004. The purpose was to block entry of al Qaeda activists based in the latter country. Yemeni leaders protested the action as a violation of the Treaty of Jeddah. This 2000 treaty established a neutral zone between the two states which allows nomadic tribes to move about freely. After Yemeni president Saleh visited Riyadh to discuss the matter, the Saudis agreed to dismantle the barrier in return for increased joint border patrols to deal with smuggling and terrorist infiltration. In November 2009, Saudi forces became involved in the Yemeni government's struggle against rebels in the north, the area said to belong to the Yazidi Shiite sect. They are known as Houthis after Hussein Badr al-Din al-Houthi, their erstwhile leader. The Saudis justified their intervention by claiming that the rebels had carried out a cross-border raid in which two Saudi border guards were killed. To many observers, the Saudi attack was mostly prompted by the suspicion that Iran was behind the Shiite insurgency in North Yemen. However, the insurgents themselves say that their recourse to armed rebellion was due to the socioeconomic marginalization of their community and religious discrimination against them.

The continued survival of Saddam Hussein's regime in Iraq resulted in huge Saudi purchases of U.S. military equipment, although a $1.7 billion arms deal was cancelled in 1999 due to the economic recession. In the last few years, the purchase of U.S. arms and the stationing of 5,000 American troops on Saudi soil has drawn criticism from other Arab countries. They have even accused the kingdom of becoming a U.S. satellite. In the past, Saudi rulers have ignored such criticism. Alignment with the United States as its major ally and arms supplier has been the cornerstone of Saudi policy since World War II. However, all-out U.S. support for Israel in its conflict with the Palestinians began to erode the alliance in 2000–2001. The government authorized public anti-American demonstrations in several Saudi cities, while the crown prince and other officials angrily criticized both the Clinton and George W. Bush administrations for their lack of even-handedness in the conflict. One observer noted: "The Islamists think the Saudis have sold out to the Americans, and the Americans think they have sold out to the terrorists. Eventually this translates into an erosion of legitimacy—that if you are not satisfying the Arabs and Washington, you're on your own."[9]

The country's often difficult relationship with Iran underwent another change in 1991. The fall of the Iranian monarchy and establishment of the Islamic Republic was initially welcomed by Saudi rulers because of the new regime's fidelity to Islamic principles. But, in 1987, Iranian pilgrims attending the pilgrimage to Mecca undertook anti-Saudi demonstrations that led to a violent confrontation with police, resulting in more than 400 casualties. The two countries broke diplomatic relations; and, in 1988, Saudi Arabia established a quota system for pilgrims on the basis of one pilgrim per 1,000 population. The quota system was described as necessary to reduce congestion on the annual pilgrimages, but in fact it would limit Iran to 50,000 pilgrims and limit Iranian-inspired political activism. Iran boycotted the pilgrimage in 1988 and 1989 as a result. Although it has remained free from politically-inspired violence since then, the hajj has been adversely affected in other ways. Some 1,426 pilgrims died on July 2, 1990, in a tunnel crush, and in the following year 340 were killed in fires in the overcrowded tent city of Mina, outside Mecca. In 2004 another stampede during the devil-stoning ritual at Mina caused nearly 500 casualties, and another in January 2006 killed 363. The difference between the hajj and other large-scale public events lies in its enormous logistical problems. As the director of public safety for the Saudi government observed: "When you get 300,000 people seeking to move all at once, accidents are bound to happen and they are quickly magnified.[10]

Relations with neighboring Gulf states have also improved. Long-time border disputes with Qatar and Yemen have been resolved amicably, with demarcation through largely featureless desert territory. In the Yemeni case, the border was demarcated by a joint arbitration commission to extend from Jebel Thar to the Omani border, on the basis of the 1934 Treaty of Taif.

Now that "terrorism" has become a household word in the West, and one particularly associated with Islam, many

## Timeline: PAST

**1800**
Wahhabis seize Mecca and Medina

**1902**
Ibn Saud captures Riyadh in a daring commando raid

**1927**
Ibn Saud is recognized by the British as the king of Saudi Arabia

**1946**
Oil exports get under way

**1963**
King Saud, the eldest son and successor of Ibn Saud, is deposed in favor of his brother Faisal

**1975**
Faisal is assassinated; succession passes by agreement to Khalid

**1979**
The Great Mosque in Mecca is seized by a fundamentalist Muslim group

**1980s**
King Khalid dies; succession passes to Crown Prince Fahd; Saudi jets shoot down an Iranian jet for violation of Saudi air space

**1990s**
Saudi Arabia hosts foreign troops and shares command in the Gulf War

**2005**
February–April–First-ever nationwide municipal elections. Women do not take part in the poll.

August 1–King Abdullah Bin Abdulaziz succeeds to the throne upon the death of his half-brother, King Fahd

scholars and analysts have traced it to Wahhabism, Saudi Arabia's version of the faith. The partnership between the House of Sa'ud and the Wahhabi religious establishment has been a source of strength to the Saudi state. However, in recent years, especially since 2001, this alliance between the two forces—House of Sa'ud and Wahhabism—has become a liability for the Saudi rulers both at home and abroad. At home, it has spurred social ultraconservatism which is facing a growing resistance within society. While it is still inspiring radicalism abroad. Recent reforms enacted by King Abdullah seem intent on curtailing somewhat such ultraconservatism at home but they may not go far and fast enough, mainly because Wahhabism remains an essential pillar of the Saudi rule. Abroad,

Wahhabism is still inspiring radical movements and actions and this places the Saudi rulers in an uncomfortable position. The country is in need of substantial reforms at the institutional level as well as at the economic, political, and social levels. The monarchy is aware of that urgency but it has opted for a slow pace of change. However, the internal socioeconomic mutations underway and external pressures and challenges may create serious problems for the kingdoms, well before any meaningful reforms are enacted.

## NOTES

1. He had 24 sons by 16 different women during his lifetime (1880–1953). See William Quandt, *Saudi Arabia in the 1980's* (Washington, D.C.: Brookings Institution, 1981), Appendix E, for a genealogy.

2. George Rentz, "The Saudi Monarchy," in Willard A. Beling, ed., *King Faisal and the Modernization of Saudi Arabia* (Boulder, CO: Westview Press, 1980), pp. 26–27.

3. *Ibid.*, p. 29.

4. "Saudi Arabia's Centennial," *Aramco World*, Vol. 50, No. 1 (January–February 1999), pp. 21–22. The walls and gates were demolished in 1953 under the "relentless pressure" of modernization, but the Masmak and other structures dating from Ibn Saud's time have been preserved as museums to celebrate the nation's past.

5. The wall was torn down by his successor, King Faisal. Justin Coe, in *The Christian Science Monitor* (February 13, 1985).

6. Gordon Gaskill, "Saudi Arabia's Modern Monarch," *Reader's Digest* (January 1967), p. 118.

7. Ministry of Information, Kingdom of Saudi Arabia, *Faisal Speaks* (n.d.), p. 88.

8. David Hirst, "Corruption, Hard Times Fuel Desert Discontent," *The Washington Times* (September 29, 1999), p. 150.

9. Stephen Schwartz, *The Two Faces of Islam the House of Sa'ud from Tradition to Terror* (New York: Doubleday, 2002) pp. 64–65. A man in Jiddah was given 4,750 lashes for adultery with his sister-in-law, although the Qur'anic limit is 100.

10. Hassan M. Fattah, "Why Mecca's Pilgrims Need Engineering, Not Just Prayer," *The New York Times,* January 17, 2006. An architect in Jidda noted that 'the three main variables in managing the hajj are density, space, and time. So far all they have been dealing with is space.' *Ibid.*

# Sudan (Republic of the Sudan)

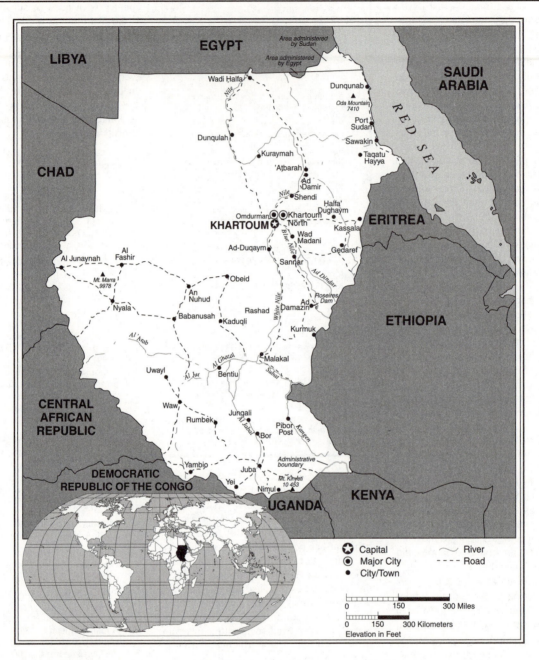

# Sudan Statistics

## GEOGRAPHY

*Area in Square Miles (Kilometers):*
892,068 (2,505,810) (about 1/4 the size
of the United States)
*Capital (Population):* Khartoum (948,000)
*Environmental Concerns:* little potable
water; threatened wildlife populations;
soil erosion; desertification
*Geographical Features:* generally flat,
featureless plain; mountains in the east
and west

*Climate:* varies from arid desert in the
north to tropical in the south

## PEOPLE

### Population

*Total:* 41,980,182
*Annual Growth Rate:* 2.15%
*Rural/Urban Population Ratio:* 68/32
*Major Languages:* Arabic (official);
various Nubian, Nilotic and other

African languages in south; English
widely used
*Ethnic Makeup:* 52% black; 39% Arab;
6% Beja; 3% others
*Religions:* 70% Sunni Muslim in
north; 25% indigenous beliefs; 5%
Christian, mostly in the south and
Khartoum

### Health

*Life Expectancy at Birth:* 51.56 years
(male), 53.54 years (female)

*Infant Mortality Rate (Ratio):* 78/1,000
live births

## Education

*Adult Literacy Rate:* 61%

## COMMUNICATION

*Telephones:* 356,100 main lines
*Daily Newspaper Circulation:* 21 per
1,000 people
*Televisions:* 8.2 per 1,000 people
*Internet Users:* 4.2 million (2008)

## TRANSPORTATION

*Highways in Miles (Kilometers):* 7,390
(11,900)
*Railroads in Miles (Kilometers):* 3,425
(5,516)
*Usable Airfields:* 61
*Motor Vehicles in Use:* 75,000

## GOVERNMENT

*Type:* transitional
*Independence Date:* January 1, 1956
(from Egypt and the United Kingdom)

*Head of State/Government:* Under
the 2005 power-sharing agreement
ending the civil war, President
Omar Hassan Al-Bashir continues
in office. In lieu of a prime minister
there are two vice-presidents, Salva
Kiir (South) and Ali Osman Taha
(North)
*Political Parties:* under the
peace accord former political
"associations" approved as parties.
They include the Popular National
Congress (PNC), Democratic
Unionist Party, Umma, National
Democratic Alliance
*Suffrage:* universal at 17

## MILITARY

*Military Expenditures (% of GDP):* 3%
*Current Disputes:* the civil war in Darfur
province has spilled across Sudan's
borders to affect neighboring states,
notably Chad, Ethiopia, Kenya, Central
African Republic, Congo and Uganda.
Some 500,000 Sudanese are presently
refugees in those countries, especially
Chad

## ECONOMY

*Currency ($U.S. Equivalent):* 2.34
Sudanese Pound = $1
*Per Capita Income/GDP:* $2,300/
$92.81 billion
*GDP Growth Rate:* 3.8%
*Inflation Rate:* 9%
*Unemployment Rate:* 18.7%
*Labor Force:* 11.92 million
*Natural Resources:* petroleum; small
reserves of iron ore; copper; chromium
ore; zinc; tungsten; mica; silver; gold
*Agriculture:* cotton; groundnuts; sorghum;
millet; wheat; gum arabic; sesame;
sheep
*Industry:* cotton ginning; textiles; cement;
edible oils; sugar; soap distilling;
shoes; petroleum refining; armaments
*Exports:* $7.5 billion (primary partners
China, Japan, Saudi Arabia)
*Imports:* $8.963 billion (primary partners
China, Saudi Arabia, United Arab
Emirates

## SUGGESTED WEB SITE

http://lcweb2.loc.gov/frd/cs/sdtoc.html

# Sudan Country Report

**S**udan is the largest country on the African continent. It extends from its northern border with Egypt and the Libyan and Nubian Deserts southward deep into tropical Africa. Its territory includes the Blue and White Nile Rivers, which join at Khartoum to form the Nile, Egypt's lifeline.

The name of the country underscores its distinctive social structure. Centuries ago, Arab geographers named it Bilad al-Sudan, "Land of the Blacks." The northern half, including Khartoum, is Arabic in language, culture, and traditions, and Islamic in religion. However, the admixture of Arab and African peoples over 2,000 years has produced a largely black Arab population.

Southern Sudan is the home of a large number of black African tribes and tribal groups, the largest being the Dinka. Other important ones are the Shilluk, Nuer, and in western Sudan the Azande and Bor. They make up approximately 30–35 percent of the total population. About 5 percent are Christian.

The two halves of Sudan have little or nothing in common. The country's basic political problem is how to achieve unity between these two different societies, which were brought together under British rule to form an artificial state.

## HISTORY

The ancient history of Sudan, at least of the northern region, was always linked with that of Egypt. The pharaohs and later conquerors of Egypt—Persians, Greeks, Romans, and eventually the Arabs, Turks, and British—periodically attempted to extend their power farther south. The connection with Egypt became very close when the Egyptians were converted to Islam by invading armies from Arabia, in the seventh century A.D. As the invaders spread southward, they converted the northern Sudanese people to Islam, developing in time an Islamic Arab society in northern Sudan. Southern Sudan remained comparatively untouched, because it was isolated by the geographical barriers of mountain ranges and the great impassable swamps of the Nile.

The two regions were forcibly brought together by conquering Egyptian armies in the nineteenth century. The conquest became possible after the exploration of sub-Saharan Africa by Europeans. After the explorers and armies came slave traders and then European fortune hunters, interested in developing the gold, ivory, diamonds, timber, and other resources of sub-Saharan Africa.

The soldiers and slave traders were the most brutal of all these invaders, particularly in southern Sudan. In fact, many of the slave traders were Muslim Sudanese from the north. The Civil War between the Islamic north and the Christian/animist south began essentially in 1955 before independence and continued intermittently until 2005. However its roots in the nineteenth-century experiences of the southerners, as "memories of plunder, slave raiding and suffering" at the hands of slavers and their military allies were passed down from generation to generation.[1]

## THE ORIGINS OF THE SUDANESE STATE

The first effort to establish a nation in Sudan began in the 1880s, when the country was ruled by the British as part of their protectorate over Egypt. The British were despised as foreign, non-Muslim rulers. The Egyptians, who made up the bulk of the security forces assigned to Sudan, were hated for their arrogance and mistreatment of the Sudanese.

In 1881 opposition to the British and their Egyptian cohorts led to the emergence of a religious leader, Muhammad

Ahmad, who announced that he was the Mahdi ("Guided One") who would return to earth to announce the Day of Judgment and rid Sudan of its foreign rulers. He then called for a *jihad* against Anglo-Egyptian rule.

Sudanese by the thousands flocked to join the Mahdi. His warriors, fired by revolutionary zeal, defeated several British-led Egyptian armies. In 1885, they captured Khartoum, and, soon thereafter, the Mahdi's rule extended over the whole of present-day Sudan. For this reason, the Mahdi is remembered, at least in northern Sudan, as Abu al-Istiqlal, the "Father of Independence."[2]

The Mahdi's rule did not last long; he died in 1886. His chief lieutenant and successor, the Khalifa Abdallahi, continued in power until 1898, when a British force armed with guns mowed down his spear-carrying, club-wielding army. Sudan was ruled jointly by Britain and Egypt from then until 1955. Since the British already ruled Egypt as a protectorate, for all practical purposes joint rule meant British rule.

Under the British, Sudan was divided into a number of provinces, and British university graduates staffed the country's first civil service.[3] But the British followed two policies that have created problems for Sudan ever since it became independent. One was "indirect rule" in the north. Rather than developing a group of trained Sudanese administrators who could take over when they left, the British governed indirectly through local chiefs and religious leaders. The second policy was to separate southern from northern Sudan through "Closed Door" laws, which prohibited northerners from working in, or even visiting, the south.

Sudan became independent on New Year's Day 1956, as a republic headed by a civilian government. The first civilian government lasted until 1958, when a military group seized power "to save the country from the chaotic regime of the politicians."[4] But the military regime soon became as "chaotic" as its predecessor's. In 1964, it handed over power to another civilian group. The second civilian group was no more successful than the first, as the politicians continued to feud, and intermittent conflict between government forces and rebels in the southern region turned into all-out civil war.

In 1969, the Sudanese Army carried out another military coup, headed by Colonel Ja'far (or Gaafar) Numeiri. Successive Sudanese governments since independence, including Numeiri's, have faced the same basic problems: the unification of north and south, an economy hampered by inadequate transportation and few resources, and the building of a workable political system. Numeiri's record in dealing with these difficult problems is one explanation for his

longevity in power. A written Constitution was approved in 1973. Although political parties were outlawed, an umbrella political organization, the Sudan Socialist Union (SSU), provided an alternative to the fractious political jockeying that had divided the country before Numeiri.[5]

Numeiri's firm control through the military and his effectiveness in carrying out political reforms were soon reflected at the ballot box. He was elected president in 1971 for a six-year term and was re-elected in 1977. Yet broad popular support did not generate political stability. There were many attempts to overthrow him, the most serious in 1971 and 1976, when he was actually captured and held for a time by rebels.

One reason for his survival may be his resourcefulness. After the 1976 coup attempt, for example, instead of having his opponents executed, he invited them and other opposition leaders to form a government of national unity. One of Numeiri's major opponents, Sadiq al-Mahdi, a great-grandson of the Mahdi and himself an important religious leader, accepted the offer and returned from exile.

## DEVELOPMENT

Although the country ranks near the bottom of the Arab world economic ladder, its oil production and exports mainly to China, its principal defender internationally in the on-going Darfur conflict, have improved its financial status. According to official government estimates, current oil production is 536,000 barrels per day (bpd). Reserves are estimated at 5 billion barrels. While wealth is unevenly distributed and mostly centered in Khartoum, Darfur and other outlying provinces, including the war-ravaged South, have seen little economic progress.

Numeiri's major achievement was to end temporarily the Civil War between north and south. An agreement was signed in 1972 in Addis Ababa, Ethiopia, mediated by Ethiopian authorities, between his government and the southern Anya Anya resistance movement. The agreement provided for regional autonomy for the south's three provinces, greater representation of southerners in the National People's Assembly, and integration of Anya Anya units into the armed forces without restrictions.

## THE COUP OF 1985

Numeiri was reelected in 1983 for a third presidential term. Most of his political opponents had apparently been reconciled with him, and the army and state security

forces were firmly under his control. It seemed that Sudan's most durable leader would round out another full term in office without too much difficulty. However, storm clouds were brewing on the horizon. Numeiri had survived for 16 years in power largely through his ability to keep opponents divided and off balance by his unpredictable moves. From 1983 on, however, his policies seemed designed to unite rather than divide them.

The first step in Numeiri's undoing was his decision to impose Islamic law (*Shari'a*) over the entire country. The impact fell heaviest on the non-Muslim southern region. In a 1983 interview, Numeiri explained that his goal from the start of his regime was "to raise government by the book [i.e., the Qur'an] from the level of the individual to that of government." If the Sudanese, with their numerous ethnic and cultural differences and the country's vast size, were governed properly by God's Book, they would provide an example of peace and security to neighboring countries.

In Numeiri's view, the application of Islamic restrictions on alcohol, tobacco, and other prohibited forms of behavior was appropriate to Sudanese Muslims and non-Muslims alike, since "Islam was revealed to serve man and all its legislation has the goal of regulating family, social, and individual life and raising the level of the individual."[6]

The new draconian measures were widely resented, particularly in the south, where cigarettes and home-brewed beer were popular palliatives for a harsh existence. When Numeiri continued his "Islamic purification" process with a re-organization of Sudanese administration into several large regions in order to streamline the cumbersome bureaucracy inherited from the British, the southerners reacted strongly. Consolidation of three autonomous provinces into one directly under central-government control was seen by them as a violation of the commitment made to regional autonomy that had ended the Civil War. An organized guerrilla army, the Sudan People's Liberation Army (SPLA), resumed civil war under the expert leadership of U.S.-trained Colonel John Garang. The rebels' new strategy was not only to oppose government troops but also to strike at development projects. Foreign workers in the newly developed oil fields in southwestern Sudan were kidnapped or killed; as a result, Chevron Oil Company halted all work on the project.

A crackdown on Islamic radical groups, particularly the Muslim Brotherhood, added to Numeiri's growing list of opponents. Members of the Brotherhood had

(US Agency for International Development/AED. www.USAID.gov)
The attainment of political stability is important to Sudanese development. Strengthening educational opportunities for students is a fundamental need that will pay future dividends to the people and government.

been active in implementing Islamic law as the law of the land, but Numeiri felt that they had gone too far. By late 1984, it appeared that the president had angered or alienated everybody in the country, all for different reasons.

In the end, it was the failure of his economic policies rather than anything else that brought about Numeiri's fall. The International Monetary Fund imposed strict austerity requirements on Sudan in 1984 as a prerequisite to a $90 million standby loan to enable the country to pay its mounting food and fuel bills. The food bills were aggravated by famine, the fuel bills by the necessity to import almost all fuel requirements. The IMF insisted on drastic budget cuts, devaluation of currency, and an end to subsidies on basic commodities. If Numeiri had been able to carry out these reforms, he would have stood a chance of restoring the country to solvency and his own rule to respectability. Protests turned to riots, mainly over the end of price subsidies and a consequent 33 percent increase in the prices of such necessities as bread, sugar, and cooking oil. Other protests erupted over the application of Islamic law, especially the ban on alcohol, which brought thousands of Sudanese into the streets shouting "We want beer! We want beer!"

Numeiri's departure for the United States to seek further economic help triggered a general strike in 1985. A genuine national movement arose, uniting students and professionals with the urban poor, all demanding that Numeiri resign. Fearing anarchy or an uprising by young army

officers, the senior military leaders moved quickly, took over the government, and ordered Numeiri deposed. Crowds in Khartoum shouted, "Numeiri the butcher is finished; the country belongs to the people."

The new military government, headed by General Abd al-Rahman Swareddahab, a highly respected senior officer, promised to hold elections within a year to restore civilian rule and to revive political parties. That promise was kept: In 1986, elections were held for a new People's Assembly. Two revived pre-Numeiri parties, the Umma and the Democratic Unionist Party (DUP), won the majority of seats, with the National Islamic Front emerging as a strong third party. Sadiq al-Mahdi, head of the Umma, automatically became prime minister; his principal rival, DUP leader Ahmed Ali al-Mirghani, was chosen as president. The new prime minister chose a coalition cabinet to begin the arduous process of starting the democratic process after 15 years of Numeiri.

But the euphoria over the departure of "Numeiri the Butcher" soon gave way to the realization that the problems that had daunted him remained unresolved. They included heavy foreign indebtedness, a weak economy, inefficient agricultural production, an inadequate transportation system, party and personal rivalries, and extreme distrust between north and south in the divided Sudan.

## INTERNAL PROBLEMS

The al-Mahdi government had no more success than its predecessors in resolving Sudan's endemic political disunity.

Efforts to limit the application of Islamic law throughout the country were blocked by the National Islamic Front (NIF) in 1988. The Civil War then heated up. SPLA success in capturing the principal towns in the south led the DUP to sign a separate agreement with the rebels for a cease-fire. The People's Assembly rejected the agreement, and the DUP then withdrew from the government.

Faced with the imminent collapse of civilian authority, the armed forces again seized power, in Sudan's fourth military coup since independence. The army moved after food shortages and soaring inflation, fed by war costs of $1 million a day, led to riots in Khartoum and other cities. A Revolutionary Council, headed by Lieutenant General Omar Hassan al-Bashir, suspended the Constitution and arrested government leaders.

In 1992, Bashir appointed a 300-member National Transitional Assembly to lay the groundwork—at least in theory—for a return to civilian rule. Its members included military leaders (those who sat on the ruling Revolutionary Council), provincial (state) governors, and some former government leaders. Its primary function was to implement Council decrees during the transitional period; however, it could also initiate legislation.

The regime also sought to broaden its popular base through the establishment of local elections. The elections were held in two stages, the first stage being the election of people's congresses (at the village and town level); in the second stage of the process, the congresses then elected provincial legislatures. Due to the Civil War, the southern region remained unrepresented.

The gradual return to representative government in the 1990s improved Sudan's image internationally. Elections were held in 1996 for a 400-member National People's Assembly and to choose a president. Not surprisingly, Bashir was elected president; he received 75.5 percent of the 5.5 million votes cast. (The south was excluded from the election process.) The leader of the NIF, Hassan al-Tourabi, then allied with Bashir, was elected Speaker of the newly-formed National Assembly; his party held the majority of seats.

In June 1998, the regime enacted a number of constitutional reforms. They allow political parties to form, although they are to be registered officially as "associations." Freedoms of speech, assembly, and the press are guaranteed under the reforms, although political parties that receive foreign funding or "go beyond the bounds of religion" can be proscribed.

In 1998 and 1999, the regime called on political opponents to return and help build a "new democratic Sudan." Several did so. They included Numeiri and Sadeq al-Mahdi. However, rivalry between Bashir and Turabi, which came to a head in 1999, halted the restoration of representative government. Turabi presented constitutional amendments to the Assembly in December which included abolishing the position of prime minister and making the president impeachable by a two-thirds vote in the Assembly.

On December 12, however, the embattled president struck back. He declared a three-month state of emergency, suspended the Constitution and the Assembly, and dismissed his entire cabinet. In January 2000, he removed all state governors from office and appointed a new cabinet, with most of the ministries now held by his own supporters. "God willing with this team we will guide Sudan toward peace," he told the nation in a public address.

During this transitional period Turabi formed a political "association" (so named because political parties remain banned). It was called the Popular National Congress (PNC). It boycotted the 2000 elections on grounds they had been "cooked and pre-arranged" by the Bashir regime under the state of emergency. Subsequently Turabi was suspended as Speaker and charged with complicity with the SPLA, mainly because he had signed an agreement with its leaders. This agreement called for an end to the civil war and recognition of Sudan's religious and cultural pluralism. Former Sudanese president Jaafar al-Numeiri, invited to return after years of exile in Egypt, ran against the president as an independent, receiving 9 percent of the popular vote. Despite the boycott and low voter turnout Bashir was re-elected by 86 percent of the popular vote. Turabi was released from jail in 2005. He has continued to press the regime for changes in its adamant

insistence on the full observance of Islamic law. In May 2010, he was arrested again after another harsh criticism of President Bashir following the presidential elections of the previous month in which Bashir was declared winner with 68 percent of the vote. The election had come in the wake of Bachir's indictment by the International Criminal Court for war crimes and crimes against humanity Darfur. The court issued an arrest warrant against him right before the elections.

## THE CIVIL WAR

The government gained some ground against rebels in the Civil War in late 1991, when the SPLA split into contending factions. One faction, led by Lieutenant Rick Machar, accused SPLA commander John Garang of a dictatorial reign of terror within the organization. The split followed ethnic lines when Nuer troops of Machar's faction invaded Dinka territory; the Dinkas are Garang's main supporters. Some 100,000 Dinkas fled their homeland during the fighting. Sudan government forces took advantage of internal SPLA rivalry to capture several important southern towns during an offensive in March 1992.

The ethnic killings of Nuers and Dinkas, along with famine (which has been intensified by the SPLA infighting), led other African states and, in late 1993, the United States to attempt to mediate and bring the two factions together as a prelude to ending the Civil War. But even the presence of former U.S. president Jimmy Carter as mediator failed to bridge the differences separating the two SPLA leaders. The major differences between southerners and northerners—imposition of Islamic law on non-Muslims, revenue sharing among regions, states' rights and powers versus those of the national government—seemed insurmountable.

In the late 1990s, the National Islamic Front, renamed the National Congress Party in an effort to soften its Islamist image, won almost complete control over the Revolutionary Council. The security forces, the judiciary, and the universities were purged of moderate or liberal staff members and replaced by NIF militants. In 1991, the regime had bowed to NIF pressure and issued an edict making Islamic law the "law of the land" in both north and south Sudan. As a result, the Civil War intensified.

In 1997, the government signed peace agreements with several SPLA factions after rebel successes threatened to win the entire southern region. The agreements specified a four-year autonomy period for the south. At the end of the period, the

population could choose between independence and integration on the basis of equality with the Muslim north.

Early in 2003 the peace talks were renewed, this time in Kenya and under joint Libyan-Egyptian sponsorship. But many questions remained to be resolved. They included allocation of a fair proportion of oil revenues to southerners (where the oil fields are located), the nature of the proposed transitional government, and restitution to families of southerners kidnapped and sold into slavery.

After three years of off-and-on intense negotiations, effectively mediated by Kenya's Gen. Lazaro Sumbeiyo, SPLA chief John Garang and President Bashir signed in 2005 a far-reaching agreement to end Africa's longest civil war. The war had lasted half a century and caused 2 million casualties. Sumbeiyo's mediation was critical in moving the process forward.

Following the peace agreement Garang was named vice-president for the southern region, the first southerner to hold a cabinet post. Shortly thereafter he was killed in a plane crash, but the peace pact held as Salva Kiir, another former SPLA leader, succeeded him. With the peace pact in place, Kiir's government has increasingly taken on the appearance of a sovereign state. Thus it issues its own visas, sets internal policies and budget, and carries on external trade, most of it via Uganda (which also manages its mobile phone network). Southern schools are increasingly replacing Arabic with English as the language of instruction. With elections scheduled for 2009 and a referendum on separation or unification with the North in 2011, the South's separate attachment to East Africa rather than the Islamic North looms as a distinct possibility. However, in October 2007 the national unity government was fractured by the withdrawal of the Peoples' Liberation Movement, one of the southern political parties participating in the peace pact. Its leaders said that the Bashir government has not implemented the agreement, nor has it agreed on sharing of power and allocation of oil revenues. The agreement had called for a joint command of northern and southern troops to be in place by July 2007. Instead, some 16,000 northern soldiers are dug in the border areas, notably Abyei province, where many oil wells are located. With world attention focused on Darfur, a miscalculation by either side could ignite a renewal of the civil war, with tragic consequences mainly for the south. The parliamentary and presidential elections originally scheduled for 2009, finally took place in April 2010. President Bashir was reelected and in the south, where separate elections were held, Salva Kiir, leader of the Sudan People's Liberation Movement, also won reelection with 92.99 percent of the votes. Many observers pointed to several flaws in the electoral process and most importantly the decision of many opposition figures and parties to boycott the vote. In the south, most political forces seemed more interested in the planned referendum in 2011 that will decide whether the country will remain united or will split in two.

## WAR IN DARFUR

Unfortunately the resolution of the north-south civil war did not extend to Darfur, Sudan's westernmost and poorest province. Several rebel groups that had operated independently of the SPLA during the war summarily rejected the peace agreement. The government then began using an armed militia known as the *janjaweed* which undertook a systematic campaign against the Darfur population which was accused of supporting the rebel groups. Villages were torched, crops destroyed, women raped and families driven from their homes to become refugees. By 2005 it was estimated that the janjaweed had killed 200,000 people and driven 2.4 million across the border into neighboring countries, the majority into Chad. As the conflict escalated the UN Security Council was forced into action. In addition to several resolutions, it imposed an arms freeze and sanctions on the Sudanese government. Under this pressure the government reluctantly agreed to a 26,000-member peacekeeping force recruited principally from African Union member states. Some 7,000 peacekeepers arrived in Darfur in 2006, but before the full peacekeeping force could be mobilized, one of the rebel factions stormed its base in the dusty village of Haskanita and killed ten peacekeepers. With the rebels split into numerous factions and the janjaweed continuing their attacks in the province, prospects for peace seemed dim. The conflict seemed to flare up again in February 2010, following a government cease-fire agreement—thanks to Qatari mediation in Doha—with one rebel group, the Justice and Equality Movement (JEM) and a government declaration that the war in the region to be over. According to the deal, the JEM will become a party that will be offered seats in the government.[7]

## THE ECONOMY

Although the attainment of political stability is important to Sudanese development, much depends on building the economy and sharing its resources equitably across the country. The Sudanese economy is largely dependent on agriculture. The most important crop is cotton. Until recently, the only other Sudanese export crop of importance was gum arabic.

Because Sudan has great agricultural potential, due to its rivers, alluvial soils, and vast areas of unused arable land, Numeiri had set out in the 1970s to develop the country into what experts told him could be the "breadbasket" of the Middle East. To reach this ambitious goal, some cotton plantations were converted to production of grain crops. The huge Kenana sugar-refinery complex was started with joint foreign and Sudanese management; the long-established Gezira cotton scheme was expanded; and work began on the Jonglei Canal, intended to drain a vast marshy area called the Sudd ("swamp") in the south, in order to bring hundreds of thousands of acres of marshlands under cultivation. But the breadbasket was never filled. Mismanagement and lack of skilled labor delayed some projects, while others languished because the roads and communications systems needed to implement them did not exist.

Almost the only positive news out of ravaged Darfur is economic rather than political or conflict-oriented. In June 2007 a UN Environmental Program report noted that water shortages were creating conflict conditions affecting all segments of the population. Subsequently an Egyptian-born geologist and his team, using remote sensing, reported the discovery of a Massachusetts-sized subsurface aquifer, the remains of a 5,000-year-old Saharan lake but still having a water potential. By drilling 1,000 wells, the geologist reported, the aquifer could meet water needs for some 3.5 million Darfuris, once its existence was scientifically confirmed.

## FREEDOM

The 1998 Constitution guarantees full civil rights for all citizens and re-establishes a multi-party political system as had been the case before Bashir's coup. Although the National Assembly has been reinstated, the state of emergency imposed after the coup still limits political activity.

It may be that oil, rather than agriculture, holds the key to Sudan's economic growth and indirectly its internal peace. Oil was discovered by Chevron in the southwestern region in the 1970s. The two oil fields there were being developed when the north-south war resumed. In 1984, three foreign oil workers were killed by rebels in an attack on the Bentiu facility, and Chevron withdrew and closed down its entire installation.

In the late 1990s, a temporary halt to the Civil War made resumption of oil exploration feasible. A consortium of three foreign oil companies (Talisman of Canada and the state oil companies of China and Malaysia), along with the Sudan National Oil Company, built a 936-mile, $1.2 billion pipeline from the former Chevron fields near Haglig northeast to Port Sudan. The pipeline was completed in less than a year. Exports from the Port Sudan refinery had reached 320,000 bpd by 2005.

In April some 60 countries pledged $4.5 billion for reconstruction of the southern provinces, including $765 million from the European Commission. It would be used for food, refugee resettlement, schools, roads, and hospitals. The total cost of reconstruction was estimated to be $7.9 billion. The U.S. contribution would be $1.7 billion; however this was to be contingent on resolution of the Darfur conflict.

Although it was criticized for supporting a repressive government with oil revenues, enabling it to purchase new weaponry, Talisman officials insisted that they were helping the Sudanese people to meet urgent social needs.

U.S. hostility toward Sudan as a supporter of terrorism led Congress in 2001 to pass a law prohibiting foreign oil companies working there from raising capital or trading in U.S. financial markets to finance their oil operations. Most of them denounced the action as interference in their business operations. However the Darfur conflict, from a humanitarian viewpoint, has led a number of American states to ban investment of their state pension funds. Florida was the first state to do so, in 2007, divesting some $5 billion of its $150 billion pension fund, the third largest in the United States.

## FAMINE

The Sudanese people traditionally have lived in a barter economy, with little need for money. Huge budget deficits and high prices for basic commodities hardly affect the mass of the population. But the Civil War and a 12-year drought cycle in the sub-Saharan Sahel region, which includes Sudan, have changed their subsistence way of life into one of destitution.

The drought became critical in 1983, and millions of refugees from Ethiopia and Chad, the countries most affected, moved into temporary camps in Sudan. Then it was Sudan's turn to suffer. Desperate families fled from their villages as wells dried up, cattle died, and crops wilted. By 1985, an estimated 9 million people, half of them native Sudanese, were dying of starvation. Emergency food supplies from many countries poured into Sudan; but due to inadequate transportation, port delays, and diversion of shipments by incompetent or dishonest officials, much of this relief could not be delivered to those who most needed it. Bags of grain lay on the docks, waiting for trucks that did not come because they were immobilized somewhere else, stuck in the sand or mired in the mud of one of Sudan's few passable roads.

## ACHIEVEMENTS

The Sudanese economy grew a record 11 percent in 2006, largely due to oil sales to China and Chinese investments. China has become the country's largest export market, with trade estimated at $55 billion. The first major Chinese-built development project, a hydroelectric plant at Meroe, began operations in 2007. It was built at a cost of $1.8 billion. However, these achievements did not affect the bulk of the population, most of which live below the poverty line. A fall of the GDP growth rate to 3.8 percent in 2009, along with the unsettling internal conflicts, will curtail of the impact of any achievement.

Heavy rains in the rainy season regularly washed out sections of track of Sudan's one railroad, the only link with remote provinces other than intermittent air drops. By 1987, it was estimated that 2,000 children a day were dying from malnutrition-related diseases.

Prodded into action in 1989, after a drought-related famine had caused 250,000 deaths, the United Nations organized "Operation Lifeline Sudan," a consortium of two of its agencies (Unicef and the World Food Program) and 40 humanitarian nongovernmental organizations (NGOs). Humanitarian aid averaging $1 million a day reduced the number of Sudanese requiring emergency relief in the 1990s. However, prolonged drought and the ongoing Civil War increased their numbers significantly in 2000. As of January 2001, the World Food Program (WFP) was feeding 1.7 million people in Sudan, most of them in the provinces of Darfur, Kordofan, Equatoria, and Jonglei. A ban on cattle imports due to outbreaks of foot-and-mouth disease elsewhere added to the misery of southerners, many of whom have only their cattle herds as their assets.

These difficulties have been compounded by the periodic ban on relief flights imposed by the government and requisitioning of food stocks, sometimes by the military, but also by the SPLA or local militias. The Sudanese military's policy forcibly removing villagers from oil-field areas and using food as a weapon,

along with rape, forced labor, and abduction of southern youths to be taken to Khartoum as slaves or household servants for Muslim families, has turned a civil war into one of extermination of people.

## FOREIGN POLICY

Aside from the internal devastation of the Civil War, Sudan's somewhat unwitting involvement in events outside its borders has affected its economic survival as well as its political stability. Under President Bashir, Sudan followed a pan-Arabist foreign policy undergirded by a wish to become a modern Arabo-Islamic state and a key link between the Arab world and Africa. The country sided with Iraq during the Gulf War, and consequently 300,000 Sudanese expatriate workers were expelled from the Arab states in that area. Their return put further strain on the weak economy and eliminated $445 million annually in worker remittances, which had been an important source of revenue. However, before and even after the Gulf War of 1991, Bashir was able to obtain from many Arab countries (especially Saudi Arabia, Kuwait and Gulf states) financial assistance and diplomatic support. The regime's reinstatement of Parliament and gradual steps toward representative government helped to improve Sudan's relations with its neighbors. Diplomatic relations were restored with Egypt and Eritrea in 2000. A treaty with Uganda withdrew Sudanese support for the Lord's Resistance Army, an opposition force to the Ugandan government.

Sudan's identification with international terrorism led the UN Security Council to approve *Resolution 1044* in 1996. It imposed economic sanctions on the country. The United States put into place its own sanctions after Sudanese nationals were implicated in the 1993 bombing of the World Trade Center building in New York.

In August 1998, the Clinton administration's firm belief that Sudan was a major sponsor of international terrorism led to the bombing of the Al-Shifa pharmaceutical plant near Khartoum. The plant, one of six in the country, produced drugs, medicines, and veterinary medications. In January it had been granted a $199,000 contract to ship 100,000 cartons of Shifazole (an antibiotic used to treat parasites in animals) to Iraq. The shipment was to be made for humanitarian purposes; hence, it would be exempt from UN-imposed sanctions on that country. But the United States claimed that the shipment would include a chemical that could be used to manufacture the nerve gas UFX. Subsequent investigation proved that the Al-Shifa plant was involved exclusively with production of pharmaceuticals and that the United States had erred in

### Timeline: PAST

**1820**
An Egyptian province under Muhammad Ali

**1881**
Mahdi rebellion against the British and Egyptians

**1898**
The British recapture Khartoum; establishment of joint Anglo-Egyptian control

**1955**
The Civil War begins

**1956**
Sudan becomes an independent republic

**1969**
Numeiri seizes power

**1980s**
Numeiri is overthrown in a bloodless coup; millions of people die of starvation; the Civil War resumes in the south

**1990s**
The regime institutes systematic slavery

### PRESENT

**2000s**
Resolution of the Civil War in 2005 and establishment of a regional government in the South, with a referendum on autonomy or independence scheduled for 2011

The Darfur conflict leads to UN decision in 2006 to send 26,000 peace-keeping troops

The government and two main rebel groups in Darfur sign in 2006 the Darfur Peace Agreement (DPA)

The International Criminal Court (ICC) issues in March 2009 an arrest warrant for President Bashir on charges of war crimes and crimes against humanity in Darfur

The government and the Justice and Equality Movement, the main Darfur rebel group sign in February 2010 a peace accord; President Bashir declares the Darfur war over

President Bashir wins re-election in April 2010, in the first presidential vote since 1986

The ICC issues, in July 2010, a second arrest warrant for President al-Bashir for genocide

bombing it. Since then the Sudanese government has preserved the ruined plant as a showcase symbolizing its mistreatment at the hands of the world's only superpower.

However, Sudan's internal problems remain a major obstacle to better relations with the outside world. The North-South conflict, the Darfur situation and the ICC's indictment of President Bashir have prevented the normalization of relations with many countries. It is important to note though, even in these conditions, many countries have continuously provided humanitarian assistance to Sudan, especially in the famine years of the 1980s and 1990s, and in the wake of the attacks against, and displacement of, hundreds of thousands of people in the Darfur region.

By far the best relation Sudan has had with foreign countries has been that with China. Their bilateral economic relations have boomed in recent years, especially in the oil business. China is the biggest trading partner of Sudan. In exchange for petroleum purchase and exploration deals, China has provided Sudan weapons and relatively cheap consumer products. Furthermore, as a permanent member of the UN Security Council, China has been a major diplomatic asset to Sudan.

## NOTES

1. Dunstan Wai, *The African-Arab Conflict in the Sudan* (New York: Africana Publishing, 1981), p. 32.

2. *Ibid.,* p. 31. Southerners's view of the Mahdi is not as favorable; in the South, the Mahdi's rule was as cruel as the Egyptian.

3. Peter M. Holt, *The History of the Sudan,* (London: Weidenfeld and Nicolson, 1979), p. 123.

4. *Ibid.,* p. 171.

5. Harold D. Nelson, ed., *Sudan, A Country Study* (Washington, D.C.: American University, Foreign Area Studies, 1982), p. 199. The SSU is defined as "a grand alliance of workers, farmers, intellectuals, business people and soldiers."

6. The text of the Darfur Peace Agreement can be found at www.sudantribune.com/IMG/pdf/Darfur_Peac_Agreement-2.pdf

7. Kristen Chick, "Darfur Conflict Flares After Sudan President Bashir Declares War Over," *Christian Science Monitor* (February 25, 2010). Online at www.csmonitor.com/World/terrorism-security/2010/0225/Darfur-conflict-flares-after-Sudan-President-Bashir-declares-war-over. Consulted on 2010.

## SUDAN INTERNET NEWS SOURCES

Sudan Views: http://sudanviews.net/
SudaneseOnline: http://sudaneseonline.com/
South Sudan News Agency: www.southsudannewsagency.com/
SPLM Website: www.splmtoday.com/

# Syria (Syrian Arab Republic)

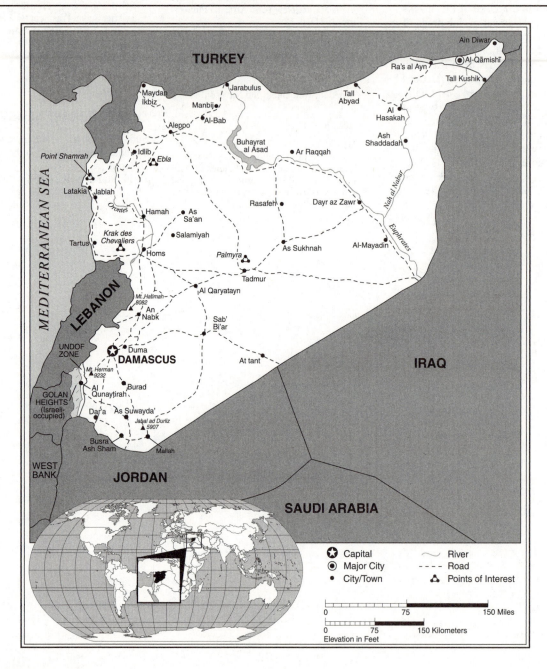

# Syria Statistics

## GEOGRAPHY

*Area in Square Miles (Kilometers):*
71,500 (185,170) (about the size of
North Dakota)

*Capital (Population):* Damascus
(1,669,000)

*Environmental Concerns:* deforestation;
overgrazing; soil erosion;
desertification; water pollution;
insufficient potable water

*Geographical Features:* primarily
semiarid and desert plateau;
narrow coastal plain; mountains in
the west

*Climate:* predominantly desert;
considerable variation between the
interior and coastal regions

## PEOPLE

### Population

*Total:* 22,198,110 (plus 20,000 Arabs,
18,000 Druze and 2,000 Alawites in
the Israeli-occupied Golan Heights)

*Annual Growth Rate:* 1.954%

*Rural/Urban Population Ratio:* 47/53

*Major Languages:* Arabic, Kurdish,

various minority languages, e.g. Aramaic, Hebrew

*Ethnic Groups:* Arabs 90%, Kurds 9.7%, Armenian and other Christians 2.3%

*Religions:* 74% Sunni Muslim; 16% Alawite, Druze, and other Muslim sects; 10% Christian and Jewish

### Health

*Life Expectancy at Birth:* 72 years (male); 77 years (female)

*Infant Mortality Rate (Ratio):* 16.14/1,000 live births

*Physicians Available (Ratio):* 1/953 people

### Education

*Adult Literacy Rate:* 76.9%

*Compulsory (Ages):* 6–12

## COMMUNICATION

*Telephones:* 3.633 million main lines

*Daily Newspaper Circulation:* 19 per 1,000 people

*Televisions:* 49 per 1,000 people

*Internet Users:* 3.565 million (2008)

## TRANSPORTATION

*Highways in Miles (Kilometers):* 25,741 (41,451)

*Railroads in Miles (Kilometers):* 1,650 (2,750)

*Usable Airfields:* 100

*Motor Vehicles in Use:* 353,000

## GOVERNMENT

*Type:* republic but essentially an authoritarian state ruled by the Alawite minority since 1963, first under President Hafez al-Assad and currently by his son and successor

*Independence Date:* April 17, 1946 (from a League of Nations mandate under French administration)

*Head of State/Government:* President Bashar al-Assad; Prime Minister Muhammad al-Utri

*Political Parties:* in 2003 the former single-party Ba'th (Syrian branch) formed the National Progressive Front (NPF), an umbrella political organization which includes the Syrian Arab Socialist Union (SASU), the Socialist Unionist Democratic Party, the Syrian Communist Party (2 branches) and the Syrian Socialist Nationalist Party (SSNP). There are several unrecognized parties which operate outside the system, one of which represents the Kurdish minority

*Suffrage:* universal at 18

## MILITARY

*Military Expenditures (% of GDP):* 5.9%

*Current Disputes:* Syria contests Israel's annexation of the Golan Heights and Jewish settlements there, but has taken no aggressive action since the 1973 war. A longtime border dispute with Jordan was settled recently and awaits formal demarcation

## ECONOMY

*Currency ($U.S. Equivalent):* 51.7 Syrian pounds = $1

*Per Capita Income/GDP:* $4,600/ $54.99 billion

*GDP Growth Rate:* 1.8%

*Inflation Rate:* 3.8%

*Labor Force:* 5.772 million

*Natural Resources:* petroleum; phosphates; chrome and manganese ores; asphalt; iron ore; rock salt; marble; gypsum; hydropower

*Agriculture:* wheat; barley; cotton; lentils; chickpeas; olives; sugar beets; beef; mutton; eggs; poultry; milk

*Industry:* petroleum; textiles; food processing; beverages; tobacco; phosphate-rock mining

*Exports:* $6.9 billion (primary partners Iraq, Italy, Germany)

*Imports:* $6.6 Billion (primary partners Saudi Arabia, China, Egypt)

## SUGGESTED WEB SITE

http://lcweb2.loc.gov/frd/cs/sytoc.html

# Syria Country Report

The modern Syrian state is a pale shadow of ancient Syria, which at various times in its history was a great kingdom, incorporating the lands of present-day Lebanon, Israel, Iraq, Jordan, and a part of Turkey within its boundaries. Ancient Syria was also a part of the great civilization centered in Mesopotamia. Recent discovery by archaeologists of a 6,000-year-old city at Hamonkar, in northeastern Syria near the Iraqi and Turkish borders, has pushed back the start of urban design to centuries earlier than that of the Sumerians.

Syrian kings figure prominently in the Old Testament as rivals to those of Israel and Judah. One of these kings, Antiochus, divided the empire of Alexander the Great. Antiochus's kingdom dominated the Near East prior to the establishment of the Roman empire, with Syria as its center.

Syria also figured prominently in the expansion of Islam. After the death of Prophet Muhammad, his successors, called *caliphs,* expanded Islamic rule over a territory greater than Rome. They moved their capital from Mecca to Damascus. The Umayyad Caliphate spread the Arabic language and Islamic culture from Morocco to the western border of India. Due to its centrality, Arab geographers and cartographers termed Syria *Bilad ash-Sham* (land of the rising, or Levant in French), whence the sun rose over the lands of Islam.

Modern Syria is a country with artificial borders determined by agreement between France and Britain after World War I. The country's current boundaries are with Turkey, Iraq, Jordan, Israel, and Lebanon. (The only one of these boundaries in dispute is the Golan Heights, which was seized and annexed by Israel in the 1970s.) The border with Turkey is defined by a single-track railroad, perhaps the only case in the world of a railroad put to that use. Syria's other borders are artificial lines established by outside powers for their own convenience.

Syria's political system was established by outside powers. Since becoming independent in 1946, the Syrians have struggled to find a political system that works for them. Syrian political instability stems from the division of the population into separate ethnic and religious groups. The Syrians are an amalgamation of many different ethnoreligious groups that have settled in the region over the centuries. The majority of the population are Sunni Muslim Arabs. The Alawis form the largest minority group. Although the Alawis are Muslims, the Sunni Muslims distrust them—not because of religion, but because of the secret nature of their rituals and because, as a minority they are very clannish. The next-largest minority are the Druze who also live in Israel and Lebanon in great numbers. They are nominally Muslims, but their (secret) rituals include Christian liturgical elements such as the Eucharist.

(Damascus Online/Ayman Haykal (DAMA001))

Dome of the Eagle (Qubbat Al-Nisr) is considered one of the architectural highlights of the Omayad Mosque in Damascus.

During the Umayyad rule, Damascus became a great center of learning and culture. The Caliph Abd al-Malik built the great Umayyad Mosque on the site of a Byzantine church which overlays a Roman temple and below it an Aramean shrine, testaments to the incredible age of the world's oldest city in continuous use, which Mark Twain called a type of immortality and the Prophet Muhammad (PBUH) refused to enter, saying that man should only enter Paradise once.

## FREEDOM

The 1973 constitution defines Syria as a socialist, popular democracy with press freedom and other civil rights. The late President Hafez al-Assad disregarded most of these rights and ruled by martial law. His successor briefly restored press freedom and allowed political parties to form, although the Ba'th remained dominant. Unfortunately the withdrawal of Syrian forces from Lebanon and other factors prompted a reversal. In 2007 a number of prominent advocates of political reform were arrested and given long prison terms. Some were released later, but the absence of genuine political opening leaves the risk of political arrests constant.

The Syrian Druze community was divided when Israel occupied the Golan Heights, where the majority lived. Since then, Druze families have had to resort to megaphone communication across the artificial border, which is monitored by UN peacekeepers but with access essentially controlled by Israel. Under Israeli rules students and clerics may do so, but Druze wives, although they consider themselves Syrian citizens, may not. Over the decades of Israeli occupation and annexation only a handful of these wives have been able to visit their families on the Syrian side.

The largest non-Arab minority is the Kurds, some 1.7 million, forming 9 percent of the population. They are Sunni Muslims, forming part of the large Kurdish population spread over mountainous areas in eastern Turkey, northern Iraq and Iran. In 1962 some 120,000 Kurds were stripped of citizenship by the Syrian government, allegedly for advocating an independent Kurdish state. In 2005, President Bashar al-Assad, faced with a political crisis due to Syria's alleged involvement in the murder of Lebanon's ex-Prime Minister Rafik Hariri and the resulting international fallout, agreed formally to restore citizenship to the Syrian Kurds in the near future. (Currently some 300,000 Kurds are classified as "foreigners" and carry red ID cards in lieu of passports.)

Syria also has small but long-established Christian and Jewish communities. The Alawi regime, itself a minority (15 percent) of the population, allows them full exercise of their religious rights and services. Some Christian communities still use the ancient Aramaic language in their liturgy, an example being the village of Qamishli, near the Turkish border.

Although Syrian cities are slowly becoming more homogeneous in population, the different communities still constitute a majority in certain areas. Thus, Alawis make up 60 percent of the population of the northern coast. The Druze predominate in Jabal Druze, near the Lebanese border, and in that part of the Golan Heights still under Syrian control. Kurds are found mostly north of Aleppo and eastward toward the Turkish border.

## HISTORY

Syria's greatest period was probably that of the Umayyad caliphs (A.D. 661–750). These caliphs were rulers of a vast Islamic empire. The first Umayyad caliph, Mu'awiya, is considered one of the political geniuses of Islam. He described his political philosophy to a visitor as follows:

I apply not my lash where my tongue suffices, nor my sword where my whip is enough. If there be one hair binding me to my fellow men I let it not break. If they pull I loosen; if they loosen I pull.[1]

The Umayyads were overthrown in 750 A.D. by a rival group with Persian backing, and the caliphate capital was moved from Damascus to Baghdad. From then on until Syria became an independent republic in the 20th century, its destiny was controlled by outside forces.

After the Ottoman Turks had established their empire and expanded their rule to the Arab lands of the Middle East, Syria became an Ottoman province governed by a pasha. His main responsibilities were to keep order and collect taxes, with a specified amount remitted to the Sultan's government in Constantinople. The balance was his to keep as compensation for his unpaid appointment. Of the three historically important cities of Ottoman Syria—Aleppo, Palmyra, and Damascus—the third gave its name to the province. The term "Syria" did not come into use until after World War I when it was adopted by France for its League of Nations mandate.

Syria was ruled by the Ottoman Turks for four centuries as a part of their empire. It was divided into provinces, each governed by a pasha. In mountain areas such as Lebanon, then part of Syria, the Ottomans delegated authority to the heads of powerful families or leaders of religious

168

communities. They recognized each of these confessional communities as a *millet,* a Turkish word meaning "nation." The religious head of each millet represented the millet in dealings with Ottoman officials and was allowed to manage the community's internal affairs. The result was that Syrian society became a series of sealed compartments. The millet system has disappeared, but its effects have lingered to the present.

### The French Mandate

In the nineteenth century, as Ottoman rule weakened and conflict developed among Muslim, Christian, and Druze communities in Syria, the French began to intervene directly in Syria. French Jesuits founded schools for Christian children. In 1860, French troops intervened to protect the Christian Maronites from massacres by the Druze. The French forces were withdrawn after the Ottoman government agreed to establish a separate Maronite region in the Lebanese mountains. This arrangement brought about the development of Lebanon as separate from Syria. The Christians in Syria were less fortunate. About 6,000 of them were slaughtered in Damascus before Ottoman troops restored order.[2] Many were saved by the intervention of the Algerian exile Emir Abd al-Qadir and his soldiers.

In the years immediately preceding World War I, numbers of young Syrian Christians and some Muslims were exposed through mission schools to ideas of nationalism and human rights. A movement for Arab independence from Turkish rule gradually developed, centered in Damascus and Beirut. After the start of World War I, the British convinced Arab leaders to revolt against the Ottoman government. The Arab army recruited for the revolt was led by Emir Faisal, the second son of Sharif Husayn of Mecca, leader of the powerful Arab Hashimite family, and the Arab official appointed by the Ottomans as "Protector of the Holy Shrines of Islam." Faisal's forces, along with a British army, drove the Ottomans out of Syria. In 1918, the emir entered Damascus as a conquering hero, and in 1920 was proclaimed king of Syria.

Faisal's kingdom did not last long. The British had promised the Arabs independence in a state of their own, in return for their revolt. However, they had also made secret agreements with France to divide the Arab regions of the defeated Ottoman Empire into French and British protectorates. The French would govern Syria and Lebanon; the British would administer Palestine and Iraq. The French sent an ultimatum to Faisal to accept French rule. When

he refused, a French army marched to Damascus, bombarded the city, and forced him into exile. (Faisal was later made king of Iraq under a British protectorate.)

What one author calls the "false dawn" of Arab independence was followed by the establishment of direct French control over Syria.[3] The Syrians reacted angrily to what they considered betrayal by their former allies. Resistance to French rule continued throughout the mandate period (1920–1946), and the legacy of bitterness over their betrayal affects Syrian attitudes toward outside powers, particularly Western powers, to this day.

During the French colonization, which attempted, without success, to divide the country into small religious and ethnic entities, the Syrians remained strongly attached to Arab unity and Arab independence, first in Syria, then in a future Arab state.[4]

## INDEPENDENT SYRIA

Syria became independent in 1946. Pressure from the Syrian nationalists, the United States, the Soviet Union, and Britain forced the French to leave both Syria and Lebanon.

The new republic began under adverse circumstances. Syrian leaders had little experience in government; the French had not given them much responsibility and had encouraged personal rivalries with their divide-and-rule policy. The Druze and Alawi communities feared that they would be under the thumb of the Sunni majority. In addition, the establishment in 1948 of the State of Israel next door caused great instability in Syria. The failure of Syrian armies to defeat the Israelis was blamed on weak and incompetent leaders.

For two decades after independence, Syria had the reputation of being the most unstable country in the Middle East. There were four military coups between 1949 and 1954 and several more between 1961 and 1966. There was also a brief union with Egypt (1958–1961) which ended in an army revolt.

One reason for Syria's chronic instability was that political parties were simply groups formed around individuals. At independence, the country had many such parties. In 1963, one party, the Ba'th, acquired control of all political activities. Since then, Syria has been a single-party state.

## THE BA'TH PARTY

The Ba'th Party (the Arabic word *ba'th* means "resurrection, renaissance, or rebirth") began in the 1940s as a political party dedicated to Arab unity. It was founded by two

(Library of Congress (3b03523u))
In 1920, following the successful expulsion of the Ottoman government from Syria in 1918, Emir Faisal was named king of Syria.

Damascus schoolteachers, both French-educated: Michel Aflaq, a Greek Orthodox Christian, and Salah Bitar, a Sunni Muslim. In 1953, the Ba'th merged with another political party, the Arab Socialist Party. Since then, the formal name of the Ba'th has been the Arab Socialist Resurrection Party.

The Ba'th was the first Syrian political party to establish a mass popular base and to draw members from all social classes. Its program called for freedom, Arab unity, and socialism. The movement for Arab unity led to the establishment of the branches of the party in other Arab countries, notably Iraq and Lebanon. The party appealed particularly to young officers in the armed forces and attracted strong support from the Alawi community, because it called for social justice and the equality of all Syrians.

The Ba'th was instrumental in 1958 in arranging a merger between Syria and Egypt as the United Arab Republic (U.A.R.). The Ba'thists had hoped to undercut their chief rival, the Syrian Communist Party, by the merger. But they soon decided that they had made a mistake. The Egyptians did not treat the Syrians as equals but as junior partners. Syrian officers seized control and expelled the Egyptian advisers. The U.A.R ended in 1961.

For the next decade, power shifted back and forth among military and civilian factions of the Ba'th Party. The process had little effect on the average Syrian, who liked to talk about politics but was wary, with good reason, of any involvement. Gradually, the military faction gained preeminence and, in 1970, Lieutenant General Hafez al-Assad, the defense minister of one of the country's innumerable previous governments, seized power in a bloodless coup.[5]

## HAFEZ AL-ASSAD

Syria is formally a presidential republic, in the sense that the head of state has extensive powers, which are confirmed in the Constitution approved in 1973. He decides and executes policies, appoints all government officials, and commands the armed forces. He is also head of the Ba'th Party. Under the Constitution, he has unlimited emergency powers "in case of grave danger threatening national unity or the security . . . of the national territory" (Article 113), which only the president can determine.

Hafez al-Assad ruled Syria for nearly three decades, becoming in the process the longest-serving elected leader of any Arab state. He was first elected in 1971 (as the only candidate), and thereafter for five consecutive seven-year terms, the last in 1999. Over the years he broadened the political process to some extent, establishing a People's Assembly with several small parties as a token opposition in the Legislature. In 1990, elections were held for an enlarged, 250-member Assembly. Ba'th members won 134 seats to 32 for the opposition; the remainder were won by independents. Assad then approved the formation of a National Progressive Front, which included the independents. However, mindful of Syria's long history of political instability in the years before he took office, he decreed that its only function would be approval of laws issued by the Ba'th Central Committee.

### Syria's Role in Lebanon

Assad's position was strengthened domestically in the 1970s due to his success (or perceived success) in certain foreign-policy actions. The Syrian Army fought well against Israel in the October 1973 War, and Syria subsequently received both military and financial aid from the Soviet Union as well as Arab states. The invitation by the Arab League for Syria to intervene in Lebanon, beginning with the 1975–1976 Lebanese Civil War, was widely popular among Syrians. They never fully accepted the French action of separating Lebanon from Syria during the mandate period, and they continue to maintain a proprietary attitude toward Lebanon. Assad's determination to avoid conflict with Israel led him

in past years to keep a tight rein on Syrian-based Palestine Liberation Organization (PLO) operations. The al-Saiqa Palestinian Brigade was integrated into the Syrian Army, for example. However, Assad's agreement to join a Middle East conference with other Arab states and Israel in 1991 resulted in the release of all PLO activists held in detention in Syria.

When the Lebanese Civil War broke out in 1975, Assad pledged that he would control the Palestinians in Lebanon. He sent about 2,000 al-Saiqa guerrillas to Beirut in early 1976. A peacekeeping force approved by the Arab League for Lebanon included 30,000 regular Syrian troops. For all practical purposes, this force maintained a balance of power among Lebanese factions until the Israeli invasion of June 1982. It then withdrew to the eastern Biqa' Valley, avoiding conflict with Israeli forces and providing sanctuary to Palestinian guerrillas escaping from Beirut.

Syria made a number of attempts to broker a peace agreement among the various Lebanese factions. However, all of them failed, owing in large measure to the intractable hostility separating Muslim from Christian communities and intercommunal rivalries among the militias. In 1987, faced with a near-total breakdown in public security, Assad ordered 7,000 elite Syrian commandos into West Beirut. Syrian forces maintained an uneasy peace in the Lebanese capital until 1989, when they were challenged directly by the Christian militia of General Michel Aoun, who refused to accept Syrian authority and declared himself president. Syrian forces surrounded the Christian enclave and, early in 1990, mounted a massive assault, backed by heavy artillery, that finally broke the Christian resistance. Aoun took refuge in the French Embassy and then went into exile.

Syrian troops in Lebanon were reduced in stages after the end of the Lebanese civil war. However the assassination of Lebanon's former Prime Minister, Rafik Hariri, in February 2005 and the alleged involvement of Syrian intelligence agents

and government officials in the murder triggered massive demonstrations in Lebanon demanding the withdrawal of the remaining Syrian troops. Essentially peaceful demonstrations, the "Cedars of Lebanon" movement which developed led to UN Security Council *Resolution 1559*, requiring troop withdrawal and an international investigation. While the Syrian government denied any involvement and questioned the reliability of witnesses appearing before the investigating committee, it withdrew its remaining troops and closed the offices of the much-feared Syrian intelligence service (the *mukhabarat*) which had ruled Lebanon for more than 20 years.

### Internal Opposition

Opposition to the Hafez al-Assad regime was almost nonexistent in the 1990s. A major cause for resentment among rank-and-file Syrians, however, was—and still is—the dominance of the Alawi minority over the government, armed forces, police, and intelligence services. The main opposition group was the Syrian branch of the Muslim Brotherhood (a Sunni organization spread throughout the Arab world). The Brotherhood opposed Assad because of his practice of advancing Alawi interests over those of the Sunni majority. Its main stronghold was the ancient city of Hama, famed for its Roman waterwheels. In 1982, Assad's regular army moved against Hama after an ambush of government officials there. The city was almost obliterated by tanks and artillery fire, with between 7,000 to 30,000 casualties, according to various reports. Large areas were bulldozed as a warning to other potentially disloyal elements in the population.

The "lessons of Hama" have not been forgotten. The calculated violence of the attack was meant not only to inflict punishment but to provide a warning for future challengers. It did have a positive result. In ensuring the survival of his regime, Assad guaranteed political stability, along with prosperity for the largely Sunni merchant class.

Assad's control over the various levers of power, notably the intelligence services, the security police, and the military, ensured his rule during his lifetime, despite his narrow support base as head of a minority group. After Hama, no organized opposition group challenged his authority. As a result, he was able to give Syria the political stability that his predecessors had never provided.

Hafez al-Assad died on June 10, 2000 and his younger son, Bashar, was elected to succeed him on June 25 by the People's Assembly, confirmed by 97.5 percent of voters in a nationwide referendum. The Syrian Constitution, which precludes anyone under age 40 from serving as president, was conveniently amended by lowering the minimum age to 34 years.

Syria's new leader was trained as an opthalmologist in Britain and had little experience in national politics before being summoned back to replace his elder brother Basil (killed in an auto accident in 1994) as the heir-apparent. His only public post was that of commander of the Republican Guard. After his election to the presidency (he was the only candidate, like his father), Bashar became head of the armed forces and of the Ba'th Regional Command.

Bashar brought fresh air into a moribund political system and a stagnant economy. He began by enforcing the rule requiring retirement at age 60, which is mandatory for the military but had never been adhered to. As a result, many senior commanders were forced to retire. They included Hafez al-Assad's long-serving chief of staff and the head of the mukhabarat. In March 2002, the entire cabinet resigned, as the president continued to turn to new faces to strengthen political support and help liberalize the economy. Bashar also changed the composition of the Ba'th Regional Command, bringing in younger army commanders as well as some women. In other essentially cosmetic changes, private universities were established to supplement, and revitalize, the ailing state system, and in 2002 private banks were allowed to form. By mid-2003 six such banks were in operation. According to regulations, they must be capitalized at $25.5 million with no more than 49 percent foreign ownership.

In March 2003, elections were held for a new Peoples' Assembly (Parliament). The National Progressive Front, a 7-party coalition dominated by the Ba'th, won 167 seats to 83 for independent (non-party) candidates. Almost the same configuration resulted from the 2007 parliamentary elections which were followed by the almost automatic renewal of President Assad's seven-year term.

A new law proposed in February 2006 would allow political parties to form outside the Ba'th. The government also announced it would restore Syrian citizenship to its Kurdish minority. And in January 2006 five prominent opposition political prisoners were released, including Riad Seif and Mahmoud al-Homsi, former legislators who had been stripped of their parliamentary immunity due to their public demands for political reform and an end to government corruption. These actions were in large measure Bashar's response to an opposition statement, "the Damascus Declaration" issued in October 2005. It was described as a "blueprint" for reforming the political process. Its backers included a broad range of normally fractious groups, such as Communists, Kurdish nationalists, exiles and the London-based Muslim Brotherhood. The Declaration came after the brief "Damascus Spring of 2001–2002," when "salons" were allowed to form for meetings and political discussion in members' homes. However, the salons were ordered closed and human rights activists arrested in a government crackdown in 2002. As a prominent Syrian intellectual noted, "Suddenly people are not sure where the red lines on freedom of speech are any more."[6]

Syrian popular support for the aging president grew in the 1990s, as he continued to resist accommodation with Israel, while other Arab states were establishing relations or even recognizing Israel as Jordan did. This broader support enabled Assad to loosen the reins of government. At the start of his fourth term he included several Sunni ministers in his cabinet. Political prisoners were released, most of them Muslim Brotherhood members. In 1999, he ordered a general amnesty for 150,000 prisoners, most of whom had been jailed for smuggling, desertion from the armed forces, or economic crimes.

## THE ECONOMY

At independence, Syria was primarily an agricultural country, although it had a large merchant class and a free-enterprise system with considerable small-scale industrial development. When it came to power, the Ba'th Party was committed to state control of the economy. Agriculture was collectivized, with land expropriated from large landowners and converted into state-managed farms. Most industries were nationalized in the 1960s. The free-enterprise system all but disappeared.

Cotton was Syria's principal export crop and money earner until the mid-1970s. But with the development of oil fields, petroleum became the main export. Syria produced enough oil for its own needs until 1980. However, the changing global oil market and the reluctance of foreign companies to invest in Syrian oil exploration under the unfavorable concession terms set by the government have hampered development. Oil production, formerly 580,000 barrels per day, fell to 340,000 bpd in the mid-1990s. It increased to 450,000 bpd in 2000 and 550,000 bpd in 2001, due largely to imports of Iraqi oil for further export through the Kirkuk-Banias pipeline. However, due to the invasion of Iraq in 2003, oil production fell again, reaching 375,000 in 2009.

Unrest among the Kurdish population, in whose territory the oil fields are located, has deterred the search for new oil resources. Lacking new discoveries and major foreign investment, the industry may decline in the coming years.

Agriculture, which in 2009 accounted for 17.7 percent of gross domestic product and employed 17 percent of the labor force, benefited in the early 1990s from expanded irrigation, which brought additional acreage under cultivation. Production of cotton, the major agricultural crop, reached a record 1.1 million tons in 2000, with 270,000 tons exported. However, production fell to an estimated 700,000 in 2009.

The end of Syria's special relationship with the Soviet Union due to the breakup of that country in 1991 encouraged a modest liberalization of the economic system. A prominent exiled businessman who had been one of Assad's biggest critics returned in 1993 to set up a retail store chain similar to London's Marks & Spencer, taking advantage of new tax exemptions and other incentives. However economic growth in the early 1990s was hampered by a recession at the end of the decade. It was compounded by population growth at an explosive 3.4 percent rate, foreign debts of $10–13 billion (mostly to the former Soviet Union) and an unfortunate mixture of too many government workers and landless peasants in the labor force. The unemployment level at that time was 30 percent. The association agreement with the European Union negotiated in 2004 has encouraged the regime to liberalize the foreign investment laws and simplify tax regulations.

Bashar al-Assad's accession to the presidency has been most successful in economic change. Unfortunately this has not been matched by a broadening of the political system toward more representative government. But in December 2000 private banks were allowed to open, ending 40 years of state control over banking and foreign exchange. Tariffs and other restrictions on foreign investment were ended and foreign exchange bureaux legalized. Foreigners were allowed to buy and own property, and as a result grand hotels, residential subdivisions and even malls have become a common feature in Damascus and other cities.

As the economy started to pick up slightly, the unemployment started to decline. In 2008 it was 10.9 percent and in 2009 8.5 percent, in spite of a slow down of growth (1.8 percent only) due to the global economic crisis and its effect on oil prices and foreign investment. Bashar's economic reforms included lowering lending interest rates, opening private banks, cutting down subsidies on some items (e.g., gasoline and cement), and creating the Damascus Stock Exchange. However, in spite of these liberalization steps, the state still controls the economy and the investment environment remains constrained. The World Bank's Ease of Doing Business ranks Syria 143rd in 2010 out of 183 countries, up from 138th in 2009. In the Middle East and North Africa region, it ranked 17th, with only Iraq and Djibouti doing worse. The 2009–2010 report of the Global Competitiveness Index (GCI) published by the World Economic Forum, ranked Syria 94th out of 130 countries (it declined by 16 ranks since 2008).[7] Given that Syria's oil income and production are substantially affected by external factors and by dwindling reserves, and given that its agricultural sector is directly affected by climatic conditions and recurring drought, economic recovery and growth may have to rely on serious and sustained reforms and on improving the overall private investment environment.

## FOREIGN RELATIONS

Syria's often prickly relations with its neighbors and its opposition to Israel have made the country the "odd man out" in the region at various times. Syria's hostility to the rival Ba'thist regime in Iraq resulted in periodic border closings and a shutdown in shipments of Iraqi oil through Syrian pipelines to refineries on the Mediterranean coast in the 1980s. The border was closed definitively after Syria sided with Iran during its war with Iraq and remained so in the Gulf War, as Syrian troops formed part of the coalition that drove Iraqi forces out of Kuwait. The UN sanctions on Iraq brought the two Arab neighbors closer together. The border was reopened in 1997, and the new president removed all restrictions on travel to Iraq in 2001. In February, the two countries signed a free-trade agreement and, in August, Syrian prime minister Muhammed Moru made the first official visit to Baghdad of any Syrian government leader since 1979.

Syria's role as an alleged major sponsor of international terrorism has adversely affected its relations with Western countries for years. In 1986, a number of these countries broke diplomatic relations after the British discovered a Syrian-funded plot to blow up an Israeli airliner at Heathrow Airport in London, England. Syria sent troops to support the U.S.-led Coalition in the Gulf War, despite its close economic relationship with Iraq. Following the September 11, 2001 attacks on the United States by al Qaeda terrorists, Syria provided intelligence information on its network. However, Syria's continued support of anti-Israeli organizations such as Hamas and Hezbollah have tarnished its image abroad, notably in the United States. After the U.S. invasion and occupation of Iraq, Bush administration policymakers charged that its open border with that country enabled weapons and terrorists to enter and thus delay the reconstruction of Iraq. In December 2003 Congress passed the Syria Accountability Act which bans exports of dual-use items (those which have both civilian and military applications). In March 2004 Bush ordered the imposition of economic sanctions in implementation of the act.

Syria's inclusion on the Department of State list as a state supporter of terrorism had been based on the harboring of groups engaged in violence, usually against Israel but also against Yassir Arafat's Palestinian organization. The groups included Hamas, the Popular Front for the Liberation of Palestine (PFLP), and Islamic Jihad. However, the Assad government was careful not to allow them to launch anti-Israeli operations from Syrian territory. The September 11, 2001, terrorist attacks on the United States brought a change in the equation. President Bashar denounced the terrorist attacks and criticized Osama bin Laden and his al Qaeda network for giving Islam a bad name. However, he declared that the Palestinian-Israeli conflict ultimately bore responsibility for the terrorism.

The 1993 Oslo agreements between Israel and the Palestinians and the 1994 Jordan-Israel peace treaty encouraged Assad to begin serious discussions with the Israelis for a settlement of the Golan Heights issue. Talks began with the Rabin government, but were broken off after the election of Benjamin Netanyahu as Israel's prime minister. His defeat in the 1999 elections made possible the revival of negotiations, inasmuch as incoming prime minister Ehud Barak had stressed settlement of the Golan as part of his 15-month plan for regional peace.

Syrian and Israeli representatives met in January 2000 in the resort town of Shepherdstown, West Virginia, with then-president Bill Clinton serving as moderator. Their talks ended inconclusively, as the Syrian and Israeli positions remained far apart on such issues as the Golan Heights. However, the death of Hafez al-Assad made the pursuit of a peace treaty with Israel less urgent for the new Syrian president. Its priorities of necessity have concentrated on internal reform and revitalization of the economy. Furthermore, the prospects for peace negotiations were set back in September 2007 when Israel carried out an aerial strike against a military site in northern Syria suspected of housing a nuclear reactor that was not yet operational.

## PROSPECTS

By the summer of 2010, Syria seemed to be slowly coming out of the isolation it suffered due to the assassination of former Lebanese prime minister Hariri. The fallout from the assassination and the resulting UN investigation into Syria's involvement placed Bashar in an awkward position. In October 2005 the chief UN prosecutor, Detlev Mehlis, named the president's brother Maher and his brother-in-law, Asef Shawkat, who are respectively head of the presidential guard and the chief of intelligence, as prime suspects. Four Lebanese security agents formerly on the Syrian payroll were arrested, and Syria was given 6 months to surrender these officials for questioning. Failure to do so would result in punitive sanctions. As if on cue, Syrian Interior Minister Gen. Ghazi Kenaan, former head of military intelligence in Lebanon, committed suicide following publication of the investigative report.

Whether these developments will have a long term effect on Syria's relations with Lebanon and on its own internal dynamics remains an open question. Bashar's deft balancing act in the U.S-Iraq imbroglio and other regional crises suggests the opposite. Syria's potential role in stabilizing Iraq was underscored in May 2007, when a

U.S. Congress delegation headed by House Speaker Nancy Pelosi visited the country for direct talks with Assad. In the same month, U.S. Secretary of State Condoleezza Rice met Syria's foreign minister Walid Muallem, the first contact at this level between the two countries in two years. This was followed in March 2009 by the first high-level U.S. diplomatic mission to Syria for nearly four years and in February 2010, the United States appointed an ambassador to Syria after a five-year break. In July 2008, President Bashar was welcomed by French President Nicolas Sarkozy in Paris, signaling the end of the diplomatic isolation of Syria by the West after the Hariri assassination three years earlier.

Possibly as a result of these developments, Syria closed its border with Iraq in October. Under new Syrian rules, Iraqis wishing to take refuge there must apply for visas at the Syrian embassy in Baghdad. In spite of these overtures, the overall normalization of relations with the West has been very slow, notably due to the regional issues and conflicts which affect Syria's relations with the concerned parties. In fact, in May 2010, the Obama administration decided to renew the economic sanctions imposed on Syria by the Bush administration in 2004. The reasons invoked by President Obama include Syria's pursuit of weapons of mass destruction and missile programs; arming of Hezbollah with Scud missiles; and undermining U.S. stabilization and reconstruction efforts in Iraq.

Syria, like all states of the region, has been trying to find the right balance between assuring its security in an unstable region marred by foreign intervention, while at the same time taking meaningful steps to reassure the outside world and bring hope of relative change to the domestic forces seeking political and economic progress.

A 2007 Assad speech was marked by a new Syrian confidence about its role in regional affairs. He said that "in the east we see the resistant Iraq, in the west the resistant Lebanon, in the south the resistant Palestinian people. We in Syria are not in the middle but the heart of the resistance."[8]

To counterbalance its difficult relations with the Western powers, Syria has recently started developing and nurturing relations with Iran, which also finds itself in an almost similar situation, and a rising regional player, Turkey, which has been developing substantial economic ties with Syria and other regional states, and has been at the forefront on critical issues, such as the Palestinian question and the Iran-West show-down on the nuclear weapons' program. Because Turkey is a member of NATO and a potential economic bridge to Europe, Syria hopes to gain from this newly formed relationship.[9]

## NOTES

1. The statement is found in many chronicles of the Umayyads. See Richard Nyrop, ed., Syria, A Country Study (Washington, D.C.: American University, Foreign Area Studies, 1978), p. 13.

2. Philip Khoury, *Urban Notables and Arab Nationalism: The Politics of Damascus 1860–1920* (Cambridge, England: Cambridge University Press, 1983), pp. 8–9.

3. Umar F. Abd-Allah, *The Islamic Struggle in Syria* (Berkeley, CA: Mizan Press, 1983), p. 39.

4. According to John F. Devlin, the "Syrians had long seen themselves as Arabs . . . who considered the Arab world as rightly a single entity." John F. Devlin, *Syria: Modern State in an Ancient Land* (Boulder, CO: Westview Press, 1983), p. 44.

5. He was barred from attending a cabinet meeting and then surrounded the meeting site with army units, dismissed the government, and formed his own. Devlin, Syria: Modern State in an Ancient Land, Op. Cit., p. 56.

6. Helena Cobban, "Waiting For War In Damascus: Syria Has Been Opening Up. A War Will Shut It Down," *Boston Review,* February/March 2003. Online at www .bostonreview.net/BR28.1/cobban.html. Consulted on July 11, 2010.

7. Syria's detailed report of the World Bank's Doing Business 2010 can be found at www .doingbusiness.org. The Global Competitiveness Index rating can be found at www .weforum.org/en/initiatives/gcp/Global% 20Competitiveness%20Report/index.htm. Consulted on July 11, 2010.

8. Quoted by Hugh Naylor, "Syrians vote for a sense of security," *Christian Science Monitor,* May 29, 2007. Consulted on July 12, 2010.

9. For more on this, see Stephen Starr, "Syria's New Best Friend," Blog Post on Le Monde Diplomatique, June 14, 2010. Online at http://mondediplo.com/blogs/ syria-s-new-best-friend. Consulted on July 12, 2010.

# Tunisia (Republic of Tunisia)

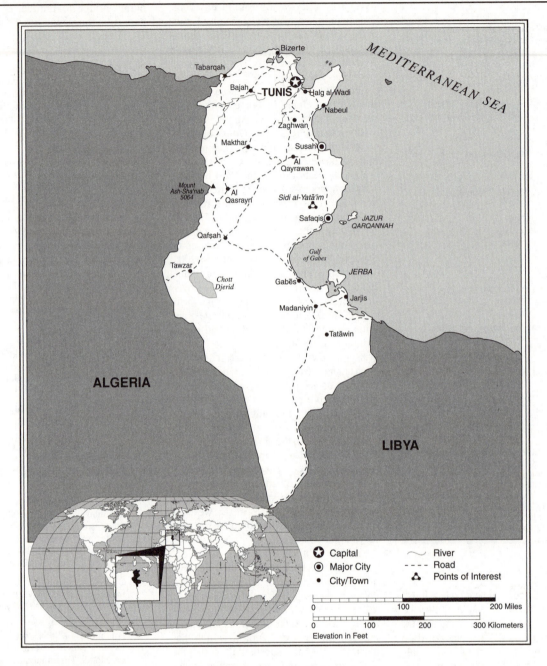

# Tunisia Statistics

## GEOGRAPHY

*Area in Square Miles (Kilometers):*
63,153 (163,610) (about the size of Georgia)

*Capital (Population):* Tunis (1,200,000)

*Environmental Concerns:* hazardous-waste disposal; water pollution; limited fresh water resources; deforestation; overgrazing; soil erosion; desertification

*Geographical Features:* mountains in north; hot, dry central plain; semiarid south merges into Sahara

*Climate:* hot, dry summers; mild, rainy winters; desert in the south; temperate in the north

## PEOPLE

### Population

*Total:* 10,486,339

*Annual Growth Rate:* 0.98%

*Rural/Urban Population Ratio:* 33/67

*Major Languages:* Arabic; French

*Ethnic Makeup:* 98% Arab-Berber; 1% European; 1% others

*Religions:* 98% Muslim; 1% Christian; less than 1% Jewish

### Health

*Life Expectancy at Birth:* 73.98 years (male); 77.8 years (female)

*Infant Mortality Rate:* 22.57/1,000 live births

**Education**

*Adult Literacy Rate:* 74.3%
*Compulsory (Ages):* 6–16

## COMMUNICATION

*Telephones:* 1,313,000 main lines
*Daily Newspaper Circulation:* 45 per 1,000 people
*Televisions:* 156 per 1,000 people
*Internet Service Provider:* 1 (2000)

## TRANSPORTATION

*Highways in Miles (Kilometers):* 14,345 (23,100)
*Railroads in Miles (Kilometers):* 1,403 (2,260)
*Usable Airfields:* 32
*Motor Vehicles in Use:* 806,493

## GOVERNMENT

*Type:* republic

*Independence Date:* March 20, 1956 (from France)
*Head of State/Government:* President Zine El Abidine Ben Ali; Prime Minister Mohammed Ghannouchi
*Political Parties:* Constitutional Democratic Rally (RCD), official ruling party, other approved parties include Green Party for Progress (PVP), Liberal Socialist Party (PSL), Movement for Democratic Socialism (MDS), Progressive Democratic Party. An-Nahda (Renaissance), an Islamist party, remains outlawed
*Suffrage:* universal at 18

## MILITARY

*Military Expenditures (% of GDP):* 1.5%
*Current Disputes:* none

## ECONOMY

*Currency ($U.S. Equivalent):* 1.211 dinars = $1

*Per Capita Income/GDP:* $7,900/ $81.71 billion
*GDP Growth Rate:* 4.4%
*Inflation Rate:* 4.6%
*Unemployment Rate:* 14.1%
*Labor Force:* 3,660,000
*Natural Resources:* petroleum; phosphates; iron ore; lead; zinc; salt
*Agriculture:* olives; dates; oranges; almonds; grain; sugar beets; grapes; poultry; beef; dairy products
*Industry:* petroleum; mining; tourism; textiles; footwear; food; beverages
*Exports:* $19.22 billion (primary partners Germany, France, Italy)
*Imports:* $23.23 billion (primary partners France, Germany, Italy)

## SUGGESTED WEB SITES

www.cia.gov/cia/ publications/factbook/ index.html
www.tunisiaonline.com

# Tunisia Country Report

Tunisia, the smallest of the North African countries, is less than one tenth the size of Libya, its neighbor to the east. However, its population is nearly twice the size of Libya's.

Tunisia's long coastline has exposed it over the centuries to a succession of invaders from the sea. The southern third of the country is part of the Sahara Desert; the central third consists of high, arid plains. Only the northern region has sufficient rainfall for agriculture. This region contains Tunisia's single permanent river, the Medjerda.

**DEVELOPMENT**

Associate membership in the European Union has resulted in a number of advantages to Tunisia. One important one is favorable terms for its agricultural exports. Privatization of some 140 state-owned industries, a liberal investment code and tax reform have made possible a GDP growth rate averaging 4.5 to 5 percent annually.

The country is predominantly urban. There is almost no nomadic population, and there are no high mountains to provide refuge for independent mountain peoples opposed to central government. The Tunis region and the Sahel, a coastal plain important in olive production, are the most densely populated areas. Tunis, the capital, is not only the dominant city but also the hub of government, economic, and political activity.

## HISTORY

Tunisia has an ancient history that is urban rather than territorial. Phoenician merchants from what is today Lebanon founded a number of trading posts several thousand years ago. The most important one was Carthage, founded in 814 B.C. It grew wealthy through trade and developed a maritime empire. Its great rival was Rome; after several wars, the Romans defeated the Carthaginians and destroyed Carthage. Later, the Romans rebuilt the city, and it became great once again as the capital of the Roman province of Africa. Rome's African province was one of the most prosperous in the empire. The wheat and other commodities shipped to Rome from North African farms were vitally needed to feed the Roman population. When the ships from Carthage were late due to storms, lost at sea, or seized by pirates, the Romans suffered hardship. Modern Tunisia has yet to reach the level of prosperity it had under Roman rule.

The collapse of the Roman Empire in the fifth century A.D. affected Roman Africa as well. Cities were abandoned; the irrigation system that had made the farms prosperous fell into ruin. A number of these Roman cities, such as Dougga, Utica, and Carthage itself, which is now a suburb of Tunis, have been preserved as historical monuments of this period.

Arab armies from the east brought Islam to North Africa in the late seventh century. After some resistance, the population accepted the new religion, and from that time on the area was ruled as the Arab-Islamic province of *Ifriqiya*. The Anglicized form of this Arabic word, "Africa," was eventually applied to the entire continent.

The Arab governors did not want to have anything to do with Carthage, since they associated it with Christian Roman rule. They built a new capital on the site of a village on the outskirts of Carthage, named Tunis. The fact that Tunis has been the capital and major city in the country for 14 centuries has contributed to the sense of unity and nationhood among most Tunisians.[1]

The original Tunisian population consisted of Berbers, a people of unknown origin. During the centuries of Islamic rule, many Arabs settled in the country. Other waves of immigration brought Muslims from Spain, Greeks, Italians, Maltese, and many other nationalities. Tunisia also had a large community of Jews, most of whom emigrated to the State of Israel when it was founded in 1948. The blending of ethnic groups and nationalities over the years has created a relatively homogeneous and tolerant society, with few of the conflicts that marked other societies in the region.

From the late 1500s to the 1880s, Tunisia was a self-governing province of the Ottoman Empire. It was called a regency because its governors ruled as "regents" on behalf of the Ottoman sultan. Tunis was already a well-established, cosmopolitan city when it became the regency capital. Its rulers, called beys, were supported by an Ottoman garrison and a corsair fleet of fast ships that served as auxiliaries to the regular Ottoman navy. The corsairs, many of them Christian renegades, ruled the Mediterranean Sea for four centuries, raiding the coasts of nearby European countries and preying on merchant vessels, seizing cargoes and holding crews for ransom. The newly independent United States was also affected, with American merchant ships seized and cargoes taken by the corsairs. In 1799, the United States signed a treaty with the bey, agreeing to pay an annual tribute in return for his protection of American ships.

In the nineteenth century, European powers, particularly France and Britain, began to interfere directly in the Ottoman Empire and to seize some of its outlying provinces. France and Britain had a "gentleman's agreement" about Ottoman territories in Africa—the French were given a free hand in North Africa and the British in Egypt. In 1830, the French seized Algiers, capital of the Algiers Regency, and began to intervene in neighboring Tunisia in order to protect their Algerian interests.

The beys of Tunis worked very hard to forestall a French occupation. In order to do this, they had to satisfy the European powers that they were developing modern political institutions and rights for their people. Ahmad Bey (1837–1855) abolished slavery and piracy, organized a modern army (trained by French officers), and established a national system of tax collection. Muhammad al-Sadiq Bey (1859–1882) approved in 1861 a written Constitution which had a declaration of rights and provided for a hereditary (but not an absolute) monarchy under the beys. The Constitution worked better in theory than in practice. Provincial landowners and local chiefs opposed the Constitution because it undermined their authority. The peasants, whom it supposedly was designed to protect, opposed the Constitution because it brought them heavy new taxes, collected by government troops sent from Tunis. In 1864, a popular rebellion broke out against the bey, and he was forced to suspend the Constitution.

In 1881, the French army invaded and occupied all of Tunisia, almost without firing a shot. The French said that they had intervened because the bey's government could not meet its debts to French bankers and entrepreneurs, who had been lending money for years to keep the country afloat. There was concern also about the European population. Europeans from many countries had been pouring into Tunisia, ever since the bey had given foreigners the right to own land and set up businesses. However, another major reason for taking over Tunisia was the need to protect France's next-door colony, Algeria. It was also partly for that same reason that France took control of Morocco (west of Algeria) a few years later. Both, Tunisia and Morocco were placed under French protectorate, another guise for colonialism.

The bey's government continued under the French protectorate, but it was supplemented by a French administration, which held actual power. The French collected taxes, imposed French law, and developed roads, railroads, ports, hospitals, and schools. French landowners bought large areas and converted them into vineyards, olive groves, and wheat farms. For the first time in 2,000 years, Tunisia exported wheat, corn, and olive oil to the lands on the other side of the Mediterranean.

Because Tunisia was small, manageable, and primarily urban, its society, particularly in certain regions, was influenced strongly by French culture. An elite developed whose members preferred the French language to their native Arabic. They were encouraged to enroll their sons in Sadiki College, a European-type high school set up in Tunis by the French to train young Tunisians and expose them to Western subjects. After completing their studies at Sadiki, most were sent to France to complete their education in such institutions as the Sorbonne (University of Paris). The experience helped shape their political thinking, and on their return to Tunisia a number of them formed a movement for self-government that they called Destour (*Dustur* in Arabic), meaning "Constitution." The name was logical, since these young men had observed that independent countries such as France based their sovereignty on such a document. They were convinced that nationalism, "in order to be effective against the French, had to break loose from its traditional power base in the urban elite and mobilize mass support."[2] In 1934, a group of young nationalists quit the Destour and formed a new party, the Neo-Destour. The goal of the Neo-Destour Party was Tunisia's independence from France. From the beginning, its leader was Habib Bourguiba.

## HABIB BOURGUIBA

Habib Ben Ali Bourguiba, born in 1903, once said he had "invented" Tunisia, not historically but in the sense of shaping its existence as a modern sovereign nation. The Neo-Destour Party, under Bourguiba's leadership, became the country's first mass political party. It drew its membership from shopkeepers, craftspeople, blue-collar workers, and peasants, along with French-educated lawyers and doctors. The party became the vanguard of the nation, mobilizing the population in a campaign of strikes, demonstrations, and violence in order to gain independence. It was a long struggle. Bourguiba spent many years in prison. But eventually the Neo-Destour tactics succeeded. On March 20, 1956, France ended its protectorate and Tunisia became an independent republic, led by Habib Bourguiba.

A Constitution was approved in 1959 that established a "presidential republic"—that is, a republic in which the elected president has great power. Bourguiba was elected president in 1957.

Bourguiba was also the head of the Neo-Destour Party, the country's only legal political party. The Constitution provided for a National Assembly, which is responsible for enacting laws. But to be elected to the Assembly, a candidate had to be a member of the Neo-Destour Party. Bourguiba's philosophy and programs for national development in his country were often called Bourguibism. It was tailored to the particular historical experience of the Tunisian people. Since ancient Carthage, Tunisian life has been characterized by the presence of a strong central government able to impose order and bring relative stability to the people. The predominance of cities and villages over the countryside reinforced this sense of order. The experience of Carthage, and even more so that of Rome, set the pattern. "The beys continued the pattern of strong order while the

French developed a strongly bourgeois, trade-oriented society, adding humanitarian and some authoritarian values contained in French political philosophy."[3] Bourguiba considered himself the tutor of the Tunisian people, guiding them toward moral, economic, and political maturity.

In 1961, Bourguiba introduced a new program for Tunisian development that he termed "Destourian Socialism." It combined Bourguibism with state planning for economic and social development. The name of the Neo-Destour Party was changed to the Destour Socialist Party (PSD) to indicate its new direction. Destourian Socialism worked for the general good, but it was not Marxist; Bourguiba stressed national unanimity rather than class struggle and opposed communism as the "ideology of a godless state." Bourguiba took the view that Destourian Socialism was directly related to Islam. He said once that the original members of the Islamic community (in Muhammad's time in Mecca) "were socialists . . . and worked for the common good."[4] For many years after independence, Tunisia appeared to be a model among new states because of its stability, order, and economic progress. Particularly notable were Bourguiba's reforms in social and political life. Islamic law was replaced by a Western-style legal system, with various levels of courts. Women were encouraged to attend school and enter occupations previously closed to them, and they were given equal rights with men in matters of divorce and inheritance.

Bourguiba strongly criticized those aspects of Islam that seemed to him to be obstacles to national development. He was against women wearing the veil, polygyny, and ownership of lands by religious leaders, which kept land out of production. He even encouraged people not to fast during the holy month of Ramadan, because their hunger made them less effective in their work.

There were few challenges to Bourguiba's leadership. His method of alternately dismissing and reinstating party leaders who disagreed with him effectively maintained Destourian unity. But in later years Bourguiba's periodic health problems, the growth of an Islamist movement, and the disenchantment of Tunisian youth with the single-party system raised doubts about Tunisia's future under the PSD.

The system was provided with a certain continuity by the election of Bourguiba as president-for-life in 1974, when a constitutional amendment was approved specifying that at the time of his death or in the event of his disability, the prime minister would succeed him and hold office pending a general election. One author observed: "Nobody is big enough to replace Bourguiba. He created a national liberation movement, fashioned the country and its institutions."[5] Yet he failed to recognize or deal with changing political and social realities in his later years.

The new generation coming of age in Tunisia was deeply alienated from the old. Young Tunisians increasingly protested their inability to find jobs, their exclusion from the political decision-making process, the unfair distribution of wealth, and the lack of political organizations. It seemed as if there were two Tunisias: the old Tunisia of genteel politicians and freedom fighters; and the one of alienated youths, angry peasants, and frustrated intellectuals.

The division between these groups was magnified by the growth of an Islamist movement which Bourguiba equated with rejection of the secular, modern Islamic society that he created. The Islamic Tendency Movement (MTI) emerged in the 1980s as the major Islamist group. MTI applied for recognition as a political party after Bourguiba had agreed to allow political activity outside of the Destour Party and had licensed two opposition parties. But MTI's application was rejected.

## THE END OF AN ERA

In 1984, riots over an increase in the price of bread signaled a turning point for the regime. For the first time in the republic's history, an organized Islamist opposition challenged Bourguiba, on the grounds that he had deformed Islam to create a secular society. Former Bourguiba associates urged a broadening of the political process and formed political movements to challenge the Destour monopoly on power. Although they were frequently jailed and their movements proscribed or declared illegal, the Islamists continued to press for political reform.

As Bourguiba's mental state deteriorated, his actions became increasingly irrational. He would appoint a cabinet minister one day and forget the next that he had done so. Opposition became an obsession with him. The two legal opposition parties were forced out of local and national elections by arrests of leaders and a shutdown of opposition newspapers. The Tunisian Labor Confederation (UGTT) was disbanded, and the government launched a massive offensive against the Islamists.

The repression was directed by General Zine el-Abidine Ben Ali, the minister of the interior, regarded by Bourguiba as one of the few people he could trust. There were mass arrests of Islamist militants, most of them belonging to the MTI. Under the leadership of Rachid Ghannouchi, it reorganized later as Ennahda (Renaissance) party, opted for a peaceful and legal strategy and sought recognition by the state unsuccessfully.

Increasingly, it seemed to responsible leaders that Bourguiba was becoming senile as well as paranoid. "The government lacks all sense of vision," said a long-time observer. "The strategy is to get through the day, to play palace parlor games." A student leader was more cynical: "There is no logic to [Bourguiba's] decisions; sometimes he does the opposite of what he did the day before."[6]

A decision that would prove crucial to the needed change in leadership was made by Bourguiba in September 1987, when he named Ben Ali as prime minister. Six weeks later, Ben Ali carried out a bloodless coup, removing the aging president under the 1974 constitutional provision that allows the prime minister to take over in the event of a president's "manifest incapacity" to govern. A council of medical doctors affirmed that this was the case. Bourguiba was placed under temporary house arrest in his Monastir villa, but he was allowed visitors and some freedom of movement within the city until his death on April 6, 2000 at age 96.

## NEW DIRECTIONS

President Ben Ali (elected to a full five-year term in April 1989) initiated a series of bold reforms designed to wean the country away from the formal one-party system. Political prisoners were released under a general amnesty. Prodded by Ben Ali, the Destour-dominated National Assembly passed laws ensuring press freedom and the right of political parties to form as long as their platforms are not based on language, race, or religion. The Assembly abolished the constitutional provision establishing the position of president-for-life, which had been created expressly for Bourguiba. Henceforth Tunisian presidents would be limited to three consecutive terms in office, but Ben Ali later enacted another amendment which ended term limit. In October 2009, he will be seeking a fifth term with almost no challenging opposition.

Ben Ali also undertook the major job of restructuring and revitalizing the Destour

Party. In 1988, it was renamed the Constitutional Democratic Rally (RCD). Ben Ali told delegates to the first RCD Congress that no single party could represent all Tunisians. He said that there can be no democracy without pluralism, fair elections, and freedom of expression. However, all of these have been missing since he took over.

Elections in 1988 underscored Tunisia's fixation on the single-party system. RCD candidates won all 141 seats in the Chamber of Deputies, taking 80 percent of the popular vote. Two new opposition parties, the Progressive Socialist Party and the Progressive Socialist Rally, participated but failed to win more than 5 percent of the popular vote, the minimum needed for representation in the Chamber. MTI candidates, although required to run as independents because of the ban on "Islamic" parties under the revised election law, dominated urban voting, taking 30 percent of the popular vote in the cities. However, the winner-take-all system of electing candidates shut them out as well.

Local and municipal elections have confirmed the RCD stranglehold on Tunisian political life. In the 1995 local and municipal council elections, RCD candidates won 4,084 out of 4,090 contested seats, with 92.5 percent of Tunisia's 1,865,401 registered voters casting their ballots.

Efforts to mobilize an effective opposition movement earlier were hampered when Ahmed Mestiri, the long-time head of the Movement of Socialist Democrats (MDS), the major legal opposition party, resigned in 1992. In the 1994 elections, the only opposition party to increase its support was the former Tunisian Communist Party, renamed the Movement for Renewal. It won four seats in the Chamber.

## ACHIEVEMENTS

With domestic electric demand rising at the rate of 77 percent annually, the country has moved rapidly to add new power plants. The new Rades plant, powered by a combination of diesel fuel and natural gas, went into operation in mid 2003; it increases national output from 2000 megawatts (mw) to 2,480. Some 94 percent of Tunisian homes now have electric power.

After the election the Chamber of Deputies was enlarged from the present 144 to 160 deputies. Twenty seats would be reserved for members from opposition parties. In the presidential election, Ben Ali was re-elected for a third term and again in

1999 for a fourth term. In the latter election he faced modest opposition, and as a result his victory margin was a "bare" 99.44 percent.[7]

The Chamber was enlarged again in time for the 1999 elections, this time to 182 seats, to broaden representation for Tunisia's growing population. The results were somewhat different from the previous election. The RCD won 148 seats to 13 for the MDS, the largest opposition party. However, opposition parties all together increased their representation from 19 seats to 34.

In May 2002, through a referendum, president Ben Ali ended the presidential term limit and changed the maximum age for a president from 70 to 75. This allowed him, at age 67, to run for—and win—a fourth term in 2004 with 94.5 percent of the votes. In 2009, he won a fifth term, at age 73, with 89.62 percent of the votes. According to the constitution, this should be his last term.

In the 2009 parliamentary elections, the presidential party, RCD, obtained 84.59 percent of the votes, which automatically gave it 75 percent of the seats.

## THE ECONOMY

The challenge to Ben Ali lies not only in broadening political participation but also in improving the economy. After a period of impressive expansion in the 1960s and 1970s, the growth rate began dropping steadily, largely due to decreased demand and lowered prices for the country's three main exports (phosphates, petroleum, and olive oil). Tunisia is the world's fourth-ranking producer of phosphates, and its most important industries are those related to production of superphosphates and fertilizers.

Problems have dogged the phosphate industry. The quality of the rock mined is poor in comparison with that of other phosphate producers, such as Morocco. The Tunisian industry experienced hard times in the late 1980s with the drop in global phosphate prices; a quarter of its 12,000-member workforce were laid off in 1987. However, improved production methods and higher world demand led to a 29 percent increase in exports in 1990.

Tunisia's oil reserves are estimated at 1.65 billion barrels. The main producing fields are at El Borma and offshore in the Gulf of Gabes. New offshore discoveries and a 1996 agreement with Libya for 50/50 sharing of production from the disputed Gulf of Gabes oil field have improved oil output, currently about 4.3 million barrels annually.

Tunisia became an associate member of the European Union in 1995, the

first Mediterranean country to do so. The terms of the EU agreement require the country to remove trade barriers over a 10-year period. In turn, Tunisian products such as citrus and olives receive highly favorable export terms in EU countries. The EU also provides technical support and training for the economic Mise A Nouveau (Upgrading and Improvement) program intended to enhance productivity in business and industry and compete internationally.

Tunisia's political stability—albeit one gained at the expense of human rights—and its economic reforms have made it a favored country for foreign aid over the years. During the period 1970–2000 it received more World Bank loans than any other Arab or African country. Its economic reform program, featuring privatization of 140 state-owned enterprises since 1987, liberalizing of prices, reduction of tariffs and other reforms, is lauded as a model for development by international financial institutions.

The country's political stability and effective use of its limited resources for development have made it a favored country for foreign aid. Since the 1970s it has received more World Bank loans than any other Arab or African country. The funding has been equitably distributed, so that 60 percent of the population are middle class, and 80 percent own their own homes.

Tunisia's social policies helped raise living conditions within the region, and wise economic policies have maintained a relatively good growth rate which averaged around 5 percent over the past decade. Due to the global economic recession, especially in Europe, Tunisia's main export market, that rate declined to 4.7 percent in 2008 and is expected to decline further in 2009.

One of the biggest challenges Tunisia faces is unemployment which remains high at 15 percent, most particularly among the the youth—35 percent of whom are without jobs.

## THE FUTURE

Tunisia's progress as an economic beacon of stability in an unstable region has been somewhat offset by a decline in its long-established status as a successful example of a secular, progressive Islamic state. Following President Ben Ali's ouster of his predecessor in 1987, he proclaimed a new era for Tunisians, based on respect for law, human rights, and democracy. Tunisia's Islamic nature was reaffirmed by such actions as the reopening of the venerable Zitouna University in Tunis, a center for Islamic scholarship, along with its counterpart in Kairouan. But like other Islamic countries, it has not been free from the scourge of militant Islamists.

Militant Islam, represented by al-Qaeda and its various subsidiary organizations, has not entirely spared Tunisia despite its government's extreme repression of Islamist groups. In April 2003 a bomb attack on the ancient Jewish synagogue on Djerba Island, a popular tourist destination, killed 17 people, striking a blow at the country's important tourist industry. Subsequently, in 2007, a plan to attack the American and British embassies in Tunis was uncovered and thwarted in a series of gun battles between militants and security forces, with 12 militants and 2 security officers killed. The plan had been developed by members of the Salafist Group for Preaching and Combat (GSPC), an Algerian group which has joined al-Qaeda in January 2007 and renamed itself al-Qaeda in the land of the Islamic Maghreb.

Tunisia has become an increasingly closed society. The press is heavily censored. Telephones are routinely tapped. More than 1,000 Ennahda members have been arrested and jailed without trial.

The regime's repression of Islamist groups, even moderate nonviolent ones, has changed its former image as a tolerant, progressive Islamic country. The Tunisian League for Human Rights, oldest in the Arab world, has been shut down from time to time by the government. Until recently opposition leaders were given no coverage in the mainstream press, and press censorship remains routine.

Following his "tainted" election victory in 1999, Ben Ali announced a new program designed to provide full employment by 2004. Called the 21–21 program, it would supplement an earlier 26–26 one that had brought the public and private sectors together to end poverty and increase home ownership, notably among the poor. In his address announcing the new program, Ben Ali stated: "Change comes from anchoring the democratic process in a steady and incremental progress aimed at avoiding setbacks or losing momentum."[8]

Ironically, Ben Ali government's ruthless crackdown on Islamist parties, beginning with the ban on Al-Nahda after its success in the 1989 elections and continuing up to the present, has generated a largely non-violent but politically effective opposition, particularly among university students. To some extent, the radicalization of Tunisian youth stems from anger over U.S. wars in Iraq and Afghanistan, as is the case elsewhere in the Arab world. But heavy-handed government methods used in the crackdown are also a factor. In 2004 six youths were given 19-year jail sentences for downloading bomb-making instructions on the Internet, after a trial described as unfair by human rights lawyers. (The six were released in 2006). But as the leader of the Tunisian Journalists' Union commented in launching a hunger strike by opposition leaders on the eve of the 2005 World Summit on Information Society, which was held in Tunisia, "It is the only means open to protest, because the authorities have closed all other avenues of dialogue and negotiation."[9]

The government's harsh and restrictive policies were eased somewhat in 2004–2006. New measures included approval for the International Committee of the Red Cross to visit Tunisian prisons and a limiting of censorship of newspaper and magazine articles. But any return to Tunisia's traditionally open, secular society as formed by Habib Bourguiba seems doubtful. A senior Tunisian university professor publicly questioned the moderating of repressive government policies: "Is the government able to endorse secular regulations and rules of law? Is the secular leadership strong enough to resist an Islamic (sic) uprising? And would this be an invitation to danger or a credible and reliable step toward a liberal system?"[10]

## NOTES

1. Harold D. Nelson, ed., *Tunisia: A Country Study* (Washington, D.C.: American University, Foreign Area Studies, 1979), p. 68.

2. *Ibid.,* p. 42.

3. *Ibid.,* p. 194. What Nelson means, in this case, by "authoritarianism" is that the French brought to Tunisia the elaborate bureaucracy of metropolitan France, with levels of administration from the center down to local towns and villages.

4. *Ibid.,* p. 196.

5. Jim Rupert, in *The Christian Science Monitor* (November 23, 1984).

6. Louise Lief, in *The Christian Science Monitor* (April 10, 1987).

7. Mamoun Fandy, in *The Christian Science Monitor* (October 25, 1999).

8. Georgie Ann Geyer, in *The Washington Post* (October 23, 1999).

9. "Hunger for Change," *The Economist,* November 12, 2005.

10. Quoted by Jill Carroll, "Secular Tunisia may face new, younger Islamist challenge," *The Christian Science Monitor,* October 10, 2007, p. 1.

## Timeline: PAST

**264–146 B.C.**
Wars between Rome and Carthage, ending in the destruction of Carthage and its rebuilding as a Roman city

**800–900**
The establishment of Islam in Ifriqiya, with its new capital at Tunis

**1200–1400**
The Hafsid dynasty develops Tunisia as a highly centralized urban state

**1500–1800**
Ottoman Turks establish Tunis as a corsair state to control Mediterranean sea lanes

**1881–1956**
French protectorate

**1956**
Tunisia gains independence, led by Habib Bourguiba

**1974**
An abortive merger with Libya

**1987**
Bourguiba is removed from office in a "palace coup;" he is succeeded by Ben Ali

**1990s**
Tunisia's economic picture brightens; Ben Ali seeks some social modernization; women's rights are expanded

## PRESENT

**2000s**
Political closing continues and President Ben Ali secures a fifth term in office

# Turkey (Republic of Turkey)

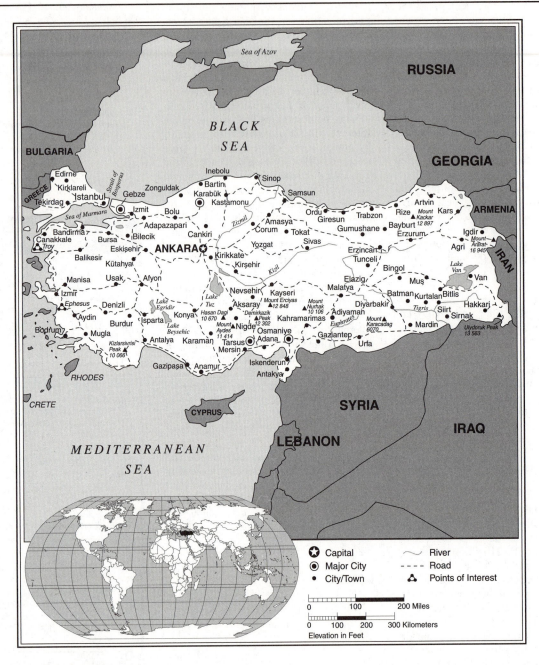

# Turkey Statistics

## GEOGRAPHY

*Area in Square Miles (Kilometers):*
301,303 (780,580) (about the size of Texas)

*Capital (Population):* Ankara (3,763,591)

*Environmental Concerns:* water and air pollution; deforestation; threat of oil spills from Bosporus ship traffic

*Geographical Features:* mostly mountains; a narrow coastal plain; a high central plateau (Anatolia)

*Climate:* temperate; hot, dry summers and mild wet winters along coasts; much drier and more extreme in temperatures in interior plateau and mountains

## PEOPLE

### Population

*Total:* 77,804,122 (2010)
*Annual Growth Rate:* 1.272%
*Rural/Urban Population Ratio:* 29/71

*Major Languages:* Turkish; Kurdish; Arabic

*Ethnic Makeup:* 80% Turk; 17% Kurd; 3% others

*Religions:* 99% Muslim (about 79% Sunni, 20% Shi'a); 1% others

## Health

*Life Expectancy at Birth:* 70 years (male), 75 years (female)

*Infant Mortality Rate:* 24.84/1,000 live births

*Physicians Available (Ratio):* 1/1,200 people

### Education

*Adult Literacy Rate:* 86%
*Compulsory (Ages):* 6–16

## COMMUNICATION

*Telephones:* 17,502,000 main lines
*Daily Newspaper Circulation:* 44 per 1,000 people
*Televisions:* 171 per 1,000 people
*Internet Users:* 24.483 million (2008)

## TRANSPORTATION

*Highways in Miles (Kilometers):* 265,295 (426,951)
*Railroads in Miles (Kilometers):* 5,404 (8,697)
*Usable Airfields:* 121
*Motor Vehicles in Use:* 4,320,000

## GOVERNMENT

*Type:* republican parliamentary democracy
*Independence Date:* October 29, 1923 (successor state to the Ottoman Empire)

*Head of State/Government:* President Abdullah Gul (elected August 2007) Prime Minister Erdogan continues in office; Prime Minister Recep Tayyip Erdogan
*Political Parties:* Justice and Development Party (AKP), majority party. There are some 49 opposition parties, the principal ones being Motherland (ANAP), Democratic Left Party (DSP), Republican Peoples' Party (CHP), Social Democratic Peoples' Party (SHP)
*Suffrage:* universal at 18

## MILITARY

*Military Expenditures (% of GDP):* 5.3%
*Current Disputes:* periodic conflict with Iraq-based Kurdistan Workers Party (PKK), which formerly sought independence for Turkish Kurdistan but in recent years fought for autonomy and specific national rights for Kurds in that region. While Turkey is not directly affected by the conflict between Armenia and Azerbaijan over the Armenian enclave of Nagorno-Karabagh, its support for Azerbaijan

as a Muslim country has resulted in the closing of the Armenian-Turkish border.

## ECONOMY

*Currency ($U.S. Equivalent):* 1.4 liras = $1
*Per Capita Income/GDP:* $8,900/ $608 billion
*GDP Growth Rate:* −5.6%
*Inflation Rate:* 6.5%
*Unemployment Rate:* 14.5%, plus 4% underemployment
*Labor Force:* 25,300,000, plus 1,200,000 Turks working abroad
*Natural Resources:* antimony; coal; chromium ore; mercury; copper; borate; sulfur; iron ore; meerschaum; arable land; hydropower
*Agriculture:* tobacco; cotton; grains; olives; sugar beets; pulse; citrus; livestock
*Industry:* textiles; food processing; automobiles; mining; steel; petroleum; construction; lumber; paper
*Exports:* $102.2 billion (primary partners Germany, Britain, Italy)
*Imports:* $140.8 billion (primary partners Germany, Italy, Russia)

# Turkey Country Report

Except for a small area in extreme Southeastern Europe called Thrace, the Republic of Turkey comprises the large peninsula of Asia Minor (Anatolia), which forms a land bridge between Europe and Asia. Asiatic Turkey is separated from European Turkey by the Bosporus, a narrow strait connecting the Black Sea with the Aegean Sea and the Mediterranean Sea via the Sea of Marmara. Throughout history, the Bosporus and the Dardanelles, at the Mediterranean end, have been important strategic waterways, fought over by many nations.

Except for the Syrian border, Asiatic Turkey's borders are defined by natural limits, with seas on three sides and rugged mountains on the fourth. European Turkey's frontiers with Greece and Bulgaria are artificial; they fluctuated considerably in the nineteenth and twentieth centuries before the Republic of Turkey was established.

Modern Turkey occupies a much smaller area than did its predecessor, the Ottoman Empire. The Ottoman Turks were the dominant power in the Middle East for more than five centuries. After the defeat of the empire in World War I, Turkey's new leader, Mustafa Kemal Ataturk, turned away from the imperial past, limiting the

new republic to territory with a predominantly Turkish population. Since then, Turkey has not attempted to annex land beyond its natural Anatolian borders—with two exceptions. One was the Hatay, a coastal province that includes the important port of Iskenderun (Alexandretta) and the city of Antakya (ancient Antioch). France, which controlled Syria under a mandate from the League of Nations after World War I, ceded the Hatay to the new Turkish Republic after a plebiscite in which the Turkish majority in the population had voted to join it. (The cession has yet to be formally recognized by Syria, but for all practical purposes the Hatay is part of Turkey's territory.)

The second exception is Cyprus. This island republic has a Greek majority in the population, but a significant minority (20 percent) are Turkish Cypriots, descended from Turkish families that settled there when Cyprus was Ottoman territory. Although it is a sovereign state, fear of violence against the Cypriot Turks and of annexation of the Island by Greece (known as Enosis), led Turkish forces to occupy the northern third of the island in 1974 and declare the birth of an independent Turkish Cypriot state. They have been there since

then, with no agreement as yet on reunification of Cyprus. Some years ago, the Turkish government officially recognized the area under its control as the Republic of Northern Cyprus, but no other country has done so.

Asia Minor has an ancient history of settlement. Most of the peninsula is a plateau ringed by mountains. The mountains are close to the coast; over the centuries, due to volcanic action, the coastline became cracked, with deep indentations and islands just offshore. The inland plateau has an area of arid steppe with dried-up salt lakes at the center, but most of it is rolling land, well suited to agriculture. Consequently, people settled in small, self-contained villages at an early period and began to cultivate the land. Over the centuries, nomadic peoples migrated into Asia Minor, but the geographical pattern there did not encourage them to remain nomadic.

In terms of national unity, the modern Turkish state has not had the thorny problem of ethnic conflicts—with two important exceptions. One is the Armenians, an ancient Christian people who ruled over a large part of what is now eastern Turkey many centuries ago. With the outbreak of World War I the Ottoman government aligned itself with Germany against Britain, France, and its old enemy Russia. Following a declaration of war, the Czarist government invited Armenians living in Ottoman territory to revolt against the Sultan's rule. A small minority did so, and the "Young Turks," a military triumvirate that effectively governed the empire used the pretext of an "armed Armenian revolutionary uprising" to eliminate its entire Armenian population. In what is usually described as the first 20th century genocide, approximately 800,000 Armenians were uprooted from their towns and villages and deported to Syria and other nearby Ottoman territories. The deportations were carried out under harrowing conditions, and few survived. Those who did, settled elsewhere. The memories of the deportations and massacres were kept alive, passed on from generation to generation and there is a constant call by Armenians and others around the world for Turkey to acknowledge the genocide.

Since the establishment of the Turkish republic, successive governments have consistently disclaimed responsibility for the actions of its Ottoman predecessor. In the 1970s and 1980s an Armenian terrorist organization, the Secret Army for the Liberation of Armenia (ASALA), carried out a series of attacks on Turkish diplomats abroad, killing 30 of them. However, when violence proved unproductive, Armenian community leaders undertook a lobbying campaign with the U.S. government and European governments to encourage them to put pressure on Turkey for an admission of its indirect responsibility for the deportations and deaths, since they had been carried out by its predecessor. This persistent lobbying finally brought results. In March 2001, the U.S. House of Representatives approved a resolution calling on Turkey to "recognize publicly the Armenian genocide." A similar resolution was approved in April by the European Parliament, the deliberative body of the European Union.

Perhaps prodded by such actions as a resolution by the French National Assembly on the Armenian genocide, the Turkish government in 2005 inaugurated a first-ever national debate on its predecessor's actions toward the Armenians. The murder in January 2007 of Hrant Dink, ethnic Armenian editor of the bilingual newspaper *Argos,* by a teenage Turkish gunman, underscored the narrow line followed by some people in Turkey between patriotism and extreme actions against minorities, particularly the Armenians. External pressure on Turkey from many sources to admit a degree of responsibility for the massacres as a successor to the Ottoman state, as a precondition for EU membership, probably contributed to this latest act of anti-Armenian violence.[1]

Ironically Dink had been given a 6-year suspended sentence in 2005 for "insulting Turkey and Turkishness" in a column in which he urged an end to hatred between the two peoples. His funeral, in January 2007, marked a rare move toward reconciliation, as Armenian spiritual and political leaders attended and thousands of mourners marched carrying plaques that read, "We are all Armenians." But as Dink had argued before his murder, admission of an element of guilt in the massacres would have to come from unfettered debate among the Turks themselves, rather than as the result of external pressures and Congressional resolutions.[2] The latter came to a head in October 2007 when the Foreign Affairs Committee of the House of Representatives approved a resolution condemning Turkey for genocide in the case of more than a million Armenians killed during World War I, when the Ottoman Empire was at war with Russia. A similar resolution was passed by the same committee on March 4, 2010 recommending that the United States recognize the killings as genocide. Just as in 2007, the resolution generated furious resentment in Turkey. (At this writing the 2010 resolution had not been brought before the full House for a vote, just like the 2007 one, an indication that the national interest, maintaining good relations with its important Turkish ally, has priority).

The other exception to Turkish homogeneity is the Kurds, who make up 17 percent of the population officially but may be closer to 20 percent. There are also Kurdish populations in Iraq, Syria, and Iran, but Turkey's Kurds form the largest component of this nation without a state, one of the last large ethnic communities in the world which does not enjoy self-rule. Their fierce spirit of independence have led to periodic uprisings against the governments that rule them. In Turkey, the Ataturk regime crushed Kurdish rebellions in the 1920s, and from then on, Kurds were officially referred to as "Mountain Turks." Until the 1980s, Turkey's Kurds were considered an unimportant, albeit economically deprived, population group. Many emigrated to the cities or abroad, mainly to Germany and the Netherlands. Turkey's Kurdish population is concentrated in its southeastern region and its provincial capital, Diyarbakir. During the 15-year guerrilla war between the Turkish army and security forces and the Kurdish PKK nationalist movement, some 35,000 civilians and militants were killed and over a million villagers displaced, most fleeing to Turkish cities or such foreign countries as Germany.

## DEVELOPMENT

The loans pledged by the IMF and World Bank to resolve Turkey's economic crisis require the country to maintain a 4% budget surplus, excluding interest on foreign debts. Inflation and the loss of purchasing power have made that objective almost impossible to reach. A new tracking system that requires an official personal identification number (PIN) for transactions over $3,000 or to hold a bank or stock account should reduce cheating and create a financial database. It will also provide for more equitable tax collection.

In addition to those in Cyprus, there are two other important populations of ethnic Turks outside of Turkey. They are in Bulgaria and western (Greek) Thrace. Those in Bulgaria make up about 10 percent of the population. In the 1980s, they were suppressed by the Communist Bulgarian regime as foreigners and Muslims, although they had lived in peace with their neighbors for centuries. About one third fled to Turkey as refugees. This forced assimilation policy was reversed after the fall of the Communist regime, and most of them have now returned to their Bulgarian homes.

There are also about 120,000 ethnic Turks in Greek Thrace, left over from the forced exchange of Greek and Turkish populations in 1922. However, they have never been granted Greek citizenship and are discriminated against in various ways. In 1990, the Greek government unilaterally abrogated the 1923 Treaty of Lausanne, which, among other things, guaranteed the Turkish minority the right to choose its own religious leaders. They are mostly small farmers, forming a close-knit group mainly due to their religious separateness. Perhaps because of the republic's long-standing policy of not expanding its territory, the turks in Greek Thrace have had little contact with those living in the adjoining Turkish vilayet (province) of Edirne.

An estimated 20 percent of Turkey's population are *Alevis,* a blanket term for various Muslim communities whose Islamic rituals and beliefs differ from those of the Sunni majority. Some are Shi'as; others have ethnic and religious affinities with the Alawis, who currently rule Syria, and live close by in the Hatay and other areas near the Syrian border. Other Alevis form compact communities in such small Anatolian towns as Sivas, Corum, and

Archway on Temple of Hadrian in Ephesus, Turkey, which dates back to 128 A.D.

Kahramanras, and Istanbul has a substantial Alevi population. Alevi rituals incorporate music and dancing into their services. They have no religious leaders, but each Alevi community has a *dede* ("old man") who directs community affairs. One observer said of them, "They claim to live according to the inner meaning of religion (*batin*) rather than by external (*zahir*) demands . . ., prayer, the fast in Ramadan, *zakat* and *hajj* are alien."[3]

A small population of Assyrian Christians, 6,000 in all, is still found in southeastern Turkey in Kurdish territory, remnants of their deportation along with the Armenians during the first World War and offshoots of the much larger Assyrian community in Iraq. In 2005, for the first time in their history under the republic, they were allowed to observe publicly their New Year celebration (Akito), presumably due to Turkey's continued efforts to polish its image and its commitment to democratic change in the run-up to its application for membership in the European Union.

In the years of the Ottoman Empire, a large Jewish population settled in Turkey's lands, invited there from Spain after their expulsion from that country by its Christian rulers. Nearly every Ottoman city had its Jewish quarter and synagogue. But with the establishment of Israel and the rise of Turkish nationalism, the great majority of Jews left Turkey. Small Jewish communities still survive in Ankara, Istanbul, and Antakya. Most of the country's synagogues have become architectural museums, beautifully designed monuments to the multiethnic, multireligious Ottoman past. However, radical Islamist violence, aimed at destabilizing secular Muslim regimes, reached Turkey in late 2003 with the suicide bombing of two Istanbul synagogues along with a branch of Britain's Barclay's Bank. The synagogues were attacked during Shabbat prayers, killing 25 worshippers and injuring several hundreds more, mostly Muslims on the street outside the buildings.

## HISTORY: A PARADE OF PEOPLES

The earliest political unit to develop in the peninsula was the Empire of the Hittites (1600–1200 B.C.), inventors of the two-wheeled chariot and one of the great powers of the ancient Near East. Other Asia Minor peoples made important contributions to our modern world through their discoveries and inventions. We are indebted to the Lydians for our currency system. They were great warriors but also great traders, developing a coinage based on gold and silver to simplify trade exchanges. The gold was panned from the Pactolus River near their capital of Sardis. It was then separated from other metals by melting through capellation—mixing the particles with salt, heating in an earthenware container, and finally smelting until ready to mint. The Lydian king, Croesus (561–547 B.C.), who ruled when Lydian trade was at its peak, has become a familiar figure, "rich as Croesus" as a result of this process.[4]

Following the collapse of the Roman Empire in the fifth century A.D., Asia Minor became the largest part of the East Roman or Byzantine Empire, named for its capital, Byzantium. The city was later renamed Constantinople, in honor of the Roman emperor Constantine, after he had become Christian.

## The Ottoman Centuries

Nomadic peoples from Central and western Asia had wandered for many centuries westward in search of water, pasturage, a safe place for their families and other reasons. Their main artery of travel was the fretwork of trails and caravan routes known collectively as the Silk Road. It dates back to 1500 B.C., but the name was coined by a 19th century German geographer. In addition to nomads on the move, it served as the main trade link between Europe and China via the Middle East. Such great Chinese discoveries and inventions as the crossbow, gunpowder, lock-gates, drive-belts, the mechanical clock, spinning wheels, and well-drilling techniques. A major reason for its decline and gradual abandonment resulted from a combination of China's retreat into self-isolation and Columbus's voyage of discovery. The latter made possible the development by Portugal and Spain of seaborne trade routes, themselves ironically made possible by the discovery, by an unknown, probably Chinese inventor, of the maritime compass.

Among these nomadic peoples were the ancestors of the Turks of today. They settled mostly along the borders of Christian Byzantine and Islamic lands in what is today the Turkish Republic's territory, formerly called Asia Minor, or Anatolia (Turkish Anadolu). Others settled in northwest Persia. Although divided and subdivided into clans and families, they had from early on a strong sense of unity as a nation. They were also early converts to Islam. Its simple faith and requirements appealed to them more than did Christian ritual, and they readily joined Islam's battles as *Ghazis,* "warriors for the faith." Asia Minor, having been wrested from the Greeks by the Turks, also gave the Turks a strong sense of identification with that particular place. To them it was Anadolu (Anatolia), "land of the setting sun," a "sacred homeland" giving the Turks a strong sense of national identity and unity.[5]

The Ottomans were one of many Turkish clans in Anatolia. They took their name from Osman, a clan leader elected because of certain qualifications considered ideal for a Ghazi chieftain—wisdom, prudence, courage, skill in battle, and justice, along with a strong belief in Islam.[6] Osman's clan members identified with their leader to such an extent that they called themselves *Osmanlis,* "sons of Osman," rather than *Turks,* a term they equated with boorish, unwashed peasants.

Although the Ottomans started out with a small territory, they were fortunate in that Osman and his successors were extremely able rulers. Osman's son, Orkhan, captured the important Greek city of Bursa, across the Sea of Marmara from Constantinople (modern-day Istanbul). It became the first Ottoman capital. Later Ottoman rulers took the title of sultan to signify their temporal authority over expanding territories. A series of capable sultans led the Ottoman armies deep into Europe. Constantinople was surrounded, and on May 29, A.D. 1453, Mehmed II, the seventh sultan, captured the great city amid portents of disaster for Christian Europe.[7]

The North African corsair city-states of Algiers, Tripoli, and Tunis, which owed nominal allegiance to the sultan but were in practice self-governing, aligned their swift fleets with his from time to time in the contest with European states for control of the Mediterranean. On two occasions his armies besieged Vienna, and during the rule of Sultan Sulayman I, a contemporary of Queen Elizabeth I of England, the Ottoman Empire was the largest and most powerful in the world.

One reason for the success of Ottoman armies was the Janissaries, an elite corps recruited mostly from Christian villages and converted to Islam by force. Janissary units were assigned to captured cities as garrisons. Those in Constantinople enjoyed special privileges. They had their own barracks and served on campaigns as the sultan's personal guard. Invading Ottoman armies were preceded by marching bands of drummers and cymbal players, like the bagpipers who marched ahead of Scottish armies. These Janissary bands made such terrifying noises that villagers fled in terror at their arrival, while enemy forces surrendered after hearing their "fearsomely loud sounds, like an alarm."[8]

Another factor that made the Ottoman system work was the religious organization of non-Muslim minority groups as self-governing units termed *millets,* a Turkish word meaning "nations." Each millet was headed by its own religious leader, who was responsible to the sultan for the leadership and good behavior of his people. The principal millets were the Christians and Jews. Although Christians and Jews were not considered equal to Muslims, they were under the sultan's protection. Armenian, Greek, and Jewish merchants rendered valuable services to the empire due to their linguistic skills and trade experience, particularly after the wars with Europe were replaced by peaceful commerce.

## The "Sick Man of Europe"

In the eighteenth and nineteenth centuries, the Ottoman Empire gradually weakened, while European Christian powers grew stronger. European countries improved their military equipment and tactics and began to defeat the Ottomans regularly. The sultans were forced to sign treaties and lost territories, causing great humiliation, since they had never treated Christian rulers as equals before. To make matters worse, the European powers helped the Greeks and other Balkan peoples to win their independence from the Ottomans.

The European powers also took advantage of the millet system to intervene directly in the Ottoman Empire's internal affairs. French troops invaded Lebanon in 1860 to restore order after civil war broke out there between the Christian and Druze communities. The European powers claimed the right to protect the Christian minorities from mistreatment by the Muslim majority, saying that the sultan's troops could not provide for their safety.

**FREEDOM**

In preparing for eventual EU membership Turkey has made a number of reforms and amendments to its 1923 Constitution. The death penalty was eliminated in 2001 and prison conditions substantially improved for those incarcerated. The 1926 Civil Code has been updated to give women equal rights in matters of divorce, property ownership and the workplace. But the controversial Article 301, which makes insulting Turkish national identity or "Turkishness" a crime has yet to be repealed. It has been used recently not only against Dink but also to convict writers of international stature such as Orhan Pamuk. In 2008 several amendments were made to article 301 by parliament, including the requirement of the approval of the minister of justice to file a case; it also changed the crime from insult to "Turkishness" to insult to the "Turkish nation."

Sultans in the nineteenth century tried to reform in the Ottoman system. They suppressed the Janissaries, who by then had become an unruly mob, and organized a modern army equipped with European weapons, uniforms, and advisers. Sultan Mahmud II issued an imperial decree called *Tanzimat* (literally, "reordering"). It gave equal rights under the law to all subjects, Muslims and non-Muslims alike, in matters such as taxation, education, and property ownership. Provincial governors were directed to implement its provisions. In one province, Baghdad, the governor, Miidhat Pasha, established free schools and hospitals, invited foreign missionaries to develop a Western-style curriculum for these schools, reduced taxes, and restored public security in this traditionally unruly border province.

Subsequently Midhat Pasha was appointed grand vizier (e.g., prime minister) by the new sultan, Abdul Hamid II. In 1876, prodded by Russian and British threats of a takeover, the sultan agreed to Midhat Pasha's urgings and issued a Constitution, the first such document in the empire's history. It would limit the sultan's absolute power by establishing an elected Grand National Assembly (GNA), which would represent all the classes, creeds, and ethnic, and linguistic groups within the empire. (The GNA survived the fall of the empire and was reborn as the Legislature of the Turkish Republic.)

However, the forces of reaction, represented by the religious leaders, the sultan's courtiers, and the sultan himself, were stronger than the forces for reform. Abdul-Hamid had no real intention of giving up the absolute powers that Ottoman sultans had always had. Thus, when the first Grand National Assembly met in 1877 and the members ventured to criticize the sultan's ministers, he dissolved the Assembly.

Because it was increasingly falling under the financial control of the European powers, it was unable to enact effective reforms, and it was losing territory in disastrous wars, the Ottoman Empire became known as the "Sick Man of Europe" in the second half of the 1800s and the European states plotted his death.

But the Sick Man's death was easier to talk about than to carry out, primarily because the European rulers distrusted one another almost as much as they disliked the sultan. If one European ruler seemed to be getting too much territory, trade privileges, or control over the sultan's policies, the others would band together to block that ruler.

### World War I: Exit Empire, Enter Republic

During World War I, the Ottoman Empire was allied with Germany against Britain, France, and Russia. Ottoman armies fought bravely against heavy odds but were eventually defeated. A peace treaty signed in 1920 divided up the empire into British and French protectorates, except for a small part of Anatolia that was left to the sultan. The most devastating blow of all was the occupation by the Greeks of western Anatolia, under the provisions of a secret agreement that brought Greece into the war. It seemed to the Turks that their former subjects had become their rulers.

At this point in Turkey's fortunes, however, a new leader appeared. He would take it in a very different direction. This new leader, Mustafa Kemal Ataturk, had risen through the ranks of the Ottoman Army to become one of its few successful commanders. He was largely responsible for the defeat of British and Australian forces at the Battle of Gallipoli, when they attempted to seize control of the strategic Dardanelles (Straits) in 1915.

Mustafa Kemal took advantage of Turkish anger over the occupation of Anatolia by foreign armies, particularly the Greeks, to launch a movement for independence. It would be a movement not only to recover the Anatolian homeland but also for independence from the sultan.

The Turkish independence movement began in the interior, far from Constantinople. Mustafa Kemal and his associates chose Ankara, a village on a plateau, as their new capital. They issued a so-called National Pact stating that the "New Turkey" would be an independent republic. Its territory would be limited to areas where Turks were the majority of the population. The nationalists resolutely turned their backs on Turkey's imperial past.

The Turkish War of Independence lasted until 1922. It was fought mainly against the Greeks. The nationalists were able to convince other occupation forces to withdraw from Anatolia by proving that they controlled the territory and represented the real interests of the Turkish people. The Greeks were defeated in a series of fierce battles; and eventually France and Britain signed a treaty recognizing Turkey as a sovereign state headed by Mustafa Kemal.

## THE TURKISH REPUBLIC

The Turkish republic has passed through several stages of political development since it was founded. The first stage, dominated by Mustafa Kemal, established its basic form. "Turkey for the Turks" meant that the republic would be predominantly Turkish in population; this was accomplished by rough surgery, with the expulsion of the Armenians and most of the Greeks. Mustafa Kemal also rejected imperialism and interference in the internal affairs of other countries. He once said, "Turkey has a firm policy of ensuring [its] independence within set national boundaries."[9] Peace with Turkey's neighbors and the abandonment of imperialism enabled Mustafa Kemal to concentrate on internal changes. By design, these changes would be far-reaching, in order to break what he viewed as the dead hand of Islam on Turkish life. Turkey would become a secular democratic state on the European model. A Constitution was approved in 1924, the sultanate and the caliphate were both abolished, and the last Ottoman sultan went into exile. Religious courts were also abolished, and new European law codes were introduced to replace Islamic law. An elected Grand National Assembly was given the responsibility for legislation, with executive power held by the president of the republic.

The most striking changes were made in social life, most bearing the personal stamp of Mustafa Kemal. The traditional Turkish clothing and polygyny were outlawed. Women were encouraged to work, were allowed to vote (in 1930), and were given equal rights with men in divorce and inheritance. Turks were required to have surnames; Mustafa Kemal took the name *Ataturk,* meaning "Father of the Turks."

Mustafa Kemal Ataturk died on November 10, 1938. His hold on his country had been so strong, his influence so pervasive, that a whole nation broke down and wept when the news came. Ataturk's mausoleum in Ankara, the Anit Kabir, is the place most frequently visited by Turkish schoolchildren. His portrait hangs in every public place, even in barber shops, and his image appears on every bank note in the new currency issued in January 2005.

Ismet Inonu, Ataturk's right-hand man, succeeded Ataturk and served as president until 1950. Ataturk had distrusted political parties; his brief experiment with a two-party system was abruptly cancelled when members of the officially sponsored "loyal opposition" criticized the Father of the Turks for his free lifestyle. The only political party he allowed was the Republican People's Party (RPP). It was not dedicated to its own survival or to repression, as are political parties in many single-party states. The RPP based its program on six principles, the most important, in terms of politics, being *devrimcilik* ("revolutionism" or "reformism"). It meant that the party was committed to work for a multiparty system and free elections. One author noted, "The Turkish single party system was never based on the doctrine of a single party. It was always embarrassed and almost ashamed of the monopoly [over power]. The Turkish single party had a bad conscience."[10]

Agitation for political reforms began during World War II. Later, when Turkey applied for admission to the United Nations, a number of National Assembly deputies pointed out that the UN Charter specified certain rights that the government was not providing. Reacting to popular demands and pressure from Turkey's allies, Inonu announced that political parties could be established. The first new party in the republic's history was the Democratic Party, organized in 1946. In 1950, the party won 408 seats in the National Assembly, to 69 for the Republican People's Party. The Democrats had campaigned vigorously in rural areas, winning massive support from farmers and peasants. Having presided over the transition from a one-party system with a bad conscience to a two-party one, President Inonu stepped down to become head of the opposition.

## MILITARY INTERVENTIONS

Modern Turkey has struggled for decades to develop a workable multiparty political system. An interesting point about this struggle is that the armed forces have seized power three times, and three times they have returned the country to civilian rule.

Ataturk deliberately kept the Turkish armed forces out of domestic politics. He believed that the military had only two responsibilities: to defend the country in case of invasion and to serve as "the guardian of the reforming ideals of his regime."[11] Since Ataturk's death, military leaders have seized power only when they believed that the civilian government had betrayed the ideals of the founder of the republic.

The first military coup took place in 1960, after a decade of rule by the Democrats. Army leaders charged them with corruption, economic mismanagement, and repression of the opposition. After a public trial, the three top civilian leaders were executed. The military leaders reinstated civilian rule in 1961. The Democratic Party was declared illegal, but other parties were allowed to compete in national elections. The new Justice Party, successor to the Democrats, won the elections but did not win a clear majority. As a result, the Turkish government could not function effectively. More and more Turks, especially university students and trade union leaders, turned to violence as they became disillusioned with the political system. As the violence increased, the military again intervened, but it stopped short of taking complete control.

In 1980, the armed forces intervened for the third time, citing three reasons: failure of the government to deal with political violence which pitted right wing militants against those of the left; inability of the civilian government to rule and the revival of radical Islamism which they viewed as a total surrender of the secular principles established by Ataturk. (The National Salvation Party advocated a return to Islamic law and organized huge rallies in several Turkish cities in 1979–1981.) The National Assembly was dissolved, the Constitution was suspended, and martial law was imposed throughout the country. The generals promised to restore parliamentary rule—but not before political violence was stopped—some 5,000 people had been killed in the years before the coup.

## RETURN TO CIVILIAN RULE

The military regime approved a new Constitution in 1982. It provided for a multiparty political system, although pre-1980 political parties were specifically excluded. (Several were later reinstated, notably the Republican People's Party, or RPP). Three new parties were allowed to present candidates for a new Grand National Assembly (GNA), and elections were scheduled for 1983. However, the party least favored by the generals, the Motherland Party (ANAP), ran an American-style political campaign, using the media to present its candidates to the country. It won handily. Its leader, Turgut Ozal, became the first prime minister in this phase of Turkey's long, slow progress toward effective multiparty democracy.

Ozal, an economist by profession, had served as minister of finance under the military government in 1980–1982. In that capacity, he developed a strict austerity program that stabilized the economy. But the prime ministership was another matter, especially with five generals looking over his shoulder. The Motherland Party's popularity declined somewhat in 1986–1987, a decline that owed more to a broadening of the political process than to voter disenchantment.

On September 6, 1987, the country took a significant step forward—although some analysts viewed it as sideways—toward full restoration of the democratic process. Voters narrowly approved the restoration of political rights to about 100 politicians who had been banned from party activity for 10 years after the 1980 coup: The vote was 50.23 percent "yes" to 49.77 percent "no" in a nationwide referendum. The results surprised many observers, particularly the most prominent political exiles, former prime ministers Suleyman Demirel of the Justice Party and Bulent Ecevit,

leader of the banned Republican People's Party. They had expected a heavy vote in their favor. Prime Minister Ozal's argument that the nation should not return to the "bad old days" before the 1980 coup, when a personal vendetta between these two leaders had polarized politics and paralyzed the economy and there were several dozen murders a day, had clearly carried weight with the electorate.

Thus encouraged, Ozal scheduled new elections for November 1, 1987, a year ahead of schedule. But in October, the Constitutional Court ruled that a December 1986 electoral law was invalid because it had eliminated the primary system, thereby undermining the multiparty system. The elections were held on November 29 under new electoral guidelines. The Motherland Party won easily, taking 292 of 450 seats in the GNA. The Social Democratic Populist Party (SHP), a newcomer to Turkish politics, ran second, with 99 seats; while True Path (DYP), founded by Demirel to succeed the Justice Party, ran a distant third, with 59.

The Motherland Party's large parliamentary majority enabled Ozal to have himself elected president to succeed General Evren in 1989. Although the Turkish presidency is largely a ceremonial office, Ozal continued to run the country as if it were not, with less successful results than those he had attained during his prime ministership. As a result, popular support for his party eroded. In the October 1991 elections for a new National Assembly, candidates of the opposition True Path Party won 180 seats to 113 for the Motherland Party, taking 27 percent of the popular vote, as compared to 24 percent for the majority party. The Social Democratic Populist Party garnered 20 percent of the vote, followed by the Islamic Welfare Party (Refah), whose growing strength was reflected in its 16 percent support from voters.

Lacking a majority in the Assembly, the DYP formed a coalition government with the SHP in November 1991. Party leader Suleyman Demirel became prime minister. The DYP-SHP coalition improved its political position in local elections early in 1992, when its candidates won a majority of urban mayorships. In July of that year, the ban on political parties existing before the 1980 military coup was lifted; most of them had been incorporated into new parties, but the Republican People's Party, founded by Ataturk, reentered the political arena. It drew a number of defections from Assembly members, due in large part to the charismatic appeal of its leader, Deniz Baykal; as a result, the coalition was left with a shaky six-vote majority in the Legislature.

## HEALTH/WELFARE

Improved prison conditions is an important pre-requisite for Turkey's membership in the European Union. A hunger strike by inmates protesting these conditions in 2001 led to 31 deaths. Also in 2001, parliament adopted a new Civil Code which established full equality of men and women in the family; it also replaced 'husband' and 'wife' from its terminology with 'spouses'.

President Ozal died in April 1993, abruptly ending the long political feud between him and Demirel that had weakened government effectiveness. Demirel succeeded him as president. The DYP elected Tansu Ciller, a U.S.-educated economist and university professor, as Turkey's first woman prime minister, one of two in the Muslim world (the other was Benazir Bhutto of Pakistan).

Ciller's first two years in office were marked by economic difficulties; rising popularity of the Islamist tendency, spearheaded by Refah; and intensified violence by Kurdish nationalists of the Workers' Party of Kurdistan (PKK), in the southeastern region. Nevertheless, her government, a coalition of the DYP and the Republican People's Party, representing the center left and the center right, seemed to be governing effectively in at least some respects. By early 1995, the army had regained control of much of the southeast from PKK forces, and in March, agreement was reached for a customs union with the European Union. Municipal elections in June also favored the ruling coalition. It won 61.7 percent of Council seats against 17.4 percent for Refah candidates and 13.4 percent for those of ANAP.

The collapse of the coalition government in September came as a surprise to most observers. Republican People's party head Deniz Baykal had set certain terms for continuation of his party's alliance with DYP. These included repeal of a strict antiterrorism law, which had drawn international condemnation for its lack of rights for detained dissidents; tighter controls over the Islamists; and a pay raise of 70 percent for public workers to offset inflation. When these terms were rejected, he withdrew his party from the coalition.

Elections in December 1995 brought another shock, with Refah winning 158 seats to 135 for True Path and 132 for ANAP. For the first time in modern Turkish history, an Islamist party had won more seats in the Grand National Assembly than its rivals. Refah leader Necmettin Erbakan was named Turkey's first Islamist prime minister, taking office in April 1996. However, his party lacked a clear majority in the Assembly. As a result, coalition government became necessary. Erbakan's cabinet included ministers from the three major parties, and Ciller became foreign minister.

The septuagenarian Erbakan initially brought a breath of fresh air into the country's stale political system. With his round face and Italian designer ties, he seemed more like a Turkish uncle than an Islamist. During his year in office, his government reaffirmed traditional secularism, state socialism, and other elements

of the legacy of Ataturk. The government also stressed NATO membership in its foreign policy and continued the drive for an economic and customs union with the European Community begun by its predecessors.

With Refah's victory at the polls, Turkey's military leaders believed that the party was determined to dismantle the secular state founded by Ataturk and replace it with an Islamic one. In 1997, they demanded Erbakan's resignation. Inasmuch as they have final authority over political life under the 1980 Constitution, Erbakan had no choice. After his resignation, the state prosecutor filed suit to outlaw Refah on the grounds that its programs were intended to impose Islamic law on Turkish society. The court agreed and Erbakan was barred from politics for five years.

President Demirel then named ANAP leader Mesut Yilmaz to head a caretaker government. But he also resigned following a no-confidence resolution in the Grand National Assembly (GNA).

In the April 1999 GNA elections, however, a relatively new party, Democratic Left (Demokratik Sol Parti, DSP), surprised observers by winning a clear majority of seats. A strong pro-nationalist party, Nationalist Action (MHP), ran second, with 18 percent of the popular vote, winning 130 seats. The Virtue Party, reformed from the ruins of Refah, finished with 102 seats and 15 percent of the popular vote.

Virtue then set out to distance itself from radical Islamism. Unfortunately, the "new image" of Virtue did not convince the country's military and civilian leaders, who were adamant in their defense of Ataturk's legacy. In July 2000, an appeals court upheld a one-year jail sentence imposed on Erbakan, and the following year the Constitutional Court, the country's highest court, banned Virtue as a political party. The action came over the objections of many political leaders, including Ecevit. Despite the ban, Virtue deputies in the GNA were allowed to keep their seats, as independents.

In August 2001, yet another Islamic political party was formed. The new party, Justice and Development (AKP), included many former Virtue leaders, such as the charismatic ex-mayor of Istanbul, Recep Tayyip Erdogan. He had been banned from politics for five years in 1998 for criticizing the country's nonadherence to traditional Islam, but he was released under the 2000 amnesty law for political prisoners.

The debate between Islamists and secularists over Turkey's identity is far from being resolved. In May 2001, the debate

shifted to the presidency. Ecevit had proposed a change in the constitution to allow Suleyman Demirel, the incumbent, to run for a second term but to reduce his term to five years rather than seven. Demirel's election was seen as a sure thing, once the GNA had accepted the proposed changes. However, a majority of deputies rejected the proposal. Their candidate, Ahmet Cevdet Sezer, chief judge of the Constitutional Court, was elected to the largely ceremonial post on the third ballot by a 60 percent margin.

Sezer continued his predecessor's active participation in national politics, using his presidential veto power to block passage of GNA laws he considered harmful to the public. One was a measure that would mandate dismissal of government employees suspected of separatism or Islamist tendencies. This action put him at odds with Ecevit who was serving then as prime minister for the fourth time.

In the November 3, 2002 parliamentary elections, and following the collapse of the DSP-MHP-ANAP coalition led by Ecevit, AKP, led by Recep Tayyip Erdoğan, won 34.3% of the vote which gave it a substantial majority (363 seats). The incumbent parties had failed to win enough votes to remain in parliament. The Republican People's Party, (CHP) was the only other party to win more than the required 10% of the vote; with 10.69%, it acquired 178 seats. However, this was not enough to prevent the formation of Turkey's first single party government since 1987; it did however produce Turkey's first two-party parliament in 48 years.

The AKP's electoral victory and rising popularity thereafter were partly due to people's resentment toward the previous political class and its ineptitude, and to how deeply rooted is Islam in Turkish society. In spite of various claims by the nationalist/secular opposition forces, the Erdoğan government reassured the Turkish people by enacting economic reforms, supporting business and the democratic process and maintaining Turkey's commitment to pursuing membership in the European Union.

AKP's dominance of the political scene was emphasized in the 2007 presidential elections which followed the end of Sezer's term. The party nominated Foreign Minister Abdullah Gul for the position, which requires confirmation by the GNA. However public opposition and the concern of military leaders that Gul, who is a devout Muslim and whose wife wears the Islamic headscarf, would lead the country away from Ataturk's secular state, led to his failure to obtain sufficient support in the Assembly. The election was postponed until August, when under parliamentary

## ACHIEVEMENTS

Improvement in Turkey's educational system is a necessary requirement for EU membership. A 1997 law requires children to complete 8 years of primary school, and a World Bank grant of $250 million guarantees attendance through allowances of $15–$20 per child for poor families. A number of new universities have been established, both public and private, with most courses given in English.

rules Gul was elected by 339 votes, more than the required simple majority. In his acceptance speech Gul emphasized his commitment to a secular republic and Turkey's commitment to EU membership.

One EU requirement is that of a reduction in the powers of the National Security Council. The 10-member body, composed of the president, four cabinet ministers, and the five top military commanders, sets the agenda for all important issues, even laws, before they may be debated by the GNA. The order for dismissal of government employees for their "Islamist" beliefs was originally issued as a directive to the GNA by the council. It did not go into effect because Sezer refused to sign it, not as a council member but in his capacity as president.

Turkey has come a long way since then in trying to neutralize the political power security forces and the military. What seems to have emboldened the AKP and its leader in their reform momentum was their reconfirmation in office following a major victory in the 2007 parliamentary elections. The AKP won 47% of the vote and two opposition parties won over 10% share each—enough to maintain their presence in parliament. The Republican People's Party (CHP) won 20%, and the right-wing Nationalist Action Party (MHP) received 14% of the vote.

The nationalist/secular forces—both civilian and military—sought very hard to stop that momentum by accusing the governing party of planning to turn the country into an Islamist state, thereby breaking away from republic and secular principles of country. They took their case to the Constitutional Court seeking a ban on the party. However, the Court rejected, in March 2008, a call by the chief prosecutor to ban the AKP and 71 of its members. There have also been serious allegations that members of the military were involved in plots to overthrow the government. As a result, a formal investigation was started in 2009 and led to the arrest of more than 200 people (20 in March 2010 alone) suspected of involvement in a plot to overthrow the

government. The arrested included active-duty and retired military officers and government employees. These events may have two possible implications: one is the full de-politicization of the Turkish military—i.e., taking away their long-standing power to intervene in politics; and two, the danger of a serious conflict between the two most powerful forces in the country, the Islamists and the military, as had happened in Algeria in the 1990s.

Capitalizing on the support of the European Union for substantive reform (as a necessary condition for membership consideration) and on the popular support they enjoy, Prime Minister Erdoğan and his party indicated in March 2010 that they would seek to amend the constitution in a fundamental way in several areas, including the Constitutional Court, the way judges are appointed and the rules on political parties so as to make it harder to ban political parties based on political or ideological disagreements.

## THE "KURDISH PROBLEM"

Ataturk's suppression of Kurdish political aspirations and a separate Kurdish identity within the country effectively removed all traces of a "Kurdish problem" from national consciousness during the first decades of the republic. From the 1930s to the 1970s, the Kurdish areas were covered by a blanket of silence. Posters in Diyarbakir, the regional capital, proclaimed Ataturk's message: "Happy is he who says he is a Turk."

However, the general breakdown in law and order in Turkey in the late 1970s led to a revival of Kurdish nationalism. The Workers' Party of Kurdistan (PKK), founded as a Marxist-Leninist organization, was the first left-wing Kurdish group to advocate a separate Kurdish state. It was outlawed after the 1980 military coup; some 1,500 of its members were given jail sentences, and several leaders were executed for treason.

The PKK then went underground. In 1984, it began a campaign of guerrilla warfare. Its leader, Abdullah ("Apo") Ocalan, had won a scholarship in political science at Ankara University. While there, he became influenced by Marxist ideology and went into exile in Syria. There, and with Syrian support and financing, he called for a "war of national liberation" for the Kurds. Prior to the 1991 Gulf War, PKK guerrillas mounted mostly cross-border attacks into Turkey from bases in northern Lebanon, where they came under Syrian protection. But with Iraq's defeat and the establishment of an autonomous Kurdish region in northern Iraq, the PKK set up bases there to supplement its Lebanese bases.

Use of these bases posed a problem for Iraq's Kurdish leaders. On the one hand, they were committed to the cause of Kurdish sovereignty. But the cross-border raids brought Turkish retaliation, endangering their hard-won freedom from the long arm of Saddam Hussein's government. In 1992, after the raids had brought on massive Turkish counterattacks, they announced that they no longer supported the PKK and would not allow their territory to be used for its attacks on Turkish villages and police and army posts.

However, the momentum of the conflict left little maneuvering room for the groups involved. Turkey imposed martial law on its eastern provinces, and Turkish forces carried out large-scale raids on PKK bases in northern Iraq, seriously hampering PKK effectiveness. Ocalan called a unilateral cease-fire in 1993, but the Turkish government said that it would not deal with terrorists. The PKK then resumed the conflict, which by 2000 had claimed 40,000 lives, the majority of them villagers caught between security forces and the guerrillas. Some 3,000 villages had been destroyed and 2 million Kurds made refugees.

Yet despite Turkey's huge military superiority, its struggle with the PKK remained a stalemate until 1999. Syria meanwhile had expelled Ocalan after the Turks had threatened to invade its territory under the international "right of hot pursuit." The PKK leader went first to Italy. The Ecevit government demanded his extradition, but the Italians refused, on grounds that their laws forbid extradition to countries that have the death penalty. However, by this time Ocalan had become a huge embarrassment to his hosts. He left Italy for Greece and was finally given sanctuary in the Greek Embassy in Nairobi, Kenya.

Acting on a tip from Greek intelligence, Turkish commandos abducted Ocalan from the embassy and placed him in solitary confinement on an island in the Sea of Marmara. He was then tried for treason. Although the Turkish government insisted that the trial was an internal matter, UN and European Union observers were permitted to attend it.

Testifying in his own defense, Ocalan said that he had learned his lesson. He renounced violence as a "mistaken policy" and asserted that he would work as a loyal citizen toward the goal of peace and brotherhood. "We want to give up the armed struggle and have full democracy, so the PKK can enter the political arena," he said. "I will serve the state because now I see that it is necessary." The court was unconvinced, and on June 29, Ocalan was sentenced to death. The criminal appeals court, the only one in the Turkish legal system, upheld his conviction on appeal.

Ocalan's death sentence was commuted to life imprisonment in 2002, after the GNA had abolished the death penalty as a pre-requisite for EU membership. In May 2005, however, the European Court of Human Rights ruled 11–6 that his trial had not been conducted as an impartial and independent tribunal and thus violated European conventions on human rights. Since Turkey has signed this convention, defying the decision held serious implications for the country's membership application. Prime Minister Erdoğan then stated that "whether this case is opened or not, the matter is a closed one for the nation's conscience." Most Turks agreed with him.

With Ocalan jailed, the PKK went into semi-hibernation for several years. In 2006 it resumed the conflict, mainly because the government had not implemented its pledged commitments to greater Kurdish rights. In May 2007 a number of government forces and PKK militants were killed in cross-border attacks mounted from bases in Iraqi Kurdistan. Using the "right of hot pursuit" as justification, Turkey reacted by invading the Kurdish-controlled northern Iraq and fought the PKK force with the hope that the movement would stop its violent attacks in Turkey proper. The invasion led to many deaths on both sides, but no one was sure whether it would halt the PKK violent actions in Turkey's territory.

## FOREIGN POLICY

Other than friction with the U.S. Congress and with France over the Armenian issue, Turkey has been consistently a Western ally in its foreign policy. Since the end of the 1991 Gulf War, it allowed U.S. and British planes to be based at its Incirlik air base from where they protected the Kurdish and Shi'a populations from Saddam Hussein's regime. The agreement, code-named Operation Provide Comfort, was approved at six-month intervals by the GNA until 2003, when the U.S. invasion and occupation of Iraq made it unnecessary.

Turkey's relations with Iraq have always been complex and have had a negative effect on the Turkish economy, with an estimated loss of $40 billion from the cutoff in Iraqi oil exports. With the overthrow of Saddam Hussein in March 2003, the pipeline from Kirkuk to the Turkish port of Ceyhan was reopened briefly but then closed due to sabotage. In March 2010 Iraq and Turkey agreed to renew an accord to operate an oil pipeline from northern oil fields near Kirkuk to the Turkish Mediterranean port of Ceyhan.

Turkey's long-established friendship with the U.S. as its major ally, maintained through two world wars and many minor conflicts, underwent a severe strain when U.S. forces invaded Iraq in 2003. During the countdown to the invasion, the GNA refused permission for American troops to enter Iraq from its territory. Despite threats that the Bush administration would reduce U.S. aid, the Turks held firm, preferring to work through the UN to force Saddam Hussein to expose and remove his presumed weapons of mass destruction. As things turned out, the aid was maintained at the same level.

Turkey's relatively independent posture in foreign policy has been marked by agreements with Iran and Israel for training of its airforce pilots. The country reached agreement with Israel in April 2001 for water deliveries, as a part of its "water for peace" program for the Middle East. Under the terms of the agreement, Israel would receive 50 million cubic meters annually of water from the Tigris and Euphrates Rivers. Both of them rise in Turkey. However, serious tensions developed between Israel and Turkey starting with Ankara repeatedly criticizing Israel for its offensive in Gaza in December 2009 and January 2010, which devastated the besieged Palestinian territory and left 1,400 people dead. Another source of tension in 2009 was a popular fictional Turkish television series "Valley of the Wolves," which depicted Israeli intelligence agents as running operations in Turkey to kidnap babies and convert them to Judaism. Tensions increased further when Israeli Deputy Foreign Minister Danny Ayalon summoned Turkish ambassador Ahmet Oguz Celikkol on January 11, 2010 to complain about the television show. The Turkish ambassador was reportedly treated in an undiplomatic and demeaning way by his host in front of the news media. The Turkish government reacted strongly to the humiliation of the ambassador.

The Cyprus issue, which has divided Turkey and Greece ever since Turkish troops occupied the northern part of the island republic in 1974, moved toward a solution in 2004 as Greek and Turkish Cypriot leaders began serious negotiations under UN sponsorship. Although Turkish Cypriots approved unification in a plebiscite, the Greek Cypriot community rejected it. In February 2006 the Turkish government issued new proposals that would remove all restrictions on freedom of goods transfers, exchange of families and sharing of services in the divided island. If agreed to by the UN and the Greek community it would end the Turkish zone's economic isolation and expand Cyprus's present EU membership to a single Greek-Turkish entity.

The country has also improved its links with the newly independent Turkish-speaking countries of Central Asia. Turkey was the first country to recognize the independence of Kazakhstan and Azerbaijan. In 2000, the government signed a 15-year agreement with Azerbaijan for imports of natural gas from the Shaykh Deniz field, offshore in the Caspian Sea. Another important agreement between Turkey, Georgia, Azerbaijan, and Kazakhstan has initiated construction of the thousand-mile oil pipeline from Baku, Azerbaijan, to Ceyhan (Adana) on Turkey's Mediterranean coast.

In its bid for accession to the European Union and other aims, Turkey has presented itself more as a European country than a Middle Eastern one. Its domestic and foreign policies reflected this tendency, notably secularism, republicanism, and shared security interests with the West. However, in the last few years, due to important domestic policy initiatives and new foreign policy positions and actions, some observers have started to wonder whether Turkey is rediscovering its natural environment, the Middle East, and is moving away from its close association with the West as a result of both domestic changes, notably the consolidated rule of the AKP, and some rebuffs in its relations with both Western Europe and the United States.

"In fact, with Turkey cultivating ever closer ties with the Iranian regime, overcoming past enmities with Syria, engaging Hamas in Palestine, and quarrelling with Israel, the debate has only grown more heated on whether Turkey's 'activism' in the Middle East may perhaps provide even stronger evidence than domestic, political, and societal dynamics of the country's drift away from the West."[12]

Turkey's new activism in the Middle East and in Central Asia may be best understood as part of its effort to adapt to the post-Cold War environment and its risks and opportunities. It is also a moment when Turkey may be redefining its identity in light of both internal and external changes. However, this redefinition is not likely to weaken Turkey's resolute ambition to be fully integrated in Europe and to maintain special security ties with both Europe and the United States. Its own security and livelihood depend on these two aims.

## THE ECONOMY

Turkey has a relatively diversified economy, with a productive agriculture and considerable mineral resources. Cotton is the major export crop, but the country is the world's largest producer of sultana raisins and hazelnuts. Other important crops are tobacco, wheat, sunflower seeds, sesame and linseed oils, and cotton-oil seeds. Opium was once an important crop, but, due to illegal exportation, poppy growing was banned by the government in 1972. The ban was lifted in 1974 after poppy farmers were unable to adapt their lands to other crops; production and sale are now government-controlled.

Mineral resources include bauxite, chromium, copper, and iron ore, and there are large deposits of lignite. Turkey is one of the world's largest producers of chromite (chromium ore). Another important mineral resource is meerschaum, used for pipes and cigarette holders. Turkey supplies 80 percent of the world market for emery, and there are rich deposits of tungsten, perlite, boron, and cinnabar, all important rare metals.

Turkey signed a customs agreement with the European Union in 1996. The agreement eliminated import quotas on Turkish textiles and slashed customs duties and excise taxes on Turkish imports of manufactured iron and steel products from the European Union.

The agreement was intended as a first step toward full membership in the EU. However, the accession process has been delayed by the resistance of some EU members, such as France and Germany, as well as by Turkey's slow pace of political and economic reforms and its financial crisis of 2000–2001.

The "liquidity crisis" that nearly overwhelmed the Turkish economy in 2001 resulted from a combination of factors. Ironically, one of them was the economic-reform program introduced by the Ecevit government to meet EU requirements. Corruption in economic and fiscal management was another factor, while a third grew from the public dispute between Sezer and Ecevit over privatization of state-owned enterprises. The feud between the two leaders, plus the slow pace of privatization, led to a fiscal crisis in November 2000. The liquidity crisis followed, with a run on foreign-currency reserves in the Central Bank as worried Turks and foreign investors rushed to retrieve their funds. The bank lost $7.5 billion in reserves in a two-day period. The government's stop-gap decision to end currency controls and allow the Turkish lira to float caused it to lose nearly 50 percent of its value. In December, 10 banks collapsed; they included Ihlas Finans, the country's largest Islamic bank. (Under Turkish banking laws, deposits in such banks, which are interest-free under Islamic prohibitions against usury, are not covered by federal deposit guarantees. Consequently, 200,000 depositors lost their life savings.)

The crisis was averted temporarily when the International Monetary Fund agreed "in principle" to provide $5 billion in emergency aid. However, the IMF's insistence on fiscal reform as a precondition brought on another crisis in March–April 2001. The government then appointed Kermal Dervis, a Turkish-born World Bank economist, as minister of the economy. He was charged with bringing economic order out of fiscal chaos. His reform package included a 9 percent limit on government expenditures and a hiring freeze in the bloated public sector. But despite $16 billion in loans from the IMF and the World Bank, the economy continued to slide downward, with gross domestic product down 11.8 percent for 2001.

In recent years the Dervis reform package has led to a remarkable turnaround in Turkey's economic growth. GDP shot up to 8 percent in 2004 and 2005 before leveling off to 5.2 percent in 2007. Inflation also dropped to 9.8 percent, the first in single digits since 1972. Other reform measures, notably reduced subsidies on certain agricultural crops, generated more than $4.5 billion in savings after they were instituted. Privatization of state-owned industries, another pre-requisite for EU membership, has been slow. However state ownership of DHY, the national airline, was reduced to 49 percent in 2005, and private participation in management plus a $3 billion modernization program has resulted in the airline's being named Europe's fastest-growing—and most punctual—in 2006.

The country has a fairly large skilled labor force, and Turkish contractors have been able to negotiate contracts for development projects in oil-producing countries, such as Libya, with partial payment for services in oil shipments at reduced rates. The large Turkish expatriate labor force, much of it in Germany, provided an important source of revenue through worker remittances.

The 2008–2009 global economic slowdown caused by the financial crisis directly affected Turkey's economic performance. The GDP growth rate declined from 5.2% in 2007 to 0.9% 2008 and an estimated −6% in 2009. The direct cause of this decline was a decreased demand for Turkish products which led to a high current account deficit and a high external debt. When Turkey manages to weather this substantial slowdown, its bright economic prospects will return. Because of the possibility of joining the EU, foreign direct investment will continue (its value in 2009 was estimated to be $180 billion). The privatization of public enterprises, which has already brought in $39 billion in revenue to the state, is likely to continue and the current process of judicial reform will consolidate this positive trend. Furthermore, the oil flow from Iraq to the port of Ceyhan and through the Baku-Tbilisi-Ceyhan

## Timeline: PAST

**330**
The founding of Constantinople as the Roman Christian capital, on the site of ancient Byzantium

**1453**
The capture of Constantinople by Sultan Mehmed II; the city becomes the capital of the Islamic Ottoman Empire

**1683**
The Ottoman Empire expands deep into Europe; the high-water mark is the siege of Vienna

**1918–1920**
The defeat of Ottomans and division of territories into foreign protectorates

**1923**
Turkey proclaims its independence

**1960**
The first military coup

**1980s**
Military coup; civilian rule later returns; the government imposes emergency rules

**1990s**
The Kurdish problem intensifies; Alawi and Kurdish social unrest; thousands die as earthquakes devastate Turkey

**2000s**
Serious financial crise threated the nation; Turkey continues to try to meet requirements for EU membership

**2002**
Death sentence is abolished
Justice and Development Party (AKP) wins landslide victory in parliamentary elections

**2005**
EU membership negotiations officially launched after intense bargaining

**2007**
AKP wins parliamentary elections

**2009**
Turkey and Armenia agree to normalize relations
The government increases Kurdish language rights and reduces the military presence in the mainly-Kurdish southeast

## PRESENT

**2010s**
70 members of the military are arrested over alleged military coup plot. Thirty-three officers are charged with conspiring to overthrow government.

pipeline—which started in 2006—along with new planned gas pipelines from several central Asia countries to Europe through Turkey will increase revenue. The banking and financial systems of Turkey did not suffer much from the global financial crisis mostly because of the stringent reforms enacted after the 2001 crisis, but if the general economic slowdown persists, these sectors may as well feel the effect, especially if investor confidence is negatively affected. Economic growth is likely to be negative or very small in 2010 due to unchanged global indicators, but the biggest threat to Turkey's economy might end up being any serious and sustained political instability.

## NOTES

1. "The killing (of Dink) is the ultimate result of increasing nationalism, isolationism, and increasing animosity toward minorities that the European Union has fueled in its handling of Turkey's membership process." Can Baydarol, quoted in Sebnem Arsu and Susanne Fowler, "Turkish Gunman Said to Confess to Killing Armenian Editor," *The New York Times,* January 21, 2007.

2. The center of this ultra-nationalism and anti-Armenian feeling is the Black Sea port of Trabzon; the gunman and eight others implicated in the plot came from there. A prison therapist who works there observed that "Black Sea people are dynamic, restless, energetic and have strong heroic feelings. Their environment . . . creates a greater potential for reaction to social issues, intolerance toward the Other, superiority toward minorities. . ." Ali Sarkoglu, quoted in Sebnem Arsu, *The New York Times,* Feb. 21, 2007.

3. Martin van Bruisenessen, "Kurds, Turks and the Alevi Revival in Turkey," *Middle East Report* (July–September 1996), p. 7.

4. John Noble Wilford, "The Secrets of Croesus' Gold," *The New York Times* (August 15, 2000). Online at www.nytimes.com. Consulted on August 9, 2010. Another Asia Minor ruler, King Midas of Phrygia, was said to have the "golden touch" because everything he touched (including his daughter) turned to gold; he has angered the gods, it seemed.

5. Lord Kinross, *The Ottoman Centuries: The Rise and Fall of the Turkish Empire,* (New York: William Morrow, 1977).

6. *Ibid.,* p. 25.

7. An American astronomer, Kevin Pang, advanced the proposal that the fall of the Byzantine capital was preceded by a "darkening of the skies" and other portents of doom related to the eruption of the volcano Kuwae, in the New Hebrides, in 1453. See Lynn Teo Simarski, "Constantinople's Volcanic Twilight," *Aramco World* (November/December 1996), pp. 8–13.

8. It is said that the marching bands at football games and parades in our society apparently derive from Janissary bands of drummers and cymbal players who marched ahead of invading Ottoman armies.

9. V. A. Danilov, "Kemalism and World Peace," in A. Kazancigil and E. Ozbudun, eds., *Ataturk, Founder of a Modern State* (Hamden, CT: Archon Books, 1981), p. 110.

10. Maurice Duverger, *Political Parties* (New York: John Wiley, 1959), p. 277.

11. C. H. Dodd, *Democracy and Development in Turkey* (North Humberside, England: Eothen Press, 1979), p. 135.

12. Emiliano Alessandri, "The New Turkish Foreign Policy and the Future of Turkey-EU Relations," Paper prepared for the Istituto Affari Internazionali (IAI), Rome, Italy, February 2010, p. 3. Online at www .iai.it/pdf/DocIAI/iai1003.pdf. Consulted on April 1, 2010.

# United Arab Emirates

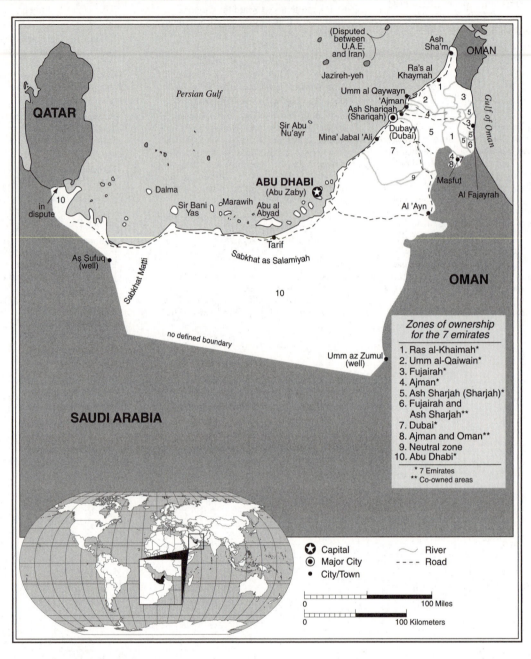

Zones of ownership for the 7 emirates
1. Ras al-Khaimah*
2. Umm al-Qaiwain*
3. Fujairah*
4. Ajman*
5. Ash Sharjah (Sharjah)*
6. Fujairah and Ash Sharjah**
7. Dubai*
8. Ajman and Oman**
9. Neutral zone
10. Abu Dhabi*

* 7 Emirates
** Co-owned areas

Capital
Major City
City/Town
River
Road

0    100 Miles
0    100 Kilometers

# United Arab Emirates

## GEOGRAPHY

*Area in Square Miles (Kilometers):* 31,992 (82,880) (about the size of Maine)
*Capital (Population):* Abu Dhabi (799,000)
*Environmental Concerns:* lack of natural freshwater; desertification; oil pollution of beaches and coastal waters
*Geographical Features:* flat, barren coastal plain merging into rolling sand dunes of vast desert; mountains in the east

*Climate:* hot, dry desert; cooler in the eastern mountains

## PEOPLE

### Population

*Total:* 4,975,593 (note: 2005 census included 1,606,079 non-nationals, but 2007 estimates suggest a higher figure)
*Annual Growth Rate:* 3.561%
*Rural/Urban Population Ratio:* 16/84

*Major Languages:* Arabic; Persian (Farsi); English; Hindi
*Ethnic Makeup:* 19% Emirati; 23% other Arab and Iranian; 50% South Asian; 8% East Asian and Westerner
*Religions:* 96% Muslim (80% Sunni, 16% Shi'a); 4% Hindu, Christian, and others

### Health

*Life Expectancy at Birth:* 73 years (male); 79 years (female)

192

*Infant Mortality Rate (Ratio):* 12.3/1,000 live births

### Education

*Adult Literacy Rate:* 77.9%

### COMMUNICATION

*Telephones:* 1.508 million main lines
*Daily Newspaper Circulation:* 135 per 1,000 people
*Televisions:* 18 per 1,000 people
*Internet Users:* 2.922 million (2008)

### TRANSPORTATION

*Highways in Miles (Kilometers):* 3,002 (4,835)
*Railroads in Miles (Kilometers):* none
*Usable Airfields:* 35
*Motor Vehicles in Use:* 400,000

### GOVERNMENT

*Type:* federation of 7 emirates-Abu Dhabi, Ajman, Dubai, Fujairah, Ras al-Khaimah, Sharjah, Umm al-Qaiwain
*Independence Date:* December 2, 1971 (from the United Kingdom)
*Head of State/Government:* Federal Supreme Council of Emirate Rulers-president is Shaykh Khalifa Bin Zayd al-Nuhayyan, ruler of Abu Dhabi
*Political Parties:* none, but in 2006 a Federal National Council of 40 members, 20 appointed by emirate Rulers and 20 elected by an "electoral college" of 6,689 UAE citizens, including 1,189 women, was established as an advisory body
*Suffrage:* none

### MILITARY

*Military Expenditures (% of GDP):* 3.1%
*Current Disputes:* Iranian occupation of Greater and Lesser Tunbs Islands contested by UAE. Boundary with Oman formally demarcated in 2000

### ECONOMY

*Currency ($U.S. equivalent):* 3.673 dirhams = $1
*Per Capita Income/GDP:* $49,700/ $231.3 billion
*GDP Growth Rate:* −3.5%
*Inflation Rate:* 10%
*Labor Force:* 3.168 million (74% of those in age group 15–64 are non-nationals)
*Natural Resources:* petroleum; natural gas
*Agriculture:* dates; vegetables; watermelons; poultry; dairy products; fish
*Industry:* petroleum; fishing; petrochemicals; construction materials; boat building; handicrafts; pearling
*Exports:* $174 billion (primary partners Japan, South Korea, Thailand)
*Imports:* $141 billion (primary partners Britain, China, United States)

### SUGGESTED WEB SITE

http://lcweb2.loc.gov/frd/cs/aetoc.html

# United Arab Emirates Country Report

The United Arab Emirates (U.A.E.) is a federation of seven independent states with a central governing Council located on the northeast coast of the Arabian Peninsula. The states—called emirates, from the title of their rulers—are Abu Dhabi, Ajman, Dubai, Fujairah, Ras al-Khaimah, Sharjah, and Umm al-Qaiwain. They came under British "protection" in the 1800s and came from Great Britain by treaty in 1971. At that time, they created the federal union. From its modest beginnings, the U.A.E. has come to play an important role in Middle East affairs, because of its oil wealth.

Abu Dhabi, the largest emirate, contains 87 percent of the UAE's total land area. The federal capital is also named Abu Dhabi, but Dubai, capital of the second largest emirate, is a larger city, with a population of approximately 1 million. Dubai has the U.A.E.'s only natural harbor, which has been enlarged to accommodate super-tankers. Abu Dhabi, Dubai, and Sharjah produce oil; Sharjah also has important natural-gas reserves and cement. Fujairah port is a major entrepôt for shipping. The other emirates have little in the way of resources and have yet to find oil in commercial quantities.

The early inhabitants of the area were fishermen and nomads. They were converted to Islam in the seventh century A.D., but little is known of their history before the sixteenth century. By that time, European powers, notably Portugal, had taken an active interest in trade with India and the Far East. Gradually, other European countries, particularly the Netherlands, France, and Britain, challenged Portuguese supremacy. As more and more European ships appeared in Arabian coastal waters or fought over trade, the coastal Arabs felt threatened with loss of their territory. Meanwhile, the Wahhabis, militant Islamic missionaries, spread over Arabia in the eighteenth century. Wahhabi agents incited the most powerful coastal group, the Qawasim, to interfere with European shipping. European ships were seized along with their cargoes, their crews held for ransom. To the European countries, this was piracy; to the Qawasim, however, it was defense of Islamic territory. Ras al-Khaimah was their chief port, but soon the whole coast of the present-day U.A.E. became known as the Pirate Coast.

Piracy lasted until 1820, when the British, who controlled India and thus dominated Eastern trade, convinced the principal chiefs of the coast to sign a treaty ending pirate activities. A British naval squadron was stationed in Ras al-Khaimah to enforce the treaty. In 1853, the arrangement was changed into a "Perpetual Maritime Truce." Because it specified a *truce* between the British and the local chiefs, the region became known as the Trucial Coast, and the territory of each chief was

### DEVELOPMENT

Huge oil revenues (over 33 percent of GDP) have enabled the UAE to maintain perhaps the world's highest per capita income and accumulate a substantial foreign trade surplus despite the disparity of wealth among the member emirates. With oil and gas reserves expected to be used up within a century, Abu Dhabi and Dubai, the major producers, have emphasized large-scale urban development along with such non-oil sector projects as the world's largest drydock.[1]

termed a "trucial state." A British garrison was provided for each ruler, and a British political agent was assigned to take charge of foreign affairs. Britain paid the rulers annual subsidies; in most cases, it was all the money they could acquire. There were originally five Trucial States (also called emirates); Sharjah and Ras al-Khaimah were reorganized as separate emirates in 1966.

The arrangement between Great Britain and the Trucial States worked smoothly for more than a century, through both world wars. Then, in the 1960s, the British decided—for economic and political reasons—to give up most of their overseas colonies, including those in the Arabian

Peninsula, which were technically protectorates rather than colonies. In 1968, they proposed to the Trucial Coast emirs that they join in a federation with Bahrain and Qatar, neighboring oil-producing protectorates. But Bahrain and Qatar, being larger and richer, decided to go it alone. Thus, the United Arab Emirates, when it became independent in 1971, included only six emirates. Ras al-Khaimah joined in 1972.

## PROBLEMS OF INTEGRATION

Differences in size, wealth, resources, and population have hampered U.A.E. integration since it was formed. Another problem was poor communications. Until recently, one could travel from emirate to emirate only by boat, and telephone service was nonexistent. A combination of economic growth and technology (for example the Internet and cell phones), have produced full integration and rapid communication between the seven emirates.

Despite full integration there are certain internal disagreements among the emirates, particularly in the areas of joint economic planning and allocation of development funds for projects. One result is the unnecessary duplication of ports and international airports, as each emirate wishes to have its own access to the outside world. Also several borders remain undemarcated—that between Ras al-Khaimah and Umm al-Qaiwain and Sharjah's border with Oman's Musandam Peninsula.

The U.A.E. federal system, as defined in the 1971 Constitution, consists of a Supreme Council of Rulers of the seven emirates; a Council of Ministers (cabinet) appointed by the president of the Council; and a unicameral Federal National Assembly of 40 members appointed by the ruling emirs on a proportional basis, according to size and population. A stabilizing factor in the U.A.E. system was the leadership of Shaykh Zayed of Abu Dhabi, president of the Council of Rulers from its inception

until his death in 2004. The federal capital is located in Abu Dhabi, the largest and richest emirate. The ruler of Dubai, the second largest of the emirates, serves as vice-president. Other unifying features of the U.A.E. are a common commercial-law code, currency, and defense structure. The sharing of revenues by the wealthy emirates with the less prosperous ones has also helped foster U.A.E. unity.

The 1979 Iranian Revolution, which seemed to threaten the U.A.E.'s security, accelerated the move toward the centralization of authority over the defense forces, the abolition of borders, and the merging of revenues. In 1981, the U.A.E. joined with other states in the Gulf Cooperation Council (GCC) to establish a common-defense policy toward Iran. The U.A.E. also turned to the United States for help; the two countries signed a Defense Cooperation Agreement in 1994. Under the agreement, a force of several hundred U.S. military personnel is stationed in the emirates to supervise port facilities and air refueling for American planes patrolling the no-fly zone in southern Iraq.

Early in 2001, the U.A.E. joined with other GCC members in a mutual-defense pact, the first in the region. With support from the United States, the pact would increase the current rapid-deployment force from 5,000 to 22,000. Each GCC member would contribute to the force in proportion to its size and population.

The September 11, 2001, terrorist attacks on the United States intensified the importance of increased security for oil operations on the part of Abu Dhabi and Dubai, the chief oil-producing U.A.E. states. The Federal Council supported the newly formed international coalition against terrorism in a public statement, and the U.A.E. withdrew its recognition of the Taliban as the legitimate government of Afghanistan. The U.A.E. initially backed U.S. efforts in the UN to force disclosure of Iraq's alleged weapons of mass destruction. Prior to the U.S. invasion of that country, another Arab satellite all-news TV channel, Al-Arabiya, began operating in the U.A.E. to supplement Qatar's Al-Jazeera station.

The governments of the emirates themselves are best described as patriarchal. Each emir is head of his own large "family" as well as head of his emirate. The ruling emirs gained their power a long time ago from various sources—through foreign trade, pearl fishing, or ownership of lands. In recent years, they have profited from oil royalties to maintain their positions as heads of state.

Disagreements within the ruling families have sometimes led to violence or

"palace coups," there being no rule or law of primogeniture. The ruler of Umm al-Qaiwain came to power when his father was murdered in 1929. Shaykh Zayed deposed his brother, Shaykh Shakbut, in 1966, when the latter refused to approve a British-sponsored development plan for the protectorate. In 1987, Shaykh Abd al-Aziz, the elder brother of the ruler of Sharjah, attempted to overthrow his brother on the grounds that economic development was being mishandled. The U.A.E. Supreme Council mediated a settlement, and Abd al-Aziz retired to Abu Dhabi.

Sharjah, the third largest of the emirates (1,165 square miles), has a well-developed structure of ports, industries and manufacturing to supplement its meager oil resources. As of 2007, it accounted for over 50 percent of U.A.E industrial output. Much of this output comes from oil-based chemical industries, and due to its ample supply of natural gas its some 300 public utility vehicles have been converted to use this fuel. The emirate currently has three free foreign trade zones and as a result has become a major global trade center.

The other emirates are less fortunate. Ajman and Umm al-Qaiwain are essentially coastal ports, with some agricultural development inland. Ras al-Khaimah's sole resource is aggregate, used in making cement. The oil refinery in Fujairah, opened in 2001, refines some 105,000 barrels per day (bpd) and its bunkering port, largest in the region, can accommodate supertankers of up to 90,000 deadweight tons.

## AN OIL-DRIVEN ECONOMY

In the past, the people of the Trucial Coast made a meager living from breeding racing camels, some farming, and pearl fishing. Pearls were the main source of cash. However, twentieth-century competition from Japanese cultured pearls ruined the Arabian pearl-fishing industry.

In 1958, Shaykh Zayed, then in his teens, led a party of geologists into the remote desert near the oasis of al-Ain, following up the first oil-exploration agreement signed by Abu Dhabi with foreign oil companies. Oil exports began in 1962, and from then on the fortunes of the Gulf Arabs improved dramatically. Production was 14,200 barrels per day in 1962; by 1982, it was 1.1 million bpd, indicating how far the country's oil-driven economy had moved in just two decades. Oil reserves are approximately 98 billion barrels, while gas reserves are 205 trillion cubic feet— 10 percent of global reserves.

## ACHIEVEMENTS

The rapid development of Islamic banks, those which observe shari'a law governing Islamic finance but replace interest payments and charges with "handling fees," has brought about the establishment particularly in Dubai of a body of legal scholars authorized to issue fatwas (seals of Islamic approval) governing bank establishment and investments. Their particular legal instrument is the *sukuk* (Islamic bond), which covers credit cards, Islamic mortgages and other investments. Dubai Ports World used a sukuk in its purchase of the P & O line and in its aborted attempt to buy security in U.S. East Coast ports.

Backed by almost unlimited oil wealth, Abu Dhabi and Dubai are engaged in a not-too-friendly competition for cultural and commercial supremacy. Dubai has a significant headstart, but in 2006 Abu Dhabi began construction of a $27 billion project which will include hotels, art galleries, a maritime museum and other cultural facilities, a sort of "cultural xanadu" for the Arab world. Not to be outdone, Dubai has its Dubailand theme park, while Sharjah's University City boasts an American-funded university as well as its own university, founded in 1997 and endowed with an outstanding foreign faculty.

The bulk of hydrocarbon production and reserves is in Abu Dhabi. Dubai, not content with second place in U.A.E. development, launched a Strategic Development Plan in 1998, intended to increase its non-oil income to $20,000 per capita by 2010. Its government earlier had established a free-trade zone in the port of Jebel Ali. It provides 100 percent foreign ownership, full repatriation of capital and profits, and a 15-year exemption from corporate and other taxes. By 1996, more than 1,000 companies had located in the zone. Since 2000 this free-trade zone has been supplemented by another in Dubai, linked globally with foreign markets through the Internet.

The ruling family in Dubai is also quietly investing in foreign real estate, with over $1 billion invested abroad. In 2004 it purchased Madame Tussaud's Wax Works in London along with a major stake in Daimler/Chrysler, and in 2005 it acquired several large properties in New York City. Early in 2006 Dubai Ports World, based in Dubai and presently owner of the British P & O (Peninsular and Oriental Navigation Company) line, temporarily purchased a controlling interest in six major U.S. ports. Although the purchase was legitimate and the U.A.E is a close U.S. ally in the war against terrorism, the outcry in Congress (which had not been consulted by the Bush administration before the purchase agreement had been negotiated) over the alleged sale of port security to an *Arab* country was such that Dubai Ports World cancelled the agreement. As one columnist noted, "this Dubai ports deal has unleashed nativist, isolationist mass hysteria, a kind of collective mania we haven't seen in decades."[2]

Although they are not blessed with the vast petroleum-based wealth of Abu Dhabi and Dubai, the other emirates do have some important economic assets. Liquefied natural gas (LNG) was discovered in Sharjah in 1992, and by 2001 its onshore Kahaif and Sajaa fields were producing 40 million cubic feet per day, sufficient to meet domestic needs.

The U.A.E.'s dependence on foreign workers, who comprise approximately 80 percent of the labor force, has been an obstacle to self-sufficiency and diversification. In October 1996, a strict new residency law governing foreign labor was approved by the Supreme Council. The law limits both immigration numbers and length of stay; it is aimed particularly at low-level Asian workers. As a result, some 400,000 "guest workers"—approximately 15 percent of the total foreign population— left the federation.

The U.A.E. celebrated its silver anniversary in December 1996 with a 69-ton birthday cake. An even larger one, 50 feet long by 6 feet across, was unveiled in 1998 for the country's children. Dubai has at present the world's tallest skyscraper, tallest hotel, an enormous Disney-style theme park, strip malls and other components of Western urbanism, in what was once a tiny Gulf trading port. Sinbad the Sailor, the legendary Arab traveler who supposedly lived there, would be amazed if he returned and saw the changes in his ancient anchorage.

## NOTES

1. Matt Gross, "The Frugal Traveller: Dubai," *The New York Times,* May 20, 2007.

2. David Brooks, "Kicking Arabs in the Teeth," *The New York Times,* February 24,

2006. As other observers have pointed out, the U.A.E. was the first Middle East government to accept the U.S. Container Security Initiative to screen containers before they proceed to U.S. ports and has agreed to U.S. Energy Department requests to ban nuclear materials from shipment from its ports.

## Timeline: PAST

**1853, 1866**
Peace treaties between Great Britain and Arab shaykhs establishing the Trucial States

**1952**
Establishment of the Trucial Council under British advisers, the forerunner of federation

**1971**
Independence

**1973**
The U.A.E. becomes the first Arab oil producer to ban exports to the U.S. after the Yom Kippur War

**1979**
Balanced federal Assembly and cabinet are established

**1990s**
The U.A.E. reduces its dependence on oil revenues; the free-trade zone proves a success

## PRESENT

**2001**
The U.A.E. supports the International coalition against terrorism

**2004**
UAE President Sheikh Zayed Bin-Sultan Al Nahyan dies and is succeeded by his son, Sheikh Khalifa

The UAE signs Trade and Investment Framework Agreement with The United States and began negotiations for a Free Trade Agreement

**2006**
Sheikh Maktoum bin Rashid al-Maktoum, UAE PM and Vice-President and ruler of Dubai, dies and is succeeded by his brother, Sheikh Mohammed bin Rashid al-Maktoum

First-ever national elections in which a small number of hand-picked voters elected half of the members of advisory Federal National Council

Dubai Ports World relinquishes control of terminals at six major American ports after a big controversy is raised in the United States

**2008**
France is awarded the right to set up a permanent military base in Abu Dhabi

**2010**
Burj Khalifa Tower, the world's tallest building, opens in Dubai

Palestinian militant leader Mahmoud al-Mabhouh is killed in a Dubai hotel, in a hit widely blamed on Israel and meticulously documented through video surveillance tapes

# Yemen (Republic of Yemen)

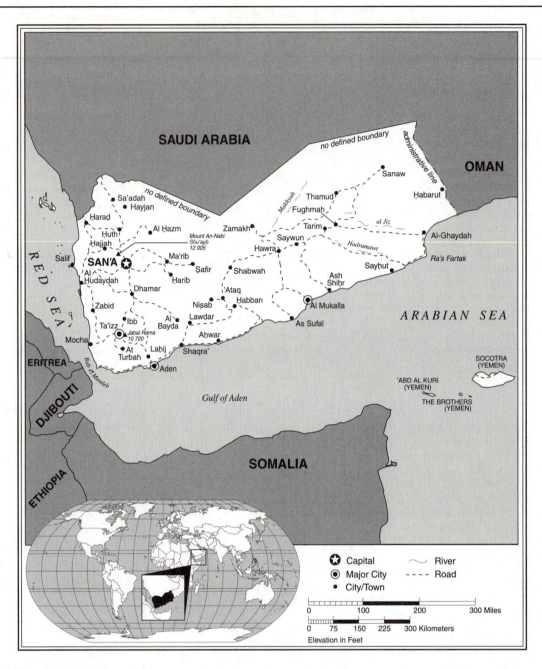

# Yemen Statistics

## GEOGRAPHY

*Area in Square Miles (Kilometers):*
203,796 (527,970) (about twice the size of Wyoming)

*Capital (Population):* San'a (political capital) (972,000); Aden (economic capital) (562,000)

*Environmental Concerns:* limited freshwater supplies; inadequate potable water; overgrazing; soil erosion; desertification

*Geographical Features:* a narrow coastal plain backed by hills and mountains; dissected upland desert plains in the center slope into desert

*Climate:* mostly desert; hot, with minimal rainfall except in mountain zones

## PEOPLE

### Population

*Total:* 23,495,361
*Annual Growth Rate:* 2.713%
*Rural/Urban Population Ratio:* 66/34
*Major Language:* Arabic
*Ethnic Makeup:* predominantly Arab;

small Afro-Arab, South Asian, and European communities

*Religions:* nearly 100% Muslim; small numbers of Christians, Jews, and Hindus

### Health

*Life Expectancy at Birth:* 61.35 years (male); 65.47 years (female)
*Infant Mortality (Rate):* 56.77/1,000 live births

### Education

*Adult Literacy Rate:* 50%
*Compulsory (Ages):* 6–15

## COMMUNICATION

*Telephones:* 1.117 million
*Televisions:* 6.5 per 1,000 people
*Internet Users:* 370,000 (2008)

## TRANSPORTATION

*Highways in Miles (Kilometers):* 44,303 (71,300)
*Railroads in Miles (Kilometers):* none

*Usable Airfields:* 50
*Motor Vehicles in Use:* 510,000

## GOVERNMENT

*Type:* republic, formed by merger of former Yemen Arab Republic and People's Democratic Republic of Yemen
*Independence Date:* formally united May 22, 1990 (date of merger)
*Head of State/Government:* President Ali Abdullah Saleh; Prime Minister Ali Muhammad Mujawar
*Political Parties:* General Peoples' Congress, majority Party; Islah, main opposition party; others include Yemen Socialist Party (YSP), Nasserist Union Party, Ba'th Party
*Suffrage:* universal at 18

## MILITARY

*Military Expenditures (% of GDP):* 6.6%
*Current Disputes:* none

## ECONOMY

*Currency ($U.S. Equivalent):* 197 rials = $1
*Per Capita Income/GDP:* $900/$26.54 billion
*GDP Growth Rate:* 3.8%
*Inflation Rate:* 19%
*Labor Force:* 6.641 million
*Unemployment Rate:* 35%
*Natural Resources:* petroleum; fish; rock salt; marble; small deposits of coal, gold, lead, nickel, and copper; fertile soil in west
*Agriculture:* grain; fruits; vegetables; qat; coffee; cotton; livestock; fish
*Industry:* petroleum; cotton textiles and leather goods; food processing; handicrafts; aluminum products; cement
*Exports:* $5.5 billion (primary partners China, India, Thailand)
*Imports:* $7.12 billion (primary partners United Arab Emirates, Saudi Arabia, Switzerland)

# Yemen Statistics

The Republic of Yemen occupies the extreme southwest corner of the Arabian Peninsula. It consists of three distinct regions, which until 1990 had been separated geographically for centuries and divided politically into two states: the Yemen Arab Republic (North Yemen, or Y.A.R.) and the People's Democratic Republic of Yemen (South Yemen, or P.D.R.Y.). Until the twentieth century, the entire area was known simply as Yemen; with the merger of the two states, it has resumed its former geographic identity. The former Y.A.R.'s territory consists of two distinct regions: a hot, humid coastal strip, the Tihama, along the Red Sea, and an interior region of mountains and high plains that shade off gradually into the bleak, waterless South Arabian Desert.

Yemeni territory also includes Socotra, a remote island 550 miles from Aden, and two other small islands, Abd al-Khuri and the Brothers, which lie off the African coast of Somalia. Socotra is the only world habitat for Dragon's Blood trees, which produce cinnabar resin, and of some 850 other plants that exist nowhere else.

The Yemeni interior is very different not only from the Tihama but also from other parts of the Arabian Peninsula. It consists of highlands and rugged mountains ranging up to 12,000 feet. At the higher elevations, the mountain ridges are separated by deep, narrow valleys, usually with swift-flowing

streams at the bottom. The ample rainfall allows extensive use of terracing for agriculture. The main crops are coffee, cereals, vegetables, and qat (a shrub whose leaves are chewed as a mild narcotic).

This part of Yemen has been for centuries the home of sedentary peoples who have formed a stable, stratified society living in villages and small cities. These groups have been the principal support for the Shi'a Zaidi Imams, whose rule was the political nucleus of Yemen from the ninth century A.D. to the establishment of the republic in 1962. The Yemeni political capital, San'a, is located in these northern highlands.

The former P.D.R.Y., almost twice the size of its neighbor but less favored geographically, consists of the port and hinterland of Aden (today Yemen's economic capital); the Hadhramaut, a broad valley edged by desert and extending eastward along the Arabian Sea coast; the Perim and Kamaran Islands, at the south end of the Red Sea; and Socotra Island.

Until the recent discoveries of oil, South Yemen was believed to have no natural resources. The dominant physical feature is the Wadi Hadhramaut. It is one of the few regions of the country with enough water for irrigation. Except for Aden, the area has little rainfall; in some sections, rain may fall only once every 10 years. Less than 2 percent of the land is cultivable.

In ancient times, the whole of Yemen was known to the Greeks, Romans, and other peoples as Arabia Felix ("Happy Arabia"), a remote land that they believed to be fabulously wealthy. They knew it as the source of frankincense, myrrh, and other spices as well as other exotic products brought to Mediterranean and Middle Eastern markets from the East. In Yemen itself, several powerful kingdoms grew up from profits earned in this trade. One kingdom in particular, the Sabaeans, also had a productive agriculture based on irrigation. The water for irrigation came from the great Marib Dam, built around 500 B.C. Marib was a marvel of engineering, built across a deep river valley. The Sabaean economy supported a population estimated at 300,000 in a region that today supports only a few thousand herders.

The Sabaeans were followed by the Himyarites whose rulers were converted to Christianity by wandering monks in the second century A.D. The Himyarites had contacts with Christian Ethiopia across the Red Sea and for a time were vassals of Ethiopian kings. An Ethiopian army invaded South Arabia but was defeated by the Himyarites in A.D. 570, the "Year of the Elephant" in Arab tradition, so called because the Ethiopian invaders were mounted on elephants. (The year was also notable for the birth of Muhammad, the Prophet of Islam.)

## DEVELOPMENT

Although Yemen is the poorest Arab country in terms of GDP, per capita income, and other factors, it has significant oil resources plus major port and bunkering facilities in Aden.

The rise in world oil prices in recent years brought in much needed extra cash but did not bring about prosperity. Internal political instability, particularly in the north, and the country's vulnerability to terrorism, continue to affect economic progress. The country has a good potential in agricultural production, but it imports around 70 percent of its food needs.

Sabaeans and Himyarites ruled long ago, but they are still important to Yemenis as symbols of their long and rich historical past. The Imams of Yemen, who ruled until 1962, used a red dye to sign their official documents in token of their relationship to Himyarite kings. (The word *Himyar* comes from the same root as *ahmar*, "red.")

The domestication of the camel and development of an underground irrigation system of channels (*falaj*) made this civilization possible. Ships and camel caravans brought the frankincense, myrrh, and musk from Socotra and silks and spices from India and the Far East to northern cities in Egypt, Persia, and Mesopotamia. Aden was an important port for this trade due to its natural harbor and its location at the south end of the Red Sea.

Yemenis were among the first converts to Islam. The division of the Yemenis into mutually hostile Sunni and Shi'a Muslims took place relatively early in Islamic history. Those living in the Tihama, which was easily accessible to missionaries and warriors expanding the borders of the new Islamic state, became Sunnis, obedient to the caliphs (the elected "successors" of Muhammad). The Yemeni mountaineers were more difficult to reach; when they were converted to the new religion, it was through the teachings of a follower of Shi'at Ali, "Party of Ali," those who felt that Muhammad's son-in-law Ali and his descendants should have been chosen as the rightful leaders of the Islamic community. Yemenis in Aden and the Hadhramaut, as well as those in the Tihama, became Sunni, creating the basis for an intra-Yemeni conflict, which still exists.

Yemen was the home of a small Jewish community for at least 2,500 years, dating back to the time of the Babylonian captivity. Although its members were excluded from all professions, except silversmithing, and were required to wear identifying clothing and sidecurls, the community lived side by side with Muslims without incident. After the establishment of Israel

in 1948, 48,000 Jews were airlifted to the new Jewish state. Some 24,000 others left Yemen for Israel in later years. Today only 300 Jews remain in Yemen.

## THE ZAIDI IMAMATE

In the late ninth century A.D., a feud among certain nominally Muslim groups in inland Yemen led to the invitation of a religious scholar living in Mecca to come and mediate in their dispute. (Use of an outside mediator was common in Arabia at that time.) This scholar brought with him a number of families of Ali's descendants who sought to escape persecution from the Sunnis. He himself was a disciple of Zaidi, Ali's great-grandson. He settled the feud, and, in return for his services, he was accepted by both sides of the conflict as their religious leader, or Imam. He and his successor Imams, 111 in all, established the Zaidi Imamate in north Yemen, a theocratic state of sorts which lasted until 1962.

The first Zaidi Imam had some personal qualities that enabled him to control the unruly mountain people and bend them to his will. He was a shrewd judge of character, using his knowledge and his prestige as a member of the family of Ali to give personal favors or to give his power of *baraka* (special powers from God) to one group or withhold it from another. He had great physical strength. It was said of him that he could grind corn with his fingers and pull a camel apart barehanded. He wrote 49 books on Islamic jurisprudence and theology, some of which are still studied by modern Yemeni scholars. He was also said to bring good (or bad) fortune to a subject merely by a touch or a glance from his piercing black eyes.[1]

In a reversal of the ancient process whereby South Arabian merchants carried goods to the far-flung cities of the north, from the late 1400s on, the towns of the bleak Arabian coast attracted the interest of European seafaring powers as way stations or potential bases for control of their expanding trade with the East Indies, India, and China. Aden was a potentially important base, and expeditions by Portuguese and other Europeans tried without success to capture it at the time. In 1839, a British expedition finally succeeded. It found a town of "800 miserable souls, huddled in huts of reed matting, surrounded by guns that would not fire," or so the American traveler Joseph Osgood described the scene.

Under British rule, Aden became an important naval base and refueling port for ships passing through the Suez Canal and down the Red Sea en route to India.

For many British families bound for India, Aden was the last land, with the last friendly faces, that they would see before arriving many days later in the strange wonderland of India. The route through the Suez Canal and down the Red Sea past Aden was the lifeline of the British Empire. In order to protect Aden from possible attack by hostile peoples in the interior, the British signed a series of treaties with their chiefs, called shaykhs or sometimes sultans. These treaties laid the basis for the South Arabian Protectorates. British political agents advised the rulers on policy matters and gave them annual subsidies to keep them happy. One particular agent, Harold Ingrams, was so successful in eliminating feuds and rivalries that "Ingrams's Peace" became a symbol of the right way to deal with proud, independent local leaders.

In the 16th century A.D. the Ottoman Turks had seized control of the Tihama and the port of Aden. However fierce Zaidi resistance forced them to withdraw. Subsequently an Ottoman military expedition reconquered coastal Yemen and it became an Ottoman province. However Ottoman control was tenuous at best and did not sit well with the mountain peoples. A Yemeni official told a British visitor: "We have fought the Turks, the tribes . . . and we are always fighting each other. We Yemenis submit to no one permanently. We love freedom and we will fight for it."[2]

The Ottoman occupation sparked a revolt. The Ottoman forces were unable to defeat the mountain peoples, and in 1911, they signed a treaty that recognized Imam Yahya as ruler in the highlands. In return, the Imam recognized the Ottoman rule in the Tihama. At the end of World War I, the Ottomans left Yemen for good. The British, who then controlled most of the Middle East, signed a treaty with Imam Yahya, recognizing his rule in all Yemen.

The two Yemens followed divergent paths in the twentieth century, accounting in large measure for the difficulties they faced in incorporating into a single state. North Yemen remained largely uninvolved in the political turmoil that engulfed the Middle East after World War II. Imam Yahya ruled his country as an absolute monarch with a handful of advisers, mostly tribal leaders, religious scholars, and members of his family. John Peterson notes that the Imamate "was completely dependent on the abilities of a single individual who was expected to be a competent combination of religious scholar, administrator, negotiator, and military commander."[3] Yahya was all of these, and his forceful personality and ruthless methods of dealing with potential opposition (with just a touch of magic) ensured his control over the population.

Yahya's method of government was simplicity itself. He held a daily public meeting (*jama'a*) seated under an umbrella outside his palace, receiving petitions from anyone who wished to present them and signing approval or disapproval in Himyarite red ink. He personally supervised tax collections and kept the national treasury in a box under his bed. The Imam distrusted the Ottomans, against whom he had fought for Yemeni independence, and refused to accept their coinage. He also rejected the British currency because it represented a potential foreign influence.

Yahya was determined to keep foreign influences out of Yemen and to resist change in any form. Although Yemen was poor by the industrial world's standards, it was self-sufficient, free, and fully recognized as an independent state. Yahya hoped to keep it that way. He even refused foreign aid because he felt that it would lead to foreign occupation. But he was unable to stop the clock entirely and to keep out all foreign ideas and influences.

Certain actions that seemed to be to his advantage worked against him. One was the organization of a standing army. In order to equip and train an army that would be stronger than tribal armies, Yahya had to purchase arms from abroad and to hire foreign advisers to train his troops. Promising officers were also sent for training in Egypt, and upon their return, they formed the nucleus of opposition to the Imam.

In 1948, Imam Yahya was murdered. He had alienated not only army officers who resented his repressive rule but also leaders from outside the ruling family who were angered by the privileges given to the Imam's sons and relatives. However, the coup conspirators were unsure of their goals. Crown Prince Ahmad, the Imam's eldest son and heir, was as tough and resourceful as his 80-year-old father had been.[4] He gathered support from leaders of other clans and defeated the rebellion.

Imam Ahmad (1948–1962) ruled as despotically as his father had ruled, but the walls of Yemeni isolation inevitably began to crack. Unlike Yahya, Ahmad was willing to modernize a little. Foreign experts came to design and help build the roads, factories, hospitals, and schools that the Imam felt were needed. Several hundred young Yemenis were sent abroad for study. Those who had left the country during Imam Yahya's reign returned. Many Yemenis emigrated to Aden to work for the British and formed the nucleus of a "Free Yemen" movement.

In 1955, the Imam foiled an attempted coup. Other attempts, in 1958 and 1961, were also unsuccessful. The old Imam finally died of emphysema in 1962, leaving his son, Crown Prince Muhammad al-Badr, to succeed him.

## THE MARCH TO INDEPENDENCE

The British wanted to hold on to Aden as long as possible because of its naval base and refinery. It seemed to them that the best way to protect British interests was to set up a union of Aden and the South Arabian Protectorates. This was done in 1963, with independence promised for 1968. However, the British plan proved unworkable. In Aden, a strong anti-British nationalist movement developed in the trade unions of dock workers and refinery employees. This movement organized a political party, the People's Socialist Party, strongly influenced by the socialist, anti-Western, Arab nationalist programs of President Gamal Abdel Nasser in Egypt.

The party had two branches: the moderate Front for the Liberation of Occupied South Yemen (FLOSY) and the Marxist National Liberation Front (NLF). About all they had in common was their opposition to the British and the South Arabian sultans, whom they called "lackeys of imperialism." FLOSY and the NLF joined forces in 1965–1967 to force the British to leave Aden. British troops were killed and bombs damaged the refinery. By 1967, Britain had had enough and signed a treaty granting independence to South Yemen under a coalition government made up of members of both FLOSY and the NLF.

Muhammad al-Badr held office for a week and then was overthrown by a military coup. Yemen's new military leaders formed a Revolution Command Council and announced that the Imam was dead. Henceforth, they said, Yemen would be a republic. It would give up its self-imposed isolation and would become part of the Arab world. But the Revolution proved to be more difficult to carry out than the military officers had expected. The Imam was not dead, as it turned out, but had escaped to the mountains. The mountain peoples rallied to his support, helping him to launch a counterrevolution. About 85,000 Egyptian troops arrived in Yemen to help the republican army. The coup leaders had been trained in Egypt, and the Egyptian government had not only financed the Revolution but also had encouraged it against the "reactionary" Imam.

For the next eight years, Yemen was a battleground. The Egyptians bombed villages and even used poison gas against civilians in trying to defeat the Imam's

forces. But they were unable to crush the people hidden in the mountains of the interior. Saudi Arabia also backed the Imam with arms and kept the border open. The Saudi rulers did not particularly like the Imam, but he seemed preferable to an Egyptian-backed republican regime next door.

After Egypt's defeat by Israel in the 1967 Six-Day War, the Egyptian position in Yemen became untenable, and Egyptian troops were withdrawn. It appeared that the royalists would have a clear field. But they were even more disunited than the republicans. A royalist force surrounded San'a in 1968 but failed to capture the city. The Saudis then decided that the Imam had no future. They worked out a reconciliation of royalists and republicans that would reunite the country. The only restriction was that neither the Imam nor any of his relatives would be allowed to return to Yemen.

Thus, in 1970, two "republics" had come into existence side by side. The Yemen Arab Republic was more of a tribal state than a republic in the modern political sense of the term. Prior to 1978, its first three presidents either went into exile or were murdered, victims of rivalry within the army. Colonel Ali Abdullah Saleh, a career army officer, seized power in that year and was subsequently chosen as the republic's first elected president. He was reelected in 1983 and again in 1988 for consecutive five-year terms. With unification, he became the first head of state of all Yemen.

Saleh provided internal stability and allowed some broadening of the political process in North Yemen. A General People's Congress (GPC) was established in 1982. A Consultative Council, elected by popular vote, was established in 1988 to allow some citizen input into legislation. Saleh displayed great skill in balancing tribal and army factions and used foreign aid to develop economic projects such as dams for irrigation to benefit highland and Tihama Yemenis alike.

## SOUTH YEMEN: A MARXIST STATE

With the British departure, the South Arabian Federation collapsed. Aden and the Hadhramaut were united under Aden political leadership in 1970 as the People's Democratic Republic of Yemen. It began its existence under adverse circumstances: Britain ended its subsidy for the Aden refinery, and the withdrawal of British forces cut off the revenues generated by the military payroll.

But the main problem was political. A power struggle developed between FLOSY and the NLF. The former favored moderate policies, good relations with other Arab states, and continued ties with Britain. The NLF were Marxists and by 1970 had won. FLOSY leaders were killed or went into exile. The new government set its objectives as state ownership of lands, state management of all business and industry, a single political organization with all other political parties prohibited, and support for antigovernment revolutionary movements in other Arab states, particularly Oman and Saudi Arabia.

During its two decades of existence, the P.D.R.Y. modeled its governing structure on that of the Soviet Union, with a Presidium, a Council of Ministers, a Supreme People's Legislative Council, and provincial and district councils, in descending order of importance. In 1978, the ruling (and only legal) political party took the name Yemen Socialist Party, to emphasize its Yemeni makeup.

Although the P.D.R.Y. government's ruthless suppression of opposition enabled it to establish political stability, rivalries and vendettas among party leaders led to much instability within the ruling party. The first president, Qahtan al-Sha'bi, was overthrown by radicals within the party. His successor, Salim Rubayyi Ali, was executed after he had tried and failed to oust his rivals on the party Central Committee. Abd al-Fattah Ismail, the country's third president, resigned in 1980 and went into exile due to a dispute over economic policies. Ali Nasir Muhammad, the fourth president, seemed to have consolidated power and to have won broad party support, until 1986, when he tried to purge the Central Committee of potential opponents. The people of the interior, who formed Muhammad's original support base, stayed out of the fighting. After 10 days of bloody battles with heavy casualties, the president's forces were

defeated. He then went into exile and was convicted of treason in absentia. He returned to Yemen in 1996 after the end of the Civil War and the reunification of the "two Yemens."

## UNIFICATION

Despite their natural urge to unite, the two Yemens were more often at odds with each other than united in pursuing common goals. This was due in part to the age-old highland-lowland, Sunni-Shi'a conflict that cut across Yemeni society. But it was also due to their very different systems of government. There were border clashes in 1972, 1975, and 1978–1979, when the P.D.R.Y. was accused of plotting the overthrow of its neighbor. (A P.D.R.Y. envoy brought a bomb hidden in a suitcase to a meeting with the Y.A.R. president, and the latter was killed when the bomb exploded.)

Improved economic circumstances and internal political stability in both Yemens revived interest in unity in the 1980s, especially after oil and natural-gas discoveries in border areas promised advantages to both through joint exploitation. In May 1988, President Saleh and Prime Minister al-Attas of the P.D.R.Y. signed the May Unity Pact, which ended travel restrictions and set up a Supreme Yemeni Council of national leaders to prepare a constitution for the single Yemeni state.

In 1989, the P.D.R.Y. freed supporters of former President Ali Nasir Muhammad. Early in 1990, the banks, postal services, ports administration, and customs of the two republics were merged, followed by the merger under joint command of their armed forces.

Formal unification took place on May 22, 1990 and Ali Abdullah Saleh was unanimously chosen as the republic's first president, with a four-member Presidential Council formed to oversee the transition. A draft constitution of the new republic established a 39-member Council of Ministers headed by P.D.R.Y. prime minister al-Attas, with ministries divided equally between North and South. In a national referendum in May 1991, voters approved the new all-Yemen Constitution.

Elections were scheduled for November 1992 but were postponed until April 1993 after the elections committee protested that insufficient time had been allocated for voter registration, preparation of candidate lists, drawing of constituency borders, and campaigning.

The campaign itself was marred by violence, much of it directed at officials of the Yemen Socialist Party by tribal opponents of unification or others who feared that the election would result in greater

influence for the more liberal, ex-Marxist Southerners in the government. In 1992, an economic crisis also hit the country; in December people took to the streets protesting price increases and a 100 percent inflation rate.

The Constitution provided for a 301-member Parliament. When the elections for the new parliament were held, President Saleh's General People's Congress won 147 seats, just shy of a majority. The elections were carried out in open democratic fashion. A coalition government was formed in May 1993 between the General People's Congress (GPC), the Yemen Socialist Party, Islah, and Islamist party, which ran third in the balloting. However, rivalry between the former political elites of North and South, plus differences in outlook, continued to impede progress toward full unification. Early in 1994, Ali al-Beidh, Yemen Socialist Party (YSP) leader and vice president of the ruling coalition, presented a set of 18 demands whose acceptance was a prerequisite for his return to the government. They were rejected by President Saleh, and civil war broke out in May 1994. Initially, the South Yemeni forces had the better of it, but the larger and better-equipped army of the North, moving slowly southward, surrounded Aden and captured the city after a brief siege. Vice-President al-Beidh fled into exile, effectively depriving the rebellion of its chief leader, and his Yemen Socialist Party was excluded from the governing coalition, although it was allowed to exist as a political party.

The end of the Civil War, more or less on North Yemen's terms, offered Saleh another opportunity to unify the country. The first step was the restoration of representative government. A 1992 law was reinstated to require political parties to have 5,000 or more members, plus offices in each of the fourteen governorates. Elections for the National Assembly in 1993 resulted in a solid majority for the GPC, winning 239 seats to 62 for the main opposition Islah Party. This balance of seats remained unchanged in the more recent

Assembly elections, which took place in tandem with the 1999 and 2006 presidential elections.

What struck outside observers about the election was its faithful adherence to political democracy. The entire process was supervised by the Supreme Election Commission, established by law as an independent body with balanced political representation. Despite having one of the lowest literacy rates in the world, Yemenis participated with enthusiasm and in great numbers, illiterate voters being assisted by literate volunteers to mark their ballots inside the curtained polling booths. Ballots were tabulated by hand by representatives of the Supreme Election Council, prompting an American observer to ask why "they didn't use voting machines and computers. They said they would not trust such a system because it would not be transparent."[5]

In 1999 the electorate approved by referendum a constitutional amendment to allow two consecutive terms for an incumbent president. As a result President Salih unanimously won his first full term, with no opposition. In September 2006 he was elected for a second full term. This time he had opposition, winning 77.2 percent of the votes to 21.8 percent for his chief opponent, former legislator Faisal Bin Shamlan. Among other reasons advanced for the decline in Salih's support were public perceptions of government corruption and over-centralization of the civil service. After his election Salih promised to deal directly with these issues.

In September 1999, Yemen's first direct presidential election marked a milestone in the slow progress of the state toward representative government. Prior to the election, the Constitution was amended to allow an incumbent to serve for two consecutive five-year terms. Although he was nominated by both his own party and the opposition Islah Party, President Ali Abdullah Saleh faced opposition for the first time in a presidential election. Admittedly the opposition consisted of token, unknown candidates, and

Saleh won reelection with ease. However, despite its flawed nature, the election underlined the president's popularity among his people.

Although on the surface Yemen seems to offer fertile ground for Islamic radicalism due to its poverty, its high unemployment rate, and its divisions between a tribal north and a Marxist south, until recently no homegrown radical Islamist movement existed there. Following the withdrawal of Soviet troops from Afghanistan in 1989, a large number of Afghan resistance fighters (*mujahideen*) and Muslim volunteers from other countries who had gone to Afghanistan to defend Afghanistan fled to Yemen. At the end of 1994, one mujahideen group, Aden-Abyan Islamic Jihad, carried out a number of bombings and kidnappings of foreign tourists and oil company employees. Government forces captured most of its members in 1999 and 10 were sentenced to death. They were executed in 2000.

## THE ECONOMY

Discoveries of significant oil deposits in the 1980s should have augured well for Yemen's economic future. Reserves are estimated at 1 billion barrels in the Marib basin and 3.3 billion in the Shabwa field northeast of Aden, with an additional 5.5 billion in the former neutral zone shared by the two Yemens and now administered by the central government. Yemen also has large deposits of natural gas, with reserves estimated at 5.5 trillion cubic feet.

Unfortunately, the political conflicts of the 1990s had a negative effect on these rosy prospects. The Gulf War, in which Yemen supported Iraq against the U.S-led coalition, caused Saudi Arabia to deport some 850,000 Yemeni workers. The Civil War in 1994 seriously damaged the infrastructure, requiring some $200 million in repairs to schools, hospitals, roads, and power stations.

In ancient times, Yemen, particularly in the South, had a flourishing agriculture based on monsoon rains, supplemented by a sophisticated system of small dams and canals and centered in the Wadi Hadhramaut. But long neglect and two decades of disastrous Soviet-style state-farm management adversely affected agricultural production.

In 2006 Salih launched an ambitious anti-corruption program intended to enable Yemen to qualify for funds under the Bush administration's Millennium Challenge Account (MCA). The program ties aid to reform benchmarks. With oil resources expected to be used up in 15 years and the water table well below normal due

to drought, MCA funds would make a significant difference to one of the world's poorest countries economically. Other MCA requirements include anti-corruption measures and strict procurement rules for government contracts. As a first step, in December 2006 the National Assembly approved formation of a National Supreme Anti-Corruption Authority to expedite economic reform.

As the result of its efforts Yemen was on schedule for admission to the MCA's Threshold Program, which will enable it to receive stopgap funds to speed up the reform program. And in 2007 Britain and the Gulf Arab states jointly pledged $4.7 billion over a 4-year period in recognition of the fact that Yemen was underfunded as a developing country.

## FOREIGN RELATIONS

Prior to unification with South Yemen, North Yemen's geographical isolation and tribal social structure limited its contact with other Arab states. South Yemen's Marxist regime, in contrast, actively attempted to subvert the governments of its neighbors. Reunification has brought better and closer relations with these states. In 1995, the flags of Yemen and Oman flew side by side on their newly demarcated common border, based on a 1992 agreement to accept UN mediation.

Yemen's relations with Saudi Arabia have followed an uneven course. Yemeni workers in the kingdom were deported en masse after the Gulf War, due to Yemeni support for Iraq. The action was a severe blow to the Yemeni economy, as 20 to 25 percent of the national budget had come from expatriate-worker remittances. In 1995, with the aid of mediators from Syria, the two neighbors reconfirmed the 1934 Treaty of Taif that had demarcated their common border. However, concern on the part of the Saudi government with the infiltration of Islamic fundamentalist militants across the border led to the construction of security barriers on the Saudi side.

The range of anti-U.S. terrorism reached Yemen in October 2000, when the U.S. Navy destroyer *Cole* was attacked while it was in Aden Harbor for refueling. Seventeen Americans were killed in the attack, which was carried out by several men in a small boat packed with explosives. A number of the attackers were later arrested but later escaped. Early in 2004 they were recaptured by security forces. One of them was Jamal Badawi, described as Yemen's most dangerous terrorist. Two turned themselves in later when offered amnesty in return for pledging to renounce violence. The remainder are still at large, including Badawi.

## Timeline: PAST

**A.D. 500**
Collapse of the Marib Dam, destroying the flourishing Himyarite civilization

**890**
Establishment of the Zaidi Imamate in highland Yemen

**1517, 1872**
Yemen is occupied by the Ottoman Turks; it eventually becomes an Ottoman province

**1839**
The capture of Aden by a British naval expedition

**1882–1914**
South Arabian protectorates are established by the British

**1934**
Yemen is recognized as an independent nation under Imam Yahya

**1962**
A revolution overthrows Imam al-Badr; a military group proclaims a republic in North Yemen

**1962–1969**
Civil war between supporters of Badr and Egyptian backed republicans; protectorates merge with Aden Crown Colony

**1967**
British forces withdraw from Aden; the National Liberation Front proclaims South Yemen an independent republic

**1980s**
Major oil and natural-gas discoveries

**1990s**
The two Yemens unite on May 22, 1990; free elections are held on April 27, 1993; civil war in 1994

## PRESENT

**2000**
U.S. destroyer Cole is attacked in Aden harbor; seventeen US sailors killed

**2002**
French Supertanker Limburg is attacked and badly damaged off Yemen's coast

**2004**
Start of northern rebellion led by dissident cleric Hussein al-Houthi. Al-Houthi is killed by the Houthi, rebellion goes on

**2006**
President Saleh is re-elected

Major reform plan is announced to deal with economic crisis and dwindling oil reserves

**2007**
Rebel leader Abdul-Malik al-Houthi accepts ceasefire, but violence continues

Peaceful protest and secession movement begins in the south

**2008**
Al-Qaeda attack on US embassy in capital Sana'a kills 18 people

**2009**
In a deal with al-Qaeda, the government releases 176 Islamist suspects

Clashes between northern rebels and Saudi security forces along the border. Saudi forces intervene and regained control of territory seized by Yemeni rebels.

Yemeni al-Qaeda branch claims to be behind the failed attack on U.S. airliner by the Nigerian "underwear bomber"

**2010**
Northern rebels agree to a new cease-fire

---

Following the September 11, 2001, terrorist attacks in the United States, the Yemeni government declared its willingness to join the international anti-terror coalition. It arrested 20 Yemenis suspected of having been trained in al Qaeda camps in Afghanistan before returning to their own country.

To underscore Yemen's cooperation, Prime Minister Abdul-Kader Bajammal indicated that 4,000 Yemenis trained in such camps had been expelled. In January 2003 the government signed a contract with Canada's Nexen Corporation, one of the foreign firms engaged in developing its oil resources

for patrol boats, surveillance equipment and anti-terrorism training for the Yemeni security services. However, the equipment arrived too late to prevent the kidnapping and murder of three American medical missionaries in Ibb province, near San'a. The murdered missionaries had founded a Baptist hospital there in the 1960s which served 40,000 poor Yemenis annually. Their attacker, after his arrest, said he had acted to "cleanse the country of infidels."

The kidnapping of an Islah Party official in January 2003, along with the missionaries' murder, marked a growing division between the people and the government, due essentially to the latter's U.S. alignment. In 2005 a previously-unknown organization called Believing Youth, formed probably in 2004, began an uprising from secret bases in the far north of the country. After a 3-year conflict which has resulted in some 4,000 deaths on both sides, mediators from Qatar established a ceasefire agreement in June 2007. The rebels agreed to surrender their heavy weaponry, and in return the government will release rebel prisoners, pay for reconstruction of villages ravaged in the fighting, and provide homes for displaced villagers.

## NOTES

1. Robin Bidwell, *The Two Yemens* (Boulder, CO: Westview Press, 1983), p. 10.

2. Quoted in Robert Stookey, *Yemen: The Politics of the Yemen Arab Republic* (Boulder, CO: Westview Press, 1978), p. 168.

3. John Peterson, "Nation-building and Political Development in the Two Yemens," in B. R. Pridham, ed., *Contemporary Yemen: Politics and Historical Background* (New York: St. Martin's Press, 1985), p. 86.

4. Bidwell, The Two Yemens, op. cit., p. 121.

5. Quoted in Ginny Hill, "Millions in aid linked to Yemeni Reform," *Christian Science Monitor*, Feb. 26, 2007.

# The Western Sahara    Whose Desert?

It is a fearsome place, swept by sand-laden winds that sting through layers of clothing, scorched by 120°F temperatures, its flat, monotonous landscape broken occasionally by dried-up *wadis* (river beds). The Spanish called it Rio de Oro, "River of Gold," in a bitter jest, for it has neither. Rainfall averages two to eight inches a year in a region twice the size of Colorado but without mountains, only rolling dunes swept constantly by sand-laden winds that fill tents, clothing and food with gritty particles of sand. The region had no name until the twentieth century; it was simply the "western" part of the Sahara. For a brief period in the eleventh century A.D. a Berber tribal confederation, the Almoravids, rode out of the territory to find a powerful Islamic sultanate in Morocco and Spain. But after they were overthrown by another tribal confederation, the Almohads, the Western Sahara reverted to political obscurity.

As a political entity, the Western Sahara resulted from European colonization in Africa in the late nineteenth century. Britain and France had a head start in establishing colonies. Spain was a latecomer. By the time the Spanish joined the race for colonies, little was left for them in Africa. Since they already controlled the Canary Islands, off the West African coast, it was natural for them to claim Rio de Oro, the nearest area on the coast.

In 1884, Spain claimed Rio de Oro and its adjoining region, Saguia al-Hamra, in a note to other European powers. The Spanish claim was based on the principle that "occupation of a territory's coast entitled a colonial power to control the interior."[1] But Spanish rights to the Saharan interior clashed with French claims to Mauritania and efforts to control the independent Sultanate of Morocco to the north. After the establishment of a joint Franco—Spanish protectorate over Morocco in 1912, Rio de Oro and Saguia al-Hamra were recognized as a single Spanish colony, with its boundaries fixed with the French colony of Mauritania on the south and east and Morocco to the north. The nomads of the Western Sahara now found themselves living within fixed boundaries defined by outsiders.

The Spanish moved very slowly into the interior. The entire Western Sahara was not "pacified" until 1934. Spain invested heavily in the development of the important Western Sahara phosphate deposits but did little else to develop the colony. The Spanish population was essentially a garrison community, living apart from the Sahrawis, the indigenous Saharan population, in towns or military posts. A few Sahrawis went to Spain or other European countries, where they received a modern education; upon their return, they began to organize a Saharan nationalist movement. Other Sahrawis traveled to Egypt and returned with ideas of organizing a Saharan Arab independent state. A real sense of either a Spanish Saharan or an independent Sahrawi identity was slow to emerge.[2]

Serious conflict over the Spanish Sahara developed in the 1960s. By that time, both Morocco and Mauritania had become independent. Algeria, the third African territory involved in the conflict, won its independence after a bloody national liberation war against France. All three new states were highly nationalist and were opposed to the continuation of colonial rule over any African people, particularly Muslim peoples. They encouraged the Sahrawis to fight for liberation from Spain, giving arms and money to guerrilla groups and keeping their borders open.

However, the three states had different motives. Morocco claimed the Western Sahara on the basis of historical ties dating back to the Almoravids, plus the oath of allegiance sworn to Moroccan sultans by Saharan chiefs in the nineteenth and twentieth centuries. Kinship was also a factor; several important Saharan families have branches in Morocco, and both the mother and the first wife of the founder of Morocco's current ruling dynasty, Mulay Ismail, were from Sahrawi families.

The Mauritanian claim to the Spanish Sahara was based not on historical sovereignty but on kinship. Sahrawis have close ethnic ties with the Moors, the majority of the population of Mauritania. Also, Mauritania feared Moroccan expansion, since its territory had once been included in the Almoravid state. A Saharan buffer state between Mauritania and Morocco would serve as protection for the Mauritanians.

Algeria's interest in Spanish Sahara was largely a matter of support for a national liberation movement against a colonial power. The Algerians made no territorial claim to the colony. Algeria's foreign policy has rested on two pillars since independence: the right to self-determination of subject peoples and the principle of self-determination through referendum. Algeria consistently maintains that the Saharan people should have these rights.

In the 1960s, Spain came under pressure from the United Nations to give up its colonies. After much hesitation, the Spanish announced in August 1974 that a referendum would be held under UN supervision to decide the colony's future.

The Spanish action brought the conflict to a head. King Hassan II declared that 1975 would mark the restoration of Moroccan sovereignty over the territory. The main opposition to this claim came from Polisario (an acronym for the Popular Front for the Liberation of Saguia al-Hamra and Rio de Oro, the two divisions of the Spanish colony). This organization, formed by Saharan exiles based initially in Mauritania, issued a declaration of independence, and Polisario guerrillas began attacking Spanish garrisons, increasing the pressure on Spain to withdraw. In October 1975, King Hassan announced that he would lead a massive, peaceful march of civilians, "armed" only with Qur'ans, into the Spanish Sahara to recover sacred Moroccan territory. This "Green March" of half a million unarmed Moroccan volunteers into Spanish territory seemed an unusual, even risky, method of validating a territorial claim, but it worked. In 1976, Spain reached agreement with Morocco and Mauritania to partition the territory into two zones, one-third going to Mauritania and two-thirds to Morocco. The Moroccan zone included the important phosphate deposits.

The Polisario rejected the partition agreement. It announced the formation of the Sahrawi Arab Democratic Republic

(S.A.D.R.), "a free, independent, sovereign state governed by a national democratic system, of a unionist orientation, progressive and of Islamic faith, on the base of the free popular will founded at the beginnings of the democratic option."[3]

In the early stages of the war, Polisario tactics of swift-striking attacks from hidden bases in the vast desert were highly effective against the Moroccan and Mauritanian occupation forces. Mauritania withdrew from the war in 1978 when a military coup overthrew its government. The new Mauritanian rulers signed a peace treaty with Polisario representatives. Morocco, not to be outdone, promptly annexed the Mauritanian share of the territory and beefed up its military forces. A fortified "Sand Wall," which was built in stages from the former border with Rio de Oro down to the Moroccan—Mauritanian border and in 1987 extended about 350 miles to the Atlantic Ocean, providing the Moroccan Army with a strong defensive base from which to launch punitive raids against its elusive foe. The new segment also cut off the Polisario's access to the sea; Polisario raiders had begun to intercept and board fishing vessels in attempts to disrupt development of that important Moroccan resource and to bring pressure on foreign countries (such as Spain) that use the fishing grounds to push Morocco toward a settlement.

Although a large number of member states of the Organization of African Unity (OAU) subsequently recognized the Sahrawi Republic, Morocco blocked its admission to the OAU, on the grounds that it was part of Moroccan territory. However, the drain on Moroccan resources of indefinitely maintaining a 100,000-man army in the desert led King Hassan II to soften his obduracy, particularly in relation to Algeria. With both countries affected by severe economic problems and some political instability, a rapprochement became possible in the late 1980s. Diplomatic relations were restored in 1988 and in 1989, Morocco joined Algeria, Libya, Tunisia, and Mauritania in the creation of the Arab Maghrib Union (known by its French acronym UMA). The new regional organization aimed at integrating all five states in the future.

Algeria's preoccupation with internal affairs and the withdrawal of Algerian and Libyan financial aid placed the Polisario in a difficult position. Two of its founders, Omar Hadrami and Noureddine Belali, defected in 1989 and acknowledged Moroccan sovereignty over the territory. A 1990 amnesty offer by King Hassan for all Polisario members and Saharan exiles was accepted by nearly 1,000 persons; these included S.A.D.R.'s foreign minister, Brahim Hakim.

Later, Polisario leaders reached an agreement in principle with the king to settle the dispute by referendum. Participants in the referendum would be limited to the original inhabitants of the territory. But with the Moroccan Army entrenched behind its Sand Wall and the Polisario in control of the open desert, there was little chance for the implementation of the referendum.

UN mediation produced a formal cease-fire in 1991 until a referendum is organized. A UN observer force, the Mission for the Referendum in the Western Sahara (MINURSO), proceeded to the territory to supervise voter registration. By that time, thousands of Moroccan settlers had moved there to take advantage of free land, housing, and other inducements offered by the government to help "Moroccanize" the country's newest province. The new residents changed the population balance, thereby complicating registration procedures. Morocco insisted that they should be eligible to vote in the referendum. A further complication arose from the fact that some 140,000 of the original inhabitants included in the 1974 Spanish census had become refugees in Algeria.

In May 1995, the UN Security Council, prodded by Algeria and Sahrawi activists, approved *Resolution 995,* which called for prompt registration of voters in the territory under the supervision of MINURSO. By December 1998, 147,000 voters were registered. However, the Moroccan government insisted that 85,000 others, belonging to three Saharan tribes residing there in the past, should be included in the registration rolls. Former U.S. secretary of state James Baker was appointed as a "high-profile" UN envoy to mediate between Morocco and the Polisario to resolve the registration deadlock and promote a final settlement for the territory.

In 2003, after several unproductive mediation efforts, Baker submitted a proposal to break the deadlock. The "Baker Plan" suggested that the referendum be postponed until 2006 and that, in the interim, the resident Sahrawi population would elect an autonomous governing body with powers limited to local and provincial affairs. Morocco rejected the plan at once while the Sahrawis first rejected it but later accepted it.

In July 2005, UN Secretary-General Kofi Annan appointed Dutch Ambassador Peter Van Walsum to replace James Baker as his personal envoy for the Western Sahara. In January 2009, UN Secretary-General Ban Ki-moon appointed former U.S. ambassador Christopher Ross, as his Personal Envoy for Western Sahara.

In 2006, Morocco proposed a "third path" to settlement: it would give the Western Sahara a special autonomy within the kingdom. The Polisario rejected the idea outright and, in spring 2007, the UN Security Council asked the two parties to negotiate directly.

The first direct negotiations brokered by the UN took place in June 2007 in Manhasset, New York; another set of negotiations took place in August. Both were inconclusive. Morocco kept insisting on a referendum that asks people to accept or reject autonomy, while the Polisario requested that the referendum offers the independence option as well.

Before the third set of negotiations took place in early January 2008, the Polisario's 12th Congress decided in mid-December 2007 that it would consider resuming its armed struggle for independence if negotiations fail. In August 2009 in Duernstein, Austria, a meeting between Moroccan and Sahrawi negotiators, which was facilitated by Christopher Ross, was inconclusive but the conflicting parties agreed to meet again.

Given Western Sahara's economic importance to Morocco and its political importance to the Monarchy, it seemed unlikely that an amicable solution is possible in the current conditions. The territory acquired a Moroccan majority in its population; its important phosphate rock deposits should give Morocco's economy a major boost when they are developed. It also offers the possibility of offshore oil discoveries, and its vast empty space could easily absorb settlers from Morocco's overcrowded cities.

On their side the Sahrawi refugees crowded into four refugee camps near Tindouf, Algeria, have developed, surprisingly, a representative democratic system with an elected parliament, a 95 percent literacy rate and a constitution guaranteeing gender equality and respect for all religions. Elected local councils undergird the parliament, and there is a high degree of volunteerism to take care of needed public services such as trash collection and food rations distribution. "We may well have developed a blueprint for an independent Western Sahara," says a tribal leader. "But we have been landless for so long, I don't know if the UN is just waiting for us to disappear, or what?"[4] Despite its recognition by 75 countries, global collective memory seems thus far to have failed to hold the SADR in its sight.

One of the key obstacles to deciding the fate of this territory is the absence of the will to do so among major international powers such as France, the United States and Spain. They all gain from the current status-quo and all stand to lose something if the situation evolves counter to Morocco's stability. These outside powers do not wish to undermine their economic and security interests by antagonizing Morocco and Algeria, two key competing regional powers.

## NOTES

1. John Damis, Conffict in Northwest Africa: The Western Sahara Dispute (Palo Alto, CA: Hoover Institution Press, 1983), p. 110.

2. *Ibid,* p. 13; the author notes that a tribal Assembly (Jama'a) was formed in 1967 for the Sahrawis but that its 43 members were all tribal chiefs or their representatives; it had only advisory powers.

3. Proclamation of The Saharawi Arab Democratic Republic, February 27, 1976. Online at www.arso.org/03-1f .htm. Consulted on August 9, 2010. For some archived public documents see www.arso.org/index.htm

4. John Thorne, "Sahara Refugees Form a Progressive Society," *Christian Science Monitor,* March 26, 2004. Online at www.csmonitor.com/2004/0326/p04s01-wome .html. Consulted on August 9, 2010.

# Middle of Where?

**The Middle East may be a crucially important region politically and economically, but try getting your hands on a decent definition of it.**

BRIAN WHITAKER

The first day of Cif's new Middle East section prompts a question that will surely exercise our commenters' brains in the months (and years?) to come: where exactly **is** the Middle East?

Most readers—I hope—can point to its general area on a map but deciding where its boundaries lie is no simple matter. Unlike Australia, say, or the Americas, the Middle East is not a self-contained land mass, nor was it ever "discovered" in the way that Australia and the Americas were.

In fact, there's very little to bind the Middle East together apart from the fact that it tends to be hot and dry. Even that is too big a generalisation. I've seen snow in Morocco and Lebanon and frost in Yemen, and once I was in Riyadh when it poured down all day.

Mention the Middle East and many people think instantly of oil. Yes, there's a lot of it, but only in certain places. Oil has made some of the inhabitants obscenely rich; others remain obscenely poor.

Mention the Middle East and many people think of wars and terror and Robert Fisk. Yes, but there are millions too who spend their lives quietly, without ever firing a shot.

Mention the Middle East and many people think of Arabs and Muslims. Yes again, but once you scratch beneath the surface there are Alawites, Armenians, Assyrians, Baha'is, Berbers, Chaldeans, Copts, Druzes, Ibadis, Ismailis, Jews, Kurds, Maronites, Sahrawis, Tuareg, Turkmen, Yazidis, Zaidis and no doubt a few others that I can't remember just at the moment.

Having travelled in most countries of the region and written about it for years, I'm still struggling to find the one elusive quality that actually defines the Middle East.

The Middle East is not so much a geographical entity as a geopolitical concept: it was invented, just over 100 years ago, by the British and the Americans. "East", of course, depends on where you're looking from and if the Chinese had got there before the British and Americans it might have become known as the Midwest.

"The Middle East" entered the English language little more than a century ago. The first person to mention it in print is thought to have been General Sir Thomas Gordon, a British intelligence officer and director of the Imperial Bank of Persia. In an article published in 1900, Gordon—who was concerned mainly with protecting British-ruled India from Russian threats—located his Middle East in Persia (present-day Iran) and Afghanistan.

Two years later, an American naval historian, Captain Alfred Mahan, also referred to "the Middle East" in an article entitled The Persian Gulf and International Relations. As an enthusiast of sea power, Mahan—not surprisingly—centred his Middle East around the waters of the Gulf.

Shortly afterwards, the term gained wider currency in Britain through a series of articles in the *Times* which appeared in 1902 and 1903, under the title The Middle Eastern Question. Written by Valentine Chirol, head of the paper's foreign department, the articles expanded Mahan's concept of the Middle East to include all land and sea approaches to India: Persia, the Gulf, Iraq, the east coast of Arabia, Afghanistan, and Tibet.

Before the discovery of oil, British interest in the Middle East was focused mainly on protecting India, the jewel in its imperial crown. To that end, in 1839, Britain had taken possession of Aden on the southern tip of Arabia, which thereafter served as a refuelling post on the route east and as a base from which to protect shipping. Until 1937, Aden continued to be ruled as part of British India. In the words of the late Lebanese writer, Samir Kassir:

> The issue of the security of the Indies route also entailed control of the Persian Gulf, a bolt-hole for pirates plying the Indian Ocean. Rather than direct rule, the British navy opted for the protectorate system, initially imposing a treaty on the sheikhs of the region, which turned the Pirate coast into the Truce coast, now the United Arab Emirates. The same approach was used in 1899 with the sheikh of the little known town of Kuwait . . . and the Sultanate of Muscat [in modern Oman].

This set a pattern that has continued to the present day. "The Middle East" (or "Near East" as Americans sometimes call it) constantly shifts its boundaries according to the preoccupations and interests of foreigners, rather than those of its inhabitants.

Perhaps the most sensible way to define "the Middle East" is to take the 22 members of the Arab League and add Israel and Iran, but even then there are anomalies. Comoros is a tiny Arab country stuck in the Indian Ocean off the coast of Mozambique, while Sudan—again, officially an Arab country—is only partly Arab. There are also arguments for and against including Turkey.

Today, the British Foreign Office usually talks about "Mena" (Middle East and North Africa), which, according to its website consists of Algeria, Bahrain, Egypt, Iran, Iraq, Israel, Jordan, Kuwait, Lebanon, Libya, Mauritania, Morocco, Oman, the Palestinian territories, Qatar, Saudi Arabia, Syria, Tunisia, the United Arab Emirates and Yemen.

The US state department's list is the same, apart from its exclusion of Mauritania. The map on its website also appears to recognise Western Sahara as a separate entity.

More recently, military considerations and the preoccupation with terrorism have led to the Middle East's boundaries being redrawn in a variety of ways. The US defence department, for instance, now talks about "Nesa" (Near East and South Asia) which starts in the west at Morocco and extends eastwards to include Bangladesh, Sri Lanka and Nepal. In 2004, President Bush also started talking about the "Greater Middle East" which, according to a document prepared for one of the G8 summits, consists of the Arab countries plus Pakistan, Afghanistan, Iran, Turkey, and Israel.

Meanwhile, the airline industry's definition of "Middle East", which has been widely adopted by others, excludes the north African countries apart from Egypt and adds Sudan. The World Bank has yet another definition which includes Malta in the Mediterranean and Djibouti on the Horn of Africa.

But please don't ask me which of these versions of the Middle East Cif will be adopting. I haven't a clue.

# Geography and the Middle East

Dona J. Stewart

Our nation's unpreparedness for the tragic events of 9/11 is well documented through formal congressional inquiry and memories of individuals on site that day. Initially, attention focused on the failure of critical rescue systems. In the weeks and months that followed, it became clear that military and educational institutions were also unprepared for this new age, in which the Middle East could no longer be defined solely in a consumption-oriented paradigm. No longer "over there" the Middle East seemed hostile, and the enemy, whoever it was, seemed to be both nowhere and everywhere.

The scarce academic experts explained the events to a fearful public, which had never heard of al-Qa'ida and could not find Afghanistan on a map. These experts, the best of whom had devoted their adult lives to study of the region, appeared in print and on talk shows, as well as at meetings in town halls, churches, and schools, in an attempt to provide the necessary context. "Security" specialists, many with no background in the region, often filled the void, emphasizing how to wage a successful "war on terror" rather than how to attack the political and sociological issues at terror's core. Political actors capitalized on the fear and broadened the conflict to Iraq, feeding anti-American sentiment and inadvertently aiding al-Qa'ida's recruitment efforts in the region.

Even our discipline faltered in its response to the events of 9/11. Certainly, geographical perspectives are needed to understand this newest national challenge. Analysis of the networks of militant Islam, the factors that shape their ideology, and the societies in which they exist would benefit from geography's deep foundation in area studies and its distinctive spatial perspective. Yet geographers were largely silent in the aftermath of the 9/11 crisis.

## A Small and Shrinking Pool

Despite the importance of the Middle East to U.S. national interests, few U.S. geographers specialize in the region. In 2005 the website of the Association of American Geographers (AAG) listed only thirty-six students and scholars with a specialization in Southwest Asia (the Middle East was not listed as an option). Although a relatively large number of Middle East geographers were trained in the 1970s, many of these scholars are nearing retirement. Whether other Middle East specialists will replace them is questionable, as departments build up technical programs rather than area studies. Many midcareer and senior Middle East geographers teach in departments that do not have doctoral programs and do not participate in training the next generation of Middle East specialists. Turkish specialists are now the largest group within Middle East geography, leading to concerns that too few students are pursuing specializations in the Arab countries of the region and Iran. When they are appointed, Middle East specialists tend to be hired more on the basis of their thematic specialty than their regional interest.

## The Decline of Area Studies

The AAG itself overlooked area studies in its official reaction to the 9/11 attacks, rushing instead for technological solutions (Cutter, Richardson, and Wilbanks 2003). In The Geographical Dimensions of Terrorism the AAG, much like the Homeland Security Administration, took the so-called spend-and-technology approach to an attempt to combat terrorism. In doing so they failed to remember that conflict and terrorism are the result of human agency and are not conducive to modeling the way natural hazards such as El Niño may be. The volume failed to offer any understanding of the societal context that has produced many of today's Middle East–based terrorist groups; the terms "Islam" and "Middle East" do not even appear in the volume's index. At no point did the AAG include an area-studies approach and incorporate perspectives of Middle East geographers. The publication of Geographical Dimensions accurately displays the decline of area studies in American geography.

Unlike political science, geography does not have a strong research tradition that focuses specifically on policy issues, foreign or domestic (with the exception of political geography). As a result, most Middle East geographers, including myself, pursued research agendas that offered limited insight into the issues surrounding 9/11. The area-studies identity of most Middle East geographers is often secondary to a thematic approach, such as urban or economic or cultural geography. A research stream focused on a key geography subfield is typically a prerequisite to a successful pretenure publishing record, but it restricts the types of research in which young scholars engage. The discipline's most nuanced and timely response to 9/11, a special issue published by the Arab World Geographer, largely featured the work of political and social geographers (AWG 2001). Here too, area studies was secondary, and the issue was specifically not cast in a regional framework.

This leads to a crucial question: Where were the voices of Middle East geographers? The decline in area studies within geography certainly plays a role in dampening their influence, but culpability also rests with ourselves: Where were we while others addressed the concerns raised after 9/11? Where is the bridge between thematic and area-studies approaches—between those who study empire and those who study the Middle East? If this bridge does not exist, it must be built. Now is the time to ask serious questions about ourselves and about the place of Middle East studies within geography.

Foremost among these should be: Can the relationship between Middle East studies and geography be strengthened and capitalized on? Three of the nation's Title VI funded National Resource Centers in Middle East studies are headed by geographers—Mike Bonine at the University of Arizona; Ian Manners at the University of Texas; and myself at Georgia State University—but Middle East geography remains weak within the discipline.

How do current publishing norms influence the types of publications produced by Middle East geographers? To achieve the publication record required for tenure, many Middle East geographers must emphasize the thematic aspects of their work over the area-studies content. Research on Cairo, for instance, becomes a case study in a paper on metropolitan restructuring, not an examination of Cairo on its own merits. As area-study perspectives within geography have diminished, placing area-studies articles in the discipline's top publications has become more challenging. In tenure reviews, interdisciplinary Middle East studies journals, alternative and supplementary publishing options for most Middle East geographers, are often not assessed as favorably as are geographical journals.

How can Middle East geographers be encouraged to engage in research on recent issues facing the region and play a more active role in current debates? For newly minted Middle East geographers who do not consider themselves political geographers, research on timely issues may be a luxury they cannot afford until after they attain tenure. Finally, the political nature of such research may intimidate researchers unless support within their department is sufficient.

# Reconceptualizing Middle East Geography

The most pertinent question remains: What is the place of Middle East geography in a post-9/11 world, within both geography and academia as a whole? The articles in this special issue of the Geographical Review exemplify some of the "new" geographical research being done on the Middle East. Though still rooted in area studies—the authors have studied the languages and cultures of the region and have spent considerable time in the field—the research issues and methods of inquiry extend well beyond those of traditional area studies. The region and/or individual country investigated is placed within frameworks that address larger processes, such as globalization, deterritorialization, or identity formation. The entire idea of the Middle East as a regional construct is in question as scholars seek to understand the articulation of the region, its religions, and other forms of identification across space and at various scales of analysis. Broadly, the articles in this issue address three major themes.

One examines the various networks—ideological, social, commercial—that link the region to other parts of the world. Joseph Hobbs's article, on the geographical dimensions of al-Qa'ida's rhetoric, gives insight into al-Qa'ida's worldview, in which the United States, Europe, and the Muslim world are engaged in a global battle over sacred space. The targeting of the United States by al-Qa'ida and the group's ability to create a successful global terror network illustrates a negative (from the U.S. perspective) outcome of globalization. Yet the region itself has long borne burdens imposed by contemporary, West-led globalization because it is marginalized from capital flows, information, communication, and commodities. In the great game of globalization, the region is a loser. Does this make al-Qa'ida's sacred geography more attractive? Petra Kuppinger examines the issue of globalization at the local level and explores the rapid construction of new spaces in greater Cairo that seem apart and disconnected—not only spatially but also conceptually—from the existing urban fabric. These new spaces are marked by Western global fashion and international architectural-design schemes. The processes creating these forms and their role in the local context exemplify the unevenness of globalization and the divergent experiences created even with respect to one city.

Identity construction, through both external and internal forces, at various levels of scale is another major theme. Ilhan Kaya investigates the creation of Turkish American identity and reminds us that the Middle East and the United States have been linked for nearly 200 years—the first Turkish immigrants arrived in 1820—and yet the level of integration of even long-time resident Muslim Americans was questioned after 9/11. His research explores the spaces in which Turkish Americanness is formed, celebrated, and passed on to future generations. Identity in Turkey is the focus of two other articles. Kyle Evered examines how globalization and regionalism have constructed an expanded Turkish national identity that crosses Turkey's borders to potentially encompass Turkic peoples to the east. Minority history and the places associated with it within the Turkish nation, officially defined as both Muslim and ethnically Turkish, is the focus of Amy Mills's article. She examines the debate over Turkish cultural identity as embedded in the landscapes of two very different Istanbul neighborhoods. Daanish Mustafa looks toward Pakistan—traditionally not considered part of the Middle East but today clearly tied to it by the networks of extremist Islamist thought—to examine the role of social capital in civil society as employed by the Jamaat-e-Islami and the Human Rights Commission in an effort to gain civil-society space.

The direct military intervention in Iraq and the policy implications for the broader Middle East that flowed from the response of the George W. Bush administration to the 9/11 attacks constitute a third theme. The advantages and limits of geographical knowledge regarding planning for U.S. military operations in Iraq is the focus of the contribution by Eugene

Palka, Francis Galgano, and Mark Corson. Although physical geographical constraints were largely anticipated and overcome, the changing calculus of human geographical factors has posed great challenges, especially for a coalition military force simultaneously carrying out military action and stability-and-support operations associated with state building. My own article examines the misconceptualization of the Middle East by the Bush administration, in both its geographical extent and its characteristics. Driven largely by ideology, this misreading of the region has had profound impacts on policy and foreign aid.

Taken together, these articles contribute to a view of the Middle East and the forces that shape it that is more nuanced than is the conventional outsider's image of the region. Even so, analysis remains suggestive rather than definitive, because only a much larger collection of voices can capture a true image of the Middle East's diversity of peoples and places. But in the richness of the tapestry they present, the authors demonstrate the insight that a commitment to the area-studies tradition in geography and related disciplines can generate.

I would like to thank the contributors, the editors, and anonymous reviewers for their participation in this special issue.

# References

Cutter, S. L., D. B. Richardson, and T. J. Wilbanks, eds. 2003. *The Geographical Dimensions of Terrorism.* New York: Routledge.

AWG [Arab World Geographer]. 2001. Forum on 11 September 2001 Events. *Arab World Geographer 4* (2). [http://users.fmg.uva.nl/vmamadouh/awg/].

Guest Editor, **DR. STEWART** is an associate professor of geography and the director of the Middle East Institute at Georgia State University, Atlanta, Georgia 30302.

# Stifled, Egypt's Young Turn to Islamic Fervor

Michael Slackman

airo—The concrete steps leading from Ahmed Muhammad Sayyid's first-floor apartment sag in the middle, worn down over time, like Mr. Sayyid himself. Once, Mr. Sayyid had a decent job and a chance to marry. But his fiancée's family canceled the engagement because after two years, he could not raise enough money to buy an apartment and furniture. Mr. Sayyid spun into depression and lost nearly 40 pounds. For months, he sat at home and focused on one thing: reading the Qur'an. Now, at 28, with a diploma in tourism, he is living with his mother and working as a driver for less than $100 a month. With each of life's disappointments and indignities, Mr. Sayyid has drawn religion closer.

Here in Egypt and across the Middle East, many young people are being forced to put off marriage, the gateway to independence, sexual activity and societal respect. Stymied by the government's failure to provide adequate schooling and thwarted by an economy without jobs to match their abilities or aspirations, they are stuck in limbo between youth and adulthood. "I can't get a job, I have no money, I can't get married, what can I say?" Mr. Sayyid said one day after becoming so overwhelmed that he refused to go to work, or to go home, and spent the day hiding at a friend's apartment.

In their frustration, the young are turning to religion for solace and purpose, pulling their parents and their governments along with them. With 60 percent of the region's population under the age of 25, this youthful religious fervor has enormous implications for the Middle East. More than ever, Islam has become the cornerstone of identity, replacing other, failed ideologies: Arabism, socialism, nationalism.

The wave of religious identification has forced governments that are increasingly seen as corrupt or inept to seek their own public redemption through religion. In Egypt, Jordan, Syria, Morocco and Algeria, leaders who once headed secular states or played down religion have struggled to reposition themselves as the guardians of Islamic values. More and more parents are sending their children to religious schools, and some countries have infused more religious content into their state educational systems.

More young people are observing stricter separation between boys and girls, sociologists say, fueling sexual frustrations. The focus on Islam is also further alienating young people from the West and aggravating political grievances already stoked by Western foreign policies. The religious fervor among the young is swelling support for Islam to play a greater role in political life. That in turn has increased political repression, because many governments in the region see Islamic political movements as a threat to their own rule. While there are few statistics tracking religious observance among the young, there is near-universal agreement that young people are propelling an Islamic revival, one that has been years in the making but is intensifying as the youth bulge in the population is peaking.

In Egypt, where the people have always been religious and conservative, young people are now far more observant and strict in their interpretation of their faith. A generation ago, for example, few young women covered their heads, and few Egyptian men made it a practice to go to the mosque for the five daily prayers. Now the hijab, a scarf that covers the hair and neck, is nearly universal, and mosques are filled throughout the day with young men, and often their fathers. In 1986, there was one mosque for every 6,031 Egyptians, according to government statistics. By 2005, there was one mosque for every 745 people and the population has nearly doubled. Egypt has historically fought a harsh battle against religious extremism. But at the same time, its leaders have tried to use religion for their own political gains. The government of President Hosni Mubarak whose wife, Suzanne, remains unveiled has put more preachers on state television. Its courts have issued what amount to religious decrees, and Mr. Mubarak has infused his own speeches with more religious references. "The whole country is taken by an extreme conservative attitude," said Mohamed Sayed Said, deputy director of the government-financed Ahram Center for Political and Strategic Studies in Cairo. "The government cannot escape it and cannot loosen it."

## Anger and Shame

Depression and despair tormented dozens of men and women in their 20s interviewed across Egypt, from urban men like Mr. Sayyid to frustrated village residents like Walid Faragallah, who once hoped education would guarantee him social mobility. Their stifled dreams stoke anger toward the government. "Nobody cares about the people," Mr. Sayyid said, slapping his hands against the air, echoing sentiment repeated in many interviews with young people across Egypt. "Nobody cares. What is holding me back is the system. Find a general with children and he will have an apartment for each of them. My government is only close to those close to the government."

Mr. Sayyid, like an increasing number of Egyptians, would like Islam to play a greater role in political life. He and many others said that the very government that claimed to elevate and emphasize their faith was insincere and hypocritical. "Yes, I do think that Islam is the solution," Mr. Sayyid said, quoting from the slogan of the Muslim Brotherhood, a banned but tolerated organization in Egypt that calls for imposing Shariah, or Islamic law, and wants a religious committee to oversee all matters of state. "These people, the Islamists, they would be better than the fake curtain, the illusion, in front of us now." Mr. Sayyid's resigned demeanor masks an angry streak. He said he and his friends would sometimes enter a restaurant, order food, then refuse to pay. They threaten to break up the place if the police are called, intimidating the owners. He explains this as if to prove he is a victim. He tells these stories with anger, and shame, then explains that his prayers are intended as a way to offset his sins. "Yeah, like thugs," he said of himself and his friends. "When we were younger, we watched the older guys do this, and then we took over. We inherited it." Mr. Sayyid, however, is no Islamic radical, combing militant websites and preaching jihad.

He could walk unnoticed in the West. He has a gap-toothed smile, rounded shoulders and a head of black hair that often shines from gel. He likes to wear jeans, and sandals with white socks. He often has a touch of a goatee, and a light shadow of calloused skin—barely noticeable—runs from his hairline to the middle of his forehead. The shadow is his prayer mark, or zebibah, which he has earned from pressing his head into the ground each time he bows in prayer. Like most religious young people, Mr. Sayyid is not an extremist. But with religious conservatism becoming the norm—the starting point—it is easier for extremists to entice young people over the line. There is simply a larger pool to recruit from and a shorter distance to go, especially when coupled with widespread hopelessness.

"There are lots of psychological repercussions and rejection from society," said Hamdi Taha, a professor of communications at Al Azhar University who runs a government-aligned charity that stages mass weddings for older low-income couples. "This is actually one of the things that could lead one to terrorism. They despair. They think maybe they get nothing in this world, but they will get something in the other life."

# Obstacles to Marriage

In Egypt and in other countries, like Saudi Arabia, governments help finance mass weddings, because they are concerned about the destabilizing effect of so many men and women who can not afford to marry. The mass weddings are hugely festive, with couples, many in their late 30s and 40s, allowed to invite dozens of family members and friends. Last year, Mr. Taha said, he had

about 6,000 applications for help—and managed to aid 2,300 men and women. In Idku, a small city not far from Alexandria on Egypt's north coast, Mr. Taha's charity staged a wedding for more than 65 couples; 200 others received help but decided not to take part in the collective wedding late last year. The couples were ferried to an open-air stadium in 75 cars donated by local people. They were greeted by a standing-room-only, roaring crowd, flashing neon lights, traditional music, the local governor and a television celebrity who served as the master of ceremonies for the event. "They are encouraging the youth to settle down and preventing them for doing anything wrong," said Mona Adam, 26, as she watched her younger sister, Omnia, marry. "Any young man or woman aspires to have a home and a family."

Across the Middle East, marriage is not only the key to adulthood but also a religious obligation, which only adds to the pressure—and the guilt. "Marriage and forming a family in Arab Muslim countries is a must," said Azza Korayem, a sociologist with the National Center for Social and Criminal Studies. "Those who don't get married, whether they are men or women, become sort of isolated." Marriage also plays an important financial role for families and the community. Often the only savings families acquire over a lifetime is the money for their children to marry, and handing it over amounts to an intergenerational transfer of wealth. But marriage is so expensive now, the system is collapsing in many communities. Diane Singerman, a professor at American University, said that a 1999 survey found that marriage in Egypt cost about $6,000, 11 times annual household expenditures per capita. Five years later, a study found the price had jumped 25 percent more. In other words, a groom and his father in the poorest segment of society had to save their total income for eight years to afford a wedding, she reported.

The result is delayed marriages across the region. A generation ago, 63 percent of Middle Eastern men in their mid- to late 20s were married, according to a recent study by the Wolfensohn Center for Development at the Brookings Institution and the Dubai School of Government. That figure has dropped to nearly 50 percent across the region, among the lowest rates of marriage in the developing world, the report said. In Iran, for example, 38 percent of the 25- to 29-year-old men are not married, one of the largest pools of unattached males in Iranian history. In Egypt, the average age at which men now marry is 31. And so, instead of marrying, people wait and seek outlets for their frustrations.

Mr. Sayyid lives with his mother, Sabah, who is 45, and who divorced shortly after he was born. He now spends most of his time behind the wheel of a Volkswagen Golf, listening to the Qur'an. At home, the radio is always on, always broadcasting the Qur'an. Two books are on a small white night table beside Mr. Sayyid's bed, a large Qur'an and a small Qur'an. As a young woman, Sabah, whose family did not want her last name used, never covered herself when she walked the streets of Sayeda Zeinab, the teeming, densely populated neighborhood known for its kebab and sweets. But now, she makes a pilgrimage each year to Mecca, wears loose fitting Islamic clothing that hides her figure, and she fasts twice a week. "We pull each other," said Sabah, who cannot read or write and so has learned about Islamic ideas from her son. She said that her son taught her that the Prophet Muhammad said that even if you could not read, looking at the Qur'an was like reading it. So she does just that and flips the pages, admiring the artistry of Arabic script.

## Dashed Expectations

Mr. Sayyid's path to stalemate began years ago, in school. Like most Egyptians educated in public schools, his course of study was determined entirely by grades on standardized tests. He was not a serious student, often skipping school, but scored well enough to go on to an academy, something between high school and a university. He was put in a five-year program to study tourism and hotel operations. His diploma qualified him for little but unemployment. Education experts say that while Egypt has lifted many citizens out of illiteracy, its education system does not prepare young people for work in the modern world. Nor, according to a recent Population Council report issued in Cairo, does its economy provide enough well-paying jobs to allow many young people to afford marriage.

Egypt's education system was originally devised to produce government workers under a compact with society forged in the heady early days of President Gamal Abdel Nasser's administration in the late 1950s and '60s. Every graduate was guaranteed a government job, and peasant families for the first time were offered the prospect of social mobility through education. Now children of illiterate peasant farmers have degrees in engineering, law or business. The dream of mobility survives, but there are not enough government jobs for the floods of graduates. And many are not qualified for the private sector jobs that do exist, government and business officials said, because of their poor schooling. Business students often never touch a computer, for example. On average, it takes several years for graduates to find their first job, in part because they would rather remain unemployed than work in a blue-collar factory position. It is considered a blow to family honor for a college graduate to take a blue-collar job, leaving large numbers of young people with nothing to do.

"O.K., he's a college graduate," said Muhammad el-Seweedy, who runs a government council that has tried with television commercials to persuade college graduates to take factory jobs and has provided training to help improve their skills. "It's done. Now forget it. This is a reality." But more widespread access to education has raised expectations. "Life was much more bearable for the poor when they did accept their social status," said Galal Amin, an economist and the author of "Whatever Happened to the Egyptians?" "But it is unimaginable when you have an education, to have this thought accepted. Frustration opens the door to religiosity."

In many ways, that is true of Mr. Sayyid. "What do you think? Of course I am bored," Mr. Sayyid said, trying not to let go of the forced smile he always wears when he talks about his stalled life. "When I get closer to God, I feel things are good in my life." He insists that it did not bother him that he never found a job in a hotel. "No one who prays wants a corrupt job in a hotel," he said, referring to the pork and alcohol served at such establishments but which are prohibited under Shariah. Later he admitted, "Yes, of course I wanted to work in tourism."

## Finding Solace in Religion

Zagazig is a medium-size city about an hour north of Cairo, surrounded by the farm land of the Nile Delta region. Laila Ashour works here as a volunteer in a clinic run by the Islamic Preaching Organization. Originally, it aimed to provide medical services to the poor, but it quickly expanded and also helps poor young couples start their lives together by providing furniture, appliances and kitchenware.

Ms. Ashour is 22 years old, a university graduate in communications. There was a time she dressed and acted like her friends, covering her head with a scarf but wearing blue jeans and bright shirts. She flirted with young men on the street, and dreamed of being a television producer. Today, Ms. Ashour dresses in a loose black gown called an abaya, and covers her head, all but her eyes, with a black piece of clothing over her face called a niqab. When she goes outside she wears black gloves as well. Even in this conservative town, she looks like a religious fundamentalist. What she is, is hurt. "I realized that people don't help you," Ms. Ashour said. "It is only God that helps you." She was engaged to Mustafa, whose last name she will not disclose, for more than two years. The plan was for Mustafa and his family to take a year or two to construct and furnish an apartment. But Mustafa's father had no money left after setting up two older sons, and the young man was unable to raise enough money to finish the construction. Ms. Ashour wanted to help, secretly, but she has been unable to find a paying job. When her mother told her to end the engagement, something snapped, and she sought solace in increasingly strict religious practice. "Everything is God's will," she said, explaining why she decided to take on the niqab. "Everything is a test."

The despair extends to rural Egypt, always a traditional, religious environment, but one that ambitious young people long to escape. In the village of Shamandeel, not far from Zagazig, it took Walid Faragallah six years after graduating with a degree in psychology to find a job in a factory, and his pay was less than $50 a month. That is an average period of waiting—and average pay—for new entries in the job market. Mr. Faragallah kept that job for a year, and recently found another factory job for $108 a month, two hours from his home. "It brings us closer to God, in a sense," Mr. Faragallah said, speaking of the despair he felt during the years he searched for work. "But sometimes, I can see how it does not make you closer to God, but pushes you toward terrorism. Practically, it killed my ambition. I can't think of a future." His parents built him an apartment so that he would not have to wait to marry. The apartment has been empty for years, though now, at 28 and with his new job, he said he hoped he could support a wife. "I tell them, my friends still in university, not to dream too much," Mr. Faragallah said one day while sitting on the balcony of the empty apartment he hopes to one day share with a family.

Back in Cairo, every Friday, the Muslim day of prayer, Mr. Sayyid's mother cooks him something special, so that when he returns from the mosque he has something to look forward to. "I am worried about him," she said. "What can he do?" There is a mosque a few steps from the front door of their house. But an Islamic tradition holds that the farther you walk to the mosque the more credit earned with God. So every Friday, Mr. Sayyid walks past the mosque by his home, and past a few more mosques, before he reaches the Sayeda Zeinab mosque. "By being religious, God prevents you from doing wrong things," Mr. Sayyid said, revealing his central fear and motivation, that time and boredom will lead him to sin. "This whole atmosphere we live in is wrong, wrong."

# Fighting for the Soul of Turkey

## Can an Islamic nation founded on secularism continue to survive the politics of faith?

Adnan R. Khan

In Turkey, even the winds have meaning. There is the *samiel,* a hot dry wind from the south associated with destruction; there's the *lodos,* the moist, warm southwesterly that brings with it lethargy and a tendency toward laissez-faire; then there's the *karayel* and *poyraz,* winds from the north forecasting storms and warning people to take shelter. The winds change often—as they are currently doing in Turkish politics.

After a spring season in which the Islamic-leaning Justice and Development Party (AKP) and secularists, including the army, faced off over the appointment of Abdullah Gul as the country's new president, the standoff led to early elections on July 22. The AKP won a resounding victory, garnering nearly half of the popular vote—a 14 per cent jump from its previous election results. Then, last Tuesday, Gul, a devout Muslim and AKP member, finally won the presidency after three parliamentary votes—in the face of yet another warning from the military. All that has set off a political debate in Turkey virtually unparalleled in its history, with the Islamist movement emboldened, and secularists, who lay claim to Turkey's founding principles, on the defensive. "How the Turkish experiment will unfold," says Soli Ozel, professor of political science at Bilgi University in Istanbul, "is not going to be important just for Turkey itself, but it will have repercussions."

The biggest danger now is whether Gul's accession to the presidency, a powerful position not only symbolically but also in practical and political terms, will deepen the divides within Turkish society. Some observers in the European Parliament had hoped the AKP, led by Prime Minister Recep Tayyip Erdogan, would choose a less divisive figure, someone without Islamist roots such as secular-minded Koksal Toptan, the newly elected speaker of parliament. The decision to push through Gul, they fear, may be a sign that the AKP knows it has a stranglehold on the levers of Turkish power.

What that means for the future of Turkey, a key member of NATO, remains to be seen. From Washington's perspective, the benefits of having an Islamic nation with a functioning, Western-style secular democracy as a crucial ally are immeasurable. The fact that Turkey's entire government structure is now dominated by a single party with far-reaching Islamic appeal represents a powerful symbol that the Bush administration can wield in its mission to democratize the Muslim world. And in what almost seemed like a gift to U.S. Republicans, Pakistan's ambassador to Turkey wrote in a recent commentary piece that his government, led by beleaguered President Pervez Musharraf, views Turkey as a model for reform in Pakistan. (Conservative Muslims in his country and in neighbouring Afghanistan see things differently: they consider Turkey an apostate Muslim nation. "Turks?" many say with open contempt. "Those aren't real Muslims.")

But to use the word "Islam" in any Turkish political context is misleading: the fact remains that Turkey is anything but a democratic Muslim country. Officially, it is a secular state—militantly secular in the same vein as France, with religion constitutionally banned from playing any role in politics, education and even, in some cases, society itself. Political parties with even a mildly religious platform are not permitted, and a religious education from any of the state-controlled madrasas is not recognized by universities. Alcohol laws are more liberal than in most Western nations, and any attempt to tighten them up is met with cries of Islamicization by secularists (though some bar owners have complained that since the AKP took power, alcohol licences are harder to come by).

Will that change now that religion reigns in Turkey's presidential palace? There is some evidence to support that possibility. During the AKP's first term in power, restrictions on religious education were loosened and the subsequent full-time enrollment rate in madrasas jumped from 3,000 to 4,950, while the number of part-time students doubled to 130,000. During the same period, the AKP attempted to amend laws to make religious education the equivalent of a high school diploma, but the proposals were vetoed by then-president Ahmet Necdet Sezer, a secularist. With Sezer now making way for the more religiously minded Gul, and the religious education issue back on the parliamentary agenda, many fear the amendments will be pushed through soon.

Those who sense an Islamist agenda behind the AKP's pro-secular rhetoric point to this sort of political manoeuvring as evidence. But it's still unclear what Erdogan's plan is. If his power base is any indication, a trend toward religious conservatism would be natural: the majority of Turks who voted for the AKP are from low-income, traditionalist segments of society. Where the party garnered the least support was in the Aegean coastal region bordering Greece, historically the richest and most secular region in Turkey.

In Istanbul's conservative Fatih district, many residents view the AKP's electoral success as a victory for Islam. "I didn't vote for Erdogan," says Neset Ugurlu, a street vendor selling knick-knacks from a wooden cart. "I voted for my religion." The sentiment is widespread in Fatih, a district famous for the 15th-century mosque at its heart, shops selling religious paraphernalia that surround it, and the predominance of bearded men and covered women. The addition of Gul as president has further emboldened Turkey's conservative Muslims, many of whom are looking to the AKP to put the Islam back in what they consider an Islamic nation.

But what does Islamicization really mean? If it's seen as a Pakistani-style nurturing of radical or fundamentalist religion, then no, the AKP is not taking Turkey toward Islamicization. But if it means removing some of the barriers to religion erected by the secular principles of the Turkish constitution, then yes, there is that in the AKP's agenda.

This is perhaps the most controversial issue facing Gul. "The president is constitutionally bound to uphold the *values* of the Turkish state," says Oktay Vural, deputy chairman of the Nationalist Movement Party (MHP). "The presidency is not a political office. Political responsibility rests on the government side. Gul should separate himself from his party affiliation and the AKP should not see him as their president." According to

Vural, the president is not a "notary public" who simply rubber-stamps laws passed in parliament. Gul should be prepared to oppose the AKP when the need arises—in other words, when Turkey's secular principles are threatened.

Whether or not he'll play that role is anybody's guess. "But we should remember," says Hugh Pope, a senior analyst with the International Crisis Group, "Gul will have seven years as president. He'll find his own balance. I think rather than obsess over his Islamist past, we should welcome this new era of Turkish politics. In the 1990s, the government couldn't even get a law passed." Now, after decades of struggling through inert coalition governments and military coups, Turkey is finally getting a taste of single-party rule, with a unified government.

What concerns people like Oktay Vural, though, is that for the first time in Turkish politics one party now controls all the executive branches of government. "That is our main concern," he says. "In Turkey, unfortunately, the political executive [the cabinet and the presidency] has a lot of power: it heavily influences the judiciary and the media. This is a problem in our democracy we have to solve—without checks and balances, it is difficult to predict how the government will act."

The AKP has promised to make necessary changes to Turkey's democracy—reducing the veto power of the president, for example, so that some crucial issues are decided by referendums rather than the whims of a single person. The test of the government's true intentions may be whether it follows through on those promises, or if it instead bows to Islamist tendencies. "So, we have then in this particular set-up the seeds of transformation in the country," says Ozel, "or the seeds of paralysis. And we will see which one we'll obtain."

# In Algeria, a Tug of War for Young Minds

Michael Slackman

Algiers—First, Abdel Malek Outas's teachers taught him to write math equations in Arabic, and embrace Islam and the Arab world. Then they told him to write in Latin letters that are no longer branded unpatriotic, and open his mind to the West. Malek is 19, and he is confused. "When we were in middle school we studied only in Arabic," he said. "When we went to high school, they changed the program, and a lot is in French. Sometimes, we don't even understand what we are writing." The confusion has bled off the pages of his math book and deep into his life. One moment, he is rapping; another, he recounts how he flirted with terrorism, agreeing two years ago to go with a recruiter to kill apostates in the name of jihad.

At a time of religious revival across the Muslim world, Algeria's youth are in play. The focus of this contest is the schools, where for decades Islamists controlled what children learned, and how they learned, officials and education experts here said. Now the government is urgently trying to re-engineer Algerian identity, changing the curriculum to wrest momentum from the Islamists, provide its youth with more employable skills, and combat the terrorism it fears schools have inadvertently encouraged.

It appears to be the most ambitious attempt in the region to change a school system to make its students less vulnerable to religious extremism. But many educators are resisting the changes, and many disenchanted young men are dropping out of schools. It is a tense time in Algiers, where city streets are crowded with police officers and security checkpoints and alive with fears that Algeria is facing a resurgence of Islamic terrorism. From 1991 to 2002, as many as 200,000 Algerians died in fighting between government forces and Islamic terrorists. Now one of the main terrorist groups, the Salafist Group for Preaching and Combat, or G.S.P.C., has affiliated with Al Qaeda, rebranding itself as Al Qaeda in the Islamic Maghreb.

There is a sense that this country could still go either way. Young people here in the capital appear extremely observant, filling mosques for the daily prayers, insisting that they have a place to pray in school. The strictest form of Islam, Wahhabism from Saudi Arabia, has become the gold standard for the young. And yet, the young in Algiers also appear far more

socially liberal than their peers in places like Egypt and Jordan. Young veiled women walk hand in hand, or sit leg to leg, with young men, public flirtations unthinkable in most other Muslim countries. The two natures of the country reflect the way in which Algerian identity was cleaved in half by 132 years of French colonial rule, and then again by independence and forced Arabization. Once the French were driven out in 1962, the Algerians were determined to forge a national identity free from Western influence. The schools were one center of that drive. French was banned as the language of education, replaced by Arabic. Islamic law and the study of the Qur'an were required, and math and science were shortchanged. Students were warned that sinners go to hell, and 6-year-olds were instructed in the proper way to wash a corpse for burial, education officials said.

There is a feeling among many Algerians that they went too far. "We say that Algeria's schools have trained monsters," said Khaoula Taleb Ibrahim, a professor of education at the University of Algiers. "It is not to that extent, but the schools have contributed to that problem." Over the years, the government has pushed back, reintroducing French, removing the most zealous religious teachers and trying to revise the religious curriculum. Seven years ago, a committee appointed by the president issued a report calling for an overhaul of the school system—and it died under intense political pressure, mostly from the Islamists and conservatives, officials said. But this year, the government is beginning to make substantive changes. The schools are moving from rote learning—which was always linked to memorizing the Qur'an—to critical thinking, where teachers ask students to research subjects and think about concepts. Yet the students and teachers are still unprepared, untrained and, in many cases, unreceptive. "Before, teachers used to explain the lesson," Malek said. "Now they want us to think more, to research, but it's very difficult for us." Malek says he hopes to graduate from high school next year and now wants to join the military, just like his father. He is a long way from being the person who had accepted what he says the terrorist recruiter told him—that soldiers, like his own father, are apostates and should be killed. His resolution lasted for three days, until his imam found out and persuaded him not to go. But the call to jihad still tugs at him. In his world, jihad, or struggle, is a duty for Muslims, but as Malek explains, the challenge is who will convince young people of the proper form that struggle should take. "They really convince you," he said of the extremists. Then later, with great sincerity, he asked: "Can you help me? I want to go to New York and rap."

# The Family

In Algeria, your sense of identity often depends on when you went to school. Hassinah Bou Bekeur, 26, enjoys watching the Saudi satellite channels and the news in Arabic. She watches with her mother and four younger sisters in one room. But her father, Nasreddin, 60, stays in another room so he can watch in French, the language of his education. "He is not very strict," she said of her father, with a touch of affection and disappointment in her voice. "We have more awareness of religion now." She took the veil when she was 20; one sister did so at 17, and another sister at 15. The youngest, Zeinab, is only 12 and does not yet wear the veil. The veil is a symbol of the distance between father and children. While Mr. Bou Bekeur studied the Qur'an, Islam was not the cornerstone of his identity. He says he even drank alcohol—which is prohibited by Islam—until 1986. "I never knew that," said Amal, his 17-year-old daughter, and then with a smile, she waved her fist at her father and said, "I will kill you." The Bou Bekeur family illustrates the outcome of Algeria's school-based Arabization project. The family is close but the generation gap is extraordinary. It is not solely the result of schooling—but the history of the education system here helps explain the distance between the generations. It begins with occupation and schools designed to train people for a French-run system. Even after independence, the schools needed to continue to train in French because the government needed managers and experts to replace those French citizens who had left the country, officials here said. In 1971, officials said, the Arabization project began in earnest, when French was prohibited as a language of education. But there were not enough educators qualified to teach in Arabic, so Algeria turned to Egyptians, Iraqis and Syrians—not realizing, officials say now, that many of those teachers had extreme religious views and that they helped plant the seeds of radicalism that would later flourish in a school system where Arabization became interchangeable with Islamization. In the Bou Bekeur house that meant children far more religious than their father—and their mother. "The foundation of religion, I learned in school," said Mr. Bou Bekeur's son, Abdel Rahman, 25. "We pray more than them and we know religion better than them," he said of his father's generation. "We are more religious. My father used to drink. I never drank. My father asked me if it was O.K. to take a car loan. I told him, no, it is haram," forbidden in Islam. So his father did not take the loan. His father is a quiet man in a house of strong-willed people. He can barely help his children with their homework, because his Arabic is poor. And he worries about their future, and the future of his country. "Now they are at a crossroads," Mr. Bou Bekeur said of his children and their generation. "Either they go to the West, or stay with this and become extremists."

The children do not respond to such remarks. They often give their father a kind of sad, knowing smile, as though they have done the best that they can with him, and are pleased with the progress he has made. The family lives in a small pink villa, inherited from Mr. Bou Bekeur's father, who was killed fighting the French. Mr. Bou Bekeur's wife, Naima, is 48, and of a different generation altogether. She was among the first to go through the state-sponsored Arabization process. She said she remembered having a teacher from Egypt who was supposed to teach academic subjects in Arabic—but provided her first real lessons in religion. Mrs. Bou Bekeur started serving lunch, homemade couscous. The family was sitting in the main living room on big brown couches, as Mr. Bou Bekeur scratched away at one of his French crossword puzzles. Hassinah wore orange velour pants, an orange velour top and a large pink scarf that covered her head and was pinned beneath her chin. The conversation shifted, with Hassinah complaining that men were treated better at home than women. "The boys don't have to wash the dishes. Why?" she said. "Why the difference? If I had a boy or girl, I would treat them equal. Women are supposed to work all day and come home and clean and cook—no way," she fumed, her hands firmly on her knees. Mr. Bou Bekeur seemed pleased. "Women have more opportunities today than they used to. Women can participate in sports and still be respected," he said in his naturally soft voice. "No," Hassinah said, gently, shaking her head at her father. "My way of thinking is more influenced by religion. My religion tells me 'no, that's not right.' " Zeinab, the 12-year-old, was seated in the corner, headphones on, humming a song by Beyoncé, and smiling as she did homework.

# Malek and Friends

Four years ago, Amine Aba, 19, one of Malek's best friends, decided it was time to take his religion more seriously, to stop listening to music, to stop dancing, to stop hanging around with Malek—most of which he accomplished most of the time. "Muslim countries have been influenced by the Europeans," Amine said, explaining why he thought he had not been religious enough for most of his life. "We have neglected our religion," he said. "Like us," said Malek, who was nearby with a new buddy, Muhammad Lamine Messaoudi, a baby-faced 18-year-old with a bit of a paunch and a constant smile. The two burst into nervous laughter. Malek, Amine and Lamine are each dealing with the forces shaping their world in slightly different ways. Amine has chosen religion; Malek, who has gelled hair and a slight stutter, has taken a middle road of religion, girls and rap; and Lamine appears a sentry of the left, interested in beer, girls and, he hopes, a life in France. Each has felt the push and pull of the political-ideological fight going on in Algerian schools, between those who want to maintain the status quo and those who hope to reopen a window to the West. The messages the young men receive through teachers and the curriculum are still, almost uniformly, aimed at reinforcing their Arab-Islamic identity. But that is changing, slowly, and not without a fight. "We would never have imagined Algeria could one day be faced with violence that would come from Islam," said Fatiha Yomsi, an adviser to the minister of education.

Students go to school amid subdued tension because many educators do not like the changes that are coming. "He is an Islamist. He would not shake my hand before," Ms. Yomsi said as she introduced an Arabic teacher during a morning tour of Al Said Hamdeen high school here. Then as she walked around, she pointed out the front line in the struggle, keeping boys and girls together in class. "You see, all these classes are mixed," she said. "It is very important. We fought for this. That is why I am targeted for death." At stake are the identities of young people like Malek, Amine and Lamine—and their futures.

The young men focused on trying to pass their exams, because Algiers is full of examples of those who have not. More than 500,000 students drop out each year, officials said—and only about 20 percent of students make it into high school. Only about half make it from high school into a university. A vast majority of dropouts are young men, who see no link between work and school. Young women tend to stick with school because, officials said, it offers independence from their parents. Algeria's young men leave school because there is no longer any connection between education and employment, school officials said.

The schools raise them to be religious, but do not teach them skills needed to get a job. This is another cause for extremism, and it is one reason the police do nothing to stop so many young men from illegally selling everything from deodorant to bread at makeshift stands. "These stands are illegal, but they let them do it as a matter of security and because of unemployment—instead of them going out and carrying weapons," said Muhammad Darwish, a social studies teacher in the Muhammad Bou Ras middle school, as he passed masses of young men selling on the street. Malek, Amine and Lamine are all trying to avoid ending up like a vast majority of their friends—selling on the street. Lamine and Malek try to study. But they say that is only because if they fail the exams, they cannot get into the military—and if they cannot get into the military, they will have no status in Algeria. They have focused on the science curriculum. But their hearts do not seem to be in it. "They don't let you like education here," Lamine said. Malek met Amine when Amine's family moved into the walled and guarded compound for military families where Malek already lived. It is beside the Casbah, the old Arab quarter, where streets wind up and down hills that fall from the mountains to the sea. That was four years ago, and the young men became friends, going together to the mosque where they practiced the traditional way of reciting the Qur'an aloud. But as Amine grew more religious, Malek began to drift away from him, in part out of concern for his father. "The military and a beard don't go together," he said. Malek shaved his beard and started to spend all his free time with Lamine, a very quiet young man with a shaved head. One of their favorite spots to relax is the monument to those killed in the war against the French. The concrete monument soars more than 300 feet into the sky, with three ramps sweeping up to an apex.

The sky was blue, the wind heavy and the clouds white on a May day when Malek dropped to the pavement and began to break dance, his feet in the air, his shoulders pressed to the ground. Suddenly Algerian rap played from Lamine's cellphone as they danced and laughed—until they stopped. Amine wrapped his arm around Malek's shoulder and they recited the Qur'an, their voices carrying through the wind. Lamine stood by, silently. "I only have 25 days until the test; I have to go home," Amine said. "My mother will be mad at me if I don't study." After he left, Lamine was asked how he felt about Amine. He has frequently teased him, suggesting that they go together to the bar for a beer. Lamine does not go with Malek to pray, talks often about drinking alcohol and said that two years ago he was arrested trying to sneak onto a ship to get to France. "He's O.K.," Lamine said. "I'd like to be like him. I'd like to be religious someday, too."

# The Future of Iraq: The Decline of Violence, the Rise of Politics

KIMBERLY KAGAN

## Baghdad

I have made four trips to Iraq since May 2007. I have walked through markets in Baghdad escorted by U.S. soldiers, visited the outposts where they live with their Iraqi army partners, talked with school children playing soccer in the street, seen newly renovated housing in war-torn neighborhoods, and eaten in the homes of local and tribal leaders who have helped our soldiers fight Al Qaeda in Iraq. This morning, a weekday in July 2008, I am doing something I have never done before: visiting the headquarters of a small Iraqi political party to learn about its campaign for the upcoming provincial and national elections.

The visit was not on the original itinerary of the group of military analysts with whom I am traveling. The party's leader, a member of parliament whom we met several days ago, invited us to his headquarters, our schedule permitting. We have cancelled a morning's worth of meetings in order to see something new.

And so I step out of a Humvee onto a quiet, semi-residential street in central Baghdad, lined with trees that shade us from the bright sun. The only U.S. military personnel in sight are our escorts. We Americans are incongruously dressed in the body armor and helmets required outside the Green Zone, while our host, who comes out to greet us, is wearing a fine suit. We look as ridiculous in our protective gear as we would if we dressed like this to walk into a foreign embassy just off 16th Street in Washington.

The member of parliament—whom I choose not to name; he survived an assassination attempt years ago that killed members of his family—escorts us into the building. His party is secular and nonsectarian. There were 70 founding members at its first meeting, he says, before the 2005 elections. Today the party has over 10,000 members and headquarters in most of Iraq's major cities. Our friend holds his party's single seat in the Council of Representatives, a body of 275 legislators, in which the dominant forces are Prime Minister Nuri al-Maliki's Dawa party, Abd al-Aziz al-Hakim's Islamic Supreme Council of Iraq (ISCI), and the Sadrist Trend.

Our host gives us a brief tour of the headquarters. It is strikingly familiar, reminiscent of hundreds of town and county election headquarters in the United States. A widescreen television in the large conference room displays news continuously. A freshly photocopied stack of flyers sits in an anteroom, explaining the party's position on the strategic agreement between Iraq and the United States that is the subject of intense debate throughout the country. Party officials responsible for different districts of Baghdad plan to distribute the flyers door to door over the weekend, assisted by staff and volunteers. They are preparing another round of flyers for next week. Nearby, young men and women sit at a bank of computers writing and designing the party's newspaper and laying out the advertisements that pay for its production. The color photographs in today's edition highlight a recent event sponsored by the party's youth committee: an awards ceremony for school children who have gotten top grades this academic year.

Our tour of the various sections, from the youth committee to the women's committee, lasts ten minutes. Then our host whispers that it's time for chai. We sit down to drink tea in the party's formal conference room, perched on the gold-hued couches that Iraqi officials think are elegant. Extra chairs are brought in from all over the building in order to seat the 30 party members who have come to discuss politics with us. Roughly half of them are in their twenties, like the bright and earnest recent college graduates one finds working for any U.S. election campaign. The young men are awkwardly dressed in suits; a few of them, daringly, do not wear the customary moustache—a bold statement of their post-Saddam outlook.

I am one of seven women in the room, which is a record number for me in Iraq, whether with Iraqis or with U.S. forces. The older women, well dressed in suits and headscarves, are senior officials in the party. The young women's outfits vary, and show a range of interpretations of traditional Muslim dress. Most wear headscarves. One beautiful young woman has covered her hair with a chic, regal, purple scarf glinting with beads, coordinated perfectly with her colorful, tailored long skirt. The headscarf brings out her perfectly made-up eyes. Her image is modern and elegant, whereas her equally modern companion dresses more casually—a pair of jeans, a blouse, and a translucent pink headscarf. Another twenty-something, in a lace-trimmed blouse and long skirt, shakes her uncovered hair, which is long and highlighted.

We sip our tea and discuss the upcoming provincial elections. The party leader proudly takes out a folder containing the results of last week's poll, which the party commissioned from an independent firm. He has very high name recognition, strong favorable ratings, and low unfavorable ratings. If these continue until Iraq's national elections in 2009, he thinks he will retain his seat in parliament, and the party may gain a few more.

We are guests, so we ask our questions first. We discuss the party and its campaign, national issues such as foreign investment in Iraq, and foreign affairs including the Iranian nuclear program. We ask what they tell people when they go door to door: Why should anyone join and vote for their party? One older woman answers, We are religious people, but we are not a religious party. Any Iraqi can join, regardless of sect. We stand for all Iraqis. She says this gravely, and it does not seem a platitude.

These party members are hardly naive, despite their optimism. They have experienced politically driven and sectarian violence. The headquarters is surrounded by low, concrete barriers to protect it from vehicle bombs. After the party signed a lease for its first headquarters in Baghdad in 2005, the homeowner reneged on the agreement for fear that his property would be bombed, so the party moved.

I ask the young people why they have joined the party, and whether they hope to have careers in politics. One young man, who has been to college, explains that many young Iraqis have not had a proper education. He has joined the party and its youth committee to help improve Iraqi education, recruit good teachers, and ensure that all young people can not only read and write, but also acquire the skills that they will need to pursue their careers in a high-tech world. This is important, he insists, not only for the young people themselves, but also for the future of Iraq's economy, which must be able to compete in the global market. Another young man will not pursue a career exclusively in politics, but believes that when he enters the business world his political connections will come in handy.

The young woman with highlighted hair is frankly ambitious. She intends to have a political career and hopes to be a high party official someday—so she can better help the people, she adds as an afterthought. The older woman seated next to the party leader smiles wryly at this comment and cleans her spectacles so no one will notice her expression. She is evidently the high official that the young woman aspires to replace.

This could be the future of Iraq. These people have a strong vision of what their country can become, and are working to bring it to fruition in their lifetimes. They are not alone. In fact, 502 political parties have registered to participate in the provincial elections that officials anticipate will be held in December. Iraq's electoral commission, which determines whether parties are legitimate, rejected only 17 applications.

Five hundred parties are a lot. Forty registered in Basra alone, and if each runs a full slate of candidates (provincial councils have around 30 members), the ballot will look like a phone book. The proliferation of parties is not entirely desirable. Were they to join together in legislative and electoral coalitions, they might compete more directly with the larger parties. Iraqi politics tends to be noisy, chaotic, and unpredictable.

But the key point is, it is politics. Over the past year, the struggle for power in Iraq has shifted from military conflict to political competition. Iraq's leaders—Sunni, Shia, Turkmen, and Kurd—are thinking ever less about how to use armed might to seize or retain control of all or part of the country and ever more about winning votes. For all its drawbacks, the proliferation of political parties is an enormous advance toward stable, nonsectarian, or at least cross-sectarian politics.

Until now, Iraqi politics has been dominated by clerical parties attempting to function as monolithic blocs. An alliance between the ISCI and Maliki's Dawa party dominated Shia politics, challenged only by the Sadrist Trend. The Iraq Islamic party (IIP) represented Iraq's Sunni Arabs. The two Kurdish parties functioned largely as a bloc. The resulting parliamentary politics was simple, because there were really only three moving parts. It was also dysfunctional, because the Arab parties reflected the most hardline sectarian views of a minority of their constituents much more than the moderate views of the majority. The breaking of this sectarian political logjam would be an epochal event in Iraq, and it appears to be well underway.

The prime minister's decision to clear Basra of militias in March, followed by operations to clear Sadr City and Amara, has transformed the Iraqi political environment no less than the security environment. Iraqi forces, supported by the coalition, shattered the Sadrist and Iranian-controlled leadership of Moktada al-Sadr's Mahdi army, of the criminal Shia gangs Iranian agents were cynically paying and using, and even of the Special Groups more tightly controlled by Iran. Iraqi and coalition forces killed hundreds of militia fighters and leaders, and thousands more fled, many leaving Iraq. Iranian-backed militias initially fought very hard in Basra and Sadr City, but then broke completely. By the time Iraqi forces moved into Amara, the remaining Shia militants had no stomach for a fight.

Maliki ordered the Basra operation on his own, against the advice of coalition commanders. The initial operation, inadequately planned and prepared, looked very ugly. The coalition rushed assistance to Basra in the form of planning staff, intelligence and air assets, and military advisers—but no combat formations. The Iraqi military also rushed reinforcements to the city, including the Quick Reaction Force of the 1st Iraqi Army Division based in Anbar. That formation, with a high proportion of Sunnis, marched into combat against Shia militias in an overwhelmingly Shia city—and were received as liberators. And after the initial setbacks, the Iraqi soldiers fought hard. The process was repeated in Sadr City, although coalition forces initially did play a significant role in direct combat in order to stop the rocket attacks on the Green Zone. Once that was accomplished, the Iraqis cleared the rest of Sadr City on their own, with the same mix of enablers the coalition had provided in Basra (albeit on a larger scale).

These surprising successes—which resulted from Maliki's initiative and occurred over initial coalition objections—have raised Maliki's stature in Iraq to a level never before seen. The change is palpable. Talking to Sunni sheikhs recently, I found a new tolerance for Maliki, whom they now see as someone who is at least sometimes willing to take on his own constituency for the good of the country. Many Sunni Arab leaders remain angry about Maliki's advisers' sectarian tendencies, but for the first time in my experience, Sunni Arabs are distinguishing between the prime minister and those around him.

Maliki himself—and even some of those "evil advisers"—learned interesting lessons from Basra. Hardline Shias in government have long feared the re-creation of a Sunni-dominated Iraqi army that could become, at least in their minds, a sectarian coup force. That is one of the chief reasons for early Shia efforts to seize control of the Ministry of the Interior, which oversees the National Police and the provincial Iraqi Police: Since the Shia believed they were preparing for sectarian civil war, it made sense to develop an independent Shia paramilitary force. But when the chips were down in Basra, it was not the interior ministry or the police that came to Maliki's rescue, but the Iraqi army—in the person of Defense Minister Abdul Qadr, a Sunni, and the Anbar-based Quick Reaction Force, which reinforced the city. Maliki and some of his advisers have taken note of that fact, and relationships even within the most senior governmental ranks have been shifting.

The destruction of the Sadrist Trend not only as a paramilitary force, but also as a cohesive political force, has also had profound consequences. Sadr himself did not stir from Iran while his loyalists were being hammered by Iraqi and coalition forces. Many of his movement's leaders were captured, killed, or driven off. The government's declaration that no political party would be allowed to compete in the elections without disarming its militia has broken up the Sadrist Trend as a political movement as well. Sadrist leaders who remain in Iraq are running as independents or joining other parties. Some say that they will re-form a Sadrist political movement after the elections, but it will almost certainly be a far weaker force than the one that gripped Baghdad with fear for so long.

Among Iraq's Sunni Arabs, tension with the central government remains high, but electoral politics are beginning to overshadow that tension. In Anbar, the leaders of the Awakening movement that helped defeat Al Qaeda in Iraq have formed a powerful political party. They mean to defeat the Iraq Islamic party and become the voice of Anbar. The IIP is responding to the challenge in various ways—some legitimate, and some less so. Everyone in Iraq thinks that one party or another will try to rig or steal the elections. Everyone I talked to said it would be best if there were an American soldier standing by every ballot box. They're probably right on both counts. But no one suggested that they did not intend to abide by the results of the elections. Of course, every party is confident that it will win.

Iraq's ethno-sectarian wounds have not healed—one might best say that they are starting to scab over. Tensions remain high along the Arab-Kurdish fault line in Ninewa, Kirkuk, and Diyala Provinces. Sectarian tensions are also high between Sunni and Shia Arabs in Diyala and in and around Baghdad. Nor are the Iraqi security forces quite as ready to take full responsibility for keeping the precarious peace as some of Iraq's leaders suppose. Flush with success and eager to appear strong and independent as elections approach, some of Iraq's leaders exaggerate their own capabilities, something that complicates our negotiations for a strategic partnership, among other things.

But even the most extreme of these hubristic Shia advisers strongly favor a partnership with the United States. "Iraq is flying west," one of them told me over a dinner of rice, kabobs, and *masghouf* (a fish dish). The debate over the details of the military arrangements for 2009 has overshadowed a much more important point, he said, echoing the comments of the young people at the party headquarters we visited: Iraq wants American help of every kind. The security arrangements must be seen within the context of this larger partnership, he added. Like American politicians, of course, he and the rest of Iraq's leaders have to figure out how to sell any specific agreement to the parliament—and to the voters. That makes negotiations difficult, but it is also the strongest possible sign of hope in Iraq.

The whole purpose of the surge was to transform the conflict over power in Iraq from a military to a political struggle. We and the Iraqis have accomplished that goal—for now. But the most critical period in the birth of a new Iraq lies ahead. America can stand beside this fractious and sometimes violent young state whose people are now passionate about democracy. Or we can abandon them to their enemies, to their own fears and insecurities, and to the fragility of their months-old efforts at real reconciliation. It is a weighty choice, but not a hard one for anyone who has seen the vision of a possible future Iraq.

**KIMBERLY KAGAN** is the president of the Institute for the Study of War and the author of *The Surge: A Military History* (forthcoming).

# Saudi Arabia: Reality Check

**The recent meeting between the US vice-president, Dick Cheney, and Saudi Arabia's King Abdullah confirmed the solid relations between Riyadh and Washington. Most Saudis, however, care more about the situation at home, under a new ruler who claims to want to change society and the role of women, to combat poverty and to promote greater freedom.**

ALAIN GRESH

When the deputy minister of information asked me in 2002, "Will you talk about Saudi Arabia objectively?" the question seemed almost menacing. A few years later, journalists enjoy much greater freedom to travel across the country and meet anyone they wish, even intellectuals the authorities have forbidden to speak to the press.

This time a female journalist in the Jeddah head office of the English language *Saudi Gazette* asked: "Will you talk about Saudi Arabia objectively?" She wore a headscarf and the lower part of her face was concealed, but there was nothing timid about her attitude or the way she forced me on the defensive. She had just upset the authorities by publishing an article on choppy relations between Saudi Arabia and Libya; they put diplomatic relations on hold for several months. She was covering the Organisation of the Islamic Conference (OIC) summit meeting in Mecca, talking to heads of state and political leaders.

So how do I answer the question? How can I be sure of giving an objective picture of a country that is culturally so different, with so much regional diversity and so many identities? The language is not an obstacle for me, but how am I to rise above deep prejudice and facile simplification?

However eager I may be to highlight social and political change, progress and growing debate, the facts can't be disregarded. Saudi Arabia has a set menu for foreign journalists. They meet political leaders well versed in empty language, westernised academics and business executives who speak English and share the visitors' world view. These encounters result in articles that all say the same thing. So how to give a true account?

Islam is at the core of Saudi Arabia, influencing its way of life and its world outlook. Superficial observation may suggest that Wahhabism is adequate as an all-encompassing description. But the country is home to religious schools representing a wide range of traditions, including Sufis, and has a lively Shia minority. Far from being uniform, even Sunni Wahhabism has its own internal debate and discord, which has developed in recent years. But to appreciate the diversity, one must listen carefully to men and women who operate inside another system of values, use different words from ours, and are understandably wary of the western media which they consider, sometimes rightly, to be hostile to Islam.

Saudi Arabia, which has just joined the World Trade Organisation, is surfing on a wave of rising oil prices. Earnings in 2005 reached almost $0.5bn a day. The prosperity and economic drive is palpable. The value of the stock market doubled in 2004, doing just as well last year, and it now represents a source of income for many families. By December 5.7 million Saudis had spent almost $2bn on shares in the national oil company Yanpet (at Yanbu).

The upper and middle classes are reasonably accessible to westerners. But we know almost nothing about the others, especially the poor, whose existence the government has finally acknowledged. There are 6.3 million immigrants (to 19.7 million Saudis), and they represent most of the workforce.

It is hard to grasp the scale of social problems. Without detailed statistics, a trade union movement or even the beginnings of indigenous social sciences, it is difficult to assess poverty, although the press provides unexpected help. Over recent years—more since King Abdullah came to the throne on 1 August 2005—the newspapers have started to provide regular cover of unemployment, poverty, prostitution and drugs. The Aids epidemic has prompted several public initiatives; on 1 December, World Aids Day, health workers were spotted handing out leaflets in Jeddah.

Will the durable influx of oil revenue enable the country to solve problems in the labour market, education and healthcare? The first challenge will be to find work for everyone, especially tens of thousands of young people and the growing number of women looking for jobs. Their demands and frustrations will be important in the future.

The spectacle in the streets of Riyadh on Wednesday evenings is impressive. There are thousands of listless youths with nowhere to go, in the absence of theatres, cinemas or anywhere to meet females. They are obviously bored, all the more since the internet and satellite television have opened their eyes to international culture. It is hardly surprising that problems of delinquency and drug addiction are rising. At the weekend some seek an outlet in Bahrain, the island kingdom connected to Saudi Arabia by a gigantic bridge; 11 million travellers crossed it in 2004 and the number increases steadily. They go in search of entertainment they cannot find at home.

Some youths, and not necessarily the most underprivileged, have chosen a more dangerous route. In the 1980s many answered the call to arms in Afghanistan, responding to appeals by their own government and assisted by the United States. Their younger brothers followed, outraged by massacres in Bosnia or Chechnya, and trained in the Taliban camps. Several thousand more are now in Iraq.

They originally took up arms to fight the Soviet or US enemy but some subsequently turned against the Saudi regime, particularly after it appealed for US help in August 1990, after the Iraqi invasion of Kuwait. Since then there has been more talk of extremism, jihad and the role of Islam, particularly after May 2003 when a wave of attacks hit the kingdom. The final communiqué of the OIC conference in Mecca, on 7 and 8 December, stated that "Islam is a religion of moderation (*wassatiyyah*) which rejects bigotry, extremism and fanaticism".

Sheikh Salman al-Awdah, one of Saudi Arabia's most popular preachers, embodies this change more than anyone. During Ramadan his daily broadcast on the MBC satellite channel proved a huge success, particularly as he did not restrict himself to religious matters. He addressed more personal topics such as beauty, prompting criticism from conservatives. We met him outside his house, on his return from the afternoon prayer meeting he leads in a nearby mosque. In the hall a private tutor was instructing the sheikh's three young children: "Education is the most important thing," said al-Awdah. His office is sparsely furnished with a prayer mat, a bookcase and some drawings of trees hanging on the wall.

His charisma was apparent as he prepared unroasted coffee, dates and chocolates, all part of Saudi "tradition and civilisation", as he put it. Al-Awdah was one of the clerics behind the *sahwa* (awakening) movement. At the end of the 1980s and through the 1990s it contributed to renewing Islam, enabling it to wrest the initiative from the liberals and modernists who seemed to have gained the upper hand at the beginning of the 1980s.

With the first Gulf war, in 1990–91, the focus shifted from culture to politics, and the *sahwa* turned its attention to relations with the US and the situation in Saudi Arabia. The authorities finally arrested al-Awdah in 1994 and he spent five years in prison. He has changed since, though it is hard to say whether it is because of his detention, the suicidal tendencies of the jihadists, the 9/11 attacks or the more liberal attitude adopted by Abdullah, then crown prince, well before he came to the throne. Although he is still deeply attached to his dogma, the sheikh's sermons are more moderate.

He was critical of the warlike spin that some put on religious texts, and said: "The Qur'an offers guidance on relations with non-Muslims, but ordinary people sometimes misread words or take them out of context. In the *sura* entitled 'Muhammad', verse 4 reads: 'If you encounter those who disbelieve, you may strike the necks.' But it is impossible to understand this passage outside the context of war. Here 'encounter' means to fight. We should remember the history of Islam. At the time of the prophet . . . Muslims were under attack. But they had a guide and did not seek vengeance, as it was contrary to the teaching of Islam. Do you know how many people were killed in the fighting during the 23 years he preached? Between 250 and 300 in 20 battles. Nowadays the tiniest skirmish claims many more victims."

In July 2003 al-Awdah took part in the first national dialogue instigated by Abdullah. He met Shia religious leaders in public, a brave gesture because many Sunnis see them as heretics, even as non-Muslims.

Sheikh Abdul Aziz al-Gassim is another example of the same tolerant attitude. He contributed to the *sahwa* but has since gone further along the road towards reform. The French academic Stéphane Lacroix refers to him, among others, as an "Islamo-liberal", but most of those concerned reject the term, reluctant to distance themselves from the Islamic consensus. Al-Gassim is an inspiration to the young, who after flirting with radicalism, are now looking for ways of mixing Islam and political liberalism.

He runs a law firm which publishes studies on law and sharia. He spoke calmly but with conviction: "The most important [change] is that religious matters are now open to debate. The state has always wanted to control the religious institution, now it is keen to open it to the outside world. All the more so because the death of Sheikh bin Baz and Sheikh bin Uthaimeen, two ulema of undisputed authority, created a vacuum that no one else can fill. It makes it more difficult for the authorities to use the institution (as they did in 1990 when they appealed for US military assistance) because it has less credibility. The Council of Grand Ulema had to agree to some of its members retiring, before their death, which was unheard of."

Khaled works at the ministry of religious affairs. He runs an advertising agency and works as a journalist in his spare time. He belongs to a new generation of orthodox Muslims who seek change. A year and a half ago, with friends, he started Al-Sakina (tranquillity), an internet-based campaign aimed at young people who had yielded to radical ideas.

"We have had 63,000 hours' debate involving 1,000 people. We managed to change 590 of them to different degrees. Most of the time discussions are anonymous, for obvious reasons of security. Some of those involved are scared. We explain the concept of jihad, what sharia means, and the attitude Muslims should adopt to others. Unfortunately even liberals sometimes see everything in black and white. According to them, we have to choose between liberal values and Islam. But we disagree. We are Muslims and liberals." However, it is hard to convert people to dialogue. The fifth national dialogue forum, "Us and the others: a national vision for interacting with international cultures", was set up by Abdullah when he was still crown prince. The meeting in Abha in December brought together several dozen intellectuals and heads of NGOs and religious bodies. For the first time the discussions were broadcast live on television.

"We will have to start by learning to talk to each other," said Suhayla Zayn al-Abidin, shortly before she left for the conference. "It's not for us to decide who is *kafir* [an unbeliever] and who is not. Only God can decide that." Critics have accused her of being secular, tantamount to being an atheist. Yet it would be difficult to find anyone more traditional, both politically— she condemns "Zionist plots"—and in her respect for religious rules. But when she starts talking about women's rights there is no stopping her.

"Islam", she says, "gives women substantial rights, more rights than western women have. But traditions and patterns of thought that have nothing to do with religion are predominant in Saudi Arabia. Women are entitled to use their money. That was already the case with the wives of the prophet. They carried out transactions without consulting him, but we need a tutor (*mahram*). What we demand is a return to true Islam. The government is on our side. The resistance comes from society."

The position of women is changing, but Saudi Arabia is still lagging. Nowhere else is there such rigid gender segregation. Only a tiny proportion of women are in work and, for many formalities, they need to be assisted by their father or husband. Still, some real progress has been made over the past two years. Women can obtain an identity card without their *mahram*'s authorisation. They are also better represented in business and lead official delegations on foreign visits.

The recent election at the Jeddah chamber of commerce and industry was a historic moment. The vote was originally set for September but, after his accession, the new king postponed it several times so that women candidates could compete. Two months later than planned, despite a hostile campaign by several imams, two women were elected (out of 12 representatives). The minister for trade and industry appointed two more women to sit on the board (out of six appointed members).

Dr Hatoon al-Fassi, a liberal intellectual, was delighted. She works at the university but has been banned from teaching for the past five years, without knowing why. She is a regular contributor to the press and speaks English and French. She spoke about her trips to France, where she decided to wear a headscarf when travelling abroad. She said: "We have a positive opinion of the new king, who has made some important gestures. On coming to the throne he met two women's groups, about 40 people on each occasion. The first group was of officials from the ministry of education, the second of intellectuals. They came to swear a *baya* [oath of allegiance]. It was unprecedented and they even broadcast parts of the ceremony on television."

Saudi society is growing more transparent and problems of marital violence are slowly surfacing. A report published by the National Human Rights Association noted that out of 5,000 cases brought to its attention, a third concerned marital violence, now reported in the press. Newspapers in Jeddah have started reporting cases of mothers abandoning their newborn babies, a disturbing trend.

Although the scope of social debate is broadening, political change is proving more erratic. It depends on the goodwill of the king, but the rules of political process are so vague that any gains may be lost tomorrow. The municipal elections are a good example of uncertainty. After being announced several times in recent years the elections were finally held between February and April last year in the regions, with voters electing half the representatives on the 178 municipal councils. The authorities appointed the other half.

The Eastern Province witnessed the liveliest campaign. Qatif, an old port on the Gulf, is a Shia political and religious stronghold. A total of 148 candidates competed in five constituencies. Out of 120,000 potential voters, 44,000 registered and 35,000 voted, one of the best showings. This area, which is close to Iraq, has longstanding political traditions, in contrast to the rest of the kingdom. In the 1950s all the political trends that affected Iraq also left their mark here: Arab nationalism, communism and Islamism.

"I polled 24,000 votes," said Jafar al-Shayeb, a Shia and a successful candidate. "The election campaign was very short, but the preparations lasted longer. Some local committees made a genuine effort to explain to people how to register and vote. They picked them up at the mosque to register or took them to the polling station. About 100 meetings were held locally. In our constituency, at Tarut, we had three debates featuring the candidates. Each one presented his platform, then the public was able to ask questions. The authorities did not meddle with the vote at all."

But once the poll ended all over the country, it took eight months to publish the regulations governing council proceedings and their largely advisory prerogatives. Two weeks later the government appointed the remaining members of the municipal councils, in many cases selecting public figures on the basis of their ability. The council in Qatif elected al-Shayeb to chair proceedings (the mayor is appointed). Elsewhere the appointed mayor also chairs council meetings.

Sheikh Hassan al-Saffar wears the white turban of Shia dignitaries. Though youthful in appearance he can look back on a long career as an activist. He fled in 1980, after the Shia insurrection that followed the 1979 Iranian revolution. He only came home in 1995 after signing an agreement with the monarchy. His freedom of movement has improved but he is still subject to changes in the political climate. Some of his books are published in Saudi Arabia, others only in Lebanon.

Al-Saffar emphasised his concern at the discrimination the Shia community still suffers. "It must end. The national dialogue certainly removed some barriers between Sunni and Shia but we went no further than debate. There is a lot of pressure from conservatives in the religious institution to oppose such meetings. Sometimes on our side too. I have met important Sunni sheikhs, such as Salman al-Awdah. He has adopted a positive attitude and I think he has changed. But he is under pressure from the conservatives and he does not want to lose the influence he enjoys. We need joint initiatives to facilitate change, both among the Sunni and Shia."

He concluded: "We are not advocating rapid change. We have no desire to turn the country into another Algeria. But the authorities must allow the groups to voice their concerns, creating a situation more conducive to reform. They must establish rules for political life and let in any forces that wish to take part, which in turn will make them act more responsibly. For the time being there is no definite project and the few positive signals we have seen are no more than ink marks on paper."

Many intellectuals and militants share this gloomy outlook. At the end of 2003 a largely Islamist group published an appeal for constitutional reform. Professor Abdullah al-Hamed, one of the group's spokesmen, acknowledges that the aim was to assert their existence as an independent movement. He said: "We were asking for a shift from an absolute to a constitutional monarchy. The Riyadh appeal was a call for tolerance, unity and humanitarian values. It was mainly the work of people inspired by Islam, because I thought it was important that a religious group in favour of democracy should state its case. The aim was to pull the rug out from under the feet of those calling for the overthrow of the regime and to quell the violence. We consider that a state cannot be Islamic unless it is democratic and governed by a constitution."

But did the calls for constitutional reform go too far in the eyes of the authorities? The movement, formed in 2002–03 with the tacit support of the crown prince, paid a high price for its appeal.

The poet Ali al-Domaini said: "They had no right to arrest us, because we had not broken any laws. They disregarded the rights of the defence and the police even confiscated from our prison cells the texts we had prepared for our defence. Fortunately our families had copies. Then the judge insisted on the trial being on camera." The first day of proceedings prompted articles in the press that were highly critical of the government. Some were posted on the internet.

Three members of the group received heavy prison sentences: six years for Professor Matruk al-Falih (an Arab nationalist), seven years for Hamed (an Islamist) and nine for Domaini (a former communist). None had committed a crime, none had fomented violence; all had advocated peaceful reform.

Why did the crown prince allow this to happen? The most common explanation highlights the power struggle within the regime and the difficulty Abdullah had establishing his authority. The question is whether, now that he is on the throne, his position is any stronger, boosted by his enormous popularity (his decision to drop the title "His Majesty" and the custom of kissing his hand was much appreciated).

"After our release," said al-Domaini, "we wanted a private meeting with the king. We wanted to establish a stronger relationship with him, to encourage him to carry on along the still uncertain road to reform. We were only able to see him in public".

"Each of us spoke briefly to say we were travelling along the same road to reform, hand in hand, heart to heart. The sovereign replied that we were good citizens, that we were his brothers and his sons." Al-Domaini hopes he will soon be able to obtain a passport and travel again.

# Fearful of Restive Foreign Labor, Dubai Eyes Reforms

Jason DeParle

They still wake before dawn in desert dormitories that pack a dozen men or more to a room. They still pour concrete and tie steel rods in temperatures that top 110 degrees. They still spend years away from families in India and Pakistan to earn about $1 an hour. They remain bonded to employers under terms that critics liken to indentured servitude.

But construction workers, a million strong here and famously mistreated, have won some humble victories.

After several years of unprecedented labor unrest, the government is seeking peace with this army of sweat-stained migrants who make local citizens a minority in their own country and sustain one of the world's great building booms. Regulators here have enforced midday sun breaks, improved health benefits, upgraded living conditions and cracked down on employers brazen enough to stop paying workers at all.

The results form a portrait of halting change in a region synonymous with foreign labor and, for many years, labor abuse.

Many rich countries, including the United States, rely on cheap foreign workers. But no country is as dependent as the United Arab Emirates, where foreigners make up about 85 percent of the population and 99 percent of the private work force. From bankers to barbers, there are 4.5 million foreigners here, compared with 800,000 Emirati citizens, according to the Ministry of Labor. About two-thirds of the foreigners are South Asians, including most of the 1.2 million construction workers.

The labor agitation came as a surprise in this city of glass towers and marble-tiled malls where social harmony is part of the marketing plan and political action can seem all but extinct. But when thousands of migrant construction workers walked off the job last year, blocking traffic and smashing parked cars, it became clear that the non-natives were restless.

"I'm not saying we don't have a problem," said Ali bin Abdulla Al Kaabi, the Emirates' labor minister, who was appointed by the ruling sheiks to upgrade standards and restore stability. "There is a problem. We're working to fix it."

Change here is constrained by rival concerns of the sort that shape the prospects of workers worldwide. Like many countries, only more so, the United Arab Emirates needs the foreign laborers but fears their numbers. The recent focus on the workers' conditions still leaves them under close watch, segregated from the general population, with no right to unionize and no chance at citizenship.

"We want to protect the minority, which is us," Mr. Kaabi said.

Among those buffeted by recent events is Sami Yullah, a 24-year-old pipe fitter from Pakistan, who arrived four years ago. Like many workers, he paid nearly a year's salary in illegal recruiter's fees, despite laws here that require employers to bear all the hiring costs. In exchange, he was promised a job building sewer systems at a monthly salary of about $225, nearly twice what he earned at home.

Mr. Yullah found the work harder and more hazardous than he had expected. Two co-workers were killed on the job, he said, and two others injured, when they fell through a manhole. Conditions at the workers' camp where he lived, rudimentary at best, disintegrated when his employer let the water and electricity lapse. Then a problem even more basic arose: the company stopped paying the workers.

The owner kept saying, "Wait a minute, I will get some money," said Mr. Yullah, who joined about 400 co-workers last year in walking off the job. "He was taking advantage of us."

In a break with past practice, Mr. Kaabi's Labor Ministry backed the workers. Tapping a company bank guarantee, it restored the camp utilities and paid some of the back wages. It barred the company, Industrial and Engineering Enterprises, from hiring more workers, leading it to close its Emirates operation. And it helped workers like Mr. Yullah, who is still owed nearly six months' back pay, find new jobs.

By global standards, punishing a company that does not pay its workers may seem modest, but Mr. Yullah recognized it as something new.

"The company cheated me," he said. But the labor office is standing with the laborers.

The United Arab Emirates is a rags-to-riches story on a nation-state scale. Until the discovery of oil in the late 1950s, there was little here but Bedouins and sand. To extract the oil and build a modern economy, the rulers imported a multinational labor force that quickly outnumbered native Arabs.

An ethos of tolerance has prevailed, with churches, bars and miniskirts co-existing with burqas. But the construction workers who build hotel rooms that rent for $1,000 a night and malls that sell shoes for $1,000 a pair live segregated lives outside of this prosperous, cosmopolitan world.

They rise before dawn in distant camps, work six days a week at guarded sites and return by bus with time to do little but eat or sleep. Their sheer numbers inspire unease. When the film "Syriana" was released here, the government cut a scene of violent labor protest.

Sonapur, a camp a half-hour's drive into the desert from Dubai, houses 50,000 workers and feels like an army base. Two- and three-story concrete-block buildings stretch across the horizon, throngs of South Asian laborers fill the streets and desert dust fills the air. Even at midnight the camp roars. Buses ferry workers to third-shift jobs. Earthmovers work the perimeter, breaking ground for more dorms.

Building skyscrapers is inherently dangerous, especially in the heat. Until the government recently began insisting on summer sun breaks, one Dubai emergency room alone was reporting thousands of heat exhaustion cases each month. In a rare count, Construction Week, a local trade publication, canvassed foreign embassies and estimated that nearly 900 foreign construction workers died in 2004, though it could not say what percentage of the deaths were work-related.

The government does not track job-related injuries and deaths, though it is required by law to do so.

Standing on Sonapur's sand-blown streets, some workers count their blessings. "The work here is no problem," said Dinesh Bihar, 30, whose $150 salary is four times what he made when he left India.

Some workers count their debts. "I was so eager to come to Dubai, I didn't ask questions," said Rajash Manata, who paid placement fees of nearly $3,800, thinking his salary would be six times higher than it is. "I blame myself."

Some workers simply count the days until they see their families again.

"Three years, four months," said Cipathea Raghu, 37, when asked how long it had been since he had seen his 10-year-old daughter and 12-year-old son. "They're always saying, 'Daddy please, come, when will you come?' " he said.

"Tension, tension," he added, pointing to his heart.

Several years of quickening protests, mostly over unpaid wages, peaked in March 2006, when hundreds of workers went on a rampage near the unfinished Burj Dubai, which is being built as the world's tallest building. Eight months later, Human Rights Watch, a New York-based advocacy group, accused the Emirates of "cheating workers."

For a country courting tourists and investors—and a free trade pact with the United States—the report stung. "If the U.A.E. wants to be a first-class global player, it can't just do it with gold faucets and Rolls-Royces," said Sarah Leah Whitson, the Middle East director for Human Rights Watch. "It needs to bring up its labor standards."

Mr. Kaabi, 39, took office in late 2004, with what he describes as a mandate to do just that, for ethical and practical purposes, a departure from the Labor Ministry's earlier focus on processing employer requests for more foreign hires. "A healthy worker will provide more effective labor—period," he said in an interview.

He created the summer sun breaks, from 12:30 to 3 P.M. He pledged to increase the number of inspectors to 1,000, from roughly 100, though progress has been slow. And he publicly punished companies caught failing to pay their workers.

The most notable action involved the Al Hamed Development and Construction Company, which was run by a well-connected sheik. After hundreds of workers blocked traffic in Dubai, Mr. Kaabi ordered the company to pay nearly $2 million in fines and temporarily froze the company's ability to hire new workers.

"A beautiful message was sent: everybody follows the rules," Mr. Kaabi said.

Acting separately, the emirate of Abu Dhabi has strengthened health benefits and subsidized what is meant to be a model labor camp. Still much about the workers' lives remains unchanged, including the frequent need to pay high recruiting fees. Mr. Kaabi said that practice was hard to police, since it often occurred in the workers' home countries. Workers remain tied to specific employers and cannot, without permission, change jobs. And unions remain off limits. Mr. Kaabi said allowing unions would give foreign labor bosses a chokehold on the economy.

"God forbid something happens between us and India and they say, 'Please, we want all our Indians to go home,' " he said. "Our airports would shut down, our streets, construction. No. I won't do this."

In July, the government ended a four-day strike at a gas processing plant by sending in the armed forces. There continue to be press accounts of worker suicides.

Faced with complaints about low wages and difficult work, Mr. Kaabi repeats a point often made here: Many workers face greater hardships at home for less pay. "We don't force people to come to this country," Mr. Kaabi said. "They're building a whole new life for their families. Some come from backgrounds so impoverished," he said, "they don't know how to use the toilet; they will sit and do it on the ground."

But Ms. Whitson of Human Rights Watch said, "That's what exploitation is—you take advantage of someone's desperation."

Perched bare-chested on his bunk after a day in the sun, Sadiq Batcha, an 18-year veteran of labor camp life, was of two minds about the recent militancy. "People who did strikes were justified to a certain extent," he said.

At the same time, Mr. Batcha, 40, said his monthly salary of $250 was more than twice what he could make back home in an Indian fishing village. He had built a house, given his sister a dowry of $2,500, allowing her to marry, and sent his children to a private, English-speaking school. "If strikes are made legal, the company will lose money, and eventually we'll lose our jobs," he said.

Then with his eyes heavy at 9:30 P.M., Mr. Batcha excused himself. An alarm would sound in six hours and he was eager for sleep.

# Electoral Reform in Lebanon

Benedetta Berti

Although Lebanon's 2009 parliamentary elections were undeniably a significant step forward in the evolution of transparent and credible democratic institutions, they also illustrated that both poles of the country's multifarious governing elite are prepared to resist the kind of transformative electoral reforms long advocated by civil society activists.

## Background

Lebanon's consociational political system distributes fixed allotments of executive and legislative power among the country's main sectarian groups. The offices of president, prime minister, and parliament speaker are respectively reserved for Maronite Christians, Sunni Muslims, and Shiite Muslims. Seats in parliament are divided among nearly a dozen communities by quota, half for various Christian denominations and half for Muslim sects. Although the 1989 Taif Accord that brought an end to Lebanon's 15-year civil war called for the abolition of political sectarianism in principle, in practice it preserved the confessional power-sharing system, revising only the respective allotments of each community.

The raison d'etre of Lebanon's power-sharing system is to provide each group with a political safeguard against domination by the others—not insignificant in a region where multi-confessional states have frequently fallen victim to mono-confessional authoritarian regimes—but it has several well-known flaws.

The most serious is that it turns the state into an arena for sectarian conflicts to develop and play out, rather than a platform for national integration and reconciliation. A second consequence of institutionalizing sectarian divisions within the political system is that it strengthens the power of confessional leaders.

The constitution does not specify a particular electoral system for filling seats in parliament. Under Lebanon's majoritarian block vote and multi-member district electoral system, each voter is allowed to cast as many votes as the number of seats allocated in his/her electoral district. Each seat is then won by the candidate who is awarded the highest number of electoral preferences within his own confessional group.[1] Changes to Lebanon's electoral system over the years have mainly been limited to redrawing district boundaries to the benefit of ascendant political forces. During the Syrian occupation, districts were gerrymandered so that most Christian seats were elected in majority non-Christian districts.

The structural foundations of political sectarianism are further entrenched by a range of procedural attributes of its electoral system that work to the advantage of confessional leaders by enabling vote-buying and undermining the secrecy of the vote.

## The Boutros Commission

In August 2005, the government appointed a National Commission for a New Electoral Law, comprised of academics, lawyers, and civil society activists, under the chairmanship of Fouad Boutros. In collaboration with the United Nations Development Program and various domestic and international NGOs, the Boutros Commission formulated a draft law outlining an array of electoral reforms that meet with broad consensus.

Although the draft law was released in May 2006,[2] it languished for over two years as a result of the July-August 2006 Israeli military campaign in Lebanon and subsequent outbreak of an eighteen-month political crisis, during which the Hezbollah-Amal Shiite bloc and Michel Aoun's predominantly Christian Free Patriotic Movement (FPM) tried unsuccessfully to topple the ruling March 14 coalition through a campaign of mass protests.

The crisis escalated from peaceful protests to armed confrontation in May 2008, when Hezbollah reacted to a government attempt to shut down its communication network by seizing parts of West Beirut controlled by Sunni militiamen loyal to the late Rafiq Hariri's Future Movement, sparking the worst episodes of violence since the civil war. To solve the conflict, the parties met in Doha, Qatar, and agreed to the formation of national unity government, a compromise candidate for president, and "to examine and discuss" the Boutros Commission draft law.[3]

Over the summer, the Lebanese MPs debated each provision of the draft law. The result was a new parliamentary electoral law (PEL), approved in September, that discarded the most crucial reforms recommended by the Boutros Commission. The discrepancies between the two are revealing.

## Structural Reforms

The most sweeping proposal of the Boutros Commission was the introduction of a mixed system of electing the 128-member parliament. Although confessional quotas would remain the same, 51 representatives were to be chosen with a proportional system at the *muhafaza* (governorate) level, while the other 77 deputies would be selected according to the current majoritarian system at the *qada* (small administrative district) level. The introduction of proportional representation would work to the advantage of nonconfessional groups that don't have enough support within any one confessional group to win election. The Communist party, for example, is very influential in Lebanese intellectual life, but has never won a seat in parliament.

The PEL failed to adopt the commission's proposal to introduce proportional representation. Instead, it retained the system as is, while revising the demarcation of electoral districts. The new law replaces the 14 electoral districts established by the 2000 PEL with 26 smaller districts that largely coincide with the existing *qadas*.[4]

This provision was adopted to ensure that the proportion of Christian candidates elected in majority Christian districts is roughly en par with the proportions for other sects. Under the previous electoral law, 38 of 64 Christian seats were in majority Muslim districts, while only 8 of 64 Muslim seats were in majority Christians districts. Under the new law, just 17 Christian seats are in Muslim districts.[5] The creation of more numerous and smaller districts also reduces the ability of political coalitions to win large blocs of seats with a narrow majority of the vote, making seat allocation somewhat more proportional.[6]

However, the increased number of mono-confessional electoral districts also has the effect of further strengthening sectarian dynamics,[7] as it is no longer necessary for candidates to appeal outside of their own confessional constituencies to win election. Rather than reducing the role sectarianism of in politics, the new law arguably served to strengthen it.

Since Christians constitute only 40% of the electorate, concentrating more of their 50% allotment of parliamentary seats in mono-confessional districts also compromises the equality of votes. The average number of registered voters per seat ranged from 19,471 to 23,115 under the old electoral law,[8] but ranges from 17,845 (in the Christian district of Kesrwan) to 41,132 (in the Shiite district of Bint Jbeil) under the new one.[9]

## Procedural Reforms

The most important procedural reform in the Boutros draft law was the introduction of uniform official ballots. Under the current system, voters are allowed to use any piece of paper so long as the names of the candidate they select are clearly legible. This seemingly innocuous innovation is a critical enabler for rampant vote buying and intimidation of constituents. Political coalitions distribute their own specially tailored ballots to clients and supporters, using different colors, dimensions, and fonts for different voting blocs (e.g. particular villages and families) so that their poll monitors can trace where votes are coming from when ballots are counted. This greatly compromises the secrecy of the vote, makes it easy to ensure that the money invested in buying votes does not go to waste, and strengthens the power of local political bosses by making the "services" they provide to candidates verifiable.[10]

Although civil society activists universally agree that the introduction of a uniform official ballot is critical to the integrity

of the electoral process, the provision was rejected by fifty of seventy MPs present when it came up for a vote in parliament.[11] "Alarm bells should be going off," said Doreen Khoury, coordinator of the Civil Campaign for Electoral Reform (CCER).[12] Parliament also rejected the Boutros Commission's recommendation to count votes at the *qada* level, rather than at individual polling stations, as this would have greatly impeded the ability of party poll monitors to track bought votes.[13]

The new PEL did approve some procedural reforms proposed by the commission, such as the use of transparent ballot boxes and inking of fingers,[14] but these are of far less consequence than the rejected provisions. Ballot stuffing has *not* been the primary form of electoral fraud in Lebanon (at least not since the Syrian withdrawal in 2005).

The PEL adopted the Boutros Commission's recommendation that elections take place during one day,[15] rather than over a sequence of consecutive weeks for each region, reducing the chances for armed groups to disrupt the electoral process if initial results are unfavorable. The PEL also provided for expatriate voting, though implementation of this measure was delayed until 2013, ostensibly because the logistics were too daunting to put in place before the election.

The PEL also contained provisions for regulation of the media, which was previously unchecked. A related key achievement of the new law is to render campaign financing more transparent, by requiring candidates to account for the money they are receiving and investing in their election campaigns, and by setting ceilings for campaign-related expenditures.[16] However, despite the importance of this measure, it did little to make campaign financing more transparent.

The PEL pointedly neglected to provide for an independent electoral commission. It created a Supervisory Committee on Electoral Campaigns (SCEC), but it has authority only over campaign finance and media regulations and lacks enforcement power. The appointment of Ziad Baroud, a widely respected election expert, as interior minister was intended to compensate for the lack of an independent electoral commission, and to some extent it did—his management of the electoral process was universally praised.

## Assessing the Impact of the PEL

The most beneficial aspect of the PEL was not its content, but the fact that all major political forces agreed on it beforehand, boosting the perceived legitimacy of the electoral process. Consequently, there was little election-related violence and voter turnout was much higher than in 2005.[17] The election was also far more competitive than its predecessor. Whereas a fifth of the seats were elected uncontested in 2005, only a handful were elected uncontested in 2009.

Although the electoral reforms implemented thus far and the conduct of the election itself are positive steps toward enhancing the accountability and transparency of the system, they failed to address the core problems that undermine the integrity of the Lebanese political system. Due to the failure to introduce a national uniform ballot and an independent electoral commission with real enforcement power, vote-buying and foreign funding of candidates were still widespread practices across all political parties.[18] According to the EU team that monitored the elections, "financial resources played an excessively large role in the campaign and new regulations on spending have yet to have any notable effect on this phenomenon."[19] The rejection of the mixed-representation system and mutli-confessional districts proposed by the Boutros Commission forfeited the opportunity to further the Taif Accord's goal of moving beyond political sectarianism.

Though Interior Minister Baroud called the new PEL a "cup half full,"[20] few civil society activists would agree that the pursuit of electoral reform in Lebanon has hit the half way mark yet. Most are determined to bring public pressure to bear on the recalcitrant political establishment to change this before the 2013 elections.

# Notes

1. International Foundation for Electoral Systems (IFES), *The Lebanese Electoral System*, March 2009.

2. National Commission on the Parliamentary Electoral Law, *Parliamentary Electoral Draft Law*, 31 May 2006.

3. *The Doha Agreement*, Nowlebanon.com, 21 May 2008.

4. IFES, op. cit.

5. Democracy Reporting International, *Assessment of the Election Framework: Election Law of 2008*, December 2008.

6. Ibid.

7. Ibid.

8. In Beqaa III and Beirut I, respectively. Ibid.

9. See Ghassan Karam, *The Privileged and the Disenfranchised*, Yalibnan.com, 9 June 2009.

10. "Parlamentary Elections. Lebanon 2005," European Union Election Observation Mission, 2005.

11. Democracy Reporting International, op. cit.

12. *Talking To: Doreen Khoury*, Nowlebanon.com, 14 October 2008, www.nowlebanon.com/NewsArchiveDetails.aspx?ID=62709.

13. "Q&A's for the electoral system in Lebanon," NOW *Lebanon*, August 28, 2008, www.nowlebanon.com/NewsArchiveDetails .aspx?ID=56617.

14. Democracy Reporting International, op. cit.

15. National Commission on the Parliamentary Electoral Law, "Parliamentary Electoral Draft Law."

16. Democracy Reporting International, op. cit.

17. *Statement of the NDI Election Observer Delegation to Lebanon's 2009 Parliamentary Elections*, National Democratic Institute, June 2009.

18. "Foreign Money Seeks to Buy Lebanese Votes," *The New York Times*, 23 April 2009.

19. EU Election Observation Mission, "Lebanon Parliamentary Elections, Preliminary Report," 8 June 2009.

20. Doreen Khoury, "Lebanon's Election Law: A Cup Half Full," *The Daily Star*, 10 October 2008.

# In Sudan, No Clear Difference Between Arab and African

SOMINI SENGUPTA

Hartoum, Sudan—Abdalla Adam Khatir, 50, is from Darfur, in western Sudan.

His grandmother was an Arab, her grandfather was a member of an African tribe. He calls himself an African. As a boy in Kabkabiya, deep in the heart of Darfur, he traveled three days by camel caravan to reach the nearest town with an intermediate school. The caravan was led by an Arab, but at no point did he or his family feel unsafe. As a student here in the capital in the 1960s, he took up the banner of Arab-African unity, led by the Egyptian president Gamal Abdel Nasser. But today, Mr. Khatir finds himself wrestling with the gut-wrenching fact that, in the past two years, 102 of his relatives have been killed in Darfur by those he calls Arabs. Yet in the end, Mr. Khatir, a writer and a member of the Darfur Writers and Journalists Association, does not view this as a war between Arabs and Africans. He blames it squarely on the government in Khartoum. Its leaders, he says, have deliberately inflamed nascent ethnic divisions in a bid to stay in power.

War broke out in western Sudan in early 2003, when a rebel insurrection, frustrated by what it called the Sudan government's marginalization of Darfur, demanded economic and political reforms. The government swiftly struck back, deploying Arab militias across the region. The violence has killed tens of thousands of people and displaced around 1.5 million. Across Darfur, it was largely the villages of Africans that were torched, and with some exceptions, it was largely tribes that call themselves African that crowded into refugee camps or fled across the border to Chad. The United States and others have accused the attackers of committing "genocide," the systematic destruction of a national or ethnic group.

Juan Mendez, the United Nations Special Adviser on the Prevention of Genocide, has said that crimes against humanity and war crimes "probably occurred on a large and systematic scale." The question is how does race or ethnicity fit in. For generations, race itself has not been all that significant in Darfurian society. People regularly referred to themselves by their tribe affiliation, and rarely as just "Arab" or "African." Arabs have been in the region for almost 1,000 years, and the term has been used mostly to describe those who speak Arabic, as opposed to one of the dozens of local languages, or to those who lead nomadic, not agricultural, existences. "The implication that these are two different races, one indigenous and the other not, is dangerous," said Mahmood Mamdani, director of the Institute of African Studies at Columbia University. But the Darfur crisis has laid bare an unspoken Arab-African fault line that runs across this arid belt of Africa—from Mauritania in the west, to Sudan in the east.

Racial consciousness is, in fact, embedded in the history of central Africa. Sudan, for example, was once a center of the Arab slave trade. In Mauritania, in West Africa, blackness, which was associated with slavery, is today associated with servitude. Referring to underlying racial division, Breyten Breytenbach, the South African writer, said, "It is one of the most ambiguous problems and greatest taboos on the continent." What may have surprised everyone in Sudan was that as soon as the rebellion in Darfur began, divisions were drawn. By and large it was Arab tribes in Darfur that rallied to the government's side (some say in exchange for promises of land and power), while the government's political opponents raised the African banner and declared allegiance with the rebels. Those lines could harden even more.

The racial character given to the fighting in Darfur by the government and the rebels has found many willing listeners—and the appeal to racial solidarity could extend itself to Chad or further afield to Niger or Mali, where the competition between farmers and nomadic herders could turn even uglier. "There's been a long-running effort to suppress recognition of racial tension," argued Salih Booker, executive director of Africa Action, a Washington-based advocacy group. "It is something the continent has to grapple with." But racial chauvinism, once let loose in a society, can be hard to put back in the bottle. And its effects can be murderous. It is foolish, said Mr. Khatir, for any Sudanese to consider himself an Arab. "We are not Arabs, not Sudanese—not even those who are telling themselves they are Arabs," he said. "I am an African," he added, "who has absorbed Arab and Islamic culture. The way I see it, our people, Arab tribes and African tribes, are victims of the national policies of this government. We are all victims."

# Change They Can Believe In

**To make Israel safe, give Palestinians their due.**

WALTER RUSSELL MEAD

Reviving the Middle East peace process is the worst kind of necessary evil for a U.S. administration: at once very necessary and very evil. It is necessary because the festering dispute between the Israelis and the Palestinians in a volatile, strategically vital region has broad implications for U.S. interests and because the security of Israel is one of the American public's most enduring international concerns. It is evil because it is costly and difficult. The price of engagement is high, the chances for a solution are mixed at best, and all of the available approaches carry significant political risks. A string of poor policy choices by the Bush administration made a bad situation significantly worse. It inflamed passions. It weakened the position of moderate Israelis and Palestinians alike. And it reduced the U.S. government's credibility as a broker.

Even without the damaging aftermath of eight misspent years, the Israeli-Palestinian dispute will not be easily settled. Many people have tried to end it; all have failed. Direct negotiations between Arabs and Jews after World War I foundered. The British tried to square the circle of competing Palestinian and Jewish aspirations from the time of the 1917 Balfour Declaration until the ignominious collapse of their mandate in 1948. Since then, the United Nations, the United States, and the international community have struggled with the problem without managing to solve it. No issue in international affairs has taxed the ingenuity of so many leaders or captured so much attention from around the world. Winston Churchill failed to solve it; the "wise men" who built NATO and the Marshall Plan handed it down, still festering, to future generations. Henry Kissinger had to content himself with incremental progress. The Soviet Union crumbled on Ronald Reagan's watch, but the Israeli-Palestinian dispute survived him. Bill Clinton devoted much of his tenure to picking at this Gordian knot. He failed. George W. Bush failed at everything he tried. This is a dispute that deserves respect; old, inflamed, and complex, it does not suffer quick fixes.

As Kissinger has famously observed, academic politics are so bitter because the stakes are so small. In one sense, this is true of the Israeli-Palestinian dispute as well: little land is involved. The Palestine of the British mandate, today divided into Israel proper and the occupied territories of Gaza and the West Bank, was the size of New Jersey. In 1919, its total population was estimated at 651,000. Today, the territory counts about 5.4 million Jews and about 5.2 million Arabs. Two diasporas in other parts of the world—some 7.7 million Jews and 5.2 million Palestinians—believe that they, too, are entitled to live there.

But the conflict is about more than land; many people on both sides feel profoundly that a compromise would be morally wrong. A significant minority of Israelis not only retain a fervent attachment to the land that makes up the Eretz Yisrael of the Bible but also believe that to settle and possess it is to fulfill a divine decree. For these Jews, it is a sin to surrender land that God has given them. Although most Israelis do not share this belief with dogmatic rigor, they would be reluctant to obstruct the path of those seeking to redeem the Promised Land.

It may be difficult for outsiders to understand the Palestinians' yearning for the villages and landscapes lost during the birth of Israel in 1948. The sentiment is much more than nostalgia. The Palestinians' national identity took shape in the course of their struggle with Zionism, and the mass displacement of Palestinians resulting from Israel's War of Independence, or the *nakba* ("catastrophe" in Arabic), was the fiery crucible out of which the modern Palestinian consciousness emerged. The dispossessed Palestinians, especially refugees living in camps, are seen as the bearers of the most authentic form of Palestinian identity. The unconditional right of Palestinians to return to the land and homes lost in the *nakba* is the nation's central demand. For many, although by no means all, Palestinians, to give up the right of return would be to betray their people. Even those who do not see this claim as an indispensable goal of the national movement are uneasy about giving it up.

## A Tale of Two Peoples

The conflict is not just fiendishly hard to resolve; history and culture make it difficult for both the Israelis and the Palestinians to make the necessary choices. The two peoples had very different experiences in the twentieth century, but both have been left with a fractured national consciousness and institutions too weak to make or enforce political decisions.

For the Israelis, determining the relationship between religion, ethnicity, and citizenship is a perpetually difficult question. Is the return of the Jews to their ancestral home a basically secular objective with religious overtones, like the goals of other independence movements among minorities in the Ottoman Empire, including the Greeks and the Armenians? Or is it a fundamentally religious project? Other countries face similar questions, but the issue is particularly acute for Israel given its position as the world's only Jewish state.

Another complication is that although the Jews are an old people, the Israelis are a young one. Jews have come to Israel from very different societies and cultures and from all over the world, bringing very different expectations, and they have established a political society as varied and fragmented as their respective histories. Ashkenazim and Sephardim, Orthodox and ultra-Orthodox, secular socialists and secular liberals, post-Soviet Russians: this diversity—with the tensions it brings heightened by the pressure of Israel's existential anxieties—is reflected in the country's political landscape. A predictable combination of weak governments and explosive politics hinders decisive official action: more than most, Israel's leaders must keep looking over their shoulders to gauge public opinion.

Israeli society is also traumatized, both by the attempted extermination of Europe's Jews in the Holocaust and the phenomena associated with the Holocaust: the failure of Jewish assimilation, centuries of persecution before the Enlightenment, the world's ghastly betrayal of desperate refugees from Nazi Germany seeking countries to take them in. Jews arriving in Israel from the Muslim world brought their own history of betrayal, discrimination, and victimization—culminating in what for many was a flight every bit as frightening and impoverishing as anything the Palestinians experienced. Having gotten to what seemed like the last refuge on earth, they then had to listen to calls for its destruction and endure wave after wave of attack. This is not a people that can easily trust. Nor is it one among which discussions of national security can always be conducted in tones of calm reason.

## History has left both the Israelis and the Palestinians with a fractured national consciousness and weak institutions.

The situation among the Palestinians is surprisingly similar. From its inception, Palestinian nationalism has shifted uneasily between the religious and the secular. Are the Palestinians a distinct national society of Muslims and Christians? Are they part of the worldwide *umma* (Muslim community)? Part of a broader Arab nation? Even though the traumatic experiences of the twentieth century gave Palestinians of all political and religious leanings a common identity and history—perhaps the strongest in the Arab world, outside Egypt—basic definitional questions continue to haunt their national consciousness.

Historically, Palestine was a complex region with many subcultures, and the gradual transformation of the Levant throughout the nineteenth century accentuated its diversity. Christians, Druze, and Jews amounted to about one-fifth of the population. The cities and the coastal plain were dominated by agriculture, European commercial interests, and the cultural and political ferment of the late Ottoman period. Jerusalem, where Muslims lived as a minority among Christians and Jews, followed its own direction, with notable Arab families—some of whose names remain prominent in Palestinian politics today—exercising important leadership in much of the area. Peasant communities were oriented toward smaller towns and regional centers such as Nablus. Everywhere, ancient tribal divisions and family rivalries complicated the picture further.

Palestinian history was turbulent in the twentieth century. The nationalist movement against the British culminated not in independence but in the uprooting of half of Palestine's Arab population. Some of the displaced settled in refugee camps; others moved in with relatives in the countryside, as earlier generations had done during previous periods of political tension or economic recession; others still became refugees within the borders of the new state of Israel. The numbers are disputed, but estimates suggest that about 276,000 refugees fled to the West Bank, between 160,000 and 190,000 went to Gaza, and about 100,000 crossed into Jordan. Another 175,000 or so, mostly from the northern Galilee, are estimated to have fled to Lebanon and Syria.

After this, Palestinian society grew even more complex. From 1948 to 1967, the majority of Palestinians lived under Jordanian rule in the West Bank or Jordan itself, and Gaza was under Egyptian administration. Their economic and social conditions in these areas, as well as in Lebanon and Syria, varied tremendously. In Gaza, virtually everyone was a refugee and impoverished. In the West Bank, refugees were scattered in camps among traditional communities of Palestinians still living on ancestral land. Many of the Jerusalem notables survived with their influence relatively intact, despite losing all their property on the Israeli side of the Green Line. In Jordan and to a lesser extent Syria, Palestinians integrated into their host societies. In Lebanon, they had their ups and downs and now live largely in ghettos with restricted educational opportunities, few economic prospects, and no chance at political participation. Two additional diasporas developed: one, of mostly well-educated Palestinians working as professionals in the Persian Gulf and elsewhere; the other, a smaller group of political and military leaders who later were driven out of Jordan (in 1971) and Lebanon (in 1982) and left Tunisia (in 1994, following the Oslo accords). Partly because of this history, Palestinian society has splintered into many different political, religious, and ideological factions.

In the absence of a state—or, rather, in the presence of so many different states, none run by Palestinians—Palestinian political life is chaotic. There is no common educational system and no effective institutions, parliamentary or otherwise, through which consensus can be built and enforced. The tragic division of the Palestinians into a "Hamastan" in Gaza and a "Fatahstan" in the West Bank is only one expression of the nation's splintered politics and institutional brittleness. Palestinians in Jordan, Lebanon, and Syria and in the broader diaspora will be essential constituencies when the time comes to enforce the security guarantees Israel will need once a Palestinian state is created. Yet they have no say in the election of the representatives who will negotiate the peace deal on their behalf, and their interests are not necessarily the same as those of the Palestinians in Gaza or the West Bank.

Like the Jews, the Palestinians experienced the twentieth century as a time of betrayal by the international community. The League of Nations awarded Palestine as a mandate to the United Kingdom under terms that explicitly called for the establishment of a Jewish national home but required to consultation with the people of Palestine. The United Nations authorized the territory's partition in 1947—again making fundamental decisions about the future of Palestine over the heads of its inhabitants. Since then, the Palestinians have been exploited at virtually every turn, not least by various Arab leaders.

The twentieth century taught both the Jews and the Palestinians that the international community's grand moral claims are mostly hollow, that great powers are cynical and brutal, that international politics is a blood sport, and that, at the end of the day, a people can depend only on itself. And both survived thanks to dogged persistence, violent struggle, and a refusal to accept defeat. The Jews clawed their way out of the ruins of Europe to build a state and then turned it into a regional superpower despite repeated efforts by others to destroy it. The Palestinians created a national movement in the face of disaster, asserted themselves by armed struggle, defended their independence in the harsh world of Middle East power politics, and succeeded in placing their cause on the international community's agenda. Both peoples trust their own instincts much more than they do the promises of any single power or of all the world's powers together. They distrust each other because they know how tough and even how ruthless each of them had to be to survive. And they both understand, as no others can, the bitterness and the intimacy of the unique situation they share.

## What Is to Be Done?

The incoming U.S. administration of Barack Obama faces a daunting task. It needs to develop a Middle East peace strategy that makes a clear break with the past, that is politically sustainable at home and abroad, that offers real hope for a final resolution, and that in the meantime can bring benefits to the two peoples, the wider region, and the United States itself. But Washington will have only limited options. American public opinion strongly and consistently favors a pro-Israel orientation for U.S. foreign policy, and Israel's friends in the United States can mobilize broad support on short notice. Decades of intensive diplomacy and scholarship have already delineated the possible solutions to the dispute. The outlines of a settlement—regarding borders, security, refugees, and water rights—are reasonably well understood by all parties, and Obama cannot do much to change them. He cannot expand the Holy Land to give each people the territory it wants; he cannot create another Temple Mount, or Noble Sanctuary, to give each side its own holy site; he cannot move the al Aqsa Mosque away from the Western Wall.

Still, Washington can change the way that a peace deal is framed and thus make it more appealing to both sides. The Obama administration needs to accomplish a kind of Copernican shift in perception: looking at the same sun, moon, planets, and stars that others have seen, it must reconceptualize the relations among them. In the past, U.S. peacemakers have had an Israel-centric approach to the negotiating process; the Obama administration needs to put Palestinian politics and Palestinian public opinion at the center of its peacemaking efforts.

## Washington needs to put Palestinian politics and Palestinian public opinion at the center of its peacemaking efforts.

This will fall well short of a revolution. The United States' goals, and many of its policies, will not change. Its relationship with Israel will stay strong; if anything, it will deepen. But despite their military weakness and their political factiousness, the Palestinians hold the key to peace in the Middle East. And if the United States hopes to create a more secure and stable environment for Israel, it must sell peace to Israel's foes.

Only clear support for a peace treaty by a solid majority of Palestinians—in Gaza, the West Bank, and the diaspora—will bring Israel the security it craves and deserves. When, as will inevitably happen after a deal, armed gangs seek to disrupt the peace, much in the way that Irish ultranationalists continued to fight the British long after Ireland achieved independence, the Palestinian public will have to condemn the violence and support crackdowns by Palestinian authorities. U.S. negotiators during the Clinton administration, assuming that Yasir Arafat, then chair of the Palestine Liberation Organization, controlled Palestinian public opinion, reduced the matter of clinching Palestinian support for peace to getting Arafat's signature on the dotted line. This was a very damaging mistake. Now, the United States must focus on swaying Palestinian public opinion in favor of peace—especially since current Palestinian leaders have none of Arafat's power or prestige.

This will take work. U.S. diplomacy has for too long overestimated the appeal of a two-state solution among Palestinians and in the broader Arab world. Some polls suggest that a majority of Palestinians in the occupied territories would accept such an outcome—or, rather, would have accepted it some years ago—but there has never been much enthusiasm for the proposal. A two-state solution has been even less popular with the diaspora, and today, even some of the proposal's most vocal Palestinian backers, such as the well-respected author and scholar Sari Nusseibeh, are moving away from it.

Not surprisingly, support for the proposal has been strongest in the West Bank and particularly among the relatively prosperous West Bankers and Palestinian Jerusalemites who are not refugees. For such Palestinians, a two-state solution might be a wrenching compromise, but it has its attractions. For those in the camps, and especially those in Gaza, a territory virtually without resources and with few economic prospects under even the most favorable conditions, a two-state solution has fewer charms. The Israelis get security, the Palestinian elite gains power and resources, but impoverished refugees and the diaspora are left out in the cold as new flags fly over the same old camps.

Back in the 1990s, Israeli critics of the Oslo process were fortified by the Palestinians' only partial support for a two-state solution. Would the newly formed Palestinian National Authority have the moral authority, the political will, and the administrative capacity to provide Israel with adequate security against those hard-line rejectionist Palestinians who were sure to repudiate the agreement? In the absence of an effective Palestinian partner, might the agreement—which called for the withdrawal of Israeli forces and settlers from the West Bank—undermine Israel's security? Such doubts are still voiced loudly in Israeli politics today, and they continue to complicate the task of any Israeli leader seeking serious negotiations.

But those doubts are not just an obstacle to peace; they indicate a way forward for the United States. To a very important degree, Israeli and Palestinian interests are linked. A peace agreement that does not address central Palestinian concerns will lack the legitimacy in Palestinian public opinion that is necessary to make peace real—that can give the Palestinian state the authority and support it needs to enforce the peace and protect Israel's security. Unless the Palestinians get enough of what they want from the settlement, the Israelis will not get enough of the security they seek.

This linkage offers a historic opportunity for the Obama administration to improve the chances for peace and to align the United States with key Palestinian aspirations without moving away from or against Israel. To address the Palestinians' concerns about a two-state solution does not mean favoring the Palestinians over the Israelis; it means addressing the justifiable concerns of both thoughtful Palestinians and thoughtful Israelis about the future of their countries. No agreement can offer Israel perfect security—and neither could permanent occupation of the West Bank—but an agreement that does not command sustained support among the Palestinians cannot offer Israel much improvement over its current situation. This means that any deal must address the issues of greatest concern to the dispossessed refugees, who best embody Palestinian nationalism and remain the ultimate source of political legitimacy in Palestinian politics. Although some of the most contentious issues dividing the two parties are zero-sum ones, in which any Israeli gain represents a Palestinian loss, and vice versa, significant elements of a compromise solution are not zero-sum. Indeed, by bringing new resources to the table, the United States can make peace more attractive to both parties and ease the path to compromise on even the zero-sum issues for both Israeli and Palestinian leaders.

## Addressing the Palestinians' concerns does not mean favoring the Palestinians over the Israelis.

When he reiterates the United States' support for an independent, viable Palestinian state with borders based on the Green Line, that is, the pre-1967 borders (with minor and mutually-agreed-on modifications), Obama must go further than his predecessors. He must overcome the skepticism created by the Bush administration's empty rhetorical support for a Palestinian state. He must declare that the United States is committed not only to an independent Palestine but also to acknowledging the wrongs the Palestinians have suffered, compensating them for those, and otherwise ensuring a dignified future for every Palestinian family.

To give substance to this pledge, the Obama administration should consult with a wide range of Palestinian groups and other interested parties in order to develop recommendations for concrete U.S. proposals that address key Palestinian issues. In consultation with U.S. allies in Europe (especially Germany and the United Kingdom, which have special historical interests and ties in the region) and elsewhere, the Obama administration should present an agenda that substantially enhances the value of a two-state solution to both the Israelis and the Palestinians and mount a determined diplomatic effort to reinvigorate direct negotiations between the parties.

# Finally

What the Palestinians want from peace is, first of all, an acknowledgment of the injustices they have suffered. Israeli and Palestinian scholars have documented many incidents during Israel's War of Independence in which massacres or threats of violence caused Palestinians to flee. Most Palestinians who left their homes and villages to protect themselves and their families were never allowed to return, and much of their property was confiscated by the new Israeli government. It is not a crime for civilians to flee combat, and international law recognizes the right of such people to return to their homes. Enforcing that right has been a centerpiece of U.S. policy in Bosnia, so why, the Palestinians ask, should they be treated any differently? This is a legitimate grievance, and the United States must lead the international community in reckoning with it fully and frankly. Any diplomatic effort hoping to build a secure peace with the Palestinians' support must address this issue.

That said, it would be as unfair to place all responsibility for the Palestinian refugee problem on Israel as it is to overlook the injustices the Palestinians suffered. The Israelis argue that the War of Independence was a fight for survival: here were survivors from Hitler's death camps suddenly facing not only the Palestinians but also the armies of five Arab states. Self-defense, the Israelis argue, justified their actions during and after the war. And although most Israelis acknowledge that wrongs were committed, almost all charge that, faced with similar choices, their critics would have done the same or worse. They are right. The responsibility for the *nakba* cannot simply be laid at Israel's door.

The United Nations' failure to provide elementary security for both the Arab and the Jewish inhabitants of Palestine as the British withdrew was the immediate cause of both communities' suffering in the late 1940s—of the initial clashes between them, of the accelerating spiral of violence, of the Arab armies' entry into the conflict, and then of the prolonged period of hostility. Modern Israel should acknowledge and account for its part in those tragic events, but the international community at large must accept the ultimate responsibility for the *nakba,* solemnly acknowledging the wrongs done and sincerely trying to compensate Palestinian refugees today.

## Paying One's Dues

The U.S. government should build on this historical reality to craft an international body that can assume all claims arising from the Israeli-Palestinian conflict, adjudicate them in accordance with existing international precedents and law, and pay appropriate compensation to the claimants. Claims would include the losses suffered by Palestinians as well as those sustained by Jews forced to flee their homes in the region, but the system should be set up so that Jewish and Palestinian claimants do not compete for limited funds. This entity should be funded by the international community, with Israel making a substantial payment as part of whatever negotiated legal agreement creates the new body.

The expense will be significant; according to the Aix Group, an economic forum comprising Israeli, Palestinian, and international economists and policymakers, the total potential costs of compensation to Palestinian refugees can be estimated at $55–$85 billion. The Obama administration should work with U.S. allies and partners to fund the claims authority. The United States' contribution should be appropriately large, in order to demonstrate Washington's renewed determination to lead the effort to resolve the Israeli-Palestinian conflict. The exact U.S. contribution should be determined as part of Washington's diplomatic effort to establish and fund the claims organization, but one possible model might look to a division of responsibilities in which the United States, Europe, Israel, member states of the Organization of the Islamic Conference, and the rest of the world (principally Japan, other East Asian countries, and other countries with strong interests in resolving the conflict, such as Australia, Canada, and Norway) would each assume a roughly equal share of the financial cost involved in funding a combination of compensation and humanitarian programs for the victims of the conflict. Under this program, the United States would make the largest contribution of any single country (with the possible exception of Israel), but the burden would also be widely shared among the many states that are concerned with stability and justice in this vital part of the world.

Although the certification and payment of claims will require complex procedures, and although the payment of compensation should be part of a multistage implementation of a final and comprehensive peace agreement between the Israelis and the Palestinians, the claims entity should begin to review and certify claims while negotiations are still under way. As quickly as the legal and institutional frameworks can be agreed on and established, refugees ought to be able to submit their claims, and those claims should be assessed and certified in a timely fashion. This will help assure the refugees that justice will be done and that the conclusion and implementation of a comprehensive peace agreement would result in tangible benefits.

## The Right of Return

The right of return is one of the tough zero-sum questions that will need to be settled in final-status negotiations between the Israelis and the Palestinians. Like the sensitive matter of the holy sites in Jerusalem, this issue is one of the most contentious; it has already been extensively tackled in various informal and "track-two" discussions, and neither side is likely to make an official final offer until very late in the process. Logically, Palestinian acceptance of a two-state solution would imply significant limits on the exercise of the right of Palestinian refugees (and their descendants and heirs) to move within the pre-1967 borders of Israel; if five million Palestinians entered Israel, the Jewish state would have an Arab majority. But it is one thing to draw logical conclusions and another for the Palestinian nation to make a deliberate and serious judgment that painful compromise on this point offers the best road to a just and humane future for the nation as a whole.

As the Palestinian nation grapples with these choices, the United States and the international community can take a number of steps to help the Palestinians make their decision. The key is to assure the Palestinians that the refugees and their heirs will be given several viable options. Palestinians who choose not to exercise their right of return or whose right is in some way restricted in the final Israeli-Palestinian agreement should be substantially compensated by the international community (including Israel) to acknowledge that the right to return is indeed a right and that its loss or restriction entitles the holder to just compensation.

Additionally, the United States and its partners around the world should take steps to ensure that at the end of the process, no Palestinian is stateless and all Palestinians enjoy full economic, social, and political rights. Programs need to be designed to integrate Palestinians in the diaspora into the communities in which they now live, allow them to emigrate within or from the Middle East, and ensure appropriate opportunities for them. Such programs should in no way prejudice negotiations on the right of return, but as Palestinians await the outcome of those talks, the world community must move decisively to create dignified choices for them.

The effort to provide a future for the Palestinians should not be restricted to Arab countries. The United States, Canada, Australia, and European countries, as well as other states around the world, should be prepared to offer immigration visas to Palestinians. Developing countries that agree to receive Palestinians should receive appropriate assistance from the international community; the citizens of poor countries should not feel that their governments are diverting resources in order to house newcomers. Countries such as Jordan and Syria, which have already set the example, should receive compensation as recognition for their past efforts.

## The Architecture of Peace

The Obama administration will also need to address the structural imbalance of the peace process. Negotiations are front-loaded in favor of the Israelis; by recognizing Israel from the outset, the Palestinians concede Israel's core demand and receive only the right to start talking. The Palestinians have to put the most valuable card in their hand on the table, while the Israelis can keep all their best cards to themselves. At the back end, however, the imbalance is reversed. Here, it is Israel that has to make key concessions: withdrawing from territory, dismantling settlements and military posts, recognizing the Palestinian state. Now, it is Israel who must lay down the cards—and trust and hope that the Palestinians will reciprocate by providing Israel with the security it craves. (The Palestinians face unpleasant choices at the end also: negotiating over the right of return and agreeing on borders will inevitably disappoint many refugees. However, the Palestinians will reap the rewards of any concessions on these issues once the new state gains control of its territory; the Israelis will still be living in hope that the Palestinians will continue indefinitely to cooperate on security issues.)

This basic imbalance had a serious and negative impact on Middle East negotiations during the Clinton administration. Once Arafat played the recognition card, he needed quick progress on the negotiations and concrete results on the ground to maintain his political position among the Palestinians; Israel, having already gained what it saw as the biggest benefit available, was reluctant to move on to a stage in which it would have to make painful concessions in return for uncertain results. The outcome, amply detailed in Dennis Ross' painstaking and thoughtful memoir, was a relationship between the parties that led to progressively diminishing trust, weakened the political position of peace advocates among the Israelis and the Palestinians alike, and ultimately led to the collapse of the peace process and political victories for hard-liners in both camps.

As the Obama administration moves to rebuild the momentum for peace, it needs to address the imbalances that complicate what would under any circumstances be a tortuous process. It must bring the obligations of and the benefits accruing to the parties into better balance as the negotiations move forward. The Palestinians need from the outset some clearer commitments on both the duration of the talks and the benefits that would result from any agreement; the Israelis need greater assurance that a future Palestinian state would have both the necessary means and the incentives to deliver on security.

For both parties, solid commitments from the international community on many of the issues that matter most could give the process new credibility and help build the public support needed to make it possible. One goal of the Obama administration should be to develop a package along these lines that encourages Palestinian groups that now reject recognition of Israel to come under the tent; that way, in the next round of negotiations, the Palestinians could present a unified bargaining team broadly representative of key Palestinian political tendencies. Making a peace deal more attractive to the Palestinians and bringing rejectionist political groups into the process would help address Israel's concerns about future relations between the two states. Another goal should be to further assuage Israeli concerns by making payments and benefits to the Palestinians conditional on the Palestinians' full implementation of the agreement's terms. This means that a future Palestinian state

would have to meet its security obligations in order to continue to benefit from the provisions of the accord.

The Obama administration should also take steps to build broad public support for a compromise peace in Israel. Once again, it will need support from friends and allies, especially in Europe.

# Being Copernicus

Even when Copernicus put the sun at the center of the solar system, he did not forget that he was living on earth. In the same way, shifting Washington's attention toward the Palestinians' concerns would not—and should not—mean turning away from Israel. A refocusing of the United States' approach to the peace process would also offer Israel substantial long-term benefits. A decision by the international community to assume the ultimate moral and financial responsibility for the Palestinians' plight would give Israel an opportunity to close the book on Palestinian claims once and for all. Developing and helping fund a mechanism that would also compensate Israeli refugees from the Arab world would address the impression widely shared among Israelis that many states have a one-sided approach to refugee issues. And by making the Palestinians' commitment to peaceful coexistence a key test of the peace process, the Obama administration would be placing the focus where many Israelis think it belongs.

## A new approach could offer Israel substantial long-term benefits.

The Obama administration should engage with Israel seriously and candidly to determine what else the United States and its allies can do to help Israel take the risks and make the sacrifices required to give peace a chance. Support for Israel runs very deep among Americans, and it is likely to increase as Israel moves closer to a settlement with the Palestinians. The Obama administration needs to harness that support to help the Israeli government take steps on the sensitive questions of the status of Jerusalem and the status of the territories, steps that an increasing number of Israeli politicians acknowledge must be taken.

The prospect of a just settlement for the Palestinians and an end to the occupation would also open the door to a new age in European-Israeli relations. The United States is not the only country with a stake in bringing this dispute to an end. Washington should work with its EU partners to come up with major new incentives that would convince Israel that the benefits of peace outweigh the costs. The United States should press its NATO allies for conditional assurances that an Israeli-Palestinian agreement would open the alliance's doors to the Jewish state. Closer coordination with and greater support for Israel on the part of key EU countries on Iran policy should also follow. The EU should work closely with the United States to ensure that a comprehensive Israeli-Palestinian agreement leads to the recognition of Israel by the members of the Arab League and the normalization of relations between them. Membership for Israel in the Western European and Others Group at the United Nations should also accompany the agreement. The EU should welcome both Israel and the Palestinian state into the European single market as quickly and as thoroughly as possible, providing assistance to both states as necessary.

The Obama administration need not choose the Israelis over the Palestinians or the Palestinians over the Israelis. But it must engage with both sides more deeply than past U.S. administrations have done and use the full power of the U.S. presidency to develop a comprehensive peace strategy. This is one of the most difficult challenges the new president will face, but real progress is possible. At the very least, Obama can change the terms of the debate in the Middle East—which in itself would be no mean achievement.

**WALTER RUSSELL MEAD** is Henry A. Kissinger Senior Fellow for U.S. Foreign Policy at the Council on Foreign Relations.

From *Foreign Affairs,* Vol. 88, No.1, January/February 2009, pp. 59–76. Copyright © 2009 by Council on Foreign Relations. Reprinted by permission. www.ForeignAffairs.com

# Western Sahara Poser for UN

JACOB MUNDY

Morocco serves as the backdrop for such Hollywood blockbusters as *Gladiator, Black Hawk Down* and *Body of Lies*. The country's breathtaking landscapes and gritty urban neighbourhoods are the perfect setting for Hollywood's imagination.

Unbeknown to most filmgoers, however, is that Morocco is embroiled in one of Africa's oldest conflicts—the dispute over Western Sahara. This month the UN Security Council is expected to take up the dispute once more, providing US President Barack Obama with an opportunity to assert genuine leadership in resolving this conflict. But there's no sign that the new administration is paying adequate attention.

The story of Western Sahara would make quite a movie. There was high diplomatic intrigue when Moroccan troops occupied the territory, after Spain abandoned its long-time colony as Generalissimo Franco lay dying in 1975. The subsequent war between Morocco and the Algerian-supported Polisario Front, which sought Western Saharan independence, furnished plenty of action sequences in the desert. There is also the real human tragedy of the Western Saharan refugees, who have languished in exile for more than three decades.

In 1991, the Security Council created the UN mission in Western Sahara, MINURSO, whose mandate has been ritually reauthorized ever since. MINURSO's original task was to organise a referendum in Western Sahara in which the residents would vote up or down on self-determination. Morocco, on the other hand, lobbied that tens of thousands of Moroccans be counted, a demand that Polisario resisted.

It was not until 1997, when former UN Secretary-General Kofi Annan called in former US Secretary of State James Baker as envoy that the debate got unstuck. However, the deadlock ensued once more in 1999 when Morocco's new king, Mohammed VI, dropped all support for a referendum. Baker resigned—in part due to the (at best) weak support of the Security Council for his mandate.

Morocco's latest stance is that Rabat share power in Western Sahara with indigenous groups. An autonomy proposal Morocco advanced in 2007 is in fact a credible starting point for negotiations aimed at a power sharing agreement. But Polisario will not discuss power sharing until Morocco recommits to a referendum on self-determination.

It has long been assumed in Western capitals that the Western Sahara question will be resolved through power sharing, but such a solution cannot simply be imposed. Only a negotiated settlement can bring about comprehensive peace.

But the UN does not push effectively for negotiations. Indeed, in rolling over MINURSO's mandate year after year, the Security Council seems to hope that one party or the other will give in—an attitude that favours the more powerful actor, Morocco, a state that is closely allied with Security Council members France and the US.

The last thing the world needs is more de facto partisanship from the ostensibly neutral Security Council. Peace in Western Sahara will require that both Morocco and Polisario accept something they do not like. Polisario must accept that the achievement of a comprehensive power sharing agreement with Morocco is a prerequisite for a referendum. Morocco, on the other hand, must commit to a self-determination referendum as a necessary condition for power sharing talks. How to cut the Gordian knot?

The new man in charge of MINURSO is Christopher Ross, former US ambassador to Algeria and Syria. Ross can boast of fluency in Arabic and an extensive background in North African affairs.

Instead of waiting for conditions to ripen, the new envoy should, at the next round of negotiations, secure the commitment of the parties—in writing—to a strong Security Council resolution calling for both a negotiated political solution and a referendum. This approach not only balances the interests of the parties but it also unblocks the mutual suspicion currently stalling talks.

If one side or the other refuses to sign, the Security Council must be willing to wield the weapon of shame and name names. The Obama administration should back Ross to the hilt as enforcer of the UN's writ.

Western Sahara is not a problem of imagination that needs a Hollywood producer or two. It is a problem of political will. With strong, consistent leadership from the US, inside and outside the Security Council, Morocco and the Polisario Front can be put on the right track toward peace.

---

JACOB MUNDY is a PhD candidate in the Institute of Arab and Islamic Studies at the University of Exeter. He is coauthor of the forthcoming *Western Sahara: War, Nationalism and Conflict Irresolution*.

# Responding to a Nuclear Iran

CHRISTOPHER HEMMER

What should American foreign policy be if current efforts to discourage Iran from developing nuclear weapons fail? Despite the recent resumption of high-level contacts between Iran and the International Atomic Energy Agency, and the potential for stronger action by the United Nations Security Council, an Iranian nuclear weapon remains a distinct possibility. The current debate regarding US policy toward Iran revolves around the relative merits of a preventive military strike, including the possibility of seeking regime change in Tehran, versus a policy that focuses on diplomacy and economic sanctions to dissuade Iran from pursuing a nuclear bomb. This debate, however, risks prematurely foreclosing discussions regarding a wide-range of foreign policy options should diplomacy and sanctions fail to persuade Tehran to limit its nuclear ambitions.

The choices America would face if Iran developed nuclear weapons are not simply between preventive military action and doing nothing. The calculations America would face are not between the costs of action versus the costs of inaction. A nuclear-armed Iran will certainly pose a number of challenges for the United States. Those challenges, however, can be met through an active policy of deterrence, containment, engagement, and the reassurance of America's allies in the region.

## American Interests

The United States has three strategic interests in the Persian Gulf: maintaining the flow of oil onto world markets, preventing any hostile state from dominating the region, and minimizing any terrorist threat. Given these interests, the challenges posed by a nuclear-armed Iran need to be addressed by a policy that minimizes the threat to key oil production and transportation infrastructure and negates any Iranian bid for regional hegemony. Additionally, any action taken toward Iran has to be weighed against the potential impact it may have with regard to the global war on terrorism and ongoing US initiatives related to nation-building in Iraq and Afghanistan. Moreover, such a policy needs to be executed in a manner that avoids any nuclear threat to the United States or its allies.

The end-state the United States should be working toward, as a result of these strategic interests, is an Iran that is an integral part of the global economy, at peace with its neighbors, and not supportive of terrorist organizations. While America's strategic interests do not include the proliferation of democracy, any acceptable end-state will likely require some measure of democratic reform. Given the fact that anti-Americanism and anti-Zionism are an integral part of the Islamic Republic's identity, some measure of regime evolution will be required in an effort to advance America's long-term interests.[1]

## The Perils of a Preventive Strike

Any attempt to disarm Iran through the use of military options would in all likelihood damage America's interests in the region. While a military option might inflict significant damage on Iran's infrastructure by damaging or destroying its nuclear weapons program, disrupting its regional ambitions, and possibly serving as a deterrent to future proliferators, the likely costs would far outweigh the benefits.

First, any military action against Iran would send seismic shocks through global energy markets at a time when the price of oil is already at record highs. Since Iran relies heavily on the income derived from oil exports, it is unlikely that it would withhold petroleum from global markets. Iran may, however, threaten to disrupt the flow of traffic through the Strait of Hormuz or sponsor attacks on key oil infrastructure on the territory of America's Gulf allies. Such actions could hurt the US economy and potentially bolster Iranian revenue by raising the price of oil. While it is true that the world market would eventually adjust to such actions, as James Fallows has noted, that is a bit like saying eventually the US stock market adjusted to the Great Depression.[2] Any direct military action against Iran could also have a significant impact on America's war on terrorism. Such action would only serve to confirm many of Osama bin Laden's statements that the United States is at war with the world of Islam. This charge would be difficult to counter, given the fact that the United States has looked the other way for years with regard to Israel's nuclear program, accepted India as a legitimate nuclear-state, and is negotiating with North Korea regarding its nuclear ambitions.

Any military action against Iran would also undermine America's nation-building efforts in Iraq and Afghanistan, due to possible Iranian retaliation in both countries. While Iranian efforts toward stabilizing these two states have been sporadic at best, and purposely obstructive at worst, there is little reason to doubt that Iran could make achieving US objectives in Iraq and Afghanistan far more difficult. Although mostly bluster, there is some truth to former Iranian President Ali Rafsanjani's argument that as long as American troops maintain a formidable presence on Iran's borders, "it is the United States that is besieged by Iran."[3] The same holds true regarding Iran's ties to Hezbollah and its presence in Lebanon. By targeting Iran's nuclear program the United States would unwisely encourage Iranian escalation in a number of these arenas.

Military strikes against Tehran would also undermine Washington's long-term goal of seeing reform movements succeed in Iran. If the history of military incursions and the Iranian nation teach us anything it is the fact that intervention is likely to solidify support for the current regime. The idea that the Iranian people would react to a military strike by advocating the overthrow of the existing regime is delusional.[4] Instead the likely outcome of any direct military incursion would be the bolstering of the current regime.

Moreover, any preventive attack, no matter how effective, is only a temporary fix. First, such a campaign will eliminate only that portion of Iran's nuclear program known to intelligence agencies. Even after the extensive bombing campaign of the 1990–1991 Gulf War, subsequent inspections discovered large parts of Iraq's unconventional weapons programs that were previously unknown. More importantly, even if such an attack succeeded in eliminating significant facets of Iran's nuclear program, it would do little toward discouraging Iran from rebuilding those assets. Thus, even after a fully successful denial campaign, the United States, in a number of years, would likely face the prospect of having to do it all over again.

## The Problem with Regime Change

Given the limits of any preventive strike, perhaps the United States should not restrict its goal in Iran to simply nuclear disarmament, but opt instead for the broader objective of regime change. If successful, regime change in Iran could provide for a number of benefits. It may eliminate the Iranian threat of interrupting the flow of oil from the region; it would also send a strong message to potential proliferators about the costs of similar actions; it might diminish Iran's support for terrorism; even possibly eliminate the threat of official Iranian meddling in Iraq and Afghanistan; and could potentially curtail Iran's nuclear ambitions.

The reason a policy advocating regime change is a bad idea, given its potential benefits, is the fact that such a policy is beyond America's means. While the United States certainly possesses the capability to eliminate the regime in Tehran, as the invasion of Iraq has shown, eliminating the present leadership is the easy part of regime change. The more difficult and costly challenge is installing a new government. With America's resources already overly committed in Afghanistan and Iraq, taking on a new nation-building mission in a country far larger and in some ways far more nationalistic than Iraq would be the epitome of strategic overreach.

Additionally, one of the few scenarios where Iran might use its nuclear capability would be if Tehran believed that the United States intended to exercise forcible regime change. A

nuclear strike against any American presence in the region might be seen by the leadership in Tehran as its last hope for survival. It goes without saying that once any government has crossed the nuclear threshold, forcible regime change by an external actor is no longer a viable option. The threat of nuclear retaliation would simply be too great. Indeed, this is probably the most important reason why states such as Iran and North Korea desire nuclear weapons. Does this mean that the United States should therefore seek regime change before Iran develops its nuclear capability? No; even without nuclear weapons, forcible regime change in Iran and the ensuing occupation would entail too great a commitment of resources on the part of the United States. Pursuing regime change in Iran as a response to its nuclear program would be akin to treating a brain tumor with a guillotine. The proposed cure is worse than the disease.

## A Better Policy: Deter, Contain, and Engage

Fortunately, US policy options for dealing with a nuclear Iran are not limited to preventive military strikes, regime change, or doing nothing. A more promising option would have four key components. First, deter Iran from ever using its nuclear weapons. Second, prevent Iran from using its nuclear status to increase its influence in the region. Third, engage Iran in a meaningful way that encourages the creation of a government friendly to the United States and its regional allies, one that does not sponsor terrorism. Finally, such a policy should reassure US allies in the region that America's commitment to their security is steadfast. This four-pronged strategy would do a better job of protecting American interests in the region than any military strike or forcible regime change.

### *Deter*

America's overriding concern regarding Iran's nuclear weapons program is that these weapons are never used against the United States or its allies. Fortunately, the strategy of nuclear deterrence can go a long way in resolving this problem. The threat of annihilation as the result of an American retaliatory strike can be a powerful deterrent. As the United States and the Soviet Union discovered during the Cold War and as India and Pakistan have recently learned, the threat of nuclear retaliation makes the use of such weapons problematic.

The central question in any debate over America's policies toward a nuclear Iran is whether or not the regime in Tehran is deterrable. If in fact it is, then deterrence is a less costly and risky strategy than prevention. Proponents of the preventive use of military force argue, as did the alarmists in the late 1940s with regard to the Soviet Union and in the early 1960s about China, that Iran is a revolutionary state seeking to export its destabilizing ideology. For these analysts Iran is often depicted as a regime of religious zealots that cannot be deterred because they are willing to accept an apocalyptic end to any conflict.[5]

While Iran's track record with regard to its foreign policy does indicate a regime that is hostile to America, nothing would indicate that Iran is beyond the realm of nuclear deterrence.

The bulk of the revolutionary fervor demonstrated by the Islamic Republic during its infancy died during the long war with Iraq. Moreover, the power of nuclear deterrence lies in the fact that precise calculations and cost and benefit analyses are not needed given the overwhelming costs associated with any nuclear exchange. Iranian leaders are rational enough to understand that any use of nuclear weapons against the United States or its allies would result in an overwhelming and unacceptable response.

What about President Mahmoud Ahmadinejad talking of wiping Israel off the map or the former President Rafsanjani declaring that while Israel could not survive a nuclear war, the Islamic world could survive a nuclear exchange? Fears related to such rhetoric need to be viewed in a historical context. Similar arguments were made about the Soviets and Chinese as they developed their nuclear arsenals. The fear of many Cold War hawks was that the Kremlin was run by ideologues. Wasn't it a fact that they did not shirk while watching 25 million of their own killed in World War II; nor did they flinch while millions more were murdered in internal purges? This demonstrated, many argued, that the Soviet leadership would be impervious to the logic of mutually assured destruction. Indeed, at times Mao Tse-Tung offered strikingly similar rhetoric to that coming out of Tehran today. He also boasted about how China could afford to lose millions in a nuclear exchange and still emerge victorious.[6] Such worries turned out to be baseless with regard to the Soviets and the Chinese, and such rhetoric proved to be just that, rhetoric. While the bizarre views and hostile statements coming from Iran's current President are cause for concern, one must also be cognizant of the fact that the President of Iran is not the commander-in-chief of the armed forces and, in reality, has little influence over the nuclear program. The Supreme Leader does, however, and Ayatollah Ali Khameni has distanced himself from the most bellicose of Ahmadinejad's rhetoric.

To counter these ominous tirades one could look to more reassuring statements, such as Supreme Leader Khameni's argument that nuclear weapons are un-Islamic.[7] More enlightening, however, than comparing dueling quotes, is an examination of what Iran has done in terms of its foreign policy. Iran has shown itself to be pragmatic in its actions to protect national interests, foregoing the activities one associates with a religiously driven revolutionary state.

Following the collapse of the Soviet Union, contrary to expectations, Iran did not seek to export its revolution to parts of the former Soviet Union, understanding that their national interest lay in forging a solid and profitable relationship with Russia. Iran even went so far as to dismiss the war in Chechnya as an internal Russian matter. Similar calculations of national interests led Iran to support Christian Armenia over Muslim Azerbaijan. Following the 1991 Gulf War, Iran did not push for a Shia revolution in Iraq, fearing that the outcome would probably be too dangerous and destabilizing. Following its isolation during the Iran-Iraq War Iran worked vigorously to improve relations with its Gulf neighbors.[8]

But does Tehran's antipathy toward the United States and Israel outweigh its long-term national interests? No; indeed, during the Iran-Iraq War Tehran was willing to engage in arms shipments with the United States and Israel in an effort to further its war against Iraq. Given the difficulties the Iranians had with the Taliban, Tehran has also been fairly supportive of the American intervention in Afghanistan, to include offering the United States the use of its airfields and ports.[9] While Tehran was less supportive of America's subsequent intervention in Iraq, the leadership was astute enough to recognize the benefits associated with the destruction of Saddam Hussein's regime. The point of these examples is not to discount any policy differences that Washington has with Tehran, but to stress that Iran is not run by ideologues, rather by a group of pragmatists devoted to protecting Iranian interests. Leaders who are rational enough to understand that the use of nuclear weapons against America would not be in their national interests.

There has also been a good deal of international media reports related to the fear that Iran might provide nuclear weapons to terrorist organizations. Ironically, the very use by Iran of surrogate terrorist organizations, rather than more overt attacks, is evidence that Tehran is sensitive to the calculations associated with the strategy of deterrence. It is also an affirmation that the Iranian leadership is attempting to minimize the risks to its foreign policy objectives. Such acts argue strongly against any possibility that Iran might provide terrorist organizations with nuclear weapons. Any move of this nature carries with it a great amount of risk; Iranians would lose control over the employment of the weapons while still having to worry that they might be blamed and targeted for response.[10]

## Contain

The second pillar of US strategy toward a nuclear Iran should be a policy of containment, to be certain that Iran does not succeed in exercising its nuclear capability as a tool of coercive diplomacy against US or allied interests in the region. Given Iran's perception of itself as the historically preeminent power in the region, Tehran can be expected to continue its policy attempting to increase its regional influence at the expense of the United States.

How would the possession of a deliverable nuclear weapon impact Tehran's foreign policy agenda? One possibility is that a nuclear Iran might be more, rather than less, restrained in its regional agenda. If any of Iran's actions are driven by a sense of insecurity with regard to America's intentions (or the threat created by a nuclear Pakistan or Israel, even the possibility of a resurgent Iraq), the security that Tehran would gain from having its own nuclear deterrent could make the nation's leadership less worried about the regional balance of power. Moreover, possession of a nuclear weapon would certainly increase the attention other world-powers paid Iran. The leadership in Tehran would have to continually worry that if any crisis developed involving another nuclear power the potential foe might opt for a preemptive attack on Iranian nuclear facilities. The fear that even a limited conflict might escalate into a nuclear exchange could make Tehran more cautious across the entire spectrum of conflict.

While such pressures may play a limited role in Iran's decisionmaking, it would be unwise for the United States to put too much faith in such possibilities. First, Iran's regional behavior is only partially driven by security fears. Even if Iran believed there was no threat from the United States, its status as a potential regional hegemon gives it incentive to increase its role in regional affairs. Second, while a limited amount of learning related to nuclear crisis management did take place during the Cold War, it took the United States and the Soviets a number of crises to fully appreciate these lessons.[11] Although the existence of this Cold War record might enable Iran to learn such lessons more quickly, the limits of vicarious learning offer ample reasons to doubt that Iran will internalize these dictums without experiencing similar crises.

The result is that Iran can probably be expected to continue furthering its regional agenda in an attempt to increase its stature and diminish that of the United States. At least initially, any increased nuclear capability will likely embolden rather than induce caution on the part of Iran's leadership. Having gone to great lengths and paid significant costs to develop its nuclear capabilities, Iran is likely to continue testing the regional and international waters. Such efforts are bound to create challenges for the United States and its allies. The good news is that nuclear weapons have proven to be poor tools for coercive diplomacy, especially against states that already possess nuclear weapons or who may be allied with a nuclear power. Nuclear weapons have proven to be extraordinarily effective at two tasks: deterring the use of such weapons against other nuclear powers or their allies, and deterring states from directly challenging the vital interests of a nuclear power. Beyond these two critical tasks, however, nuclear weapons have not proven particularly useful as diplomatic tools of intimidation. For the United States and its allies, a policy of containment against Iranian attempts to expand its influence in the region is the correct foreign policy strategy. Certainly, such a strategy far outweighs any policy based on preventive war.

## Engage

To advance America's long-range goal of an Iran that is part of the global economy, at peace with its neighbors, and not supporting terrorism, Washington would be better served by engaging Iran rather than attempting to isolate it. A policy of engagement could take two forms: the establishment of direct diplomatic relations and the encouragement of Iran's involvement in the global economy.

The United States broke diplomatic ties with Iran in April 1980, during the hostage crisis. The establishment of direct diplomatic ties between the United States and Iran, however, should not be seen as any form of a reward to Iran or as approval of Iranian policies. Nor should the reestablishment of formal relations be seen as the final stage in some sort of grand bargain. Instead, diplomatic relations should be viewed as part of the normal business of conducting America's foreign policy. There is little reason to doubt that Iran would portray any US initiative to reestablish diplomatic relations as a victory, as Tehran did with the recent moves by the Bush Administration to engage in direct talks related to the situation in Iraq. America should not let fear of such a reaction stand in the way of any initiative that would advance America's long-term security interests.

Over the years the United States has found that it needs diplomatic relations with hostile states as well as with allies. Such relationships were maintained throughout the Cold War with the Soviet Union, despite numerous crises and conflicts. In the case of Iran the absence of direct governmental links makes it more difficult to deter and contain Iran. Obviously, Iran would have to concur in the reestablishment of any form of diplomatic relations.

Given the number of domestic challenges the Islamic Republic is facing, most notably a tremendous growth in its youthful population, combined with the incompetence and corruption that has marked its stewardship of the Iranian economy, it is hard to imagine that this regime can continue to avoid collapse without significant reform.[12] At the same time, there is little reason to expect that a democratic revolution is imminent. The reform movements that seemed so promising in the late 1990s have largely been defeated. The best strategy for revitalizing these movements is to encourage Tehran's involvement in the world economy, as opposed to further attempts at isolation. Increasing the Iranian people's exposure to the world economy is much more likely to increase motivation and expand the resources available to any future reform movement. Iran's eventual inclusion in the World Trade Organization is one of the carrots currently being held out to Iran as part of ongoing negotiations regarding its nuclear program. Such incentives may advance America's long-term foreign policy goals in the region even if those efforts fail to negate Iran's development of a nuclear weapon.

Potential economic sanctions against Iran related to its nuclear program need to be carefully addressed. Iran's stagnant economy, as well as its reliance on the international energy market, make it acutely vulnerable to economic sanctions.[13] While the threat of sanctions may be useful in dissuading the development of nuclear weapons, it is less clear that the actual imposition of sanctions would advance US foreign policy interests. While economic sanctions might extract a high toll on the Iranian economy, the reality is that the political effect that accompanies such sanctions often strengthens, rather than undermines, a regime. Sanctions tend to increase a government's control over the country's economic activity, thereby starving potential opponents of resources. Sanctions can also create a "rally round the flag" effect that permits a regime to blame international hostility for the state's internal weaknesses.[14]

In the case of a nuclear Iran, sanctions are only likely to be useful under a fairly stringent set of circumstances. To significantly impact Iran's economy, any sanctions regime would have to be multilateral and include at a minimum the United States, European Union, Russia, and China. Sanctions would also have to be properly targeted against the leadership of the current regime and not structured in such a manner as to inflict indiscriminate damage to Iran's economy. Finally, penalties inflicted by the sanctions need be directly attributable to the regime's development of nuclear weapons.

Creating sanctions that meet these requirements would not be easy. The importance of Iran as a market for Russia and an energy supplier to China makes any sanctions regime a tough sell in Moscow and Beijing. The complicated and often opaque nature of Iranian domestic politics also presents a challenge to the development of "smart sanctions." Finally, given the distrust that exists in Iran regarding the history of external interventions, it is doubtful that any sanctions regime would be interpreted as anything except another attempt to interfere in internal politics. In all likelihood, the United States would be better off by not making sanctions the focal point for its policies regarding a nuclear Iran. Engagement has often proven to be a surer path to regime evolution than economic isolation.[15]

# Reassure Iran's Neighbors

The final portion of a US strategy toward a nuclear-armed Iran should focus on convincing Iran's neighbors that the American commitment to their security remains strong. If the United States wants regional powers to resist Iranian attempts at expanding its influence, then Washington needs to bolster security ties in the region. Improving security cooperation with Iran's neighbors could advance a number of American interests beyond simple containment. Such efforts could also help increase the security of the oil infrastructure in the region, as well as expand intelligence cooperation related to international terrorism.

A more definite US security commitment to Iran's neighbors may also decrease the chance that the development of a nuclear weapon would increase the threat of nuclear proliferation in the region. Egypt, Turkey, and Saudi Arabia have been cited as states likely to respond to any Iranian nuclear capability with increased nuclear programs. Egypt, however, has been able to tolerate a nuclear Israel for more than 30 years, as well as accommodate Libya's weapons programs. Given that historical precedent, it is unlikely that an Iranian bomb would dramatically change Cairo's calculations. Similarly, Turkey's membership in the North Atlantic Treaty Organization and its desire to join the European Union are likely to dissuade Ankara from attempting to join the nuclear fraternity. Saudi Arabia and the other members of the Gulf Cooperation Council, however, would more than likely attempt to strengthen security ties with the United States in an effort to bolster their position against a nuclear Iran.

Part of America's strategy regarding regional allies needs to focus on assuring individual states that as long as Iran is contained, the United States will not take any preventive military action. While the Gulf States certainly would prefer that Iran not develop nuclear weapons, it is also important to recognize that they fear any US-Iranian conflict more than they fear the prospect of a nuclear Iran.[16] America's most promising strategy toward a nuclear-armed Iran should be the development of a security architecture based on deterrence and containment.

# Conclusion

The United States should be under no illusions regarding the problems that a nuclear-armed Iran would present. The challenges that development would pose for American interests in the region would be monumental and lasting. The strategy of deterrence, containment, engagement, and reassurance provides the framework for achieving America's long-term regional objectives. Such a strategy would minimize disruptions to the international flow of oil, blunt Iran's attempts at regional hegemony, stabilize US efforts in Afghanistan and Iraq, and aid in countering the global war on terrorism. Ultimately, it will provide the time that reformers in Iran need to recast the Iranian government from within. It is this reformation of Iran's government that will offer the best guarantee for preserving America's interests in the region.

When US diplomat George Kennan proposed the doctrine of containment against the Soviet Union at the outset of the Cold War, he argued that Soviet diplomacy was:

> At once easier and more difficult to deal with than the diplomacy of aggressive leaders like Napoleon and Hitler. On the one hand it is more sensitive to contrary force, more ready to yield on individual sectors of the diplomatic front when that force was felt to be too strong, and thus more rational in the logic and rhetoric of power. On the other hand it cannot be easily defeated or discouraged by a single victory on the part of its opponents. . . . [I]t can be effectively countered not by sporadic acts which represent the momentary whims of democratic opinion, but only by intelligent long-range policies.[17]

Admittedly, the Iran of today is quite different than the Soviet Union of the 1940s. It represents what is at best a regional rather than a global challenge, and its distinctive Persian and Shia ideologies are likely to have limited appeal abroad. These differences aside, Kennan's insight still applies. Iranian nuclear ambitions can best be deterred by means of an intelligent long-range foreign policy, not the threat of military intervention.

# NOTES

1. On regime evolution versus regime change, see Richard N. Haass, "Regime Change and Its Limits," *Foreign Affairs,* 84 (July/August 2005), 68.

2. James Fallows, "The Nuclear Power Beside Iraq," *The Atlantic Monthly,* May 2006, 32.

3. Quoted in Kamram Taremi, "Iranian Foreign Policy Towards Occupied Iraq, 2003–2005," *Middle East Policy,* 12 (Winter 2005), 42.

4. For examples of those who argue that decisive military action against Iran could cause a favorable regime change, see Arthur Herman, "Getting Serious About Iran: A Military Option," *Commentary,* 122 (November 2006), 28–32 and Norman Podhoretz, "The Case for Bombing Iran," *Commentary,* 123 (June 2007), 17–23.

5. For example, see Bernard Lewis, "August 22," *Wall Street Journal,* 8 August 2006, A10; William Kristol, "It's Our War," *The Weekly Standard,* 24 July 2006; Charles Krauthammer, "The Tehran Calculus," *The Washington Post,* 15 September 2006, A19; and Efraim Inbar, "The Need to Block a Nuclear Iran," *Middle East Review of International Affairs,* 10 (March 2006), 85–105.

6. On the comparison between Iran's rhetoric on nuclear weapons and earlier statements from Mao, see Ray Takeyh, "Confronting

Iran: Take Ahmadinejad with a Grain of Salt," *The Los Angeles Times,* 19 November 2006, M1.

7.  Kenneth M. Pollack, *The Persian Puzzle: The Conflict Between Iran and America* (New York: Random House, 2004), 237; and Michael Eisenstadt, "Deter and Contain: Dealing with a Nuclear Iran" in Henry Sokolski and Patrick Clawson, eds., *Getting Ready for a Nuclear-Ready Iran* (Carlisle, Pa.: US Army War College, Strategic Studies Institute, October 2005), 227–29.

8.  See Ray Takeyh, *Hidden Iran: Paradox and Power in the Islamic Republic* (New York: Times Books, 2006), 59–82; Robert O. Freedman, "Putin, Iran, and the Nuclear Weapons Issue," *Problems of Post-Communism,* 53 (March/April 2006), 41; and Mohsen M. Milani, "Iran: The Status Quo Power," *Current History,* 104 (January 2005), 30–36.

9.  Pollack , 346–47.

10. For a discussion of the issues involved in deterring states from supplying nuclear weapons to terrorists, see Caitlin Talmadge, "Deterring a Nuclear 9/11," *Washington Quarterly,* 30 (Spring 2007), 21–34.

11. Joseph S. Nye, Jr., "Nuclear Learning and U.S.-Soviet Security Regimes," *International Organization,* 41 (Summer 1987), 389–90.

12. Ray Takeyh and Nikolas K. Gvosdev, "Pragmatism in the Midst of Iranian Turmoil," *Washington Quarterly,* 27 (Autumn 2004), 33–56; Ali Gheissari and Vali Nasr, "The Conservative Consolidation in Iran," *Survival,* 47 (Summer 2005), 175–90; and Jahangir Amuzegar, "Iran's Theocracy under Siege," *Middle East Policy,* 10 (Spring 2003), 135–52.

13. Kenneth Pollack and Ray Takeyh, "Taking on Tehran," *Foreign Affairs,* 84 (March/April 2005), 20–34; and Abbas Milani, "U.S. Foreign Policy and the Future of Democracy in Iran," *Washington Quarterly,* 28 (Summer 2005), 41–56.

14. See, for example, Meghan L. O'Sullivan, *Shrewd Sanctions: Statecraft and State Sponsors of Terrorism* (Washington: Brookings Institution Press, 2003), especially 284–320.

15. Haass, 71.

16. Judith S. Yaphe and Charles D. Lutes, *Reassessing the Implications of a Nuclear-Armed Iran* (Washington: National Defense Univ., Institute for National Strategic Studies, McNair Paper #69, August 2005), 19.

17. X [George Kennan], "The Sources of Soviet Conduct," *Foreign Affairs,* 25 (July 1947), 575.

**DR. CHRISTOPHER HEMMER** received his doctorate from Cornell University. He currently serves as an Associate Professor of International Security Studies at the Air War College. He is the author of *Which Lessons Matter? American Foreign Policy Decision Making in the Middle East, 1979–1987.*

From *Parameters,* by Christopher Hemmer, (37:3) Autumn 2007, pp. 42–43. Published by U.S. Army War College. Reprinted by permission.

# China through Arab Eyes: American Influence in the Middle East

CHRIS ZAMBELIS AND BRANDON GENTRY

The significance of Beijing's hosting of the second annual China-Arab Cooperation Forum—an event bringing together key envoys from 22 Arab nations under the auspices of the Arab League and their Chinese counterparts—went largely unnoticed in the western media. According to Chinese and Arab news reports, however, the conference, held in May and June 2006, was a success on many levels. As Chinese and Arab dignitaries agreed to greatly strengthen and expand economic, energy, and cultural ties to unprecedented levels over the course of the twenty-first century, Chinese President Hu Jintao, speaking warmly of the blossoming Sino-Arab relationship, stated, "China thanks the Arab states for supporting China in relation to Taiwan and human rights issues and will as always support the just cause of the Arab states and people."[1] For his part, Arab League Secretary-General Amr Moussa reaffirmed the League's support of the "One China" principle, declaring, "The world has but one China, and we only visit a China with Beijing as its capital."[2]

Despite its lack of publicity, the forum represents another significant effort by the People's Republic of China (PRC) in recent years to strengthen its ties to the Arab world and the greater Middle East.[3] Beijing is finding an array of potential partners in the region looking to harness China's economic and political momentum for their own reasons. Incumbent autocratic regimes throughout the Middle East seek to bolster their respective positions and lessen their dependence on the United States through closer ties to Beijing. Middle Eastern business leaders are eager to reap the profits of lucrative partnerships with Chinese investors. And recent public opinion polls indicate that the people of the Middle East are desperate to see an end to what is widely perceived as a destructive US regional hegemony.

Consequently, as China's global influence increases, Beijing looks to the Middle East—where it historically has held a low profile—to establish a political, economic, and cultural foothold in the energy-rich and strategically central region. In so doing, the PRC poses a multifaceted challenge to the United States, whose presence and influence in the region have long been a cornerstone of American geopolitical strategy.[4] Indeed, a growing Chinese presence in the Middle East may someday convince long-standing US allies in the region to reorient their strategic relationships away from Washington toward Beijing, dramatically transforming the strategic landscape in the process.

The most obvious motivation underpinning the PRC's new engagement strategy is the need to secure vital energy resources required to sustain China's dynamic economic growth amidst increasingly unstable international energy markets. Having ceased to be a net oil exporter in the early 1990s, China currently imports approximately 60 percent of its oil from the Middle East.[5] Major Chinese state-owned oil concerns such as the China Petroleum and Chemical Corporation (Sinopec) have made impressive inroads in recent years with key energy producers such as Saudi Arabia and Iran. The China National Petroleum Corporation (CNPC) is busy in Sudan, while the China National Offshore Oil Corporation (CNOOC) has established itself in Algeria and elsewhere in the region. Moreover, China's unprecedented domestic growth over the last two decades has come at a high social and environmental cost; a reliance on coal has resulted in severe ecological damage and an alarming rise in respiratory diseases affecting those living in large cities and heavily industrialized areas, causing China to seek cleaner-burning energy sources such as petroleum and natural gas.[6]

China is also eager to gain access to untapped consumer markets for its exports and lucrative investment opportunities. The 2006 China-Arab Cooperation Forum included a commitment to expand and diversify trade volumes between China and the Arab countries to over $100 billion within the next five years, up from the current figure of just over $50 billion—approximately 40 percent of which is oil-related.[7] Furthermore, then-Chinese Foreign Minister Li Xiaoxing and Arab League Secretary-General Amr Moussa pledged to forge closer contacts in counterterrorism and security cooperation, technology and aid transfers, and cultural exchanges, expanding the dimensions of Sino-Arab cooperation beyond energy and business.

Apart from its economic dimension, Beijing's growing interest in the Middle East should also be considered in a geopolitical context. As an emerging diplomatic and military force on the international stage, China is intent on projecting power outside its immediate East Asian sphere of influence and matching its rival India's impressive efforts in the region.[8] Cultivating strong relations with the Arab world and the greater Middle East constitutes a key pillar of this strategy, stabilizing China's global presence and enhancing its image as a major economic power. In addition to forging closer ties to the Arab world, Beijing is shoring up its position in Iran and Pakistan, as well as with the former Soviet republics of Central Asia.[9] Given China's significant economic and energy interests in Iran, Beijing sees the international diplomatic controversy concerning the Iranian nuclear program as a crucial test of its global leverage, especially vis-à-vis the United States.[10] Washington's preoccupation with the escalating violence and instability in Iraq and Afghanistan, as well as the Iranian nuclear crisis—combined with widespread popular opposition to the United States—provide Beijing with a historic window of opportunity to enhance its position.

# Arab Resentment and Chinese Opportunism

Much has been said about China's successful Middle East diplomacy. Beijing offers prospective partners many tangible benefits. In return for investment and development aid, China's profile in the region has grown significantly in recent years, most notably in countries such as Egypt, Saudi Arabia, and others firmly entrenched in long-standing political, military, and economic alliances with the United States.

China's potential as a source of lucrative investment receives the most attention, as well as its willingness and ability to fund large-scale infrastructure and economic development programs in countries and regions that are considered too risky by other investors, or that have been deemed pariahs by the international community due to human rights concerns, such as Sudan.[11] Many Arab countries look to China as a successful political and economic development model worthy of emulation. China is widely regarded in the Arab world as a developing country that has charted its own unique path toward economic development and modernization, a point frequently touted by Beijing.[12] This perception is attractive to societies where the legacy of harsh colonial governance and foreign interference in local and regional affairs by the West continues to shape recent memory and influence perceptions. Consequently, the Chinese system of state-led economic development provides an alternative to the US system, with its emphasis on the principles outlined by the World Bank and the International Monetary Fund (also known as the "Washington Consensus") and its insistence on implementing strict neo-liberal free market formulas and related policy prescriptions.

An often overlooked aspect of Beijing's success in projecting influence and power in the Arab world transcends economics and stems from the generally positive perceptions of China that prevail in the region—both at the state and grassroots levels. These positive perceptions are crucial to facilitating closer Sino-Arab bilateral and multilateral contacts and cooperation and cannot be underestimated. Indeed, rightly or wrongly, Arabs in varying degrees see China as a potential strategic partner able to counter the influence of an increasingly unpopular United States. Initial Arab hopes for the emergence of a credible check on American influence in the Middle East and across the globe in the shape of the European Union or a rejuvenated post-Soviet Russia have failed to materialize. In this context, China is widely perceived as the only credible alternative to US hegemony.[13]

Facilitating China's emergence as a major power in the Middle East is the fact that American credibility in the region is currently at an abysmal low. Deep-seated opposition to the US-led wars in Iraq and Afghanistan—and, most recently, the widespread belief that Washington is preparing to attack Iran over its nuclear program—top the list of regional grievances. Arabs and Muslims also harbor deep resentment toward the United States for its unwavering support of Israel primarily due to Israel's continued occupation of Palestinian land. Washington's reluctance to jumpstart the long-dormant Middle East peace process bolsters regional perceptions that the United States will always side with Israel against the rest of the Middle East. The November 2007 talks at Annapolis, for example, were widely regarded in the Middle East as a photo-op for a lame-duck president in search of positive headlines amid the violence and instability in Iraq and Afghanistan, with no real progress being made on substantive issues aside from agreements between Israelis and Palestinians to hold regular talks.[14] The United States then withdrew a UN Security Council resolution supporting efforts by the Israelis and Palestinians to reach a final agreement by the end of 2008 after Israel voiced concerns about aspects of the resolution, further strengthening the perception that Washington unceasingly bends to the will of Israel.[15]

Continuing US diplomatic, military, and economic support for autocratic regimes in Egypt, Jordan, Morocco, and Saudi Arabia—regimes which many Arabs believe to be oppressive, illegitimate, and incompetent—is also a major source of bitterness, especially given Washington's stated commitments to supporting genuine political reform in the region. American criticism of the January 2006 elections in Palestine that elevated Hamas—elections which were widely regarded as free and fair by international observers—is also indicative of what Arabs see as hypocrisy. Additionally, most Arabs find messages emphasizing the virtues of democracy and freedom to be condescending and misguided, especially when US officials maintain highly publicized contacts with regional leaders known for their systematic repression of freedom of expression and dissent.[16] Such diplomatic activity confirms the widespread belief that Washington is not serious about supporting genuine political reform and democracy in the region and is instead intent on maintaining the status quo.

Interestingly, China's plans for expanded influence resonate among democratic reform-minded Islamist opposition groups, including the banned *Al-Ikhwan al-Muslimeen* (Muslim Brotherhood) in Egypt, who see China's rise as a possible check on unbridled US power. Despite being outlawed, the Muslim Brotherhood is on the forefront of democratic opposition politics in Egypt.[17] It is against this background that China senses a historic opportunity to boost its position in a region firmly planted in the US strategic landscape.

Contrary to widespread opinions in US foreign policy, academic, and media circles, much of the negative Arab perceptions of the United States are not rooted in a popular Arab or Muslim aversion to American culture or society. On the contrary, public opinion polls demonstrate that Arabs hold American culture and values—especially those of individual freedom and democracy—in high-esteem. Arabs do, however, strongly oppose US foreign policy in the Middle East, and many wish to see US presence and influence in the region greatly reduced, at least in their current forms.[18] Consequently, China represents a potential check on what Arabs see as an overbearing and destructive American influence.

Beijing has begun to skillfully exploit Arab dissatisfaction with US policies, at times aggressively criticizing American moves in the Middle East. For instance, in a statement appearing in the 1 February 2007 edition of *People's Daily,* China's Director of the State Administration for Religious Affairs, Minister Ye Xiaowen, issued a strong criticism of the Bush Administration's conduct in the war on terrorism. Among other things, he specifically pointed to President George W. Bush's use of the term "crusade" to characterize the upcoming "war on terror" following the 11 September 2001 attacks, and painted the President's use of terms such as "Islamic fascism" as an attack against Islam.[19]

In its calculated criticism of American rhetoric and conduct in the war on terrorism, China seeks to portray itself to Arabs and Muslims as a friendly and positive alternative to US hegemony, essentially relying on "soft power" to plead its case.[20] White House rhetoric as described in the *People's Daily* article evoked strong opposition to the United States in the Middle East, confirming in the minds of many Arabs and Muslims the perception that America was determined to exploit the 11 September attacks as a pretext to wage a war of imperial conquest against Muslim countries and Islam. China's criticism of US rhetoric enhances its image as a friend to Arabs and Muslims, despite Beijing's dismal record on human and religious rights regarding its own ethnic Uighur Muslim minority community.

## Perceptions of China

Most Arab states see China as a potential strategic partner worth engaging beyond the traditional trade and business spheres. This is especially true in countries the United States considers vital strategic partners, such as Egypt, Saudi Arabia, Kuwait, Morocco, and Oman. As is the case elsewhere in the world since the demise of the Soviet Union, many in the Middle East are concerned about the prevailing unipolar, US-dominated geopolitical landscape and welcome the emergence of a counterbalance to American power. The robust US military footprint in the region, first established during the 1991 Persian Gulf War, brings these issues to light for key regional allies who feel they have no other options but to rely on Washington for political, economic, and military support. This holds especially true for regional powerbrokers such as Egypt and Saudi

Arabia. Despite Cairo and Riyadh's close strategic relations with Washington, both regimes resent US pressure to initiate political liberalization programs in the post-9/11 era, as well as American criticism of their domestic human rights records. The same applies for other authoritarian Arab regimes with close ties to Washington, such as Morocco and Jordan.[21]

Consequently, incumbent Arab autocrats find common ground and a useful ally in Beijing. China is more than willing to offer development funding and financial investment in return for preferential access to regional energy reserves and investment opportunities, and does so without making human rights or political reform demands. China's extensive and controversial relationship with Sudan, despite international condemnation of Khartoum's policies toward Darfur, is a case in point.[22] Likewise, ruling autocratic regimes in the Middle East are eager to offer Beijing their full support regarding Taiwan and the "One China" principle, as well as its position on Tibet and other domestic controversies. Given Beijing's experience with US criticism of its own record on political freedom and human rights and its vocal stance against foreign interference in its internal affairs, it is clear why the convergence of interests on these issues helps facilitate close Sino-Arab contacts at the state level.

Regional leaders and intellectuals also point to China's conservative approach to political and economic development and modernization as a model worth adopting and a viable alternative to US and western-inspired reform models—models which are often perceived as instruments of western imperial control and exploitation. China is seen as a developing country that is succeeding while building its own independent path, not one dictated by Washington or by US-backed international institutions. Arab regimes, many of which are grounded in semi-socialist models of economic policy and are accustomed to a much higher level of state-controlled economic policy than exists in the United States, chafe at perceived American efforts to impose an economic system, free-market capitalism, which many Arab leaders feel is ill-suited to Arab society at this stage. The fact that China is successfully pursuing an economic course driven by a highly centralized economic model is attractive to leaders throughout the Middle East.

Beijing's effective public diplomacy also plays an important role in bringing China closer to governments in the Middle East. China often emphasizes the historic ties between the Arab world and Chinese civilization—ties stretching back to the Silk Road era—as well as the great contributions of both cultures to mankind. This kind of historical rhetoric resonates throughout the Middle East on both the state and local levels. For example, Beijing frequently highlights its relations with the region during the height of Arab nationalism and the Non-Aligned Movement in the early 1960s and regularly praises Arab states for being among the first to establish diplomatic relationships with the People's Republic of China.[23]

Regional governments must balance their staunch pro-US strategic orientation amidst popular discontent and deep-seated resentment toward American foreign policy against the background of growing domestic political opposition, including democratic reform-minded Islamist movements calling for revolutionary change. Arabs deeply resent long-standing US support for authoritarian regimes in the Middle East, the wars in Iraq and Afghanistan, and US support for Israel. It is therefore in the interest of regional governments to court Beijing, an American rival and potential peer competitor, since closer Sino-Arab relations enhance public perceptions that Arab regimes are in fact acting on their own discretion and not as instruments of US foreign policy.

# Grassroot Views of China

Currently, China enjoys generally positive perceptions all over the world. According to a recent BBC public opinion poll in which citizens of 27 countries were asked which nations had the most positive global influence, China ranked sixth behind Canada, Japan, the European Union, France, and Great Britain. Russia and the United States lagged behind, while Iran and Israel occupied the bottom two spots on the list.[24] The findings indicate that those countries most dependent on "soft power" as a means of leveraging influence tend to garner the most positive perceptions. Not surprisingly, soft power, in the form of economic aid, investment, and political support, is the cornerstone of China's greater Middle East strategy.

Until fairly recently, China's role as an active and constructive player in Middle East diplomacy had been peripheral at best. Despite this, surveys of Arab public opinion indicate that Arabs tend to view China in a very positive light. These sentiments stem in part from nostalgic feelings of solidarity dating back to the height of Arab nationalism and China's preeminent role bolstering international Third World solidarity and anticolonial movements, which entailed support for popular Arab nationalist causes. In this context, local perceptions of China mirror those of the former Soviet Union based on the role it played in supporting Arab nationalism and other regional movements.

These sentiments prevail despite the fact that strategic concerns are driving Beijing's regional policies and not ideological affinities, as might have been the case decades ago during the height of Soviet power and influence. At the same time, China's vocal support for the Palestinian cause and willingness to challenge the United States on a host of regional issues provide Arabs with a sense of hope. For instance, Beijing's refusal to bow to US pressure regarding the participation of Hamas representatives during the 2006 China-Arab Cooperation Forum is one example of China's popular allure in the region.

Recent public opinion polls indicate that Arabs see the United States and Israel—perceived as a surrogate of US power—as the gravest threats to the region. In contrast, Arabs are not threatened by China. Instead, they see an emerging China as a potential opportunity and a welcomed force that should be harnessed to the fullest extent possible. A 2006 Arab public opinion poll conducted by Zogby International and the Brookings Institution showed that China, second only to France, is the country most Arabs would like to see emerge as a superpower. The United States placed fifth in the same poll, behind France, China, Pakistan, and Germany.[25] The Zogby-Brookings poll, however, indicates that Arabs would prefer to live in the United States instead of the PRC, and also feel that America provides more freedom for its citizens. Arabs would also prefer to see their family members study in the United States.[26] Such responses bolster the notion that even though China would be a preferred superpower, owing to its perceived support of popular Arab and Muslim positions, its policy of noninterference in domestic affairs, and its lack of a colonial legacy in the region, Arabs still admire the American culture of personal and political freedom.

Despite China's lackluster record on human rights and civil liberties—to include systematic oppression of the minority ethnic Uighur Muslim community—Arabs would prefer to see a Chinese, as opposed to an American, hegemon. This suggests that popular perceptions of Beijing's potential as a positive force in the minds of Arabs transcend nostalgic sentiments and ideology and are rooted in calculated strategic thinking based on the premise that a strong China can rival the United States, thus benefiting the region as a whole. China's critical stance toward the war in Iraq, US efforts to curtail Iran's nuclear program, and the crisis in Sudan, coupled with its traditionally vocal support for the Palestinian struggle for an independent state, all enhance its stature in the region as a partner worth courting. This is the case despite the PRC's controversial defense ties with Israel.

# Sino-Israeli Ties

The governments of China and Israel appear eager to see Sino-Israeli economic and cultural relations expand. China represents a highly lucrative market for Israel, while Israel is a source of high-technology goods and services for China.[27] Though Beijing is keen on enhancing its standing amongst the Arab states and Iran, the regime is also hesitant to alienate Israel, forcing the PRC to conduct a delicate diplomatic balancing act in the region.

Beijing's historic support for the Palestinian nationalist cause delayed the development of the Sino-Israel relationship for nearly half a century. As the Cold War drew to a close, however, diplomatic relations between Israel and the PRC were established in 1992, with Israel opening a consulate in Shanghai in 1994. Throughout the 1990s, China and Israel cultivated a diplomatic and economic relationship grounded in cultural and economic cooperation and exchange. Trade agreements were signed in October 1992. In 1993 the two powers signed an agricultural memorandum of understanding, resulting in the subsequent creation of Sino-Israeli cooperative agricultural institutions in China, and a cultural exchange agreement.[28]

The Sino-Israeli economic relationship has flourished since the early 1990s. In 1992, annual trade between the two countries was approximately $50 million. By 2005, annual trade had grown to nearly $3 billion.[29]

Today, China is Israel's largest Asian economic partner, with Sino-Israeli trade representing the world's sixth-largest bilateral trade relationship. In November 2006, China's charge d'affaires of the PRC's embassy to Israel, Zhang Xiao'an, announced at an economic conference held in Tel Aviv that "we expect the [Sino-Israeli trade] volume to reach $5 billion by 2008."[30]

The arms trade is a critical aspect of the Sino-Israeli relationship. Much has been written about the transfer of Israeli arms to China, which began in the early 1990s and continues today, despite significant pressure placed on Israel by the United States to cease the transfer of advanced defense platforms and technology to the Chinese military. Israel and the United States have clashed repeatedly over arms sales to China, based primarily on America's concerns that advanced Israeli platforms will contribute to China's military advantage over Taiwan and US forces operating in the Pacific. Given China's history of providing weapon systems to Iran and US rivals in the region and beyond, there is legitimate concern that advanced Israeli weapons and technology could, by way of Beijing, end up in the hands of America's opponents on the battlefield.

American disapproval has repeatedly failed to stop Israel's transfer of weapons to China. In 2000, the United States blocked the sale of the Phalcon early warning radar system.[31] Following this incident, Israel promised to be more discerning in its sale of weapon systems to Beijing, but in 2004 the United States had to force Israel to abandon a deal in which China would receive spare parts for advanced Harpy Killer unmanned drones.[32] Though Israel temporarily suspended its arms sales to China, in March 2006 Israel's Ministry of Defense announced that these sales had resumed.[33]

It would appear that Israel is willing to risk angering the United States, as Beijing, flush with hard currency and eager to improve its military posture in East Asia and beyond, is willing to pay top dollar for advanced Israeli weapons. Beijing seems also willing to risk Arab disapproval. Meanwhile, Arab regimes are willing to overlook Sino-Israeli ties in return for closer economic and political relations with China. This is mainly due to the PRC's repeated rhetorical and diplomatic support for Palestine and the Middle East peace process, as well as the recognition by Arab nations that the Sino-Israeli relationship is grounded on little more than economics.

## Hard Realities

Though regional governments are eager to facilitate China's emergence as an influential presence in the Middle East, these same regimes also understand Beijing's severe limitations in terms of its ability to act as a credible counterweight to the United States in the near future. Ruling autocrats are well aware that their own strategic interests continue to be best served through close ties to America and understand that Beijing has a vital interest in friendly and constructive relations with Washington.[34] America is China's single largest trading partner, with annual trade estimated to reach $300 billion by 2010. In fact, the PRC is nowhere near matching previous Soviet involvement in the region in the political and military spheres, and there is little evidence indicating that it intends to challenge the United States in this regard in the foreseeable future.

Given the current trajectory of Sino-Arab relations and the reality of Chinese intentions and capabilities, Arab hopes for reaping the benefits of a strategic partnership with China are as likely to bring disappointment as they are continued optimism. For instance, the PRC's efforts to expand its military capabilities,

to include developing the ability to project power outside of its immediate East Asian sphere of influence in a sustained manner, are well-documented. Beijing is far from achieving the ability to challenge the United States in the Middle East, even in a limited capacity. Moreover, Chinese strategists are busy navigating the complex geopolitics of East Asia, namely Taiwan, Japan, the Korean Peninsula, and increasingly Central and South Asia, not to mention the robust US military presence in the Pacific.

Given this background, it is unlikely that China will redirect its military focus toward the Middle East in the foreseeable future. In reality, so long as energy and goods originating in the region continue to reach China, Beijing is likely to acquiesce to the US-dominated status quo. There is also evidence that the expansion of Beijing's influence in some developing countries is evoking resentment. For example, growing concerns are the influx of cheap Chinese consumer goods undermining local producers and sellers, questionable labor practices employed by many Chinese firms in their hiring practices, and poor treatment of local workers.[35] In recent years, Chinese workers in Sudan, Nigeria, Pakistan, and elsewhere have increasingly been targeted by militant groups angered by the growing Chinese presence.

Nevertheless, Arab leaders continue to see the utility of cultivating closer relations with Beijing both for domestic and international consumption in the hope of facilitating greater Chinese inroads into the region. Increasingly, leaders throughout the Middle East are coming to realize that they can no longer depend solely on the United States as a patron—the political costs are getting higher as the American military presence in the region grows, and popular discontent is becoming more hazardous to the life of the regimes. In this context, closer ties to China provide a safety valve, a way for the regimes to positively address their images as American puppet states while continuing to reap the benefits of political and economic support from a powerful regional actor.

## Conclusion

The burgeoning Sino-Arab relationship is poised to develop and expand in the twenty-first century, providing tremendous benefits on many levels to all parties involved. More robust Chinese inroads into the Middle East are being encouraged by both state actors and local public opinion, thus facilitating stronger ties across social, political, economic, and cultural sectors. Although the United States is certain to retain its preeminent position in the region in the foreseeable future, Arabs are increasingly optimistic regarding the rise of China. Beijing will continue to harness this momentum to enhance its position in the Middle East and will be able to count on many willing partners eager for an alternative to the United States.

China will continue to rely on soft power to enhance its image and influence in the Middle East. As Beijing becomes more confident, it is also likely to leverage its growing influence in the form of more ambitious diplomatic objectives impacting the region, and ultimately the US presence. Though China's strategy does not pose a direct near-term threat to American hegemony, Washington cannot afford to ignore the unavoidable truth of the Arab world's growing interest in China's potential.

As America's popularity and influence in the greater Middle East wane, Beijing watches and waits, eager and increasingly able to establish a greater presence in this vital region.

# NOTES

1. Xinhua News Agency, "Hu Vows to Cement China-Arab Cooperation," 1 June 2006.

2. Xinhua News Agency, "Interview: AL Chief Hails Arab-Sino Relations," 27 May 2006.

3. The term "greater Middle East" generally refers to the countries of the Arab world, together with Pakistan, Afghanistan, Iran, Israel, and Turkey.

4. Flynt Leverett and Jeffrey Bader, "Managing China-U.S. Energy Competition in the Middle East," *The Washington Quarterly,* 29 (Winter 2005–06), 187–201.

5. Julian Madsen, "China's Policy in the Gulf Region: From Neglect to Necessity," *Power and Interest News Report,* 27 October 2006.

6. For an overview of China's environmental crisis, see The World Bank, *Cost of Pollution in China: Economic Estimates of Physical Damages* (Washington: The World Bank, February 2007), http://go.worldbank.org/FFCJVBTP40.

7. Xinhua News Agency, "China, Arab States to Hold First Oil Meeting," 1 June 2006.

8. Although China's growing inroads into the greater Middle East attract the most attention, its rival India also seeks to enhance its position as an emerging global power by expanding its presence in the strategically vital region. See C. Christine Fair, "India and Iran: New Delhi's Balancing Act," *The Washington Quarterly,* 30 (Summer 2007), 145–59.

9. For more details on the development of China's relations with Iran, see J. Brandon Gentry, "The Dragon and the Magi: Burgeoning Sino-Iranian Relations in the 21st Century," *The China and Eurasia Forum Quarterly,* 3 (November 2005), 111–25. For an overview of China's strategic interests in Central Asia, see Xuanli Liao, "Central Asia and China's Energy Security," *The China and Eurasia Forum Quarterly,* 4 (November 2006), 61–69.

10. Dingli Shen, "Iran's Nuclear Ambitions Test China's Wisdom," *The Washington Quarterly,* 29 (Spring 2006), 55–66.

11. See 1 November 2006 "Appeal by Amnesty International to the Chinese Government on the Occasion of the China-Africa Summit for Development and Cooperation," www.amnesty.org/en/report/info/AFR54/072/2006.

12. Anouar Abdel-Malek, "China's Message to the Arabs," *Al-Ahram Weekly On-line* (Cairo), 708 (16–22 September 2004).

13. See report based on presentation by Dr. Mamoun Fandy, "Energy Security: Implications for U.S. China-Middle East Relations, China vs. U.S.: A View from the Arab World" (Houston, Tex.: Rice University, James A. Baker III Institute for Public Policy, 18 July 2005), www.rice.edu/energy/publications/docs/SIIS_MFANDY_ChinaUSArabWorld_071805.pdf.

14. See "Annapolis: Not-So-Great Expectations," *The Economist Online,* 28 November 2007, www.economist.com/displayStory.cfm?story_id=10202105&fsrc=RSS.

15. Shlomo Shamir, "U.S. Withdraws UN Annapolis Resolution After Israel Objects," *Haaretz* (Tel Aviv), 3 December 2007.

16. Leon Hadar, "Innocent Abroad: Karen Hughes's Mission Impossible," *The American Conservative,* 19 December 2005.

17. Discussions with members and supporters of the Egyptian Muslim Brotherhood by Chris Zambelis, Cairo, Egypt, February and March 2006. In general, democratic reform-minded Islamist opposition groups such as the Egyptian Muslim Brotherhood see China as a positive force based on its perceived potential to check US power in the Middle East and elsewhere in the world.

18. See "Arab Attitudes Towards Political and Social Issues, Foreign Policy and the Media," public opinion poll conducted by Shibley Telhami and Zogby International, October 2005, www.bsos.umd.edu/sadat/pub/unweighted.htm.

19. "Islam as a Political Issue in China," *Asia Times Online,* 10 February 2007.

20. For more details on the central role of "soft power" in Chinese diplomacy, see Joshua Kurlantzick, *Charm Offensive: How China's Soft Power is Transforming the World* (New Haven, Conn.: Yale Univ. Press, 2007).

21. Chris Zambelis, "The Strategic Implications of Political Liberalization and Democratization in the Middle East," *Parameters,* 35 (Autumn 2005), 87–102.

22. Yitzhak Shichor, "China's Darfur Policy," *China Brief* (Jamestown Foundation), 7 (5 April 2007).

23. Abdel-Malek.

24. "In total 28,389 citizens in Argentina, Australia, Brazil, Canada, Chile, China, Egypt, France, Germany, Great Britain, Greece, Hungary, India, Indonesia, Italy, Kenya, Lebanon, Mexico, Nigeria, Philippines, Poland, Portugal, Russia, South Korea, Turkey, United Arab Emirates, and the United States were interviewed between 3 November 2006 and 16 January 2007. Polling was conducted for the BBC World Service by the international polling firm GlobeScan and its research partners in each country. In 10 of the 27 countries, the sample was limited to major urban areas. Given that country ratings were given by half-samples, the margin of error per country ranges from +/−3.1 to 4.9 percent." "Israel and Iran Share Most Negative Ratings in Global Poll," BBC World Service poll, 6 March 2007, www.globescan.com/news_archives/bbccntryview/.

25. "2006 Annual Arab Public Opinion Survey" (Washington: Brookings Institution, Saban Center for Middle East Policy, 8 February 2007), http://brookings.edu/views/speeches/telhami20070208.pdf.

26. Ibid.

27. Yoram Evron, "Sino-Israeli Relations: Opportunities and Challenges," *Strategic Assessment,* 10 (August 2007).

28. See overview of Sino-Israeli relations on the official statement of the Embassy of the People's Republic of China in Israel.

29. Xinhua News Agency, "China and Israel—The Best is Yet to Come," 13 July 2006.

30. Xinhua News Agency, "China-Israel Trade Volume Ranks No. 1 Amongst Israel's Asian Trade Partners," 8 November 2006.

31. P. R. Kumaraswamy, "Israel-China Relations and the Phalcon Controversy," *Middle East Policy,* 12 (Summer 2005), 93–103.

32. Miles A. Pomper, "U.S., Israel Seek to Cut Deal on China Arms Sales," *Arms Control Today,* July/August 2005, www .armscontrol.org/act/2005_07-08/IsraelChina_ArmsSales.asp.

33. Alon Ben-David, "Israel to Resume Security Exports to China," *Jane's Defence Weekly,* 8 March 2006.

34. Wang Jisi, "China's Search for Stability with America," *Foreign Affairs,* 84 (September/October 2005), www .foreignaffairs.org/20050901faessay84504/wang-jisi/china-s-search-for-stability-with-america.html.

35. James Traub, "China's African Adventure," *The New York Times Magazine,* 19 November 2006.

**Mr. Chris Zambelis** is an associate with Helios Global, Inc., a political and security risk analysis firm. He is a graduate of New York University and has a master's in Foreign Service from Georgetown University.

**Mr. Brandon Gentry** specializes in Middle East politics and political movements as an associate at Helios Global, Inc. He received his undergraduate degree in History from the College of William and Mary and his master's in Middle Eastern Studies from the University of Texas at Austin.

From *Parameters,* by Chris Zambelis and Brandon Gentry, Spring 2008, pp. 60–72. Published by U.S. Army War College. Reprinted by permission.

# The Human Rights of Women and Social Transformation in the Arab Middle East

Hayat Alvi

Although recently much attention has been paid to signs of reform and liberalization in the Arab world, there is also considerable evidence of trends in regressive social transformation. One such manifestation is the prevailing attitudes and social policies that continue to deny women their fundamental human rights and freedoms. Arab women continue to suffer major deficiencies in both oil-rich and poorer Arab countries.

There are growing forces of resistance in the Arab world to one of the major factors of progressive social transformation, the human rights of women. Two interrelated variables account for such resistance to the incorporation of women's human rights into domestic agendas: (1) the ideological and attitudinal variables; and (2) the empirical realities.

The ideological/attitudinal-based resistance[1] is due to two factors: first, to a dangerous trend observable in the Arab/Islamic world toward extreme regression, as opposed to progression. The second factor has more to do with cultural and nationalistic attitudes, which engender a degree of suspicion towards, and perhaps outright rejection in principle of, anything perceived as Western-modeled human development programs. Such suspicious attitudes are particularly aimed at women's human rights issues.

The empirical realities are mostly derived from the groundbreaking *Arab Human Development Report 2002* (AHDR)[2] and the *AHDR 2003*. Specifically, the empowerment of women, one of the three deficiencies[3] that the *AHDR 2002* identifies in the Arab region's overall human development diagnosis, is closely examined. The analysis of women's empowerment focuses on general health and nutrition indicators, education, employment, political participation, human welfare, and domestic policies and whether or not they address the rights and freedoms of women. Egypt serves as a case study, while other Arab countries are also given as examples.

It is important to note that the empirical realities reflect the glaring deficiencies in the human rights of women in the Arab world often because of the ideological/attitudinal resistance to women's empowerment. Hence, the two levels of analysis (i.e. ideological/attitudinal variables and empirical realities) are interrelated and interdependent. Clearly, without ideological and attitudinal changes regarding women's rights, there cannot be positive empirical changes in the status of women.

Moreover, without positive empirical changes in the status of women, there can be no progressive social transformation for the societies as a whole.

## Social Transformation: Trends of Extreme Regression

Social transformation may involve changes in social structures, labor relations, urbanization, attitudes, beliefs, views, and values, freedoms and rights, the quality of education, competitive and comparative advantages, and effective governance. The process may also involve political transformation. According to Samuel Huntington, political transformation correlates with modernization: "Modernization in practice always involves change in and usually the disintegration of a traditional political system."[4] Moreover, modernization can be defined as "a change in the attitudes, values, and expectations of people from those associated with the traditional world to those common to the modern world."[5] This process requires economic development and social mobilization. Huntington asserts that social mobilization refers to "changes in the aspirations of individuals, groups, and societies," and economic development refers to "changes in their capabilities."[6] Most of the Arab/Islamic world is characterized by coexisting religious and political authoritarianism, rendering socio-political changes in traditional systems more difficult. In fact, traditions are deeply entrenched, as reflected in the region's social policies.

### Ideological Trends

Usually, a country's social policies represent the prevalent attitudes and ideologies of that society. Generally, the social policies of the Arab/Muslim world are based on religion (Islam) in one way or another. The religious influence on social policies can be subtle or clearly identifiable, depending on the country's national political ideology. If it is a theocracy, like Saudi Arabia or Iran, then religion plays a far more prominent role in social policymaking.

The Arab/Muslim world finds itself in a struggle in dealing with change. There are forces trying to pull society in the historically traditional direction, hence rejecting those elements that are deemed by them to be "un-Islamic." Such unacceptable elements are usually perceived to be from Western origins. There are also the opposing modernists, referred to as reformists. These elements generally aspire to secularize and modernize political and social systems. Then there are various moderate elements found in between. They would like to harmonize the two opposing forces: the orthodox and the reformists. The idea is to be progressive and modern without compromising one's socio-cultural heritage, beliefs, and identity.

Post-Cold War trends in the Arab/Muslim world indicate one of three directions of transformation: regression, stagnation (or a static situation), and progression.

Progressive social transformation is imperative for making adjustments to the changes and challenges of modernity. Stagnation is a motionless state, in other words, there is no movement toward any direction. However, some traditional societies have opted for *regressive* transformation in reaction to the demands and forces they face, hence going in the *reverse* direction, instead of moving forward. Regressive transformation involves an attempt to return to the past in an effort to preserve one's cultural, linguistic, religious, and socio-historical heritage. In that case, an appeal is made to stimulate cultural and religious irredentism in order to persuade the masses sharing a common ethnic or religious identity that their identity and beliefs are being threatened, and the only way to preserve and protect them is by reverting to the beliefs and practices of the past. This is the way proposed to conquer the challenges and pressures of globalization.

Such has been the trend in the Islamic world, epitomized by the fierce ideological competition among Islamists in response to the 1979 Soviet invasion of Afghanistan, which unleashed an orthodox Islamic militancy that, aside from accepting modern military technology, has wholly rejected symbols of modernization. The Islamic religious establishment has adopted similar positions, preaching to the masses ideas and principles that are marked departures from the true spirit of Islam, as well as from the spirit of tolerance and learning observed during earlier Islamic history by prominent Muslim jurists, scholars, and institutions.

What the traditional Islamic establishment calls for today is more reminiscent of the patriarchal attitudes, practices, and beliefs that actually *predate* Islam, in many cases rendering to contemporary Islamic societies an anachronistic medieval aura, totally incompatible with modernity. Intellectual discourse and rational thinking or reasoning are discouraged, even reviled by the ultra-orthodox establishment. In this case, such societies may be headed toward extreme regression.

The early 20th century marked the collapse of the Ottoman Empire. As post-colonial nation-states evolved in the Middle East, the institution of the *ulama* had to be suppressed and controlled by the new governments. This marks the beginning of the stagnation of what once was progressive Islamic discourse. This stagnation constitutes the suppression of intellectualism and religious revival in the form of progressive reinterpretation of Islamic principles and laws. The status quo established by the newly formed governments, which were typically dictatorial at least in this regard, precipitated this stagnation. In fact, economies stagnated along with socio-cultural, religious, and educational institutions. The leader's whim was the rule of the day, which proved detrimental to the region's development. Consider the alarming statistic in the *Arab Human Development Report 2002* (AHDR): the GDP in all Arab countries combined stood at $531.2 billion in 1999—less than that of a single European country, Spain ($595.5 billion).[7]

During the era between the coming of Islam and the 20th century there were many times when Islamic history was imbued with the spirit of tolerance, greater scrutiny of religious laws and of leadership, profound scientific and intellectual achievements, and interfaith dialogue. This period of Islamic history was very progressive in the context of its time, but it did not last.

Although many Islamic movements in the modern era claim that they are trying to reinstate this seemingly progressive segment of Islamic history, in reality they propose extreme regression in the direction of the *pre*-Islamic era. Ultra-orthodox Islamic movements and ideologies, such as Wahhabism, the Taliban, Salafiyya, and branches of the Muslim Brotherhood, Islamic Jihad, Deobandism, and their offshoots, try to replicate pre-Islamic social structures and apply them to the modern era. These social structures encompass a male-dominated authoritarianism entrenched in an ultra-orthodox, literal implementation of socio-religious policies.

Despite their supposed passion for "justice," wherein the weak and oppressed would be rescued by the strong and virtuous following the laws of religion, such groups and ideologies see nothing wrong with the use of force against even the downtrodden in order to exact their compliance and/or achieve political goals. Furthermore, their attitudes and behavior towards women and religious minorities have been nothing less than disgraceful. In reality, then, they are not far from resembling the pre-Islamic pagan Arab societies, characterized by fierce authoritarianism and victimization of weaker tribes and of women. The only difference now is that these groups and ideologies have been using Islam as a pretext for their socio-religious authoritarianism.

There are numerous examples of Islamic groups and ideologies that are in extreme regression, such as Wahhabism, the Salafi movement, and various Islamist militant groups.[8] In comparison, those individuals, groups, and institutions promoting progression are typically marginalized and suppressed. Therefore, a new contemporary Islamic renaissance, which would strive to reconcile the challenges of modernization and globalization with Islam, has yet to take place. The religious authorities in the Arab/Muslim world are hard at work resisting the pressures for reform, reinterpretation, and liberalization by promoting authoritarianism in religion. The public appears to be reinforcing these beliefs and practices.

Especially since the September 11th attacks against the United States, the Muslim world has experienced a strong sense of insecurity, affected by the perception of being under siege because of the "war on terrorism." The siege is often interpreted as not so much a war on terrorism as it is a war against Islam and the Muslim world. The fundamental beliefs and principles of the Muslim world are perceived to be threatened, which also means, since Islam prescribes the believers' way of life, the Muslims' entire lifestyle is perceived under threat. Add to that the fact that Islam is a very visible faith, in terms of dress code, congregational prayers, and the like, which fuel the Muslims' sense of being vulnerable targets to racism, prejudice, and racial profiling by the authorities, especially in the West. The end result is a resurgence of—and further entrenchment in—one's Islamic beliefs and lifestyle, in order to secure them from the looming threats the modern world poses to them.

## Authoritarianism in Arab/Islamic Societies

Although the psychological impact of the September 11th attacks and subsequent "war on terrorism" on Arabs and Muslims has been severe, these developments were not the primary catalysts that precipitated this trend of authoritarianism. Throughout the twentieth century the Arab/Islamic world has faced a major challenge in adjusting to the forces of modernization, and more acutely globalization. The more traditional societies have wed many of their traditional tribal and/or cultural customs and practices with Islam. These societies have been particularly resistant to the forces of modernization, especially involving the empowerment of women and certain judicial processes and penal codes. At the same time, the Arab Middle East has long been characterized by political authoritarianism that has traditionally excluded not only women, but any opposition groups.

## Religious Authoritarianism

The spread of religious authoritarianism can be attributed in no small part to Saudi Arabia. Despite its vast oil wealth and high-tech conveniences, Saudi Arabia remains the most draconian society in terms of Islamic social policy. Saudi practices and beliefs resemble the primitive *pre-Islamic* Arab customs and mentalities more than mainstream Islam. The Saudi interpretation of authoritarian Islam, then, is actually an example of extreme regression towards pre-Islamic times, far from embracing the real spirit and essence of Islam which promote tolerance. The Taliban of Afghanistan took this approach to such extremes that even the Saudis had to ask them to tone down their excessively violent enforcement of Islam.

Like Marxist movements in the West, radical Islamists have developed the concept of cultural hegemony as a way to seek control over societies. By gaining control of schools, media, clerical circles, social networks, and the overall direction of discourse, they seek to impose their respective versions of Islamic ideology, which they are totally convinced constitutes the only true and accurate interpretation of Islamic law. Other ideologies that differ from theirs or even open debate are wrong and must be purged.

The Saudi effort to export Wahhabism is an international version of this struggle, which was called a cultural war (kulter kampf) in nineteenth-century Germany. Saudi Arabia's oil wealth gives it the means to gain enormous influence and to fund mosques, schools, and other institutions which spread its version of Islam. The result has been a regression in countries as widespread as Nigeria, Sudan, and Afghanistan, among others. Even in the West, within each Muslim community, this struggle is going on with the Islamists and especially Wahhabi groups having a powerful effect on these evolving societies. In all these cases, the effect is particularly pronounced on matters concerning the rights, freedoms, and available choices possessed by women and girls specifically.

Take France as an example of this struggle in which regressive forces often seem to be determining the direction of events. By April 2004, France had expelled five Muslim clerics spreading extremist interpretations of Islam. In the most recent case, Abdelkader Bouziane was deported "for advocating wife beating, stoning, and other medieval Islamic views at odds with the principles of the modern French state."[9] Even in this case, there is a common link between Bouziane and Saudi Arabia, as he had spent six months in the kingdom before settling and preaching in Venissieux, France. According to a report in the American news program "60 Minutes," "In the [poorer areas where Muslims live], the fundamentalist voices are growing stronger. They are now targeting the disaffected youth in the ghettos. Many of the mosques there are filled with fundamentalist preaching."[10] French-Muslim relations have been further exacerbated due to the recent government ban of Islamic headscarves worn in public schools. But for this to happen there must be in the first place a prevailing view of normative Islam in which women must wear such garments.

The problem that many Western countries, like France, are facing stems from the paucity of well-trained clerics who can properly relate to Muslims living in Western cultures. Many mosque congregations in the West must rely on importing imams from Islamic countries. Numerous such imams espouse "fundamentalist beliefs that grate against Europe's more tolerant societies."[11] Muslim congregations in America and Canada often have the same problems. The current struggle in both Western and Islamic societies is to confront the forces of religious authoritarianism and ideological hegemony, both of which seriously threaten the human rights of women.

In the Muslim ghettos of France, crimes against women have been on the rise. Gangs of young men may rule the streets, in communities where male-dominated Arab traditions and growing religious fundamentalism dictate social policies. According to the "60 Minutes" report, "It's gotten so bad that, today, most of the young women only feel safe if they are covered up, or if they stay at home. Girls who want to look just like other French girls are considered provocative, asking for trouble."[12] Rape and gang rape have become common, and the victims are usually ostracized due to the stigma of dishonor upon losing one's virginity. A descendent of Algerian immigrants, Samira Bellil, was gang raped in one of the French ghettos. According to the report, "When Bellil's family discovered that she had been raped, they weren't sympathetic. They threw her out onto the streets."[13] Moreover, statistics show that "at least 70,000 young women have come under pressure to accept arranged marriages, according to France's Commission for Integration."[14] Consequently, there exists a growing dichotomy between the male-dominated traditions among the Muslim population in France, and secular, modernist Western social norms and policies that characterize French and European culture.

As a result, the image of male-dominated Arab societies in and outside of the Middle East region continues to be perceived as anachronistic and grossly authoritarian. This is the case not only in terms of socio-cultural policies, but also in the area of politics. Aside from the damage suffered by the image of Muslims and Arabs as well as the possibility that such norms might be imposed on the local communities, there is the danger that the West might accept such practices as proper, normative, and traditional Islam.

## Political Authoritarianism

Political authoritarianism has been entrenched in the Arab region, and in most cases continues to exclude women from fair and free political participation. Although a handful of Arab countries recently have made some adjustments to their political systems so as to allow women and opposition groups to participate, the Arab Middle East as a whole is still a long way off from democratizing. Politics remains a male-dominated profession, and the ratio of women politicians to men is significantly small, especially compared to other developing regions.

Bahrain and Morocco have made some positive changes in terms of including women in politics, and in January 2003 Egypt appointed the first woman judge. In Qatar, the first woman cabinet minister has been appointed. However, the all-male Kuwaiti parliament still opts to exclude women from political processes. Indeed, only about 15 percent of Kuwaiti citizens can vote.[15] The Kuwait Information Office states that "on May 16, 1999, the Amir unexpectedly issued a decree allowing women the right to vote and to hold public office."[16] But it does not mention that the Kuwaiti parliament rejected the decree and women still do not have the right to vote. Although on May 16, 2004, the Council of Ministers approved a new women's suffrage bill, in May 2005 the plan to approve women's suffrage was postponed. The Islamist and conservative elements in parliament abstained from voting, which led to the postponement of the vote on the bill.

The struggle for democratization and enfranchisement across the board in the Arab Middle East is ongoing. In each country the political competition between ruling parties and various opposition groups representing diverse ideologies and platforms has been fierce, and at times violent. In such a scenario, women's human rights and empowerment issues become marginalized. It becomes the task of individual activists and nongovernmental organizations (NGOs) working for women's human rights issues, along with occasional external pressures for reform, to bring respective governments to make appropriate policy changes. Hence, the process has been very gradual. As long as the plight of women remains out of public view,

the regimes in the region proceed with business as usual. Once the plight of women is publicized, often dramatically, then the governments try to make what are usually cosmetic changes.

Yet this strategy is very damaging for their societies. The *2002 AHDR* elaborates on this issue of the "freedom deficit":

> While de jure acceptance of democracy and human rights is enshrined in constitutions, legal codes and government pronouncements, de facto implementation is often neglected and, in some cases, deliberately disregarded. In most cases, the governance pattern is characterized by a powerful executive branch that exerts significant control over all other branches of the state, being in some cases free from institutional checks and balances. Representative democracy is not always genuine and sometimes absent. Freedoms of expression and association are frequently curtailed. Obsolete norms of legitimacy prevail.[17]

Very seldom do governments in the Arab/Islamic world try to go against the religious establishment. Overall, since there is no separation of religion and politics in Islam, issues like social transformation and reform will almost always be politicized and "religionized" in varying degrees. But restrictions on freedom also suit the interests of the regimes themselves. This combination of pressure from the religious leadership, a highly conservative society, and regime interests has a devastating force that is very hard for any internal force to compete with or even counter.

## Islam versus Liberalism

It is not in the scope of this paper to examine the inherent contradictions between authoritarianism and individualism in Islamic theology and law.[18] What warrants investigation here is the incompatibility of the current authoritarian trends observable in Arab/Islamic societies with modernization and progress. The current trends indicate a clash between Islam and liberalism, that is, individualism. Liberal democracy and ideals seemingly have secured a predominant position as the modern global ideology since the collapse of the Soviet Union. Despite the countless emphases on individualism and individual accountability in Islamic theology, the religious establishment in Islamic societies has called for authoritarianism, orthodoxy, and greater social compliance. More often than not, the voices of the liberal reformists in the Islamic world have been marginalized, and in many cases those advocating progressive reforms have faced threats from religious zealots.

Such behavior of the religious establishment, which usually attempts to assert its own authority in order to maintain the status quo of the power hierarchy, undermines individualism. This results in the denial of liberal ideals like tolerance, and especially that of individual choices and freedoms. The pressures of social compliance and conformity are exerted zealously, at the behest of the religious establishment. These pressures are also enforced at the familial level, usually in the context of a patriarchal authority. This authoritarian framework allows parents to impose decisions on their children in matters concerning what would normally be the individual's personal choice.

The trend in Islamic societies that has been most harmful to individualism seems to be institutionalized totalitarianism enforcing compliance with religious obligations, such as prayers, fasting, dress codes, gender segregation, and the like, all of which further erodes individual choices and freedoms, and only promotes intolerance. The most dangerous manifestation of this extreme authoritarianism is the institution of the so-called religious police, better known as the department of the "Promotion of Virtue and Prevention of Vice" (*Amr Bil Maruf wa Nai Al Munkar*) employed in Saudi Arabia and Iran, and in Afghanistan during the Taliban era.

## *Exclusive versus Inclusive Policies*

The socio-political policies of most countries in the Middle East region have been policies of exclusion rather than inclusion. The former (i.e., exclusive policies) coincides with regression. The latter coincides with progressive development. By exclusion it is meant that a number of laws and policies exclude certain social groups from benefiting from rights that are granted to others in society. For example, citizenship, residency, and immigration laws in various Middle Eastern countries continue to be exclusive. In particular, they penalize women for marrying non-nationals, even Arab men from other countries in the region. Only recently Egypt changed its citizenship laws to recognize the children of women married to non-Egyptians as Egyptian nationals. However, the bureaucratic procedures for this status change are so taxing that the print media have questioned whether it is even worth the trouble.

A great deal of exclusive policies stem from religious influences on policymakers and political institutions. For example, screening books and the media by censors, and banning items, are often decisions made by religious institutions on the grounds of religious sensitivities. Consequently, religious authorities decide what is included in and excluded from public access. Political authorities do the same with regard to the print and broadcast media. State-run newspapers and TV channels are subject to the decisions of the political authorities regarding what to include and exclude in the dissemination of news and information. Governments have also been trying to control the flow of information on the Internet. Exclusive policies, then, tend to predominate within the region.

## Rejection of Western Ideas

Surprisingly, resistance to progressive change does not come from only the mullahs and orthodox religious establishment. Many highly educated intellectuals in the Arab/Islamic world have succumbed to their inherently suspicious attitudes and mentalities regarding social reforms. For example, in December 2002, a panel discussion was held at an American university in the Middle East. The topic was the *2002 Arab Human Development Report* (AHDR), and two of its authors served as the panelists in addition to two scholars who critiqued the report. The authors of the AHDR concluded that the Middle East region suffers from three major deficits: (1) a deficit of knowledge, (2) a deficit of women's empowerment, and (3) the suppression of freedoms and rights.

One of the panelists who critiqued the report responded to the findings with a suggestion that women's empowerment is not a priority, since wealth and power can trickle down to them once there is sufficient economic growth and prosperity by means of implementing economic reforms and liberalization. Quoting him directly:

> It could be argued, for instance, that the question of women's empowerment should not have been included . . . [as a problem] calling for priority action. For improving the status of Arab women is better regarded as an outcome rather than as a condition of human development. Women's empowerment is bound to increase [from] . . . improvements in general economic, social, and political conditions rather than [through] women's solutions, political decisions, or legislation.[19]

The audience also reacted to the report's UNDP sponsorship. Some in the audience felt that this was Western-sponsored research, and it gives Western-modeled advice for progressive change in the Arab Middle East, and therefore, should be rejected. Specifically, a renowned Egyptian economist, Galal Amin, remarked that: "the [AHDR] adopted criteria for human development which are directly copied from the West," while disregarding cultural sensitivities.[20]

The two authors of the AHDR responded to these reactions by pointing out that the formula for human development is *universal,* not Western per se. Responding to Galal Amin, Nader Fergany, the lead author of the AHDR, said, "Human rights are the crowning achievement of the human race," adding that the cultural issue should not be taken too far.[21]

Moreover, Rima Khalaf-Hunaidi, a coauthor of the AHDR, challenged the suggestion that economic growth will take care of women's empowerment, and therefore the latter need not be a priority for development in the Arab world. She retorted:

> On women's empowerment . . . Dr. Issawy said that maybe it shouldn't be a priority, and maybe economic growth will solve it. Ladies and gentlemen, look at our region. You'll see that countries with the highest per capita income are countries where women suffer most. They are countries who have voted to deprive women of their rights. They are countries where women do not have even citizenship, and women are deprived of the basics. So I do not think that economic growth and development in and of itself will solve the women's disempowerment issue, and I actually believe that it is something that we should give priority for, not only because it's a human rights issue, and because women should be entitled to equal citizenship, because I actually believe that a society deprived of half its citizens will find it extremely difficult to move forward.[22]

What is ironic is that women's rights were in fact a priority in the early Islamic period, as the first legal injunction in the Qur'an protected females from infanticide (see Surah 81: 1-14).[23] It seems that this is conveniently overlooked by many in the region who feel threatened by women's empowerment. Today, the promotion of women's empowerment is often viewed as a Western

**Table 1**  Life Expectancy (years), the Arab Region

| Males | | Females | |
|---|---|---|---|
| **1950–55** | **1990–95** | **1950–55** | **1990–95** |
| 40.5 | 62.6 | 42.6 | 65.2 |

Source: *The Arab Human Development Report 2002.*

**Table 2**  Infant Mortality (per thousand) in Egypt

| | Year | Males | Females | Urban | Rural | Total |
|---|---|---|---|---|---|---|
| **EGYPT** | 2000 | 55 | 54.5 | 43.1 | 61.8 | 43.5 |

Source: *The Arab Human Development Report 2002.*

**Table 3**  Maternal Mortality Ratio (MMR) per 100,000 Live Births, 1985–99

| Country | MMR |
|---|---|
| Bahrain | 46 |
| Kuwait | 5 |
| UAE | 3 |
| Qatar | 10 |
| Libya | 75 |
| Saudi Arabia | N/A |
| Lebanon | 100 |
| Oman | 14 |
| Tunisia | 70 |
| Jordan | 41 |
| Algeria | 220 |
| Syria | 110 |
| Egypt | 170 |
| Morocco | 230 |
| Sudan | 550 |
| Yemen | 350 |
| Djibouti | N/A |

Source: *The Human Development Report 2002: Deepening Democracy in a Fragmented World.*

cultural import that threatens to demolish the male-dominated power structure. Furthermore, those societies that are in extreme regression do not hesitate to use violence to exact compliance. They are examples of *coercive* social transformation in the reverse direction. In such scenarios, women are usually the first to be punished, and the last on the priorities list, if listed at all.

## Empirical Realities

Some of the afflictions that continue to plague women in the Arab Middle East include poverty, illiteracy, poor health and nutrition, inequality and discrimination in various spheres of life, and serious deficiencies in human development in general. This is especially the case for women in Arab countries not endowed with oil wealth. The *AHDR 2002* provides some statistics with regard to women's human development. Table 1 illustrates the life expectancy figures for females and males in the Arab region.

According to Table 1, the life expectancy of males in the Arab region rose by 22.1 years over a period of 40 years. The life expectancy of females in the Arab region increased by 22.6 years for the same period. According to the *AHDR 2002,* the global average increase in the difference between the life expectancy of males and females is by 4 years.[24] This indicates room for improvement for women's life expectancy in the Arab world since, according to the figures, the gender difference in the increase is only 2.6 years [i.e. 65.2 years females—62.6 years males for the 1990–95 period]. One way to do so, as the *AHDR* mentions, is by reducing maternal mortality rates in the region [see Table 3].

Looking at our case study, Egypt, the life expectancy of males for the period 1950–55 was 41.2 years, and for the period 1990–95 it was 62.4 years, an increase by 21.2 years. For Egyptian females, in the years 1950–55, the life expectancy was

43.6 years, and for 1990–95, it was 64.8 years, an increase by 21.2 years.[25] The gender difference for life expectancy in Egypt is 2.4 years for the 1990–95 period. Table 2 provides Egypt's infant mortality rates per thousand.

Although Egypt has seen some improvements in reducing infant mortality rates over the last few decades, by development standards its rates still appear relatively high, in two-digit figures. For the year 1998, Qatar had the lowest figures for male and female infant mortality, at 10.2 and 8.2 respectively. Kuwait's 1996 infant mortality rates were surveyed at 11.9 for males and 10.6 for females. Thus, Qatar and Kuwait had the lowest rates for male and female infant mortality for the period covering the survey analysis, according to the *AHDR 2002.* Yemen had the highest infant mortality rates for the year 1997: 98.4 for males, and 80.0 for females.[26]

The *AHDR 2002* says, "High maternal mortality is a key health challenge facing most Arab countries."[27] The *AHDR* explains that more than half of the countries in the Arab Middle East indicate maternal mortality ratios (MMR) higher than 75 per 100,000 live births, and "as many as a third have an MMR exceeding 200 per 100,000 live births."[28] Given the vast oil wealth of the Gulf Arab countries, the MMR should be much lower than they stand today. The United Arab Emirates (UAE) and Kuwait are the only two Arab countries that have reduced their MMR to global standards: a maximum of five per 100,000 live births.[29] Table 3 provides the MMR figures for the Arab region.

## Table 4  Malnutrition in Infants, 1990–97, and in Children under Five Years of Age, 1995–2000

| Country | Infants with Low Birth Weight (%) | Severely Underweight* | Wasting Moderate & Severe* | Stunting Moderate & Severe* |
|---|---|---|---|---|
| Algeria | 9.0 | 3.0 | 9.0 | 18.0 |
| Bahrain | 6.0 | 2.0 | 5.0 | 10.0 |
| Egypt | 10.0 | 3.0 | 6.0 | 25.0 |
| Iraq | 15.0 | 6.0 | 10.0 | 31.0 |
| Jordan | 10.0 | 1.0 | 2.0 | 8.0 |
| Kuwait | 7.0 | 3.0 | 11.0 | 24.0 |
| Lebanon | 10.0 | 0.0 | 3.0 | 12.0 |
| Libya | 7.0 | 1.0 | 3.0 | 15.0 |
| Morocco | 9.0 | 2.0 | 4.0 | 23.0 |
| Oman | 8.0 | 4.0 | 13.0 | 23.0 |
| Occupied Palestinian Territory | 8.6 | 6.2 | 1.7 | 9.1 |
| Qatar | — | — | 2.0 | 8.0 |
| Saudi Arabia | 7.0 | 3.0 | 11.0 | 20.0 |
| Sudan | 15.0 | 11.0** | 13.0** | 33.0** |
| Syria | 7.0 | 4.0 | 9.0 | 21.0 |
| UAE | 6.0 | 3.0 | 15.0 | 17.0 |
| Yemen | 19.0 | 15.0 | 13.0 | 52.0 |

*Percentage of under-five children.

**Data for a year or period other than those specified in the heading, or differ from the standard definition, or refer to only part of the country.

Source: *The AHDR 2002.*

From Table 3 we can see that Sudan and Yemen have the highest figures for MMR, at 550 and 350 respectively. Also, out of fifteen Arab countries for which we have data, seven have 3-digit MMR figures, and six have double-digit MMR figures. This is a reflection of the major deficiencies in women's health care, especially concerning reproductive health. Five of the countries listed (Bahrain, Qatar, Libya, Oman, and Algeria) have substantial oil wealth, yet they have double-digit MMR figures, except for Algeria's alarming 3-digit MMR (220), which may be due to its ongoing civil war.

Women's health deficiencies are further reflected in nutritional data, which are related to the MMR status described above. Nutritional data are important, because, as George Kent points out, "Women have special nutritional vulnerabilities. For example, iron-deficiency anemia is widespread among women in developing countries, and it leads to high levels of maternal mortality."[30] Women also play a primary role in providing nutrition, care, and health to children. According to Professor Kent, "There is much empirical evidence that societies in which women have status closer to men are likely to suffer less malnutrition, and that women as active agents can have profound effects." Thus far, the Arab Middle East has not met such standards of development, particularly because of the unequal status of women. Analyzing nutrition levels

of women and children is one way to measure the status of women. Table 4 examines malnutrition in infants in the Arab countries.

Yemen has the highest percentage of infants with low birth weight, at 19 percent, followed by Iraq and Sudan, both 15 percent. Egypt has 10 percent of infants with low birth weight. The UAE and Bahrain have the lowest percentage, both 6 percent. Yemen again leads in the category of severely underweight children of less than five years of age, comprising 15 percent. Lebanon records zero cases of severely underweight children under five. Yemen has the highest percentage of children under five suffering from stunting malnutrition, standing at 52 percent. Jordan and Qatar have the lowest rates of stunting malnutrition among under-five children, both 8 percent.

These figures are very telling. Why is it that such a wealthy country as Saudi Arabia has failed to eliminate malnutrition in the form of severely underweight children? In fact, Saudi Arabia and Egypt share the same percentage, 3 percent, in this category, whereas Lebanon, which has suffered a vicious civil war, is showing no cases of severely underweight children. One can argue that Lebanon has allowed more freedoms and empowerment of women, compared to Saudi Arabia and to some extent Egypt. Also, Lebanon does not share the same levels of poverty and population dilemmas as Egypt.

**Table 5** Percentage of Pregnant Women with Anemia

| Country | Percentage of Pregnant Women with Anemia 1975–1991 |
|---|---|
| Algeria | 42 |
| Bahrain | — |
| Egypt | 24 |
| Iraq | 18 |
| Jordan | 50 |
| Kuwait | 40 |
| Lebanon | 49 |
| Morocco | 45 |
| Oman | 54 |
| Qatar | — |
| Saudi Arabia | — |
| Sudan | 36 |
| Syria | — |
| Tunisia | 38 |
| UAE | — |
| Yemen | — |

Source: *The AHDR 2002.*

**Table 6** Education in the Arab Region: Adult Illiteracy Rates (%), 1999

| Country | Number of Illiterate Adults (million) | Males | Females | Both |
|---|---|---|---|---|
| Egypt | 19.4 | 33.9 | 57.2 | 45.4 |
| Bahrain | 0.1 | 9.5 | 17.8 | 12.9 |
| Jordan | 0.3 | 5.5 | 16.6 | 10.8 |
| Arab Region | 57.7 | 26.9 | 51.0 | 38.7 |

Source: *The AHDR 2002.*

**Table 7** Employment: Labor Force Participation Rate in Economic Activity (%), 1997

| Country | Males | Females | Both |
|---|---|---|---|
| Egypt | 51.4 | 22.1 | 37.0 |
| Qatar | 72.0 | | |
| Mauritania | | 39.9 | |
| Oman | | 8.6 | |
| Libya | 43.0 | | |

Source: *The AHDR 2002.*

Table 5 provides data for pregnant women with anemia.

From Table 5 it is evident that the percentage of pregnant women with anemia is considerably high, especially in the oil-rich country of Oman (54 percent). Iraq had the lowest percentage (18 percent) prior to the 1991 Gulf War. Egypt has 24 percent of pregnant women with anemia. Lebanon and Jordan have very high percentages, 49 percent and 50 percent respectively. This is an indication of inadequate nutrition of women. There may be numerous reasons for this, among them educational deficiencies, poor health care, lack of awareness about the nutritional value of foods, and lack of awareness about health and nutrition during prenatal, pregnancy, and postnatal stages. Education is a major factor, and, in fact, some Arab countries have high female illiteracy rates.

For example, Egypt suffers from terrible illiteracy rates. Table 6 shows the illiteracy statistics in the Arab region.

Looking at the data in Table 6, we see that Egypt has a considerably high illiteracy rate, particularly among females, in fact, more than half of the female population. Bahrain and Jordan have comparatively lower illiteracy rates, but for an oil-rich country like Bahrain, the 17.8 percent female illiteracy rate is excessively high. In addition, *none* of the Arab countries has single-digit percentages for adult illiteracy of females. That is an alarming statistic! The gender-based employment ratio is also rather unbalanced, as Table 7 indicates.

From Table 7 it is evident that Egypt has a serious discrepancy in the male-female labor force ratio, a difference of 29.3 percentage points, and this most likely does not account

for females who are considered heads of households and those involved in the informal economy. Qatar has the highest male labor force percentage, 72 percent; while Libya has the lowest male percentage, 43 percent. Mauritania has the highest female labor force percentage, 39.9 percent; Oman has the lowest female percentage, 8.6 percent.

Rounding up what has been assessed so far, we see that the Arab region has failed to empower women. In 1998, the Human Development Index (HDI) ranking of the Arab region was 0.64; Egypt's rank was 0.62.[31] Kuwait earned the highest rank, 0.84; while Djibouti, Mauritania, and Yemen all ranked 0.45, the lowest in the region.[32] In comparison, what is considered high ranking of the HDI is 0.91, and the world rank is 0.71.[33]

Moreover, although a considerable number of Arab countries have signed major international human rights conventions, many have failed to ratify them, and/or they have not implemented them. The *AHDR 2002* does not provide a gender-based analysis of political participation in the Arab region, but it does provide a list of countries that have signed/ratified human rights conventions. For instance, Egypt is a member state (MS) for the Convention on the Elimination of All Forms of Racial Discrimination (CERD), the Convention on the Elimination of All Forms of Discrimination against Women (CEDAW), and the Convention on the Rights of the Child (CRC). Clearly, the empirical realities pertaining to women illustrate that the articles and conditions of these conventions have not been implemented in Egypt.

Oman is a member state for the CRC, but none of the other conventions. The Occupied Palestinian Territories are not signatories to any of the conventions. Qatar is a member state for CERD and CRC, but that is all. Saudi Arabia is a member state for CERD and CRC, and, according to the *AHDR 2002,* it ratified the CEDAW in September 2000. However, Saudi Arabia ratified only certain portions of CEDAW, rather than all of it. The Saudis rejected any part of the CEDAW provisions that they perceived as conflicting with Islamic law. In any case, with its repressive social policies still in place, Saudi Arabia is unequivocally and grossly violating the CEDAW provisions. Syria and the UAE are member states for CRC, but not for CEDAW.

There is one more item of empirical evidence that must be examined, and it involves the *AHDR 2003* survey which compares Arab attitudes towards the three main deficiencies that were ascertained in the *2002 AHDR.* Four Arab countries—Algeria, Egypt, Jordan, and Morocco—were targeted for field surveys measuring their attitudes towards the three deficiencies. The survey results show that "Arabs value knowledge and good governance strongly but *take an ambivalent stand on gender equality* "[34] (emphasis added). Furthermore, the results of the survey indicate the following:

Arabs . . . expressed the highest level of rejection of authoritarian rule (a strong leader who does not have to bother with parliament and elections).

On the empowerment of women, the Arabs came third in rejecting that 'a university education is more important for a boy than for a girl' while expressing the highest approval that 'when jobs are scarce, men should have more right to a job than women.'

In other words, Arabs stood for gender equality in education but not in employment. In human development terms, *Arabs expressed support for building the human capabilities of women but not for their utilization.*[35] (Emphasis added)

These empirical realities about the Arab Middle East show that there is substantial reluctance to fully embrace the empowerment and human rights of women.

## Conclusion

Progressive social transformation is what the Middle East region needs to undertake in order to adjust accordingly to the dynamic global and regional changes of the modern era. Regressive social transformation, especially cloaked in religion, is wholly counterproductive and not conducive to the modern world. No change at all, or stagnation, is defeatist. It precludes a given society from keeping up with the pace and scope of change in the world, and hence, the rest of the world will pass it by and leave the stagnant society in the dust.

The Middle East region contains a variety of classifications for social transformation. In fact, there are even variations at the regional, national, and grassroots levels. Two things the Arab

countries in the Middle East region have in common—with a few exceptions—are the following: (1) coping with change is an extremely gradual and complicated process; and (2) social transformation is highly "religionized" and politicized. The reasons for this are multifaceted, but mostly pertain to ideological/ attitudinal factors and pervasive authoritarianism.

Prevailing attitudes, even among many of the educated classes, indicate strong suspicion and rejection of any ideas perceived to be Western-modeled. In fact, many in the Arab region even exhibit forms of denial regarding the poor status of women. Mention of the disenfranchisement and disempowerment of women in the Arab Middle East is often dismissed as Western propaganda to give the region, and Arab culture in particular, a negative image. There are also many within the Arab region who simply do not consider women's empowerment and human rights as important. Other priorities take precedence, and, as some have suggested, once these priorities are fulfilled, the status of women would automatically improve.

The empirical realities illustrate serious deficiencies in the status of women, even in the oil-rich Gulf Arab countries. The health, nutrition, human welfare, education, employment, and general human development indicators reveal startling contradictions, wherein their wealth should not render such poor results pertaining to women's health and development. The empirical realities are even worse for women in the poorer countries in the Arab region. As the AHDR 2002 has emphasized, the Arab Middle East ranks among the lowest in the development spectrum of developing countries. In certain areas of human development, only South Asia and SubSaharan Africa rank lower than the Arab world.

Arab and Muslim women, as well as conscionable and supportive men, now face the unenviable tasks of reversing the ideological trend of extreme regression; persuading their respective societies that women's empowerment and human rights are important for overall human development and should be top priorities; and working to significantly improve the human development indicators that specifically pertain to women. It is evident from the current ideological, attitudinal, and empirical realities that the struggle to empower women and realize their human rights in the Arab world will continue to be a formidable, complicated endeavor.

## Notes

1. The ideological/attitudinal level of analysis is based on general observations and inferences drawn from classroom discussions with Egyptian students, public lecture series in Cairo, the Arab press and media, and analyses of current ideological trends in the Islamic world.

2. The *AHDR 2002*, published by the United Nations Development Program (UNDP), is the first ever UNDP Human Development Report that focuses specifically on the Arab Middle East, and it is written by Arab scholars.

3. The other two deficiencies are the knowledge deficiency and the freedom/human rights deficiency.

4. Samuel Huntington, *Political Order in Changing Societies* (London: Yale University Press, 1996), p. 35.

5. *Ibid.,* p. 34.

6. *Ibid.*

7. *The Arab Human Development Report 2002: Creating Opportunities for Future Generations* (New York: United Nations Development Program, 2002), p. 85.

8. Depending on the circumstances, a number of Islamic militant groups are also suppressed and under tremendous scrutiny from law enforcement authorities, mainly to keep political opposition in check, as well as to protect countries from potential terrorist threats. Egypt, which relies heavily on its tourism industry, is an example of a state that closely monitors and suppresses the activities of Islamic militants, who have in the past killed not only tourists, but also Egypt's former President Anwar Al Sadat.

9. Craig S. Smith, "France Is Struggling to Suppress Extremist Muslim Clerics," *The New York Times* online, April 30, 2004. Online at www.nytimes.com/2004/04/30/world/france-is-struggling-to-suppress-extremist-muslim-clerics.html?scp=4&sq=&st=nyt.

10. Christiane Amanpour, "The New French Revolution," *60 Minutes, CBS News,* May 16, 2004, accessed from <www.cbsnews.com/stories/2004/05/1 3/60minutes>.

11. Smith, "France Wrestles with Radical Islam."

12. Amanpour, "The New French Revolution."

13. *Ibid.*

14. *Ibid.*

15. *Democratization,* The Kuwait Information Office, accessed from <www.kuwait-info.org/democratization.html>.

16. *Ibid.*

17. *The AHDR 2002, op. cit.,* p. 2.

18. For more information about this topic, see Khaled Abou El Fadl's book, *Speaking in God's Name: Islamic Law, Authority and Women* (Oxford: Oneworld Publications, 2001).

19. Dr. Ibrahim El Issawy, panel discussion: "The 2002 Arab Human Development Report," *English Public Lecture Series*, December 16, 2002, The American University in Cairo, Egypt.

20. Dr. Galal Amin, panel discussion: "The 2002 Arab Human Development Report," *English Public Lecture Series,*

December 16, 2002, The American University in Cairo, Egypt. Written question from Galal Amin asked by panel moderator to the panelists in his absence.

21. Dr. Nader Fergany, panel discussion: "The 2002 Arab Human Development Report," *English Public Lecture Series,* December 16, 2002, The American University in Cairo, Egypt.

22. Dr. Rima Khalaf-Hunaidi, panel discussion: "The 2002 Arab Human Development Report," *English Public Lecture Series,* December 16, 2002, The American University in Cairo, Egypt.

23. Surah 81 *"Takwir"* or "The Folding Up" (early Meccan), verses 8-9 say: "When the female (infant) is buried alive, is questioned—for what crime she was killed."

24. *The AHDR 2002,* p. 38.

25. *Ibid.,* p. 143.

26. *Ibid.,* p. 145.

27. *Ibid.,* p. 40.

28. *Ibid.*

29. *Ibid.*

30. George Kent, "A Gendered Perspective on Nutrition Rights," *Agenda,* 51, 2002, p. 43.

31. *The AHDR 2002.*

32. *Ibid.*

33. *Ibid.*

34. *The Arab Human Development Report 2003: Building a Knowledge Society* (New York: UNDP, 2003), p. 19.

35. *Ibid.*

**HAYAT ALVI** is an Assistant Professor of Political Science at the American University in Cairo, specializing in the Middle East and South Asian regions. She is the author of *Regional Integration in the Middle East: A Comparative Analysis of Inter-Arab Economic Cooperation* (Lewiston, NY: Edwin Mellen Press, 2007) and "Reconstruction in Post-Taliban Afghanistan: Women and Education" *Resources for Feminist Research,* Vol. 30, No. 3/4 (Spring/Summer 2004).

From *Middle East Review of International Affairs (MERIA) Journal,* by Hayat Alvi, vol. 9, No. 2, (June 2005) pp. 142–160. Copyright © Interdisciplinary Center (IDC) Herzliya. Reprinted by permission of Global Research in International Affairs (GLORIA) Center, Herzliya, Israel.

# Glossary of Terms and Abbreviations

**A'ayan** In Arabic, collective name for noble families in Palestine during the British Mandate.

**Abd** In Arabic, "slave" or "servant" (of God) commonly used in personal names (Gamal Abd al-Nasir).

**Abu** In Arabic, "father of," commonly used in names.

**Alawi** (Nusayri), a minority Muslim community in Syria, currently in power under the Assad family. It is nominally Shi'a but has separate liturgy and secret rites, with some non-Muslim festivals. The Alevi in Turkey are unrelated but follow some of the same rituals.

**Aliyah** In Hebrew, "ascent" or "rising up," term used to describe the return of Jews to Palestine from the Diaspora.

**Allah** God, in Islam.

**Al-Qaeda** In Arabic, "the Base," name of the violent Islamist organization founded by Osama bin Ladin.

**Ashkenazi** In Hebrew/German, name for Jews who emigrated from northern/eastern Europe to Palestine/Israel.

**'Ashura** In Arabic, the 10th day of the Islamic month of Muharram, marking for Shi'a Muslims the death and martydom of Hussain, Muhammad's grandson.

**Ayatollah** "Sign of God," the title of highest rank among the Shi'a religious leaders in Iran and elsewhere.

**Baraka** ("blessing"), given by God or a holy person.

**Ba'th** In Arabic, full name; (in English), Arab Socialist Resurrection Party—the dominant and ruling party in Syria and formerly in Iraq. In the latter country it was the only legal party from 1968 to 2003.

**Bey** In Turkish, a commander in the Ottoman army; also used for the heads of the Ottoman Regency of Algiers and Tunisia prior to the French conquest.

**Bilad al-Makhzan** In Arabic, in the Maghrib (North Africa) land under the control of a central authority (e.g. the sultans of Morocco).

**Bilad al-Siba'** In Arabic land of dissidence, not under central control.

**Caliph** In Arabic, *khalifa;* agent, representative, or deputy; in Sunni Islam, the line of successors to Muhammad.

**Chador** In Persian, a full-length body covering for women, usually black, which completely conceals the female form. In some Arab countries something similar is called abaya but the chador does not have sleeves and does not close in the front. The woman holds it closed by hand.

**Colon** Settler, colonist (French), a term used for the French population in North Africa during the colonial period (1830–1962).

**Dar al-Islam** "House of Islam," territory ruled under Islam. Conversely, *Dar al-Harb,* "House of War," denotes territory not under Islamic rule.

**Diaspora** In Hebrew, the dispersal of Jews outside Palestine on a more or less permanent basis, beginning with the destruction of Jerusalem by the Roman emperor Titus in 70 C.E.

**Druze (or Druse)** An offshoot of Islam that has developed its own rituals and practices and a close-knit community structure; Druze populations are found today in Lebanon, Jordan, Syria, and Israel.

**Emir (or Amir)** A title of rank, denoting either a patriarchal ruler, provincial governor, or military commander. It is used for rulers of some Arabian Peninsula states.

**Faqih** In Arabic, jurist specializing in Islamic law.

**Fatwa** A legal opinion or interpretation delivered by a Muslim religious scholar-jurist; a religious edict.

**Fida'i** (Feda'iy, plural Fida'iyun or Fedayeen) In Arabic, individual willing to fight for a community cause such as resistance to occupation or tyranny, even at the cost of self-sacrifice.

**Fiqh** In Arabic, Islamic law or jurisprudence.

**GCC (Gulf Cooperation Council)** Established in 1981 as a mutual-defense organization by the Arab Gulf states. Membership: Bahrain, Kuwait, Oman, Qatar, Saudi Arabia, and United Arab Emirates. Its aims was extended to economic cooperation in view of future integration Headquarters: Riyadh.

**Gush Emunim** In Hebrew, "Bloc of the Faithful," a radical Zionist movement.

**Hadith** The compilation of sayings and decisions attributed to Prophet Muhammad that serve as a model and guide to conduct for Muslims. Hadith is also considered important in understanding the Qur'an and in matters of Islamic jurisprudence.

**Hajj** Pilgrimage to Mecca, one of the Five Pillars of Islam.

**Halakhah** In Hebrew, the legal system in Judaism, based on the Talmud and Torah.

**Halal** In Arabic, any action approved by fiqh (q.v.). It is an object or an action that is permissible or legal in Islam. The opposite is Haraam.

**Haluzin** "Pioneers" in Hebrew, early Zionist settlers there.

**Hamas** "Zeal" in Arabic, acronym for Movement of the Islamic Resistance, a radical organization founded 1988, which currently holds the majority in the Palestinian legislature elected in 2006.

**Hanbali, Hanafi** In Arabic, two of the four schools of legal interpretation in Islam.

**Haram al-Sharif** In Arabic, Noble Sanctuary, collective name for the Dome of the Rock and al-Aqsa Mosque in Jerusalem. It is believed to be the location of Prophet Muhammad's ascent to heaven.

**Haredim** In Hebrew, "Tremblers," Ultra-Orthodox Jews. The term is derived from a verse in Isaiah.

**Hijab** In Arabic, head scarf worn by Muslim women and covering the entire hair. It is not obligatory in most Muslim states.

**Hijrah (Hegira)** The Prophet Muhammad's emigration from Mecca to Medina in A.D. 622 to escape persecution; the start of the Islamic calendar.

**Hizb** In Arabic, party.

**Ibadi** A militant early Islamic group that split with the majority (Sunni) over the question of the succession to Muhammad. Their descendants form majorities of the populations in Oman and Yemen.

**Ihram** In Arabic, the seamless white cloth worn by all Muslims making the hajj. This white clothing is meant to make everyone appear the same, in total equality before God. It is also the sacred state which a Muslim must be in while performing the pilgrimage. It is attained by performing cleansing rituals and wearing the prescribed white clothing attire.

**Ijma'** In Arabic, consensus (of the community), used in decision-making when neither Qur'an nor hadith seem to apply.

**Imam** In Arabic, religious leader, prayer-leader of a congregation. It can also refer to the descendants of Ali who are regarded by Shi'a Muslims as the rightful successors to Muhammad.

**Intifada** In Arabic, "resurgence," referring to the uprising of Palestinians against Israeli occupation of the West Bank and Gaza Strip.

**Islam** In Arabic, "submission," i.e. to the Will of God as revealed to Muhammad in the Qur'an. It refers to the religion handed down through Prophet Muhammad.

**Jahiliyya** The "time of ignorance" of the Arabs before Islam. Sometimes used by Islamic fundamentalists today to describe secular Muslim societies, which they regard as sinful.

**Jamahiriyya** Popular democracy (as in Libya).

**Jihad** In Arabic, "struggle"; the term basically refers to efforts by individuals to reform bad habits or shortcomings in the practice of the faith, either within themselves or the larger Islamic community. This is known as the "Greater Jihad" (al-Jihad al-Akbar). The "Smaller Jihad" (al-Jihad al-Asghar) refers to war waged in the defense of the Muslim community and Islam. It is meant only as a defensive action.

**Jumu'a** In Arabic, Friday. Salat al-Jumu'a refers to the Friday communal prayer, held in a mosque (jama').

**Kabbala** In Hebrew, traditions of mysticism in Judaism.

**Khan** A title of rank in eastern Islam (Turkey, Iran, etc.) for military or clan leaders.

**Khedive** Viceroy, the title of rulers of Egypt in the nineteenth and twentieth centuries who ruled as regents of the Ottoman sultan.

**Kibbutz** A collective settlement in Israel in which members of the collective society share possessions and cooperate in all areas of production, consumption and education.

**League of Arab States (Arab League)** Established in 1945 as a regional organization for newly independent Arab countries.

**Maghrib** In Arabic, West and sunset. It also refers to the North Africa region (where the sun sets from a Middle East vantage point). The countries of the Maghrib are Algeria, Morocco, Libya and Tunisia.

**Mahdi** In Arabic "The Guided One," the Messiah, who will appear on earth to reunite the divided Islamic community and announce the Day of Judgment. In Twelver Shi'a Islam (mainly in Iran and Iraq) he is the twelfth and Last Imam (al-Mahdi al-Muntazir) who disappeared 12 centuries ago but is believed to be in a state of occultation (suspended between heaven and earth).

**Majlis** In Arabic, literally, "assembly," used traditionally for a ruler's weekly public meetings with subjects to hear complaints. Today, it refers to legislature or council.

**Maliki** A school of Islamic legal interpretation.

**Mandates** An arrangement set up under the League of Nations after World War I for German colonies and territories of the Ottoman Empire inhabited by non-Turkish populations. The purpose was to prepare these populations for eventual self-government under a temporary occupation by a foreign power, which was either Britain or France. In reality, it served as a guise for colonization in the sole interest of the occupier.

**Millet** In Arabic, "Nation," a non-Muslim population group in the Ottoman Empire recognized as a legitimate religious community and allowed self-government in internal affairs under its own religious rules.

**Muezzin** A prayer-caller, the person who announces the five daily obligatory prayers from the minaret of a mosque.

**Mufti** A legal scholar empowered to issue legal opinion known as fatwa. Usually one mufti is designated as the Grand Mufti of a particular Islamic state or territory.

**Mujahid (plurial Mujahideen)** In arabic, a person who engages in the Small Jihad, i.e., armed defense against attack on the Muslim community or Islam. It also refers to Muslim fighters against Muslim governments perceived to have failed their societies.

**Mullah** In Arabic, Farsi, a religious cleric, especially in Iran.

**Muslim** (see Islam) In Arabic, one who follows the religion of Islam.

**OAPEC (Organization of Arab Petroleum Exporting Countries)** Established in 1968 to coordinate oil policies—but not to set prices—and to develop oil-related inter-Arab projects, such as an Arab tanker fleet and dry-dock facilities. Membership: all Arab oil-producing states. Headquarters: Kuwait.

**OIC (Organization of the Islamic Conference)** Established in 1971 to promote solidarity among Islamic countries, provide humanitarian aid to Muslim communities throughout the world, and provide funds for Islamic education through construction of mosques, theological institutions of Islamic learning, etc. Membership: all states with an Islamic majority or significant minority. Headquarters: Saudi Arabia.

**OPEC (Organization of Petroleum Exporting Countries)** Established in 1960 to coordinate global oil policies of members. A majority of its 13 member states are in the Middle East. Headquarters: Vienna.

**Polisario** A national resistance movement in Western Sahara that opposes annexation by Morocco and is fighting to establish an independent Saharan Arab state, the Sahrawi Arab Democratic Republic (SADR).

**PSD (Parti Socialiste Destourien)** The dominant political party in Tunisia since independence and until recently the only legal party.

**Qadi** In Arabic (also kadi) an Islamic judge, one who administers the Islamic law (shari'a)

**Qanat** In Arabic, an underground tunnel used for irrigation.

**Qiyas** In Arabic, reasoning by analogy, one of the four sources of decision-making by the Islamic scholars (*ulema*), after the Qur'an, hadith and ijma'.

**Qur'an** In Arabic, the book compiled from God's revelations to Muhammad via the Angel Gabriel that form the basis for Islam.

**Quraysh** The group of clans who made up Muhammad's community in Mecca.

**Shafi'i** In Arabic, a school of Islamic legal interpretion.

**Shari'a** "The Way," the corpus of the sacred laws of Islam as revealed to Muhammad in the Qur'an. The sacred law is derived from three sources, the Qur'an, Sunna (q.v.), and hadith (q.v.).

# Glossary of Terms and Abbreviations

**Sharif**  In Arabic, holy, a term applied to members of Muhammad's immediate family and descendants through his daughter Fatima and son-in-law Ali.

**Shaykh**  In Arabic, also sheikh, sheik; title of a tribal leader, religious group leader or prominent Muslim personality, especially in the Gulf states.

**Shi'a**  Commonly, but incorrectly, *Shiite*. Originally meant "Party," i.e., of Ali, those Muslims who supported him as Muhammad's rightful successor. Today, broadly, the principal Islamic minority sect.

**Shura**  an advisory council set up by an Islamic organization or appointed by a ruler to advise on national issues.

**Sunnah**  In Arabic, "custom," the habits and practices of the Prophet Muhammad as recorded by his companions and family. Collectively they constitute the ideal behavior enjoined on Muslims.

**Sunnis**  The majority in the Islamic community.

**Suq (Souk)**  In Arabic, a public weekly market in Arab rural areas.

**Sura**  In Arabic, a chapter in the Qur'an.

**Taliban**  "Students"; originally used for students in Islamic madrasas (schools), the term acquired political significance with the rise to power in Afghanistan of this extreme Wahhabi-inspired Islamist movement.

**Talmud**  In Hebrew, "study," Jewish scripture containing the options and statements of the rabbis of Palestine and Babylonia in the 1st–5th centuries C.E. and their interpretations.

**Taqiyya**  Dissimulation, concealment of one's religious identity or beliefs in the face of repression.

**Tawhid**  In Arabic, belief in the absolute oneness of God; the central tenet in Wahhabism (q.v.)

**Torah**  In Hebrew lit., "teaching", the Pentateuch, the first 5 books of Jewish scripture (Old Testament) plus the law of Moses.

**U.A.R. (United Arab Republic)**  The name given to the short-lived union of Egypt and Syria (1958–1961).

**Ulema**  The corporate body of Islamic religious scholars, and jurists.

**Umma**  The worldwide community of Muslims.

**UNHCR (United Nations High Commission for Refugees)**  Established in 1951 to provide international protection and material assistance to refugees worldwide. UNHCR has several refugee projects in the Middle East.

**UNIFIL (United Nations Interim Force in Lebanon)**  Formed in 1978 to ensure Israeli withdrawal from southern Lebanon. After the 1982 Israeli invasion, UNIFIL was given the added responsibility for protection and humanitarian aid to the people of the area. Headquarters: Naqoura, Lebanon.

**United Nations Peacekeeping Forces**  Various military observer missions formed to supervise disengagement or truce agreements between the Arab states and Israel. They include UNDOF (United Nations Disengagement Observer Force). Formed in 1974 as a result of the October 1973 Arab-Israeli War and continued by successive resolutions. Headquarters: Damascus.

**UNRWA (United Nations Relief and Works Agency for Palestine Refugees)**  Established in 1950 to provide food, housing, and health and education services for Palestinian refugees who fled their homes after the establishment of the State of Israel in Palestine. Headquarters: Vienna. UNRWA maintains refugee camps in Lebanon, Syria, Jordan, the occupied West Bank, and the Gaza Strip. It has also assumed responsibility for emergency relief for refugees in Lebanon displaced by the Israeli invasions and by the Lebanese Civil War.

# Bibliography

## SOURCES FOR STATISTICAL REPORTS

U.S. State Department, Background Notes (2008–2009).
The World Factbook (2009).
World Statistics in Brief (2009).
World Almanac (2009).
The Statesman's Yearbook (2009).
Demographic Yearbook (2009).
Statistical Yearbook (2009).

## CRADLE OF ISLAM

Jonathan Bloom & Sheila Blair, *Islam: A Thousand Years Of Faith and Power* (New Haven: Yale University Press, 2002). Textual companion to the PBS Documentary *Islam: Empire of Faith*.

Richard Bonney, *Jihad: From Qur'an to Bin Laden* (New York: Palgrave MacMillan, 2004).

Richard Bulliett, *The Case for Islamic-Christian Civilization* (New York: Columbia Univ. Press, 2004).

Edmund Burke III & David Yaghoubian, *Struggle and Survival in the Modern Middle East* (Berkeley: University of California Press, 2006, 2nd ed.).

B. Jill Carroll, *A Dialogue of Civilizations: Gulen's Islamic Ideals . . .* Foreword by Akbar Ahmed. (Somerset NJ: The Light, 2007.)

Juan Cole, *Sacred Space and Holy War: The Politics, History and Culture of Shiite Islam* (London: I.B. Tauris, 2005).

Patricia Crone, *God's Rule: Government and Islam, Six Centuries of Medieval Islamic Political Thought* (New York: Columbia Univ. Press, 2004).

Farhad Daftary, *The Assassins: Legends, Myths of the Ismailis* (London: I.B. Tauris, 1997).

Lawrence Davidson, *Islamic Fundamentalism: An Introduction* (Westport CT: Greenwood Press, Rev. ed, 2003).

Harm De Blij, *Why Geography Matters: Three Challenges Facing America* (New York: Oxford, 2005).

Faisal Devji, *Landscapes of the Jihad: Militancy, Morality, Modernity* (Ithaca: Cornell Univ. Press, 2005).

Fawaz Gerges, *Journey of the Jihadist: Inside Islamic Militancy* (New York: Harcourt Brace, 2006).

M.A.S. Abdel Haleem, *The Qur'an: A New Translation* (Oxford, UK: Oxford Univ. Press, 2004).

Abdellah Hammoudi, *A Season in Mecca: Narrative of a Pilgrimage* translated by Pasali Ghazaleh (New York: Hill & Wang, 2005).

Robert Irvin, *The Alhambra* (Cambridge: Harvard University Press, 2004).

Zachary Karabell, *Peace Be Upon You: The Story of Muslim, Christian and Jewish Coexistence* (New York: Knopf, 2007).

Hugh Kennedy, *When Baghdad Ruled the Muslim World* (Cambridge: Perseus Books Group, 2004).

Ibn Khaldun, *The Muqaddimah: An Introduction to History,* translated by Franz Rosenthal, abridged and edited by N.J. Dawood with Introduction by Bruce Lawrence (Princeton: Princeton Univ. Press, 2005).

Hans Kung, *Islam: Past, Present, and Future.* Translated by John Bowden (New York: Oneworld, 2007) third in a series on the Abrahamic religions.

Ira M. Lapidus, *A History of Islamic Societies* (Cambridge: Harvard Univ. Press, 2004).

Jacob Lassner, *The Middle East Remembered: Forged Identities, Competing Narratives* (Ann Arbor: University of Michigan Press, 2002).

Makers of the Muslim World, A monograph series: Maribel Fierro, *Abd al-Rahman III, The First Cordoban Caliph;* Chase Robinson, *'Abd al-Malik;* Shahzad Bashir, *Fazlallah Astarabadi and the Hurufis;* Usha Sanyal, *Ahmad Riza Khan Barelwi: In the Path Of the Prophet;* Sunil Sharma, *Amir Khusraw: The Poet of Sultans And Sufis* (New York: One World/Oxford Univ. Press, 2005).

Mansoor Moaddel, *Islamic Modernism, Nationalism and Fundamentalism* (Chicago: Univ. of Chicago Press, 2005).

Helen Nicholson, *God's Warriors: Crusaders, Saracens and the Battle For Jerusalem* (Oxford, UK: Osprey Publishers, 2005).

F. E. Peters, *Muhammad and the Origins of Islam* (Albany, NY: SUNY Press, 1994).

Ramadan, Tariq, *In the Footsteps of the Prophet: Lessons from the Life Of Muhammad* (New York: Oxford, 2007).

Ahmad Rashid, *Taliban: Militant Islam* (New York: New York University Press, 2001).

Lawrence Rosen, *The Culture of Islam* (Chicago: University of Chicago Press, 2002).

Olivier Roy, *Globalized Islam* (London: Hurst, 2004).

Richard L. Smith, *Ahmad al-Mansur, Islamic Visionary* (New York: Pearson/Longman, 2006).

Azzam Tamimi, *Rachid Ghannouchi: A Democrat Within Islamism* (New York: Oxford University Press, 2006), biography of the founder of Tunisia's En Nahda movement.

## THEATER OF CONFLICT

### Israeli-Palestinian Conflict

Warren Bass, *Support Any Friend: Kennedy's Middle East and the Making of the U.S.–Israel Alliance* (New York: Oxford University Press, 2003).

Yossi Beilin, *The Path to Geneva: The Quest for a Permanent Agreement, 1996–2004* (New York: RDV Books/Akaskic Books, 2004).

Shlomo Ben-Ami, *Scars of War, Wounds of Peace: The Israeli-Arab Tragedy* (New York: Oxford, 2006).

Peter Bergen, *The Osama bin Laden I Know . . .* (New York: Free Press, 2006).

Jeremy Bowen, *Six Days: How the 1967 War Shaped the Middle East* (New York: St. Martin's Press, 2005).

Robert Bowker, *Palestinian Refugees: Mythology, Identity and the Search for Peace* (Boulder CO: Lynne Rienner, 2003).

John K. Cooley, *An Alliance Against Babylon: The U.S., Israel, and Iraq* (London: Pluto Press, 2005).

Joyce Davis, *Martyrs: Innocence, Vengeance and Despair In the Middle East* (New York: Palgrave MacMillan, 2003).

Charles Enderlin, *Shattered Dreams: The Failure of the Peace Process in the Middle East, 1995–2002* (New York: Other Press, 2003).

Avner Falk, *Fratricide in the Holy Land . . .* (Madison: University of Wisconsin Press, 2003).

Gregory Harms, *The Palestinian-Israeli Conflict: A Basic Introduction.* with Todd M. Ferry. (London: Pluto Press, 2006).

## Bibliography

Bruce Lawrence, ed., *Messages to the World: The Statements of Osama Bin Laden.* Translated by James Howarth. (New York: Verso, 2005).

Sari Nusseibeh, *Once Upon a Country: A Palestinian Life* (New York: Farrar, Straus & Giroux, 2007).

Dennis Ross, *The Missing Peace . . .* (New York: Farrar, Straus & Giroux, 2004).

Gilad Sher, *Just Beyond Reach: Israeli-Palestinian Negotiations 1999–2001* (Tel Aviv: Frank Cass, 2005).

A.J. Sherman, *Mandate Days: British Lives in Palestine, 1918–1948* (Baltimore: Johns Hopkins University Press, 1997).

David Shipler, *Arab and Jew: Wounded Spirits in the Promised Land* (London: Penguin Books, 2002).

Clayton Swisher, *The Truth About Camp David . . .* (New York: Nation Books, 2004).


## Other Conflicts

Gilbert Achcar, *The 33-Day War.* With Michael Warshawski (New York: Paradigm Publishers, 2006).

Rick Atkinson, *An Army at Dawn: The War in North Africa, 1942–1943* (New York: Henry Holt, 2002).

Thomas Barnett, *The Pentagon's New Map: War and Peace In the 21st Century* (New York: Putnam, 2004).

James A. Baker III and Lee H. Hamilton, co-chairs, *The Iraq Study Group Report* (New York: Vantage Books, 2006). Report to the president and congress by a study group commissioned to study the Iraq invasion and occupation and make policy recommendations.

Jason Burke, *Al-Qaeda* (London: I.B. Tauris, 2003).

Rajiv Chandrasekaran, *Imperial Life in the Emerald City: Inside Iraq's Green Green Zone* (New York: Knopf, 2006).

Richard Clarke, *Against All Enemies: Inside America's War On Terror* (New York: Free Press, 2004).

Anthony Cordesman, *The Iraq War . . .* (see under Iraq listing).

James Turner Johnson and George Weigel, *Just War and the Gulf War* (Washington, D.C.: Ethics and Public Policy Center, 1991).

Rashid Khalidi, *Resurrecting Empire: Western Footprints and America's Perilous Path in the Middle East* (Boston: Beacon Press, 2004).

Anatol Lieven & John Hulsman, *Ethical Realism: A Vision for America's Role in the Modern World* (New York: Pantheon Books, 2006). Chapter 5, "The Way Forward," deals with Middle East Conflicts as U.S. foreign policy issues.

Matthew Levitt, *Targeting Terror: U.S. Policy Toward Middle East State Sponsors and Terrorist Organizations* (Washington DC: Washington Institute for Near East Policy, 2002).

Hugh Miles, *Al-Jazeera, The Inside Story* (New York: Grove Press, 2005).

Michael O'Hanlon, *Defense Strategy for the Post-Saddam Era* (Washington DC: Brookings Inst. Press, 2005).

Michael B. Oren, *Power, Faith and Fantasy: America in the Middle East 1776 to the Present* (New York: W.W. Norton, 2007).

Lawrence G. Potter & Gary Sick, eds., *Iran, Iraq and the Legacies of War* (New York: Palgrave MacMillan, 2004).

David R. Woodward, *Hell in the Holy Land: World War I in the Middle East* (Lexington KY: University of Kentucky Press, 2006).

Steven Yetiv, *Explaining Foreign Policy: U.S. Decision-making and the Persian Gulf War* (Baltimore: Johns Hopkins Univ. Press, 2004).


## ALGERIA

Ahmed Aghrout and Mohamed Redha Bougherira, *Algeria in Transition: Reforms and Development Prospects* (New York: Routledge-Curzon, 2004).

Anne-Emmanuelle Berger, *Algeria in Others' Languages* (Ithaca, NY: Cornell University Press, 2002).

Mounira Charrad, *States and Women's Rights: The Making of Postcolonial Tunisia, Algeria, and Morocco* (Berkeley: University of California Press, 2001).

Steven A. Cook, *Ruling but Not Governing: The Military and Political Development in Egypt, Algeria, and Turkey* (Baltimore: Johns Hopkins University Press, 2007).

Abder-Rahmane Derradji, *A Concise History of Political Violence in Algeria, 1954–2000: Brothers in Faith, Enemies in Arms* (Lewiston, NY: E. Mellen Press, 2002).

Bradford L. Dillman, *State and Private Sector in Algeria: The Politics of Rent-Seeking and Failed Development* (Boulder, CO: Westview Press, 2000).

Martin Evans and John Phillips, *Algeria: Anger of the Dispossessed* (New Haven, CT: Yale University Press, 2007).

Jane E. Goodman and Paul A. Silverstein, eds., *Bourdieu in Algeria: Colonial Politics, Ethnographic Practices, Theoretical Developments* (Lincoln: University of Nebraska Press, 2009).

Jonathan K. Gosnell, *The Politics of Frenchness in Colonial Algeria, 1930–1954* (Rochester, NY: University of Rochester Press, 2002).

Jeremy Keenan, *The Lesser Gods of the Sahara: Social Change and Contested Terrain Amongst the Tuareg of Algeria* (London: Frank Cass, 2004).

Ranjana Khanna, *Algeria Cuts: Women and Representation, 1830 to the Present* (Stanford, CA: Stanford University Press, 2008).

John W. Kiser, *The Monks of Tibhirine: Faith, Love, and Terror in Algeria* (New York: St. Martin's Press, 2002).

Nelli Kopola, "The Construction of Womanhood in Algeria: Moudjahidates, Aishah Radjul, Women as Others and Other Women." Thesis (doctoral), (Stockholm University, Dept. of Political Science, 2001).

Ricardo René Laremont, *Islam and the Politics of Resistance in Algeria, 1783–1992* (Trenton, NJ: Africa World Press, Inc., 2000).

James D. Le Sueur, *Algeria Since 1989: Between Terror and Democracy* (New York: Zed Books, 2010).

Andrea Liverani, *Civil Society in Algeria: The Political Functions of Associational Life* (New York: Routledge, 2008).

Patricia M. E. Lorcin, ed., *Algeria & France, 1800–2000: Identity, Memory, Nostalgia* (Syracuse, NY: Syracuse University Press, 2006).

Miriam R. Lowi, *Oil Wealth and the Poverty of Politics: Algeria Compared* (New York: Cambridge University Press, 2009).

Benjamin MacQueen, *Political Culture and Conflict Resolution in the Arab World: Lebanon and Algeria* (Carlton, Vic.: Melbourne University Publishing, 2009).

Margaret A. Majumdar, *Transition and Development in Algeria: Economic, Social and Cultural Challenges* (Bristol, UK: Intellect, 2005).

James McDougall, *History and the Culture of Nationalism in Algeria* (New York: Cambridge University Press, 2006).

Phillip Chiviges Naylor, *Historical Dictionary of Algeria* (Lanham, MD: Scarecrow Press, 2006).

Khaled Nezzar, *Bouteflika, L'homme Et Son Bilan* (Algiers: Editions APIC, 2003).

Jennifer Noyon, *Islam, Politics and Pluralism: Theory and Practice in Turkey, Jordan, Tunisia and Algeria* (London: Royal Institute of International Affairs, Middle East Program, 2003).

Andrew J. Pierre and William B. Quandt, *The Algerian Crisis: Policy Options for the West* (Washington, DC: Carnegie Endowment for International Peace: Distributed by the Brookings Institution, 1996).

Hugh Roberts, *The Battlefield Algeria, 1988–2002: Studies in a Broken Polity* (New York: Verso, 2003).

John Ruedy, *Modern Algeria: The Origins and Development of a Nation* (Bloomington: Indiana University Press, 2005).

Judith Scheele, *Village Matters: Knowledge, Politics & Community in Kabylia, Algeria* (Rochester, NY: James Currey, 2009).

Joshua Samuel Schreier, "From Jewish Regeneration to Colonialism: The Ideology and Practice of Civilizing in France and Algeria, 1815–1870." Thesis (PhD.), (New York University, Graduate School of Arts and Science, 2003).

Paul A. Silverstein, *Algeria in France: Transpolitics, Race, and Nation* (Bloomington: Indian University Press, 2004).

Benjamin Stora, *Algeria, 1830–2000: A Short History* (Ithaca, NY: Cornell University Press, 2001).

Frédéric Volpi, *Islam and Democracy: The Failure of Dialogue in Algeria* (Sterling, VA: Pluto Press, 2003).

Isabelle Werenfels, *Managing Instability in Algeria: Elites and Political Change Since 1995* (New York: Routledge, 2007).

## BAHRAIN

Hamad Bin Isa Al Khalifah, *First Light: Modern Bahrain and Its Heritage* (New York: Columbia University Press, 1994).

Anthony H. Cordesman, *Bahrain, Oman, Qatar, and the UAE: Challenges of Security* (Boulder, CO, Westview Press, 1997).

Timothy R. Insoll, *The Land of Enki in the Islamic Era: Pearls, Palms, and Religious Identity in Bahrain* (London: Kegan Paul, 2005).

Glada Lahn, *Democratic Transition in Bahrain: A Model for the Arab World?* (London: Gulf Centre For Strategic Studies, 2004).

Fred H. Lawson, *Bahrain: The Modernization of Autocracy* (Boulder, CO: Westview Press, 1989).

Andrew Wheatcroft, *The Life and Times of Shaikh Salman Bin Hamad Al-Khalifa: Ruler of Bahrain, 1942–1961* (New York: Kegan Paul, 1995).

## EGYPT

Genevieve Abdo, *No God But God: Egypt and the Triumph of Islam* (New York: Oxford University Press, 2002).

Ahmed Belal et al., *Bedouins by the Lake: Environment, Change, and Sustainability in Southern Egypt* (Cairo: American University in Cairo Press, 2009).

Beth Baron, *Egypt as a Woman: Nationalism, Gender and Politics* (Berkeley: University of California Press, 2005).

Robert Bowker, *Egypt and the Politics of Change in the Arab Middle East* (Northampton, MA: Edward Elgar, 2010).

Douglas J. Brewer, *Egypt and the Egyptians* (New York: Cambridge University Press, 2007).

Steven A. Cook, *Ruling but Not Governing: The Military and Political Development in Egypt, Algeria, and Turkey* (Baltimore: Johns Hopkins University Press, 2007).

Rabab El-Mahdi and Philip Marfleet, eds., *Egypt: The Moment of Change* (New York: Zed Books, 2009).

Mine Ener, *Managing Egypt's Poor and the Politics of Benevolence* (Princeton, NJ: Princeton University Press, 2003).

Michael Ezekiel Gasper, *The Power of Representation: Publics, Peasants, and Islam in Egypt* (Stanford, CA: Stanford University Press, 2009).

Maria Golia, *Cairo: City of Sand* (London, UK: Reaktion Books, 2007).

Arthur Goldschmidt, *A Brief History of Egypt* (New York: Facts on File, 2008).

Benjamin H. Hary, *Translating Religion: Linguistic Analysis of Judeo-Arabic Sacred Texts from Egypt* (Leiden, Netherlands: Brill, 2009).

Amy J. Johnson, *Reconstructing Rural Egypt* (Syracuse NY: Syracuse University Press, 2003).

Agnieszka Paczyńska, *State, Labor, and the Transition to a Market Economy: Egypt, Poland, Mexico, and the Czech Republic* (University Park: Pennsylvania State University Press, 2009).

Bruce K. Rutherford, *Egypt after Mubarak: Liberalism, Islam, and Democracy in the Arab World* (Princeton, NJ: Princeton University Press, 2008).

Dina Shehata, *Islamists and Secularists in Egypt: Opposition, Conflict, and Cooperation* (New York: Routledge, 2010).

Leila Simona Talani, *From Egypt to Europe: Globalisation and Migration across the Mediterranean* (New York: Tauris Academic Studies, 2010).

Sherifa Zuhur, *Egypt: Security, Political, and Islamist Challenges* (Carlisle, PA: Strategic Studies Institute, U.S. Army War College, 2007).

## IRAN

Reza Abedini and Hans Wolbers, *New Visual Culture of Modern Iran* (West New York, NJ: Mark Batty Publisher, 2006).

Fariba Adelkhah, *Being Modern in Iran* (New York: Columbia University Press, 2000).

Arshin Adib-Moghaddam, *Iran in World Politics: The Question of the Islamic Republic* (New York: Columbia University Press, 2008).

Reza Afshari, *Human Rights in Iran: The Abuse of Cultural Relativism* (Philadelphia: University of Pennsylvania Press, 2001).

Kamran Scot Aghaie, *The Martyrs of Karbala: Shi'i Symbols and Rituals in Modern Iran* (Seattle: University of Washington Press, 2004).

Hamid Algar, *Roots of the Islamic Revolution in Iran: Four Lectures* (Oneonta, NY: Islamic Publications International, 2001).

Parvin Alizadeh, Hassan Hakimian, and Massoud Karshenas, *The Economy of Iran: Dilemmas of an Islamic State* (London/New York: I. B. Tauris; distributed by St Martins Press, 2000).

Faisal bin Salman Al-Saud, *Iran, Saudi Arabia and the Gulf: The Transformation of Great Power Politics* (London: I. B. Tauris, 2003).

Mohammad Javad Amid and Amjad Hadjikhani, *Trade, Industrialization and the Firm in Iran: The Impact of Government Policy on Business. Culture and Society in Western and Central Asia* (New York: I. B. Tauris, 2005).

Elena Andreeva, *Russia and Iran in the Great Game: Travelogues and Orientalism* (New York: Routledge, 2007).

Ali M. Ansari, *Confronting Iran: The Failure of American Foreign Policy and the Next Great Crisis in the Middle East* (New York: Basic Books, 2006).

_____, *Iran under Ahmadinejad: The Politics of Confrontation* (Abingdon, Oxon: Routledge, 2007).

Peter Avery, *The Spirit of Iran: A History of Achievement from Adversity* (Costa Mesa, CA: Mazda Publishers, 2007).

## Bibliography

Fakhreddin Azimi, *The Quest for Democracy in Iran: A Century of Struggle against Authoritarian Rule* (Cambridge, MA: Harvard University Press, 2008).

Hassan Bashir and Seyed Ghahreman Safavi, *The Roots of the Islamic Revolution in Iran: Economical, Political, Social and Cultural Views* (London: BookExtra, 2002).

Lois Beck and Guity Nashat, *Women in Iran from 1800 to the Islamic Republic* (Urbana: University of Illinois Press, 2004).

Stephanie Cronin, *Reformers and Revolutionaries in Modern Iran: New Perspectives on the Iranian Left* (New York: Routledge-Curzon, 2004).

Elton L. Daniel, *The History of Iran* (Westport, CT: Greenwood Press, 2001).

David R. Farber, *Taken Hostage: The Iran Hostage Crisis and America's First Encounter with Radical Islam* (Princeton, NJ: Princeton University Press, 2004).

Nematallah Fazeli, *Politics of Culture in Iran: Anthropology, Politics and Society in the Twentieth Century* (London/New York: Routledge, 2006).

Babak Ganji, *Politics of Confrontation: The Foreign Policy of the USA and Revolutionary Iran* (New York: Tauris; distributed by Palgrave Macmillan, 2006).

Ali Gheissari and Vali Nasr, *Democracy in Iran: History and the Quest For Liberty* (New York: Oxford, 2006).

Mark J. Gasiorowski and Malcolm Byrne, *Mohammad Mosaddeq and the 1953 Coup in Iran* (Syracuse, NY: Syracuse University Press, 2004).

David Patrick Houghton, *U.S. Foreign Policy and the Iran Hostage Crisis* (New York: Cambridge University Press, 2001).

Jane Mary Howard, *Inside Iran: Women's Lives* (Washington, DC: Mage Publishers, 2002).

Roger Howard, *Iran Oil: The New Middle East Challenge to America* (New York: I. B. Tauris; distributed by Palgrave Macmillan, 2007).

Alireza Jafarzadeh, *The Iran Threat: President Ahmadinejad and the Coming Nuclear Crisis* (New York: Palgrave, 2007).

Farideh Koohi-Kamali, *The Political Development of the Kurds in Iran: Pastoral Nationalism* (New York: Palgrave Macmillan, 2003).

Mahnaz Kousha, *Voices from Iran: The Changing Lives of Iranian Women* (Syracuse: Syracuse University Press, 2002).

Trita Parsi, *Treacherous Alliance: The Secret Dealings of Israel, Iran, and the United States* (New Haven: Yale University Press, 2007).

Lawrence G. Potter and Gary Sick, *Iran, Iraq, and the Legacies of War* (New York: Palgrave Macmillan, 2004).

Hamideh Sedghi, *Women and Politics in Iran: Veiling, Unveiling, and Reveiling* (New York: Cambridge University Press, 2007).

Mehdi Semati, *Media, Culture and Society in Iran: Living with Globalization and the Islamic State* (New York: Routledge, 2008).

Kerim Yildiz and Tanyel B. Taysi, *The Kurds in Iran: The Past, Present and Future* (Ann Arbor, MI: Pluto, 2007).

## IRAQ

J. M. Abdulghani, *Iraq & Iran: The Years of Crisis* (Baltimore, MD: Johns Hopkins University Press, 1984).

Thabit Abdullah, *A Short History of Iraq: From 636 to the Present* (New York: Pearson/Longman, 2003).

Tariq Ali, *Bush in Babylon: The Recolonisation of Iraq* (New York: Verso, 2003).

Yasmin Husein Al-Jawaheri, *Women in Iraq: The Gender Impact of International Sanctions* (New York: I. B. Tauris, 2008).

Ali A. Allawi, *The Occupation of Iraq: Winning the War, Losing the Peace* (New Haven, CT: Yale University Press, 2007).

James Carroll, *Crusade: Chronicles of an Unjust War* (New York: Metropolitan Books/Henry Holt, 2004).

Christopher Catherwood, *Churchill's Folly: How Winston Churchill Created Modern Iraq* (New York: Carroll & Graf Publishers, 2004).

Larry Jay Diamond, *Squandered Victory: The American Occupation and the Bungled Effort to Bring Democracy to Iraq* (New York: Times Books, 2005).

Gwynne Dyer, *After Iraq: Anarchy and Renewal in the Middle East* (New York: Thomas Dunne Books/St. Martin's Press, 2008).

Richard A. Falk, Irene L. Gendzier, and Robert Jay Lifton, *Crimes of War: Iraq* (New York: Nation Books, 2006).

James M. Fallows, *Blind into Baghdad: America's War in Iraq* (New York: Vintage Books, 2006).

Edmund Ghareeb and Beth Dougherty, *Historical Dictionary of Iraq*, (Lanham, MD: Scarecrow Press, 2004).

Michael M. Gunter, *The Kurdish Predicament in Iraq: A Political Analysis* (New York: St. Martin's Press, 1999).

_____. *The Kurds Ascending: The Evolving Solution to the Kurdish Problem in Iraq and Turkey* (New York: Palgrave Macmillan, 2008).

Michael Heazle and Iyanatul Islam, *Beyond the Iraq War: The Promises, Pitfalls and Perils of External Interventionism* (Northampton, MA: Edward Elgar, 2006).

Eric Herring and Glen Rangwala, *Iraq in Fragments: The Occupation and Its Legacy* (Ithaca, NY: Cornell University Press, 2006).

Stanley Hoffmann, *Gulliver Unbound: America's Imperial Temptation and the War in Iraq* (Lanham, MD: Rowman & Littlefield Publishers, 2004).

Shams Constantine Inati, *Iraq: Its History, People, and Politics* (Amherst, NY: Humanity Books, 2003).

Laura Sjoberg, *Gender, Justice, and the Wars in Iraq: A Feminist Reformulation of Just War Theory* (Lanham, MD: Lexington Books, 2006).

Gareth R. V. Stansfield, *Iraq: People, History, Politics* (Cambridge: Polity, 2007).

David Thomas, *Christians at the Heart of Islamic Rule: Church Life and Scholarship in 'Abbasid Iraq. The History of Christian-Muslim Relations* (Leiden, Netherlands: Brill, 2003).

Sophie Thomashausen, *Humanitarian Intervention in an Evolving World Order: The Cases of Iraq, Somalia, Kosovo, and East Timor* (Pretoria, South Africa: Africa Institute of South Africa, 2002).

Kenneth R. Timmerman, *The Death Lobby: How the West Armed Iraq* (New York: Houghton Mifflin, 1991).

Charles Tripp, *A History of Iraq* (Cambridge: Cambridge University Press, 2007).

W. Thom Workman, *The Social Origins of the Iran-Iraq War* (Boulder, CO: Lynne Rienner Publishers, 1994).

Kerim Yildiz, *The Kurds in Iraq: Past, Present and Future* (Ann Arbor, MI: Pluto, 2007).

Sherifa Zuhur, "Iraq, Women's Empowerment, and Public Policy." Letort papers. (Strategic Studies Institute, U.S. Army War College, 2006).

## ISRAEL

Edward Abboud, *Invisible Enemy: Israel, Politics, Media, and American Culture* (Reston, VA: VOX Publishing Company, 2003).

Majid Al Haj, "Immigration and Ethnic Formation in a Deeply Divided Society the Case of the 1990s Immigrants from the Former Soviet Union in Israel," *International Studies In Sociology and Social Anthropology*, vol. 91, 2004.

Irvine H. Anderson, *Biblical Interpretation and Middle East Policy: The Promised Land, America, and Israel, 1917–2002* (Gainesville: University Press of Florida, 2005).

Lisa Anteby Yemini, *Les Juifs Ethiopiens En Israël: Les Paradoxes Du Paradis* (Paris: CNRS éditions, 2004).

Alan Arian, *Politics in Israel: The Second Republic* (Washington, DC: CQ Press, 2005).

Gawdat Bahgat, *Israel and the Persian Gulf: Retrospect and Prospect* (Gainesville: University Press of Florida, 2005).

Smadar Bakovic, *Tall Shadows: Interviews with Israeli Arabs* (Lanham, MD: Hamilton Books, 2006).

Simeon D. Baumel, *Sacred Speakers: Language and Culture among the Haredim in Israel* (New York: Berghahn Books, 2006).

Joel Beinin and Rebecca L. Stein, *The Struggle for Sovereignty: Palestine and Israel, 1993–2005* (Stanford, CA: Stanford University Press, 2006).

Gadi Ben-Ezer, *The Ethiopian Jewish Exodus: Narratives of the Migration Journey to Israel 1977–1985* (New York: Routledge, 2002).

Danny Ben-Moshe and Zohar Segev, *Israel, the Diaspora, and Jewish Identity* (Portland, OR: Sussex Academic Press, 2007).

Guy Ben-Porat, *Israel Since 1980* (Cambridge: Cambridge University Press, 2008).

Francis A. Boyle, *Palestine, Palestinians and International Law* (Atlanta, GA: Clarity Press, 2004).

Ahron Bregman, *A History of Israel* (New York: Palgrave Macmillan, 2003).

Ronet Chacham, *Breaking Ranks: Refusing to Serve in the West Bank and Gaza Strip* (New York: Other Press, 2003).

Julia Chaitin, *Inside-Out: Personal and Collective Life in Israel and the Kibbutz* (Lanham, MD: University Press of America, 2007).

Yoel Cohen, *The Whistle-blower of Dimona: Israel, Vanunu and the Bomb* (New York: Other Press, 2003).

N. R. M. De Lange and Miri Freud-Kandel, *Modern Judaism: An Oxford Guide* (New York: Oxford University Press, 2005).

Alain Dieckhoff, *The Invention of a Nation: Zionist Thought and the Making of Modern Israel* (New York: Columbia University Press, 2003).

Els van Diggele, *A People Who Live Apart: Jewish Identity and the Future of Israel* (Amherst, NY: Prometheus Books, 2003).

Eran Kaplan, *The Jewish Radical Right: Revisionist Zionism and Its Ideological Legacy. Studies on Israel* (Madison: The University of Wisconsin Press, 2005).

Rebecca B. Kook, *The Logic of Democratic Exclusion: African Americans in the United States and Palestinian Citizens in Israel* (Lanham, MD: Lexington Books, 2002).

Baruch Kimmerling and Joel S. Migdal, *The Palestinian People: A History* (Cambridge: Harvard University Press, 2003).

Michael M. Laskier, *Israel and the Maghreb: From Statehood to Oslo* (Gainesville: University Press of Florida, 2004).

Dan Leon, *Who's Left in Israel?: Radical Political Alternatives for the Future of Israel* (Portland, OR: Sussex Academic Press, 2004).

Michelle Mart, *Eye on Israel: How America Came to View the Jewish State as an Ally,* (Albany: State University of New York Press, 2006).

Nur Masalha, *The Bible and Zionism: Invented Traditions, Archaeology and Post-Colonialism in Palestine-Israel* (New York: Zed Books; Distributed by Palgrave Macmillan, 2007).

_____. *The Politics of Denial: Israel and the Palestinian Refugee Problem* (Sterling, VA: Pluto Press, 2003).

Nur Masalha, ed., *Catastrophe Remembered: Palestine, Israel, and the Internal Refugees: Essays in Memory of Edward W. Said, 1935–2003* (New York: Zed Books; Distributed by Palgrave Macmillan, 2005).

Deborah Dash Moore and S. Ilan Troen, *Divergent Jewish Cultures: Israel and America. Studies in Jewish Culture and Society* (New Haven, CT: Yale University Press, 2001).

Riad M. Nasser, *Palestinian Identity in Jordan and Israel: The Necessary 'Other' in the Making of a Nation* (New York: Routledge, 2005).

Ilan Pappe, *A History of Modern Palestine: One Land, Two Peoples* (Cambridge UK: Cambridge University Press, 2004).

Trita Parsi, *Treacherous Alliance: The Secret Dealings of Israel, Iran, and the United States* (New Haven: Yale University Press, 2007).

Shany Payes, *Palestinian NGOs in Israel: The Politics of Civil Society* (New York: Tauris Academic Studies; distributed by St. Martin's Press, 2005).

Gideon Rahat, *The Politics of Regime Structure Reform in Democracies: Israel in Comparative and Theoretical Perspective* (Albany: State University of New York Press, 2008).

Uri Ram, *The Globalization of Israel: Mcworld in Tel Aviv, Jihad in Jerusalem* (New York: Routledge, 2008).

Bernard Reich, *A Brief History of Israel* (New York: Facts on File, 2005).

Naftali Rothenberg, et al., *Jewish Identity in Modern Israel: Proceedings on Secular Judaism and Democracy* (Jerusalem, Israel: The Van Leer Jerusalem Institute, 2002).

Shlomo Sharan, *Israel and the Post-Zionists: A Nation at Risk* (Portland, OR: Sussex Academic Press, 2003).

Ira Sharkansky, *Governing Israel: Chosen People, Promised Land, & Prophetic Tradition,* (New Brunswick, NJ: Transaction Publishers, 2005).

Rebecca L. Stein, *Palestine, Israel, and the Politics of Popular Culture* (Durham: Duke University Press, 2005).

Sandy M. Sufian and Mark LeVine, *Reapproaching Borders: New Perspectives on the Study of Israel-Palestine* (Lanham, MD: Rowman & Littlefield Publishers, 2007).

Sarah S. Willen, *Transnational Migration to Israel in Global Comparative Context* (Lanham, MD: Lexington Books, 2007).

Oren Yiftachel, *Ethnocracy: Land and Identity Politics in Israel/Palestine* (Philadelphia: University of Pennsylvania Press, 2006).

## JORDAN

Betty S. Anderson (Betty Signe), *Nationalist Voices In Jordan: The Street and the State* (Austin: University of Texas Press, 2005).

Julia Droeber, *Dreaming of Change: Young Middle-Class Women and Social Transformation In Jordan* (Leiden, Netherlands: Brill, 2005).

Egbert Harmsen, *Islam, Civil Society and Social Work: Muslim Voluntary Welfare Associations in Jordan between Patronage and Empowerment*, ISIM dissertations (Leiden, Netherlands: ISIM: Amsterdam University Press, 2008).

Warwick M. Knowles, *Jordan Since 1989: A Study in Political Economy* (New York: I. B. Tauris, 2005).

Russell E. Lucas, *Institutions and the Politics of Survival in Jordan: Domestic Responses to External Challenges, 1988–2001* (Albany: State University of New York Press, 2005).

## Bibliography

Riad M. Nasser, *Palestinian Identity in Jordan and Israel: The Necessary 'Other' in the Making of a Nation* (New York: Routledge, 2005).

Philip Robins, *A History of Jordan* (Cambridge: Cambridge University Press, 2004).

Jillian Schwedler, *Faith in Moderation: Islamist Parties in Jordan and Yemen* (New York: Cambridge University Press, 2006).

Dona J. Stewart, *Good Neighbourly Relations: Jordan, Israel and the 1994–2004 Peace Process* (New York: Tauris Academic Studies, 2007).

## KUWAIT

Abdulkarim Al-Dekhayel, *Kuwait: Oil, State and Political Legitimation* (Dryden, NY: Ithaca Press, 2000).

Salwa Alghanim, *The Reign of Mubarak Al-Sabah: Shaikh of Kuwait, 1896–1915* (New York: I. B. Tauris, 1998).

Frederick Fallowfield Anscombe, *The Ottoman Gulf: The Creation of Kuwait, Saudi Arabia, and Qatar* (New York: Columbia University Press, 1997).

Gökhan Bacik, *Hybrid Sovereignty in the Arab Middle East: The Cases of Kuwait, Jordan, and Iraq* (New York: Palgrave Macmillan, 2008).

Lori Plotkin Boghardt, *Kuwait Amid War, Peace and Revolution: 1979–1991 and New Challenges* (New York: Palgrave Macmillan, 2007).

Jerry M. Long, *Saddam's War of Words: Politics, Religion, and the Iraqi Invasion of Kuwait* (Austin: University of Texas Press, 2004).

Anh Nga Longva, *Walls Built on Sand: Migration, Exclusion, and Society in Kuwait* (Boulder, CO: Westview Press, 1997).

Nadeya Sayed Ali Mohammed, *Population and Development of the Arab Gulf States: The Case of Bahrain, Oman and Kuwait* (Burlington, VT: Ashgate, 2003).

Haya Mughni, *Women in Kuwait: The Politics of Gender* (London: Saqi, 2001).

Helen Mary Rizzo, *Islam, Democracy, and the Status of Women: The Case of Kuwait* (New York: Routledge, 2005).

B. J. Slot, *Mubarak Al-Sabah: Founder of Modern Kuwait 1896–1915* (London: Arabian Publishing Ltd., 2005).

Mary Ann Tétreault, *Stories of Democracy: Politics and Society in Contemporary Kuwait* (New York: Columbia University Press, 2000).

Deborah L. Wheeler, *The Internet in the Middle East: Global Expectations and Local Imaginations in Kuwait* (Albany: State University of New York Press, 2006).

## LEBANON

Abdul-Rahim Abu-Husayn, *The View from Istanbul: Lebanon and the Druze Emirate in the Ottoman Chancery Documents, 1546–1711* (New York: Centre for Lebanese Studies & I. B. Tauris, 2004).

Marijean Boueri, et al., *Lebanon A to Z: A Middle Eastern Mosaic* (Exeter, N.H.: Publishing Works, 2005).

Chalabi, Tamara, *The Shi's of Jabal 'Amil and the New Lebanon* (New York: Palgrave MacMillan, 2006).

Kail C. Ellis, ed., *Lebanon's Second Republic: Prospects for The 21st Century* (Gainesville: University Press of Florida, 2002).

Raghid El-Solh, *Lebanon and Arabism: National Identity and State Formation* (London: I. B. Tauris, 2004).

David Grafton, *The Christians of Lebanon: Political Rights In Islamic Law* (London: I. B. Tauris, 2003).

Simon Haddad, *The Palestinian Impasse in Lebanon: The Politics of Refugee Integration* (Brighton, UK: Sussex Academic Press, 2003).

Ahmad Nizar Hamzeh, *In The Path of Hizbullah* (Syracuse, NY: Syracuse University Press, 2004).

Claude Boueiz Kanaan, *Lebanon 1860–1960: A Century of Myth and Politics* (London: Saqi, 2005).

Samir Khalaf, *Civil and Uncivil Violence in Lebanon: A History of the Internationalization of Communal Conflict* (New York: Columbia University Press, 2002).

Sandra Mackey, *Lebanon: A House Divided* (New York: W. W. Norton, 2006).

Augustus R. Norton, *Hezbollah*, (Princeton, NJ: Princeton University Press, 2006).

Elizabeth Picard, *Lebanon, A Shattered Country: Myths and Realities of the Wars in Lebanon* (New York: Holmes & Meier, 2002).

Raghīd El-Solh, *Lebanon and Arabism: National Identity and State Formation* (New York: The Centre for Lebanese Studies & I. B. Tauris, 2004).

Naim Qassem, *Hizbullah: The Story from Within,* translated from the Arabic by Dalia Khalil (London: Saqi Books, 2005).

Margaret Lowrie Robinson, *Season of Betrayal* (Suffern, NY: Tatra Press, 2006).

Nawaf Salem, ed., *Options for Lebanon* (London: I. B. Tauris, 2004).

## LIBYA

Ali Abdullatif Ahmida, *Forgotten Voices: Power and Agency in Colonial and Postcolonial Libya* (London: Routledge, 2005).

_____, *The Making of Modern Libya: State Formation, Colonization, and Resistance* (Albany: State University of New York Press, 2009).

Ines Kohl, *Beautiful Modern Nomads: Bordercrossing Tuareg between Niger, Algeria and Libya* (Berlin: Reimer, 2009).

Luis Martinez, *The Libyan Paradox* (New York: Columbus University Press, 2007).

Khalil I. Matar & Robert W. Thabit, *Lockerbie and Libya: A Study in International Relations* (Jefferson, NC: Mcfarland & Company, 2003).

Amar Obeidi, *Political Culture in Libya* (Leonia, NJ: Curzon Press, 2000).

Yehudit Ronen, *Qaddafi's Libya in World Politics* (Boulder, CO: Lynne Rienner Publishers, 2008).

Ronald Bruce St. John, *Historical Dictionary of Libya* (Lanham, MD: Scarecrow Press, 2006).

_____, *Libya: From Colony to Independence* (Oxford: Oneworld, 2008).

Dirk J. Vandewalle, *A History of Modern Libya* (New York: Cambridge University Press, 2006).

_____, ed., *Libya Since 1969: Qadhafi's Revolution Revisited* (New York: Palgrave Macmillan, 2008).

## MAURITAINIA

Anthony G. Pazzanita, *Historical Dictionary of Mauritania* (Lanham, MD: Scarecrow Press, 2008).

Mohameden Ould-Mey, *Global Restructuring and Peripheral States: The Stick and the Carrot in Mauritania* (Lanham, MD: Littlefield Adams Books, 1996).

## MOROCCO

Fatima Agnaou, *Gender, Literacy and Empowerment in Morocco* (New York: Routledge, 2004).

Jamila Bargach, *Orphans of Islam: Family, Abandonment, and Secret Adoption in Morocco* (Lanham, MD: Rowman & Littlefield Publishers, 2002).

Sahar Bazzaz, *Forgotten Saints: History, Power, and Politics in the Making of Modern Morocco* (Cambridge, MA: Harvard University Press, 2010).

Cynthia Becker, *Amazigh Arts in Morocco: Women Shaping Berber Identity* (Austin: University of Texas Press, 2006).

Abdesselam Cheddadi, *Éducation et Culture au Maroc : Le Difficile Passage à la Modernité* (Casablanca: Le Fennec, 2003).

Shana Cohen, and Larabi Jaïdi, *Morocco: Globalization and Its Consequences* (New York: Routledge, 2006).

Brian T. Edwards, *Morocco Bound: Disorienting America's Maghreb, from Casablanca to the Marrakech Express* (Durham, NC: Duke University Press, 2005).

Moha Ennaji, *Multilingualism, Cultural Identity, and Education in Morocco* (New York: Springer Science, 2005).

Abdellah Hammoudi, *Master and Disciple: The Cultural Foundations of Moroccan Authoritarianism* (Chicago, IL: University of Chicago Press, 1997).

Stacy E. Holden, *The Politics of Food in Modern Morocco* (Gainesville: University Press of Florida, 2009).

Marvine Howe, *Morocco: The Islamist Awakening and Other Challenges* (New York: Oxford University Press, 2005).

Stephen O. Hughes, *Morocco under King Hassan* (Dryden, NY: Ithaca Press, 2001).

Azzedine Layachi, *State, Society and Democracy in Morocco: The Limits of Associative Life* (Washington, DC: Center for Contemporary Arab, 1998).

Haim Malka and Jon B. Alterman, *Arab Reform and Foreign Aid: Lessons from Morocco* (Washington, DC: CSIS Press, Center for Strategic and International Studies, 2006).

David A. McMurray, *In and Out of Morocco: Smuggling and Migration in a Frontier Boomtown* (Minneapolis: University of Minnesota Press, 2001).

Carol Miller, et al., *Women's Employment in the Textile Manufacturing Sectors of Bangladesh and Morocco* (Geneva: United Nations Research Institute for Social Development, 2002).

Maâti Monjib, *Islamists Versus Secularists: Confrontations and Dialogues in Morocco: Values, Democracy, Violence, Freedom, Education* (Rabat, Morocco: IKV PAX, 2009).

Rachel Newcomb, *Women of Fes: Ambiguities of Urban Life in Morocco* (Philadelphia: University of Pennsylvania Press, 2009).

Raphael Chijioke Njoku, *Culture and Customs of Morocco* (Westport, CT: Greenwood Press, 2006).

Thomas K. Park and Aomar Boum, *Historical Dictionary of Morocco* (Lanham, MD: Scarecrow Press, 2006).

C. R. Pennell, *Morocco: From Empire to Independence* (Oxford: Oneworld, 2003).

Fatima Sadiqi, *Women, Gender, and Language in Morocco* (Leiden, Netherlands: Brill, 2003).

James N. Sater, *Civil Society and Political Change in Morocco* (New York: Routledge, 2007).

James N. Sater, *Morocco: Challenges to Tradition and Modernity* (New York: Routledge, 2010).

Daniel J. Schroeter, *The Sultan's Jew: Morocco and the Sephardi World* (Stanford, CA: Stanford University Press, 2002).

Susan Slyomovics, *The Performance of Human Rights in Morocco* (Philadelphia: University of Pennsylvania Press, 2005).

Lise Storm, *Democratization in Morocco: The Political Elite and Struggles for Power in the Post-Independence State* (New York: Routledge, 2007).

Haïm Zafrani, *Two Thousand Years of Jewish Life in Morocco* (Jersey City, NJ: Ktav, 2005).

Malika Zeghal, *Islamism in Morocco: Religion, Authoritarianism, and Electoral Politics* (Princeton, NJ: Markus Wiener Publishers, 2008).

Gregory White, *A Comparative Political Economy of Tunisia and Morocco: On the Outside of Europe Looking In* (Albany: State University of New York Press, 2001).

# OMAN

Dionisius A. Agius, *In the Wake of the Dhow: The Arabian Gulf and Oman* (Dryden, NY: Ithaca Press, 2002).

Calvin H. Allen, *Oman: The Modernization of the Sultanate* (Boulder, CO: Westview Press; Croom Helm, 1987).

Calvin H. Allen and W. Lynn Rigsbee, *Oman under Qaboos: From Coup to Constitution, 1970–1996* (London: Frank Cass, 2000).

Isam Al-Rawas, *Oman in Early Islamic History* (Dryden, NY: Ithaca, 2000).

John Duke Anthony, Donald S. Abelson, and John Peterson, *Historical and Cultural Dictionary of the Sultanate of Oman and the Emirates of Eastern Arabia* (Metuchen, NJ: Scarecrow Press, 1976).

John Beasant, *Oman: The True-Life Drama and Intrigue of an Arab State* (Edinburgh: Mainstream Publishing, 2002).

J. R. L. Carter, *Tribes in Oman* (London: Peninsular Pub.: distributed by Scorpion Publications, 1982).

Raghid El-Solh, *The Sultanate of Oman, 1914–1918* (Chicago, IL: Garnet/Ithaca, 1999).

Hussein Ghubash, *Oman: The Islamic Democratic Tradition* (New York: Routledge, 2006).

Juliet Highet, *Frankincense: Oman's Gift to the World* (London, UK: Prestel Publishing, 2006).

Miriam Joyce, *The Sultanate of Oman: A Twentieth Century History* (Westport, CT: Praeger, 1995).

Joseph A. Kechichian, *Oman and the World: The Emergence of an Independent Foreign Policy* (Santa Monica, CA: Rand, 1995).

Elham Manea, *Regional Politics in the Gulf: Saudi Arabia, Oman, Yemen* (London: Saqi, 2005).

Hubert Moyse-Bartlett, *The Pirates of Trucial Oman* (London: Macdonald & Co., 1966).

Beatrice Nicolini and Penelope-Jane Watson, *Makran, Oman, and Zanzibar: Three-Terminal Cultural Corridor in the Western Indian Ocean, 1799–1856* (Leiden, Netherlands: Brill, 2004).

John Peterson, *Oman's Insurgencies: The Sultanate's Struggle for Supremacy* (London: Saqi, 2007).

Uzi Rabi, *The Emergence of States in a Tribal Society: Oman under Sa'Id Bin Taymur, 1932–1970* (Portland, OR: Sussex Academic Press, 2006).

Carol J. Riphenburg, *Oman: Political Development in a Changing World* (Westport, CT: Praeger, 1998).

Marc Valeri, *Oman: Politics and Society in the Qaboos State* (New York: Columbia University Press, 2009)

_____, *Le Sultanat D'Oman: Une Révolution en Trompe-L'œil* (Paris: Karthala, 2007).

Unni Wikan, *Behind the Veil in Arabia: Women in Oman* (Chicago, IL: University of Chicago Press, 1991).

John Craven Wilkinson, *The Imamate Tradition of Oman* (New York: Cambridge University Press, 1987).

Paul Yule and C. Bergoffen, *Studies in the Archaeology of the Sultanate of Oman* (Rahden/Westf: Verlag Marie Leidorf, 1999).

# Bibliography

## QATAR

Frederick. F. Anscombe, *The Ottoman Gulf: The Creation of Kuwait, Saudi Arabia, and Qatar* (New York, Columbia University Press, 1997).

Anthony. H. Cordesman, *Bahrain, Oman, Qatar, and the UAE: Challenges of Security* (Boulder, CO: Westview Press, 1997).

Jill Crystal, *Oil and Politics in the Gulf: Rulers and Merchants in Kuwait and Qatar* (New York: Cambridge University Press, 1995).

Steven Dorr and Bernard Reich, *Qatar* (Boulder, CO: Westview Press, 2000).

Holger Kapel, *Atlas of the Stone-Age Cultures of Qatar* (Aarhus, Denmark: Aarhus University Press, 1967).

Zekeriya Kursun, *The Ottomans in Qatar: A History of Anglo-Ottoman Conflicts in the Persian Gulf* (Istanbul: Isis Press, 2002).

Habibur Rahman, *The Emergence of Qatar* (New York: Routledge, 2006).

Rosemarie S. Zahlan, *The Making of the Modern Gulf States: Kuwait, Bahrain, Qatar, The United Arab Emirates, and Oman* (Dryden, NY: Ithaca Press, 1998).

## SAUDI ARABIA

Askar H. Al-Enazy, *The Creation of Saudi Arabia: Ibn Saud and British Imperial Policy, 1914–1927* (New York: Routledge, 2010).

Hamid Algar, *Wahhabism: A Critical Essay* (Oneonta, NY: Islamic Publications International, 2002).

Madawi Al-Rasheed, *A History of Saudi Arabia* (New York: Cambridge University Press, 2010).

_____, *Contesting the Saudi State: Islamic Voices from a New Generation* (New York: Cambridge University Press, 2007).

Anthony Cave Brown, *Oil, God and Gold: The Story of Aramco and the Saudi Kings* (Boston, MA: Houghton Mifflin, 1999).

Anthony Cordesman, *Saudi Arabia Enters the Twenty-first Century* (New York: Praeger, 2003, 2 vols).

David Dean Commins, *The Wahhabi Mission and Saudi Arabia* (New York: I. B. Tauris, 2006).

Toby Craig Jones, *Desert Kingdom: How Oil and Water Forged Modern Saudi Arabia* (Cambridge, MA: Harvard University Press, 2010).

Sean Foley, *The Arab Gulf States: Beyond Oil and Islam* (Boulder, CO: Lynne Rienner, 2010).

Steffen Hertog, *Princes, Brokers, and Bureaucrats: Oil and the State in Saudi Arabia* (Ithaca, NY: Cornell University Press, 2010).

Fouad N. Ibrahim, *The Shi'is of Saudi Arabia* (London: Saqi, 2006).

Joshua Craze and Mark Huband, eds., *The Kingdom: Saudi Arabia and the Challenge of the 21st Century* (New York: Columbia University Press, 2009).

David E. Long, *Culture and Customs of Saudi Arabia* (Westport, CT: Greeenwood Press, 2005).

Sebastian Maisel and John A. Shoup, *Saudi Arabia and the Gulf Arab States Today: An Encyclopedia of Life in the Arab States* (Westport, CT: Greenwood Press, 2009).

Tim Niblock and Monica Malik, *The Political Economy of Saudi Arabia* (New York: Routledge, 2007).

Mohamed A. Ramady, *The Saudi Arabian Economy: Policies, Achievements and Challenges* (New York: Springer, 2005).

Frederic Wehrey, *Saudi-Iranian Relations Since the Fall of Saddam: Rivalry, Cooperation, and Implications for U.S. Policy* (Santa Monica, CA: Rand, 2009).

George Rentz, *The Birth of the Islamic Reform Movement in Saudi Arabia: Muhammad Ibn 'Abd Al-Wahhāb (1703/4–1792) and the Beginnings of Unitarian Empire in Arabia* (London: Arabian Pub., 2004).

Robert Vitalis, *America's Kingdom: Mythmaking on the Saudi Oil Frontier* (Stanford, CA: Stanford University Press, 2009).

James Wynbrandt and Fawaz A. Gerges, *A Brief History of Saudi Arabia* (New York: Facts On File, 2004).

## SUDAN

Mohamed A. Abusabib, Art, *Politics, and Cultural Identification in Sudan* (Uppsala, Sweden: Uppsala Universitet, 2004).

Korwa G. Adar, et al., *Sudan Peace Process: Challenges and Future Prospects* (Pretoria, South Africa: Africa Institute of South Africa, 2004).

Stephanie Beswick, *Sudan's Blood Memory: The Legacy of War, Ethnicity, and Slavery in Early South Sudan* (Rochester, NY: University of Rochester Press, 2004).

Janice Patricia Boddy, *Civilizing Women: British Crusades in Colonial Sudan* (Princeton, NJ: Princeton University Press, 2007).

Millard Burr and Robert O. Collins, *Revolutionary Sudan: Hasan Al-Turabi and the Islamist State, 1989–2000* (Leiden, Netherlands: Brill, 2003).

Francis Deng and Mohammed Khalil, *Sudan's Civil War—The Peace Process Before and After Machakos* (Lansing: Michigan State University Press, 2004).

Alexander De Waal, *Famine That Kills: Darfur, Sudan* (New York: Oxford University Press, 2005).

Abdullahi A. Gallab, *The First Islamist Republic: Development and Disintegration of Islamism in the Sudan* (Burlington, VT: Ashgate, 2008).

Omer Awadella Ali Gasmelseid, "Federalism as Conflict-Management Device for Multiethnic and Multicultural Societies: The Case of Sudan." Thesis (doctoral). (Helbing & Lichtenhahn, Universität, Fribourg, 2005, 2006).

Amir H. Idris, *Conflict and Politics of Identity in Sudan* (New York: Palgrave Macmillan, 2005).

Douglas Johnson, *The Root Causes of Sudan's Civil War* (Bloomington: Indiana University Press, 2002).

Ruth Iyob and Gilbert M. Khadiagala, *Sudan: The Elusive Quest for Peace* (Boulder, CO: Lynne Rienner Publishers, 2006).

Jok, Madut Jok, *Sudan: Race, Religion and Violence* (Oxford: Oneworld, 2007).

Mansour Khalid, *War and Peace in Sudan: A Tale of Two Countries* (New York: Kegan Paul International, 2003).

Susan M. Kenyon, *Five Women of Sennar: Culture & Change in Central Sudan* (Long Grove, IL: Waveland Press, 2004).

Ann Mosely Lesch, *The Sudan: Contested National Identities* (Bloomington: Indiana University Press, 1980).

Richard Lobban, Robert S. Kramer, and Carolyn Fluehr-Lobban, *Historical Dictionary of the Sudan* (Lanham, MD: Scarecrow Press, 2002).

Gabriel Meyer and James Nicholls, *War and Faith in Sudan* (Grand Rapids, MI: W. B. Eerdmans Publishing Company, 2005).

Salma Ahmed Nageeb, *New Spaces and Old Frontiers: Women, Social Space, and Islamization in Sudan* (Lanham, MD: Lexington Books, 2004).

Donald Petterson, *Inside Sudan: Political Islam, Conflict, and Catastrophe* (Boulder, CO: Westview Press, 2003).

Gerard Prunier, *Darfur: The Ambiguous Genocide* (Ithaca, NY: Cornell University Press, 2007).

Øystein H. Rolandsen, *Guerrilla Government: Political Changes in The Southern Sudan during the 1990s* (Uppsala, Sweden: Nordic Africa Institute, 2005).

Samuel Totten and Eric Markusen, *Genocide in Darfur: Investigating the Atrocities in the Sudan* (New York: Routledge, 2006).

Gabriel Warburg, *Islam, Sectarianism, and Politics in Sudan Since the Mahdiyya* (Madison: University of Wisconsin Press, 2003).

Karin Willemse, *One Foot in Heaven: Narratives on Gender and Islam in Darfur, West-Sudan* (Leiden, Netherlands: Brill, 2007).

B. Yongo-Bure, *Economic Development of Southern Sudan* (Lanham, MD: University Press of America, 2007).

## SYRIA

John Borneman, *Syrian Episodes* (Princeton, NJ: Princeton University Press, 2006)

Jennifer Marie Dueck, *The Claims of Culture at Empire's End: Syria and Lebanon under French Rule* (New York: Published for the British Academy by Oxford University Press, 2010).

Jubin M. Goodarzi, *Syria and Iran: Diplomatic Alliance and Power Politics in the Middle East* (New York: Tauris Academic Studies, 2006).

Raymond Hinnebusch, et al., *Syrian Foreign Policy and the United States: From Bush to Obama* (St. Andrews, UK: University of St. Andrews, Centre for Syrian Studies: distributed by Lynne Rienner, 2010).

Fred H. Lawson, ed., *Demystifying Syria* (London: Saqi and The London Middle East Institute, 2009).

Flynt Leverett, *Inheriting Syria: Bashar's Trial by Fire* (Washington, DC: Brookings Institution Press, 2005).

Robert G. Rabil, *Syria, the United States, and the War on Terror in the Middle East* (Westport, CT: Praeger Security International, 2006).

Volker Perthes, *Syria under Bashar al-Assad: Modernization and the Limits of Change* (New York: Oxford University Press, 2004).

Patrick Seale, *Asad of Syria: The Struggle for the Middle East* (Berkeley: University of California Press, 1989).

Samir Seifan, *Syria on the Path to Economic Reform* (St. Andrews, UK: University of St. Andrews, Centre for Syrian Studies: Distributed by Lynne Rienner Publishers, 2010).

John A. Shoup, *Culture and Customs of Syria* (Westport, CT: Greenwood Press, 2008).

Aurora Sottimano and Kjetil Selvik, *Changing Regime Discourse and Reform in Syria* (St. Andrews, UK: University of St. Andrews, Centre for Syrian Studies, Distributed by Boulder: Lynne Rienner, 2009).

Lisa Wedeen, *Ambiguities of Domination: Politics, Rhetoric and Symbols in Contemporary Syria* (Chicago, IL: University of Chicago Press, 1999).

Eyal Zisser, *Commanding Syria: Bashar al-Asad and the First Years in Power* (London: Tauris, 2007).

## TUNISIA

Christopher Alexander, *Tunisia: Stability and Reform in the Modern Maghreb* (New York: Routledge, 2010).

Eva Bellini, *Stalled Democracy: Capital, Labor and the Paradox of State-Sponsored Development* (Ithaca, NY: Cornell University Press, 2002).

Andrew Borowiec, *Taming the Sahara: Tunisia Shows a Way While Others Falter* (Westport, CT: Praeger, 2003).

Mohamed Elhachmi, *The Politicization of Islam: A Case Study of Tunisia* (Boulder CO: Westview Press, 1998).

Derek Hopwood, *Habib Bourguiba of Tunisia: The Tragedy of Longevity* (New York: St. Martin's Press, 1992).

Stephen J. King, *Liberalization against Democracy: The Local Politics of Economic Reform in Tunisia* (Bloomington: Indiana University Press, 2003).

Kenneth J. Perkins, *History of Modern Tunisia* (Cambridge, UK: Cambridge University Press, 2004).

Azzam Tamimi, *Rachid Ghannouchi: A Democrat within Islamism* (New York: Oxford University Press, 2001).

## TURKEY

Morton Abramowitz. *The United States and Turkey: Allies in Need* (New York: Century Foundation Press, 2003).

Sina Aksin, *Turkey from Empire to Revolutionary Republic: The Emergence of the Turkish Nation from 1789 to the Present* (New York: New York University Press, 2007).

Bülent Aras, *Turkey and the Greater Middle East* (Istanbul: Tasam Publications, 2004).

Yildiz Atasoy, Turkey, *Islamists and Democracy: Transition and Globalization in a Muslim State* (New York: I. B. Tauris; distributed by Palgrave Macmillan, 2005).

Alison Burrell and A. J. Oskam, *Turkey in the European Union: Implications for Agriculture, Food and Structural Policy* (Oxfordshire, UK: CABI Publishing, 2005).

Soner Çagaptay, *Islam, Secularism and Nationalism in Modern Turkey: Who Is a Turk?* (London; New York: Routledge, 2006).

Ali Çarkoglu and Barry M. Rubin, *Religion and Politics in Turkey* (London; New York: Routledge, 2006).

Steven A. Cook, *Ruling but Not Governing: The Military and Political Development in Egypt, Algeria, and Turkey* (Baltimore, MD: Johns Hopkins University Press, 2007).

William M. Hale, *Turkey, the U.S. and Iraq* (London: Saqi, 2007).

Metin Heper, *Historical Dictionary of Turkey* (Lanham, MD: Scarecrow Press, 2002).

_____. *The State and Kurds in Turkey: The Question of Assimilation* (New York: Palgrave Macmillan, 2007).

Christopher Houston, *Islam, the Kurds and the Turkish Nation-State* (New York: Oxford, 2001).

Muammer Kaylan, *The Kemalists: Islamic Revival and the Fate of Secular Turkey* (Amherst, NY: Prometheus Books, 2005).

Stephen Larrabee, *Turkish Foreign Policy in an Age of Uncertainty* (Santa Monica, CA: Rand, 2002).

Bernard Lewis, *The Emergence of Modern Turkey* (New York: Oxford University Press, 2002).

Guenter Lewy, *The Armenian Massacres in Ottoman Turkey: A Disputed Genocide* (Salt Lake City: University of Utah Press, 2005).

Andrew Mango, *Ataturk: The Biography of the Founder of Modern Turkey* (New York: Overlook Publishing, 2000).

Omer Taspinar, *Kurdish Nationalism and Political Islam in Turkey: Kemalist Identity in Transition* (New York: Routledge, 2005).

Jenny B. White, *Islamist Mobilization in Turkey: A Study in Vernacular Politics* (Seattle: University of Washington Press, 2002).

M. Hakan Yavuz, *The Emergence of a New Turkey: Democracy and the AK Parti* (Salt Lake City: University of Utah Press, 2006).

## Bibliography

## UNITED ARAB EMIRATES

Frank A. Clements, *The United Arab Emirates* (Santa Barbara, CA: ABC-Clio, 1998).

Christopher M. Davidson, *The United Arab Emirates: A Study in Survival* (Boulder, CO: Lynne Rienner Publishers, 2005).

Sayed Hamid A. Hurreiz, *Folklore and Folklife in the United Arab Emirates* (London: Routledge-Curzon, 2002).

Joseph Kechichian, ed., *A Century in Thirty Years: The United Arab Emirates* (Washington, DC: Middle East Policy Council, 2000).

Andrea B. Rugh, *The Political Culture of Leadership in the United Arab Emirates* (New York: Palgrave Macmillan, 2007).

Ahmed M. Salah Ouf, *Urban Conservation Concepts for the New Millennium in the United Arab Emirates* (Al Ain, UAE: Zayed Center for Heritage and History, 2000).

## YEMEN

Reuben Ahroni, *Jewish Emigration from the Yemen, 1951–1998: Carpet without Magic*, (Richmond, UK: Curzon, 2001).

Madawi Al-Rasheed and Robert Vitalis, *Counter-Narratives: History, Contemporary Society, and Politics in Saudi Arabia and Yemen* (New York: Palgrave Macmillan, 2004).

Steven Charles Caton, *Yemen Chronicle: An Anthropology of War and Mediation* (New York: Hill and Wang, 2005).

Janine A. Clark, *Islam, Charity, and Activism: Middle-Class Networks and Social Welfare in Egypt, Jordan, and Yemen* (Bloomington: Indiana University Press, 2004).

Marta Colburn, *The Republic of Yemen: Development Challenges in the 21st Century* (London: Stacey International, 2002).

William J. Donaldson, *Sharecropping in the Yemen: A Study of Islamic Theory, Custom, and Pragmatism* (Leiden, Netherlands: Brill, 2000).

Paul Dresch, *A History of Modern Yemen* (Cambridge; New York: Cambridge University Press, 2000).

Caesar Farah, *The Sultan's Yemen: Nineteenth Century Challenges to Ottoman Rule* (New York: I. B. Tauris, 2002).

Isaac Hollander, *Jews and Muslims in Lower Yemen: A Study in Protection and Restraint, 1918–1949* (Leiden, Netherands: Brill, 2005).

Leila Ingrams, *Yemen Engraved: Foreign Travellers to the Yemen, 1496–1890* (London: Kegan Paul International, 2000).

Clive Jones, *Britain and the Yemen Civil War, 1962–1965: Ministers, Mercenaries and Mandarins: Foreign Policy and the Limits of Covert Action* (Brighton, UK: Sussex Academic Press, 2004).

Kamil A. Mahdi, Anna Würth, and Helen Lackner, *Yemen into the Twenty-First Century: Continuity and Change* (Dryden, NY: Ithaca Press, 2007).

Trevor Hugh James Marchand, *Minaret Building and Apprenticeship in Yemen* (Richmond, UK: Curzon, 2001).

Jillian Schwedler, *Faith in Moderation: Islamist Parties in Jordan and Yemen* (New York: Cambridge University Press, 2006).

Gabriele Von Bruck, *Islam, Memory, and Morality in Yemen: Ruling Families in Transition* (New York: Palgrave Macmillan, 2005).

## REGIONAL STUDIES

Ibrahim M. Abu-Rabi', *Contemporary Arab Thought: Studies in Post-1967 Arab Intellectual History* (London: Pluto Press, 2003).

Christiane Bird, *A Thousand Sighs, a Thousand Revolts: Journeys In Kurdistan* (New York: Random House, 2004).

Edmund Burke III & David Yaghoubian, eds., *Struggle and Survival in the Modern Middle East* (Berkeley: Univ. of California Press, 2005, 2nd ed.).

Adeed Dawisha, *Arab Nationalism in the Twentieth Century* (Princeton: Princeton University Press, 2003).

Raymond Hinnebusch and Anoushirvan Enteshami, eds., *The Foreign Policies of Middle Eastern States* (Boulder, CO: Lynne Rienner, 2002).

Maya Jasanoff, *Edge of Empire: Lives, Culture and Conquest In the East, 1750–1850* (New York: Knopf, 2005).

Robert W. Olson, *Turkey's Relations With Iran, Syria, Israel and Russia 1991–2000: The Kurdish and Islamist Questions* (Costa Mesa, CA: Mazda Publishers, 2001).

Robert Rabil, *Embattled Neighbors: Syria, Israel and Lebanon* (Boulder, CO: Lynne Rienner, 2003).

Barry Rubin, *The Tragedy of the Middle East* (Cambridge, UK: Cambridge University Press, 2003).

Colin Thubron, *Shadow of the Silk Road* (New York: Harper Collins, 2007).

John Waterbury, *The Nile Basin National Determinants and Collective Action* (Princeton: Princeton University Press, 2002).

Richard Zachs, *The Pirate Coast* (New York: Hyperion, 2005) Deals with the U.S. in North Africa

Rosemarie Said Zahlan, *Making of the Modern Gulf States* (Chicago, IL: Garnet/Ithaca, 1999).

## WOMEN'S STUDIES

Anita Amirrezvani, *The Blood of Flowers* (Boston: Little, Brown, 2007).

Lois Beck and Guity Nashat, *Women in Iran from 1800 to the Islamic Republic* (Urbana: University of Illinois Press, 2004).

Mounira M. Charrad, *States and Women's Rights: The Making of Post-Colonial Tunisia, Algeria and Morocco* (Berkeley: University of California Press, 2003).

Shirin Ebadi, *Iran Awakening: A Memoir of Revolution and Hope* with Azadeh Moaveni. (New York: Random House, 2006).

Jennifer Heath, *The Scimitar and the Veil: Extraordinary Women of Islam* (Hidden Spring Press, 2004).

Barbara Hodgson, *Dreaming of East: Western Women and the Exotic Allure of the Orient* (New York: Greystone, 2005).

Norma Khouri, *Honor Lost: Love and Death in Present-Day Jordan* (New York: Atria Press, 2003).

Jean Said Makdisi, *Teta, Mother and Me: Three Generations of Arab Women* (New York: W.W. Norton, 2006).

Rene Melammed, *Heretics or Daughters of Israel? The Crypto-Jewish Women of Castile* (New York: Oxford University Press, 2002).

Azadeh Moaveni, *Lipstick Jihad: A Memoir of Growing Up Iranian in America and American in Iran* (New York: Public Affairs Press/Perseus Books, 2005).

Haya al-Mughni, *Women in Kuwait: The Politics of Gender* (London: Al-Saqi, 2001).

Dalia Sofer, *The Septembers of Shiraz* (New York: Ecco Press, 2007 (two novels about Iran by expatriate Iranian women writers).

## LITERATURE IN TRANSLATION

Suad Amiry, *Sharon and My Mother-in-Law: Ramallah Diaries* (New York: Pantheon Books, 2004).

Peter Cole, ed. and translator, *The Dream of the Poem: Hebrew Poetry From Muslim and Christian Spain, 950–1492* (Princeton: Princeton University Press, 2007).

Elias Khoury, *Gate of the Sun,* translated by Humphrey Davies (New York: Archipelago Books, 2005) (stories told by Palestinians in refugee camps).

Tahar Ben Jalloun, *This Blinding Absence of Light* (New York: Penguin, 2006).

Leila Lalami, *Hope and Other Dangerous Pursuits* (New York: Harvest Press, 2006).

Bernard Lewis, *Music of a Distant Drum* (Princeton: Princeton University Press, 2002).

O.Z. Livanelli, *Bliss* (New York: St. Martin's Press, 2002). Translated from the Turkish by Cigdem Aksoy Fromm. A novel.

Paul Lunde & Caroline Stone, translators, *From the Meadows of Gold: Mas'udi* (New York: Penguin, 2007).

Naguib Mahfouz, *The Dreams,* translated from the Arabic by Raymond Stack (Cairo: A.U.C. Press, 2004).

Hisham Matar, *In The Country of Men* (New York: Dial Press, 2006) A novel about Libya.

Amos Oz, *A Tale of Love and Darkness,* translated from the Hebrew by Nicholas de Lange (New York: Harcourt Brace, 2004).

Holly Payne, *The Weaver's Knot* (New York: Penguin Books, 2002). A novel about a famous female weaver in Lycia, Turkey.

## CURRENT EVENTS

To keep up to date on rapidly changing events in the contemporary Middle East and North Africa, the following materials are especially useful:

*Africa Report* Bimonthly, with an "African Update" chronology for all regions.

*Africa Research Bulletin* (Exeter, England) Monthly summaries of political, economic, and social developments in all of Africa, with coverage of North–Northeast Africa.

*The Christian Science Monitor* 1 Norway St., Boston, MA; weekly Mon-Fri, extensive regional coverage with periodic in-depth articles and reports.

*Current History, A World Affairs Journal* At least one issue per year is usually devoted to the Middle Eastern region.

*The Economist* U.S. edition, 1111 West 57th St., New York, NY; weekly except Sunday.

*Middle East Economic Digest* (London, England) Weekly summary of economic and some political developments in the Middle East–North African region generally and in individual countries. Provides special issues from time to time.

*The Nation* 33 Irving St., New York, NY; weekly news magazine, liberal-leftist in approach.

*SaudiAramco World* Published in Houston, TX by Saudi American Oil Company. Bimonthly, with extensive coverage of social-cultural life in the Islamic lands of the Middle East and elsewhere.

*Tikkun* 22 Shattuck Lane, Berkeley, CA, bimonthly magazine of the Jewish left, edited by Michael Lerner, distinguished scholar-rabbi.

*World Press Review* Shrub Oak, NY; monthly magazine with articles from the world press, translated into English.

## PERIODICALS

*The Economist* 25 St. James's Street London, England.

*The Middle East and North Africa* Europa Publications 18 Bedford Square London, England. A reference work, published annually and updated, with country surveys, regional articles, and documents.

*The Middle East Journal* 1761 N Street, NW Washington, D.C. 20036. This quarterly periodical, established in 1947, is the oldest one specializing in Middle East affairs, with authoritative articles, book reviews, documents, and chronology.

*New Outlook* 9 Gordon Street Tel Aviv, Israel. A bimonthly news magazine, with articles, chronology and documents. Reflects generally Israeli leftist peace-with-the-Arabs views of the movement Peace Now with which it is affiliated.

# Index

# Index

# Index

# Index

# Index

# Index